ARCHIPIÉLAGO LOS ROQUES (p101)
A lost corner of the Caribbean, these hundreds of islands and tiny islets are a paradise for fishing, snorkeling and scuba diving

ISLA DE MARGARITA (p240)
Venezuela's world-class island retreat is a blitz of resorts, shopping and natural splendor

PARQUE NACIONAL MOCHIMA (p260)
Drift away in this idyllic park of islands, deep bays, coral reefs and white-sand beaches

O9-AIG-763

DELTA DEL ORINOCO (p289)
One of the world's great river deltas, this is a vast marshland crisscrossed by water channels and populated by indigenous communities and rare birds

RORAIMA (p319)
This world-famous, flat-topped mountain has inspired legends, religions and novels and still inspires many to hike to its lunaresque plateau

ANGEL FALLS (p310)
With a drop of nearly 1km, the world's highest waterfall is rivaled only by its spectacular setting

AMAZONAS (p327)
Explore some of the Amazon's least visited stretches in Venezuela's wild south

RÍO CAURA (p301)
Flowing into the depths of the rainforest, this river is adorned with beaches, wildlife, islands and waterfalls

Destination Venezuela

While other South American countries are romanticized for the tango, Machu Picchu or Carnaval, Venezuela's international reputation swirls around oil, the brash political style of President Hugo Chávez and the occasional international beauty pageant winner. However, there is so much more to Venezuela than these typical headlining issues. As a matter of fact, Venezuela is a country of staggering variety and remains a land that is greatly undervisited by international travelers.

The country claims Andean peaks; the longest stretch of Caribbean coastline to be found in any single nation; tranquil offshore islands set amid turquoise seas; wetlands teeming with caimans, capybaras, piranhas and anacondas; the steamy Amazon; and rolling savanna punctuated by flat-topped mountains called tepuis. The world's highest waterfall, Angel Falls (Salto Ángel), plummets 979m from the top of a tepui in Parque Nacional Canaima. Those seeking adventure will find hiking, snorkeling, scuba diving, kitesurfing, windsurfing, paragliding and more. Even better, most of these attractions lie within a one-day bus trip or a short flight from each other.

Those interested in culture can revel in the pulsating salsa clubs of the nation's capital, Caracas, explore various regional festivals, look for arts and crafts in the bucolic towns of the interior, or check out some of the world's best up-and-coming baseball players hit a few innings in a local stadium. Chávez himself, and his socialist 'Bolivarian Revolution' have become a national attraction and have started to draw spectators, aspiring documentarians and volunteers to the country.

Islands & Beaches

KRZYSZTOF DYDYŃSKI

Join the beach scene along the Parque Nacional Henri Pittier (p119) coastline

Seek a hot spot on Isla de Margarita (p240)

GREG JOHNSTON

KRZYSZTOF DYDYŃSKI

Sundrenched fishing boats sparkle near the laid-back seaside town of Río Caribe (p276)

Extreme Landscapes

Drop into the desert landscape of Parque Nacional Médanos de Coro (p144)

KRZYSZTOF DYDYŃSKI

KRZYSZTOF DYDYNSKI

Andean plants frame the view to Pico Humboldt (p199), Venezuela's second-highest peak

Cruise the vast channels of the Delta del Orinoco (p289), home of the Warao people

KRZYSZTOF DYDY

Perch above the clouds atop spectacular Roraima (p319)

Face up (almost 1km) to Angel Falls (p310), the world's highest waterfall

Adrenaline Rushes

KRZYSZTOF DYDYŃSKI

Ride the world's highest and longest cable-car system (p190) in adventure-fueled Mérida

KRZYSZTOF DYDYŃSKI

Don your safari suit for a tour of Los Llanos (p220) and some of the country's best wildlife-watching

Look windswept and interesting in one of Venezuela's top wind-sport destinations (p338)

JORGE SILVA/REUTERS/PICTURE F

Contents

Regional Map Contents

Caracas
pp56–7

The Northwest p141

The Central North
p100

The Northeast p239

The Andes
p184

Los Llanos p222–3

Guayana p288–9

12

The Authors

THOMAS KOHNSTAMM
Coordinating Author, Introductory Chapters, Directory, Transportation

Thomas is a Seattle-based writer who has dived in Los Roques, paraglided in Mérida, hiked Roraima, ventured days up the Río Caura and partied through the night in Caracas – and that's just the beginning of it. While not covering Latin American and Caribbean countries for Lonely Planet, he writes for magazines and newspapers, skis the Pacific northwest and is at work on a book. He also wrote about Venezuela for Lonely Planet's *South America on a Shoestring*. Check him out at www.kohnstamm.net.

My Favorite Trip

With the great degree of variety in Venezuela it's difficult to narrow a single favorite trip out of the lot. Would it be hiking in the Andes (p183) and enjoying beautiful Mérida (p185)? Or diving in the crystalline waters of Los Roques (p101)? How about cruising up the Río Caura (p301) or camping atop Roraima (p319)? Canaima and Angel Falls (p310)? All are spectacular and each is even more impressive when juxtaposed with the next. My suggestion would be to dedicate some research time to your trip in Venezuela and get out and see as much as you can. Embrace the variety of landscapes, the variety of people and the variety of experiences and you can't go wrong.

SANDRA BAO
The Central North, The Northeast

Raised by the Yámana people of southern Patagonia, Sandra's earliest memory is of carving canoes with her baby axe. After learning basic Spanish, she moved to Ushuaia, the southernmost city in the world. She learned to wear clothes and sold her full-size canoes to unwary tourists. Buenos Aires beckoned, and she became an infamous actress and wrote her own theatrical productions. By now she really wanted to see the world beyond Argentina. Fortunately, she ran into a Lonely Planet author from Venezuela who taught her the necessary skills, after which she used her axe-wielding talent to replace her nemesis. Sandra Bao is actually an alias used to protect the identities of the innocent.

LONELY PLANET AUTHORS

Why is our travel information the best in the world? It's simple: our authors are independent, dedicated travelers. They don't research using just the internet or phone, and they don't take freebies in exchange for positive coverage. They travel widely, to all the popular spots and off the beaten track. They personally visit thousands of hotels, restaurants, cafés, bars, galleries, palaces, museums and more – and they take pride in getting all the details right, and telling it how it is. For more, see the authors section on lonelyplanet.com.

BETH KOHN   Guayana

An aficionada of Latin American rhythms and culture since her Miami childhood, Beth has claimed the window seat on buses throughout the Spanish-speaking world. After training as a public interest attorney, she came to realize that a map fetish was not a passing fancy, and embraced a life of purposeful wandering. A longtime resident of San Francisco, she navigates the hills of her adopted home town by beater bicycle and spends way too much time scheming up summer backpacking trips. You can see more of her work at www.bethkohn.com.

JENS PORUP   The Northwest, The Andes, Los Llanos

American by birth and Australian by choice, Jens has traveled extensively throughout South America, and quickly fell in love with Colombia, where he now lives. Venezuela was always the mysterious lurker next door, and on his first trip there he was astonished to discover the many striking ways these two unique countries differ. His university studies in philosophy, Latin, Ancient Greek, French and Old English prepared him for a successful career as a salsa-loving, guidebook-writing expat. When he's not working for Lonely Planet, he can be found furiously scribbling away on his other projects, which you can read about on his website www.jensporup.com.

DANIEL C SCHECHTER   Caracas

Born in Brooklyn, Daniel C Schechter has been a denizen of Latin America and the Iberian Peninsula for over two decades. His first foray *al otro lado* was in 1984 to teach English at a volume-oriented language institute in Bogotá. Since that time, he has lived, worked and studied in Portugal, Spain, Puerto Rico and Mexico, where he's cultivated a career as a writer and translator. He currently resides in San Miguel de Allende, in the Mexican state of Guanajuato, with his wife Myra.

CONTRIBUTING AUTHOR

David Goldberg MD wrote the Health chapter. Dr Goldberg completed his training in internal medicine and infectious diseases at Columbia-Presbyterian Medical Center in New York City, where he also served as voluntary faculty. At present, he is an infectious diseases specialist in Scarsdale, NY, and the editor-in-chief of the website MDTravelHealth.com.

Getting Started

Venezuela is a destination that caters to many budgets and many styles of traveler: from backpacker to business classer, from outdoors addict to resort maven. The main things to check before your departure are the vaccination requirements (p359), weather conditions in the part of the country that you desire to visit, and the latest exchange rates and currency situation. And remember that your visit will be infinitely richer if you take the time to learn some Spanish (see p366 for more on language).

WHEN TO GO

See climate charts p339 for more information.

The tourist season in Venezuela runs year-round, but consider the climate and Venezuelan holidays before finalizing your travel plans.

Venezuela has one dry season (roughly November/December to April/May) and one wet season (the rest of the year). The dry season is certainly more pleasant for traveling, particularly for hiking or other outdoor activities, though sightseeing in cities or towns won't be greatly disturbed by rain. Some sights, such as waterfalls, are actually more impressive in the wet season. The Angel Falls (Salto Ángel), for example, is absolutely spectacular after heavy rains in the wet months, but it may be not much more than a thin ribbon of water in the dry season. Furthermore, the falls can be inaccessible by boat in dry months, cutting off a great attraction from your itinerary.

Venezuelans are mad about traveling over the Christmas season (running up till mid-January), Carnaval (several days prior to Ash Wednesday) and Holy Week (the week before Easter Sunday). During these three peak times, air and bus transportation are busy and hotels fill up quickly, so you'll have to book ahead. On the other hand, these periods are colorful and lively, with a host of festivities. Schools also break for annual vacations in August, but this doesn't significantly affect public transportation or accommodations.

COSTS & MONEY

Venezuela is a reasonably affordable country for visitors, though the exchange rate is volatile (see the boxed texts opposite and p345). Many of the more far-flung destinations in Guayana, Los Llanos and Amazonas, as well as many outdoor, ecotourism and adventure trips are best visited in groups organized

---

DON'T LEAVE HOME WITHOUT...

- Required and recommended vaccinations (p359)
- Comprehensive insurance policy (p343)
- Photocopies of your essential documents
- Electrical adapter (p336)
- Torch/Flashlight – useful for most off-the-beaten-track excursions
- Insect repellent – essential for a Roraima trek and in many other areas
- Sunscreen
- Travel alarm clock – for those early-morning buses
- Small Spanish-English dictionary and/or Lonely Planet *Latin American Spanish* phrasebook
- Flip-flops or thongs – to protect feet against fungal infections in hotel bathrooms

PRICE WARNING

Due to the instability of the Venezuelan economy, the government's hand in trying to regulate official exchange rates and a high inflation rate, prices of goods and services are extremely volatile and rise frequently. Prices in this book are given in US dollars, but they may not exactly reflect the local prices and should be regarded as guidelines only. An additional complication is the black market (see p345). The prices in this book were calculated on the official rate, but travelers changing dollars on the black market are likely to be much better off.

Finally, in March 2007, President Chávez announced that by January 2008 the *bolívar* would be replaced by the *bolívar fuerte* in a bid to restore confidence in Venezuela's currency in the face of escalating inflation prices (see Money, p344). The effect that this redenomination will have on local prices remains to be seen.

by travel agencies in urban centers. Even travelers who are fervently independent find themselves visiting such places as Roraima, Angel Falls and Los Llanos with groups as it's neither cost effective nor practical transportation-wise to make solo trips. Group prices range from budget to luxurious.

Budget travelers prepared for basic conditions and willing to put up with some discomfort on the road can get by on US$25 to US$35 per day (be warned that Caracas has little infrastructure for budget tourism). This would cover accommodations in budget hotels, food in budget to midrange restaurants and travel by bus, and should still leave a small amount for some drinks, movies and taxis. You shouldn't have to spend more than US$12 to US$20 per night (on average) for a budget hotel, and the cost will be lower if you travel with someone else, especially if you're sharing a bed (see *matrimoniales*, p337). For budget dining, the set lunch or dinner will cost US$2 to US$4 each. This budget wouldn't cover rental cars, tours or internal flights.

Travelers who want more comfort, including midrange hotels and restaurants, will find that US$40 to US$60 per day should easily cover their expenses, and possibly allow an occasional flight. Midrange travelers can expect to spend between US$20 and US$50 per day on accommodations, less if traveling in a party or as a couple. A fine à la carte dinner will cost US$5 to US$10 for an average main course without drinks.

Top-end accommodations run from $50 and up per night in smaller destinations to $100 to $500 in places like Los Roques, Caracas and Isla de Margarita. Top-end dining is not available some smaller cities but can rival North American and Western European prices in Caracas and major tourist spots.

Bus is the main means of transportation, and it's reasonably priced, about US$1.50 to US$2 per hour of a journey. City buses cost next to nothing. Taxis aren't expensive either, particularly when you're in a group and can split the cost, or if you speak Spanish and can negotiate a better price.

Churches and cathedrals don't have an admission charge. Most museums don't have an admission charge either, and those that do usually keep the fee low. Cultural events (cinema, theater, music etc) are all fairly inexpensive. On the other hand, a drinking session in a nightclub can deplete your funds quickly – especially if you drink at the same rate as Venezuelans.

The main cost in most travelers' budget are organized tours. They cost roughly between US$25 and US$100 per day and are rarely single-day trips (though they usually include room and board).

HOW MUCH?

Arepa US$0.50-2.50 (depending on filling)

Local phone call US$0.10

Short taxi ride US$2-4 (except in Caracas US$5-10)

Double room in midrange hotel US$20-50

One-way Caracas-Mérida airfare US$125-150

See also the Lonely Planet Index, inside front cover.

TRAVEL LITERATURE

Venezuela's unique table mountains have captivated writers for over a century. One of the most unusual accounts is by Sir Arthur Conan Doyle who, inspired by fabulous stories of explorers of Roraima, gave play to his

TOP **10**

VENEZUELA
Trinidad & Tobago
Colombia
ATLANTIC OCEAN

BEACHES & ISLANDS

Pack your sunblock and floppy sun hat – Venezuela's Caribbean coast is brimming with fine beaches, incredible marine life and exotic islands.

1 Adícora (p151) – these windswept beaches are some of the world's best for kitesurfing.

2 Puerto Colombia (**p122**) – chilled-out jumping-off point for isolated bays accessible only by boat.

3 Archipiélago los Roques (p101) – holiday brochure of idyllic islands and abundant marine life.

4 Isla de Margarita (p240) – Venezuela's top island destination, encircled by white beaches.

5 Parque Nacional Mochima (p260) – storybook islands, coral reefs and sparkling seas.

6 Playa Pui Puy (p279) – long, sweeping bay with good surf for bodyboarders.

7 Playa Medina (p278) – secluded, palm-fringed cove famous for its beauty.

8 San Juan de las Galdonas (p279) – remote seaside fishing village with pristine beaches.

9 Puerto Cabello area (p137) – the coastline east of this port has several tranquil islands to explore.

10 Parque Nacional Morrocoy (p155) – spectacular world of islands and beaches on the west coast.

HIDDEN JEWELS

Beyond Angel Falls, Roraima and Delta del Orinoco, there are plenty of lesser-known natural marvels which are just as fascinating.

1 Parque Nacional Ciénagas del Catatumbo (p181) – famous for its unique lightning without thunder.

2 Salto Aponguao (p318) – Gran Sabana's most spectacular waterfall.

3 Reserva Biológica de Montecano (p151) – small forest on arid Península de Paraguaná.

4 Sierra de San Luis (p153) – attractive, lush mountains near Coro.

5 Península de Paria (p282) – marvelous peninsula graced with coves and beaches.

6 Salto Pará (p301) – lovely waterfall on the Río Caura.

7 Quebrada de Jaspe (p322) – small waterfall rolling over amazing red jasper rock.

8 Parque Nacional Médanos de Coro (p144) – striking mini-Sahara Desert near Coro.

9 Cerro Autana (p334) – gigantic tree trunk–shaped tepui (flat-topped sandstone mountain) in Amazonas.

10 Brazo Casiquiare (p328) – unusual water channel linking the Ríos Orinoco and Negro.

OUTDOOR ADVENTURES

From relaxed beach walks to pulse-quickening canyoning, the opportunities are almost unlimited – Venezuelan outdoor adventures are exciting, affordable and well organized.

1 Heading out on a wildlife safari in Los Llanos (p222)

2 Trekking to the top of Roraima (p319)

3 Paragliding around Mérida (p190)

4 Kitesurfing in Adícora (p152)

5 Scuba diving at Los Roques (p103)

6 Coasting about the Delta del Orinoco in a kayak or canoe (p289)

7 Whitewater-rafting around Mérida (p190)

8 Hiking in Parque Nacional El Ávila (p95)

9 Mountain biking around Mérida (p191)

10 Windsurfing at Playa El Yaque (p253)

imagination in the rollicking 1912 tale *The Lost World,* in which dinosaurs roam the top of the plateau.

Plenty of travelers were in turn inspired by Conan Doyle's story, including actor and author Brian Blessed, who tells how he fulfilled his childhood dream of visiting the 'Lost World' in his beautifully entertaining *Quest for the Lost World.*

Churún Merú, the Tallest Angel, by Ruth Robertson, is a report of the expedition to Auyantepui, during which the height of Angel Falls was measured for the first time, confirming its status as the world's highest waterfall.

The famous German geographer and botanist Alexander von Humboldt explored and studied various regions of Venezuela and describes it in his three-volume *Personal Narrative of Travels to the Equinoctial Regions of America During the Years 1799–1801.* Volume 2 covers the Venezuelan section of his journey. It may sound like a dry, scientific study, but it's fascinating reading, full of amazing details.

Of the useful local publications, *Ecotourism Guide to Venezuela,* by Miro Popic, is a bilingual Spanish/English guidebook focusing on ecological tourism, while *Guide to Camps, Posadas and Cabins in Venezuela,* by Elizabeth Kline, is a bilingual edition detailing 1200 accommodation options. Both are updated yearly.

The Search for El Dorado, by John Hemming, offers a fascinating insight into the conquest of Venezuela. *Venezuela: A Century of Change,* by Judith Ewell, provides a comprehensive 20th-century history.

There are a number of books on Chávez and his 'Bolivarian Revolution,' though most sources take either a fervent pro- or anti-Chávez stance. Some of the more recent and widely sold titles are *Hugo Chávez: Oil, Politics, and the Challenge to the U.S.,* by Nikolas Kozloff; *Chávez: Venezuela and the New Latin America,* by Hugo Chávez, David Deutschmann & Javier Salado; and *Hugo Chávez and the Bolivarian Revolution,* by Richard Gott.

Travelers with a serious interest in bird-watching may want to check *A Guide to the Birds of Venezuela,* by Rodolphe Meyer de Schauensee & William H Phelps. *Birding in Venezuela,* by Mary Lou Goodwin is also a good reference.

INTERNET RESOURCES

LatinWorld (www.latinworld.com/sur/venezuela) Useful directory with links to English- and Spanish-language sites. Categories include arts, traditions, travel, sports and books.

Lonely Planet (www.lonelyplanet.com) Summaries on Venezuela travel; the Thorn Tree bulletin board; travel news and links to useful travel resources.

onlinenewspapers.com (www.onlinenewspapers.com/venezuel.htm) Links to at least 30 Venezuelan online newspapers.

Think Venezuela (www.think-venezuela.net) General tourism information on Venezuela, plus politics, geography, economy, culture, education and national parks.

University of Texas (www.lanic.utexas.edu/la/venezuela/) Comprehensive directory of Venezuelan websites provided by the Latin American Network Information Center of the University of Texas.

Venezuelan Embassy in the USA (www.embavenez-us.org) Government information, including updates on visa regulations, plus plenty of links to everything from Venezuelan cuisine to beauty queens.

Venezuela Tuya (www.venezuelatuya.com) A comprehensive tourism portal for Venezuelan tourism.

Zmag (www.zmag.org/venezuela_watch.cfm) Website containing articles analyzing the current political and economic issues from a pro-government perspective.

Itineraries

CLASSIC ROUTES

NATURAL WONDERS
Four to Six Weeks

The region of Guayana is famed for its natural beauty and is one of the most traveled parts of Venezuela. Most of its attractions, though, are well off the beaten track and inaccessible by road, and the usual way of visiting them is by tour.

Guayana's major traveler base is the colonial river port of **Ciudad Bolívar** (p293), easily accessible from Caracas by daily flights or a comfortable nine-hour bus ride. Stay a few days to stroll about the charming streets and museums, before taking a tour to **Canaima** (p312) and the famous **Angel Falls** (Salto Ángel; p310). Your next adventures might involve the vast, enchanting highlands of **Gran Sabana** (p315) and the massive table mountain of **Roraima** (p319). Tours to both can be bought in Ciudad Bolívar, or you can go by bus along a spectacular road to **Santa Elena de Uairén** (p322) and buy both tours more cheaply here.

Ciudad Bolívar is also a springboard for the **Río Caura** (p301), a lovely river 200km southwest, only accessible by tour. Guayana's other big attraction is the **Delta del Orinoco** (p289), and this trip can also be organized from Ciudad Bolívar, or you can go to **Tucupita** (p290) and shop around for a tour.

Some travelers bus to **Puerto Ayacucho** (p329) to see the upper Orinoco and Amazon basins – another off-the-beaten-track adventure and another tour.

Visiting all the listed attractions will take four to six weeks, and a large slice of your budget. Many travelers cross Guayana on their way to Brazil and just visit the main sights en route (Gran Sabana and Roraima, plus the spectacular Angel Falls). Put aside two weeks for these three sights.

CARIBBEAN COASTLINE   **Three to Four Weeks**

The longest stretch of Caribbean coastline in any single country, Venezuela's Caribbean coastline will inundate you with its wealth of beautiful beaches, islands and other natural attractions. The exquisite coral **Archipiélago Los Roques** (p101) is many people's first or last destination, easily accessible from **Caracas** (p55). West of Caracas, nestled in the eastern mountains, is the pretty German town of **Colonia Tovar** (p117). From here, it's a spectacular ride down to the lowlands. A little further west you can take one of two scenic roads up and over the coastal mountains, through the wildlife-rich cloud forests of **Parque Nacional Henri Pittier** (p119). One road emerges at the coastal village of **Puerto Colombia** (p122), surrounded by secluded beaches reached only by boat or a long hike. The other road goes to the picturesque bay of **Playa Cata** (p126).

Taking the long haul back past Caracas, **Puerto La Cruz** (p256) is the jumping-off point to explore the stunning beaches and islands of **Parque Nacional Mochima** (p260). You can hop on a ferry to Isla de Margarita here, or continue first to the historic city of **Cumaná** (p267). You may also want to take a detour southeast to the impressive **Cueva del Guácharo** (p285), or east to **Río Caribe** (p276) and the remote, undeveloped beaches nearby, including idyllic **Playa Medina** (p278). You can then take a boat from Chacopata or Cumaná to the soft, white shores of tourist mecca **Isla de Margarita** (p240).

It's possible to cover this 1450km route in three weeks at a squeeze, but if you're after rest and relaxation don't try to fit in too much. Pick and choose your destinations carefully so you can spend more time chilling out on a beach rather than sitting on a bus.

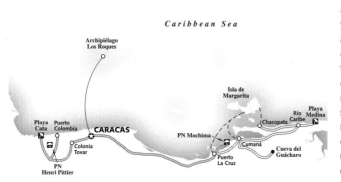

WESTERN LOOP
Three to Six Weeks

This loop covers a mixed bag of natural and cultural attractions. Starting from **Caracas** (p55), you can make the first stop in **Las Trincheras** (p135) and warm up in the world's second-hottest springs. To cool yourself down, take an hour's bus ride to **Parque Nacional Morrocoy** (p155), where you can bathe in the beautiful turquoise waters of the Caribbean.

Next port of call, **Coro** (p142), shelters some of Venezuela's best colonial architecture and is a base for the arid **Península de Paraguaná** (p147) and the lush **Sierra de San Luis** (p153), two lovely and completely different environments. Continuing west, you reach the hot, modern city of **Maracaibo** (p171), from where you can take a side trip to **Laguna de Sinamaica** (p180), where Venezuela's name was born 500 years ago.

A night bus from Maracaibo will whisk you straight to **Mérida** (p185), where you'll probably hang your hat for a week or more, taking advantage of the wide selection of adventure tours, from rafting and paragliding to mountain biking and wildlife safaris.

From Mérida, take a bus on one of Venezuela's most spectacular and dramatic mountain roads to **Valera** (p203). Take a short detour to the old town of **Trujillo** (p205) and then head northwest to **Barquisimeto** (p160), from where it's worth exploring surrounding towns noted for their fine crafts or good wine. You can then return directly to Caracas, or stop at the various regional attractions along the way.

You can do this 1975km loop comfortably by bus in three to four weeks, but you should allow an extra week or two for outdoor activities in the scenic Mérida region – it's the highlight of a fantastic circuit.

TAILORED TRIPS

VENEZUELA 101

'I have a three-week holiday – how can I see the best Venezuela has to offer?' This frequently asked question usually comes from travelers with limited time and a midrange budget; seeing Venezuela's best is easy to do if you invest in local flights and organized tours.

Stay a day or two in **Caracas** (p55) to see the museums, and then travel by air or a full-night bus ride to the Andean hot spot of **Mérida** (p185). This adventure sports region offers every kind of activity – rafting, paragliding, trekking and mountain biking – so allow a few days for some action. Also consider a four-day wildlife safari to **Los Llanos** (p220), organized from Mérida.

Next stop is **Ciudad Bolívar** (p293), where your priority is a three-day tour to the famous **Angel Falls** (p310). Back in town, take a four-day tour to the **Gran Sabana** (p315), an amazing rolling savanna dotted with table mountains and waterfalls. If you have an extra week to spare, consider a memorable trip to the top of **Roraima** (p319).

It's then time to relax on some of Venezuela's fabulous beaches, like the lovely, coral Caribbean **Archipiélago Los Roques** (p101), for two or three days. Time your flight back from the island to Caracas a few hours before your international departure and you won't even leave the airport.

HIKING VENEZUELA

Venezuela has walking for everybody, whether it's a leisurely beach stroll or a trek to a snowcapped peak.

When you arrive in Caracas, you'll find fantastic hiking territory with over 200km of well-signposted trails in **Parque Nacional El Ávila** (p95), just north of the city. More hiking awaits you in **Parque Nacional Henri Pittier** (p119), just two hours west of Caracas by bus, where there are two- or three-day treks from Turmero to Chuao, or shorter hikes. Further west along the coast, you can hike to the top of the unusual **Cerro Santa Ana** (p150), in the middle of the arid Península de Paraguaná, north of Coro.

The widest choice of hiking opportunities is around **Mérida** (p190), where you can easily spend a month tramping local mountain paths. A hike from Mérida to **Los Nevados** (p200) is one of the most popular trips, but if you need something more challenging, treks to the top of the country's highest peaks, **Pico Bolívar** (p198) and **Pico Humboldt** (p199), are the way to go.

The ultimate adventure is a trek up **Roraima** (p319) in Guayana; you need at least five days to complete the trip, plus a day or two to travel to this remote corner of the country.

Snapshot

Contemporary images of Venezuela are inseparable from the grandiose persona of President Hugo Chávez. Depending on your political slant, Chávez is either a dangerous, megalomaniacal autocrat who uses oil money to buy the votes of the impoverished masses while he consolidates power and runs the country into the ground; or he is a beacon of hope and an alternative political paradigm in the ubiquity of globalization and neo-liberalism, a man who stands up to Washington and attempts to remedy social and economic inequities that have plagued his nation and continent since colonialism. Regardless of your feelings about Chávez, he has undoubtedly transformed Venezuela from a primarily apolitical petro-state to an international political touchstone.

The sixth largest country in South America, and the northern crown of the continent, Venezuela is a land of Caribbean beaches, Andean mountains and Amazonian jungle. It is also a land of vast urban centers, massive oil refineries, glittering wealth and grinding poverty. The capital, Caracas is simultaneously home to millions of poor people stuffed into hillside shantytowns and the multimillion dollar Venezuelan fashion industry which includes cosmetics, plastic surgery, clothing design and world-renowned beauty pageant winners. While Chávez and Bush do their dance of mutual animosity, Citgo sells Venezuelan oil at 7-Elevens across the US and Venezuelans use revenues to eat at American fast-food chains, purchase Nike footwear, watch Hollywood films and keep their money at Citibank. Even with Chávez' talks of a New Socialism and bonhomie with Castro, Venezuela is no Cuba: the centrally located Caracas Hooters and the yachts off Isla de Margarita attest to that.

Oil, the battle against corruption, worsening street crime, Chávez' plans to nationalize major industries, assistance to other Latin American Leftist governments and the acrid relationship with the US are serious issues that dominate the headlines in Venezuela. On the lighter side of things, the country is enamored with baseball, beauty queens, telenovelas, music, dance and ice-cold beers (that are sold in miniature cans and bottles so that you can quickly finish them before they ever have a chance to warm up).

Whenever you think that you understand Venezuela, it will surprise you with its varied layers, facets and textures that comprise this ever-evolving nation.

FAST FACTS

Population (2006):
25.7 million

Population growth rate:
1.9%

Adult literacy: 93%

Area: 912,050 sq km

Inflation (2006): 15.8%

GDP growth rate (2006):
8.8%

Unemployment (2006):
8.9%

Number of Miss Worlds
won by Venezuelans: 5

Number of Venezuelan
baseball players in the US
major leagues: 99

History

THE FIRST FEW MILLENNIA

It is generally believed that the first inhabitants of the Americas came from Siberia across the Bering Strait, spread over the North American continent, then moved down to Central and South America in several waves of migration. There is evidence of human habitation in northwest Venezuela going back more than 15,000 years. Steady agriculture was established around the 1st millennium, leading to the first year-round settlements.

Formerly nomadic groups began to develop into larger cultures belonging to three main linguistic families: Carib, Arawak and Chibcha. By the time of the Spanish conquest at the end of the 15th century, some 300,000 to 400,000 indigenous people inhabited the region that is now Venezuela.

The warlike Carib tribes occupied the central and eastern coast, living off fishing and shifting agriculture. Various Arawak groups were scattered over the western plains and north up to the coast. They lived off hunting and food-gathering, and occasionally practiced farming.

The Timote-Cuica tribes, of the Chibcha linguistic family, were the most advanced of Venezuela's pre-Hispanic societies. They lived in the Andes and developed advanced agricultural techniques, including irrigation and terracing. They were also skilled craftspeople, as we can judge by the artifacts they left behind – examples of their fine pottery are shown in museums across the country. No major architectural works have survived, though some smaller sites in the Andean region have recently been unearthed and will be opening for tourism in the next few years.

THE SPANISH ARE COMING!

In 1498, on his third trip to the New World, Christopher Columbus became the first European to set foot on Venezuelan soil. Columbus anchored at the eastern tip of the Península de Paria, just opposite Trinidad. He originally believed that he was on another island, but the voluminous mouth of the Río Orinoco hinted that he had stumbled into something slightly larger.

A year later, explorer Alonso de Ojeda, accompanied by the Italian Amerigo Vespucci, sailed up to the Península de la Guajira, at the western end of present-day Venezuela. On entering Lago de Maracaibo, the Spaniards saw the local indigenous people living in *palafitos* (thatched huts on stilts above the water). They called the land 'Venezuela' (literally 'Little Venice'), perhaps as a sarcastic sailor joke as these rustic reed dwellings didn't exactly match the opulent palaces of the Italian city they knew. The name of Venezuela appeared for the first time on a map in 1500 and has remained to this day. Laguna de Sinamaica (p180) is reputedly the place where the first Spanish sailors saw the *palafitos,* and you can see similar huts there today.

Alonso de Ojeda sailed further west along the coast and briefly explored parts of what is now Colombia. He saw local aborigines wearing gold adornments and was astonished by their wealth. Their stories about fabulous treasures inland gave birth to the myth of El Dorado (The Golden One), a mysterious land abundant in gold. Attracted by these supposed riches, the shores of Venezuela and Colombia became the target of Spanish expeditions,

For a concise and to-the-point introduction to the country's historic, economic, societal and contemporary issues, read *In Focus: Venezuela – A Guide to the People, Politics and Culture,* by James Ferguson.

Venezuela is the only South American mainland country where Columbus landed.

John Hemming's *The Search for El Dorado* is a fascinating insight into the Spanish conquest of Venezuela and Colombia. It reads like a thriller, yet is admirably factual.

TIMELINE **14,000 BC** | **1498**

| The earliest record of human occupation in Venezuela | Christopher Columbus lands in northeastern Venezuela, the first European to see the South American continent |

an obsession with El Dorado driving them into the interior. Their search resulted in the rapid colonization of the land, though El Dorado was never found.

The Spanish established their first settlement on Venezuelan soil around 1500, at Nueva Cádiz, on the small island of Cubagua, just south of Isla de Margarita. Pearl harvesting provided a livelihood for the settlers, and the town developed into a busy port until an earthquake and tidal wave destroyed it in 1541. The earliest Venezuelan town still in existence, Cumaná (p267), on the northeast coast, dates from 1521 and is an enjoyable place to visit, even though earthquakes ruined much of the early Spanish colonial architecture.

The Explorers of South America, by Edward J Goodman, brings to life some of the adventurers who opened the continent to Europeans, from Columbus to Humboldt. Captivating reading.

Officially, most of Venezuela was ruled by Spain from Santo Domingo (present-day capital of the Dominican Republic) until 1717, when it fell under the administration of the newly created viceroyalty of Nueva Granada, with its capital in Bogotá.

The colony's population of indigenous communities and Spanish invaders diversified with the arrival of black slaves, brought from Africa to serve as the workforce. Most of them were set to work on plantations on the Caribbean coast. By the 18th century, Africans surpassed the indigenous population in number.

OUT FROM UNDER THE YOKE

With few exploited gold mines, Venezuela lurked in the shadows of the Spanish Empire for its first three centuries. The country took a more prominent role at the beginning of the 19th century, when Venezuela gave Latin America one of its greatest heroes, Simón Bolívar (see the boxed text opposite).

Francisco de Miranda lit the initial revolutionary flame in 1806. However, his efforts to set up an independent administration in Caracas ended when fellow conspirators handed him over to the Spanish. He was shipped to Spain and died in jail. Bolívar then assumed leadership of the revolution. After unsuccessful initial attempts to defeat the Spaniards at home, he withdrew to Colombia, then to Jamaica, until the opportune moment came in 1817.

The Venezuelan flag was designed by Francisco de Miranda, who, on March 12, 1806, hoisted a yellow, blue and red striped flag on his ship as he headed to Venezuela on his second attempt to initiate an independence movement. Yellow represents the land's wealth, blue the waters separating Venezuela from Spain and red the blood spilled during the independence struggle.

The Napoleonic Wars had just ended, and Bolívar's agent in London was able to raise money and arms, and recruit a small number of British Legion veterans of the Peninsular War. With this force and an army of horsemen from Los Llanos, Bolívar marched over the Andes and defeated the Spanish at the Battle of Boyacá, bringing independence to Colombia in August 1819. Four months later in Angostura (present-day Ciudad Bolívar), the Angostura Congress proclaimed Gran Colombia (Great Colombia), a new state unifying Colombia, Venezuela and Ecuador (though the last two were still under Spanish rule). The memories of the event are still alive in Ciudad Bolívar, and you can see the great mansion where the first congress debated (p294). Venezuela's liberation came on June 24, 1821 at Carabobo, where Bolívar's troops defeated the Spanish royalist army.

Though the least important of Gran Colombia's three provinces, Venezuela bore the brunt of the fighting. Venezuelan patriots fought not only on their own territory, but also in the armies that Bolívar led into Colombia and down the Pacific Coast. By the end of 1824, Bolívar and his assistants had liberated Ecuador, Peru and Bolivia. It's estimated that a quarter of the Venezuelan population died in the independence wars.

1527	1577
The town of Coro is made the first capital of colonial Venezuela	Caracas, founded in 1567 by Captain Diego de Losada, becomes the capital of Venezuela

THE SUCCESSES & FAILURES OF SIMÓN BOLÍVAR

'There have been three great fools in history: Jesus, Don Quixote and I.' This is how Simón Bolívar summed up his life shortly before he died. The man who brought independence from Spanish rule to the entire northwest of South America – today's Venezuela, Colombia, Panama, Ecuador, Peru and Bolivia – died abandoned, rejected and poor.

Simón Bolívar was born in Caracas on July 24, 1783 into a wealthy Creole family, which had come to Venezuela from Spain 200 years earlier. He was just three years old when his father died and nine years old when his mother died. The boy was brought up by his uncle and was given an open-minded tutor and mentor, Simón Rodríguez.

At the age of 16, Bolívar was sent to Spain and France to continue his education. The works of Voltaire and Rousseau introduced him to new, progressive ideas of liberalism, yet he didn't think about a political career at that stage. He married Spaniard María Teresa and the young couple sailed to Caracas to start a new life at the old family hacienda in San Mateo. Unfortunately, María Teresa died of yellow fever just eight months later. Bolívar never married again, though he had many lovers. The most devoted of these was Manuela Sáenz, whom he met in Quito in 1822 and who stayed with him almost until his final days.

The death of María Teresa marked a drastic shift in Bolívar's destiny. He returned to France, where he met with the leaders of the French Revolution, then traveled to the USA to take a close look at the new order after the American Revolutionary War. By the time he returned to Caracas in 1807, he was full of revolutionary theories and experiences taken from these two successful examples. It didn't take him long to join clandestine pro-independence circles.

Bolívar's military career began under Francisco de Miranda, but after Miranda was captured by the Spaniards in 1812, Bolívar took command. Over the following decade, he hardly had a moment's rest, as battle followed battle with astonishing frequency. He personally commanded the independence forces in 35 victorious battles, including the key Battle of Carabobo, which brought freedom to Venezuela.

Bolívar's long-awaited dream of a unified republic comprising Colombia, Venezuela and Ecuador became reality, but Gran Colombia soon began to disintegrate. As separatist tendencies escalated, Bolívar assumed dictatorship in 1828, yet this step brought more harm than good and his popularity waned. A short time later, he miraculously escaped an assassination attempt in Bogotá. Disillusioned and in bad health, he resigned from the presidency in early 1830 and decided to leave for Europe.

When he reached Santa Marta, Colombia, to board a ship bound for France, he was already very ill and depressed. He died in Santa Marta, abandoned, rejected and penniless on December 17, 1830, at the age of just 47.

GREAT COLOMBIA & GREATER PROBLEMS

Bolívar's dream of a unified republic fell apart even before he died in 1830. On his deathbed, he proclaimed: 'America is ungovernable. The man who serves a revolution plows the sea. This nation will fall inevitably into the hands of the unruly mob and then will pass into the hands of almost indistinguishable petty tyrants.' Unfortunately, he wasn't far off the mark. Gran Colombia began to collapse from the moment of its birth; the central regime was incapable of governing the immense country with its racial and regional differences. The new state existed for only a decade before splitting into three separate countries.

Following Venezuela's separation from Gran Colombia, the Venezuelan congress approved a new constitution and – incredibly – banned Bolívar from his homeland. It took the Venezuelan nation 12 years to acknowledge

1725	**1783**
Venezuela's first university, the Universidad Real y Pontificia de Caracas, is founded	National hero Simón Bolívar is born in Caracas on July 24

its debt to the man to whom it owed its freedom. In 1842, Bolívar's remains were brought from Santa Marta, Colombia, where he died, to Caracas and entombed in the cathedral. In 1876 they were solemnly transferred to the Panteón Nacional (p67) in Caracas, where they now rest in a bronze sarcophagus.

Enter the era of 'indistinguishable petty tyrants.' The post-independence period in Venezuela was marked by serious governmental problems that continued for more than a century. These were times of despotism and anarchy, with the country being ruled by a series of military dictators known as caudillos.

The first of the caudillos, General José Antonio Páez, controlled the country for 18 years (1830–48). It was a tough rule, but it established a certain political stability and put the weak economy on its feet. The period that followed was an almost uninterrupted chain of civil wars that was only stopped by another long-lived dictator, General Antonio Guzmán Blanco (1870–88). He launched a broad program of reform, including a new constitution, and assured some temporary stability, but his despotic rule triggered wide, popular opposition, and when he stepped down the country plunged again into civil war.

In the 1840s, Venezuela raised the question of its eastern border with British Guiana (present-day Guyana), claiming as much as two-thirds of Guiana, up to the Río Esequibo. The issue was a subject of lengthy diplomatic negotiations and was eventually settled in 1899 by an arbitration tribunal, which gave rights over the questioned territory to Great Britain. Despite the ruling, Venezuela maintains its claim to this day. All maps produced in Venezuela have this chunk of Guyana within Venezuela's boundaries, labeled 'Zona en Reclamación.'

Another conflict that led to serious international tension was Venezuela's failure to meet payments to Great Britain, Italy and Germany on loans accumulated during the government of yet another caudillo, General Cipriano Castro (1899–1908). In response, the three European countries sent their navies to blockade Venezuelan seaports in 1902.

THE NATIONAL SOAP OPERA

The first half of the 20th century was dominated by five successive military rulers from the Andean state of Táchira. The longest lasting and most tyrannical was General Juan Vicente Gómez, who seized power in 1908 and didn't relinquish it until his death in 1935. Gómez phased out the parliament, squelched the opposition and monopolized power.

The discovery of oil in the 1910s helped the Gómez regime to put the national economy on its feet. By the late 1920s, Venezuela was the world's largest exporter of oil, which not only contributed to economic recovery but also enabled the government to pay off the country's entire foreign debt. As in most petro-states, almost none of the oil wealth made its way to the common citizen. The vast majority of Venezuelans continued to live in poverty with little or no educational or health facilities, let alone reasonable housing. Fast oil money also led to the neglect of agriculture and to the development of other types of production. It was easier to just import everything from abroad, which worked for a while, but proved unsustainable.

Gabriel García Márquez' historical novel *The General in his Labyrinth* recounts the tragic final months of Simón Bolívar's life. It's a powerful and beautifully written work from one of Latin America's most celebrated literary figures.

A moving film directed by Diego Rísquez, *Manuela Sáenz: La Libertadora del Libertador* (2000) jumps between an old woman in a plague-ridden Peruvian town and her former life as the feisty mistress of Simón Bolívar.

Tensions rose dangerously during the following dictatorships, exploding in 1945 when Rómulo Betancourt, leader of the left-wing Acción Democrática (AD) party, took control of the government. A new constitution was adopted in 1947, and noted novelist Rómulo Gallegos became president in Venezuela's first democratic election. The inevitable coup took place only eight months after Gallegos' election, with Colonel Marcos Pérez Jiménez emerging as the leader. Once in control, he smashed the opposition and plowed oil money into public works and built up Caracas. He superficially modernized the country but the mushrooming development did not heal the country's economic and social disparities, nor the bitter resentment that lingered from the coup.

THE BOOM/BUST CYCLE

Pérez Jiménez was overthrown in 1958 by a coalition of civilians and navy and air-force officers. The country returned to democratic rule and Rómulo Betancourt was elected president. He enjoyed popular support and actually completed the constitutional five-year term of office – the first democratically elected Venezuelan president to do so. Since then, all changes of president have been by constitutional means, although the last decade has seen a few hiccups.

During the term of President Rafael Caldera (1969–74), the steady stream of oil money flowed into the country's coffers keeping the economy buoyant. President Carlos Andrés Pérez (1974–79) benefited from the oil bonanza – not only did production of oil rise but, more importantly, the price quadrupled following the Arab-Israeli war in 1973. In 1975 Pérez nationalized the iron-ore and oil industries and went on a spending spree; imported luxury goods crammed shops and the nation got the impression that El Dorado had finally materialized.

In the late 1970s, the growing international recession and oil glut began to shake Venezuela's economy. Oil revenues declined, pushing up unemployment and inflation, and once more forcing the country into foreign debt. The 1988 drop in world oil prices cut the country's revenue in half, casting

> Written with an insider's knowledge by the prominent Venezuelan novelist, historian and politician Arturo Uslar Pietri, *Half a Millennium of Venezuela* provides a comprehensive record of the country's events, from the Spanish conquest to modern times.

VENEZUELA'S BLACK GOLD

Oil is Venezuela's principal natural resource and the heart of its economy. Discovered here in 1914, it soon turned Venezuela from a poor debtor nation into one of South America's richest countries. Until 1970, Venezuela was the world's largest oil exporter, and though it was overtaken by Middle Eastern countries, its oil production has expanded year after year.

As cofounder of the Organization of the Petroleum Exporting Countries (OPEC), Venezuela was influential in the fourfold rise in oil prices introduced in 1973–74, which quadrupled the country's revenue. On this strength, Venezuela borrowed heavily from foreign banks to import almost everything other than oil. Predictably, oil has overshadowed other sectors of the economy.

Today Venezuela is the world's fourth-largest oil producer, and the state oil company Petróleos de Venezuela Sociedad Anónima (PDVSA) is one of the world's biggest oil corporations. Oil provides 80% of Venezuela's export revenues, yet this dependence on oil leaves Venezuela vulnerable to fluctuations in the global economy. The main oil deposits are beneath and around Lago de Maracaibo, but other important reserves have been discovered and exploited in Los Llanos and Delta del Orinoco.

1821	1849
Bolívar's victory in the Battle of Carabobo seals the independence of Venezuela	Rich lodes of gold are found in Guayana, generating one of the world's greatest gold rushes

The gripping film *Amaneció de Golpe* (1999), directed by Carlos Azpúrua, portrays Venezuelan political unrest in the early 1990s. It tells how military man Hugo Chávez led an unsuccessful coup against then-president Carlos Andrés Pérez.

doubt on Venezuela's ability to pay off its debt. Austerity measures introduced in 1989 by Pérez Jiménez (elected for the second time) triggered a wave of protests, culminating in the loss of more than 300 lives in three days of bloody riots known as 'El Caracazo.' Further austerity measures sparked protests that often escalated into riots. Strikes and street demonstrations continued to be part of everyday life.

To make matters worse, there were two attempted coups d'état in 1992. The first, in February, was led by paratrooper Colonel Hugo Chávez. Shooting throughout Caracas claimed more than 20 lives, but the government retained control. Chávez was sentenced to long-term imprisonment. The second attempt, in November, was led by junior air-force officers. The air battle over Caracas, with war planes flying between skyscrapers, gave the coup a cinematic, if not apocalyptic, dimension. The Palacio de Miraflores, the presidential palace, was bombed and partially destroyed. The army was called to defend the president, and this time more than 100 people died.

Corruption, bank failures and loan defaults plagued the government through the mid-1990s. In 1995, Venezuela was forced to devalue the currency by more than 70%. By the end of 1998, two-thirds of Venezuela's 23 million inhabitants were living below the poverty line. Drug-trafficking and crime had increased and Colombian guerrillas had dramatically expanded their operations into Venezuela's frontier areas.

The 1999 constitution changed the country's name from República de Venezuela to República Bolivariana de Venezuela, requiring replacement of everything bearing the name, from coins and banknotes to passports and the coat of arms.

VEERING TO THE LEFT

There is nothing better in political theater than a dramatic comeback. The 1998 election put Hugo Chávez, the leader of the 1992 failed coup, into the presidency. After being pardoned in 1994, Chávez embarked on an aggressive populist campaign: comparing himself to Bolívar, promising help (and handouts) to the poorest masses and positioning himself in opposition to the US-influenced free-market economy. He vowed to produce a great, if vague, 'peaceful and democratic social revolution.'

Since then, however, Chávez' 'social revolution' has been anything but peaceful. Shortly after taking office, Chávez set about rewriting the constitution. The new document was approved in a referendum in December 1999, granting him new and sweeping powers. The introduction of a package of new decree laws in 2001 was met with angry protests, and was followed by a massive and violent strike in April 2002. It culminated in a coup d'état run by military leaders sponsored by a business lobby, in which Chávez was forced to resign. He regained power two days later, but this only intensified the conflict.

Shot by two Irish documentary filmmakers, Kim Bartley & Donnacha O'Briain, who were inside the presidential palace during the coup d'état of April 2002, *The Revolution Will Not Be Televised* contains compelling firsthand footage of the events.

While the popular tensions rose, in December 2002 the opposition called a general strike in an attempt to oust the president. The nationwide strike paralyzed the country, including its vital oil industry and a good part of the private sector. After 63 days, the opposition finally called off the strike, which had cost the country 7.6% of its GDP and further devastated the oil-based economy. Chávez again survived and claimed victory.

THE CHÁVEZ ERA

National politics continued to be shaky until Chávez won a 2004 referendum and consolidated his power. Emboldened by greater political support and his pockets swollen by high oil prices, Chávez quickly moved to expand his influence beyond the borders of Venezuela, reaching out to other Leftist leaders in Bolivia,

1908–35	1914
Venezuela experiences a period of tyrannical dictatorial rule under General Juan Vicente Gómez	The first oil well is sunk in Lago de Maracaibo, precipitating the oil boom and completely changing Venezuela

Argentina, Cuba, Uruguay, Chile and Brazil. He has openly allied himself with Cuba's Fidel Castro, supported the successful Leftist candidacy of Bolivia's Evo Morales and Leftist candidates in Peru and Mexico who did not win office. Not afraid to make his opinion heard, Chávez also called former Mexican President, and free-trade supporter, Vicente Fox a 'puppy dog of the (US) empire.'

Chávez hopes to establish a Latin American political bloc to offer an alternative to US hegemony in the region. He made an international reputation for himself with his outspoken opposition to US president George W Bush and the proposed Free Trade Area of the Americas (FTAA) at the 2005 Summit of the Americas in Mar del Plata, Argentina.

In 2005, shortly after Caracas hosted the 6th World Social Forum, Chávez started a highly publicized and dubiously intentioned program to provide reduced-priced heating oil for impoverished people in the US. The program was expanded in 2006 to include four of New York City's five boroughs, providing 25 million gallons of fuel for low-income New Yorkers at 40% off the wholesale price. While the program obviously aided hundreds of thousands of poor New Yorkers, it was used as a political jab to Chávez' enemy Bush.

In 2006, Chávez announced Venezuela's bid to win the Latin American and Caribbean nonpermanent seat on the UN Security Council. The US encouraged other nations to vote for Guatemala instead. Chávez tried to get China to intervene by offering discounted oil, but the voting arrived at

HUGO CHÁVEZ: THE EARLY YEARS

Hugo Chávez Rivas was born on July 28, 1954 in a small village in Los Llanos. The second son of two schoolteachers, he is of mixed indigenous, African, and Spanish descent. At an early age, Chávez was sent to Sabaneta to live with his paternal grandmother. There, Chávez pursued hobbies such as painting, singing and baseball. He was later forced to relocate to the town of Barinas to attend high school. At age 17, Chávez enrolled at the Venezuelan Academy of Military Sciences. After graduating in 1975 as a sub-lieutenant with a degree in Military Arts and Science, Chávez entered military service for several months. He was then allowed to pursue graduate studies in political science at Simón Bolívar University in Caracas.

Over the course of his college years, Chávez and fellow students developed a fervently left-nationalist doctrine that they termed Bolivarianism, inspired by the Pan-Americanist philosophies of 19th-century Venezuelan revolutionary Simón Bolívar and the teachings of various socialist and communist leaders. Chávez played both baseball and softball with the Criollitos de Venezuela, progressing with them to the Venezuelan National Baseball Championships in 1969. Chávez also authored numerous poems, stories and theatrical pieces.

Upon completing his studies, Chávez entered active-duty military service as a member of a counter insurgency battalion stationed in Barinas. Chávez' military career lasted 17 years, eventually rising to the rank of lieutenant colonel. He also held a series of teaching and staffing positions at the Military Academy of Venezuela, where he was first acknowledged by his peers for his oratorical style and spirited critique of Venezuelan government and society. At this time, Chávez established the Revolutionary Bolivarian Movement-200 (MBR-200). Afterwards, he rose to fill a number of sensitive high-level positions in Caracas and was decorated several times.

After an extended period of popular dissatisfaction and economic decline under the administration of President Carlos Andrés Pérez, Chávez staged an unsuccessful coup d'état on February 4, 1992. Thus, he launched a political career that will apparently endure for one or two decades or more.

1947	1998
Venezuela holds its first-ever democratic election, in which popular novelist Rómulo Gallegos becomes president	Hugo Chávez is elected president in a landslide victory

MISSION POSSIBLE

Chávez' 'Bolivarian Revolution' is known for its assistance to Venezuela's poorest citizens. The government sponsored *misiónes* are the outreach programs that transfer funds and services to these people and do a bit of social/political engineering. You will see billboards for these public works along the highways and on the sides of buildings. More and more visitors are coming to observe the *misiónes* or to volunteer with them. The following are some of the more well known and important *misiónes:*

Misión Barrio Adentro 'Inside the Neighborhood' has created free community health-care clinics in the impoverished barrios.

Misión Ribas Provides a second educational chance for some five million Venezuelan high school dropouts.

Misión Robinson Volunteers teach reading, writing and arithmetic to millions of illiterate Venezuelan adults.

Misión Sucre Offers basic education courses to the two million adult Venezuelans who had not completed their elementary-level education.

Misión Vuelta al Campo 'Return to the Countryside' aims to reverse the trend of urban migration and return the urban poor to the countryside.

Misión Vuelvan Caras 'About Face' has the lofty aim of transforming the economy from financial goals to the goal of a generally improved society that is fair to all.

Misión Zamora The controversial program that seeks to expropriate unused land and redistribute it to poor Venezuelans.

a stalemate. Panama was chosen as a consensus candidate and claimed the council seat, though Venezuela clearly felt sabotaged by the US.

On September 20, 2006, Chávez addressed the UN General Assembly. In the speech, he referred to Bush as 'the devil,' adding that Bush (who had delivered a speech to the UN the day before), had come 'to preserve the current pattern of domination, exploitation and pillage of the peoples of the world.'

The end of 2006 was enveloped in the lead-up to the December 3 presidential election. Chávez' closest challenger, Manuel Rosales, accused the president of providing impractical political favors and aid to other countries while poverty and crime increased at home, and also challenged Chávez' government-approved land takeovers (for redistribution to the landless) and the military build-up for a hypothetical US invasion. Chávez wrote Rosales off as a lackey for the US and refused to debate him on TV.

Chávez again won the national election with 63% of the vote and was thereby elected to another six-year term. The Organization of American States and the Carter Center certified the results. After his victory, Chávez promised a more aggressive turn toward socialism and, at the time of writing this book, has made moves to nationalize the telecommunications (CANTV) and electrical industries. He is also asking to eliminate the autonomy of the Central Bank and dissolve many opposition political parties and opposition media outlets. Chávez has made no secret of the fact that he plans to amend the national constitution so that he can run for president again in 2012.

1999	2006
Violent mudslides devastate the country's central coast, claiming up to 50,000 lives	Chávez wins re-election and is poised to hold power through 2012 – at least

The Culture

THE NATIONAL PSYCHE

Venezuela is proud of its national history. The War of Independence and Simón Bolívar are championed throughout the country. However, unlike some neighboring South American nations, there are few obvious defining factors of contemporary Venezuelan culture. Many attribute this to the fact that as a petrol state, Venezuela has spent much of its existence consuming from abroad (food, music, clothes, movies, furniture, cars, you name it) and not needing or bothering to produce much at home.

But just like the oil pumped out of the country, Venezuela does produce raw materials and raw talent. Two things that are produced in Venezuela, and produced quite well, are beauty queens and *béisbol* (baseball) players. Venezuelan women have won more international beauty competitions than any other country, including five Miss Worlds, four Miss Universes and countless other titles.

The North American Major League Baseball has its fair share of Venezuelan athletes, including World Series winning manager, Ozzie Guillen and pitcher Anibal Sanchez who threw a no-hitter in his rookie season. Baseball is played throughout the country too and it's common to see casual games in construction sites or along the side of highways.

The national sport goes hand in hand with the national drinks of rum and ice-cold beer. Men in Caracas tend to opt for scotch (Johnny Walker Black Label is the brand of choice) instead as they like to show their big-city sophistication.

Even in the face of deep-seated national ills and social tensions – political divisions, concerns about rising levels of crime and economic instability – Venezuelans are full of life and humor. Children are given creative, arcane or sometimes downright strange names that draw on English, Arabic and indigenous languages, and even a mix of names of landmarks like Canaima

Carmen Zubillaga won the 1955 Miss World contest for Venezuela. She was the first South American woman to win the title.

AND THE WINNER IS...MISS VENEZUELA!

Over the last 50 years, Venezuela has won more international beauty contests than anywhere else in the world. As such, it is a country afflicted with beauty-pageant fever, and has a thriving industry dedicated to finding the nation's next winner. The TV station that broadcasts the Miss Venezuela pageant pays all the costs of grooming and dressing the women selected, and their full-time training (yes, training) costs many tens of thousands of dollars each.

Here are five more facts about the beauty industry in Venezuela that may surprise you:

- Beauty queen or president – winner of Miss World in 1981, Irene Saez, was subsequently elected mayor of Chacao in Caracas and governor of Isla de Margarita. She even ran in the presidential elections of 1999 (losing to Hugo Chávez).

- Surfeit salons – Caracas lists over 900 beauty salons in the *Yellow Pages*. That works out to be one beauty salon for every two restaurants or cafés!

- Big spenders – a market research study has found that the average Venezuelan spends one-fifth of their income on personal grooming and beauty products.

- Body perfect – the plastic surgery industry in Caracas is the most profitable industry on the continent pro rata.

- Double cup – Venezuelans have twice won the annual Miss Universe and Miss World competitions simultaneously – an achievement unmatched by any other nation.

VENEZUELAN TIME & SPACE

Like many Latin Americans, Venezuelans have their own notion of time. And time-related termin-
ology here is not necessarily predictable. For example, *mañana* (literally 'tomorrow') can mean
anytime in the indefinite future. Similarly, the word *ahora* (literally 'now' or 'in a moment'), often
used in charming, diminutive forms such as *ahorita* or *ahoritica,* also has a flexible meaning. If
you're waiting for a bus and ask bystanders when it should arrive, take it easy when they reply
ahorita viene (it's coming) because this can just as easily mean in a few hour's as in a minute's
time.

Venezuelans invited to lunch also regard it as normal to arrive late. So be prepared: take a
newspaper! Many offices have a similarly flexible grasp of working hours. Don't expect to arrange anything if you arrive less than half an hour before its statutory lunch break or official
closing time.

Some Venezuelans, particularly rural dwellers, also have a different notion of space. If they
say that something you're looking for is *allí mismito* (just around here) or *cerquitica* (very close),
it may still be an hour's walk to get there. The best bet is to keep an open mind and don't be
in a rush, or you'll find yourself at odds with the local pace of life.

---

and Roraima. People are open, willing to talk and not shy about striking up
conversations with strangers – particularly in the western and Andean regions
that are known to be more extroverted and friendly. Wherever you are, you're
unlikely to be alone or feel isolated, especially if you can speak a little Spanish.
There's always a *rumba* (party) brewing somewhere. So forget schedules and
organized plans and warm up to the Venezuelan way of being.

LIFESTYLE

As with other aspects of the country, Venezuelan lifestyle has a striking
amount of variety. Venezuela holds an intriguing, if sometimes precarious,
marriage of modern and traditional. This is a phenomenon found in many
petro-states and certain members of the country have become ridiculously
wealthy, while many have watched from the sideline. During earlier oil
booms, massive amounts of consumer goods – from food, to furniture to
automobiles – were imported from abroad and gave certain sectors of the
society a modern, if not cosmopolitan, feel. Outside of the urban centers life
continued on much as usual. Tourism and the new oil boom have started
to develop some of the countryside but it is still possible to see a horse and
buggy roll alongside a Mercedes in traffic.

On the fringes of the country, nomadic indigenous groups who avoid
contact with outsiders, including even other indigenous groups, still exist.
The lives of the Ye'Kwana indigenous community near the Brazilian border
have about as much in common with Caracas fashionistas, Maracaibo oil
businessmen or Mérida mountain bikers as someone from the interior of
Senegal has with a Parisian banker; they have some political ties and speak
a version of the same language, but that's about it.

Such variety makes generalities difficult, but it is fair to say that most
Venezuelans are family-oriented and their lives are remarkably open and
public. Family life is of central importance, and at the center of this is the
mother figure. Children almost always live with their families until they are
married and will care for their aging parents, though this is changing as many
younger people are now trying to move and work abroad.

The climate and the restricted space of the majority of Venezuelan homes
create a more open, public life. Consequently, many activities takes place
outside the home: in front of the house, in the street, in a bar or at the market. Don't be surprised to see people dancing to the tune of the car stereo in

While many books have
been written on the
Yanomami culture, *Into
the Heart* (Kenneth Good
& David Chanoff, 1991) is
one of the most engag-
ing. It describes Good's
life and marriage in the
Amazonian tribe.

the streets or drinking a leisurely beer together on the sidewalk curb. And Venezuelans don't hold back in these public places either. Personal affairs are discussed loudly and without embarrassment, irrespective of who may be listening. Office employees happily gossip about private love affairs and personal problems, completely oblivious to the glares of their waiting customers.

Personal space is similarly disregarded in much of Venezuela; people waiting to use public phones will squash themselves up against the person calling, and streets and parks are filled with couples kissing passionately, blind to everyone passing around them. The exception to this rule is for gays and lesbians. Sexuality is highly stereotyped in Venezuela's macho male culture, and in this environment homosexuality tends to be swept under the carpet, except in more cosmopolitan areas like Caracas and parts of Mérida.

Noise is also a constant companion in Venezuela. Locals go undisturbed by blaring music, vehicles as noisy as tanks and horns that are used constantly, even in traffic jams. Street vendors screech at potential customers, and people converse at a volume that to outsiders can suggest a heated argument.

However, while Venezuelans are open and laid-back in their public habits, security is high priority in the home. An estimated 75% of families live below the poverty line, and a similar percentage of the population live tightly packed together in urban towns and cities. As such, it's all too common for haphazardly built *barrios* (shantytowns) to sit directly alongside opulent hillside mansions. In the resulting scramble for security, city apartment blocks have come to resemble enormous birdcages with their abundance of iron-barred windows and security fences.

> Carlos the Jackal (aka Ilich Ramírez Sánchez), the world's most notorious assassin and a member of the Popular Front for Liberation of Palestine, was born in Caracas in 1949.

Discrimination

Given that the vast majority of Venezuelans are of mixed race, it's not surprising that they profess to be a nation that doesn't judge a person by their skin color. However, under the surface there remains prejudice against the darker-skinned descendants of African slaves. The pervading ideal of beauty values light skin, blond hair and light-colored eyes – a rather sad state of affairs given that only 20% of the population are classified as 'white.' There are rarely explicit displays of racial discrimination in businesses or other public locales, but skin color is often tied to one's place in the social/economic hierarchy and people can be discriminated against on account of that.

The more openly expressed social distinction in Venezuela is by wealth and power. As in most countries, the city folk, like the *caraqueños* (Caracas locals), frequently ridicule the lower social classes as *monos* (monkeys) and deride

---

DOS & DON'TS

- Be careful when discussing politics. Showing excessive support or disdain for the Chávez government can provoke ire in the wrong company.

- Litter is a fact of life in Venezuela. Making obvious comments about the problem will only offend people. On the other side of the issue, don't litter just because you see locals doing it.

- Never show any disrespect for Bolívar – he is a saint to Venezuelans. Even sitting with your feet up on a bench in Plaza Bolívar, crossing the plaza wearing shorts, or carrying bulky parcels (or even a backpack) across the square may provoke piqued strangers to hassle you.

- If you ask for information or directions, don't bank on a correct answer. Polite campesinos (country folk) may often tell you anything just to appear helpful. Ask several people to be sure and avoid questions that can be answered by just 'yes' or 'no'; instead of 'Is this the way to…?' ask 'Which is the way to…?'

PREVENTING CHILD SEX TOURISM IN VENEZUELA *Beyond Borders*

Tragically, the exploitation of local children by tourists is becoming more prevalent throughout Latin America, including Venezuela. Various socioeconomic factors make children susceptible to sexual exploitation, and some tourists choose to take advantage of their vulnerable position.

Sexual exploitation has serious, lifelong effects on children. It is a crime and a violation of human rights.

Venezuela has laws against sexual exploitation of children. Many countries have enacted extraterritorial legislation that allows travelers to be charged as though the exploitation happened in their home country.

Responsible travelers can help stop child sex tourism by reporting it. It's important not to ignore suspicious behavior. You can report the incident to local authorities and if you know the nationality of the perpetrator, report it to their embassy.

For more information, contact the following organizations:

Beyond Borders (www.beyondborders.org) The Canadian affiliate of Ecpat. It aims to advance the rights of children to be free from abuse and exploitation without regard to race, religion, gender or sexual orientation.

Cecodap (☎ 0212-951-4079) A Venezuelan organization that works to promote and defend the rights of children and youth.

Ecpat (End Child Prostitution, Child Pornography and Trafficking of Children for Sexual Purposes; www.ecpat.org) A global network working on child-exploitation issues with over 70 affiliate organizations around the world.

---

the 'unsophisticated' ways of the campesinos (country folk). Recent political turmoil has further polarized this rich–poor mentality, and there is often deep resentment of the richer classes from the poorer sectors of society.

POPULATION

Venezuela's population density is a low 26 people per square kilometer. However the population is unevenly distributed. Seventy-five percent of Venezuelans live in towns and cities. Over one-fifth of the country's population lives in Caracas alone, while Los Llanos and Guayana are relatively empty.

About 70% of the population is a blend of European, indigenous and African ancestry, or any two of the three. The rest are full European (about 20%), African (8%) or indigenous (2%).

Of that 2% that are indigenous, there are about 24 highly diverse groups, comprising some 535,000 people that are scattered throughout the country. The main indigenous communities include the Guajiro, north of Maracaibo; the Piaroa, Guajibo, Ye'Kwana (Yekuana) and Yanomami, all in the Amazon; the Warao in the Delta del Orinoco; and the Pemón in southeastern Guayana.

Venezuela's rate of population growth stands at 2.2%, one of the highest in Latin America. It has also been the destination for significant post-WWII immigration from Europe (estimated at about one million), mostly from Spain, Italy and Portugal, but it nearly stopped in the 1960s. From the 1950s on, there has been a stream of immigrants from other South American countries, particularly Colombia. Venezuela also has some Middle Eastern communities, notably from Lebanon. Most have settled in Caracas.

Almost half of the total population of Venezuela is aged 19 or younger.

SPORTS

Soccer? What soccer? In Venezuela, baseball rules supreme. The professional baseball league is composed of eight teams: Caracas, La Guaira, Maracaibo, Valencia, Barquisimeto, Maracay, Puerto La Cruz and Cabimas. Many Venezuelans have gone on to fame and fortune in US Major League Baseball. In 2005, Ozzie Guillen (a native of Ocumare del Tuy in Miranda state), managed the Chicago White Sox to their first World Series championship in 88 years.

The biggest rivalry in the Venezuelan league is between the two top teams: Leones del Caracas and Navegantes del Magallanes (Valencia).

The next most popular sport is *baloncesto* (basketball), followed by *fútbol* (soccer), with a professional league playing August to May. In the past the national side has been prone to embarrassing defeats against fellow Latin Americans, but recent successes are slowly raising *fútbol* in the popularity stakes.

Horse races have been run in Los Llanos for centuries, but they are now run on international-style racetracks, grandstands and betting included. A more bloodthirsty spectator sport is cockfighting, and *galleras* (cockfight rings) can be found in most cities.

The Spanish *corrida* (bullfight) also found fertile soil in Venezuela, and most cities have their own *plaza de toros* (bullring). The bullfighting season peaks during Carnaval, when top-ranking matadors are invited from Spain and Latin America. Also thrilling – but bloodless – is the *coleo,* a rodeo popular in Los Llanos, in which four riders compete to bring down a bull after grabbing it by the tail from a galloping horse.

Less risky to participate in is *bolas criollas,* the Venezuelan variety of lawn bowling, each team aiming wooden balls at the smaller *mingo.* Similarly, street games of chess and dominoes have plenty of addicts throughout the country, and visitors are welcome to join in.

While not known as a South American soccer (football) powerhouse, Venezuela is trying to raise the sport's profile in the country and is host to the 2007 Copa America (American Cup).

MEDIA

Freedom of the press has become a more sensitive subject in Venezuela during recent times. President Chávez' hands-on relationship with the media has had a mixed reception, invoking some mutterings of dictatorship and muzzling of free expression.

Opposition media have had broadcasting licenses pulled or other moves to shut them down or limit antigovernment editorializing. On the other hand, the president has won the hearts of many through his use of the government-run media. He will frequently talk informally to the nation via TV appearances that can last for hours, and he hosts a regular radio program called *Aló Presidente* in which he speaks directly to the people about current issues, encouraging a feeling of inclusion and openness in his government. It is sort of like Oprah meets Fidel Castro.

Venezuelan Gustavo Cisneros is the largest shareholder in Univision, the US's leading Spanish-language television network.

RELIGION

About 95% of Venezuelans are Roman Catholics. Many indigenous groups adopted Catholicism and only a few isolated tribes still practice their ancient beliefs. Various Protestant churches in Venezuela have also gained importance, and there are small populations of Jews and Muslims.

A few curious religious cults have also spread throughout the country, including that of María Lionza (see the boxed text p165). And the country's most important holy figure is José Gregorio Hernández (see the boxed text p74). You'll see his well-attired statuettes in homes, shops and churches. Look for the black felt hat and smart suit.

To keep track of the country's current political and economic affairs, the best English-language news website is www .venezuelanalysis.com.

ARTS
Music

Music is omnipresent in Venezuela, though the country doesn't produce a lot of music of its own (and produces even less music for export). The most common types of popular music are salsa, merengue and *reggaetón* from the Caribbean and *vallenato* (popular folk music from the Colombia's Caribbean region). The king of Venezuelan salsa is Oscar D'León (1943–). He has recorded a staggering 60 albums.

North American and European pop – everything from rock to hip-hop to house – is influential among urban youth (who account for the majority of the population). *Reggaetón* is the biggest phenomenon among youth culture. The music, much of which comes from Puerto Rico, fuses hip-hop with a hybrid of reggae, dancehall (a contemporary offshoot of reggae with faster, digital beats and an MC) and traditional Latin-music beats. The music has a decidedly sexual content with a gangsta pose and rather risqué dancing. Chávez has tried to curb the influence of foreign music, mandating that 50% of all radio airplay must be Venezuelan music and, of that music, 50% must be 'traditional.' As is to be expected, few teenagers like to be told what to listen to by a politician in his 50s.

The country's most popular folk rhythm is the *joropo*, also called *música llanera*, which developed in Los Llanos (see p230). The *joropo* is usually sung and accompanied by the harp, *cuatro* (a small, four-stringed guitar) and maracas. The *joropo* song 'Alma Llanera' has become an unofficial national anthem.

Joropo apart, regional beats are plentiful. In the eastern part of the country you'll hear, depending on where you are, the *estribillo, polo margariteño, malagueñas, fulías* and *jotas*. In the west, the *gaita* is typical of the Maracaibo region, while the *bambuco* is a popular Andean rhythm. The central coast echoes with African drumbeats, a mark of the sizable black population.

European classical music emerged in Venezuela only in the 19th century. The first composers of note include José Angel Lamas (1775–1814) and Cayetano Carreño Rodríguez (1774–1836), both of whom wrote religious music. However, the most prominent figure in Venezuela's classical music was Teresa Carreño (1853–1917), a pianist and composer. Born in Caracas, she was just seven years old when she composed her first work, a polka that was performed by a military band in Caracas. At the age of nine, she held her first concert in New York.

Caracas is an exciting center of Latin pop and the 'rock *en español*' movement, which harnesses the rhythm and energy of Latin beats and combines them with international and alternative rock trends. The most famous

Caracas-born pop singer and songwriter Mayré Martínez won the first season of the reality show Latin American Idol in 2006.

RECOMMENDED LISTENING

- *The New Sound of the Venezuelan Gozadera* (Amigos Invisibles, 1998) For funky, electro-influenced Venezuelan dance music, you won't get much better than these guys.

- *Songs of Venezuela* (Soledad Bravo, 1995) Venezuelan institution Soledad Bravo has recorded more than 30 albums and taken her heartfelt voice all around the world.

- *Donde Esta el Futuro* (Desorden Publico, 1999) Features many remixed early hits for this ever-energetic ska band.

- *Inolvidable* (José Luis Rodriguez, 1997) The silky voice of 'El Puma' crooning impossibly romantic Latin ballads is enough to make icebergs melt.

- *Al Pueblo lo que es de César* (Ali Primera, 1968) Prolific folk singer of the '60s; an icon to Venezuelan revolutionaries.

- *Carreño – Piano Works* (2000) The wonderful classical works of pianist and composer Teresa Carreño, performed by Alexandra Oehler.

- *Venezuela y su Folklore: A Taste of Venezuela* (Grupo Barlovento, 1998) Broad range of traditional folk music from *joropo* to *bambuco*.

- *El Diablo Suelto: Guitar Music of Venezuela* (Sony International, 2003) A masterclass in the harp, guitar and *cuatro* (small four-stringed guitar).

product of this scene is the Grammy-winning Los Amigos Invisibles, who now reside in North America.

Dance

Given the importance of music in Venezuela, it's not surprising that dance also plays a vital role. Indeed it's all too common to hear mothers threatening their sons to learn 'or you'll never find a girlfriend!' Dancing here is more than a pastime, it's an essential social skill. Popular dances include salsa and *cumbia*.

Dances were also an integral part of ritual in Venezuela's early civilizations. These early forms merged with colonial and immigrant influences creating diverse and colorful folk dances. Such traditions are at their more energetic among black communities on Venezuela's central coast, where everybody rushes to dance when homegrown drummers spontaneously take to their instruments in the streets. The most dramatic time to see African-influenced dancing in Venezuela is during the Festival de los Diablos Danzantes in May/June (p343).

You can often see amateur folk-dance ensembles in action during annual feasts. Folk dance has sown seeds for the creation of professional groups that now promote their musical folklore to the public and abroad, such as Danzas Venezuela, founded by internationally famous folk dancer Yolanda Moreno.

Among the neoclassical dance groups, the best known is the Ballet Nuevo Mundo de Caracas, led by Venezuela's most famous ballerina, Zhandra Rodríguez. The Ballet Teresa Carreño and the Ballet Contemporáneo de Caracas (www.caracasballet.com) also perform in the neoclassical style. Contemporary dance is probably best represented by the groups Coreoarte, the Danza Hoy, the Dramo, and Acción Colectiva, whose productions can all be seen regularly in Caracas theaters (see p89) and in touring shows around the country.

Joropo can be divided into three regional subgenres: *llanero* (played with the nylon-stringed harp, the *cuatro,* and the maracas), *central* (played with a metal stringed harp, maracas, voice, and *cuatro*) and *oriental* (played with additional instruments such as guitar, mandolin and accordion).

Cinema

Venezuela's film industry is small, but has started to gain momentum in recent years. The great majority of the films are either contemporary social critiques or historical dramatizations.

The biggest smash in new Venezuelan cinema was 2005's *Secuestro Express* (Express Kidnapping) by Jonathan Jakubowicz. The film, which was criticized by the government for its harsh portrayal of the Caracas, takes a cold look at crime, poverty, violence, drugs and class relations in the capital. *Secuestro Express* broke all box-office records for a national production and was the first Venezuelan film to be distributed by a major Hollywood studio.

Those interested in learning more about Venezuelan film should track down: *Huelepega* (Glue Sniffer; Elia Schneider, 1999), which pulls no punches in its portrayal of the lives of Caracas street children, using genuine street youth, not actors, lending the film an authenticity to its nonstop, sometimes schizophrenic, action; *Amaneció de Golpe* (A Coup at Daybreak; Carlos Azpúrua, 1999), which tells the story of how Chávez burst onto the political scene; *Manuela Saenz* (Diego Risquez, 2000), which portrays the War of Independence through the eyes of Bolívar's mistress; and *The Revolution Will Not Be Televised* (Kim Bartley & Donnacha O'Briain), a documentary shot by Irish filmmakers who were inside the presidential palace during the coup d'état of 2002, which contains firsthand footage of the events and provides a deeply compelling – though unabashedly pro-Chávez – portrait of the man himself.

Venezuelan film director Fina Torres broke into international popularity with such films as 2000's *Woman on Top,* starring Penelope Cruz.

TELENOVELAS

While flicking between channels on your hotel TV, take a minute to enjoy the intense melodrama of a good ol' Venezuelan *telenovela*. These ubiquitous soap operas with their beautiful stars, hammy acting and theatrical drum rolls transfix the nation on a nightly basis. Their habitual formula is a racy mix of romance, seduction, glamour and a healthy dose of scandal.

And it works. More than 50% of Venezuelans are obsessive fans, and producers do everything they can to meet demand. It's a thriving multimillion-dollar industry, and Venezuelan soaps have been distributed all over the world (breaking rating records in foreign countries more than once). Over the last two decades Venezuela has even come to rival the two traditional *telenovela* powers, Mexico and Brazil.

Unlike ongoing European or US soaps, each *telenovela* runs for just a few months, climaxing in dramatic endings that have the power to bring the country to a standstill.

Literature

A rich world of pre-Hispanic indigenous tales, legends and stories preserved and passed from generation to generation provided invaluable information on the pre-Columbian culture for the first Spanish chroniclers. For a taste of the first chronicles narrating the early history of Venezuela, try to hunt down *Brevísima Relación de la Destrucción de las Indias Occidentales* (1552), by Fray Bartolomé de las Casas or *Elegías de Varones Ilustres de Indias* (Elegies of Illustrious Gentlemen of the Indes; 1589), by Juan de Castellanos. More analytical and comprehensive is one of the later chronicles, *Historia de la Conquista y Población de la Provincia de Venezuela* (The History of the Conquest and Population of the Province of Venezuela; 1723), by José de Oviedo y Baños.

The dawn of the 19th century saw the birth and crystallization of revolutionary trends. The first 30 years of that century were more or less dominated by political literature. Among the pivotal historical works was the autobiography of Francisco de Miranda (1750–1816). Simón Bolívar (1783–1830) himself also left an extensive literary heritage that included letters, proclamations, dissertations and also literary achievements such as *Delirio sobre El Chimborazo* (My Delirium on Chimborazo), which presents an expression of ideals for a nation fighting for its independence. Bolívar was influenced by his close friend Andrés Bello (1781–1865), the first important Venezuelan poet, who was also a noted philologist, historian and jurist.

With independence achieved, political writing gave way to other literary forms. In the 1920s, Andrés Eloy Blanco (1896–1955) appeared on the scene to become one of the best poets Venezuela has ever produced. *Angelitos Negros* (Little Black Angels) is the most popular of his numerous poems.

At the same time, several notable novelists emerged, among whom Rómulo Gallegos (1884–1969) was the most outstanding; he remains the country's internationally best-known writer. *Doña Bárbara,* his most popular novel, was first published in Spain in 1929 and has since been translated into a dozen languages. Miguel Otero Silva (1908–85) was another remarkable novelist of the period. He's best remembered for *Casas Muertas* (Dead Houses), a bestseller published in 1957.

Arturo Uslar Pietri (1906–2001) stands out as a novelist, historian, literary critic, journalist and even a politician, having been a minister and a presidential candidate. He was not only the most versatile writer in modern Venezuela, but also the most inexhaustible; since his first novel, *Lanzas Coloradas* (The Red Lances), in the 1930s, he wrote tirelessly right up until his death in 2001.

Teresa de la Parra's controversial 1924 novel *Iphigenia* so challenged the aristocracy and dictatorship of Juan Vicente Gómez that she had to go to Paris to get it published.

Internationally renowned novelist Rómulo Gallegos (1884–1969) was also Venezuela's first democratically elected president.

Other veteran Venezuelan writers include Denzil Romero (fiction novels), Salvador Garmendia (short stories), Aquiles Nazoa (humor, poetry) and Francisco Herrera Luque (historical novels). The books of Herrera Luque (1928–91) are particularly interesting as they give a profound and beautifully readable insight into Venezuela's history. His novels include *Los Viajadores de la India* (The Travelers from India), about the Spanish conquest.

The 1960s saw the start of many fresh, experimental trends in contemporary Venezuelan literature. Many writers took up magical realism, while others became more and more introspective. The increasing freedom of speech and the example of the Cuban Revolution also encouraged writers to explore the vast divides within their own oil-rich society. A ground-breaking experimental novel from the middle of the century is *El Falso Cuaderno de Narciso Espejo* (The False Notebook of Narciso Espejo), by Guillermo Meneses (1911–78); a slightly later seminal work by Adriano Gonzalez Leon (1931–) is the powerful magical-realism novel *Pais Portatil* (Portable Country), which contrasts rural Venezuela with a monstrous vision of Caracas.

Ednodio Quintero is another contemporary writer to look out for. His work *La Danza del Jaguar* (The Dance of the Jaguar; 1991) is one of several translated into other languages. Other contemporary writers worth tracking down include Carlos Noguera, Luis Brito García, Eduardo Liendo and Orlando Chirinos.

> For a biography of Venezuela's most famous poet, Andrés Eloy Blanco, plus many of his most beloved poems, visit www.los-poetas .com/b/blanco.htm (in Spanish).

Theater

Caracas has developed a strong theater tradition since it founded Venezuela's first venue, Teatro del Conde, in 1784. Several more theaters opened at the end of the 19th century in Caracas, Maracaibo, Valencia, Barquisimeto and Barcelona, all presenting a steady diet of European fare. The national theater was born only a few decades ago, with its major center in Caracas. Today, there are several dozen theatrical groups, most in Caracas. Rajatabla, tied to the Ateneo de Caracas (p89), is Venezuela's best-known theater on the international scene. Other Caracas-based groups of note include La Compañía Nacional de Teatro and the Teatro Profesional de Venezuela. It's also worth watching out for the Teatro Negro de Barlovento, formed by the black community of the central coast and taking inspiration from African roots.

Visual Arts

The history of Venezuelan art goes back before even the Spaniards. Surviving pre-Columbian works include a scattering of cave paintings in Bolívar and Amazonas states and enigmatic rock carvings, which have been found at about 200 locations throughout the country. Some of the best collections of petroglyphs can be seen on Piedra Pintada (p334), a 50m-high cliff near Puerto Ayacucho, and Parque Arqueológico Piedra Pintada (p134), near Valencia.

> Francisco Suniaga's *La Otra Isla* is a highly ac-claimed novel that takes place on Isla de Marga-rita. It is a crime story that looks at the island's development through the eyes of native islanders and German settlers.

Shuffling forward in time, the painting and sculpture of the colonial period had an almost exclusively religious character. Although mostly executed by local artists, the style was influenced by the Spanish art of the day. But when independence loomed, painting departed from strictly religious themes and began to immortalize historical events. The first artist to do so was Juan Lovera (1778–1841), whose most famous paintings can be seen in the Capilla de Santa Rosa de Lima, (p62) in Caracas.

When General Guzmán Blanco took power in the late 19th century, Venezuelan painting blossomed. The most outstanding painter in this period – and Venezuelan history as a whole – is Martín Tovar y Tovar (1827–1902), particularly remembered for his monumental works in Caracas' Capitolio

For more information
and biographies of
Venezuelan writers,
performers and artists,
visit the culture page
of the website of the
Venezuelan Embassy
in the US: www
.embavenez-us.org.

Nacional (p63). Another important 19th-century artist, Arturo Michelena (1863–98), received international recognition despite his short life. He spent much of his life in Paris, then the world's art capital. Another Venezuelan living in France, Emilio Boggio (1857–1920) acquired an international reputation for impressionist works influenced by Van Gogh.

The epic historical tradition of Tovar y Tovar was continued by Tito Salas (1888–1974), who dedicated himself to commemorating Bolívar's life and achievements in huge murals (see Casa Natal de Bolívar, p66, and the Panteón Nacional, p67).

Many claim that modern Venezuelan painting began with the unique expressionist Armando Reverón (1889–1954) and the transitional painter Carlos Otero (1886–1977). Francisco Narváez (1905–82) is commonly acclaimed as one of Venezuela's most groundbreaking modern sculptors. Porlamar's Museo de Arte Contemporáneo Francisco Narváez (p245), on Narváez' native Isla de Margarita, has the largest collection of his diverse and experimental works.

Recent Venezuelan art has been characterized by a proliferation of different schools, trends and techniques. One of the most remarkable exemplars of these movements was the painter Héctor Poleo (1918–89), who expressed himself in a variety of styles, switching easily from realism to surrealism, with some metaphysical exploration in between. Equally captivating is the expressionist painting of Jacobo Borges (1931–91), who by deforming human figures turns them into caricatures.

Jesús Soto (1923–2005) is Venezuela's number one internationally renowned contemporary artist. He was a leading representative of kinetic art (art, particularly sculpture, that contains moving parts). His large distinctive works adorn numerous public buildings and plazas in Venezuela and beyond (including Paris, Toronto and New York). The largest collection of his work is in the museum dedicated to him in Ciudad Bolívar (p298).

For a comprehensive
directory of Venezuelan
websites on just about
everything, check out
www.lanic.utexas.edu/la
/venezuela/, put together
by the Latin American
Network Information
Center of the University
of Texas.

There's a lot of activity among the current generation. Watch out for the works of Carlos Zerpa (painting), the quirky ideas of José Antonio Hernández Díez (photography, video, installations) and the emblematic paintings, collages and sculptures of Miguel von Dangel. And you'll see plenty more in the Museo de Arte Contemporáneo de Caracas (p68).

Architecture

There isn't a lot left to see of pre-Hispanic dwellings in Venezuela as many were made from perishable materials such as adobe, wood and vegetable fibers. However, the homes of remote indigenous communities in the Amazon still give a glimpse of the design of early indigenous structures.

The arrival of the Spanish brought the introduction of solid building materials such as brick and tile to Venezuelan architecture. The newly founded towns were direct reflections of the Spanish style, laid out on a square grid with the main plaza, cathedral and government house forming the center. But colonial architecture in Venezuela never reached the grandeur that marked neighbors like Colombia, Ecuador and Peru. Churches were mostly small and houses were usually undecorated, one-story constructions. Only in the last half-century of the colonial era did a wealthier merchant class emerge that built grand residences that reflected their stature. A handful of notable examples survive in Coro (see p142).

Independence initially had little impact on Venezuelan architecture, but in the 1870s a dramatic overhaul of the capital city was launched by Guzmán Blanco. He commissioned many monumental public buildings in a hodgepodge of styles, from neo-Gothic to neoclassical, largely depending on the whim of the architect in charge.

A real rush toward modernity came with oil money and culminated in the 1970s. This period was characterized by indiscriminate demolition of the historic urban fabric and its replacement by modern architecture. Many dilapidated colonial buildings fell prey to greedy urban planners. Accordingly, Venezuela's colonial legacy can be disappointing when compared to that of other Andean countries. On the other hand, Venezuela has some truly remarkable modern architecture. Carlos Raúl Villanueva, who began work in the 1930s, is considered the most outstanding Venezuelan architect. The campus of Universidad Central de Venezuela in Caracas (p71) is regarded as one of his best and most coherent designs and has been included on Unesco's Cultural Heritage list.

Environment

THE LAND

Approximately twice the size of California and the sixth largest country on the South American continent, Venezuela claims a multiplicity of landscapes. The traveler can encounter all four primary South American landscapes – the Amazon, the Andes, savannas and beaches – all in a single country.

The country has two mountain ranges. The lower Cordillera de la Costa reaches an altitude of 2725m at Pico Naiguatá, the tallest peak of the Cordillera El Ávila, which separates the valley of Caracas from the Caribbean. This mostly green and warm-to-temperate region is the most developed and populated of the country. The other, taller mountain range is the northernmost section of the great Andes mountain range. The tallest Andean point in Venezuela rises to 5000m at the Sierra Nevada de Mérida. These slopes give birth to rivers that roll down the treeless hills of the *páramos* (open highlands above about 3300m) to the downstream temperate forests before finally reaching Los Llanos (the Plains) and the lowlands around Lago de Maracaibo.

Lago de Maracaibo is the largest lake in South America and is linked to the Caribbean Sea. The region around the lake is the traditional oil-producing region of the country. While the Maracaibo basin still produces 50% of the country's oil, its significance is being displaced by drilling in other areas, such as the Orinoco river delta.

The Río Orinoco watershed embraces the sparsely populated low-lying region of Los Llanos, which is characterized by prairies with a variety of savanna and forests. Los Llanos makes up nearly a third of the country. The Río Orinoco itself runs for 2150km down to the delta's wetlands and is South America's third largest river.

South of the Orinoco lies another sparsely populated area, the Guayana region. This area, which makes up nearly half the country, includes the Río Caura watershed, the largely impenetrable Amazon rainforest, and the famous plateaus of the Guayana highlands where hundreds of tabletop mountains called tepuis (flat-topped sandstone mountains with vertical flanks) tower over the forest. The Guayana highlands are considered one of the oldest places on earth geologically. The area also holds the world's highest waterfall – the famous Angel Falls (Salto Ángel) – which plummets nearly 1km from one of the tepuis found here.

Finally, let's not forget the country's 2813km-long stretch of Caribbean coast, featuring a 900,000 sq km Caribbean marine zone with numerous islands and cays. The largest and most popular of these is Isla de Margarita, followed closely by the less-developed Archipiélago Los Roques.

WILDLIFE

Along with the variety of Venezuelan landscapes you will encounter is the amazing diversity of wildlife. One of the best places on earth to see biodiversity is in the Guayana region, where dramatic contrasts in geology and altitude have produced a huge range of habitats for a diverse selection of plants and animals. The finest example is the 'lost worlds' atop the tepuis, where flora and fauna is isolated from the forest below and from the other tepuis, and therefore there has developed independently from its surroundings. Some of the tabletop habitats have been isolated for millions of years and many of the species found on the tops of tepuis exist only on their particular summit. For example, half of the plant species found on Roraima do not exist anywhere else in the world.

The Río Orinoco's watershed is one of the largest and most complex fresh-water ecosystems on earth. It's home to more than 1000 fish species – more than Europe and North America combined.

Parques Nacionales de Venezuela, edited by Oscar Todtman, is a review of Venezuela's 43 national parks. It showcases some wonderful photography, but lacks the more practical information a traveler needs to get around.

Animals

Again, diversity is the key word when it comes to describing Venezuela's fauna. There are 341 species of reptiles, 284 species of amphibians, 1791 species of fishes, 351 species of mammals and many butterflies and other invertebrates. More than 1360 species of birds – approximately 20% of the world's known species – reside in the country, and 46 of these species are endemic. The country's geographical setting on a main migratory route makes it a bird-watcher's heaven.

The evergreen forests of the Cordillera de la Costa are a good place to look for sloths, monkeys and marsupials, and are a definite must for bird-watchers, who will delight in such rare species as Venezuela's endemic parakeets, screamers (*Anhimidae* family), trogons, rare thrushes and many species of toucan and toucanet. Parque Nacional El Ávila (p95), north of Caracas, provides an excellent starting point to search for hummingbirds, parakeets and fruit-eaters, among the more than 300 species identified there. West of Caracas, Parque Nacional Henri Pittier (p119) is another birder's paradise with some 582 bird species. Further west, in the Golfete de Cuare fauna refuge (p156), you can spot one of the country's largest flamingo colonies. If you visit the Cueva del Guácharo (p285), 12km east from Caripe, you can't miss the unique *guácharo* (oilbird). This blind bird is about half a meter long, has reddish-brown feathers and curved beak and lives in the caves. The Andes are home to the endangered South American bear or spectacled bear, plus many birds including curassows, quetzals, owls, hawks and a small population of the recently reintroduced Andean condor.

Along the Caribbean coastline and on the islands you will spot many water-birds including the colorful scarlet ibis. At some of the islands you may also see endangered parrots, such as the *cotorra cabeciamarilla* (yellow-shouldered parrot) – look for its green feathers and yellow face. Although this bird has become nearly extinct in the Caribbean, Isla de Margarita (p240) is home to one of the largest remaining populations. Dolphins are abundant along Venezuela's coastline, and around Archipiélago Los Roques (p101) you will be surprised by the health and vitality of the reefs and the abundant marine life that rivals any of the better-known diving destinations in the Caribbean. Endangered green sea turtles nest on the archipelago and in the Parque Nacional Península de Paria (p282) on the eastern mainland coast.

The seasonally flooded plains of Los Llanos (p220) are among Venezuela's best places to spot wildlife. You have a good chance of seeing capybaras (locally known as *chiguire*), spectacled caimans, monkeys, giant anteaters, armadillos, anacondas, piranhas, ocelots and even the elusive jaguar. Birds flock here by the millions: it's one of the planet's most important bird-breeding reserves, with well over 350 species including waterfowl species such as ibises, herons, jacanas and egrets. Seed-eating birds, macaws, raptors and the strange *hoatzin* – a prehistoric-looking bird with punky yellow feathers on its head – all make their home here. South of Lago de Maracaibo, within the Parque Nacional Ciénagas del Catatumbo, you can find howler monkeys, spectacled caimans, endemic river dolphins and many birds including ospreys, kingfishers, herons, masked ducks and ibises. Manatees and otters are also found here, but are notoriously hard to spot. In the Delta del Orinoco (p289) you can expect some of the species found in the Llanos.

The Guayana region contains many rare, unique and endangered species, including the endemic birds of the tepuis (such as the amazing Cock of the Rock with its brilliant orange crest), jaguars, pumas, otters, harpy eagles and tapirs (the biggest mammal in the country). It's also home to the native, endangered Orinoco crocodile, which grows up to 8m long and is the largest crocodile in the Americas.

The Birds of Venezuela 2003, by Stephen L Hilty, is a must for bird-watchers. Similarly, A Guide to the Birds of Venezuela, by William H Phelps and Rodolphe Meyer de Schauensee, was the first of its kind and remains a classic.

The anaconda (from the Tamil word meaning 'elephant killer') is the largest snake on earth. Its average length is 3m to 4m, but specimens as long as 11m have been found.

Leslie Pantin's beautifully illustrated Genio y Figura de la Fauna Venezolana describes Venezuela's fauna and includes folktales in Spanish.

Plants

Venezuela boasts 650 types of vegetation and thousands of plant species in several major habitats. Tropical lowland rainforests still cover a very large part of the country. Cloud forests are confined to the mountain slopes between 1000m and 2800m above sea level, and are a primary feature of Parque Nacional Henri Pittier (p119) and the Parque Nacional Sierra Nevada (p198). Dry forests are found mainly on the larger Caribbean islands and in the hills between Coro and Barquisimeto. The coasts and islands feature mangrove forests. Grasslands and savannas are mainly on the plains and in Parque Nacional Canaima (see the boxed text below). Finally, you can see the Mérida *páramos*, highland meadows that are found just above the cloud forests.

The national flower, the Flor de Mayo (May Flower; *Cattleya mossiae*), is just one of the more than 25,000 species of orchid found in Venezuela's forests; its sensuous pink flower blossoms in May. Another Venezuelan specialty is the *frailejón (Espeletia)*, a typical plant of the *páramos*; it has pale green leaves coated in white velvety fur, which are arranged in a rosette pattern around a thick trunk. The *frailejón* can grow to more than 3m tall and its yellow flowers bloom from September to December.

Otto Huber's Ecological Guide to the Gran Sabana provides excellent information on the environmental features of Parque Nacional Canaima, including lists of animals and plants.

If you drive along the Caracas–Valencia highway between December and April, you are likely to see the splendid yellow blossoming of Venezuela's national tree, the *araguaney* (trumpet tree). Endemic to Roraima is the little carnivorous *Drosera roraima*, which is found in the humid areas atop of the tepui and has intense red leaves with sticky tentacles that catch insects. When visiting the Gran Sabana, look along the main road for the *morichales* (palm groves), which are groups of *moriches* (oily palms) that grow along waterways or in flood-prone areas. These are very common in the eastern plains of the Llanos as well. The adult plant features a 15m-tall trunk dotted with fan-shaped leaves, which are used by indigenous people for construction. The palm's reddish fruit serves as a local food source.

NATIONAL PARKS

Venezuela's national parks offer a diverse landscape of evergreen mountains, beaches, tropical islands, coral reefs, high plateaus and rainforests. The national parks are the number one destination for tourism within the country. Canaima, Los Roques, Mochima, Henri Pittier, El Ávila and Morrocoy are the most popular parks. While some parks, especially those in coastal and marine zones, are easily accessible and tend to be overcrowded by locals during holiday periods and weekends, others remain unvisited. A few of the parks offer tourism facilities, but these are generally not very extensive. For some parks, such as Morrocoy, you'll need to get a permit and pay a small fee for camping. Always ask about safety when going camping.

PARQUE NACIONAL CANAIMA

Comprising 30,000 sq km in the remote southeastern corner of the country, Parque Nacional Canaima (p310) was declared a World Natural Heritage Site by Unesco in 1994 for its outstanding natural features that include cloud forest, savanna, rivers, huge waterfalls, *moriche* palm groves, shrub lands, swamp forests and, most notably, the extraordinary geologic formations called tepuis. Tepuis are the remains of mighty sandstone plateaus; these tabletop habitats have been isolated for millions of years, allowing the development of unique flora and fauna that attracts research scientists from around the world. The highest of the tepuis is the legendary Roraima (2810m), which is located in the eastern sector of the park. The park is also home to the world's highest waterfall – the famous Angel Falls (Salto Ángel) – which descends nearly 1km from Auyantepui in the western sector of the national park.

NOTABLE NATIONAL PARKS

Protected Area	Features & Activities	Best Time to Visit	Page
Parque Nacional Archipiélago Los Roques	mangrove coastline embraced by the Caribbean's turquoise waters; secluded cays with white-sand beaches & coral reefs; extraordinary diving & snorkeling; fishing; sailing, windsurfing & kitesurfing; marine biological station; green turtle nesting area abundant marine life; birds (over 90 species)	year-round	p101
Parque Nacional Canaima	arguably 'the jewel in the crown' with Angel Falls; hiking the tepuis & Roraima; wildlife-watching: jaguars, anteaters, Cock of the Rock, harpy eagles, tapirs	year-round	opposite & p310
Parque Nacional Guatopo	rainforest & mountains embrace a freshwater reservoir; camping; walking trails; park ranger at La Macanilla; Hacienda La Elvira; wildlife: 50 species of bats, eight species of marsupials, howlers & capuchins, monkeys, armadillos, jaguars, harpy eagles	year-round	p109
Parque Nacional Henri Pittier	steep, forested mountains rolling into Caribbean beaches; wildlife-watching: birds (500 species, 22 endemic), monkeys, sloths, snakes	late June for Fiesta de San Juan	p119
Parque Nacional Mochima	hills with dry tropical forest penetrating deep-water beaches on the east coast; rainforest inland; diving & snorkeling; rafting; camping; wildlife: dolphins, abundant marine life, marine birds, iguanas	year-round	p260
Parque Nacional Morrocoy	palm-fringed cays with sandy beaches protected by mangroves & coral reefs on the western coast; diving & snorkeling; camping; Golfete de Cuare fauna refuge; wildlife: abundant marine life, birds, alligators, large scarlet ibis colonies	September	p155
Parque Nacional Sierra Nevada	snowy mountains of the Andes descend into temperate & tropical forest; hiking & biking; Venezuela's tallest mountain Pico Bolivar (5001m); wildlife: spectacled bears & Andean condors (both endangered), deers, ocelots ocelots, *frailejón* endemic plants	year-round	p198

Some 50% of the country is protected under national law as Areas Under Special Administration (ABRAEs). Most of these protected territories are considered national parks and natural monuments, though some are designated under categories such as wildlife refuges, forests and biosphere reserves.

Inparques (Instituto Nacional de Parques Nacionales; www.inparques.gov.ve in Spanish), an autonomous institute attached to the Ministry of Environment, was created to manage the national parks and natural monuments. Unfortunately the park authorities lack the funding, equipment, personnel and enforcement capacity to fully manage this huge territory. Some parks do require permits, and there is usually an Inparques office in most main towns, or posts at the national parks themselves, which can provide information. Other types of protected lands are managed by other organizations designated by the Ministry of Environment.

ECOTOURISM OPPORTUNITIES

Venezuela's incredible variety of natural attractions and biodiversity makes it an understandably attractive destination for nature lovers. Most of the country's important features fall inside one of Venezuela's protected areas. Many of the country's 43 indigenous groups live on or near protected areas as well.

There are more than 1000 posadas or lodges in natural areas that provide accommodations for nature tourists, ranging from the most rustic camps to very comfortable lodges. A growing number of tour operators include ecotourism tours and accommodations in their packages, but do be aware that not all tours marketed as 'eco' are committed to high standards of ecological conservation or to local community participation. Tour guides seldom belong to the local communities, but porters, cooks and drivers usually do. Also know that while some guides speak English and even a second foreign language, others do not, so make sure you shop around.

Perhaps the country's most successful conservation stories are in Los Llanos (The Plains), where some *hatos* (cattle ranches) have preserved their fauna and built a tourism infrastructure to make it accessible to visitors. These wildlife ecotourism reserves combine accommodations and tours, and some even have research facilities. Tours in the *hatos* usually include trucks specially outfitted for photo safaris.

In addition to these, there are many other ways travelers can experience Venezuela's ecotourism. The following are some examples of what the country can offer the ecotourist:

Campamento Nuevo Mundo (☎ 0414-825-3122, 0281-416-1599) Preserves a patch of rainforest in the south of Miranda state, and has a rustic ecolodge that provides a communal experience.

Ecochallenge (www.ecochallenge.ws) This private business monitors sharks and offers scuba-diving safaris.

Fundación Bioandina (maria@bolivar.funmrd.gov.ve) This organization has reintroduced the condor to the Venezuelan Andes. Contact it directly to learn more about the program.

Hato El Cedral (p225; ☎ 0212-781-8995, 58-212-793-6082; www.hatocedral.com) Located in the lower Llanos, this ranch is outstanding for the opportunity to see a vast number of wildlife, including over 300 bird species and a population of 20,000 capybaras.

Hato El Frio (p223; ☎ 0414-743-5329; www.elfrioeb.com) Located in the lower Llanos, 150km west of San Fernando de Apure, this wildlife refuge was established in 1974. It has its own biological station where you can see anacondas and endemic crocodiles raised in captivity.

Hato Piñero (p224; ☎ 0212-991-8935; www.hatopinero.com) In the upper Llanos, this ranch is home to more than 300 bird species and contains a herbarium featuring a diversity of floral species of the plains.

Hato Río de Agua (p280; ☎ 0294-332-215, 0294-332-0527; merle@telcel.net.ve) Located on the Peninsula de Paria, this place combines buffalo ranching, conservation and ecotourism.

Programa Andes Tropicales (☎ 0274-263-6884, 0274-263-8633; www.andestropicales.org) Rural tourism experience in the upper Andes; stay with local farming families in traditional rural lodges called *mucuposadas*.

Provita (www.wpti.org/ven.htm) Runs the Bioinsula Program (☎ 0295-416-2541; Urbanización Augusto Malavé Villalba, Av 9, Casa No 15 Boca de Río, Península de Manacao, Isla de Margarita), which targets the endangered *cotorra cabeciamarilla* (yellow-shouldered parrot). Small groups can participate in monitoring during April, July and October.

Sociedad Conservacionista Audubón de Venezuela (Map p80; ☎ 0212-992-2812, 992-3268; www.audubonvenezuela.org in Spanish; Calle Veracruz, Edificio Matisco, 1 Piso, Oficina 5, Las Mercedes, Caracas) Based in Caracas, this is one of the country's oldest environmental NGOs; it runs bird-watching tours and volunteer monitoring programs.

While the Venezuelan populace looks to the park system to protect the nation's biodiversity and provide a recreation amenity, many parks are inhabited by local indigenous and subsistence-farming communities that have lived in the parks since before they were designated as such by the government. This creates a conflict between each park's conservation needs and the local population's use of a natural resource. The greatest hope in combining conservation with economic sustainability for locals lies in a planned and responsible development of ecotourism within the protected areas.

ENVIRONMENTAL ISSUES

Far and away the most obvious environmental problem in Venezuela is waste management (or lack thereof). There is no recycling policy and dumping of garbage in cities, along roads and natural areas is common practice. Untreated sewage is sometimes dumped in the sea and other bodies of water. There continues to be a general lack of clear environmental policy and little-to-no culture of environmental stewardship outside the park areas. Much of the waste and pollution issues are a direct result of overpopulation in urban areas and a lack of civil planning and funds to cope with the rampant development.

Another major environmental issue is illegal poaching of timber, precious metals, rare plants and tropical animals that takes place in many parts of the country, including protected areas. Pet tropical birds, for example, fetch a handsome price in the US, Asia and Europe. Amazonian hardwoods are cut from the jungle and wildcat miners pan for gold in the rivers and dump their used mercury into the water.

A final major ecological concern is pollution from oil refineries, oil drilling and the general destruction wrought by industry and mining: Lago de Maracaibo has witnessed many oil spills, and much of the petroleum infrastructure is old and in need of repair. Huge strip mines create moonscapes in the once fertile lands of Guyana.

This said, there is a sector of the population – including community organizations, cooperatives, nongovernmental organizations (NGOs), universities and governmental agencies – that is working to reduce environmental degradation. Following is a list of major organizations working for the Venezuelan environment:

Conservation International (www.conservation.org) Works on conservation issues in several Latin American countries, including Venezuela.

Fundación Empresas Polar (www.fpolar.org.ve in Spanish) Leading NGO working in biodiversity, sustainable agriculture and water-management issues.

Ocean Futures Society (www.oceanfutures.org) Works on environmental issues related to coastal areas.

Planeta.com (www.planeta.com) The 'global journal of practical ecotourism' is insightful, balanced and carries a significant amount of Venezuela-specific information.

Venezuela EcoPortal (www.internet.ve/wildlife) Site focusing on ecotourism and adventure trips, but with plenty of links to general information.

Think Venezuela (www .think-venezuela.net) provides a good overview of the country's national parks - just click on the national parks link.

The website www .planeta.com has a useful directory and interactive forum promoting 'practical ecotourism' in Latin America.

Food & Drink

The Venezuelan people love to eat – and to eat well. From home-cooked corn turnovers and authentic Spanish paella to downright indulgent desserts, there is plenty for your taste buds to discover. The national cuisine is characterized by a rich fusion of indigenous and European roots. Caracas itself is an internationally renowned culinary melting pot, while the regions of Venezuela have their own peculiarities and specialties. The *costeños'* (coastal peoples') plates overflow with fish and exquisite seafood, while the Amazonian peoples have plenty of imaginative uses for the humble yucca (edible root). Wheat and trout dishes dominate in the Andes, and those bursting for a BBQ platter will adore the obscenely juicy steaks in Los Llanos.

www.venezuelatuya .com/cocina is in Spanish (or Italian), but can at least show you some photos of typical Venezuelan dishes.

STAPLES & SPECIALTIES

The Venezuelans have a saying: *lo que no mata engorda* (what doesn't kill you makes you fat), and it's true that many of their tasty common dishes appear decidedly on the fattening side, from steaks as thick as bricks to deep-fried cheese.

Many staples rely on the use of corn, especially *arepas* and empanadas, which are as common as hotdogs and hamburgers in the US. The *arepa* is a hamburger-sized corn pancake that is split and stuffed so full of juicy fillings that it takes a special talent to avoid getting it all over your face. *Areperas* (*arepa* restaurants) offer 101 fillings to choose from, but a favorite is the tasty *reina pepiada* (chicken, mayo and avocado). They're a surprisingly heavy-going, filling snack so don't be surprised if your jaw aches and you feel full by your third bite.

Deep-fried empanadas (corn turnovers) filled with meat, chicken or cheeses are also a common snack. And the sweet and greasy *cachapa* pancake is another corn-based favorite, usually with slabs of cheese and ham slapped on top. At Christmas, families lovingly prepare *hallacas*, corn dough with chopped meat and vegetables, steamed in banana leaves.

The annually updated, bilingual *Guia Gastronomica de Caracas* (Caracas Gastronomic Guide), published by Miro Popic, covers more than 600 restaurants in the capital and is a great help in discovering the local food scene. See www .miropopic.com for the latest recommendations.

But let's not get fixated on corn alone. Other Venezuelan cuisine, collectively referred to as *comida criolla,* uses plenty of rice, yam, plantain, beans and carefully prepared meat, chicken or dozens of fresh seafood varieties. The *salsas* (sauces) make generous use of *ají dulce* (small sweet peppers) and cilantro (coriander leaves used as a garnish). There's also a vast array of tropical fruits, including papaya the size of US footballs and more types of banana than you can shake a monkey at. And of course, if you're ripe for rump steak, you've come to the right place. Venezuela is famous for its cheap and abundant grill houses, serving steaks supplied in truckloads from the ranches of Los Llanos.

Spanish, Italian, Chinese and Middle Eastern restaurants are all well represented too, thanks to sizable immigrant populations, and since Venezuela is one of the most Yankified countries on the continent, expect a dense array of gringo fast-food joints.

The per capita consumption of Johnny Walker Black Label Scotch whisky in Venezuela is the highest in the world.

DRINKS

Strong espresso coffee is excellent in Venezuela. Ask for *café negro* if you want it black, for *café marrón* if you want milk, or for *café con leche* if you like it very milky. When it has more milk than coffee, it's given the tongue-in-cheek title of *tetero* (baby's bottle). For an extra kick, *café bautizado* (literally 'baptized') contains a shot of rum.

WE DARE YOU!

If you can track them down, these unusual Venezuelan dishes should give you plenty to chew on.

- *Hormigas culonas* – deep-fried Amazonian ants with big, juicy rear ends (hence the ungraceful name meaning literally 'big-bottomed'). Sometimes coated in chocolate!
- *Katara* – along the same theme, the Ye'Kwana peoples' spicy sauce is made with the heads and thorax of leaf-cutter ants and is reputedly an aphrodisiac.
- *Paticas de grillo* – don't be scared off by the name (cricket legs); this tasty dish from Lara state is actually finely shredded beef.
- *Consomé de chipi chipi* – coastal clam broth; another rumored aphrodisiac.

Given the mind-boggling variety of fruit in the country, you'll also be spoilt for choice of juices, which come as *batidos* (pure or watered down) or as *merengadas* (milk shakes). Also good for the sweet-toothed are the local drinks *chicha*, a thick milky liquid made with rice and sugar, and *papelón con limón*, sugarcane juice mixed with lemon.

Tap water is generally fine to use for brushing your teeth, but is not recommended for consumption in any part of the country. Only drink bottled water or water that has been boiled for a number of minutes.

The number one alcoholic drink is, of course, beer, sold at icy temperatures for only US$0.50 a bottle (about 0.22L) in the cheapest bars and eateries. If you ever wonder why Venezuelans don't like larger bottles, the answer is simple: the beer could get warm before you finish it. Particularly popular is the local brand Polar beer (look for the cute polar-bear logo).

Among Venezuelan spirits, rum heads the list and the smooth, dark Ron Añejo Aniversario Pampero is one of the best. Another specialty is the throat-stripping *miche*, an anise-flavored spirit made from sugarcane, similar to the Colombian *aguardiente*, and so-called in some areas. The local production of wine is small, except for some good Altagracia wines (p171).

However, it's imported whisky that wins the prize as the chic drink of choice, and upper-crust restaurants stock enough to rival any Scotch bar. Indeed, Venezuelans manage to get through about five million cases per year.

Colorful *cocteles* (cocktails) also abound: from the hugely popular *guarapita*, a fruity combination of sugarcane spirit and fresh juices that is all too easy to gulp down, to Andean *calentados*, hot toddies to warm the cockles of your heart on cold mountain nights.

Whole bottles of spirits are commonly poured over coffins (and the coffin-bearers) at Venezuelan funerals.

WHERE & WHEN TO EAT & DRINK

For a filling *desayuno* (breakfast), do what many locals do and grab something in the local *panadería* (bakery). Venezuelans take their *almuerzo* (lunch) more seriously, however. In fact, it's taken for granted that a 'lunch hour' is more likely a 'lunch two hours', and will tend to be a drawn-out social affair. For a good-value lunch, look at the *menú del día* or *menu ejecutivo*, a set meal consisting of soup and a main course. It costs just US$2 to US$5, cheaper than most à la carte dishes.

For a quick bite, grab some spit-roasted chicken from a *pollo en brasas* or a stuffed *arepa* from an *arepera* (see the boxed text p50), or markets always offer fresh local fare. Street vending is also common, though hygiene can be iffy. Particularly popular are *churro* machines, which churn out long, thin pastry sticks sprinkled with sugar.

To linger over a more sedate evening meal, visit one of the many traditional Spanish *tascas* (Spanish-style bar-restaurants) found throughout the

Restaurants and cafés automatically add 10% service charge to the bill. Upmarket restaurants, particularly in Caracas, are also notorious for not including the 16% IVA tax on the menu, so brace yourself to pay 25% more (or 35%, if you include a 10% tip).

TYPES OF RESTAURANTS

arepera – serves *arepas* (stuffed corn pancakes) and other typical dishes
charcutería – pork butcher selling hams, sausages, salamis etc
fuentes de soda – budget café serving snacks and drinks
frutería – fruit shop or place that serves fruit salads and juices
heladería – serves ice cream and sometimes fast food
lunchería – cheap restaurant serving staple food and snacks
panadería – bakery selling cakes, coffee, pastries and bread
parrillada – Argentine-style restaurant serving mixed grills
pollo en brasas – cheap restaurant/takeaway serving grilled chicken and fries
refresquería – sells soft drinks and snacks
restaurante turístico – designed to showcase regional cuisine to visitors
tasca – Spanish-style bar-restaurant, serving tapas, paella and other Spanish dishes

country. Here you can choose to chow down on tapas with the local barflies or sit down for a filling meal of succulent seafood or meats with the family. In cities, upmarket restaurants come to life from 7pm to 8pm. However, in small towns, everything may be shut by 9pm.

VEGETARIANS & VEGANS

A popular fridge magnet in Venezuela reads *'Soy vegetariano, vivo en vainitas'* (I'm vegetarian, I live on green beans). Sure enough, vegetarianism isn't a concept well grasped in a country where rump steak is king.

That said, it's relatively easy to get by in Venezuela if you don't mind a little monotony. The country has plenty of cheeses, eaten with ubiquitous staples such as *arepas* and *cachapas*. *Perico* is another filling made with scrambled eggs, tomato and onion. A popular appetizer is *tostónes* (hard plantain cakes), which generally come with vegan-friendly sauces. You can also consume a wide selection of beans, salads and fruit juices. When ordering salads, though, it's not enough to ask if it has any *carne* (meat) because chicken and fish are in a separate linguistic class and aren't necessarily considered meat – see the Useful Phrases (opposite) section for ordering tips.

In tourist haunts, there are always vegetarian pizzas, pasta and omelets available, and there are even a few dedicated vegetarian restaurants in larger cities such as Caracas. Self-catering is the safest option for vegans; markets have a great selection of fruit and vegetables.

Venezuelans are so keen on meat that in some areas they classify capybara (an aquatic rodent) as 'fish' so they can eat it through Lent and Easter.

HABITS & CUSTOMS

At all levels of society, food preparation is done with care and eating is to be savored, not hurried. Food is a central means of showing hospitality, so expect huge portions and constant refills if you're invited to somebody's house. Festivals, especially Christmas, call for displays of generosity by filling stomachs that are already fit to burst.

If somebody invites you out to eat, you can expect them to pay. Of course, the flipside is that when you invite somebody out, the bill falls to you. Before tucking in, it's polite to wish your fellow diners *buen provecho* (bon appetit), and when drinking to say *salud* (good health).

EAT YOUR WORDS

Want to know what ordering a cup of *leche de burra* (donkey's milk) or a *teta* (breast) will really bring to your table? Discover the secrets of the local cuisine by getting to know the language. For pronunciation guidelines see p366.

Useful Phrases

I'm a vegetarian.
Soy vegetariano/a. (m/f)   soy ve·khe·ta·*rya*·no/a

Do you have any vegetarian dishes?
¿Tienen algún plato vegetariano?   tye·nen al·*goon pla*·to ve·khe·ta·*rya*·no

I don't eat meat, chicken or fish.
No como carne, ni pollo ni pescado.   no *ko*·mo *kar*·ne nee *po*·yo nee pes·*ka*·do

I'm allergic to peanuts/wheat/eggs.
Soy alérgico/a al maní/trigo/huevo.   soy a·*ler*·khee·ko/a al ma·*nee/tree*·go/*we*·vo

Is this water purified?
¿Ésta agua es purificada?   es·ta *a*·gwa es poo·ree·fee·*ka*·da

Do you have a menu (in English)?
¿Tienen una carta (en Inglés)?   tye·nen oo·na *kar*·ta (en een·*gles*)

I'd like the set meal.
Quisiera el menú.   kee·*sye*·ra el men·*oo*

Does that come with salad/fries?
¿Viene con ensalada/papas fritas?   ve·e·ne kon en·sa·*la*·da/*pa*·pas *free*·tas

What do you recommend?
¿Qué me recomienda?   ke me re·ko·*myen*·da

Not too spicy please.
Sin tanto picante, por favor.   seen *tan*·to pee·*kan*·te por fa·*vor*

I didn't order this.
No pedí esto.   no pe·*dee* es·to

The bill, please.
La cuenta, por favor.   la *kwen*·ta por fa·*vor*

Thanks, that was delicious.
Gracias, estaba sabroso.   *gra*·syas es·*ta*·ba sa·*bro*·so

Menu Decoder

FOOD

aceite	(a·*say*·te)	oil
aguacate	(a·gwa·ka·te)	avocado
ají	(a·khee)	chili pepper
ajo	(a·kho)	garlic
aliño	(a·lee·nyo)	combination of spices
arepa	(a·re·pa)	small, grilled corn pancake stuffed with cheese, beef, sausage, shrimp, eggs, salad etc; Andean *arepa de trigo* is made from wheat
atún	(a·toon)	tuna
batata	(ba·ta·ta)	sweet potato
berenjena	(be·ren·khe·na)	eggplant
cachapa	(ka·cha·pa)	round, juicy corn pancake, served with cheese and/or ham
cachito	(ka·chee·to)	croissant filled with chopped ham and served hot
calabaza	(ka·la·ba·za)	squash
camarón	(ka·ma·ron)	small shrimp
cambur	(kam·boor)	banana
cangrejo	(kan·gre·kho)	crab
canilla	(kan·ee·ya)	small baguette
carabina	(ka·ra·bee·na)	Mérida version of *hallaca*
caraota	(ka·ra·o·ta)	black bean
carne de res	(kar·ne de res)	beef

casabe	(ka·sa·be)	huge, flat bread made from *yuca amarga* (bitter yucca, grated, pressed and dried); a staple in indigenous communities
cebolla	(se·bo·ya)	onion
chayote	(cha·yo·te)	choko; green pear-shaped fruit
chicharrones	(chee·cha·ro·nes)	pork cracklings
chivo	(chee·vo)	goat
chorizo	(cho·ree·zo)	seasoned sausage
chuleta	(chu·le·ta)	chop, rib steak
churrasco a la llanera	(choo·ras·ko·a·la·lya·ne·ra)	grilled steak
cochino	(ko·chee·no)	pork
coco	(ko·ko)	coconut
cordero	(kor·de·ro)	lamb
durazno	(door·az·no)	apricot
empanada	(em·pa·na·da)	crescent-shaped, deep-fried cornmeal turnover stuffed with *carne de res* (beef), *pollo* (chicken) or *queso* (cheese)
fresa	(fre·za)	strawberry
frijoles	(free·kho·les)	red beans
guanábana	(gwa·na·ba·na)	soursop
guasacaca	(gwas·a·ka·ka)	piquant sauce made of peppers, onions and seasoning
guayaba	(gwa·ya·ba)	guava
hallaca	(a·ya·ka)	corn dough with chopped pork, beef or chicken with vegetables and olives, wrapped in banana leaves and steamed; popular during Christmas
hervido	(er·vee·do)	hearty soup made of beef or chicken with root vegetables
huevo frito/revuelto	(we·vo free·to/re·vwel·to)	fried/scrambled egg
jamón	(kha·mon)	ham
langosta	(lan·gos·ta)	lobster
lau lau	(lau·lau)	catfish
lechón	(le·chon)	baked pig stuffed with its own meat, rice and dried peas
lechosa	(le·cho·sa)	papaya
lechuga	(le·choo·ga)	lettuce
limón	(lee·mon)	lemon
mamón	(ma·mon)	small, green fruit with reddish flesh
mandarina	(man·da·ree·na)	mandarin
manzana	(man·za·na)	apple
mariscos	(ma·rees·koz)	shellfish, seafood
mejillones	(me·khe·yon·es)	mussels
melocotón	(me·lo·ko·ton)	peach
melón	(me·lon)	honeydew, rock melon
milanesa	(mee·la·ne·sa)	thin steak
mondongo	(mon·don·go)	seasoned tripe cooked in bouillon with corn, potatoes and vegetables
mora	(mor·a)	blackberry
muchacho	(moo·cha·cho)	hearty roasted beef dish

naranja	(na·ran·kha)	orange
nata	(na·ta)	thick, sweet cream
natilla	(na·tee·ya)	sour-milk butter
ñame	(nya·me)	a type of yam
negro en camisa	(ne·gro·en·ka·mee·sa)	a chocolate dessert
pabellón criollo	(pa·be·yon cree·o·yo)	national dish of shredded beef, rice, black beans, cheese and fried plantain
papa	(pa·pa)	potato
papelón	(pa·be·lon)	crude brown sugar; flavoring for drinks
parchita	(par·chee·ta)	passion fruit
parrilla (parrillada)	(pa·ree·ya)	mixed grill, including steak, pork, chicken and sausages
pasapalos	(pa·sa·pa·los)	hors d'oeuvres, small snacks, finger food
pastel de chucho	(pastel·de·choo·cho)	shredded ray with plantain and cheese
patilla	(pa·tee·ya)	watermelon
pernil	(per·neel)	leg of pork
perro caliente	(pe·ro ka·lyen·te)	hot dog
piña	(pee·nya)	pineapple
plátano	(pla·ta·no)	plantain
pollo	(po·yo)	chicken
quesillo	(ke·see·yo)	caramel custard
raspao	(ras·pa·o)	sweet, flavored ice shavings
salchicha	(sal·chee·cha)	sausage
sancocho	(san·ko·cho)	vegetable stew with fish, meat or chicken
tapas	(ta·pas)	typical Spanish hors d'oeuvres, including empanadas, tortillas, *jamón serrano, camarones* (shrimp), and grilled sausage
tequeño	(te·ke·nyo)	cheese strips wrapped in pastry and deep fried
teta	(te·ta)	iced fruit juice in plastic wrap, consumed by sucking
tocineta	(to·see·ne·ta)	bacon
tomate	(to·ma·te)	tomato
tortilla	(tor·tee·ya)	omelet
tostón	(tos·ton)	fried unripe plantain
trucha	(troo·cha)	trout
yuca	(yoo·ka)	yucca (edible root)
zanahoria	(za·na·o·ree·a)	carrot

DRINKS

agua	(a·gwa)	water
aguardiente	(a·gwar·dyen·te)	sugarcane spirit flavored with anise
café	(ka·fe)	coffee
calentado	(ka·len·ta·do)	hot Andean drink with anise-flavored spirit, milk, herbs and brown sugar
cerveza	(ser·ve·sa)	beer
chicha	(chee·cha)	usually nonalcoholic drink made from corn or rice

cocuy	(ko·kooy)	sugarcane liqueur
guayoyo	(gwa·yo·yo)	weak black coffee
jugo	(khoo·go)	juice
leche	(le·che)	milk
leche de burra	(le·che de boo·ra)	Andean beverage made of *miche*, egg and (cow's) milk
miche	(mee·che)	anise-flavored sugarcane-based spirit; *aguardiente*
refresco	(re·fres·ko)	soft drink
ron	(ron)	rum
té	(te)	tea
vino blanco/tinto/ espumoso	(vee·no blan·ko/teen·to/ es·poo·mo·so)	white/red/sparkling wine

Food Glossary

arroz	(a·roz)	rice
azúcar	(a·zoo·kar)	sugar
bebida	(be·bee·da)	drink
carne	(kar·ne)	meat
comida	(ko·mee·da)	food
ensalada	(en·sa·la·da)	salad
fruta	(froo·tas)	fruit
helado	(e·la·do)	ice cream
hielo	(ee·e·lo)	ice
legumbres	(le·goom·bres)	vegetables
maíz	(ma·eez)	corn/maize
mantequilla	(man·te·kee·ya)	butter
pan	(pan)	bread
papas fritas	(pa·pas free·tas)	fries
pastel	(pas·tel)	pastry
pescado	(pes·ka·do)	fish
pimienta	(pee·myen·ta)	pepper
postre	(pos·tre)	dessert
queso	(ke·so)	cheese
sal	(sal)	salt
sopa	(so·pa)	soup
torta	(tor·ta)	cake
trigo	(tree·go)	wheat

Caracas

Spreading along a high plateau that's partitioned from the sea by towering green mountains, Venezuela's capital presents a dense urban fabric, with scores of skyscrapers sticking out of a mass of low-rise buildings like bars on a graph. Fast-paced and cosmopolitan, this progressive city nevertheless has over four centuries of history buried beneath its glass-and-concrete monuments to oil-fueled affluence, while signs of corrosion mar its patina of modernism.

Nowhere else in the country will you find such an array of cultural activity, world-class museums or eclectic cuisine, from the *arepa* joints of Sabana Grande to the haute cuisine of hubs like Las Mercedes and Los Palos Grandes. Caracas' nightlife offers clubbers, bar-hoppers and salsa aficionados the opportunity to mingle with the city's famously die-hard partiers. Commerce makes the city bustle and shopping is a vocation for many *caraqueños* (inhabitants of Caracas) who prowl glitzy malls and sprawling street markets. Complementing these attractions is an agreeable sunny climate, at 900m often described as 'eternal summer,' and a natural exuberance that pleasantly contrasts with the urban fabric. Frangipani blooms outside the metro and tiny frogs cheep from streetside trees. Caracas' northern edge abuts the steep, wooded slopes of Parque Nacional El Ávila, where miles of walking trails wind through scented forests.

Despite these obvious attractions, Caracas' grittier side predominates. Traffic is relentless, and trash and noise can be unnerving. Haphazardly built shantytowns creep up the surrounding hillsides, and poor enclaves rub shoulders with some of the ritziest zones. One constantly hears about how Caracas has declined over the past decade, and with all the warnings about crime and decay, a visit to the capital is inevitably tinged with fear. Young *caraqueños* object to these dismal depictions of their city even as they warn you not to venture into certain areas. A visit to Caracas can be an exhilarating ride, but expect some bumps along the way.

HIGHLIGHTS

- Ride the **teleférico** (cable car) to the summit of El Ávila (p95)

- Ride the *rumba* (party) through the night at the clubs and bars of **Las Mercedes** and **La Castellana** (p87)

- *Tasca*-hop in the Spanish-influenced **La Candelaria** district (p82)

- Follow the footsteps of the nation's liberator, Simón Bolívar, from cradle (Casa Natal de Bolívar) to grave (Panteón Nacional) on our **walking tour** (p72)

- Admire modern and ancient art treasures at the **Museo de Arte Contemporáneo de Caracas** (p68) and **Museo de Arte Colonial** (p67)

Panteón Nacional ★
Museo de Arte Colonial ★
Teleférico ★
La Candelaria ★
Casa Natal de Bolívar ★
Museo de Arte Contemporáneo de Caracas ★
La Castellana ★
Las Mercedes ★

- TELEPHONE CODE: 0212
- POPULATION: 6 MILLION

HISTORY

Caracas had a precarious beginning in 1560 when Francisco Fajardo of Isla de Margarita discovered the emerald valley – then inhabited by the Toromaima people. He founded a settlement named San Francisco, but was soon driven out by the indigenous inhabitants. A year later the town was resurrected, but years of bitter struggle against Toromaima attacks followed.

In 1567, a decisive conquest of the valley was ordered and 136 men led by Diego de Losada overcame a brave indigenous resistance before re-establishing the settlement once and for all on July 25. The new township was named Santiago de León de Caracas, 'Caracas' being the name of a decidedly less troublesome indigenous group that inhabited the coastal cordillera.

A decade later, provincial governor, Juan de Pimentel, chose the young town to be the capital of Venezuela. But from the beginning, Caracas was besieged by vicious pirate raids, plagues and natural disasters, including a devastating earthquake in 1641. More calamity awaited the early 1700s, when a Basque trading company called the Real Compañía Guipuzcoana was based in La Guaira and given a monopoly over trade with Spain. The company's flagrantly corrupt methods aroused widespread anger among the colonists, and the ensuing riots sowed the seeds of the independence movement.

On March 28, 1750, Caracas became the birthplace of Francisco de Miranda, and on July 24, 1783, that of Simón Bolívar. The former was to pave the way to independence; the latter was to realize that aim. On April 19, 1810, a group of councilors and notable *caraqueños* denounced the Spanish governor and formed a Supreme Junta to replace the government. The political struggle raged until July 5, 1811, when congress declared the country's independence.

The following year, on Maundy Thursday, an earthquake wrecked the town, killing some 10,000 people. The conservative clergy swiftly declared that it was a punishment from heaven for the rebellion, but the independence movement was not to be stopped. It eventually reached its aim nine years later, sealed by Bolívar's victory at the Battle of Carabobo on

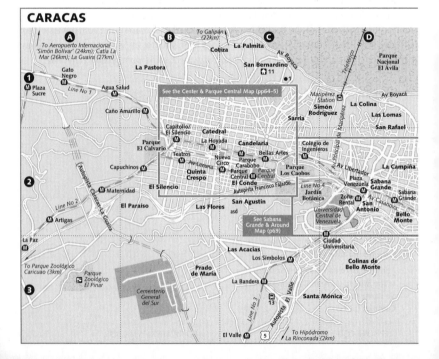

June 24, 1821. Despite this, Spain stubbornly refused to recognize Venezuela's sovereignty until 1845.

Caracas grew at a modest pace until the 1870s, when an extensive modernization program was launched by General Guzmán Blanco, known as 'El Modernizador.' His rule saw a swathe of new monumental buildings totally transform the character of the city center.

Then came the oil boom, and things began to change at breakneck speed. Oil money was pumped into modernization, transforming the bucolic colonial town into a vast concrete sprawl. Colonial buildings were demolished and their place taken by modern commercial centers and steel-and-glass towers.

Spurred on by the illusory dream of wealth, thousands of rural dwellers rushed into Caracas, but the majority never saw their share of the city's prosperity, leading a hand-to-mouth existence in *ranchos* (ramshackle huts) that covered the hills around the central districts. Over the last 50 years, the city's population has shot up from around 400,000 to over six million.

In Hugo Chávez's political ascendance – most recently in his overwhelming re-election in December 2006 – Caracas' dispossessed see the dawning of a new era when they are finally emerging from the shadowy existence of poverty and being recognized as citizens worthy of basic rights such as health care and education. Meanwhile, the much smaller segment of the population that is comfortable laments a continuation of reduced services, legal impunity and soaring crime. The contrast in perceptions will probably continue to place a wedge in serious political dialogue as the city continues to become more polarized.

ORIENTATION

Nestled in a long, narrow valley, the city spreads at least 20km from west to east. To the north looms the steep, verdant wall of Parque Nacional El Ávila, refreshingly free of human dwellings. To the south, by contrast, the city is devouring the hillsides, with modern *urbanizaciones* (suburbs) and derelict *barrios* (shantytowns) invading every reasonably flat piece of land.

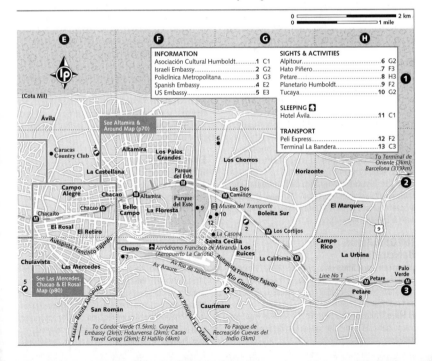

Extending eastward from El Silencio to Chacao, the central downtown area is packed with commercial centers, offices and hotels. The metro's main line (No 1) goes right along this axis. At the west end is the historic quarter (called the 'Center' in this chapter), recognizable on the map by the colonial chessboard layout of the streets. About 1.5km to the east of Plaza Bolívar is Parque Central, noted for its museums and theaters. Another 2km east is Sabana Grande, centered on a busy pedestrian mall brimming with shops and stalls. Continuing east, you come to Chacao, a commercial district good for upmarket shopping, and then to hip Altamira, which boasts scores of sophisticated restaurants and nightspots. El Rosal and Las Mercedes, south of Chacao, also cater to gourmands and night-trippers.

Maps

Fold-out maps of Caracas are sold at many book and stationery stores. One useful tool is the *Guía de Calles, Avenidas, Esquinas y Metro de Caracas*, a pocket atlas with bus and metro routes, available at Tecni-Ciencia Libros (right). Also helpful are the city maps posted near metro stations ticket booths.

To find topographical maps for the rest of Venezuela, ranging from 1:1000 to 1:250,000, visit the **Instituto Geográfico de Venezuela Simón Bolívar** (IGVSB; Map pp64–5; ☎ 546-1247; www.igvsb.gov.ve in Spanish; Office 215, Edificio Camejo, Av Este 6; ☒ 8:30am-noon & 1:30-4pm Mon-Fri).

INFORMATION
Bookstores

American Book Shop (Map p70; ☎ 285-8779; Jardín Level, Centro Comercial Centro Plaza, Los Palos Grandes; Ⓜ Altamira) Fair selection of Lonely Planet guidebooks, plus magazines in English.

El Libro Italiano (Map p69; ☎ 763-1964; Av Francisco Solano, Sabana Grande; Ⓜ Sabana Grande) Books in Italian.

El Buscón (Map p80; ☎ 993-8242; Centro Trasnocho Cultural, Centro Comercial Paseo Las Mercedes, Las Mercedes) Browse-worthy store with strong selection of Venezuelan literature (in Spanish), plus some English novels.

Librería La France (Map p69; ☎ 952-0890; Centro Comercial Chacaíto, Plaza Brión/Chacaíto; Ⓜ Chacaíto) Best selection of books in French.

Librería Alemana Oscar Todtmann (Map p69; ☎ 762-5244; Centro Comercial El Bosque, Av Libertador, Chacaíto; Ⓜ Chacaíto) Extensive choice of German-language publications.

Tecni-Ciencia Libros (Centro Comercial Ciudad Tamanaco (CCCT) (Map p80; ☎ 959-5547; fl C-2, Chuao); Centro Comercial Sambil (Map p80; ☎ 264-1765; Nivel Acuario, Av Libertador, Chacao; Ⓜ Chacao) One of Venezuela's best bookstores, with 10 branches around town. Both stores listed above include well-stocked travel sections with plenty of Lonely Planet titles.

The cheapest place to browse is the street **book market** (Map pp64–5; Plaza España a Romualda), a warren of bookstalls beneath an elevated highway featuring a haphazard range of new and secondhand books in Spanish, including some rare old editions.

Emergency

If your Spanish is not up to scratch, try to get a local to call on your behalf.

Emergency Center (ambulance, fire & police; ☎ 171)
Red Cross (☎ 541-4713)

Immigration

Onidex (Oficina Nacional de Identificación y Extranjería; Map pp64–5; ☎ 483-2070; www.onidex.gov.ve in Spanish; Av Baralt, Plaza Miranda, El Silencio; ☒ 7:30am-11:30am Mon-Fri; Ⓜ Capitolio/El Silencio) Visas and tourist cards can be extended here for up to three months (US$63). Passport, two photos and a letter explaining the purpose of the extension are required, plus the application form (available on the website by clicking 'Extranjería', then 'Prórroga de Turismo').

Internet Access

It's generally easy and inexpensive to get online in Caracas. Most shopping malls have a couple of cybercafés, and many hotels provide free access for guests. Online rates run US$0.75 to US$1 per hour, with opening hours of 8am or 9am to 9pm or 10pm daily (hours usually shorter on Sunday), unless otherwise indicated. In addition to the places listed below, most CANTV Net and Telefónica communications centers (p61) also offer online computers.

CompuMall (Map p80; Av Orinoco, Edificio Santa Ana, Las Mercedes; per hr US$1.80)

Cori@red (Map p70; Av Francisco Miranda, cnr 1a Av; Ⓜ Altamira)

Cyber Café M@dness (Map p80; Acuario Level, Centro Comercial Sambil, Av Libertador, Chacao; per hr $1.50; Ⓨ 10am-11pm; Ⓜ Chacao)

Cyber Catedral (Map pp64-5; Plaza Bolívar; Ⓨ 7am-7:30pm Mon-Sat; Ⓜ Capitolio/El Silencio)

Cyber Office 2020 (Map p69; Edificio San Germán, Calle Pascual Navarro at Av Francisco Solano, Sabana Grande; Ⓜ Plaza Venezuela)

Cyber Only Place (Map p69; Torre Lincoln, Blvd de Sabana Grande & Las Acacias; Ⓨ 8:30am-7pm Mon-Sat, 10am-4pm Sun; Ⓜ Plaza Venezuela)

Infocentro (Map pp64-5; www.infocentro.gob.ve in Spanish; Ⓨ 9:30am-4 or 5pm Tue-Sat) Biblioteca Metropolitana Simón Rodríguez (Calle Norte 4, Esq El Conde; Ⓜ Capitolio/El Silencio); Galería de Arte Nacional (Plaza Morelos, Los Caobos; Ⓜ Bellas Artes); Palacio de las Academias (Av Universidad, cnr La Bolsa; Ⓜ Capitolio/El Silencio). Product of a government initiative to give internet access to all, these centers allow anybody 30 minutes' free access. There are currently three dozen such centers at libraries and museums around town; for a full list, consult the website and click on 'Donde estamos?'

Intermanía (Map p70; 1a Transversal btwn Avs 2a & 3a; Ⓨ 9am-10:30pm Mon-Fri, 11am-10:30pm Sat & Sun; Ⓜ Parque del Este)

Las 5 Estrellas (Map pp64-5; Av Este 2, Esq Colimodio; Ⓨ closed Sun; Ⓜ Bellas Artes)

Librería Tiempo (Map p69; cnr Avs Las Palmas & Quito; Ⓜ Plaza Venezuela) Downstairs from the bookstore.

Internet Resources

Caracas Virtual (www.caracasvirtual.com in Spanish) Grab bag of useful info, from lists of taxi services to the history of chicha (sweet, milky rice beverage), plus extensive events coverage.

Guía Gastronómica de Caracas (www.miropopic.com /gastronomica in Spanish) Reviews all the city's restaurants.

Rumba Caracas (www.rumbacaracas.com in Spanish) Essential source for Caracas' endlessly varied nightlife.

Laundry

There are a few DIY lavanderías (laundrettes), but most provide full service, often the same day you drop your stuff off. A 5kg load, dried and folded, will cost US$5 or US$6. Typical

---

CARACAS IN...

Two Days
On your first morning take a trip round the historical heart of the city via our walking tour (p72), starting at Bolívar's birthplace and finishing at his tomb at the **Panteón Nacional** (p67). Once you've worked up an appetite, treat yourself to lunch at a traditional tasca (Spanish-style bar-restaurant) in **La Candelaria** (p82). In the afternoon, take your pick of the museums in Bellas Artes and don't miss the **Museo de Arte Contemporáneo de Caracas** (p68). Alternatively, it's worth the trip north to the **Museo de Arte Colonial** (p67). Finish off your day with a meal and perhaps a nightcap in the glitzy restaurants and bars of **Las Mercedes**. (p83)

On your second day, escape the urban jungle and take a trip up El Ávila mountain on the **teleférico** (cable car, p95). Once you're back on terra firma, catch a bus out to the charming colonial suburb of **El Hatillo** (p72) for some serious souvenir shopping after a meal in one of its numerous excellent restaurants. Finally, when you've deposited any bulky buys back in your hotel, those who have still got a spring in their step can enjoy a meal in upmarket **Altamira** (p84) followed by a night out in the chic clubs and bars of **Centro Comercial San Ignacio** (p86).

Four Days
If you're sticking around longer, follow the two-day itinerary, but leave El Hatillo and Altamira until your third day, spending the entire second day roaming further along the tranquil woodland paths of **Parque Nacional El Ávila** (p95). Then on your fourth day, wind down by taking a walk through the sprawling **Parque del Este** (p71) or talk to the animals at **Parque Zoológico de Caricuao** (p72).

hours are 7am to 6pm Monday to Saturday. Recommended *lavanderías*:

Lavandería Autolanka (Map pp64-5; Centro Comercial Doral, Av Urdaneta, La Candelaria; Ⓜ Parque Carabobo)

Lavandería Automática Maxi Clean (Map p70; 2a Transversal, Altamira; Ⓜ Altamira)

Lavandería Chapultepek (Map p69; Calle Bolivia, Sabana Grande; Ⓜ Plaza Venezuela) Also open Sunday morning.

Lavandería El Metro (Map p69; Calle Los Manguitos, Sabana Grande; Ⓜ Sabana Grande)

Libraries & Cultural Centers

Asociación Cultural Humboldt (Map pp56-7; ☎ 550-0464; Av Juan Germán Roscio at Av Jorge Washington, San Bernardino) The German cultural center hosts concerts, conferences and films, and also has a library of German-language publications.

Alianza Francesa (Map p69; ☎ 762-9976; www.afcaracas.org in Spanish/French; 1st fl, Edificio Centro Solano, Av Solano, Chacaíto; ⏱ 9am-12:30pm & 3-6:30pm Mon-Fri, 10am-1pm Sat; Ⓜ Chacaíto) Publications in French.

Biblioteca Nacional (Map pp64-5; ☎ 505-9125; www.bnv.bib.ve in Spanish; Av Norte 1, El Panteón; ⏱ 8:30am-5:30pm Mon-Fri, 9am-4pm Sat) Next to the Panteón Nacional, this is the best-stocked library in Caracas; it also houses the principal archives of national documents, books, newspapers and audiovisual records.

British Council (Map p80; ☎ 952-9965; www.britishcouncil.org.ve in Spanish; 3rd fl, Torre Credicard, Av Principal El Bosque, Chacaíto; ⏱ 8am-8pm Mon-Fri, 8am-4pm Sat; Ⓜ Chacaíto) Wide selection of English-language resources; check the website for upcoming events.

Centro Venezolano Americano (CVA; Map p80; ☎ 993-8422; www.cva.org.ve; Av Principal de las Mercedes) The US cultural center has many English-language publications to browse, plus movies and Spanish courses (see p73).

Medical Services

Most minor health problems can be solved in a *farmacia* (pharmacy), of which Caracas has a wide array, and one in every neighborhood takes its turn to stay open all night, easily recognizable by a neon sign reading 'Turno.' Some convenient *farmacias* include:

Farmarebajas (Map p70; ☎ 261-2337; Av Ávila, cnr Av José Félix Sosa, Altamira; Ⓜ Altamira)

Farmatodo (Map p69; ☎ 761-4812; Blvd de Sabana Grande; Ⓜ Plaza Venezuela)

Caracas has a number of public hospitals and private clinics. The latter are better equipped and offer inpatient and outpatient services; some have English-speaking doctors.

Following are reputable medical facilities:

Centro Médico de Caracas (Map pp64-5; ☎ 552-2222; Plaza El Estanque, Av Eraso, San Bernardino)

Clínica El Ávila (Map p70; ☎ 276-1111; Av San Juan Bosco at 6a Transversal, Altamira)

Clínica Instituto Médico La Floresta (Map p70; ☎ 286-3856; Av Principal de la Floresta at Calle Santa Ana; Ⓜ Altamira)

Hospital de Clínicas Caracas (Map pp64-5; ☎ 508-6111; Av Panteón at Av Alameda, San Bernadino)

Policlínica Metropolitana (Map pp56-7; ☎ 908-0100; Calle A-1, Urbanización Caurimare)

Money

Many banks have ATMs on the Cirrus and Plus networks, although extracting cash can be a hit-or-miss proposition. It is always safer to withdraw money within the bank, if possible. The following are convenient central branches:

Banco de Venezuela Center (Map pp64-5; Av Universidad, cnr Sociedad); Centro Comercial Sambil (Map p80; Nivel Acuario); La Candelaria (Map pp64-5; Av Urdaneta, cnr Candilito); La Castellana (Map p70; Av San Juan Bosco); Sabana Grande (Map p69; Av Francisco Solano, cnr Pascual Navarro)

Banesco Altamira (Map p70; Av Altamira Sur); Center (Map pp64-5; Av Universidad, cnr El Chorro); La Candelaria (Map pp64-5; Av Urdaneta, cnr El Candilito); Las Mercedes (Map p80; Calle Monterrey); Sabana Grande (Map p69; Blvd de Sabana Grande);

BBVA La Castellana (Map p70; Av San Juan Bosco, La Castellana); Parque Central (Map pp64-5; Parque Central, Torre Este); Sabana Grande (Map p69; Blvd Sabana Grande, cnr Calle San Antonio); Centro Comercial Chacaíto (Map p69; Av Francisco de Miranda)

Citibank Sabana Grande (Map p69; Centro Comercial El Recreo, Av Casanova)

The usual places to change foreign cash are *casas de cambio* (money-exchange offices), such as **Italcambio** (☎ 562-9555; www.italcambio.com in Spanish) Altamira (Map p70; Av Ávila; ⏱ 8:30am-5pm Mon-Fri, 8:30am-noon Sat); La Candelaria (Map pp64-5; Av Urdaneta); Sabana Grande (Map p69; Centro Comercial El Recreo, Av Casanova; ⏱ 10am-9pm Mon-Sat, noon-8pm Sun).

Amex (☎ 800-100-4730) offers local refund assistance for traveler's checks. For wire transfers, Western Union is represented by **Grupo Zoom** (☎ 800-767-9666; www.grupozoom.com in Spanish), with about 75 offices scattered around the city.

Post

Ipostel (www.ipostel.gob.ve in Spanish) Main Office (Map pp64-5; ☎ 862-0486; Av Urdaneta, cnr Carmelitas,

Center; 7am-7:45pm Mon-Fri, 8am-5pm Sat, 8am-noon Sun; Capitolio/El Silencio); Altamira (Map p70; Av Francisco de Miranda); La Candelaria (Map pp64-5; Plaza La Candelaria); Chacaíto (Map p80; Centro Comercial Arta, Plaza Chacaíto). Offers poste-restante service. Address letters as follows: recipient's last name capitalized and underlined, first name, Lista de Correos, Ipostel, Carmelitas, Caracas 1010.

These international courier companies operate in Caracas:

DHL (205-6000)
FedEx (205-3333)
UPS (401-4900)

Telephone & Fax

Card-operated public phones abound. Cards (US$2.40) are widely available in kiosks, pharmacies and shops. Metro stations have lots of functional phones and offer the additional advantage of being less disrupted by traffic noise.

Both **CANTV** Chacao (Map p80; Centro Comercial Sambil, Av Libertador); Las Mercedes (Map p80; CCCT, level C-1); Hotel El Conde (Map pp64-5; cnr El Conde); Parque Central (Map pp64-5) and competitor **Telefónica** (Map p69; Blvd de Sabana Grande, cnr Av Los Jabillos, Sabana Grande) have many telecommunication outlets around town called 'Centros de Comunicaciones,' which offer international and domestic calls. Most of these offer reasonably priced internet access as well.

Another widespread – though illicit – option is to use the cell phones set up on tables along the street. 'Informal' operators resell time from mobile phone plans for about US$0.15 a minute; they also sell single cigarettes, presumably for the benefit of nervous callers.

Tourist Information

Inatur (www.inatur.gob.ve in Spanish); Domestic terminal (355-1191; Maiquetía airport; 7am-8pm); International terminal (355-1060; Maiquetía airport; 7am-midnight). Note: there are no Inatur outlets in Caracas itself.
Information desk (Map pp64-5; 503-5000; Hotel Hilton Caracas, Av Sur 25 at Av Mexico, Parque Central; 24 hr) Officially for Hilton guests only, but the knowledgeable, English-speaking staff here will attend to others as well.
Inparques (Instituto Nacional de Parques Nacionales; Map p70; 273-2811; www.inparques.gob.ve in Spanish; Av Rómulo Gallegos; 8am-noon & 1:30-4pm Mon-Fri) The national parks office has a specialized library.

Travel Agencies

IVI Venezuela (Map p80; 993-6082; www.ivivene zuela.com in Spanish; Residencia La Hacienda, Av Principal de las Mercedes; 8am-6pm Mon-Fri) Offers attractive international airfares for students, teachers and people under 26 years of age; issues ISIC and ITIC cards, as well as Hostelling International cards valid for Venezuela's hostels network. IVI has agreements with hotels, restaurants and shops around the country that offer cardholder discounts (see www.isic.org for a list of these).

DANGERS & ANNOYANCES

Since the late 1980s, Caracas' crime levels have increased along with the city's rapidly growing population. Except for Chacao, Las Mercedes, Altamira and to some extent Parque Central, the rest of the city is considered a *zona roja*, a high-crime area where assaults are commonplace and police protection is minimal. In particular, locals warn you to avoid the *centro* (center) and Sabana Grande after hours. Past 9pm or 10pm at night, the streets in those zones tend to clear out, creating the sense of a de facto curfew.

Caraqueños will invariably warn you of these dangers, leaving visitors quaking with fear at the prospect of moving about the city. While such warnings should not be ignored, they also tend to reinforce the paranoiac atmosphere of the place. Like any large, chaotic city, Caracas has its hazards, but that should not deter you from exploring.

Taking certain precautions will greatly reduce any risks. Try not to look like a tourist, for example by wearing jeans instead of shorts. After dark keep off deserted streets and stick with groups of people. The best approach is to stay alert and be aware of your surroundings.

Some Caracas residents say the police are more of a threat than muggers and advise you not to ask them for any sort of assistance. Police have also been known to harass foreigners about not carrying a passport as a means of extracting a bribe, so take along a copy when you go out.

Perhaps more than street crime, traffic in Caracas is a persistent danger, especially for those on foot. Many intersections are impossible to cross safely. Never assume you have the right of way in any crossing situation. Drivers cannot be trusted to stop at red lights – it is always safer to look for a break in traffic before crossing, preferably with other pedestrians. Motorcycle taxis zip along sidewalks or against the flow of traffic to circumnavigate jams; you never know where they're coming from. Asphyxiating fumes and incessant horn honking by gridlocked vehicles are additional annoyances.

SIGHTS
The Center & Around

The historic center, where the city was born, still retains glimpses of its colonial identity. Although many original houses were replaced with new buildings in the rush toward modernization, ranging from nondescript concrete edifices to futuristic tinted-glass towers, ongoing restorations continue to unearth colonial treasures. Architectural grab bag that it is, the *centro* remains a lively and colorful area and boasts some important Bolivarian sights. Most of the places mentioned below are within reasonable walking distance of Metro Capitolio, unless otherwise noted. See p72 for a suggested route.

PLAZA BOLÍVAR

This leafy **square** (Map pp64–5) is the nucleus of the old town. It's always alive with huddled groups of *caraqueños* engaged in conversation and children feeding freshly popped corn to the black squirrels in the trees, while vendors hawk lemonade and *cepilladas* (shaved ices) on the sidelines, the whole scene shaded by African tulip trees and jacarandas. Golden cherubs gather round the fountains at each corner of the square. In the center is the obligatory monument to Bolívar – the equestrian statue was cast in Munich, shipped in pieces, and eventually unveiled in 1874 after the ship carrying it foundered on the Archipiélago de los Roques.

The plaza is a favorite stage for political visionaries and religious messiahs, who deliver their passionate speeches to a casual audience. In recent years it's been a focus for supporters of President Chávez, with stalls selling videos, paintings and photos of the red-bereted leader alongside saints and musical legends.

CATEDRAL

Set on the eastern side of Plaza Bolívar, the **catedral** (Map pp64–5; ☎ 862-4963; 8-11:30am & 4-6pm Mon-Fri, 9am-noon & 4:30-6pm Sat & Sun) started its life in the mid-16th century as a mere mud-walled chapel. A church later replaced it, only to be flattened by the 1641 earthquake. Built from 1665 to 1713, the new cathedral was

packed with dazzling gilded alters and elaborate side chapels. The wide five-nave interior, supported on 32 columns, was largely remodeled in the late 19th century. The **Bolívar family chapel** is in the middle of the right-hand aisle and can be easily recognized by a modern sculpture of El Libertador (The Liberator) mourning his parents and Spanish bride (for more on Bolívar, see the boxed text p25). Bolívar was baptized here (the baptismal font now stands in the Casa Natal de Bolívar, p66). Also take a look at the fine colonial altarpiece at the back of the chapel.

MUSEO SACRO DE CARACAS

Accommodated in a meticulously restored colonial building that stands upon the site of the old cathedral cemetery, this **museum** (Map pp64–5; ☎ 861-6562; Plaza Bolívar; admission US$0.30; 1-4pm Mon, 9am-4pm Tue-Sat) displays a modest but carefully selected collection of religious art. Duck through the low doorway into the dark, old ecclesiastical prison, where remains of early church leaders still lie in sealed niches. The Museo Sacro also stages concerts and recitals and has a delightful café inside a former chapel of the adjacent cathedral.

CONCEJO MUNICIPAL

Occupying half of Plaza Bolívar's southern side, the **city hall** (Map pp64–5; ☎ 915-1585; admission free; 9am-12:30pm & 2-4:30pm Tue-Sun) was erected by the Caracas bishops from 1641 to 1696 to house the Colegio Seminario de Santa Rosa de Lima. In 1725, the Real y Pontificia Universidad de Caracas, the province's first university, was established here. Bolívar renamed it the Universidad Central de Venezuela, the moniker it keeps to this day, though it has moved to a vast campus outside the historic center. Today the building is the seat of the Municipal Council, but part of it is open to the public.

Museo Santana, on the ground floor, has a unique 'doll's-house version' of the city's development, filled with elaborate miniature models of turn-of-the-19th-century Caracas. All the models were created by local artist, Raúl Santana. There are also grand historic paintings, banners and some fascinating ceiling murals; look for the one depicting Bolívar in the heavens.

The western side of the building houses the **Capilla de Santa Rosa de Lima**, where congress declared Venezuela's independence in

1811 (though it was another 10 years before this became a reality). The chapel has been restored with the decoration and furniture of the time.

While strolling around the courtyard, look for the reproduction of the very first Caracas map, drawn in 1578. It shows the old town when it stretched just two blocks from the plaza in each direction.

CASA AMARILLA

The 17th-century balconied mansion called the **Yellow House** (Map pp64–5), on the western side of Plaza Bolívar, was originally an infamous royal prison. Wholly revamped and painted lemon yellow (hence its name) after independence, the building was converted into a presidential residence. Today it's the seat of the Ministry of Foreign Affairs and can't be visited, but have a good look through the archway and note the well-preserved colonial appearance of its exterior.

IGLESIA SANTA CAPILLA

This neo-Gothic **church** (Map pp64-5; ☎ 860-8894; ⏱ 7am-6pm Mon-Fri, 2:30-6pm Sat, 9am-6pm Sun; Av Urdaneta, cnr Sta Capilla), one block north of Plaza Bolívar, is modeled on the Sainte Chapelle of Paris. It was ordered by General Antonio Guzmán Blanco in 1883 and built on the site of the first mass celebrated after the foundation of the town.

Illuminated by a warm light through stained-glass windows, the marble and white-washed interior has an elaborate stone altar and an unusual open-work vault. One of the treasured possessions of the church is the sizable painting *Multiplication of the Bread*, by Arturo Michelena, hanging in the right-hand aisle.

CAPITOLIO NACIONAL

As part of his mad dash toward modernization in the 1870s, Guzmán Blanco commissioned an ambitious, neoclassical seat of congress, the **National Capitol** (Map pp64-5; ☎ 483-8240; admission free; ⏱ 9:30am-noon & 2-4pm Fri-Sun), to occupy the entire block just southwest of Plaza Bolívar. The two-building complex was erected on the site of a convent, whose occupants were promptly expelled by the dictator and their convent razed.

In the central part of the northern building is the famous **Salón Elíptico**, an oval hall topped by an extraordinary domed ceiling with an all-encompassing mural, which almost seems to move as you walk beneath it. The painting, depicting the battle of Carabobo, was done in 1888 by the most notable Venezuelan artist of the day, Martín Tovar y Tovar. The southern wall of the hall is crammed with portraits of the distinguished leaders of the independence wars. In front of this wall is Bolívar's bust on top of a marble pedestal; the 1811 Act of Independence is kept in the chest inside the pedestal. It's put on public view on July 5, Independence Day.

Tovar y Tovar also left more military works of art in two adjoining halls: the **Salón Amarillo** has on its ceiling a depiction of the battle of Junín, while the **Salón Rojo** has been embellished with a scene from the battle of Boyacá.

MUSEO HISTÓRICO DEL PODER POPULAR

Recently installed on the ground level of the mayor's office, which takes up the north side of the Plaza Bolívar, the **People Power History Museum** (Map pp64-5; ☎ 863-2635; admission free; ⏱ 8:30am-5pm Mon-Fri) is 'devoted to the revolutionary process initiated by Hugo Chávez Frias.' It aims to highlight the cultural heritage of the Venezuelan people through exhibitions on the progress of social movements, achievements of revolutionary heroes and alleged crimes of US imperialism. Whether it's a genuine expression of popular concerns or yet another platform for *chavista* propaganda, you be the judge.

IGLESIA DE SAN FRANCISCO

Just south of the Capitolio Nacional, the **Church of San Francisco** (Map pp64-5; ☎ 484-5707; Av Universidad, cnr San Francisco; ⏱ 6am-noon & 3-6pm) was built in the 1570s, but was remodeled on several occasions during the 17th and 18th centuries. Guzmán Blanco, unable to resist his passion for modernizing, placed a neoclassical facade on the church to match the just-completed capitol building. Fortunately, the interior of the church didn't undergo such an extensive alteration, so its colonial character and much of its old decoration have been preserved. Have a look at the richly gilded baroque altarpieces distributed along both sidewalls, and stop at the statue of San Onofre, in the right-hand aisle. He is the most venerated saint in the church due to his miraculous powers of bringing health, happiness and a good job.

CARACAS

THE CENTER & PARQUE CENTRAL

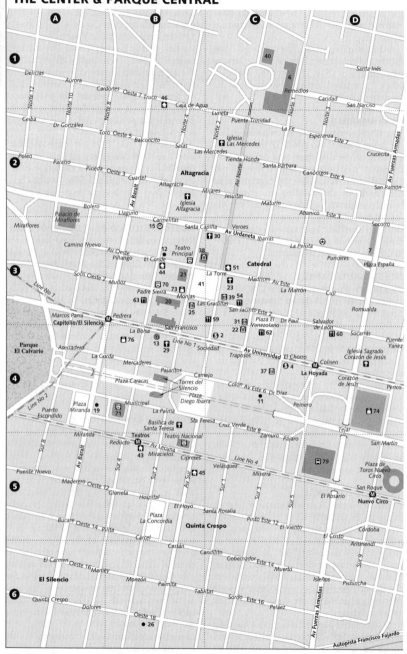

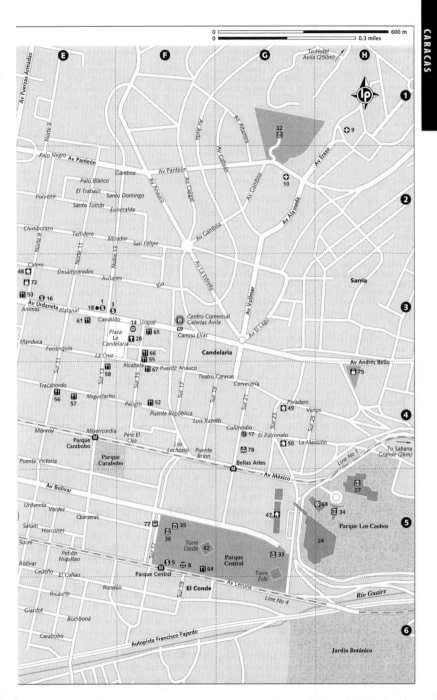

It was in this church in 1813 that Bolívar was proclaimed 'El Libertador,' and also here that his much celebrated funeral was held in 1842, after his remains had been brought from Santa Marta in Colombia, 12 years after his death.

CASA NATAL DE BOLÍVAR
Bolívar's funeral took place just two blocks from the house where, on July 24, 1783, he was born. The interior of **Bolívar's birthplace** (Map pp64–5; ☎ 541-2563; btwn Esqs San Jacinto & Traposos; admission free; ⊙ 9am-4:30pm Tue-Fri, 10am-4:30pm Sat & Sun) has been enthusiastically reconstructed. The walls are splashed with a score of huge paintings by Tito Salas depicting Bolívar's heroic battles and scenes from his life.

MUSEO BOLIVARIANO
Just a few paces north of the Casa Natal de Bolívar, this **museum** (Map pp64–5; ☎ 545-9828; btwn Esqs San Jacinto & Traposos; admission free; ⊙ 9am-4:30pm Tue-Fri, 10am-4pm Sat & Sun) has more successfully preserved its colonial style and displays a variety of independence memorabilia, from

muskets to medals and shaving sets to swords. It also has some fascinating documents and letters written by the man himself, and numerous portraits. More on the morbid side are the coffin in which the remains of Bolívar were brought from Santa Marta in Colombia, and the *arca cineraria* (funeral ark) that conveyed his ashes to the Panteón Nacional.

MUSEO FUNDACIÓN JOHN BOULTON
This small **museum** (Map pp64–5; ☎ 564-4366; www .fundaboulton.org in Spanish; 11th fl, Torre El Chorro, cnr El Chorro; admission free; ⊙ 8:30am-11:30am & 1:30-4pm Mon-Fri; Ⓜ La Hoyada) features a collection of historic and artistic objects accumulated over generations by the family of British merchant John Boulton (1805–75). Among the exhibits are paintings by Arturo Michelena, Bolívar memorabilia and a vast collection of ceramics from all over the world.

TEATRO MUNICIPAL
A striking example of General Guzmán Blanco's Euro-influenced architectural ambitions,

the **Municipal Theater** (Map pp64–5; ☎ 481-6492; Av Este 8, cnr Municipal) opened its doors in 1881 with the presentation of Giuseppe Verdi's *Il Trovatore* by the Fortunato Corvaia Italian opera company. Its sumptuous, domed interior with three tiers of balconies echoes the grandiose European opera houses of the era. After a period of deterioration, it was reinaugurated in 1998, resuming its role as a showcase for operas and plays, as well as concerts by the Municipal Symphony Orchestra of Caracas.

CUADRA BOLÍVAR

Located in the far southern section of the historic center, this was the **Bolívar family's summer house** (Map pp64–5; ☎ 481-1915; btwn Esqs Bárcenas & Piedras, Quinta Crespo; admission free; ◷ 9am-noon & 2-4pm Tue-Sun; Ⓜ Teatros), where Simón Bolívar spent much of his youth. Restored to its original appearance and stuffed with period furniture, the house is today a museum dedicated to El Libertador.

PANTEÓN NACIONAL

The entire central nave of the imposing **National Pantheon** (Map pp64–5; ☎ 862-1518; Av Norte; admission free; ◷ 9am-4pm Tue-Fri, 10am-4:30pm Sat & Sun) is dedicated to national hero Simón Bolívar, underlining the almost saint-like reverence with which he is held in Venezuela. His bronze sarcophagus is placed in the chancel, and the path to reach his tomb is covered by a ceiling filled with paintings of Bolívar's life, all done by Tito Salas in the 1930s.

No less than 140 white-stone tombs of other eminent Venezuelans are crammed into the aisles. One tomb is empty and open, symbolically awaiting the remains of Francisco de Miranda, who died in a Spanish jail in 1816 and was buried in a mass grave. There are two more empty tombs, but they are sealed. One is dedicated to Antonio José de Sucre, who was assassinated in Colombia and whose remains are in the Quito cathedral; he is considered by Ecuadorians as the liberator of their country. The other tomb commemorates Andrés Bello, a Caracas-born poet, writer and friend of Bolívar's who later went to live (and die) in Chile.

The pantheon is at the opposite, northern edge of the old town, five blocks due north of Plaza Bolívar. A church once stood on the site, but it was destroyed in the 1812 earthquake. After reconstruction, it continued as a place of worship until 1874, when Guzmán Blanco decided that it would make a suitable resting place for revered Venezuelans. The progressive president himself, who died in Paris in 1899, rests here.

IGLESIA DE LA CANDELARIA

Seven blocks east of Plaza Bolívar amidst an area steeped in Spanish flavor, this **church** (Map pp64–5; Plaza La Candelaria; Ⓜ Parque Carabobo) has richly gilded monumental retables covering the chancel's walls. The central retable dates from about 1760, while the lateral ones are modern replicas.

But the holiest place in the church for Venezuelans is doubtless the tomb of José Gregorio Hernández (see the boxed text p74), in the first chapel off the right-hand aisle. Though not canonized, José Gregorio is considered more important than many official saints whose images adorn the altars of this and other churches.

MUSEO DE ARTE COLONIAL

The **Museum of Colonial Art** (Map pp64–5; ☎ 551-4256; www.quintadeanauco.org.ve; Av Panteón, San Bernardino; admission incl 45-min tour adult/student US$2.50/1.25; ◷ 9am-11:30am & 2-4:30pm Mon-Fri, 10am-4pm Sat & Sun) is housed in an elegant country mansion known as **Quinta de Anauco**, laid out around a charming patio and enclosed by lush, shady gardens. A ball was staged here in honor of Simón Bolívar's very last night in Caracas: he was never to return alive.

When built in 1797, the mansion was well outside the historic town. Today it's just a green oasis in the inner suburb of San Bernardino, a 10-minute walk northeast of La Candelaria. (Alternatively, catch Metrobús 421 from metro Bellas Artes.) You'll be rewarded with a guided tour around meticulously restored interiors filled with carefully selected works of art, furniture and household paraphernalia. Tours depart roughly every half-hour. Chamber-music concerts are held in the adjacent former stables on Sunday.

Parque Central & Around

Parque Central is not, as you might expect, a green area, but rather a concrete complex of five high-rise residential slabs of somewhat apocalyptic appearance, crowned by two 54-story octagonal towers, the tallest in the country. You can ascend the **Torre Oeste** (West Tower; Map pp64–5) to the 49th floor for phenomenal views toward the north and west.

The Parque Central area is Caracas' art and culture hub, boasting half a dozen museums, the major performing arts center, two art cinemas and the town's most formidable theater.

The park is 1.5km southeast of Plaza Bolívar, next to the Bellas Artes metro station.

MUSEO DE ARTE CONTEMPORÁNEO DE CARACAS

Occupying the eastern end of the Parque Central complex, the **Museum of Contemporary Art** (Map pp64-5; ☎ 573-8289; Parque Central; admission free; ✆ 9am-4:45pm) is by far the best in the country, if not the continent. In a dozen halls on five levels, you'll find big, bold and sometimes shocking works by many prominent Venezuelan artists, including Jesús Soto, famous for his kinetic pieces.

There are also some remarkable paintings by such international giants as Chagall, Matisse, Monet, Leger and Miró. The pride of the museum is a collection of 100 or so engravings by Picasso, created from 1931 to 1934. Part of the exhibition space is for changing displays that showcase both locally and internationally renowned artists. There's also a pleasant café in the adjacent sculpture garden.

MUSEO DE LOS NIÑOS

The brightly colored **Children's Museum** (Map pp64-5; ☎ 575-3022; www.maravillosarealidad.com in Spanish; Parque Central; adult/child US$3.75/3.25; ✆ 9am-5pm Mon-Fri, 10am-5pm Sat & Sun) is an excellent science museum with lots of colorful, hands-on exhibits combining learning with fun for both kids and adults. There's a small planetarium too.

MUSEO DEL TECLADO

Tucked away behind the Museo de los Niños and up a flight of stairs, this little **museum** (Map pp64-5; ☎ 572-9024; Edificio Tacagua, Parque Central; admission free; ✆ 9am-noon & 2-4pm Mon-Fri) holds a collection of rare pianos and other keyboard instruments. It's also a venue for concerts and recitals Saturday at 4pm and Sunday at 11am.

COMPLEJO CULTURAL TERESA CARREÑO

Rising like a gigantic concrete bunker across the street from Parque Central (and linked to it by a footbridge), the **Complejo Cultural Teresa Carreño** (Teresa Carreño Cultural Complex; Map pp64-5; ☎ 574-9333; www.teatroteresacarreno.gob.ve in Spanish; tours US$0.30; ✆ tours 9am-5pm Tue-Sat) is a modern performing arts center. Opened in 1983, it has an enormous main auditorium, theater and side

hall that regularly host concerts, ballets, plays and recitals by local and visiting performers.

Guided tours around the complex are conducted throughout the day; call in advance if you need an English-speaking guide. At the back of the building is a small museum dedicated to Teresa Carreño (1853-1917), Venezuela's most renowned pianist (see p36).

GALERÍA DE ARTE NACIONAL & MUSEO DE BELLAS ARTES

The **National Art Gallery** (Map pp64-5; ☎ 578-1818; www.gan.org.ve in Spanish; Plaza de los Museos, Parque Los Caobos; admission free; ✆ 9am-5pm Mon-Fri, 10am-5pm Sat & Sun) has a vast collection embracing five centuries of Venezuelan artistic expression. Anything from pre-Hispanic art to mind-boggling modern kinetic pieces may be showcased here in temporary exhibitions. Designed in 1935 by Venezuelan architect Carlos Raúl Villanueva, the graceful building radiates from a neoclassical-style courtyard with a pond and weeping willow. The gallery also houses Caracas' leading art cinema (p89).

Adjoining the gallery, the **Museo de Bellas Artes** (Museum of Fine Arts; Map pp64-5; ☎ 571-1819; admission free; ✆ 9am-5pm Mon-Fri, 10am-5pm Sat & Sun) is in a more functional modern six-story building, also designed by Villanueva. The museum features mostly temporary exhibitions, and includes a little shop selling contemporary art and crafts.

You can ponder the purpose of the various works in the sculpture garden from the comfort of the garden café, while sipping on coffee and hobnobbing with local art students.

MUSEO DE CIENCIAS NATURALES

The **Natural Sciences Museum** (Map pp64-5; ☎ 577-5103; admission free; ✆ 9am-4:45pm Mon-Fri, 10:30am-5:45pm Sat & Sun), across the circle from Bellas Artes, traces the history of evolution with displays of minerals and fossils, as well as exhibits covering indigenous languages and astronomy.

Sabana Grande & Around

Though it's still an important nucleus that is packed with hotels, restaurants and shops, Sabana Grande has sadly lost luster over the past decade. Its once-pleasant pedestrian promenade, the Blvd de Sabana Grande – which extends from Plaza Venezuela to Plaza Chacaíto – has been appropriated by hundreds of unauthorized vendors in recent years,

SABANA GRANDE & AROUND

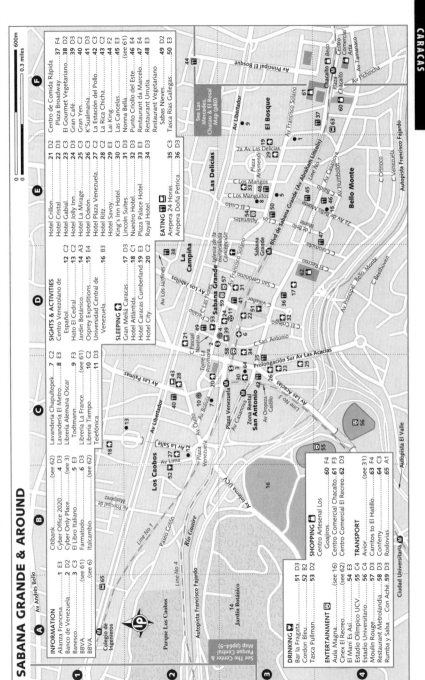

0 — 0.3 miles
0 — 600m

INFORMATION
Alianza Francesa	1 E3
Banco de Venezuela	2 D2
Banesco	3 C3
BBVA	(see 61)
BBVA	(see 6)
Citibank	4 D3
Cyber Office 2020	4 D3
Cyber Only Place	(see 3)
El Libro Italiano	5 E3
Farmatodo	6 D3
Italcambio	(see 62)
Lavandería Chapultepek	7 C2
Lavandería El Metro	8 E3
Librería Alemana Oscar Todtmann	9 F3
Librería La France	10 C2
Librería Tiempo	11 D3
Telefónica	

SIGHTS & ACTIVITIES
Centro Venezolano de Español	12 C2
Hato El Cedral	13 C2
Jardín Botánico	14 A3
Osprey Expeditions	15 E4
Universidad Central de Venezuela	16 B3

SLEEPING
Gran Meliá Caracas	17 D3
Hotel Atlántida	18 C1
Hotel Caracas Cumberland	19 E3
Hotel City	20 C2
Hotel Crillon	21 D2
Hotel Cristal	22 D3
Hotel Gabial	23 C3
Hotel Jolly Inn	24 D3
Hotel La Mirage	25 C3
Hotel Odeón	26 C3
Hotel Plaza Venezuela	27 C2
Hotel Ritz	28 C3
Hotel Savoy	29 E3
King's Inn Hotel	30 C3
Lincoln Suites	31 D3
Nuestro Hotel	32 D3
Plaza Palace Hotel	33 E3
Royal Hotel	34 D3

EATING
Arepera 24 Horas	35 C3
Arepera Doña Petrica	36 D3
Centro de Comida Rápida Plaza Broadway	37 F4
El Gourmet Vegetariano	38 D2
Gran Café	39 D3
Gran Yen	40 C2
K'Sualmania	41 D3
La Estación del Pollo	42 C3
La Rica Chicha	43 C2
Lai King	44 F2
Las Cancelas	45 E3
Nonna Bella	(see 61)
Punto Criollo del Este	46 E4
Restaurant da Marcelo	47 E4
Restaurant Urrutia	48 E3
Restaurant Vegetariano Sabas Nieves	49 D2
Tasca Rías Gallegas	50 E3

DRINKING
Bar la Fragata	51 D3
Cordon Bleu	52 B2
Tasca Pullman	53 D2

ENTERTAINMENT
Aula Magna	(see 16)
Cinex El Recreo	(see 62)
El Mani Es Así	54 E3
Estadio Olímpico UCV	55 C4
Estadio Universitario	56 C4
Moulin Rouge	57 D3
Restaurant Metrolandia	58 D3
Rumba y Salsa ... Con Aché	59 D3

SHOPPING
Centro Artesanal Los Goajiros	60 F4
Centro Comercial Chacaíto	61 F3
Centro Comercial El Recreo	62 D3

TRANSPORT
Avior	(see 31)
Carritos to El Hatillo	63 F4
Conferry	64 C3
Rodovías	65 A1

CARACAS

causing it to become strewn with trash and menaced by crime. At the time of writing, however, the vendors had been ordered to leave the boulevard, and it now remains to be seen whether the district can stage a comeback. On the boulevard's western end you'll find vestiges of the café scene that once attracted masses of strolling *caraqueños*.

JARDÍN BOTÁNICO

From Sabana Grande, it's a 10-minute walk west across hectic roads to reach the **Botanical Gardens** (Map p69; ☎ 605-3994; Av Salvador Allende, Tamanaco entrance of UCV; adult/child under 14 US$0.50/0.25; ☯ 8:30am-4pm), but inside it's a blissful escape from the madness outside. As you delve deeper into the intertwining trees, draped

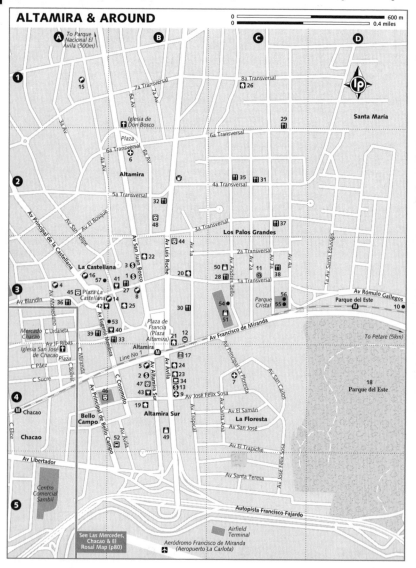

ALTAMIRA & AROUND

vines and lush plants, the traffic noise fades away and birdsong takes over. The gardens are extensive, with plants from all over the world represented.

UNIVERSIDAD CENTRAL DE VENEZUELA (UCV)

With its 85,000 students, the **UCV** (Map p69; ☎ 605-4050; www.ucv.ve in Spanish; Ⓜ Ciudad Universitaria) is Caracas' (and Venezuela's) largest university and is a hub of cultural activity.

The vast campus was designed and built all in one go in the early 1950s by Carlos Raúl Villanueva. Dotted with abstract sculptures and murals throughout its grounds by international artists like Fernán Leger, Jean Arp and Wilfredo Lam, the entire complex was declared a World Heritage Site by Unesco in 2000 for its innovative blending of art and architecture.

The excellent Aula Magna concert hall (p87), capable of seating 2700, is said to have the best acoustics in the country. US sculptor Alexander Calder contributed to this superior sound quality by hanging a set of *nubes acústicos* (acoustic clouds) from the ceiling.

Altamira & Eastern Suburbs

East of Sabana Grande lie some of Caracas' most fashionable suburbs, especially in Al-

tamira and its immediate environs. Further east, you gradually descend the social ladder, reaching a low point at Petare. Eastward from here are vast expanses of appalling *barrios*.

PARQUE DEL ESTE

Any given Sunday, there's plenty of activity within the extensive **Parque del Este** (Map p70; Av Francisco de Miranda; admission free; ☗ 5am-4:30pm Tue-Sun; Ⓜ Parque del Este), from children playing hide-and-seek among the rock gardens, to soccer games, religious groups, martial arts classes and a profusion of lycra-clad bodies jogging while chatting into cell phones. Situated on a portion of a former coffee plantation, the 82-hectare park is the largest in Caracas, and a stroll through its expanses is a botanical odyssey, with many plants and trees labeled. You can visit the snake house, aviary and cactus garden, and on weekends enjoy astral displays in the **Planetario Humboldt** (Map pp56-7; ☎ 234-9188; adult/child under 12 US\$1/0.50; ☗ shows hourly noon-4pm Sat & Sun).

LA ESTANCIA

This renovated fragment of a 220-year-old coffee **hacienda** (Map p70; ☎ 208-6463; www.pdvsa. com; Av Francisco de Miranda; admission free; ☗ 9am-5pm; Ⓜ Altamira) houses a fine museum with works by Venezuelan artists and displays on the plantation's history, as well as a graphic arts library. Property of the Simón Bolívar family until 1895, it is now owned by Petróleos de Venezuela Sociedad Anónima (PDVSA), the national oil company. Continuous guided tours of the installations are offered (English docents available), and concerts are staged in the patio on weekends.

PETARE

Founded in 1621, the independent colonial town of **Petare** (Map pp56-7; **M** Petare) has long since been swallowed by the metropolis but it still preserves some of its historic character around the restored Plaza Sucre. The eastern side of the square is occupied by the mid-18th-century **Iglesia del Dulce Nombre de Jesús**. Two blocks south of the plaza is the **Museo de Arte Popular de Petare Bábaro Rivas** (☎ 271-8335; Calle Guanche, cnr Clemente; ☺ 9am-noon & 1-5pm Mon-Fri, 10:30am-3:30pm Sat & Sun), with exhibits of folk art superbly displayed in a two-century-old house.

From the metro, take the 'Av Fco de Miranda' exit, cross over the avenue and take one of the narrow streets uphill to the plaza. Bear in mind, however, that the neighborhood, close to sprawling slums, is considered unsafe.

Southern Suburbs

The southern part of Caracas, set on rolling hills, is the most heterogeneous. Here are some of Caracas' wealthiest suburbs and also numerous pockets of ramshackle *barrios*, sometimes neighboring each other.

PARQUE ZOOLÓGICO DE CARICUAO

Caracas' main **zoo** (☎ 431-9166; Av Principal de la Hacienda, Caricuao; admission US$1; ☺ 9am-4:30pm Tue-Sun; **M** Zoológico) is situated in the beautifully kept grounds of another old coffee plantation. It has a good selection of native birds, reptiles and mammals, plus some imported felines and elephants. Most animals enjoy a fair degree of freedom in their enclosures, and some birds, including peacocks, ibises, flamingos and macaws, are almost free. Monkeys also mingle with the visitors, so keep an eye on your lunch if you don't want it disappearing up the nearest tree.

The zoo is located in the far southwestern suburb of Caricuao, 10km southwest of the center. From Metro Zoológico, it's a seven-minute walk to the zoo's entrance.

EL HATILLO

A conveniently nearby getaway for *caraqueños*, the 16th-century town of **El Hatillo** (www.elhatillo .com.ve) lived its own life for centuries until it was eventually absorbed by the burgeoning city. Its narrow streets and pretty plaza still retain many of their colonial buildings, now painted in sugary, bright colors and filled with art galleries, craft shops and restaurants (see p84).

Located 15km southeast of the city center, the little village overflows with visitors on the weekend. There's a magical atmosphere in the afternoon and early evening, when children can still be found skipping in the square and *sapitos* (tiny frogs) begin their squeaky chorus.

The biggest and best craft shop is Hannsi (p90), half a block north of the plaza, but you'll find countless other boutiques tucked away in the narrow streets. Also take a look at the parish church on Plaza Bolívar, which has a particularly well-preserved exterior, though its interior was radically (and rather controversially) modernized.

Frequent carritos (Map p69; US$0.40, 45 minutes) run to El Hatillo from Av Humboldt, just off Blvd de Sabana Grande near the Chacaíto metro station. Alternatively, Metrobús 202 leaves from near Altamira metro station on weekday mornings (until 10am) and afternoons (from 4pm).

ACTIVITIES

Hiking in Parque Nacional El Ávila (p96) is one of the more rewarding outdoor endeavors. If you'd like to join an organized group, contact one of the *centros excursionistas* (see p357).

Parque de Recreación Cuevas del Indio (☎ 273-2882; Av Principal de la Guairita; ☺ 8:30am-4pm Tue-Sun) is a favorite rock-climbing spot; local climbers flock here on the weekend. It's 9km southeast of the city center on the southern continuation of Av Principal el Cafetal.

WALKING TOUR

The national hero Simón Bolívar (see boxed text p25) is an inescapable presence in downtown Caracas, where he was born, raised and eventually entombed, and reminders of his life can be found at every corner. To take a tour of the principal sites, start at the Capitolio/El Silencio metro station, taking the 'Esq La Bolsa/Padre Sierra' exit. Cross the street and you'll find yourself at the west end of the **Palacio de las Academias** (1), with its long row

WALK FACTS

Start Metro Capitolio/El Silencio
Finish Panteón Nacional
Distance 2km
Duration 3 hours

WALKING TOUR

of arches and spires; now a branch of the city library, it once housed the national university. Proceed alongside the building's facade until you reach the **Iglesia San Francisco** (**2**; p63), where Bolívar was declared El Libertador. It was here also that his funeral took place.

It's just a short stroll two blocks east and half a block north to reach Bolívar's birthplace, the mansion **Casa Natal de Bolívar** (**3**; p66),

now a museum. Another museum dedicated to Bolívar is a few steps north: this **Museo Bolivariano** (**4**; p66) charts the independence movement with stacks of Bolivarian accoutrements. At the next corner, on the wall of an otherwise unremarkable federal building, the Liberator's words are enshrined (**5**): 'If nature opposes us, then we shall fight against her and make her obey us.' The quote was his response to the 1812 earthquake that leveled the Dominican convent which once stood here. Only the tower of that structure remains: you'll see it on the south side of the facing square, the pretty **Plaza El Venezolano** (**6**).

From here it's a block west to the city's symbolic heart, **Plaza Bolívar** (**7**; p62), presided over by Bolívar's statue and still a focal point for modern-day social revolutionaries. Continuing along the south side of the plaza, you'll find on your left the **Concejo Municipal** (**8**; p62), where Venezuela's independence from Spain was declared. Take a quick, worthwhile detour to the crisp, cream-colored **Capitolio Nacional** (**9**; p63), just southwest of the plaza. You'll see a small gatepost to your right; ask here to enter and view the Salón Elíptico, the oval seat of congress, crowned by glorious battle scenes of Bolívar et al.

Retracing your steps to the plaza and strolling across its lushly canopied length to the east side, you reach the **catedral** (**10**; p62) where Bolívar was baptized, and where his family and wife lie. You might also poke into the **Museo Sacro de Caracas** (**11**; p62), immediately south of the cathedral, for some religious art and coffee.

At this point, proceed up Av Norte, the northbound pedestrian boulevard that extends off the northeast side of the plaza. Though a bit dilapidated these days, it still makes for a pleasant tree-shaded stroll; keep an eye out for the occasional stray soccer ball. At the top of the boulevard, you'll pass under a low bridge and look up toward the **Panteón Nacional** (**12**; p67), sitting grandly at the top of several flights of steps. This is where El Libertador's extravagant tomb lies in pride of place, flanked by other great Venezuelans.

COURSES

Spanish classes are offered by the following institutes.

Centro Venezolano Americano (CVA; Map p80; ☎ 993-8422; www.cva.org.ve; Av Principal de las Mercedes) All levels offered in 16-hour modules, meeting three days per week (US$67 per module).

Centro Venezolano de Español (Ceves; Map p69; ☎ 210-5938, in USA 305-643-5092; www.ceves.org.ve; 19th fl, Torre Phelps, Plaza Venezuela; **M** Plaza Venezuela) Small groups meet 20 hours weekly for a minimum of two weeks (US$640 including lodging with Venezuelan family).

Fundación Escuela de Idiomas Modernos (Map p70; ☎ 286-4764; informacion@fundeim.org; 9th fl, Torre B, Centro Comercial Centro Plaza; **M** Altamira) This extension program of the Universidad Central de Venezuela offers Spanish for foreigners at basic and low-intermediate levels, taught by UCV professors or students (US$110, nine weeks).

TOURS

For an overview of this complex city, you might consider taking a tour. Major hotels like the Hotel Hilton Caracas and Hotel Ávila can arrange full-day tours, in English, for around US$75.

Aventura Trotamundos (Map pp64-5; ☎ 576-6160; www.trotamundos.com; 4th fl, Torre Sur, No 423, Hotel Hilton Caracas, Parque Central) offers a comprehensive Caracas tour that takes in the colonial center, as well as the modern suburbs of Altamira and La Castellana, concluding with shopping in El Hatillo or one of the city's megamalls.

For a less conventional view of Caracas, **Leo Lameda** (☎ 0412-998-1998; leosupersoul@hotmail .com; full-day tour US$50) leads walking tours, hitting some of the city's less-visited pockets, such as the central university and cemetery, while offering plenty of illuminating historical insights along the way.

For Caracas-based tour providers of other parts of Venezuela, see p356.

FESTIVALS & EVENTS

Christmas, Carnaval and Easter are celebrated with fervor in Caracas. During these times all offices close, intercity bus transportation is frantic and accommodations are scarce.

The biggest religious feast in Caracas is the **Semana Santa** (Holy Week) celebration in Chacao, which begins with the Bajada de Palmeras (literally, 'taking down of the palms') on the Friday before Palm Sunday, when hundreds of young men ascend Mt Ávila to collect royal palm fronds for the procession in a tradition that dates back over two centuries. Holy Week culminates with solemn processions on Maundy Thursday and Good Friday, concluding with the Quema de Judas (Burning of Judas) on Easter Sunday.

Traditional suburbs tend to celebrate holy days with more vigor than central districts. El Hatillo holds local feasts on several occasions during the year (May 3, July 16 and September 4), as does Petare (January 30 and 31 and the last Sunday of September).

More characteristic of Caracas are cultural events, of which the **Festival Internacional de Teatro** is the city's highlight. Held in early April of every even-numbered year, the stage fest attracts Venezuelan regional companies as well as international groups to Caracas' theaters.

The week around July 25 witnesses an increase in concerts, exhibitions and theater performances, organized to celebrate the anniversary of Caracas' foundation on July 25, 1567. The **Temporada de Danza** runs for several weeks in July and August, bringing together some of the leading national dance groups,

---

SAINT IN A SUIT

Ask Venezuelans to name their most important saint and most will answer 'José Gregorio Hernández.' Indeed, the surprisingly well-to-do image of this treasured saint is omnipresent in private homes, shrines and religious stalls. Look for the guy with a black felt hat, well-tailored suit and Charlie Chaplin moustache. It's hardly the usual get-up of saints – but don't worry, it's him. In reality, Hernández doesn't appear on the Vatican's list of saints, though he was elevated to venerable status in 1985. But this doesn't deter his faithful followers.

Born into a humble Andean family in 1864, Hernández studied medical sciences in Caracas and Paris before embarking on a brilliant career as university professor and doctor to the president. He was a passionately religious person, and distinguished himself by treating the poor without charge. He tried to dedicate himself to a monastic life on various occasions, but always returned to plough his energy into caring for the poor.

Hernández died in a car accident in 1919, and a cult soon emerged around him and spread throughout the country and beyond. Countless miracles are attributed to him, including numerous healings. Hernández was even adopted as one of the principal deities of the mysterious María Lionza cult (see p165).

plus international guests. In late October and early November, the **El Hatillo Jazz Festival** highlights major figures from across the Latin jazz spectrum.

Also see p108 for details on the festival of **Los Diablos Danzantes** in Francisco de Yare, a day trip from Caracas.

SLEEPING

Accommodations in Caracas are more expensive than elsewhere in the country. The following price breakdowns reflect that reality. All hotels listed in this chapter have rooms with private bathrooms, and most include air-conditioning and TVs.

On the whole, Caracas' budget accommodations are poor, lacking charm and located in unimpressive, sometimes unsafe areas. Most budget haunts double as love hotels (rent by the hour) and some as brothels; business is particularly brisk on Friday and Saturday. Allow time for possible hotel hunting at these times.

Caracas also has plentiful four- and five-star hotels charging hefty rates, though some top-end hotels offer temptingly low rates on weekends; ask in advance. Upmarket hotels have noiseless central air-con, instead of the rattling, dripping boxes found in budget and midrange hotels. Always have a peek at the room before booking in.

Hotel hunting can be a serious challenge during holiday periods, particularly in the Christmas season, when rooms are scarce in any price range. Few places will take phone reservations at these times, even if they have rooms available. The best strategy is to show up around check-out time (1pm) and try to look important.

The Center & Parque Central

Other than the options listed below, decent, reasonably priced accommodations are scarce in the old core of town. The cheapest places are found south of Av Lecuna, but they're often no more than scruffy shelters, renting rooms by the hour. And though the zone bustles during the day, by 8pm or 9pm everything shuts down and there's not a soul about, so you won't want to linger long outside the confines of your lodging. On the other hand, the center is perhaps the city's most human enclave, one of the few parts of town where the traffic din is surpassed by the sound of voices.

BUDGET

Hotel Inter (Map pp64-5; ☎ 564-6448; btwn Animas & Calero; s/d US$24/28; P ✗ M Parque Carabobo) Don't expect a warm welcome, but this creaky old guesthouse is recommended by travelers for its simple comforts and reasonable rates, and it's conveniently placed nearby the *tasca* (Spanish-style bar-restaurant) zone of La Candelaria.

Hotel Grand Galaxie (Map pp64-5; ☎ 864-9011; www.hotelgrandgalaxie.com in Spanish; Esq Caja de Agua; s/d US$28/38, ste with Jacuzzi US$45; ✗) This modern eight-story tower is an oddity in the otherwise rough-and-tumble Altagracia area, four blocks north of Plaza Bolívar. It's often packed with visiting employees of the nearby Education Ministry, whom you may run into at the adjacent *tasca*. Suites tend to be in better condition than the rather basic standard rooms. Weekend discounts are available.

our pick **Plaza Catedral Hotel** (Map pp64-5; ☎ 564-2111; plazacatedral@cantv.net; Plaza Bolívar; s/d incl breakfast US$28/40; ✗ M Capitolio/El Silencio) This hotel has an unbeatable position on the corner of the plaza: the best rooms have big balconies facing it. Light sleepers may opt for an interior room, however, as the cathedral's bells clang every 15 minutes. Bonuses include the hotel's top-floor restaurant, Restaurant Les Grisons (p81), and a friendly receptionist who wants to practice his English.

If these choices are full, the following are among the more acceptable options in the shabby zone near the Teatro Nacional. Both have restaurants.

Hotel El Arroyo (Map pp64-5; ☎ 484-8435; juanelarroyo@cantv.net; Av Lecuna 27; s/d US$21/38; ✗ M Teatros)

Hotel Excelsior (Map pp64-5; ☎ 545-3868; s/d US$26/35; Av Sur, btwn El Hoyo & Cipreses; ✗ M Teatros)

MIDRANGE

Hotel New Jersey (Map pp64-5; ☎ 571-4624; Av Este, cnr Paradero; s or d US$33, tr US$42; P ✗ M Bellas Artes) This basic and clean, if loopily furnished, low-rise in the somewhat easier-going section of the center near Parque Central, makes a perfectly comfortable budget choice. Rooms are relatively large and well-maintained with a cheery palette of colors and assorted decorative elements from over the decades. The attached *tasca* is usually packed with businesspeople.

Hotel Renovación (Map pp64-5; ☎ 571-0133; www .hotelrenovacion.com; Av Este 2 No 154, cnr El Patronato; s/d US$42/56; ✗ M Bellas Artes) This exceedingly narrow, orange-brick building is on the eastern

CARACAS

edge of the central grid, a relatively safe zone near the museums. The hotel has some of the city's friendlier staff, and the rooms, though basic, are zealously looked after and painted in bright primary colors. Ask for a room on one of the highest floors.

Hotel El Conde (Map pp64-5; ☎ 281-1171; fax 862-0928; cnr El Conde; s/d US$70/84; 🇽🇿 Ⓜ Capitolio/El Silencio) Just one block west of Plaza Bolívar, the Conde enjoys a privileged position, and the elegant, polished lobby with portraits of Bolívar is an attraction in itself. However, rates seem inflated for the accommodations, which sorely need an upgrade. On-the-premises restaurants and bar ensure that you won't have to venture outside after dark.

our pick Hotel Ávila (Map pp56-7; ☎ 555-3000; www.hotelavila.com.ve; Av Jorge Washington, San Bernadino; d/ste incl breakfast US$70/90; Ⓟ 🖥 🏊 Ⓜ Bellas Artes) Built by Nelson Rockefeller in the 1940s the Ávila is a throwback to a less traffic-choked age. Enjoying a secluded position at the base of the Ávila range, the grand old hotel has two ivory wings offering commanding balcony views. There's no air-con but at these cool heights the ceiling fans are more than adequate, and you'll be lulled to sleep by the chorus of tree frogs. A huge buffet breakfast is served out on the rear deck by an oval aquamarine pool. From the metro, take Metrobús 421, a 15-minute ride.

TOP END

Hotel Hilton Caracas (Map pp64-5; ☎ 503-5000; www.hiltoncaracas.com.ve; Av Sur 25 at Av México, Parque Central; r from US$135; Ⓟ 🇽🇿 🖥 🏊 Ⓜ Bellas Artes) Facing Parque Central and connected by a footbridge to the Teresa Carreño cultural complex, the five-star Hilton is one of the most-established upmarket hotels in town. Its trump cards are a convenient location for museum hopping, lofty views of the concrete jungle from the top floors, tennis courts, a couple of pools and a state-of-the-art gym. The hotel's two towers, dating from the 1960s and '80s, are linked by an arcade with travel agencies, airline offices and restaurants.

Sabana Grande & Around

Though it's not a particularly attractive or safe area, Sabana Grande still has the biggest selection of accommodations, with something in every category. There are dozens of hotels at the neighborhood's western end, near Plaza Venezuela, many doubling as trysting spots

with by-the-hour rates. Prostitution and other illicit pursuits thrive in the zone alongside all the usual legitimate activities. Heed local warnings about after-dark street crime.

BUDGET

Hotel Cristal (Map p69; ☎ 761-9131; fax 763-2118; Blvd de Sabana Grande, Pasaje Asunción, Sabana Grande; s/d US$24/28; 🇽🇿 Ⓜ Sabana Grande) Right on the boulevard, this isn't the classiest place but it has lots of spacious, serviceable rooms, some with blue balconies overlooking (and hearing) the activity below. The entrance is on a pedestrian passage that is fondly referred to as La Puñalada (The Stab), with a string of gay-oriented *tascas*.

Hotel Jolly Inn (Map p69; ☎ 762-3665; fax 761-4887; Av Francisco Solano, Sabana Grande; s/d/tr US$24/28/38; 🇽🇿 ; Ⓜ Plaza Venezuela) 'Jolly' is not the first adjective that springs to mind to describe the area nor the hotel's lobby, but upstairs are bright, basically clean rooms with lots of closet space. Expect battered furniture and well-worn carpet; streetside units are nicer but noisier.

Nuestro Hotel (Map p69; ☎ 761-5431; hostel@ospreyvenezuela.com; Calle El Colegio cnr Av Casanova, Sabana Grande; s/d/tr/q US$24/31/38/47; Ⓜ Sabana Grande) 'We're in Lonely Planet!' shouts the front wall of this self-proclaimed 'backpacker hostel.' True to form, this is a genuine haven for the international backpacker set, and travelers from Sweden to South Korea gather on the plant-drenched terrace to plot their itineraries. Plain, functional rooms are generally well-scrubbed (though the cockroach population remains undeterred). The Portuguese owners are well versed in travelers' needs, offering laundry service, luggage storage and an English-speaking driver.

Hotel Ritz (Map p69; ☎ 793-7811; cnr Avs Las Palmas & Libertad, Sabana Grande; s/d/tr US$28/31/35; 🇽🇿 Ⓜ Plaza Venezuela) A good-value choice on the west end of Sabana Grande, the Ritz matches the comfort standard of more expensive places if you don't mind ancient furniture or faded carpets. On the penthouse level, wraparound windows let the sun shine in, and comfortably firm beds somewhat compensate for the dull roar of traffic below.

Hotel Odeón (Map p69; ☎ 793-1345; Prologación Sur Av Las Acacias, cnr Av Casanova, Sabana Grande; s/d US$28/33; Ⓟ 🇽🇿 Ⓜ Plaza Venezuela) Standing at a busy intersection, this Colombian-run establishment has eight floors of starkly simple rooms and a decent café below. It's often full.

Hotel La Mirage (Map p69; ☎ 793-2733; Prolongación Sur Av Las Acacias, Sabana Grande; s/d US$28/33; P ✗ M Plaza Venezuela) At the southern end of a string of love hotels, the Mirage is a nondescript nine-story block with basically comfortable accommodations in a 'family' environment.

MIDRANGE

Royal Hotel (Map p69; ☎ 762-5494; fax 762-6459; Calle San Antonio, Blvd de Sabana Grande, Sabana Grande; s/d US$35/38; P ✗ M Plaza Venezuela) The Royal is a true haven in an unfortunate location: a trashy, rundown street preferred by drunks. The six-story structure boasts 48 well-maintained rooms with attractive wood-beam ceilings and reassuring '70s decor. With an unusually congenial staff, sociable lounge and low-lit restaurant bar, it's easy to forget the chaos outside.

Hotel Plaza Venezuela (Map p69; ☎ 781-7811; fax 781-9542; Av La Salle, Los Caobos; s/d/ste US$35/38/42; P ✗ M Plaza Venezuela) Just above the traffic hubbub on Plaza Venezuela, this relatively wholesome hotel with ground-level restaurant is favored by families and businesspeople visiting the capital. Considering the size of its rooms and captivating views, it's well worth the price and often fully booked. Soft rock is piped into the corridors but you can turn down the volume if it bugs you.

King's Inn Hotel (Map p69; ☎ 782-7112; Av Oropeza Castillo, Sabana Grande; s or d US$38, tr US$42; ✗ M Plaza Venezuela) More a sleeping facility than a hotel, this 86-room tower trades charm for neutral modern comforts. Standard-issue furniture remains unblemished and inset lighting enhances the cocoon effect. If you value your sanity, though, be sure to request a room on the parking-lot rather than the street side.

Hotel Gabial (Map p69; ☎ 793-1156; fax 781-1453; Prolongación Sur Av Las Acacias, Sabana Grande; s/d/ste US$38/40/75; P ✗ M Plaza Venezuela) An upmarket option in a sleazy district, the brick-faced Gabial is a sparkling, efficient operation, with professional, English-speaking staff. Its 95 cool, neutral units boast quiet air-con and spacious bathrooms. The cavernous restaurant-bar downstairs hosts live combos toward the weekend for a dance-oriented crowd.

Hotel Atlántida (Map p69; ☎ 793-3211; hotel atlanti@cantv.net; Av La Salle, Los Caobos; s/d/tr US$42/49/55; P ✗ M Plaza Venezuela) Somewhat secluded on a tree-lined boulevard, the secure Atlántida has a cool, modern ambience and convenient

restaurant. Slightly faded rooms get bonus points for safety deposit boxes and hairdryers. It's a few minutes' walk uphill from Plaza Venezuela through a scary tunnel; look for the squat white box with barbed-wire trim.

Hotel City (Map p69; ☎ 793-5785; fax 782-6354; Av Bolivia, Sabana Grande; s/d/ste US$54/59/63; P ✗ M Plaza Venezuela) Standing in the shadow of the pyramidal Previsora building, the City is a low-rise at just nine stories. Though not quite luxurious, it does provide upmarket comfort with friendly, service-oriented staff. Not only is it a well-maintained, comfortable nest amidst the zone's mean streets, it also allows a quick getaway: the metro station is practically on the doorstep.

Plaza Palace Hotel (Map p69; ☎ 762-4821; plaza_palace_hotel@hotmail.com; Calle Los Mangos, Las Delicias; r/ste from US$64/70; P ✗ M Sabana Grande) The Plaza Palace is a smart, businesslike hotel in a subdued enclave near the Blvd de Sabana Grande. Well-tended rooms, some boasting miniterraces, have plenty of mod cons, and there's a better-than-average restaurant on the premises.

Hotel Caracas Cumberland (Map p69; ☎ 762-9961; www.hotelescumberland.com; 2a Av Las Delicias cnr Francisco Solano, Sabana Grande; r incl breakfast US$71; P ✗ M Chacaíto) Despite the innovative cylindrical shape, this 20-year-old lodging reflects the faded swankiness of the zone, with sadly stained carpet, iridescent bedspreads and gray, unsmiling staff. On the plus side, rooms have plenty of space, and enormous hemispheric balconies afford glimpses of the Ávila range.

These hulking business hotels with restaurants are also safe bets:

Hotel Savoy (Map p69; ☎ 762-1971; www.hotel savoycaracas.com.ve; 2a Av Las Delicias cnr Francisco Solano, Sabana Grande; r US$56; P ✗ M Chacaíto).

Hotel Crillon (Map p69; ☎ 761-4411; suizotel@cantv .net; Av Libertador, cnr Av Las Acacias; r US$86; P ✗ M Plaza Venezuela)

TOP END

Lincoln Suites (Map p69; ☎ 762-8575; www.lincoln -suites.com.ve; Av Francisco Solano btwn Av Los Jabillos & Calle San Gerónimo, Sabana Grande; r/ste incl breakfast US$144/168; P ✗ 🖳) The reserved, business-class ambience of the Lincoln Suites is a world away from the chaos out the back door. The 11-story hotel offers plush, spacious suites with abstract canvasses and Ávila views, as well as a Basque-cuisine restaurant and bar. Weekends prices drop by 15%.

CARACAS

Gran Meliá Caracas (Map p69; ☎ 762-8111; www
.granmeliacaracas.solmelia.com; Av Casanova cnr Calle
El Recreo, Sabana Grande; r incl breakfast from US$211;
Ⓟ Ⓧ 🖳 🖩 Ⓜ Sabana Grande) Caracas' largest
and most luxurious hotel, the Meliá stands
in stark contrast to its blighted surroundings.
The 436-room hotel, flanked by an additional
two towers of guest apartments, has about
everything you could wish for, including a
huge fitness center with sauna, recently refurbished pool and no fewer than five restaurants.
Elegantly furnished rooms come with added
luxuries like a bathrobe and slippers and a
pillow menu.

Las Mercedes & Around

For easy access to the city's chief restaurant
and nightlife zone, you might consider staying
in Las Mercedes or El Rosal, though anything
outside the luxury category is likely to rent
rooms by the hour.

Hotel Chacao Cumberland (Map p80; ☎ 952-9833;
www.hotelescumberland.com; Av Santa Lucía, Urb El Bosque,
Chacaíto; s/d incl breakfast US$115/119; Ⓟ Ⓧ Ⓜ Chacaíto)
Around the corner from the lively Chacaíto
plaza, this is the classier younger brother to
the Caracas Cumberland a few blocks west.
The crisply designed interior gets plenty of
natural light, and abstract art jazzes up styl-
ishly furnished rooms.

Hotel Paseo Las Mercedes (Map p80; ☎ 993-9211;
www.hotelpaseolasmercedes.com; Centro Comercial Paseo
Las Mercedes, Las Mercedes; s/d incl breakfast US$137/149;
Ⓟ Ⓧ 🖩) Since so much of Caracas life re-
volves around shopping complexes, it figures
that a hotel should be part of one. Housed in
the chic mall of the same name, this has the
feel of some of the city's top-flight luxury
hotels for considerably less, and prices drop
further on weekends. Even for those not in-
clined to hang around malls, this one contains
dozens of great restaurants as well as Caracas' most cutting-edge cultural center, the
Centro Trasnocho Cultural (www.trasnocho
cultural.com).

Hotel (Map p80; ☎ 951-9268; www.thehotel.com.ve;
Calle Mohedano, El Rosal; r US$170, ste from US$228;
Ⓟ Ⓧ 🖳 Ⓜ Chacaíto) Never mind those other
hotels, this newcomer seems to say: 'we've got
the style to be *the* hotel for modern business
travelers.' Standing on the northern edge of
modish Las Mercedes, the L-shaped white
sentinel is designed for the hip young exec,
from the lobby, brimming with flat-screen
TVs and pomo knickknacks to the robotic

bellboys to the globally decorated DVD-
equipped rooms.

Altamira & Around

The upmarket district of Altamira has some
good midrange accommodations that are well
worth considering. Travelers who'd prefer
not to brave the rougher climes of Sabana
Grande and the Centro will find this a safe,
attractive area, based around a large bustling
plaza and dotted with excellent restaurants
and nightspots – all just 15 minutes from the
center by metro.

MIDRANGE

Hotel Altamira (Map p70; ☎ 267-4284; hotelaltamira@
telcel.net.ve; Av José Félix Sosa, cnr Av Altamira Sur; r US$45;
Ⓟ Ⓧ Ⓜ Altamira) Positioned away from the
plaza on a quiet street, the Altamira has fresh,
white-washed rooms with bamboo furniture.
Front-facing rooms have a small balcony,
which may not have picture-perfect views but
which do give an interesting angle on the city
looking over a small, haphazardly built *barrio* to the skyscrapers and mountain beyond.
A most cordial reception staff speak a bit of
English for Spanish-impaired guests.

Hotel La Floresta (Map p70; ☎ 263-1955; www
.hotellafloresta.com; Av Ávila, Altamira Sur; s/d US$52/59,
ste s/d from US$59/63; Ⓧ 🖳 Ⓜ Altamira) Just a few
paces away from the Montserrat, La Floresta
is a 10-story block of smallish rooms with
attached balconies; those on the north side
get a good glimpse of the mango-dotted La
Estancia estate. Focus on the view rather
than the shabby furniture, rattling air-con or
continuous horn-honking below. Ongoing
renovations should boost the comfort level. A
continental breakfast in the downstairs lounge
is on the house, though you'd be better off at
the café next door.

Hotel Residencia Montserrat (Map p70; ☎ 263-3533;
fax 261-1394; Av Ávila, Altamira Sur; s/d US$61/70, ste US$89;
Ⓟ Ⓧ Ⓜ Altamira) This seven-story box with a
checkerboard facade holds an excellent position just down from Plaza de Francia and
the metro. Accommodations consist of soccer field–size suites with kitchens and ample
balconies (the checker squares) giving oblique
views of the plaza, as well as smaller standard
rooms. All are soothingly appointed with icy
air-con.

Hotel Residencial El Cid (Map p70; ☎ 263-2611;
cumarucidhotel@cantv.net; Av San Felipe btwn 1a & 2a Transversal, La Castellana; s/d US$85/108; Ⓟ Ⓧ Ⓜ Altamira)

Setting itself apart from the rest in a non-descript zone west of the plaza, this safely enclosed hotel sports a suitably faded Spanish aristocrat theme. Apartments pack in a salon with cable TV, understocked kitchenette and bedroom with heavy colonial wood furniture and kitschy art.

TOP END

Hotel Continental Altamira (Map p70; ☎ 261-0004; www.hotel-continental.org.ve; Av San Juan Bosco, Altamira; s/d/tr incl breakfast US$108/115/123; P 🅿 🅿 M Altamira) Aside from its distinctive wing shape, the Continental looks like your average Caracas high-rise block. Pluses include friendly if addled staff; an attractive, covered patio restaurant; and astounding views from upper-level balconies. On the downside, its ample-sized rooms are sorely in need of TLC – even the cushioned chairs on the balcony seem tired.

La Posada Corporativa (Map p70; ☎ 283-4817; gerd schad@cantv.net; 8a Transversal No 2, Los Palos Grandes; r from US$120; P 🅿 🅿 🅿 M Altamira) This is a corporate retreat, though it's open to other guests when available. The imaginative creation of an economist-turned-carpenter, it's a jungly hideaway with cabins scattered through an extraordinary garden, all connected by elevated wooden walkways. With just two double rooms and three double suites, you'd better book well in advance. There's no sign outside; look for 'N2' painted on the wall.

Hotel Altamira Suites (Map p70; ☎ 285-2555; www .alsuites.com; cnr 1a Av & 1a Transversal, Los Palos Grandes; ste from US$220; P 🅿 🅿 🅿 M Altamira) A few blocks north of Plaza de Francia, this corporate hotel is designed for longer stays. Suites come in two classes but the layout is the same, with a kitchen, living room and narrow balconies. After hours, the 360 rooftop bar (p86) provides panoramic entertainment for the city's hippest clubbers.

Hotel Caracas Palace (Map p70; ☎ 771-1000; www .caracaspalace.com; Av Luis Roche, cnr Av Francisco de Miranda; r/ste US$285/550; P 🅿 🅿 🅿 🅿 M Altamira) The ex-Four Seasons is a massive piece of modernist architecture right across from the Plaza de Francia, center of Altamira's public life. The hotel has all executive features, from a wellness center with state-of-the-art treadmills to a cascading split-level pool on an elevated deck. Big-enough-to-live-in beds have seriously fluffy pillows and bathrooms are equipped with gleaming fixtures.

EATING

You could eat out three times a day for several years without ever visiting the same restaurant twice in Caracas. For more ideas, the **Guía Gastronómica de Caracas** (Caracas Gastronomic Guide; www .miropopic.com/gastronomica) is a great resource for discovering the local cuisine scene.

If you're on a budget, keep an eye out for the *menú del día* or *menú ejecutivo* (set menu with two or three courses) for US$4 to US$9. Inexpensive rotisseried chicken restaurants and *areperas* (restaurants selling *arepas* – small, thick corn pancakes) also abound. For breakfast, go to any of the ubiquitous *panaderías* (bakeries). In the evening, countless *tascas* come alive, particularly in La Candelaria and Sabana Grande (p82).

Trendy suburbs such as Las Mercedes, Altamira and La Castellana boast dozens of upmarket restaurants serving a worldwide range of delicacies. But be warned: Caracas restaurants are notorious for not including the 16.5% IVA tax in listed prices, and never the 10% service, so expect your dinner to cost 25% more (or 35% with the customary 10% tip).

With everyone devoting so much time to shopping, malls can also be substantial options, with food courts offering far more than the usual bland franchises. You'll find a particularly worthy selection at El Recreo, Centro Lido, Sambil, Ciudad Tamanaco and Paseo Las Mercedes shopping malls (p90).

Restaurants

THE CENTER & PARQUE CENTRAL

While it doesn't abound in chic restaurants, the center has plenty of low-priced eateries, many of which serve local fare known as *comida criolla*. La Candelaria, the area east of Av Fuerzas Armadas, is swamped with top-end *tascas*.

Budget

Restaurante La Atarraya (Map pp64-5; ☎ 545-8235; Plaza El Venezolano; cachapas US$3; 🕑 7am-8pm; M La Hoyada) This classic dining hall is named after a store that operated here in the 19th century, when the plaza functioned as the city market. *Comida criolla* staples like *cachapas* and roast chicken are served at the counter or in the wood-lined dining area.

Lunchería Doña Agapita (Map pp64-5; Av Sur 13 btwn La Cruz & Miguelacho; cachapas US$3.25; 🕑 8am-7:30pm Mon-Sat; M Parque Carabobo) Excellent *cachapas*

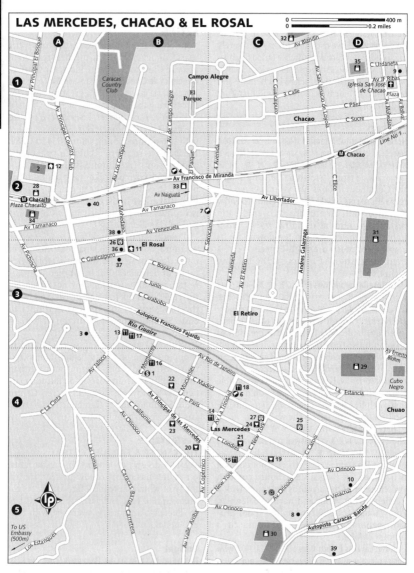

LAS MERCEDES, CHACAO & EL ROSAL

(corn pancakes) with ham and/or cheese can be had at this tiny, no-nonsense spot.

Restaurant Beirut (Map pp64–5; ☎ 545-9367; Av Este 2 btwn Salvador de León & Socarrás; combo platters US$5.50; ⏰ 11:30am-5:30pm Mon-Sat; Ⓜ La Hoyada) This atmospheric lunch place serves up northern Lebanese cuisine. If you come by on Thursday or Friday it's accompanied by belly dancing.

Restaurant Terra Park (Map pp64–5; ☎ 573-8279; Edificio Tajamar, Nivel Bolívar, Parque Central; set lunch US$5.75; ⏰ 7am-10pm Mon-Fri, 8am-7pm Sat & Sun; Ⓜ Parque Central) Bow-tied waiters shout orders at thunderous volumes at this bustling open-air Spanish restaurant on a broad, breezy ground terrace beside the Torre Oeste. It's a great place to chow down in the Parque Central; the *menú del día* will leave you contentedly stuffed.

Restaurant El Coyuco (Map pp64-5; ☎ 572-9624; Av Urdaneta, btwn Candilito & Platanal; half chicken with sides US$6; 🕚 11:30am-midnight; Ⓜ Parque Carobobo) Mouth-watering grilled chicken is what's served up in this vast, smoky dining hall on the main drag. Order your bird *con todo* for sides of yucca, salad and a *hallaquita* (mini tamale).

El Salón del Sabor (Map pp64-5; ☎ 564-9396; ground fl, Edificio Iberia, Av Urdaneta, cnr Animas, La Candelaria; 3-course menú US$7; 🕚 7am-4pm Mon-Fri; Ⓜ Parque Cara-bobo) This vegetarian lunch hall is busiest at midday, when office workers load up their trays with veggie-stuffed burritos, cream of broccoli soup and so on.

ourpick La Guayaba Verde (Map pp64-5; ☎ 415-5063; www.guayabaverde.com in Spanish; Av Este 2 btwn Tracabordo & Migelacho; set lunch US$7.50; 🕚 noon-3pm Mon-Sat; Ⓜ Parque Carobobo) Here you'll get large portions of lip-smacking Venezuelan home-cooking in a cool lime-green ambience with ceiling fans shooting you a breeze. Local gour-mands crowd the place daily to sample an ever-changing set menu (to check the week's selections, go to the restaurant's excellent blog and click on 'Menú de la Semana').

Kafta (Map pp64-5; ☎ 860-4230; Esq San Jacinto; combo platters US$8; 🕚 7am-4:30pm Mon-Sat; Ⓜ La Hoyada) This Middle Eastern eatery situated above a busy street market serves up fresh and filling platters, including some great veg-gie combos.

Midrange & Top End

Restaurant Les Grisons (Map pp64-5; ☎ 564-2111; Plaza Catedral Hotel, Plaza Bolívar; mains US$8-12; 🕚 7:30am-8:30pm Mon-Fri, 8am-2pm Sat & Sun; Ⓜ Capitolio/El Silencio) Visit this rooftop restaurant at Plaza Catedral Hotel for the excellent views rather than the unremarkable food. The Alpine posters are the only trace of the Swiss chef who departed long ago.

Padre Sierra (Map pp64-5; ☎ 482-9050; La Bolsa a Padre Sierra 18; mains US$9-14; 🕚 8am-11pm Sun-Thu, 8am-2am Fri & Sat; Ⓜ Capitolio/El Silencio) A block from Plaza Bolívar, this bright, busy restaurant serves a bit of everything, from *arepas* to steaks, even after everyone else has closed.

ourpick La Cocina de Francy (Map pp64-5; ☎ 576-9849; Av Este 2, cnr Tracabordo; mains US$9-16; 🕚 noon-7pm Mon-Sat; 📵 Ⓜ Parque Carobobo) Instead of Spanish fare, this *tasca*-style restaurant specializes in delicious Venezuelan cuisine, rooted in ances-tral recipes. Check out, for example, the *pelao guayanés*, a soulful chicken stew laced with herbs and olive oil. For dessert don't miss the *quesillo de jojoto*, a creamy corn flan.

SABANA GRANDE & AROUND

The Sabana Grande area boasts enough res-taurants, cafés and snack bars to suit any taste, though with a particularly strong selection for budgeteers. Av Francisco Solano is the area's major culinary artery.

TASCAS – THE SPANISH CONNECTION

The legacy of an early 20th–century wave of immigration from Spain and the Canary Islands, *tascas* (Spanish-style bar-restaurants) are dotted around town, but are most heavily concentrated in the Candelaria neighborhood at the east end of the center. Dozens of these informal taverns are clustered around the zone's central plaza, making *tasca*-hopping an entirely feasible activity. These places retain an extraordinary degree of Iberian character, down to the tile murals, cured hams hanging from the rafters and tie-clad waiters who cultivate that peculiarly Spanish brand of brusqueness. *Tascas* serve traditional dishes from tapas to seafood, often in a separate dining room, while most activity focuses on long, lively bars for knocking back a wee dram or three. All of the following are within easy reach of metro Parque Carabobo and all remain open from 11am or noon till 11pm or midnight.

Tasca Mallorca (Map pp64–5; ☎ 572-5974; Av Este btwn Alcabala & Puente Anauco; mains US$8-18; ⊠ Ⓜ Parque Carabobo) This smaller, cozier place has just a few tables alongside the bar.

La Cita (Map pp64–5; ☎ 572-8180; Esq Alcabala; mains US$9-13; ⊠ Ⓜ Parque Carabobo) This corner classic is one of the liveliest in the zone, with the day's seafood catch on display.

Tasca La Tertulia (Map pp64–5; ☎ 572-9757; Sur 15 btwn Alcabala & Urapal; mains US$10-23; ⊠ Ⓜ Parque Carabobo) Highlights include the *empanada de bacalao* (salt-cod tart) and baked lamb; portions are huge.

Casa Farruco (Map pp64–5; ☎ 572-9343; Av Este 2 btwn Peligro & Puente República; mains US$11-19; ⊠ Ⓜ Parque Carabobo) Decorated with beautiful tile work and ship models, this atmospheric locale offers tranquil dining upstairs and a boisterous bar downstairs. Go for the stuffed squid.

Tasca La Carabela (Map pp64–5; ☎ 578-3020; Av Urdaneta, Esq Urupal; seafood dishes US$18-20; ◷ 11am-late Mon-Sat; ⊠ Ⓜ Parque Carabobo) Time stands still in this humble spot by the plaza, where an entire wall is dominated by a wooden ship relief. Galician fare is their strong suit.

These other tascas are in Sabana Grande.

Las Cancelas (Map p69; ☎ 763-6666; 2a Calle de Bello Monte; 3-course menú US$5, paella for two US$21; Ⓜ Sabana Grande) This place breathes tradition, with a bullfighting gallery and an extraordinarily long bar, and serves some of the better paellas in town.

Tasca Rías Gallegas (Map p69; ☎ 763-0575; Av Francisco Solano 4 cnr Apamate; seafood dishes US$10-15; Ⓜ Sabana Grande) The horseshoe-shaped bar and various wood-paneled salons here overflow with chattering *caracaqueños* at lunchtime or after work.

Budget

Centro de Comida Rápida Plaza Broadway (Map p69; Blvd de Sabana Grande; ◷ 11am-7pm; Ⓜ Chacaíto) This budget food court packs in 50 or so fast-food outlets on two levels, serving everything from pad thai to tabbouleh.

Arepera 24 Horas (Map p69; Av Casanova, cnr Prolongación Sur Acacias; US$2.50-5; ◷ 24 hr; Ⓜ Plaza Venezuela) Open round-the-clock as the name suggests, this big, busy open-air joint is always good for a well-stuffed *arepa* – survey the fillings in the display case – or a big bowl of *hervido* (hearty chicken or beef boil).

Arepera Doña Petrica (Map p69; ☎ 763-1304; Av Casanova; arepas US$3-4; ◷ 24hr; Ⓜ Sabana Grande) This *arepa* restaurant, serving healthy-sized, inexpensive portions to beer-drinking locals, makes a casual introduction to the basics of Venezuelan cuisine.

Punto Criollo del Este (Map p69; ☎ 953-2536; Av Casanova; set lunch US$3.75; ◷ 6:30am-9pm; Ⓜ Sabana Grande) Though easy to overlook, this hole-in-the-wall kitchen on the east end of the district is a locally recommended purveyor of reasonably priced *comida criolla* lunches.

Restaurant Vegetariano Sabas Nieves (Map p69; ☎ 763-6712; Calle Pascual Navarro 12, Ⓜ Plaza Venezuela; buffet $3.75; ◷ 7am-5pm Mon-Fri, 8am-4pm Sat) Lunch menus change daily at this homely vegetarian spot: Monday is *comida criolla* day, Thursday there's Peruvian fare.

El Gourmet Vegetariano (Map p69; ☎ 730-7490; Av Los Jardines, La Campiña; buffet $4.25; ◷ 11:30am-2:30pm Mon-Fri; ⊠ Ⓜ Sabana Grande) Jazzier than average meatless buffets are served in this handsome, airy dining hall tucked away one block north of Av Libertador. Economical lunch packages include one side and three or four salads. Not exactly gourmet but OK.

K'Sualmania (Map p69; ☎ 762-0220; Edificio Argui, Av Los Jabillos, Sabana Grande; combo platters US$4.25; ◷ 7am-4:30pm Mon-Sat; Ⓜ Sabana Grande) Run by a corps of kinetic young women, this spiffy little Middle Eastern joint has some of the finest falafels and *tabaquitos* (stuffed grape leaves) around. The menu is helpfully illustrated on the wall.

Nonna Bella (Map p69; ☎ 952-1008; Centro Comercial Chacaíto, Blvd de Sabana Grande; pastas US$5.50-7.50; ☻ noon-midnight; Ⓜ Chacaíto) For well-prepared risottos, raviolis and pizzas, check out this pleasant open-air Italian restaurant occupying a large court in the Chacaíto shopping mall. Though it's on the slick side, the kitchen still retains the spirit of 'beautiful Grandma,' as the name translates.

La Estación del Pollo (Map p69; ☎ 793-3366; cnr Avs Casanova & Acacias; half chicken with sides US$6; ☻ noon-11pm; Ⓜ Plaza Venezuela) This popular dining hall has racks of chickens roasting over coals and attentive waiters rushing them to your table, along with the obligatory side of yucca laced with *guasacaca* sauce. Alternatively, order a *parrilla* to have steaks and sausages grilled by your table.

Restaurant da Marcelo (Map p69; ☎ 762-1451; Calle Coromoto; set lunch US$7; ☻ 11:30am-3pm Mon-Fri; Ⓜ Sabana Grande) For quality Italian fare at the lower end of the price scale, check this unpretentious place hidden down a sidestreet.

Midrange

Lai King (Map p69; ☎ 731-1053; Av Principal El Bosque, El Bosque; mains US$8-21; ☻ 11am-11pm; Ⓜ Chacaíto) Located next door to the Chinese social club, this large Chinese restaurant seems more authentic than most, judging by the number of Asian patrons. So besides lo mein and wonton soup, you can enjoy mustard greens in oyster sauce or fish-stuffed tofu. But careful how you order: portions are huge.

Gran Yen (Map p69; ☎ 793-2231; Av Las Palmas, Los Caobos; mains US$9.50-19; ☻ noon-midnight; Ⓜ Plaza Venezuela) Fronted by neon palm trees with a rainbow over the entryway, this old-school Chinese palace has a celebratory atmosphere and is invariably crowded with fans of Cantonese and Szechuan cuisine. There are lots of dim sum choices (served lunchtime only).

Restaurant Urrutia (Map p69; ☎ 763-0448; Av Francisco Solano, cnr Los Manguitos, Sabana Grande; mains US$10-19; ☻ noon-11pm Mon-Sat, noon-5pm Sun; Ⓜ Sabana Grande) Urrutia is one of the best Basque restaurants around. Shaped like a pie wedge with tables along the perimeter, it's often crowded with local office workers relaxing over a seafood meal or noshing on *pasapalos* (finger food).

LAS MERCEDES & AROUND

Eating out is a passion for *caraqueños*, and nowhere is that more obvious than in the fashionable dining district of Las Mercedes. Competition here is fierce, with 100 restaurants closely packed into a 30-block area. Unfortunately it's not a great place to walk around: SUVs and other status vehicles jam the streets and sidewalks function more as parking lots than pedestrian thoroughfares. From Chacaíto metro station, take the 'CC Expreso' exit to catch Metrobús 222 to Las Mercedes.

Budget

Restaurant Real Past (Map p80; ☎ 993-6702; Av Río de Janeiro btwn Calle Monterrey & Av Jalisco; pastas from US$3.50; ☻ 11am-10pm) Catering to students and other cash-strapped types, Real Past has some of the cheapest and most appetizing pasta and pizza around, though none of the swanky setting.

La Casa del Llano (Map p80; ☎ 991-7342; Av Rio de Janeiro; steaks US$8.50-13; ☻ 24hr) A veritable *arepa* factory, this huge no-nonsense diner sticks to traditional plains fare. Hungry locals flock here not just for the *arepas* but for charcoal-grilled steaks and hearty soups.

Midrange & Top End

our pick Mokambo (Map p80; ☎ 991-2577; Calle Madrid, cnr Monterrey; mains US$8.50; ☻ noon-midnight; 🍴) Expertly fusing Mediterranean and Caribbean elements, Mokambo has dishes you didn't know you craved – such as yucca gnocchi or octopus carpaccio – and others you know and love, like three-cheese ravioli with Kalamata olives. Dine in the cool, safari-themed interior or on the terrace, surrounded by tropical foliage.

Soma (Map p80; ☎ 993-7450; Centro Comercial Paseo Las Mercedes; salads US$9.50, set lunch US$10.50; ☻ noon-midnight Tue-Sun, 4pm-midnight Mon) Yet another component in the Trasnocho cultural center experience, Soma is a hip and minimal snack bar offering exciting, innovatively prepared salads and sandwiches and all kinds of snacks to nosh on before or after the show.

Taiko (Map p80; ☎ 993-5647; Av La Trinidad; sushi dishes US$12; ☻ noon-11pm Mon-Thu, 12:30pm-midnight Fri-Sun; 🍴) One of Caracas' first Japanese restaurants, Taiko remains a favorite for its authentically prepared sushi and sashimi in an upmarket, minimalist setting.

La Romanissima (Map p80; ☎ 993-3334; Calle New York; pastas $12-16; ☻ noon-11pm Mon-Sat, 12:30-6pm Sun;

:)) A small, romantic location perfect for an evening tête-à-tête, La Romanissima serves quality home-style Italian pasta and risottos in a mellow, low-lit environment.

La Castañuela (Map p80; ☎ 992-6668; Av La Trinidad cnr Calle París; mains US$16-21; ⏰ 11:30am-midnight; :)) Located on a particularly busy corner of Las Mercedes, this is an updated drive-up version of a traditional *tasca* with a boisterous atmosphere enhanced by freely flowing scotch and lounge singers. The waiters seem constantly in motion, toting enormous pans of paella or trays of tapas to big groups of revelers.

ALTAMIRA & AROUND

Altamira is an area dotted with upmarket restaurants, hip cafés, discos and bars, along with its neighboring suburbs of La Castellana and Los Palos Grandes.

Budget

our pick **La Ghirin Café, Dely y Restaurant** (Map p70; ☎ 286-1108; www.laghirin.com; Av Andrés Bello at 4a Transversal, Los Palos Grandes; breakfasts $3.75, sandwiches US$8.50-12; ⏰ 8am-11pm; M Altamira) Hidden from the road by a wall of palms, this open-air café is worth a stop any time of day for a criollo breakfast, five-course set lunch, or candlelit evening meal. There's a big selection of tropical fruit juices, sandwiches on homemade bread, sublime desserts – all with an emphasis on fresh, healthy ingredients and served by extremely affable waiters.

Café Il Botticello (Map p70; ☎ 266-1618; 2a Transversal, Altamira; pizzas US$5-6.50; ⏰ noon-3pm & 6-11pm Mon-Fri, 1-11pm Sun; M Altamira) Small enough to fill up fast, this unpretentious Italian bistro produces some of the best pizzas around. While you're waiting, fill your plate from the antipasto bar.

El Budaré de la Castellana (Map p70; ☎ 263-2696; Av Eugenio Mendoza, La Castellana; mains US$6-8; ⏰ 24hr; M Altamira) Conveniently located in the heart of Las Mercedes' nightlife district, 'The Griddle' makes a good pit stop between clubs. The bustling, two-level restaurant offers good *cachapas, arepas* and other Venezuelan standards.

Chef Woo (Map p70; ☎ 285-1723; 1a Av, Los Palos Grandes; combos US$6-8.50; ⏰ noon-11pm; M Altamira) This lively, neighborhood Chinese restaurant is popular for its tasty Szechuan fare and even more visited in the evening for cheap beer.

Pollo en Brasas El Coyuco (Map p70; ☎ 285-9354; 3a Av at 3a Transversal, Los Palos Grandes; half chicken & fries US$7.50; ⏰ 11:30am-11:30pm; M Parque del Este) This classic spot is often packed with locals chowing down on lusciously seasoned roasted chicken and yucca within a rustic, log cabin setting.

Restaurant El Presidente (Map p70; ☎ 283-8246; 3a Av, Los Palos Grandes; set lunch $8; ⏰ noon-4pm & 7-10pm Mon-Sat) This simple, checkered-tablecloth spot fills up quickly at noon, when locals pour in for its home-style set-lunch menus.

Midrange & Top End

El Barquero (Map p70; ☎ 261-4645; Av Luis Roche cnr 5a Transversal, Altamira; seafood US$6-13; ⏰ 11:30am-12:30am; :) M Altamira) Always busy with faithful clientele, 'The Boatman' has been serving up excellent Spanish and Galician fish and seafood dishes for many a year. There's a good list of whiskey varieties to boot.

Chirú (Map p70; ☎ 285-1960; Centro Comercial Las Cúpulas, 2a Av, cnr 5a Transversal, Los Palos Grandes; mains US$7.50-11; ⏰ noon-4pm & 7-11pm; M Parque del Este) Chirú is one of a string of modish restaurants with terrace seating at a 'gastronomic shopping mall' in a quiet corner of the Los Palos Grandes district. Their specialty is Chinese-Peruvian, or Chirú, cuisine, with things like *chupe*, an Inca-style seafood soup, and chicken seasoned with *chocle*, a maize sauce.

Catar (Map p70; ☎ 285-0649; Cuadra Gastronómica, 6a Transversal, Los Palos Grandes; mains US$12-15; ⏰ noon-10pm Tue-Sun; M Parque del Este) One of several restaurants in the culinary mall known as the Cuadra Gastronómica, Catar has aggressively eclectic food, with decor to match. The emphasis is on fresh, natural ingredients, which show up in artistically presented sandwiches, salads and carpaccios.

Restaurant La Estancia (Map p70; ☎ 261-4223; Av Eugenio Mendoza at Calle Urdaneta, La Castellana; steaks US$20; ⏰ noon-11pm; M Altamira) Famous for its grilled meats of every cut and style, La Estancia is one of the best spots in Caracas for carnivores. It's situated in a hacienda-style building with tables around a jungly courtyard.

EL HATILLO

Well known for its numerous eating outlets, the outlying colonial village of El Hatillo boasts an extraordinary variety of cuisines for adventurous palates.

Dulces Criollos (☎ 961-3198; Calle La Paz; ⏰ 8am-11pm) The sweet-toothed will have a field day in this traditional candy store on the plaza, which sells gooey cakes, jellied fruits and other local confections.

La Gorda (☎ 963-7476; Calle Santa Rosalia 32; mains US$6.50-8; ☾ noon-3:30pm & 6-10pm Mon-Fri, noon-5pm Sat & Sun) 'The fat lady' has been serving traditional Venezuelan dishes for decades. For something really special, try the *bollos pelones*, a regional variation on *hallacas* (filled corn dough steamed in banana leaves) filled with seasoned ground beef and laced with tomato sauce.

Espetería (☎ 961-5823; Calle Bolívar 9-1; kebabs US$7; ☾ noon-midnight) Madeira-style kebabs are grilled – and served – on swords at this stone-walled eatery opposite the Hannsi crafts store.

Hajillo's (☎ 961-4289; Calle Miranda; mains US$9-13; 6:30-11pm Tue-Fri, noon-midnight Sat & Sun) A block west and half a block north of the plaza, this small chef-managed restaurant offers some adventurous culinary hybrids of Venezuelan and Asian fare, with assuredly aphrodisiacal ingredients. The whitewashed plank dining room opens on lush gardens.

Kasuki (☎ 961-1342; Calle Sucre; sushi combos US$11-16; ☾ 7-11pm Tue-Fri, 1-11:30pm Sat & Sun) Chef/owner Luis Kasuki prepares Japanese cuisine that's strongly influenced by his native Sao Paulo in a stylish space located a block east and half a block north of the plaza. Gluttons should plan to dine here on all-you-can-eat Wednesday and Saturday.

Cafés

A profusion of southern European-style café/bakeries offers a good selection of pastries and cookies in their display cases. These *pastelerías* (pastry shops) invariably have Italian espresso machines and prepare excellent, strong *café negro* (black) and *café marrón* (with milk), which you can often enjoy seated at a front terrace.

Gran Café (Map p69; ☎ 763-6792; Blvd de Sabana Grande, cnr Pascual Navarro; ☾ 7am-midnight; Ⓜ Plaza Venezuela) 'It's not what it used to be,' you'll hear repeatedly in reference to the sad decay of the surrounding zone, but the Gran Café's boulevard terrace still makes a fine place to relax over coffee and croissants and people-watch for a while, hysterical warnings notwithstanding.

Panadería Noyer Deli (Map pp64-5; ☎ 541-1102; Av Norte, btwn Las Gradillas & Sociedad; ☾ 7am-7pm; Ⓜ Capitolio/El Silencio) This particularly appealing café/bakery near the Plaza Bolívar has fantastic apple strudel, among other sweet things.

Flor de Castilla (Map p70; 261-6571; Av Ávila, Altamira Sur; ☾ 7am-10pm; Ⓜ Altamira) Equipped with a fresh juice bar and front terrace seating, this makes a perfect morning coffee stop for those lodged at nearby hotels. The cannolis, éclairs and other pastries are of an especially high standard.

La Rica Chicha (Map p69; Av Libertador, cnr Av Las Palmas; chicha US$1; ☾ Mon-Fri; Ⓜ Plaza Venezuela) Just above the Hotel Ritz, a nice old man serves ice-cold *chicha* – basically rice pudding you can drink – from a big yellow thermos.

Café St Honoré (Map p70; ☎ 286-7982; Av Andrés Bello, cnr 1a Transversal, Los Palos Grandes; sandwiches US$4-5; Ⓜ Altamira) The greenery-enclosed deck at this modish bakery is perhaps the area's trendiest meeting place. Aside from amazing pastries, there are well-stuffed baguettes and breakfast specials.

Groceries & Quick Eats

Automercado Plaza's (Map p70; Centro Comercial Centro Plaza, Los Palos Grandes; ☾ 8am-9pm Mon-Sat, 8am-6pm Sun; Ⓜ Altamira) Grocery shopping for the self-sufficient.

Papa Grill (Map p70; Av Blandín, La Castellana; grills US$4; ☾ 7am-midnight; Ⓜ Altamira) For quick eats, try this stand where a wacky grillman clangs a big bell when your order's ready. The signature snack consists of grilled shredded beef on a bed of yucca, which you can garnish with various tasty sauces from a selection of squeeze bottles.

DRINKING

The youthful bar scene centers around Las Mercedes and La Castellana, while well-established *tascas* serve as more traditional drinking (and eating) venues (see the boxed text p82), particularly in Sabana Grande and La Candelaria. Due to their cheap beer, many Chinese restaurants also become popular quaffing spots toward the weekend.

Most bars open around 7pm but really liven up after 11pm, while clubs often open their doors later still.

PARQUE CENTRAL & SABANA GRANDE

Cordón Bleu (Map p69; ☎ 793-7246; Av Lima, Sabana Grande; ☾ Mon-Fri 6pm-late; Ⓜ Plaza Venezuela) Just up from Plaza Venezuela, 'the hipster bar' is a 50-year-old lounge with a retro vibe and good music. The decor reflects its earlier use as a bordello, with red plush sofas around the perimeter and kitschy art on the walls.

The breezy, upstairs terrace of the Ateneo cultural center, **La Terraza del Ateneo** (Map pp64-5; ☎ 573-4799; Ateneo de Caracas, Los Caobos; ⊗ from 9pm; Ⓜ Bellas Artes), becomes an after-hours gathering place for a diverse, arts-minded crowd in the mood for relaxed conversation and off-the-wall music. Meanwhile downstairs, the Café Rajatabla, adjacent to the famous experimental theater of the same name, is an even more laid-back, open-air affair frequented by performing arts types.

LAS MERCEDES & AROUND

A good place to start your explorations is the Paseo de las Mercedes, where much of the action unfolds.

Birras Pub & Café (Map p80; ☎ 992-4813; Av Principal de las Mercedes at Av Copérnico; ⊗ from 6pm) Appropriately named with the Italian word for beer, this stubbornly rough-around-the-edges pavement bar has its priorities right, boasting the cheapest beers around, plus an emergency fridge devoted to energy drinks to keep the *rumba* (party) rolling.

Café Boo (Map p80; ☎ 992-9354; Calle Londres at Calle New York, Las Mercedes; ⊗ from 6pm) Frequented by a college-age crowd, this tiny bar is popular for its US$1 Soleras and pleasant open-air terrace, augmented by rock videos and drinking snacks.

Wassup (Map p80; ☎ 991-0686; Calle New York btwn Calles París & Madrid, Las Mercedes; ⊗ from 6pm) This youthful, American-style bar-restaurant provides plenty of distractions for its clientele, from bands on the front terrace to dominoes to at least a dozen TVs tuned to the baseball. So why is everyone staring at their cell phones?

Auyama Café (Map p80; ☎ 991-9489; Calle Londres btwn Calles New York & Caroni, Las Mercedes; ⊗ from 5pm) The *rumba* never stops at this boisterous, open-air lounge with a broad front terrace and various brightly lit salons. It's for a slightly more mature set, who may engage in animated conversation, karaoke singing or salsa dancing (to live combos on weekends).

Samoa (Map p80; ☎ 991-6677; Av Principal de las Mercedes; ⊗ from noon) The self-proclaimed 'Island of Happy People' takes up the top level of a mock jungle hut, where groups of 20-somethings share mega cocktails through multiple straws while surf videos play continuously beneath the glare of Polynesian gods.

Maroma Bar (Map p80; ☎ 993-0513; Calle París btwn Calles Mucuchíes & Monterrey; ⊗ from 9pm Tue-Sun) The

Rasta bar. The upstairs lounge is where the real skanking goes on – a dim smoky environment where a DJ works from the front section of an old bus, pumping out a righteous blend of dub, dancehall and more commercial reggae.

Centro Comercial San Ignacio (Map p80; ☎ 263-5249; Blandín level, Centro Comercial San Ignacio, Av Blandín, La Castellana; ⊗ from 9pm; Ⓜ Chacao) Yes, it's a mall, but by night it hosts a major party scene for upper-class youth, particularly on the lower level along Av Blandín, where dozens of restaurants morph into bars, all with front terrace seating. Most popular at the moment are the Eastern-themed Suka and jet-setter franchise Whisky Bar, but you can jump in anywhere.

ALTAMIRA & AROUND

Gran Pizzería El León (Map p70; ☎ 263-6014; Plaza La Castellana; Ⓜ Altamira) This is the most famous beer-guzzling spot in Caracas – mostly thanks to its cheap prices and good pizza. It's an open-air affair on a vast terrace below towering buildings. At the weekend, you'll find a large college crowd jovially debating over row upon row of beer bottles.

Greenwich Pub (Map p70; ☎ 267-1760; cnr Avs Altamira Sur & Av José Félix Sosa, Altamira Sur; Ⓜ Altamira) This tiny, dim English pub with a rock & roll attitude really packs them in most nights. The crowd gets progressively younger and the music more up-to-date as the weekend draws near.

360° Roofbar (Map p70; ☎ 284-1874; Hotel Altamira Suites, cnr 1a Av & 1a Transversal, Los Palos Grandes; ⊗ 5pm-late; Ⓜ Altamira) This innovative open-air lounge atop the Altamira Suites attracts hip scenemakers, who come to chill out on hammocks and sofas, sip wacky cocktails and enjoy panoramic views of the city. Access is through the hotel's rear entrance on 1a Av.

El Naturista (Map p70; 2a Transversal, cnr Av San Felipe, La Castellana; ⊗ noon-midnight; Ⓜ Altamira) Nominally an *arepa* joint, after hours this turns into a major beer-drinking hangout, frequented by hippies, punks and other outlaws, despite the sign which expressly prohibits this sort of behavior.

ENTERTAINMENT

Your best bet to find out what's going on is the daily *Guía* (Guide) in the newspaper *El Universal* (www.eluniversal.com; click on 'Espectáculos'), which has brief descriptions (in Spanish) of the day's music, theater, cinema and art events. Also look out for the monthly brochure put out by the municipality of Chacao, available at various hotels and cultural venues around town. It has useful listings of events in Altamira, La Castellana and El Rosal.

For many, the nightlife is the best reason to come to Caracas. On the weekend, beautiful young things clad in designer labels swarm to Las Mercedes, El Rosal, Altamira and La Castellana. Check out the excellent website www.rumbacaracas.com (in Spanish) for up-to-the-minute trends.

Live Music

In addition to the venues listed here, check the places under Drinking and Nightclubs, many of which also host live acts, especially toward the weekend.

CLASSICAL MUSIC & BALLET

The city's major stage for concerts and ballet is Complejo Cultural Teresa Carreño (p68). Other important concert venues include the Ateneo de Caracas (p89), Museo Sacro de Caracas (p62), Museo del Teclado (p68), Teatro Municipal (p66) and Quinta de Anauco (p67).

Aula Magna (Map p69; ☎ 605-4516; Universidad Central de Venezuela; **M** Ciudad Universitaria) Check the program of this university theatre which hosts performances by the symphony orchestra, usually on Saturday afternoon and Sunday morning. Tickets can be bought from the auditorium's box office directly before the concerts.

Centro Cultural Corp Group (Map p70; ☎ 206-1149; www.corpbanca.com.ve; Torre Corp Banca, Plaza La Castellana, La Castellana; admission free–US$25; **M** Altamira) A multipurpose cultural center at the bottom of a bank building, staging an eclectic program of chamber music and jazz (theoretically listed under the 'Centro Cultural' button of their website).

ROCK & JAZZ

Juan Sebastián Bar (Map p80; ☎ 951-5575; Av Venezuela at Calle Mohedano, El Rosal; ☉ 5pm-2am Mon-Sat; **M** Chacaíto) A longtime bastion of jazz in Caracas, the club remains one of the most attractive environments anywhere for hearing jazz. If you wish, you can grab a seat right at the bandstand – there's a counter to place your drink along the front of it.

Little Rock Café (Map p70; ☎ 267-8337; 6a Av btwn 3a & 5a Transversal, Altamira; ☉ noon-midnight Sun-Wed, noon-5am Thu-Sat; **M** Altamira) In other words, something like the Hard Rock Café but smaller. Wackily decorated with images of musical icons and related paraphernalia, the club hosts rock and metal bands on the weekend, along with a pool table, burgers and TexMex food.

Moulin Rouge (Map p69; ☎ 761-1990; www.moulinrouge.com.ve in Spanish; Av Francisco López, Sabana Grande; ☉ 10pm-6am Tue-Sat; admission US$3; **M** Sabana Grande) Behind the flamboyant windmill facade is Caracas' leading venue for live alternative rock, with two environments: the performance hall and an adjacent lounge for drum-and-bass, trance and techno sessions by resident DJs. Conveniently open until the metro resumes operation.

La Cigarra (Map p70; ☎ 0414-139-7229; Av Altamira Sur, Altamira Sur; ☉ from 8:30pm Tue-Sat, from 3:30pm Sun; admission US$3; **M** Altamira) Another forum for rock and related subgenres, this very popular new pub stages a variety of acts, from reggae artists to Pantera tribute bands. For weekend gigs, there are three bands on the bill.

FOLK & TRADITIONAL

Mi Linda Llanura (Map pp64-5; Av Norte 4, cnr Padre Sierra, Centro; ☉ Thu-Sun; **M** Capitolio/El Silencio) For a taste of Los Llanos in the capital, this rooftop party terrace has ensembles playing traditional music of the plains on amplified harps and *cuatros* (small, four-stringed guitars). It's easy to find – you'll hear it from street level.

Restaurant Metrolandia (Blvd de Sabana Grande; **M** Plaza Venezuela) For something completely different, check out the terrace in front of this restaurant, just east of the Plaza Venezuela metro stop. From around 7pm to 10pm each evening, local singers clad in cowboy hats perform karaoke versions of *Vallenatos* and ballads, some quite soulfully.

Nightclubs

The hedonistic dance clubs of Caracas bear testament to Venezuelans' religious devotion to having a good time. Most clubs open from Tuesday to Saturday, but the real action cranks from Thursday to Saturday after midnight. *Caraqueños* are famed for their inexhaustible energy, and you can expect the *rumba* to roll till daybreak. Admission charges usually include the cost of a few beers. Most clubs won't let you in with sneakers or a T-shirt, so dress to impress.

LATIN DANCE

El Maní es Así (Map p69; ☎ 763-6671; Calle El Cristo at Av Francisco Solano, Sabana Grande; ☺ 11pm-5am Tue-Sun; Ⓜ Sabana Grande) This is one of Caracas' longest-standing and hottest salsa spots, where everything revolves around the dance floor and the live combos. Make an effort to catch Alfredo Naranjo y su Guajeo, an intensely rhythmic ensemble who perform here regularly.

Rumba y Salsa...Con Aché (Map p69; ☎ 761-7620; Av Francisco Solano, cnr Av Los Jabillos, Sabana Grande; ☺ from 6:30pm Tue-Sat; Ⓜ Sabana Grande) Some of the city's top *salseros* play Friday and Saturday night at this upstairs supper club.

Rumbar (Map p80; Calle New York, cnr Calle Madrid, Las Mercedes; ☺ Mon-Sat from 10pm) After they're done drinking and chatting elsewhere in the zone, people come here to dance. Salsa, merengue, *reggaetón* (a fusion of hip-hop, reggae, dancehall and traditional Latin-music beats) and on and on.

El Sarao (Map p70; ☎ 267-1660; Centro Comercial Bello Campo, Av Principal de Bello Campo, Bello Campo; admission Fri & Sat US$18; ☺ from 6pm; Ⓜ Altamira) A prime destination for middle-class *rumberos*, this narrow, subterranean space provides a continuous flow of rum and great live music. Access is through the parking garage.

ELECTRONICA

Gohka Club (Map p80; ☎ 991-4143; Calle Madrid btwn Calles Caroni & New York, Las Mercedes; ☺ from 11pm Thu-Sat) DJs, pulsing lights and smoke machines cast a hypnotic spell upon the crowds of well-heeled 20-somethings who crowd into this cavernous hall each weekend for equal doses of electronica, Latin Rock and Caribbean rhythms.

Vintage (Map p80; ☎ 262-1766; terrazza level, Centro Comercial San Ignacio; ☺ nightly). Clinging to the top-level of the San Ignacio mall's fabulous main hall, the futuristic Vintage features narrow raised dancing platforms with killer views of the city for an exclusive, flashily dressed clientele.

Cinemas

Movies are generally shown with the original soundtrack and Spanish subtitles. To find out

---

GAY CARACAS

Caracas has by far the most open gay community in what is still a relatively conservative country. When looking for gay-oriented venues, the code phrase to watch for is *'en ambiente.'* For additional options, check the websites www.vengay.com and www.rumbacaracas.com (in Spanish).

Bar La Fragata (Map p69; ☎ 762-1684; Calle Villaflor, Sabana Grande; ☺ from 6pm; Ⓜ Sabana Grande) Thumping beats and cheap booze guarantee a packed house most nights at this mostly male establishment.

Cool Café & Pub (Map p70; ☎ 265-5784; Edificio Lara, Av Eugenio Mendoza; ☺ closed Sun; Ⓜ Altamira) There's usually some performance event going on at this relaxed lounge for a mixed crowd, though the tranny cabaret acts are the biggest draw.

Copa's Dancing Bar (Map p80; ☎ 951-3947; Edificio Taeca, Calle Guaicaipuro, El Rosal; ☺ Wed & Thu from 7pm, Fri & Sat from 9:30pm; Ⓜ Chacaíto) A great spot for men and women, Copa's features a large, well-stocked bar, an eclectic musical mix and risqué shows for the weekend crowd. Thursday is girls' night.

La Cotorra (Map p80; ☎ 992-0608; Centro Comercial Paseo Las Mercedes, Las Mercedes; ☺ from 11pm Mon-Sat) One of the city's first gay bars, La Cotorra is a dark, old-school pub with a barricaded door and a conspiratorial air, appealing to a mature crowd who'd rather hear Wham! or Gloria Gaynor than electronic beats. To find it, take the escalator one level up from the cinema, turn into the parking garage, then left along the perimeter. Afterward, you could head over to the other end for the more youthful Royal Club.

Royal Club (Map p80; Nivel Cines, Centro Comercial Paseo Las Mercedes, Las Mercedes; admission US$9, open bar; ☺ 11pm-5am Thu-Sat & Mon) Entrance to this vanguard club is from the parking garage, up the ramp from the cinema level. Beyond an acclimatization zone with three bars, you cross a curtained threshold to reach the main attraction – a cavernous, strobe-lit dance space.

Tasca Pullman (Map p69; ☎ 761-1112; Edificio Ovidio, Av Francisco Solano, Sabana Grande; ☺ from 6:30pm; Ⓜ Plaza Venezuela) One of the most frequented *en ambiente* bars in Sabana Grande, the cozy Pullman has an egalitarian vibe. Though primarily a place to meet and chat, spontaneous dancing is not uncommon. Tuesday is oldies' night.

Trasnocho Lounge (Map p80; ☎ 993-1325; Centro Comercial Paseo de las Mercedes, Las Mercedes; ☺ from 7pm) The Trasnocho cultural center's minimalist bar is a place to pull up a beanbag chair, sip a martini and chill out with friends as guest DJs work their magic.

what's showing consult the local daily press or check online. Tickets are US$4 to US$5, unless otherwise noted.

The two multiplex chains run predominately Hollywood blockbusters.

Cines Unidos (☎ 0500-735-4285; www.cinesunidos .com in Spanish) La Candelaria (Map pp64-5; Centro Comercial Galerías Ávila, Av Urdaneta; Ⓜ Bellas Artes); Metrocenter (Map pp64-5; Av Universidad at Av Baralt; Ⓜ Capitolio/El Silencio); Sambil (Map p80; Centro Comercial Sambil, Av Libertador; Ⓜ Chacao)

Cinex (☎ 200-2463; www.cinex.com.ve in Spanish) Centro Plaza (Map p70; Av Francisco de Miranda, Los Palos Grandes; Ⓜ Altamira); El Recreo (Map p69; Centro Comercial El Recreo, Calle El Recreo; Ⓜ Sabana Grande); San Ignacio (Map p80; Centro Comercial San Ignacio, La Castellana; Ⓜ Chacao)

Film buffs can find a wealth of outside-the-mainstream alternatives at the following venues.

Ateneo de Caracas (Map pp64-5; ☎ 573-4099; Ⓜ Bellas Artes) See right.

Cinemateca Nacional (Map pp64-5; ☎ 576-1491; www.cinemateca.gob.ve in Spanish; Galería de Arte Nacional; admission free or US$1.75; Ⓜ Bellas Artes)

Celarg (Map p70; ☎ 285-2990; Centro de Estudios Latinoamericanos Rómulo Gallegos, Av Luis Roche, cnr 3a Transversal, Altamira; Ⓜ Altamira)

Cines Paseo (Map p80; ☎ 993-1910; www.trasnocho cultural.com in Spanish; Centro Trasnocho Cultural, Centro Comercial Paseo Las Mercedes)

Sports

Estadio Universitario (University Stadium; Map p69; ☎ 0500-226-7366; tickets US$3-10; Ⓜ Ciudad Universitaria) *Béisbol* (baseball) is the local sporting obsession. Professional-league games are played from October to February at this 25,000-seat stadium, home to the Leones de Caracas (Caracas Lions; www.leones.com in Spanish), on the grounds of the Universidad Central de Venezuela. Tickets may be purchased up to game time, usually 7:30pm Tuesday to Friday nights, 6pm Saturday and 4:30pm Sunday.

Estadio Olímpico UCV (Olympic Stadium; Map p69; Ⓜ Ciudad Universitaria) This neighboring sports complex hosts some of the Venezuela national team home soccer matches between December and March. The stadium was expanded to 40,000 capacity in order to host the Copa América in 2007.

Hipódromo La Rinconada (☎ 681-9448; Ⓜ La Rinconada) Caracas' excellent horse-racing track features racing on Saturday and Sunday afternoons

starting at 1pm. The track is 6km southwest of the center, off the Autopista del Valle.

Theater

If you'd like to catch a show – and if your Spanish is up to it – there are a dozen regular theaters in the city. Performances are generally from Thursday to Sunday, with ticket prices anywhere from US$5 to US$15 (some theaters offer discount admission on Thursday).

Serious theatergoers might plan a visit to the city in March/April of an even-numbered year, when Caracas' Festival Internacional de Teatro takes place. You'll have a chance to see some of the best theater companies from Latin America and beyond.

Following are some of the city's more reliable stages. Another good source for play info is the 'Eventos' page of www.caracasvirtual .com (in Spanish).

Ateneo de Caracas (Map pp64-5; ☎ 573-4099; Av México, Plaza Morelos; Ⓜ Bellas Artes) Next to the Complejo Cultural Teresa Carreño, this cultural center is home to the Grupo Rajatabla, the country's best-known theater company, as well as a concert hall, cinema, bookshop and several lively bars.

Celarg (Map p70; ☎ 285-2990) Two theaters highlighting works by contemporary Venezuelan playwrights.

Centro Cultural Corp Group (Map p70; ☎ 206-1149; www.corpbanca.com.ve) Stages dramas and comedies for discerning theatergoers.

Teatro Teresa Carreño (Map pp64-5; ☎ 574-9333; www.teatroteresacarreno.gob.ve in Spanish; Complejo Cultural Teresa Carreño, Los Caobos; Ⓜ Bellas Artes) See p68.

Teatro Trasnocho Cultural (Map p80; ☎ 993-1910; www.trasnochocultural.com; Centro Comercial Paseo Las Mercedes, Las Mercedes) Dedicated to pushing the boundaries of conventional theater.

SHOPPING

Caraqueños adore shopping, and the streets of La Candelaria, Sabana Grande, Chacaíto, Chacao and the historic center are all tightly packed with stores and malls to satisfy that need. As if those weren't enough, there's been an explosion of illicit outdoor street trading in recent years, as thousands of *buhoneros* – as these informal stall operators are known – clog all available pedestrian space to hawk pirated CDs and DVDs, clothing and everyday products at a fraction of shop prices. Interestingly, the phenomenon is prohibited inside the municipality of Chacao, as you'll notice when you cross the line from Blvd de Sabana Grande to Plaza Chacaíto.

Shopping Malls

To fully appreciate the national love affair with shopping, you need only visit one of Caracas' huge shopping malls. Even if you don't normally enjoy hanging around malls, it's instructive to see how they've become a sort of alternate reality to the often harsh landscape of the streets. Not only do *caraqueños* shop in malls, they also eat, get entertained, experience nightlife and even lodge there, effectively creating an idealized facsimile of city life in these temples of consumerism.

Centro Comercial Centro Plaza (Map p70; Av Francisco de Miranda, Los Palos Grandes) A magnet for Los Palos Grandes' youthful shoppers, with cafés around a large interior courtyard.

Centro Comercial Chacaíto (Map p69; Plaza Chacaíto, Chacaíto; M Chacaíto) One of Caracas' older, more established shopping complexes, alongside a bustling plaza with still more malls.

Centro Comercial Ciudad Tamanaco (Map p80; Av Ernesto Blohm, Chuao; ☉ 9am-9pm) Commonly known as CCCT, this older mall with a unique inverted pyramid design contains an exclusive hotel as well as more than 500 stores. From metro Altamira, take Metrobús 201.

Centro Comercial El Recreo (Map p69; ☎ 761-2740; Av Casanova; ☉ 10am-9pm Mon-Sat, noon-8pm Sun; M Sabana Grande)

Centro Comercial Paseo Las Mercedes (Map p80; Av Principal de las Mercedes, Las Mercedes) Includes an excellent hotel (p78) and cutting-edge arts center. From the metro Chacaíto, take Metrobús 221.

Centro Comercial San Ignacio (Map p80; ☎ 263-3953; Av Blandín, La Castellana; ☉ 10am-8pm Mon-Sat, 1-8pm Sun; M Chacao) Architecturally distinctive structure with a pair of futuristic office towers and an incredibly vast central hall; a major nightlife destination, boasting dozens of bars and clubs along the lower level.

Centro Lido (Map p80; Av Francisco de Miranda, El Rosal; M Chacaíto) In the heart of the modern business district, this has scads of exclusive shops on the four lower levels of an office tower.

Centro Comercial Sambil (Map p80; ☎ 267-2101; Av Libertador, Chacao; ☉ 10am-9pm; M Chacao) Touted as South America's largest shopping mall, this vast five-level establishment comes complete with an aquarium, museum, rooftop amphitheater and a waterfall incorporated into the front wall of the building. The corridors of this innovatively designed structure are linked by five nodes, virtually referred to as 'plazas.' Best choice for up-to-the-minute fashions, particularly footwear.

Metrocenter (Map pp64-5; btwn La Bolsa & Pedrera; M Capitolio/El Silencio) One of the few major malls in the old center of the city.

Markets

Caracas has a number of bustling markets, selling primarily everyday products or fruits and vegetables. One of the most central markets is the sprawling **Mercado de La Hoyada** (Map pp64-5; Av Fuerzas Armadas; M La Hoyada), with miles of tightly packed stalls, most selling clothing. Outside the center are **Mercado Guaicaipuro** (Map pp64-5; Av Andrés Bello, Sarria; M Bellas Artes) and the **Mercado Chacao** (Map p80; Calle 3, Chacao; M Chacao), which is three blocks north of the Chacao metro station.

Crafts

To pick up the obligatory hammocks, papier-mâché devil masks or stuffed piranhas, check out the biggest craft shop of them all at **Hannsi** (☎ 963-7184; www.hannsi.com.ve in Spanish; Calle Bolívar 12; ☉ 10am-7pm Mon-Thu, 10am-8pm Fri-Sun), in El Hatillo (p72). The narrow, winding streets around Hannsi also house numerous high-quality craft stores, so take your time to dip into them all.

Maquita (Map pp64-5; ☎ 576-8439; Av Este 2 No 112 btwn Tracabordo & Miguelacho, La Candelaria; ☉ 9:30am-6:30pm Mon-Sat; M Parque Carabobo) If you don't have time to get to El Hatillo, try the offerings at this central spot, which has good woodcarvings.

Artesanía Altamira (Map p70; ☎ 266-4727; Av Ávila, Altamira Sur; ☉ 8am-6pm; M Altamira) A veritable profusion of basket work is to be found here, along with other assorted knickknacks.

Casa Curuba (Map p70; ☎ 283-1857; Av Andrés Bello, Los Palos Grandes) Near Altamira, this high-quality store stock carved wood furniture, boxes and bowls, especially from the state of Lara.

Centro Artesanal Los Goajiros (Map p69; btwn Blvd Sabada Grande & Av Casanova; ☉ 8am-8pm; M Chacaíto) A below-street-level corridor of stalls just west of Plaza Chacaíto offers a mixed-bag of Orinoco crafts (woven hammocks and bags, carved blowguns, musical instruments) and hippie gear (Rasta caps, Guatemalan wallets).

Wednesday to Sunday, hippie artisans set up stalls in front of the Galería de Arte Nacional (p68), a great place to pick up bracelets, necklaces and popular crafts. Inside the gallery, there is a pricier modern art-and-crafts store with some exquisite wares.

Jewelry

Venezuela is a major gold producer, so keen-eyed travelers can pick up some tempting bargains. The nucleus of Caracas' gold market is the legendary central **Edificio La Francia** (Map pp64-5; Plaza Bolívar; 🕑 9am-5pm Mon-Fri, 9am-2:30pm Sat; Ⓜ Capitolio/El Silencio), which boasts 10 stories of jewelry shops, containing about 100 shops in all. It's usually brimming with eager shoppers sporting a glint in their eye, and the streets outside ring with the cries of '*compro oro, compro oro*' (I buy gold, I buy gold).

Music

For legitimately produced CDs (rather than the pirated versions that abound on the streets), try the small but well-crammed **Comercial Carrillo** (Map pp64-5; ☎ 564-4424; Av Norte 9 btwn Ánimas & Calero; 🕑 9am-6pm Mon-Sat; Ⓜ Parque Carabobo), with a voluminous collection of Venezuelan folk and other styles from around the Caribbean.

Camping & Outdoor Equipment

Corporación Verotex (Map p80; ☎ 951-3670; www .corporacionverotex.com in Spanish; 2nd fl, Centro Comercial Arta, No 2-6, Plaza Chacaíto; 🕑 10am-1pm & 2-6:30pm Mon-Fri; Ⓜ Chacaíto) Stocks a reasonable choice of camping, trekking and mountaineering equipment and is one of the cheapest retailers around.

Beco (Map p80; ☎ 952-0511; Plaza Chacaíto; 🕑 9am-8pm; Ⓜ Chacaíto) If Corporación Verotex is shut, try the camping section here, which has gas cannisters for camping stoves, tents and other equipment on the 1st floor.

GETTING THERE & AWAY
Air

The **Aeropuerto Internacional 'Simón Bolívar'** (www.aeropuerto-maiquetia.com.ve in Spanish), 26km from central Caracas, has two terminals, one for international and the other for domestic flights, separated by 400m. There's a free, though infrequent, shuttle service between the terminals.

The **international terminal** (☎ 355-3110) has a good range of facilities, including an Inatur tourist office branch (p61), five car-rental desks, half a dozen *casas de cambio,* three banks, four ATMs, post and telephone offices, restaurants and cafés, and a slew of travel agencies. The **domestic terminal** (☎ 355-2660) provides all of the same facilities.

For a list of international flight connections, see p349. For domestic connections and airline offices in Caracas, see p353. The fares for domestic flights given in the following table were a rough approximate at the time

of research; prices will vary with the airline, season and class of travel:

Destination	Single Airfare
Barcelona	US$60-70
Barinas	US$85-90
Barquisimeto	US$65-70
Carúpano	US$75-80
Ciudad Bolívar	US$90-95
Coro	US$75-90
Cumaná	US$75-80
Las Piedras	US$75-80
Maracaibo	US$65-70
Maturín	US$65-70
Mérida	US$120-150
Porlamar	US$60-85
Puerto Ayacucho	US$90-95
Puerto Ordaz	US$80-120
San Antonio del Táchira	US$120-200
Valera	US$110-120
Valencia	US$55-70

At the time of writing, the international/domestic airport tax was a hefty US$44/19 plus a further US$17.50 departure tax. In most cases, taxes will be included in your ticket price but it's always worth checking beforehand. To check for any further increases, see the airport website.

You can change your money upon arrival, but see the explanation of official/black market exchange rates first (p345). Italcambio, with several branches on the 2nd level of the international terminal, changes cash and traveler's checks and is open till midnight. Advances on Visa and MasterCard are given in the **Banco de Venezuela** (Rampa Level; 🕑 8:30am-3:30pm Mon-Fri). Otherwise try one of the ATMs on the upper level (although some foreign cards do not always work in Venezuelan ATMs; see p344). Note that airport *casas de cambio* do not change *bolívares* back into foreign currencies; if you get stuck with any, consider cashing them in for liquor or cosmetics at the duty-free shops.

To phone from the terminal, buy a phone card at a newsstand. Maiquetía has the same area code as Caracas, so just dial the local Caracas number.

Boat

Ferries run to Isla de Margarita from La Guaira, the port of Caracas, in high season and when there is sufficient demand. You can book tickets at **Conferry** (Map p69; ☎ 0501-2663-3779; www.conferry.com in Spanish; Torre Banhorient, Av Casanova, Sabana Grande; ⓧ 8am-11:30am & 2-5:30pm Mon-Thu, 8:30am-4:30pm Fri; Ⓜ Plaza Venezuela). There's no passenger service to Los Roques, only freight boats.

Bus

Caracas has three public bus terminals – two intercity stations and a central one for shorter journeys. In addition, several smaller, less chaotic private terminals cover the same destinations.

See the following bus table for standard fares and trip duration. The higher fare is for '*bus-cama*' service with seats that recline to be like beds.

TERMINAL LA BANDERA

The **Terminal La Bandera** (Map pp56-7; ☎ 693-6607; Av Nueva Granada; Ⓜ La Bandera), 3km south of the center, handles long-distance buses to anywhere in the country's west and southwest. The terminal has a **left-luggage office** (1st hr US$0.50, per hr thereafter US$0.20; ⓧ 6am-9pm Mon-Sat, 7am-7pm Sun) on the right side of the top level and a friendly Spanish-only information desk near the ticket offices.

The terminal's layout can be confusing. To get to the ticket offices, go up the ramp to the top level. Ignore the numerous touts attempting to shoo you over to their bus companies. A chart inside the entrance shows where the 40 or so bus companies go and the locations of their ticket offices, all of which are on the left side. Below is a list of the most reliable lines serving the most destinations, along with their window location numbers.

Expresos Flamingo (☎ 693-7572; 40)
Expresos Los Llanos (☎ 632-6125; 41)
Expresos Mérida (☎ 693-5559; 44)
Expresos Occidente (☎ 693-6489; 1)

All buses depart from the level directly below the ticket offices, with the exception of buses to Maracay and Valencia. To reach those, you must go to the other end of the terminal, then down one level. From the same location, por puestos (collective taxis/minibuses) travel to San Felipe, Barquisimeto and Maracay, departing as they fill.

The terminal is inconveniently not linked to La Bandera metro station, but 350m away through a chaotic, unsafe neighborhood. From the metro, take the Granada/Zuloaga

exit, cross the avenue and turn left. Leaving the terminal, go down the ramp to the left and proceed 350m, past two gas stations, and cross at the stoplight to the metro. Alternatively, you'll find secure taxis inside the station, departing from opposite the por puesto stand.

TERMINAL DE ORIENTE

The **Terminal de Oriente** (☎ 243-2606; Autopista Caracas-Guarenas) handles all traffic to the east and southeast of the country; international buses to Colombia also leave from here. The terminal is on the eastern outskirts of Caracas, on the highway to Barcelona, 5km beyond Petare (about 18km from Caracas' city center). It's accessible by local buses (20 minutes, US$0.40) from metro Petare: take the 'Av Francisco de Miranda' exit, go left to the avenue and left again to find the bus stop. A taxi from Altamira will cost about US$12. The terminal features ATMs and a helpful information desk.

TERMINAL NUEVO CIRCO

Buses servicing regional destinations (La Guaira, Los Teques, Santa Teresa, Ocumare del Tuy etc) still depart from the old central **Nuevo Circo regional bus terminal** (Map pp64-5; Av Lecuna; Ⓜ Nuevo Circo), though it's absolute chaos. Be prepared to wait in long lines and – when your bus finally arrives – to scramble on.

PRIVATE TERMINALS

Modern, comfortable buses from these smaller stations are pricier than those out of the major terminals but make up for it in convenience and straightforward access. All of the terminals listed have ATMs and snack bars.

Aeroexpresos Ejecutivos (Map p70; ☎ 266-2364; www.aeroexpresos.com.ve; Av Principal de Bello Campo, Bello Campo; Ⓜ Altamira) Services Maracay, Valencia, Barquisimeto, Maracaibo, Maturín, Ciudad Bolívar and Puerto La Cruz.

Peli Express (Map pp56-7; ☎ 239-9058; Corredor Vial Parque del Este; Ⓜ Los Dos Caminos) Has a terminal on the east side of Parque del Este, just south of the Museo del Transporte, with several lines servicing Puerto La Cruz, San Cristóbal, Mérida, Maracaibo, Barinas, Carúpano, Coro, Valencia, Cumaná and Ciudad Bolívar, among other places.

Rodovías (Map p69; ☎ 577-6622; www.rodovias .com.ve in Spanish; Av Libertador, cnr Amador Bendayan; Ⓜ Colegio de Ingenieros) Offers frequent services to Barquisimeto, Valencia, Cumaná, Carúpano, Ciudad Bolívar, Maturín and other destinations. From the metro station, it's a 150m walk east (left exiting the station).

BUSES FROM CARACAS TO MAJOR DESTINATIONS

Destination	Distance	Fare	Time
Barcelona	319km	US$10-14	5hr
Barinas	515km	US$22-25	9hr
Barquisimeto	351km	US$8-17	5½hr
Carúpano	545km	US$16-20	9hr
Ciudad Bolívar	599km	US$18-21	9hr
Coro	446km	US$17-21	9hr
Cumaná	408km	US$15-18	7hr
Guanare	425km	US$10-20	5hr
Güiria	672km	US$19	15hr
Maracaibo	684km	US$22-28	12hr
Maracay	109km	US$3.50-4.50	1½hr
Maturín	512km	US$12-16	8hr
Mérida	680km	US$17-29	13hr
Puerto Ayacucho	715km	US$23	17hr
Puerto La Cruz	333km	US$10-14	5hr
San Antonio del Táchira	857km	US$18-28	12hr
San Cristóbal	816km	US$17-28	10hr
San Fernando de Apure	404km	US$9-20	8hr
Tucupita	733km	US$21	12hr
Valencia	158km	US$4.50-5.50	3hr
Valera	585km	US$12-23	11hr

Car & Motorcycle

Driving into and out of Caracas is pretty straightforward. The major western access route is the Valencia–Caracas freeway, which enters the city from the south and joins Autopista Francisco Fajardo, the main east–west city artery, next to the Universidad Central de Venezuela. From anywhere in the east, access is by the Barcelona–Caracas freeway, which will take you directly to Autopista Francisco Fajardo.

To rent a car, you are generally better off making arrangements from home with international car-rental companies. Operators at the international terminal of Aeropuerto Internacional 'Simón Bolívar' include **Avis** (☎ 355-1190), **Hertz** (☎ 355-1197; caracas@rentamotor .com) and **Budget** (☎ 355-2782; www.budget.com.ve in Spanish). You'll find more desks of local car-rental companies in the domestic terminal. See p355 for more information on car rental.

GETTING AROUND
To/From the Airport

Caracas' main airport is at Maiquetía, near the port of La Guaira on the Caribbean coast, 26km northwest of the city center. If you only

have an overnight stop in Maiquetía, you may prefer to skip the journey into Caracas and stay the night on the coast (see p96).

Maiquetía is linked to the city by a freeway that cuts through the coastal mountain range via various tunnels and bridges. In early 2006, one of the principal bridges had to be demolished due to structural issues. At the time of writing, traffic had to take an alternate route that slowed the usual 20-minute journey by as much as an hour. The new bridge is well under way and is supposed to be completed by the time this book goes to print.

The **airport bus service** (☎ 352-4140; US$4.75) is the most economical option between Maiquetía airport and Caracas, with departures from the airport from 7am to 8:30pm. In the city, the buses depart from 5:30am to 6pm from Calle Sur 17, directly underneath Av Bolívar, next to Parque Central (Map pp64–5). Stairs connect the two levels from the playground behind the Museo de los Niños. At the airport, the bus picks up and drops off passengers by the domestic terminal only. An infrequent shuttle service connects the two terminals, but it's quicker to hike it. The bus ride normally takes 30 to 50 minutes, but until the bridge is rebuilt expect a 1½ to two-hour journey. If you travel into the city during rush hour, it's faster to get off at the Gato Negro metro station and continue by metro, although the area is considered unsafe.

The official **airport taxis** (☎ 793-9744) are black Ford Explorers with a yellow shield on the door, which line up in front of both terminals. These are widely regarded as being the most reliable: other lines are reportedly riskier to use, and armed robberies of tourists by bogus taxi drivers have occurred. Currently fares to Parque Central or Sabana Grande are a hefty US$50, to Altamira US$60. Check the correct fare with the tourist office before boarding a taxi to avoid overcharging, and confirm that the fare is in *bolívares* as opposed to dollars. The fares from the city back to the airport are generally 20% to 30% lower.

Metro

The French-built metro system (www.metro decaracas.com.ve in Spanish) is the major means of getting around Caracas. It's fast, easy to use, cheap and air-conditioned, and it provides access to most major city attractions.

The metro has four lines, with 48 stations and a total length of more than 50km. The longest line, No 1, goes east–west along the city axis. Line No 2 leads from the center southwest to the distant suburb of Caricuao and the zoo. Line No 3 runs from Plaza Venezuela, past the university and southwest to the La Rinconada horserace track. Line No 4, the newest line, parallels line 1 to the south and links lines 2 and 3. To determine which side of the tracks to use, look for the sign showing the train's final destination. On line 1, westbound platforms are marked 'Dirección Propatria,' eastbound 'Dirección Palo Grande.'

The system also includes a number of 'Metrobús' routes, buses that link some suburbs to metro stations. This means you can easily get to San Bernardino, Prados del Este, El Hatillo and other suburbs that are not reached directly by metro. The Metrobús routes are described in the appropriate sections of this chapter. All of the metro lines and Metrobús routes are marked on the Caracas maps posted in every metro station.

The metro operates daily from 5:30am to 11pm. The trains run every three to five minutes Monday to Friday, less often on weekends. Some exits close early: for example, by 10pm only the westernmost entrance of the Plaza Venezuela station remains usable.

Yellow single-ride tickets cost US$0.25 for a ride of any distance; boletos de ida y vuelta (roundtrip tickets) cost US$0.40. The transfer ticket (boleto integrado) for a combined metro-plus-bus single journey costs US$0.35.

Consider buying the **multiabono** (US$2), an orange multiple ticket which is valid for 10 metro rides; not only do you save money, but you also avoid the seemingly interminable queues at the ticket booth every time

you need to use the metro. A combined metro-plus-bus multiabono costs US$2.75. Multiabono tickets can only be purchased from ticket booths, while single and round-trip tickets are also available from vending machines.

Put your ticket into the turnstile slot, which opens and flips it back out to you to use again at your destination. Exit turnstiles conveniently display the number of rides left on your multiabono ticket.

The system moves over a million passengers a day but remains safe and orderly. At peak hours, riders queue up along painted lines on the platforms, boarding when it's their turn. Pickpockets are said to operate in the busier stations; keep your hand on your wallet and stay alert and you'll be fine.

Bus

Two kinds of buses operate on Caracas streets: city-run Metrobuses (US$0.30, see above), and privately run carritos, which are slightly more expensive. The latter are generally in worse shape, with blaring radios and beat-up seats, but go to many destinations inaccessible by metro. They can also be useful for a quick hop along the main east–west thoroughfares when you don't feel like going underground. Route destinations are posted on the windshield. Metrobuses run the same schedule as the metro while carrito lines generally stop running after 9pm.

Taxi

Identifiable by the 'Taxi' or 'Libre' sign, taxis are unmetered, so always fix the fare before boarding. A daytime taxi ride from Plaza

---

CARACAS TRAFFIC

Caracas has some of the planet's most horrendous traffic. From dawn to dusk and later, the city becomes a congested nightmare. Some two million cars jam the streets of the capital daily, with vehicles crawling at an average rate of 15km per hour. It can take an hour to get from Sabana Grande to Altamira at midday, a journey that takes under 10 minutes on the metro. The notorious gridlock leaves large sections of the city paralyzed for much of the day, and incessant horn-honking and asphyxiating fumes are facts of life. The toll on the environment – not to mention people's lungs and nerves – is disregarded.

Perhaps the root of the problem is that there is no incentive not to drive. Venezuelans enjoy some of the world's cheapest gas, a luxury that is taken for granted. Filling your tank costs less than downing an average cocktail. With driving such an inexpensive activity, new car sales are racing along, with more than 300,000 sold per year in the city. In early 2007, President Hugo Chávez belatedly addressed the problem, saying gas prices for private vehicles would increase 200% – to around US$0.10 a liter (public buses would continue to be heavily subsidized).

Bolívar to Sabana Grande or Parque Central to Las Mercedes should not cost more than US$7, Sabana Grande to Altamira US$5. Rates increase around 30% after dark.

It is recommended that you use only white cars with yellow plates and preferably those from taxi ranks, of which there are plenty, especially outside shopping malls. Alternatively, request one by calling any of the numerous companies that provide a radio service. Several companies, including **Móvil-Enlace** (☎ 577-3344), service the entire Caracas area around the clock. Other reliable services include **Taxitur** (☎ 794-1264) and **Teletaxi** (☎ 753-4155). Hotels will usually have taxi companies on standby.

Eustoquio Ferrer (☎ 0412-720-3805; ferrermiranda@ hotmail.com) is a reader-recommended, English-speaking driver with ample experience transporting foreign travelers and is a veritable font of information besides.

Locals advise you not to take 'pirate taxis' – usually 1970s-era exhaust-spewing jalopies – though they are cheaper. Another risky but relatively rapid option is to take one of the numerous *moto-taxis* (motorcycle taxis) that scoot around downtown streets, and often up onto the sidewalks to circumnavigate traffic jams. These are based at canvas-topped stands around the center and Sabana Grande.

AROUND CARACAS

This section includes only what lies between the city and the coast. For other one-day destinations out of Caracas see the Central North chapter (p99).

PARQUE NACIONAL EL ÁVILA

The steep, verdant mountain range that dominates Caracas to the north provides an easily accessible refuge from the chaos of the city. The national park stretches along about 90km of Cordillera El Ávila, which forms a natural east–west wall between the city and the sea.

A remarkable diversity of wildlife inhabits the park's varied ecosystems, which range from dry-season forest to subtundra. Birdwatchers will find hundreds of species to ogle and will likely spot flocks of green parakeets or hear the song of the great kiskadee, which Venezuelans say sounds like its local name, *cristofué* (Christ was). It may take more pa-

tience, though, to get a glimpse of a gorgeous collared trogon or groove-billed toucanet. Reptiles and snakes, both poisonous and benign, also populate the slopes, along with numerous small mammals such as armadillos, porcupines and squirrels. Early morning visitors can eavesdrop on howler monkeys conversing from the treetops. There are even a few jaguars and mountain lions roaming about the more densely vegetated patches of the northern slopes.

The southern slope, overlooking Caracas, is virtually uninhabited but is crisscrossed with dozens of walking trails. The northern face, running down to the sea, is dotted with hamlets and haciendas, yet few tourist trails are on this side. The park is crossed north–south by a few 4WD tracks and the *teleférico* (cable car).

Teleférico

Rising high above the city to the peak of El Ávila (2175m), the **teleférico** (cable car; Map pp56-7; ☎ 901-5555; www.avilamagica.com in Spanish; roundtrip adult/child under 12 & adult over 65 US$14/10.50 Mon-Fri, US$18/12 Sat & Sun; ⏰ 10:30am-8pm Sun & Tue, noon-8pm Mon, 10:30am-midnight Wed-Sat) was reopened with fanfare in 2002 after a 25-year hiatus. Built by a German company (1955–56), the old *teleférico* line consisted of two routes: the now inoperable 7.5km run from El Ávila down to Macuto on the coast, and the reconstructed 4km run from Maripérez station, next to Av Boyacá in Caracas, to Pico El Ávila.

The summit offers breathtaking views of Caracas and the Valle del Tuy beyond, and toward the north is a stunning panorama of the coastline and the Caribbean Sea stretching away to the horizon. The area around the *teleférico* station has been developed as a sort of fun park, called Ávila Mágica, with a playground, 3D cinema and an ice-skating rink, as well as several restaurants and numerous stands along the main path selling coffee, hot chocolate and snacks.

The path from the *teleférico* station leads to the circular 14-story **Hotel Humboldt**, built in 1956, an extraordinary landmark visible from almost every point in the city. It was closed when the cable car stopped running, but has been completely restored with plans for a reopening on an unspecified date. If you're curious and want to have a snoop inside, there are **tours** (adult/child US$2.50/1; ⏰ 4-6:30pm Thu & Fri, 11:30am-6:30pm Sat & Sun) of the installations.

Views are usually best before the mid- to late-afternoon clouds start snaking across the mountaintop, enveloping the complex in an eerie fog that hides objects within even a few meters. At these times it can get surprisingly chilly so be sure to pack a sweater. But when the views vanish and the cold sets in, there's always the Swiss fondue restaurant to warm up.

Regular pickup trucks (to the left as you exit the *teleférico*) carry visitors to the northern slope hamlet of **Galipán** (US$1.50, 10 min), where you'll find a string of good, inexpensive restaurants, horse rides and a couple of posadas with cabins. Galipán is also linked by covered pickup to the Cotiza neighborhood in Caracas, just west of San Bernardino (US$2, 30 min), and to Macuto on the coast (US$4.50, 1 hr). The latter ride is an unforgettable journey down a winding cobblestoned road through a series of cloud-forest villages, further down revealing astounding views of the Caribbean coast.

Carritos to Maripérez statio, labeled 'Sarria – Teleférico,' run from just north of Bellas Artes metro station.

Hiking

Of all Venezuela's national parks, El Ávila provides the best infrastructure for walkers. There are about 200km of walking trails, most of them well signposted. Half a dozen camping grounds distributed around the park are equipped with sanitary facilities, and there are many other more basic places designated for camping. Potable water is available at points along the trails.

A dozen entrances lead into the park from Caracas; all originate from Av Boyacá, commonly known as 'Cota Mil' because it runs at an altitude of 1000m. Whichever route you choose, you'll have a short ascent before you get to a guard post, where you pay a nominal park-entrance fee. The *guardaparques* (park rangers) may provide information and suggestions about routes, and you should tell them where you intend to hike. Before you come, however, pick up the useful brochure on Parque Nacional El Ávila published by ECOgraph Proyectos y Diseños, which includes a 1:25,000 map of the park. It can be found at Tecni-Ciencia Libros (p58) and other local bookstores. Keep in mind, however, that some tracks may be difficult to find and there are few distance markers.

There are plenty of options for a half- or full-day hike. One recommended way into the park is to catch a bus from the east side of Plaza de Francia in Altamira (by the Hotel Caracas Palace) to the Sabas Nieves entrance, from which it's a 300m hike up to the ranger post. From there, you can pick up an easy-to-handle nature trail along the southern slope that passes a series of streams, waterfalls and caves. Another trail from Sabas Nieves climbs the mountain, one of four main ascents to the park's highest points, Pico Oriental (2640m) and Pico Naiguatá (2765m). One of the most scenic routes is along the Fila Maestra, following the crest of the Ávila range from Pico de Ávila to Pico Naiguatá and rewarding hikers with splendid views toward both the valley of Caracas and the Caribbean sea.

Start early, as it can get extremely hot by midmorning. The dry season is from December to April, but be prepared for a few showers in the upper reaches all the same. Take rain gear and warm clothes.

LITORAL CENTRAL

The northern face of El Ávila park slopes steeply down to the sea, leaving only a narrow, flat strip of land between the foothills and the shore, referred to as the 'Litoral Central.' This strip has developed into a chain of coastal towns, including, from west to east, Catia La Mar, Maiquetía, La Guaira, Macuto, Caraballeda and Naiguatá.

Sadly, most of the area was devastated by mudslides caused by torrential rains in December 1999, with up to 50,000 people buried under the mud. Once popular seaside resorts for *caraqueños,* Caraballeda and Naiguatá were destroyed along with much of the colonial town of La Guaira, though Macuto was mostly spared. Restoration efforts have proceeded slowly and haphazardly, and it will take decades before the urban fabric is fully rebuilt, if ever.

For travelers, the zone's chief function is as an overnight alternative to Caracas near the airport. Catia La Mar, just west of the airport, has the closest lodging but little else to recommend it. A 20-minute ride in the opposite direction is Macuto, a somewhat safer, less disheveled spot with decent beaches and a string of hotels. Macuto has the additional advantage of being located at the start of a wonderful backdoor route to Caracas via the *teleférico*.

DREAMING STONES

The creation of resident artist/mountain man Zóez, **El Jardín de las Piedras Marinas Soñadoras** (Garden of Dreaming Marine Stones; ☎ 0416-628-8874; www.galipan.net in Spanish; adult/child US$4.75/3; ☙ 9am-6pm Sat & Sun, by appointment Mon-Fri) is a sort of ecological sculpture exhibit that unfolds amidst lush foliage with glimpses of the sea (from which the raw materials have been extracted). The artist's vision of nature is imbued with the female essence, and you can't go in unless there's a woman among your group. Visitors are asked to remove their footwear before entering the garden and are encouraged to interact with the sculptures, each of which has some activity associated with it: hopscotch down an embedded stone design, navigate a pebbly spiral with your eyes shut, support your partner as she attempts to tread the veins of a sloping leaf. Kids especially enjoy the participatory nature of the exhibit, and they can invent their own stone art at the end of the tour. Above the sculpture garden are **cabins** (d/tr US$70/105) for rent, each individually decorated with more rock art by the owner, and a restaurant with a lovely terrace serving 'mystic Venezuelan cuisine.'

The museum is a 15-minute drive up the road from Macuto toward Galipán. Pickup trucks bound for Galipán depart regularly from the west end of Macuto, near the Hotel Macuto, and can drop you off en route.

Sleeping & Eating

CATIA LA MAR

Il Prezzano (☎ 351-2626; ilprezzano@telcel.net.ve; Av Principal de Playa Grande; s/d/tr US$37/46/50; P ✕ 🖳) Toward Playa Grande, you'll find this hospitable lodging in an enclosed, rambling structure with attached *tasca*. Ample-sized rooms have clean tile floors and pretty bedspreads; a few upstairs units face an inner patio. Airport pickup/dropoff is an additional US$12.

Hotel La Parada (☎ 351-2148; hotel_la_parada@hotmail.com; cnr Av Principal Atlántida & Calle 10; s/d/tr incl airport transfer US$46/66/80; P ✕) Directly beneath the flight path, this makes a purely functional option, with airport pickup/dropoff included in the price, plus a small restaurant. You'll appreciate the superfriendly staff and sparkling if windowless rooms, some with bunk beds, for up to six occupants.

Buenavista Inn (☎ 352-9163; buenavistainn@hotmail.com; Av del Hotel cnr Calle 4, Urbanización Playa Grande; r US$68; P ✕ 🖳). Just around the corner from Il Prezzano, the brand new Buenavista Inn sits in a seaside suburb alongside a collection of modern residential towers. Sea breezes caress an attached terrace with hammock chairs and hanging plants. It's an efficient, securely enclosed operation, with a dozen bright, simply furnished rooms that include wireless internet and 110 cable channels. Airport transfer is available from US$14.

Hotel Eurobuilding Express (☎ 700-0700; www.hoteleuroexpress.com; Av La Armada; s/d from US$179/189; P ✕ 🖳 🖼) A flashy alternative amidst an otherwise blighted zone, the Eurobuilding is situated directly on the road departing from the terminal. Rates include shuttle to or from the airport and an ample breakfast at the hotel's Mr Grill restaurant. Half-day rates are available, too, so you can while away long hours between flights at the gym, pool and tennis courts.

MACUTO

Hotel Plazamar (☎ 339-5242; Plaza Andrés Mata, Calle 3; r Sun-Thu US$16, Fri & Sat US$19) Though basic, this friendly little guesthouse has a relaxed beachy ambience. It's right on the central Plaza de las Palomas (Pigeon Plaza, a name adopted for obvious reasons).

Hotel Colonial (☎ 339-9810; Av La Playa 48; s/d US$19/27; P ✕) This relic of a hotel on the beach promenade has rooms around a two-level arched patio. Despite the beat-up furniture, it's kept clean enough, and you can eat well at the stalls by the beach.

Posada del Hidalgo (☎ 414-8460; Av La Playa, Urbanización Alamo, Macuto; s/d/tr from US$32/39/59; P ✕) Possibly the best deal along this stretch of coast, this motel-like structure offers straightforward, if smallish, units with Andalusian hints. There's a very popular *tasca* in front serving great seafood.

Hotel Santiago (☎ 213-3500; hotelsantiago@telcel.net.ve; Av La Playa, Urbanización Alamo, Macuto; s/d US$50/65; P ✕ 🖳 🖼). This Spanish-toned lodging is owned by a Canary Islands native, and includes a fine *tasca* with open-air annex (the waiters have to cross the road to get there but they're good at it). Rooms vary in comfort, but all have good beds, soft lighting and icy air-con. Service ranges from cordial to clueless.

Hotel Olé Caribe (☎ 620-2000; www.hotelole caribe.com; Av Intercomunal, El Playón; r from US$127; Ⓟ 🔀 🖳 ⚓) For a last-night splash, the Olé Caribe will do nicely. Spectacularly perched on a hill overlooking the coast, it features large luxurious rooms, tennis courts, a sauna and a terrace restaurant by a pool with waterfall. Half-price day rates are available.

Getting There & Away

Shuttle buses travel regularly between Parque Central in Caracas and the airport (p93), from which taxis charge around US$20 to Catia La Mar or Macuto. Some hotels include airport transfer in the rate. Alternatively, buses travel the main highway between Catia La Mar and

Macuto (US$0.40), a 10- to 15-minute walk from the airport terminal. Exiting, look for the steps between the domestic and international terminals. At the top of the steps, follow the path out to the highway; you'll pass through a pedestrian control module on the way out. For eastbound Macuto buses, take the footbridge over the highway.

Another option is to go straight over the Ávila range to Caracas. Pickup trucks ply the cobblestoned road to Galipán (US$5, 50 minutes), a village on the mountain's northern slope, affording amazing views of the coast along the way. These depart from the west end of Macuto, near the Hotel Macuto. From Galipán it's another 10 minutes by pickup to the *teleférico* station down to the city. (Note: one-way fare offered only on the way down.)

The Central North

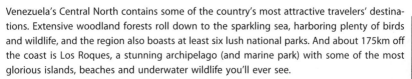

Venezuela's Central North contains some of the country's most attractive travelers' destinations. Extensive woodland forests roll down to the sparkling sea, harboring plenty of birds and wildlife, and the region also boasts at least six lush national parks. And about 175km off the coast is Los Roques, a stunning archipelago (and marine park) with some of the most glorious islands, beaches and underwater wildlife you'll ever see.

Amid the mainland's comely hills and valleys are several hidden gems. Not far from Caracas is the pretty 19th-century German town of Colonia Tovar, which lies scattered along the upper reaches of a mountainside. The second-hottest hot springs are toward the west at Las Trincheras, a well-developed miniresort. This area also claims the important battlefield of Carabobo, where national hero Simón Bolívar clinched Venezuelan independence – and which today is a focal point of national pride.

The main destination for independent travelers in this region, however, is Parque Nacional Henri Pittier. The endearing towns of Choroní and Puerto Colombia still retain their colonial feel, while the enticing beaches and coves along the park's coast (some accessible only by boat) attract heaps of both nationals and backpackers. Here too are some of the country's best festivals, heavily influenced by the days of African slavery; the occasional spontaneous party and drum session might pop up when you least expect it.

The Central North, occupying just 2.5% of national territory, is Venezuela's most developed and densely populated region and home to almost 50% of the country's population. Several places included in this chapter, such as Colonia Tovar, San Francisco de Yare and Parque Nacional Guatopo, are easy day trips out of Caracas.

HIGHLIGHTS

■ Explore the undersea wonderland of **Archipiélago Los Roques** (p101)

■ Stroll the cute German-themed town of **Colonia Tovar** (p117)

■ Rave to the sultry nighttime drumbeats in **Puerto Colombia** (p122)

■ Go bird-watching or hike to waterfalls in **Parque Nacional Henri Pittier** (p119)

■ Poach yourself silly in the hot springs of **Las Trincheras** (p135)

Archipiélago Los Roques ★

Puerto Colombia ★

Las Trincheras ★

★ Colonia Tovar

PN Henri Pittier ★

THE CENTRAL NORTH

THE CENTRAL NORTH

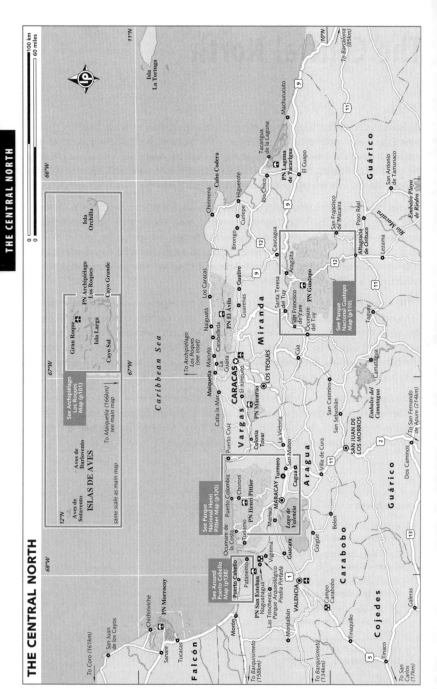

100 km
60 miles

Isla La Tortuga

ISLAS DE AVES

Aves de Sotavento

Aves de Barlovento

Isla Orchilla

See Archipiélago Los Roques Map (p101)

Gran Roque
Isla Larga
Isla Sal
Cayo Sal
Cayo Grande

PN Archipiélago Los Roques

To Archipiélago Los Roques (see inset)

To Maiquetía (166km) see main map

same scale as main map

Caribbean Sea

Cabo Codera

Chirimena

Higuerote
Curiepe

Birongo

PN Laguna de Tacarigua

Tacarigua de la Laguna

Río Chico
El Guapo

Machurucuto

Los Caracas
Guatire
Guarenas

San Francisco de Macaira

Araguita

Caucagua

Santa Teresa del Tuy
San Francisco de Yare
Ocumare del Tuy

PN Guatopo

See Parque Nacional Guatopo Map (p110)

Altagracia de Orituco
Lezama

Paso Real

To Barcelona (85km)

Guárico

San Antonio de Tamanaco

Cúa

Taguay

Miranda

Naiguatá
Carabelleda
La Guaira

Maiquetía Macuto

PN El Ávila

Catia la Mar

Puerto Cruz

Vargas

CARACAS
El Hatillo

LOS TEQUES

PN Macarao

La Victoria

San Mateo

Colonia Tovar

Puerto Colombia

Choroní

PN Henri Pittier

Maracay Turmero

Cagua

Lago de Valencia

Guacara

Güigüe

Belén

Villa de Cura

San Casimiro

San Juan DE LOS MORROS

San Sebastián

Embalse del Camatagua

Camatagua

Embalse Playa de Piedra

Río Macaira

To San Fernando de Apure (214km)

Dos Caminos

Guárico

See Parque Nacional Henri Pittier Map (p120)

Ocumare de la Costa
Tuberías
Maracá
Vigirima

Guacara

San Esteban

PN San Esteban
Naguanagua
Las Trincheras
Parque Arqueológico Piedra Pintada

See Around Puerto Cabello Map (p138)

Puerto Cabello
Patanemo

Carabobo

VALENCIA
Campo Carabobo

Montalbán

Galeras

Cojedes

Tinaquillo
Tinaco

To San Carlos (174km)

Morón

PN Morrocoy

Chichiriviche

San Juan de los Cayos

Sanare
Tucacas

Falcón

To Coro (161km)

To Barquisimeto (158km)

To Barquisimeto (134km)

ARCHIPIÉLAGO LOS ROQUES

☎ **0237 / pop 1500**

Gorgeous white-sand beaches, clear turquoise waters, amazing snorkeling and diving – these attractions all await hedonistic sun-seekers in the stunningly beautiful tropical archipelago known as Los Roques. Proclaimed a national park in 1972, this idyllic collection of small coral islands harbors rich coral reefs and comes virtually unspoilt. The archipelago's only village is the tiny Gran Roque, while most islands are uninhabited and the silence is only broken by the occasional buzz of motorboats and splash of diving pelicans. It's a much more relaxed, slow-paced and friendly place than the mainland, which seems a world away.

Los Roques lies about 160km due north off the central coast under a scorching sun and dazzlingly blue skies. Stretching 36km east to west, the archipelago consists of 42 islands big enough to bother naming, and about 250 other unnamed islets, sandbars and cays scattered around a crystal-clear, glittering lagoon brimming with marine life. The whole archipelago is around 2211 sq km in size, but Gran Roque is the focal point, being home to virtually all of its population, accommodations and transportation.

In order to preserve the habitat, protective zones have been created where tourists are not allowed or where access is limited to daytime visits. The only area with unrestricted access and the possibility of camping is the so-called Zona Recreativa, which comprises Gran Roque and the nearby islands.

All visitors to Los Roques pay the US$16 national park entry fee upon arrival (US$10 for Venezuelans). Remember that because Los Roques is a national park, visitors aren't allowed to take away animals or their products from the area. Leave sea shells for others to enjoy.

When to Go

Tourist peaks include late December and early January, Carnaval (late February to early March), Semana Santa (Holy Week, culminating in Easter) and August. Prices

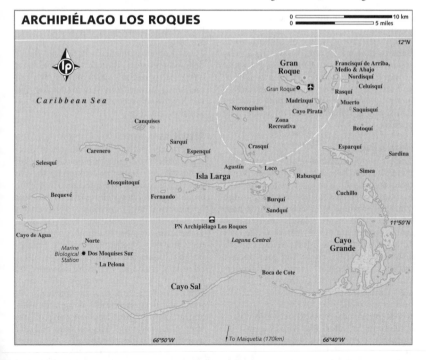

ARCHIPIÉLAGO LOS ROQUES

0 — 10 km
0 — 5 miles

12°N

Gran Roque

Francisquí de Arriba, Medio & Abajo
Nordisquí

Gran Roque

Celuisquí

Rasquí

Caribbean Sea

Madrizquí

Muerto

Noronquises

Cayo Pirata

Saquisquí

Canquises

Zona Recreativa

Botoquí

Sarquí

Crasquí

Esparquí

Carenero

Espenquí

Sardina

Selesquí

Agustín

Loco

Simea

Isla Larga

Rabusquí

Mosquitoquí

Cuchillo

Bequevé

Fernando

Burquí

Sandquí

PN Archipiélago Los Roques

11°50'N

Cayo de Agua

Norte

Laguna Central

Cayo Grande

Marine Biological Station

Dos Moquises Sur

La Pelona

Boca de Cote

Cayo Sal

66°50'W   ↑ To Maiquetía (170km)   66°40'W

are at their highest during these times, and reservations are a must. The slowest periods are May to July and September to November, when beaches are less crowded and bargaining might be possible.

The average temperature is about 82°F, with highs around 91°F in July and lows around 75°F in January. Rainfall is practically nonexistent, except for rare showers between September and January.

History

The archipelago has long been a stopping-off point for sailors, pirates and explorers. It was used as much as a thousand years ago by the indigenous peoples who temporarily inhabited the islands to catch fish, turtles and queen conch. Dos Mosquises was one of their prime staging areas.

In colonial times the islands saw a steady trail of foreigners, mostly from the Netherlands Antilles and England. In the 1920s fishermen from Isla de Margarita were attracted by the abundance of fish and gradually settled the archipelago's main island, Gran Roque, pushing out the Dutch by the 1950s. Known as *roqueños,* the fishermen's descendants now make up the majority of the local population.

Another recent influx of inhabitants is Italians, drawn here almost 20 years ago by restaurateur Vincenzo Conticello. He wrote home about the archipelago's wonders, and the rest is history. Today there are so many Italians here (most running posadas) that speaking Italian is as useful as speaking Spanish.

Flora & Fauna

The birds are a constant source of entertainment on the archipelago – from the continual rising and splashing falling of pelicans to mesmerizing frigates soaring effortlessly high overhead. Around 92 species of birds have been recorded on the islands, including 50 that migrate from North America. The only native mammal is the fishing bat, and there's also some reptiles, including four species of turtle and plenty of lizards, salamanders and iguanas. In terms of flora, the islands are sprinkled with grasses, thorny cacti, low bushes and mangroves.

But the islands' most attractive wildlife is actually underwater. The waters teem with riotously colorful fish, rays, barracudas,

---

I VAANT TO CHUPAR YOUR BLOOD!

Puri-puri are very annoying sand flies that love to feast on travelers' exotic blood. They're tiny little things that are barely visible, and you won't feel much after the first chomp – but after a while the bite will start to itch…and itch…and itch…for days on end! It's important not to scratch too much (though, frankly, this will be impossible) because it's relatively easy to pick up an infection in the tropics. If you do get seriously bitten and can't resist scratching, try going to a Venezuelan pharmacy and getting some anti-itch pills or cream. And consider covering up with clothing or repellant next time you're lined up on the beach buffet.

---

sea stars, mollusks, crabs, octopuses and lobsters, to name just a few. Any quick trip snorkeling around the archipelago's reefs will be rewarded by glimpses of everything from exquisite angelfish to the lumpish sea cucumbers. And of course the corals themselves are extraordinary, with names as exotic as their appearance, from the grooved brain coral to the orange elephant ear sponge and the devil's sea whip.

Los Roques is particularly famous for its delicious lobsters, though they have been overfished in recent years. There's now a ban on fishing lobster from May to October, but Los Roques still accounts for over 90% of national production.

Activities

The principal activity on Los Roques is relaxing, whether dozing in a hammock, cooling off in crystal-clear waters or soaking up the sun on pristine beaches. Crasquí claims one of the archipelago's longest ribbons of sand, but boat operators will most commonly drop passengers off at the islands of Francisquí and Madrizquí. There are many other beautiful beach destinations, however. One word of warning: beaches on Los Roques are shadeless and the sun is relentless, made all the more powerful by reflection off the immaculately white sand. Umbrellas often come with package deals, but you'll still need sun block, along with a hat and sunglasses. Insect repellant wards off late afternoon *puri-puri,* the region's tiny and very irritating biting flies (see above).

SNORKELING & SCUBA DIVING

Los Roques is one of Venezuela's top destinations for snorkeling. Among the best places are Boca de Cote, Crasquí and Noronquises, but there are other excellent sites closer to Gran Roque. The most popular spot is the so-called *piscina* (literally 'swimming pool') on Francisquí de Medio. You can rent snorkeling equipment in Gran Roque for about US$12 a day.

Scuba diving is also fabulous here, and there is a wealth of good places to explore. Diving is organized by several companies, including **Aquatics Dive Center** (☎ 0414-777-0196; www.scubaven ezuela.com), **Eco Challenge** (☎ 0414-291-9266; www .ecochallenge.com.ve) and **Arrecífe** (☎ 0414-249-5119; www.divevenezuela.com). Two dives generally cost from US$85 to US$100.

WIND SPORTS

Los Roques is also a top-notch spot for windsurfing of all levels. It's organized by Elias at **Vela Windsurf Center** (www.velawindsurf.com) on the island of Francisquí de Abajo, which rents equipment (US$20/35/50 per hour/half-day/day) and can provide lessons for beginners (US$40 for two hours including equipment). Get more information from Arhuna (Elias' brother) at Restaurant El Canto de la Ballena (p106) on Gran Roque. He can give you advice on the local surfing action also.

Vela Windsurf Center also rents kayaks (US$19 per day) and gives lessons in kitesurfing (US$140). For general information, inquire at **Oscar Shop** (☎ 291-9160; oscarshop@hotmail .com) by the Gran Roque airport.

OTHER ACTIVITIES

Los Roques is also renowned as one of the world's finest areas for **game fishing**, particularly for bonefish. These trips are expensive and require permits, so it's often best to arrange one in advance through a specialized company; for example, Alpitour (p356) in Caracas. In Gran Roque, **Posada Mediterráneo** (☎ 221-1130; www.posadamediterraneo.com) organizes game-fishing tours that go for US$250 to US$300 per day. Inparques (see p104) can also give you some fishing information.

You can also go **sailing** (per person per day US$150) around Los Roques on one of several sailing yachts that anchor off Gran Roque. They have cabins equipped with berths and provide meals on board, and can take you for several days around the islands. Ask at Oscar Shop for more information.

Tours

If you don't have much time or just want a quick taste of Los Roques, taking a one- or two-day tour is an easy way out. A day tour is good

---

CONSIDERATIONS FOR RESPONSIBLE DIVING

Please consider the following tips when diving, and help preserve the ecology and beauty of the archipelago's coral reefs:

- Avoid touching living marine organisms with your body or dragging equipment across the reef. Polyps can be damaged by even the gentlest contact. Never stand on corals, even if they look solid and robust. If you must hold on to the reef, touch only exposed rock or dead coral.

- Be conscious of your fins. Even without contact, the surge from heavy fin strokes near the reef can damage delicate organisms. When treading water in shallow reef areas, take care not to kick up clouds of sand. Settling sand can easily smother the delicate organisms of the reef.

- Practice and maintain proper buoyancy control. Major damage can be done by divers descending too fast and colliding with the reef. Make sure that you are correctly weighted and that your weight belt is positioned so that you stay horizontal. Be aware that buoyancy can change over an extended trip: initially, you may breathe harder and need more weight; a few days later, you may breathe more easily and need less weight.

- Resist the temptation to collect or buy corals or shells. Aside from the ecological damage, taking home marine souvenirs depletes the beauty of a site and spoils others' enjoyment.

- Ensure that you take home all your rubbish and any litter you may find as well. Plastics in particular are a serious threat to marine life. Turtles can mistake plastic for jellyfish and eat it.

- Resist the temptation to feed fish. You may disturb their normal eating habits, encourage aggressive behavior or feed them food that is detrimental to their health.

value, as it's not much more expensive than the airfare. Two-day tours give a better insight but are much more expensive as the tour companies often use upmarket accommodations.

An all-inclusive one-day tour from Maiquetía costs around US$150 to US$190, including the roundtrip flight, a boat excursion from Gran Roque to one or two of the nearby islands, lunch, soft drinks, one hour of snorkeling (equipment provided) and free time on the beach. Different operators may go to different islands and often have their own preferred snorkeling areas.

The two-day package adds an overnight stay in Gran Roque plus all meals, and it costs around US$300 to US$450 (depending on the season and posada standard). Many tours are run by the small airlines that fly to Los Roques (see p357), though plenty of travel agencies in Venezuela offer tours also. Note that tour prices don't include the US$16 entry fee to the national park.

If you plan on staying two or more days, it's often better value to go it alone. Just buy a roundtrip ticket and arrange all the rest in Gran Roque. **Oscar Shop** (☎ 291-9160; oscarshop@hotmail.com) provides boat transportation to the islands, organizes full-day boat tours, and rents out snorkeling equipment and beach chairs. It also provides general tourist information.

Try to avoid tourist peaks, when flights and accommodations are in short supply and prices are at their highest.

Getting There & Away

AIR

The Maiquetía–Los Roques one-way fare starts at around US$130 and the flight takes 40 minutes. Pack light; only 10kg of free luggage is allowed, with a charge of US$1 for every additional kilogram. There's a Los Roques airport tax of US$8. You can also fly between Los Roques and Porlamar, on Isla de Margarita (US$165 one-way, 1½ hours).

For a list of airlines servicing the archipelago, see p353.

BOAT

There are no passenger boats to Los Roques.

GRAN ROQUE

Lying on the northern edge of the archipelago, Gran Roque is the principal island and has a distinct Caribbean feel. It's small – you can walk from one end of the island's four-street fishing village to the other in less than 10 minutes. It's also a friendly place and accounts for the archipelago's biggest population, some 1500 souls in all.

Gran Roque's sandy streets, where locals walk barefoot, are lined with one-story, brightly painted concrete houses. There's also one bank, five grocery shops, a school and no less than 60 posadas. The only land vehicles you'll see are a water and garbage truck, plus maybe a golf cart or two. In contrast, the waterfront is packed with fishing boats, tour vessels and visiting yachts – all covered by a vast army of pelicans. The island also has an airstrip by the village, which handles all tourist flights.

Unlike the other islands, which are sandy and flat, Gran Roque has several massive rocky humps along its northwestern coast – the tallest is 110m – and cliffs that plunge vertically into the sea. Climb the hill crowned with an old lighthouse, known as the Faro Holandés, for sweeping views over the village, islands, coral reefs and the crystal-clear turquoise sea. The lighthouse itself was built in the 1870s and used until the early 1950s.

Information

The island's only bank, **Banesco** (☎ 221-1265; Plaza Bolívar; ☒ 8am-noon & 2-5pm Mon-Fri, 8am-2pm Sat), arranges cash advances on Visa and MasterCard with a maximum of US$375 per day (the ATM limit is US$94 per day). However, it's wise to bring cash (dollars or euro) in case your cards don't work. And note that most posadas don't take credit cards, though some will take traveler's checks.

Inparques (National Institute of National Parks; ☎ 0414-373-1004; ☒ 8am-noon & 2-6pm Mon-Fri, 8:30am-noon & 2:30-5pm Sat, 8-11:30am Sun), at the far end of village, oversees the running of the national park and can give advice on places to camp and snorkel. **Oscar Shop** (☎ 291-9160; oscarshop@hotmail.com), right by the airport, is a combination of shop, tour agency, boat operator and tourist office, all run by the knowledgeable Oscar. Upon arrival at Gran Roque, you will pass his kiosk on your way into the village.

For slow internet access there's **Enzosoft** (☒ US$9.50 per hr; 1-10pm Mon-Sat), or try the free state-sponsored Infocentro near the school. Enzosoft also has local and international telephone services. For minor ailments limp to the **medic** (☎ for emergencies 0414-326-2566; ☒ 9am-noon, 4-7pm Mon-Fri) near the school.

Sleeping

The small island village of Gran Roque has exploded with posadas over the last decade. There are now over 60 on the island, about half of them Italian-run. Most posadas will have someone meet you at the airport to escort you and your luggage (via hand cart).

Unless you're camping, accommodations will be very expensive – even in low season it's hard to find anything under US$50 for two people. Breakfast, dinner or both are often included in the price – lunch (usually sandwiches for the beach) can be available on request. In high season most posadas offer only full pension rates.

Food is also expensive, because everything except fish has to be shipped in from the mainland. You can save money by staying at a posada that offers bed only (just the cheaper ones do this in low season), while patronizing the island's few inexpensive eateries and supermarkets.

The island has an electricity and desalination plant, though there are occasional blackouts (bring a flashlight). Water should be used sparingly.

Prices listed below are for low season, when bargaining is a possibility. In high season rates increase anywhere from 30% to 70%, depending on the posada. These peak dates include late December to early January, Carnaval (late February to early March), Semana Santa (Easter) and all of August. Reservations are an absolute must during these times.

All rooms come with private bathroom unless otherwise noted. Also be aware that most prices below are per person, rather than per room.

BUDGET

Chez Judith (☎ 248-1071; chezjudith@cantv.net; r per person incl breakfast US$24; ❄) Basic but friendly family posada with dark, inexpensive rooms.

Ranchito Power (☎ 0414-141-3568; www.ranchito power.com; r per person incl breakfast US$40, bed only US$28) Tiny and simple, this six-room, Italian-run posada offers clean rooms with fan, along with a nice rooftop area in which to hang out. You'll need earplugs to block out the nearby disco at night, however.

Eva (☎ 0414-450-7581; www.posadaseva.com.ve; r per person incl breakfast US$40; ❄) Located at the far end of the village, this family-run posada is a backpacker magnet. It offers six small, simple rooms, one with shared bathroom (room 4 has a tiny garden but no air-con).

Roquelusa (☎ 0414-369-6401; r per person incl breakfast & dinner US$47) Located at the far end of the village near the Inparques office is this basic cheapie with a few rough edges, but a big plus is that all eight rooms are being converted to air-con. Opt for bed only (no meals) and prices drop.

The cheapest option in Los Roques is to camp. Camping is allowed on all the islands within the Zona Recreativa, including Gran Roque, and is free. After arrival go to the far end of the village to the Inparques office for a free camping permit. The staff will tell you which islands are open for camping and can give you other practical tips.

On Gran Roque the camping area is next to the Inparques office and set near the beach in a shady grove. Toilet and shower facilities are available at nearby posadas (Inparques has a list) for a small fee. Inparques and Oscar Shop rent tents, but the quality is iffy.

MIDRANGE

Doña Carmen (☎ 0414-291-9225; tudocar@cantv.net; r per person incl breakfast & dinner US$58; ❄) Nine decent and clean rooms, set along a colorful outdoor hallway, greet you at this long-running posada on Plaza Bolívar. All have air-con except the two fronting the beach (which come with ocean breezes instead). Your towels are folded into bird shapes.

El Botuto (☎ 0414-238-1589; www.posadaelbotuto .com; r per person incl breakfast US$60) Close to the Inparques office, this pleasant posada has six small but neat rooms, most with mosquito nets and tiny outdoor patio showers. There's a relaxing front area with shade and water views. Meals are available.

Piano y Papaya (☎ 0414-281-0104; www.pianoy papaya.com; r incl breakfast US$120) Behind the church, this bright, fresh posada has just five beautiful, spacious rooms with mosquito nets, along with a wonderful lounging area in front. It's a good deal (prices are per room, not per person), though air-con may be added and thus prices may rise. English, French and Italian are all spoken.

La Lagunita (☎ 0414-291-9151; www.posadalagunita .com; Calle La Laguna; r per person incl meals & boat tour US$75; ❄) This friendly Italian-run posada offers up seven excellent rooms with TV and safe box (room 5 is especially nice), and there's a pleasant rooftop terrace where the staff mix up free *Cuba libres* (rum and coke drinks).

THE CENTRAL NORTH

El Paraíso Azul (in Caracas ☎ 0212-953-2707; www .gentedemar.com; r per person incl breakfast US$85; ✂) Here's another Italian-run posada sporting eight clean, comfortable rooms with wonderful wood accents. It also has a sunny rooftop patio, airy bar area and excellent restaurant.

Guaripete (☎ 221-1368; www.posadaguaripete.com; r per person incl breakfast US$117) Seven pleasant rooms with fan and mosquito nets are available at this pretty, Italian-run posada, and a shady upstairs terrace comes strewn with relaxing hammocks.

El Pelicano (☎ 0414-256-2427; info@pelicano.it; r per person incl meals & boat tour US$125; ✂) Just four good, large rooms with fridge are on offer at this elegant posada located at the far end of the village.

Also recommended:

La Gaviota (☎ 0414-324-2092; www.posadalagaviota .com; r per person incl breakfast US$90; ✂) Beautiful pastel-blue posada boasting seven pleasant rooms with mosquito nets. Located next to El Canto de la Ballena restaurant.

Acuario (☎ 0414-291-9230; r per person incl meals US$92; ✂) Small Italian-run place with five no-nonsense rooms and nice front porch.

Malibú (☎ 221-1274; posadamalibu@cantv.net; r per person incl breakfast US$120, air-con extra US$25; ✂ ▢) Cool and classy posada with tasteful decor, pebbly floors, comfy lounges and general tropical feel.

TOP END

Natura Viva (☎ 221-1473; www.naturavivalosroques.com; r per person incl meals & boat tour US$150; ✂) Here's one of the island's largest posadas, with 14 stylish rooms, spa services and a beautiful rooftop terrace with sea views and boat-shaped bar.

Albacore (☎ 0414-282-6131; posadalbacora@hotmail .com; r per person incl meals & boat tour US$150; ✂) This posada has just three very comfortable rooms (including a two-level suite) with modern comforts like TV and fridge. The nearby annex has two more rooms.

Macanao Lodge (in Caracas ☎ 0212-708-9898; www .macanaolodge.com; r per person incl meals & boat tour US$200) One of Gran Roques' best, this posada has 10 beautiful rooms with high ceilings and mosquito nets. It also boasts a restaurant with sea views, along with an open yet cozy fountain courtyard.

Mediterráneo (☎ 221-1130; www.posadamediterraneo .com; r per person incl meals & boat tour US$300-400; ✂ ▢) True to its name, this spotless, whitewashed posada comes with airy Mediterranean feel. There's a great rooftop terrace, common

spaces are beautifully decorated and all rooms have a flat-screen TV.

Acuarela (☎ 221-1456; www.posadaacuarela.com; s/d incl breakfast US$335/500; ✂) This artistic posada comes with 11 gorgeous and creative rooms. It also boasts open-topped patios, an excellent (but expensive) restaurant and breezy rooftop terrace with hammocks. Prices drop after the first night. English, French and Italian are spoken.

Eating & Drinking

Since almost all posadas serve meals for their guests, there's only a handful of independent restaurants in Gran Roque.

Panadería Bella Mar (snacks under US$3; ⏱ 8am-9pm Mon-Sat) Near the school is this tiny bakery that sells cheap empanadas, sandwiches and breads. The set lunch is US$4.

Mini Lunchería Brisas de Los Roques (set menu US$7; ⏱ 6am-3pm & 5-9pm) Hole-in-the-wall cookery with just a few choices, but all cheap. Located near the Enzosoft internet café.

Aquarena Cafe (☎ 0414-131-1282; mains US$9.50-11; ⏱ 9am-1am Wed-Mon) Located near Macanao Lodge, this beachside café offers up fish, hamburgers, pizza and salads. There's beanbag seating and tables on the sand.

La Chuchera (☎ 221-1417; mains US$9.50-17; ⏱ 11am-11pm) This restaurant, located on Plaza Bolívar, plays a constant soundtrack of upbeat music. On the menu are hamburgers, pasta and fish, but pizza (including a vegetarian option) is the best choice here.

Bora la Mar (☎ 325-7814; 3-course menu US$21; ⏱ 6:30pm-midnight) Lapping waves, sandy tables and hip music make this the island's most pleasant dining experience. Watch the sun set while nibbling gourmet treats and sipping tasty cocktails – a memorable occasion.

Restaurant El Canto de la Ballena (☎ 0414-291-9020; 5-course menu US$42; ⏱ variable) This wonderfully located restaurant serves excellent food. It's open for breakfast (US$24), but its breezy wood deck is more popular in the evening, when the drinking crowd settles in.

La Gotera Art Café (☎ 221-1369; ⏱ 6pm-midnight Mon-Sat) Bean bag chairs, romantic lights, a mellow vibe and tasty drinks make this swanky beachside spot a great place to hang out.

OTHER ISLANDS

The nearest island to Gran Roque is **Madrizquí**, about 1km to the southeast. It was the favorite island among affluent *caraqueños* (peo-

---

NORDIS...QUE?

As you find your way around Los Roques, you may wonder about the islands' strange names. Many were first named by English explorers. Local fishermen preserved most of these original names but wrote them down phonetically. Then along came the linguistically correct cartographers, who changed the spelling to standard Spanish orthography. This is how Northeast Cay in English was recorded as 'Nordisky,' and eventually became 'Nordisquí.' Similarly, the Sails Cay went through 'Selesky' to 'Selesquí,' and St Luis Cay has become 'Celuisquí.'

ple from Caracas), who built summer beach houses here before the archipelago was made a national park. Connected to Madrizquí by sand bar is **Cayo Pirata**, which harbors fishing shelters known as *rancherías*. **Francisquí**, also close to Gran Roque, is actually composed of three islands, and the most popular one – Francisquí de Medio – has a casual restaurant. Beautiful and serene **Crasquí** has good snorkeling and some *rancherías*, while **Rasquí** is the only island (other than Gran Roque) with a posada.

On the island of **Dos Mosquises Sur**, at the far southwestern edge of the archipelago, is a Marine Biological Station run by the Fundación Científica Los Roques. The station, which can be visited, has breeding tanks where turtles and other endangered species are raised before being released around the archipelago. There's also a small museum here displaying archaeological discoveries from the area.

Sleeping & Eating

Wherever you stay you'll never be far from a beach, but for that ultimate castaway feeling you can stay outside Gran Roque.

Camping is free: all you need is a permit from Inparques. Permits are available for the nearby islands of Madrizquí, Cayo Pirata and Francisquí. Further away, you can also camp on Noronquises and Crasquí. You must be self-sufficient and bring all camping gear, food and water. Also don't forget your snorkeling gear, insect repellent for small biting flies, a hat and strong sun block.

Rancho Agua Clara (☎ 0414-247-3498; www.geocit ies.com/guayolosroques) This basic shelter, located

on the island of Crasquí, has a handful of beachside tents and toilet/shower facilities. Prices are US$100 per person for the first night and US$70 for each night afterwards. This price includes roundtrip boat ride, tents (with bedding provided), breakfast, dinner and beach chairs.

Rasquí Island Chalet (in Gran Roque ☎ 0414-249-9335; www.rasqui.net; per person US$182) The only posada outside Gran Roque is this idyllic place. It's located on the tiny island of Rasquí and offers just three rustic but comfortable cabins. Rates include all meals, roundtrip boat transportation and one dive lesson. In August and late December rates skyrocket to US$275 per person. For more information go to Posada Acquamarina in Gran Roque.

There are a couple of fried-fish restaurants run by fisherfolk on Crasquí. Otherwise your only formal eating option outside Gran Roque is the pleasant and casual **Restaurant Casamarina** (mains US$9.50-21; ⊙ 11am-3:30pm), located on Francisquí de Arriba. It has a great shady wood deck, but the lobster will cost you US$40 per kilo! Snorkeling equipment and umbrella rentals are available.

Getting There & Away

Oscar Shop or other boat operators in Gran Roque will take you to the island of your choice and pick you up at a prearranged time and date. Most boats leave by 9:30am, especially for destinations furthest away. Roundtrip fares per person include Madrizquí (US$6, seven minutes), the Francisquises (US$7, 10 minutes), Crasquí or Noronquises (US$14, 25 minutes) and Cayo de Agua (US$28, 1½ hours).

MIRANDA STATE

SAN FRANCISCO DE YARE
☎ 0239 / pop 22,000

Strolling around the colonial streets of this small, sleepy town, it's difficult to imagine the mayhem that reigns here annually during the Festival de los Diablos Danzantes (Dancing Devils). This colorful festival sees visitors arrive in their thousands as the village is transformed into a huge mass of frenzied, costumed revelers in devil masks dancing to the hypnotic rhythm of drums and maracas.

This famous feast has been celebrated here annually since 1742, falling on Corpus Christi (the 60th day after Easter Day, in May or June and always on a Thursday). The date is not an official Venezuelan holiday, but it is very much so in San Francisco de Yare, which spends months gearing up for the festival.

Corpus Christi is by far the best time to visit the town, but the ambience of the Diablos Danzantes is omnipresent, particularly in the weeks prior to the festival.

San Francisco de Yare lies 70km by road southeast of Caracas. The town was founded in 1714 and boasts a fine mid-18th-century church, the Iglesia de San Francisco, and some well-preserved colonial architecture.

Sights

The **Casa de los Diablos Danzantes** (Calle Rivas; admission free; ☼ 8am-noon & 2-4pm Mon-Fri), one block down from the plaza, shelters a small museum with a collection of papier-mâché devil masks and photos from previous festivals. The family living in the house to the left of the museum as

you face it can open the museum if it's closed when you arrive.

You can stop by workshops manufacturing devil masks to see the production process and buy masks at good rates. One of the best is **Artesanía El Mocho** (☎ 222-9191; Calle Rivas), led by Manuel Sanoja. It's two blocks down from the museum, above the small Bodega San Antonio. **Artesanía Morgado** (☎ 222-9345; Calle Rivas 19), one block down from the museum, is run by noted local artisan Juan Morgado.

Festival de los Diablos Danzantes

Easily one of Venezuela's most authentic and energetic festivals, the celebrations for the Festival de los Diablos Danzantes begin at noon on the Wednesday, one day prior to Corpus Christi. Crowds of devil dancers don their colorful masks and red costumes, and depart from the Casa de los Diablos Danzantes and take to the streets for the whole afternoon. In the evening they go to El Cal-

---

DANCING WITH DEVILS

The Festival de los Diablos Danzantes (Dancing Devils) is a kaleidoscopic spectacle. Up to a thousand devil dancers clad in red costumes wearing monstrous masks strut around in everything from marching movements in double file to spasmodic squirms accompanied by the stirring clamor of drums. The devil dancers take to the streets on the Wednesday, one day before Corpus Christi (held in honor of the Eucharist), and on the holy day itself. So why do the devils come out on this holiest of days?

The ceremony manifests the struggle between evil and good, and the eventual triumph of the latter. No matter how profane the devil dances look, the devils come to the church to submit themselves to the Eucharist before returning to their whirling dances. Locals believe that the dance ritual will ensure abundant crops, welfare, prosperity and protection against misfortune and natural disasters. For the devils, the dance is their religion.

The festival blends Spanish and African traditions: its origins lie in Spain, where devils' images and masks featured in Corpus Christi feasts in medieval Andalusia. But when the festival was brought to the New World in colonial times, it found a fertile soil among the black slaves, who introduced the traditional African-style masks and the rhythm of drumbeats so characteristic of their homeland. Some saw this as an act of protest against the white god, a symbol of Spanish oppression and cruelty. But the profane and the divine gradually merged, producing a striking cross-cultural ritual.

While the ceremony's African roots are palpable, the dances are not performed exclusively by blacks. Devil dances have been preserved only in areas with the heaviest import of African slaves, including the towns of Naiguatá (Vargas); Cata, Chuao, Cuyagua, Ocumare de la Costa and Turiamo (Aragua); Canoabo, Guacara, Los Caneyes, Patanemo and Tocuyito (Carabobo); Tinaquillo (Cojedes); and San Francisco de Yare (Miranda). The celebrations in Chuao and San Francisco de Yare are best known.

Dances and costumes have their own characteristics in each community, especially the papiermâché masks, which differ notably from town to town. San Francisco de Yare churns out large, elaborate masks depicting horned demons, monsters and fantastic animals painted in every color of the rainbow. Meanwhile, the masks from Chuao are smaller and painted with just three colors (white, black and red).

vario for the lengthy Velorio (Vigil), which lasts until dawn.

In the morning of Corpus Christi, the devils gather at the Casa de Los Diablos Danzantes to get the party rolling again with a short dancing session before heading for the local cemetery to pay respects to their predecessors. They then go to the parish church and continue in a joyful pageant to the Plaza de los Diablos Danzantes, four blocks from the church, where they again take to frenzied dancing.

The frolicking stops only when a church procession bringing the bishop from Los Teques arrives. This is the symbolic climax of the whole event, where good triumphs over evil for another year. A lengthy, solemn mass is celebrated on the square, with all the devils taking part. Once the mass is over, the ceremony of the Juramentación is held, in which young apprentices to devil dancers take a symbolic oath. The bishop gives God's blessing to the devils, and they all set off for the procession back to the church, carrying the image of the Holy Sacrament.

The multicolored hordes continue their dancing throughout the afternoon, wandering around the streets, stopping at makeshift street altars and visiting relatives before returning to the church at about 6pm for another procession, after which they head to El Calvario, where the celebrations conclude.

The script of the festivities differs slightly from year to year, but rest assured there will always be ritual devil dancing all over town.

Sleeping & Eating

There are no regular hotels in San Francisco de Yare, but there are accommodations options in nearby Santa Teresa del Tuy, including **Hotel Tahay** (☎ 231-7116; Calle Miranda; d US$19), and Ocumare del Tuy. There are several basic places to eat in San Francisco de Yare, especially around the cute plaza.

Getting There & Away

There's no direct transportation from Caracas to San Francisco de Yare, but you can get there easily with one connection from the Nuevo Circo regional bus terminal. Take one of the frequent buses to Ocumare del Tuy (US$1.40, 1½ hours) or Santa Teresa del Tuy (US$1.40, 1½ hours) and change at your destination. Frequent buses shuttle between Ocumare and

Santa Teresa, passing through San Francisco de Yare.

PARQUE NACIONAL GUATOPO

This national park is an important biological enclave covered by lush rainforest in the otherwise heavily developed and populated hinterland of Caracas. Thanks to the wide range of elevations and copious rainfall, the park's vegetation is varied and exuberant, and includes palms, ferns, orchids and huge trees up to 40m high.

The rich mammal world includes jaguars, pumas, tapirs, armadillos and sloths, to name just a few. Guatopo is also good for birdwatching: macaws, parakeets, woodpeckers, hummingbirds, honeycreepers and dozens of other bird species are easily spotted in the forest canopy. But keep an eye on the ground as well – there are also some poisonous snakes, including the coral snake and (the more common and dangerous) macagua.

Established in 1958, Guatopo is about 100km by road (60km as the crow flies) southeast of Caracas. The park encompasses 1225 sq km of the rugged Serranía del Interior, a mountain range that splits off the Cordillera de la Costa and winds inland. The altitude in the park ranges between 200m and 1430m above sea level. The park is also a major water source for the region, since several dams have been built around the park, creating *embalses* (reservoirs).

The climate here is wet and warm. The rainiest months are October to December, while the driest ones are March and April, but rain gear is recommended any time of the year. Insects are also plentiful, so bring repellent. The temperature ranges between 77°F and 86°F, but drops to about 59°F on the highest peaks.

Orientation

The paved road between Santa Teresa del Tuy and Altagracia de Orituco winds through the middle of the park, passing all the recreational areas and starting points for walks. Public transportation from Caracas does travel along this road sporadically, but it's infrequent and dies in the afternoon. Given that the last bus back to Caracas leaves around 3pm, a one-day trip leaves you very limited time in the park. If you decide to do this, leave very early and go directly to Agua Blanca – the best starting point for walks. Altagracia de Orituco, just

THE CENTRAL NORTH

PARQUE NACIONAL GUATOPO

beyond the park, has several hotels. Having your own transportation gives you much more flexibility.

There are some basic lodging and camping facilities in the park. The following section details the major stopovers on the route, from north to south (the exception being Hacienda La Elvira, which is accessible only from Altagracia de Orituco), along with their tourist facilities.

Bring all food and water with you. There are snacks available at Agua Blanca, but only on weekends.

Sights & Activities
LA MACANILLA

There's a *guardaparque* (park ranger) based here who can give you information about the park (7:30am to 3pm Monday to Friday, 9am to 4:30pm Saturday and Sunday), but no other services are available.

AGUA BLANCA

Thirteen kilometers on, Agua Blanca is the park's major recreational area and has a *guardaparque* and the safest camping. There's also

an intriguing reconstructed **trapiche** (traditional sugarcane mill; 7:30am-3pm Mon-Fri, 7am-4pm Sat & Sun), complete with its huge cauldrons and ladles, and you can take a bath in nearby *pozos* (ponds).

From here a 3km walking trail heads to Santa Crucita; allow up to 1½ hours to walk it at a leisurely pace. There's also another, shorter (1.5km) trail between Agua Blanca and Santa Crucita that takes just 45 minutes, running on the opposite (eastern) side of the road – so you can take a roundtrip without returning the same way.

Agua Blanca attracts day-trippers on weekends, but is usually quiet on weekdays. It has a picnic area, toilets, a guarded parking lot, a snack kiosk (open on weekends) and some accommodation options. Campamento Los Monos is a 26-bed dormitory that is reserved as a whole in advance through Caracas' Inparques office (see p61). Bring your own sheets and blankets. There are also five two-person **cabañas** (US$2.50), which are very rustic timber structures on stilts, scattered around the forest. They have no beds, so bring mats and sleeping bags. To stay at them simply check with the nearest park rangers. There's also a **camping ground** (per person US$1.40). Bring your own food and water.

SANTA CRUCITA

The next stop, Santa Crucita, is 1.5km from Agua Blanca. There is a small lagoon here, and you can pitch your tent in the unguarded grassy camping site. As well as the two trails coming here from Agua Blanca, there are two short local walking loops, one skirting around the lagoon (700m) and another one going through the nearby forest (800m).

EL LUCERO & QUEBRADA DE GUATOPO

The park's **administrative center** (🕑 7:30am-3pm Mon-Fri, 9am-4:30pm Sat & Sun) is El Lucero, 5.5km down the road from Santa Crucita. There are *guardaparques* here to provide information. Quebrada de Guatopo, 2km beyond El Lucero, has a picnic area, a creek with small waterfalls and swimming holes, and yet another (unguarded) camping ground. Again, bring your own food and water.

HACIENDA LA ELVIRA

About 26km northeast of Altagracia, this non-functioning but charming 19th-century coffee hacienda is open to visitors, and there are walks nearby. However, it's not accessible via public transportation, and even with your own vehicle it's a tricky spot to get to. From Altagracia you have to drive 8km east on the road to Paso Real and take the left turnoff north to San Francisco de Macaira. Follow this pothole-riddled road for 14km, and take the rough 4WD track branching off to the northwest and leading to La Elvira (4km). There are no accommodations here but camping is permitted. The administrative center in El Lucero can give more information, but there should be a *guardaparques* stationed here as well.

ALTAGRACIA DE ORITUCO
🕾 0238 / pop 44,000
Lying outside the national park's boundaries and a 30-minute bus ride from Agua Blanca is Altagracia de Orituco. It's an ordinary town, but big enough to have a collection of hotels and restaurants.

Buses to the park, Caracas and Barcelona depart from the intersection of Avs Ilustres Próceres and Pellón y Palacio. The **Hotel Tasca Galicia** (🕾 334-3354, s/d US$14/20; 🗷) is located

here and offers good if noisy rooms. Nearby is the **Hotel Diamante** (🕾 334-1331; d US$20; 🗷), a similar but quieter option. Four blocks down Av Pellón y Palacio is the best choice, the **Hotel Amazor** (🕾 334-1174; Calle Pellón y Palacio 16; s/d US$20/31; 🅿 🗷), with cable TV and a good restaurant.

Getting There & Away

There are hourly buses from the Nuevo Circo regional terminal in Caracas to Altagracia de Orituco (US$4.75, four hours), but they go via San Casimiro and don't pass through the park. There are also faster *camionetas* (minibuses) that run to Altagracia from about 5am to 2pm and depart when full. They go via Santa Teresa and the park, and can let you off at any point along the road. The last transportation back to Caracas leaves Altagracia around 3pm.

ARAGUA STATE

MARACAY
🕾 0243 / pop 400,000
A popular stopover for travelers heading north to the coast is this busy metropolis, the 300-year-old capital of Aragua state. There's little colonial legacy left within the city center, but it does possess a few parks and leafy plazas, including the country's largest Plaza Bolívar. Maracay is also the center of an important agricultural and industrial area, and has a palpable military presence, especially the air force.

At an altitude of about 450m, the city has a hot climate (warmer than Caracas, but more pleasant than Maracaibo), with an average temperature of 77°F and most rain falling between April and October.

Maracay is a frequent stopover en route to Parque Nacional Henri Pittier and its pretty beaches. It's a good idea to stock up on cash here if you're heading to the coast, as there are no banks there yet.

History

Founded in the mid-16th century, Maracay has long taken advantage of the valley's fertile soil, growing dozens of crops from cacao to sugarcane. It was a slow-growing town, however, and by 1900 the population had reached a mere 7000. Indeed, the city would have probably continued at this unhurried rate if it hadn't been for Juan Vicente Gómez,

THE CENTRAL NORTH

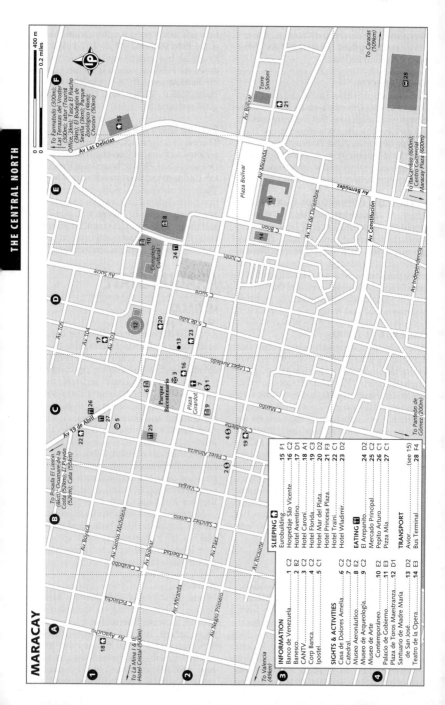

MARACAY

0 ___ 400 m
0 ___ 0.2 miles

To Caracas
(109km)

To Posada El Limón
(6km); Ocumare de la
Costa (52km); El Playón
(52km); Cata (55km)

To Femátodo (300m);
Las Terrazas del Vroster
(300m); Iatur (Tourist
Office, 2km); Tasca El Riacho
(3km); El Bodegón de
Sevilla (3km); Parque
Zoológico (4km);
Choroní (50km)

To La Mina I & II;
Hotel Cristal (500m)

To Valencia
(49km)

To ItalCambio (600m);
Centro Comercial
Maracay Plaza (600m)

To Panteón de
Gómez (200m)

probably the most ruthless of all Venezuelan caudillos. He first came here in 1899, and after seizing power in 1908, he settled in Maracay and ruled both state and country from here until his death in 1935. He set about turning the town into a city worthy of being capital, building a grandiose bullring, opera house, zoo, splendid hotels and an air-force school that became the cradle of Venezuelan aviation.

After his reign, a second wave of city development came with the freeway linking Caracas with Maracay in the 1950s. Around this time, Venezuela also developed the most powerful air force in Latin America, much of it based in Maracay. The city is still an important military base, and the unsuccessful coup of 1992 began with the rebels' planes flying to Caracas from here.

Information
INTERNET ACCESS
Internet cafés in Maracay are common.

MEDICAL SERVICES
Farmatodo (☎ 232-2049; cnr Avs Las Delicias & Urb La Soledad; ⏲ 24 hrs) A large, well-stocked pharmacy north of the center.

MONEY
Banco de Venezuela (Calle Mariño)
Banesco (Av Páez)
Corp Banca (Calle Soublette)
Italcambio (☎ 235-6945; No 110-K, 1st fl, Centro Comercial Maracay Plaza, cnr Avs Aragua & Bermúdez; ⏲ 8:30am-12:30pm & 1:30-5pm Mon-Fri, 9am-1pm Sat) Located 1.5km south of Plaza Bolívar.

POST
Ipostel (Av 19 de Abril)

TELEPHONE
CANTV (Calle Mariño; ⏲ 8am-7pm Mon-Sat) Internet access available.

TOURIST INFORMATION
Instituto Autónomo de Turismo de Aragua (latur; ☎ 242-2284; www.intur.gov.ve; Hotel de Golf Maracay, Av Las Delicias; ⏲ 8am-noon & 1-4pm Mon-Fri) Located 2km north of the center.

Sights
PLAZA GIRARDOT
The historic heart of Maracay, Plaza Girardot (for once, not Plaza Bolívar) is crowned by a large obelisk topped with a bronze eagle, erected in 1897. It commemorates the North American volunteers who joined the independence war forces led by Francisco Miranda, but were captured and hanged in 1806 by the Spaniards.

The only colonial building left by the square is the handsome **catedral** on its eastern side. The cathedral was completed in 1743 and not much has changed since. The white-washed exterior is particularly attractive when the late-afternoon sunlight strikes the facade.

MUSEO DE ARQUEOLOGÍA
An arcaded building erected by Gómez as the seat of government now houses the **archaeological museum** (Plaza Girardot; admission free; ⏲ 9am-3pm Mon-Fri, 9am-noon Sat), featuring interesting pre-Hispanic artifacts of the diverse indigenous groups living today. Keep an eye out for the stone axe and flat, deformed skulls.

CASA DE DOLORES AMELIA
Set on the northern side of Parque Bicentenario, this fine mansion was built in 1927 by Gómez for his favorite mistress, Dolores Amelia Núñez de Cáceres. Designed in the neo-Sevillan style, the building has been nicely restored, but may or may not be open during your time here. If it is, check out the patio, which is clad with glorious *azulejos* (ornamental tiles), reminiscent of the Alhambra in Granada.

SANTUARIO DE MADRE MARÍA DE SAN JOSÉ
This saintly **sanctuary** (admission free; ⏲ 8:30am-noon & 2:30-6pm Tue-Sun), one block east of Plaza Girardot, is the most revered city site. Choroní-born Madre María (1875–1967) was beatified by papal decree in 1995. Her remains were exhumed and, to everybody's shock, the corpse was allegedly intact. You can see her diminutive body in a crystal sarcophagus in the Santuario (though the face and hands are covered with masks).

PLAZA DE TOROS MAESTRANZA
This large Spanish-Moorish construction, possibly the most stylish and beautiful bullring in the country, was modeled on the one in Seville and built in 1933. It was originally called 'Calicanto,' but was then renamed in memory of César Girón, Venezuela's most famous matador, who tragically died in 1971.

A monument of him fighting a bull stands in front of the ring. If you want to have a snoop inside, try getting in through the back door on the eastern side.

MUSEO AERONÁUTICO

This is the only **aeronautical museum** (Av Santos Michelena; admission free; 9:30am-5pm Sat & Sun) in the country and well worth a look. There are about 40 aircraft on display, including four helicopters. Many are warplanes from the 1920s to the 1950s that once served in the Venezuelan air force. The collection's gem has to be a beautifully restored French Caudron G3 from the 1910s, reputedly still in perfect working order.

In the middle of the exhibition grounds is a statue of Juan Vicente Gómez: the first and only monument to the caudillo, unveiled amid great controversy in 1995.

The museum is only open on weekends. If you arrive on a weekday, enquire at the side gate at the end of Av Santos Michelena (best from 8am to 11am or 2pm to 3pm) and somebody may show you around. The soldiers at the gate may be unaware of this service, in which case politely ask them to call the supervisor (NCO).

MUSEO DE ARTE CONTEMPORÁNEO

This **contemporary art museum** (216-3854; admission free; 9am-12:30pm, 1:30-5pm Tue-Sun) stages temporary exhibitions. Enter from the building's inner side, away from the main streets.

PLAZA BOLÍVAR

At three blocks long, this pleasant, tree-filled square is the largest Plaza Bolívar in the country. It was laid out by architect Carlos Raúl Villanueva and opened in 1930. The monument to Bolívar is identical to that in Caracas.

PALACIO DE GOBIERNO

This large, ugly edifice, on the southern side of Plaza Bolívar, was once the splendid Hotel Jardín. Inaugurated in 1930 by Gómez, this playground for the rich and beautiful overshadowed all other Venezuelan hotels of the day. The place witnessed many important episodes of the country's political, social and cultural life, and Carlos Gardel once sang his nostalgic tangos here.

The hotel was closed down and remodeled as a government house in 1959, yet you can still feel the charm of the cloisters and interior gardens. If security guards refuse you entry at the front, try the back (south) gate from Av Páez.

TEATRO DE LA OPERA

Commissioned by Gómez in 1934, this **theater** (233-6043; Av Miranda at Calle Brión; box office 8:30am-noon, 2:30-6pm Mon-Fri) was intended to be the best in the country, to match the capital status of the city. An immense budget of two million *bolívares* was allotted for the structure alone. The theater was constructed swiftly, and by December 1935 (the month Gómez died) it was almost ready, missing only the imported ceiling and interior furnishings. Nonetheless, the new government halted work, and its decorations were moved to theaters in Caracas. It wasn't until 1973 that the theater finally opened. It can seat 860 people and stages a variety of visiting productions, from opera to folkloric dance.

PANTEÓN DE GÓMEZ

In typical dictator style, once Gómez had taken a firm grip of Venezuela, he set about building himself a grandiose **mausoleum** (admission free; 8am-3pm Mon-Fri, 8am-noon Sat). Finished in 1919, this rather pretentious pantheon structure is topped by a white Moorish dome, and houses the tomb of the general and members of his family. Curiously, the interior walls are covered with the kind of thanksgiving plaques normally reserved for saints, each reading 'Thanks for the favors,' and signed with initials.

Fresh flowers and lit candles are also frequently left at the tomb, evidence that Gómez is not forgotten. On the contrary, respect for Gómez has revived over recent years as a result of economic and political turmoil. The mausoleum is south of the city center, just behind the cemetery. A taxi here costs US$2.50.

PARQUE ZOOLÓGICO

At the northern city limits, this unfortunate **zoo** (Av Las Delicias; admission free; 9:30am-4:30pm Tue-Sun) is yet another of Gómez' achievements, built on one of his own estates. There's been little maintenance over the years and the only reason to come might be to encourage keepers to give the chimp a bigger cage. To get there from the city center, take the Castaño/Zoológico bus; taxis cost US$3.75.

Festivals & Events

The **Fiesta de San José**, Maracay's most important annual event, takes place over several days around March 19, the city's patron saint's day. The major *corrida* (bullfight) is celebrated during the feast, but other *corridas* are held on some Sundays in February and early March.

Maracay's Teatro de la Opera invites some groups taking part in Caracas' Festival Internacional de Teatro to perform here.

Sleeping

Maracay's cheapest accommodations are love hotels that rent rooms by the hour. Late at night take care around the bus station and in the center.

ourpick Posada El Limón (☎ 283-4925; www.posadaellimon.com; Calle El Piñal 64; dm US$12, d US$45; P ❌ 🖳 🖳) This excellent posada is run by a Dutch-Venezuelan couple. Their beautiful complex is filled with colorful mosaics and leafy patios with mountain views. Rooms are comfortable and tastefully arranged, and backpackers will appreciate the dorm or hammock option. Other pluses include a peaceful pool, wi-fi, tours, airport transfers and restaurant. It's located in the suburb of El Limón – get here via taxi (US$6 to US$8, 20 minutes from the bus station); a bus (marked 'Circunvalación') from Av Bolívar comes here, but it's infrequent.

Hotel Florida (☎ 245-4508; Calle Soblette Sur 32; d US$18; ❌) Cheap love hotel with cable TV and one-day limit – check out at 1pm, check in (for the night) at 6pm (afternoons are for lovers).

Hospedaje São Vicente (☎ 247-0321; Av Bolívar Este 3; d US$19; ❌) Sports tiny rooms set around a concrete courtyard with caged birds (including a toucan). Get a brighter upstairs room.

Hotel Mar del Plata (☎ 246-4313; Av Santos Michelena Este 23; d US$19; P ❌) Maracay's best deal and a central budget option is this peaceful hotel, which features neat rooms with hot water and cable TV.

Hotel Cristal (☎ 554-0668; Av Bolívar Oeste; s/d US$19/22; P ❌) Very impersonal hotel with large industrial hallways and spacious rooms, though avoid the gloomy ground-floor ones. It's four blocks west of Av Ayacucho, easily accessible by countless buses running along Av Bolívar.

Hotel Wladimir (☎ 246-1115; hwladimir@cantv.net; Av Bolívar Este 27; s/d US$23/31; P ❌) The plain-looking Wladimir is well kept and centrally located. Rooms are bright, neat and come with cable TV, though they're a bit outdated and front ones can be noisy.

Hotel Traini (☎ 245-5502; Av 19 de Abril; r US$32; P ❌) This reasonable option behind a security grill is clean, though it lacks personality. Prices may rise or fall depending on demand.

Hotel Caroní (☎ 554-4465; Av Ayacucho Norte 19; d US$38; P ❌) A 15-minute walk from the center, this personable hotel offers attentive service, hot showers and cable TV. Rooms are comfortable but lack any distinguishing features.

Hotel Aventino (☎ 245-7087; www.hotelaventino.com; Calle López Aveledo 15; d US$49; P ❌) This good choice looks a bit like an exotic birdcage as you enter through the extensive security bars draped with plants. The neat rooms have several button controls for the cable TV, air-con, lights and cheesy ambient music. Beds are firm.

Hotel Princesa Plaza (☎ 223-1008; www.hotelprincesaplaza.com; Av Miranda Este; d US$65; P ❌) Edging close to top-end quality, the large Princesa lies next to the 30-story brick-and-glass Torre Sindoni. It offers good-value (if a little bland) rooms with cable TV, plus little comforts like a hairdryer and laundry service.

Eurobuilding (☎ 200-1111; www.eurobuilding.com.ve; Centro Comercial Las Delicias; s/d incl breakfast US$135/146; P ❌ 🖳) This upmarket hotel lies above a swanky shopping mall filled with restaurants and boutiques. It has spacious, modern rooms with comforts like king-size beds and wi-fi, and boasts a business center, a solarium and two Jacuzzis. Enter through elevators via the lowest floor in the mall.

Eating

There are plenty of reasonably priced places to eat scattered throughout the city center. Some of the cheapest typical meals are in the Mercado Principal (try Felipe's cheap soups), open 7am to 3pm only. The city's upmarket restaurants lie along Av Las Delicias north of the city center (taxis around US$4).

El Arepanito (☎ 237-8621; Av 19 de Abril at Junín; arepas US$2.50-3.50; ❤ 8am -1am; ❌) This very popular *arepera* has a pleasant plant-filled front patio along with an air-con dining room. It also serves good pizza and cheap grilled meats, and is open 24 hours on Friday and Saturday.

Pepito Arturo (Av 19 de Abril; mains US$3.25-8; 11am-midnight) A down-to-earth, cheerful fast-food stop, Arturo's is the place to chow down on a cheap *parrilla* (mixed grill) washed down with a *batido* (fruit juice). Serves up pizza and shawarmas also.

La Mina I & II (254-2546; Av Bolívar Oeste 214; mains US$4.25-12; 8:30am-2am Sun-Thu, till 3:30am Fri & Sat) A 20-minute walk from center, this large, modern fast-food joint grills up the city's best cheap meats. Try the *pincho de lomito,* an impressive and tasty shish kebab served on a vertical hanger. Also has salad bar, good pizzas and a play area for the kids. Annex II is across street.

Pizza Mia (245-6010; Av 19 de Abril; pizzas US$5-21; 11:30am-10:30pm) This bright, modern and loud chain restaurant lies across the road from Pepito Arturo, and its long list of reasonably priced pizzas includes vegetarian options.

Las Terrazas del Vroster (232-1528; Av Las Delicias; mains US$6.50-12; 11am-11:30pm Sun-Thu, till 12:30am Fri & Sat) Located north of center near Burger King, this popular and energetic restaurant offers a good range of pizza, pasta and seafood choices. It specializes in grilled chicken, however, served with all sorts of sides.

Tasca El Riacho (242-4590; Av Las Delicias; mains US$6.50-12; 11:30am-3am) This *tasca* (Spanish-style bar-restaurant) has a huge curvaceous bar, large seating areas and a sophisticated atmosphere that comes alive in the evening. It cooks up paella, *noquis* (potato dumplings), rabbit and trout dishes and Portuguese specialties. Set meals also available.

El Bodegón de Sevilla (242-7914; Av Las Delicias; mains US$7-14; noon-late) Another traditional *tasca* is inside this cute white Spanish-style mansion. The vast menu includes a bit of everything and, of course, there's an enormous, well-stocked bar for quaffing those essential aperitifs or nibbling on tapas.

Getting There & Away

AIR

The nearest non-military airport is in Valencia, 50km to the west. **Avior** (232-8861; www.avioairlines.com; Centro Comercial Las Delicias local 30) is located in a shopping mall just above the Eurobuilding Hotel. **Santa Bárbara** (269-7170; www.santabarbaraairlines.com), at the airport, also provides services.

BUS

It's about a 20-walk from Maracay's bustling bus terminal to Plaza Bolívar, but there are frequent city buses (US$0.35) that head into the center. For transportation to El Playón and Puerto Colombia, see p122.

Destinations include Valencia (US$1.50, one hour, frequent), Caracas (US$3.25, 1½ hours, frequent), Barquisimeto (US$7, three hours), Coro (US$14, seven hours), Puerto La Cruz (US$17, seven hours), San Fernando de Apure (US$12, seven hours, frequent), Ciudad Maracaibo (US$19, 8½ hours), Bolívar (US$21, nine hours), Mérida (US$21, 11 hours) and San Cristóbal (US$19, 12 hours).

BOLÍVAR HACIENDA

The town of San Mateo, 20km east of Maracay, boasts a hacienda that once belonged to the Bolívar family. It was granted to them in 1593, after they came to settle in Venezuela from their native Spain. At the beginning of the 18th century, the Bolívars built a sugarcane mill on their land and used African slaves to work the crops, a common practice throughout the region.

In 1814 Simón Bolívar set up a military camp on the hacienda, which became the target of fierce attacks by the royalist troops. Later on, Bolívar passed through San Mateo on various occasions, including a rest stop after the battle of Carabobo in 1821, when he freed the local slaves.

During the 19th century the hacienda passed through the hands of various owners until Juan Vicente Gómez turned it into barracks in 1924.

Restored in the 1980s to its original state, the hacienda now houses two museums. The neatly displayed **Museo de la Caña de Azúcar** (admission free; 10am-4pm Tue-Sun) is centered on the original sugarcane mill. Exhibits include the

---

NO SURRENDER

The outbuildings of San Mateo's Museo Histórico Militar served as the armory during Bolívar's days, but they have been intentionally left in a state of ruin since March 25, 1814. It was here that the independence martyr Antonio Ricaurte, one of Bolívar's lieutenants, sacrificed himself to save the battle that was almost lost to the Spaniards. Closely encircled by royalists, he led them into the armory before he set fire to the entire store of gunpowder kegs, and blasted both the enemy and himself into oblivion.

mill itself and a variety of tools, implements and objects related to sugar production.

On the opposite side of the road is the affiliated **Museo Histórico Militar** (admission free; ☉ 10am-4pm Tue-Sun). This finely restored historic house, on the top of a hill, features a collection of period armor, plus the usual Bolivariana, including documents and a number of portraits.

Getting There & Away

The Bolívar hacienda is located on the old highway linking La Victoria and the town of San Mateo. Frequent buses and por puestos shuttle between the two; ask to be dropped off at El Ingenio de Bolívar, as the hacienda is commonly known.

From Caracas' La Bandera terminal, take a bus to La Victoria and from there catch a bus toward San Mateo. From Maracay get to San Mateo first, then catch a bus toward La Victoria.

LA VICTORIA

☎ 0244 / pop 120,000

Founded in 1593, Nuestra Señora de Guadalupe de la Victoria was the capital of Aragua state until 1917, when Juan Vicente Gómez moved the title to Maracay, 30km to the west.

Today it's a busy city surrounded by factories, but its historic center, particularly the area around Plaza Ribas, retains some of its old architecture and flavor. Stroll around the central streets, between Plaza Ribas and Plaza Bolívar, which are five blocks apart. Both plazas boast a church – the large 18th-century neoclassical Iglesia de Nuestra Señora de la Victoria at Plaza Ribas, and the small Iglesia de Nuestra Señora de la Candelaria at Plaza Bolívar.

If you want to stick around, head to **Hotel Hacienda El Recreo** (☎ 323-9110; hotelelrecreo@hotmail .com; Av Rivas Dávila Oeste; s/d/tr US$54/56/59; ⓟ ⓧ ⓡ), a converted sugar hacienda with 24 simple but comfortable large rooms with cable TV. The tranquil grounds are studded with palm trees and there's a restaurant and large swimming pool (plus one for the kiddies). The hotel is on the road to San Mateo, within walking distance west of Plaza Ribas.

Getting There & Away

The bus terminal is 4km east of the historic center. Local buses shuttle between the terminal and center (US$0.40).

There are frequent buses to Caracas (US$3, 1¼ hours) and Maracay (US$1, 30 minutes). Por puestos to Colonia Tovar depart regularly and wind up along a spectacular 36km mountain road (US$2.50, one hour). Sit on the right for better vistas.

COLONIA TOVAR

☎ 0244 / pop 10,000

A little piece of old Germany lost in the Venezuelan cloud forest, this tidy and scenic town of red-tile-roof cabins lies scattered on a mountainside in the Cordillera de la Costa, about 60km west of Caracas. It was founded in 1843 by a group of 376 German settlers from the Schwarzwald (Black Forest), recruited by Italian Agustín Codazzi (see the boxed text, p118).

Isolated from the outer world by the lack of roads and rules prohibiting marriage outside the colony, the village followed the mother culture, language and architecture for a century. It wasn't until the 1940s that Spanish was introduced as the official language and the ban on marrying outside the community was abandoned. And in 1963 a paved road from Caracas reached Colonia Tovar, marking a turning point in the history of the tiny town.

Today Colonia Tovar draws hordes of *caraqueños* on weekends, curious to glimpse the traditional architecture and chomp on German sausages, candied apples or strawberries and cream. The town hams up its European heritage shamelessly: waitresses sport frilly traditional garments and ye olde Gothic script (look for 'Lunchería Schmuk') is everywhere. Streets are filled with stalls selling multicolored sweets, fruit preserves, liquors and kitschy souvenirs, while markets overflow with locally grown fruits such as blackberries, apples, nectarines and plums.

Weekdays see the town deserted of tourists, but you can enjoy the town's lush surroundings and cordial inhabitants, some of whom are descendants of the original German settlers, at any time. Whenever you come, however, bring warm clothing – the temperature drops in these upper reaches of the cordillera (the town is 1800m above sea level). Colonia Tovar's average temperature is 61°F, but it's much lower at night.

Information

The village has a few banks (with ATMs), though exchanging money at the weekend can be difficult. Tour agencies (see p118) will

THE CENTRAL NORTH

A LIFE LESS ORDINARY

Swashbuckler, explorer, soldier, pirate, merchant and cartographer – it was the multitalented Italian Agustín Codazzi (1793–1858) who founded Colonia Tovar in 1843. Codazzi led an extraordinary life: at 17 he was fighting in the Napoleonic army, then took to international commerce and later managed a casino in Constantinople (now Istanbul).

When Codazzi heard that Bolívar was recruiting foreigners for a new Venezuelan army, he was the first to enroll. However, on his way south he met the French corsair Louis Aury, and together they landed on Providencia, a Colombian island. From there they ransacked Spanish galleons, reaped huge rewards, and – as a bonus – contributed to the defeat of the Spaniards.

After the war Codazzi was commissioned to draft maps of Venezuela. But after a while the Venezuelan government began to look for European migrants eager to settle and work in Venezuela to help revive the devastated economy. Codazzi set about selecting a place with acceptable climatic conditions, then returned to Europe and collected a group of several hundred German peasants (the nationality he thought most adaptable), bringing them to Venezuela and founding Colonia Tovar. By then the Venezuelan authorities had lost enthusiasm for the program, and Codazzi dedicated himself to mapping. His excellent maps are now the pride of national archives in Venezuela and Colombia.

sometimes change money and give information about the area. For internet access and telephones head to CANTV, just below the church.

Sights & Activities

Stroll about the steep, winding streets to soak up the quaint atmosphere and see some fine examples of traditional German architecture. Visit the fun and creaky **Museo de Historia y Artesanía** (☎ 251-5403; admission US$0.50; ☾ 10am-5:30pm Sat & Sun) to learn about the region's history, from grinding stones to antiquated swords to fossilized crocodile vertebrae.

Don't miss the quirky black-and-white **church**, a pretty L-shaped building with stained-glass windows and a high altar joining two perpendicular naves. The patron saint of the town, San Martín de Tours, looks down from the altar.

Pilsner lovers might appreciate a visit to the local microbrewery, **Fábrica Cerveza Tovar** (☎ 355-1889; ☾ 8am-5pm Mon-Fri, 10am-4pm Sat & Sun). Free 10-minute tours are given (in Spanish); on weekdays you can see the actual production process. It's 100m down from the church, up a short side street; look for the round sign.

For some down time consider a trip to nearby **Spa Renacer Center** (☎ 355-1504, in Caracas 0212-985-2908; www.renacerspa.com), which pampers stressed-out *caraqueños* escaping the city. A full-day visit will set you back US$120, including massage, wraps, sauna and gourmet lunch; there are also two- to five-day packages (US$145 to US$296), which include staying in

the simple but elegant rooms on the premises. A taxis to the spa from Colonia Tovar costs US$2.50.

There are various walking options around the town, including a hike up to **Pico Codazzi** (2425m), the highest peak in the area. You'll first need to reach the pass, which is 5km out of Colonia Tovar on the road toward La Victoria (walk or taxi). Here a path branches off to the right and leads up to the top, about a half-hour's walk. Hiring a guide is recommended, since it's easy to get lost.

Tours

Expediciones Rustic Tours (☎ 355-1908; rustictours@cantv.net; Av Principal) Runs local sightseeing tours into the forest, mountains and down to the coast.
Regenwald Tours (☎ 355-1662; regenwald@cantv.net; Calle Bolívar) Good source of information on local activities such as hiking, camping, paragliding and mountain biking. Also does historical tours.

Festivals & Events

Colonia Tovar hosts the annual chamber music event **Festival Internacional de Música de Cámara** (www.festivalcoloniatovar.com.ve) at the end of November.

Sleeping & Eating

Colonia Tovar is an easy day trip from Caracas, but for overnight stays there are plenty of hotels and cabañas, most with their own restaurants. Private bathrooms and hot water are the norm, and some also have heated rooms (air-con is unnecessary). The accommodations are good and stylish but not cheap. Reserve ahead for weekend stays.

Cabañas Leo (☎ 355-1623; Calle Hessen; d from US$24) One of Colonia Tovar's best deals is this small family posada with only four rooms, all boasting fridge and cable TV (kitchen extra). There's a cute grassy garden in front and concrete patio in back with views. It's located next to Cabañas Silkerbrunnen.

Cabañas Silkerbrunnen (☎ 355-1490; matildedebr eidenbach@hotmail.com; Calle Hessen; d/tr from US$35/40; P) Eighteen clean, neat rooms on flowery grounds are available at this friendly complex set into the hillside. Get them with or without kitchen. Located in a *calle ciega* (blind alley) just below the church.

Residencias Baden (☎ 251-5403; Calle El Museo; d US$42) Just six simple cabañas, some with loft and all with kitchen, spill down the mountainside at this pleasant complex. There are views, a nice grassy area below and plenty of stairs tying everything together.

Cabañas Breidenbach (☎ 355-1211; Sector El Calvario; d/tr from US$38/42, d or tr with kitchen US$47-60; P) Boasting awesome views, this large, well-tended hotel is situated just above the town center. All rooms are spacious and well furnished and come with cable TV. Splash out on a kitchen and fireplace to ward off those chilly mountain nights.

Hotel Selva Negra (☎ 355-1415; www.hotelselva negra.com; d/tr from US$67/105; P) Located to the right of the church through some big iron gates, Selva Negra is the oldest and the biggest lodge in town. It's like a little village in itself, with 44 homey, picturesque cabañas scattered along the grassy hillside, each sleeping two to five guests and boasting old-style furniture. There's a good antique-style restaurant, spa services and even an outdoor playground for the kids.

Hotel Restaurant Kaiserstuhl (☎ 355-1810; Calle Joaquín; d incl breakfast US$70; P) In the heart of town, Kaiserstuhl has 12 simple but comfortable rooms with cable TV, along with a good German restaurant served by waitresses in traditional dress.

Other good choices:

Cabañas Frida (☎ 355-1033; d US$32) Five cute cabañas, all with fridge and cable TV, are available at this small family place.

Rancho Alpino (☎ 355-1470; www.hotelranchoalpino .com; Av Principal; d from US$45) Eighteen smart rooms, some with fridge and views and all with cable TV and balcony.

Posada Die Muhle (☎ 355-1367; Sector El Calvario; d from US$47, d cabaña with kitchen & fireplace US$80) Has a motor-driven water wheel and small modern rooms. Located above the center.

Cabañas Hessen (☎ 355-1456; d US$64) Seven cute, comfy cabañas with kitchen, set on peaceful grassy grounds.

Getting There & Away

The trip from Caracas requires a change at El Junquito. In Caracas, carritos leave from the metro stop Yaguara (US$1.50, 45 minutes to 1½ hours, weekends). From El Junquito, por puesto vans take you the remainder of the journey (US$2, one hour).

If you don't want to go back the same way to Caracas (or want to continue further west), you can take an exciting ride south down to La Victoria. Over a distance of only 30km, the road descends about 1300m. Por puestos depart regularly from Colonia Tovar (US$2.50, one hour); grab a seat on the left side for better views. From La Victoria you can catch a bus to Caracas (US$2.75, 1½ hours).

PARQUE NACIONAL HENRI PITTIER
☎ 0243

Venezuela's oldest national park, created in 1937, Henri Pittier offers a gorgeous coastline for beach lovers, a huge variety of species for bird-watchers, a few trails for hikers, colonial towns for architecture buffs and rolling African drumbeats for *rumba* (party) ravers.

Named for its founder, Swiss botanist Henri Pittier, the park covers 1078 sq km of the Cordillera de la Costa, the coastal mountain range (considered the northern continuation of the great Andean system). The cordillera exceeds 2000m in some areas, then plunges down to the Caribbean coast in the north.

This mountainous region has a staircase of different zones: from Maracay, you ascend steeply through semi-dry deciduous woods to evergreen rainforest and, further up, to dense cloud forest – all over a remarkably short distance. Over the crest and descending for another hour northward to the sea, you get the same sequence in reverse, plus arid coastal scrub followed by beaches, mangroves and coconut groves at the base.

The park is famous for its birds. Almost 600 species have been identified in the park – this represents 43% of the bird species found in Venezuela and 7% of all the birds known in the world. Hardly any other park of this size

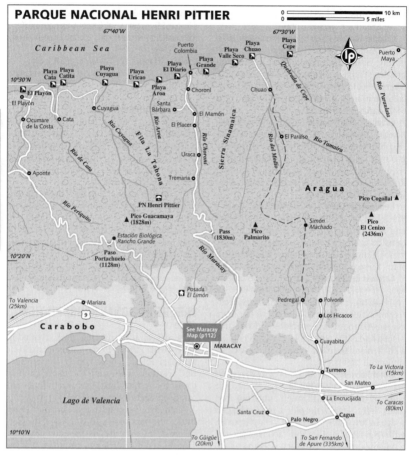

PARQUE NACIONAL HENRI PITTIER

in the world claims this diversity. An added bonus is that Paso Portachuelo (1128m) is on a bird and insect migratory route.

Estación Biológica Rancho Grande (p127) is an easy access point for bird-watchers. The animal world here is also rich and includes tapirs, deers, pumas, agoutis, peccaries, ocelots, opossums, armadillos, monkeys, snakes, frogs and bats.

Let's not forget the beaches – many splendid and secluded crescents of sand glisten along the national park's coastline. The bays are small and the beaches short but wide, some of them shaded from the relentless tropical sun by swaying coconut palms. A few beaches are accessible by road, but other more solitary coves can only be reached by boat – offering all the beauty of an easily accessible paradise, but without the crowds.

The national park is also home to various towns and villages. One of the biggest and most visited is Puerto Colombia, at the end of the eastern road. It's the park's main tourist destination and offers the widest choice of services. El Playón, toward the end of the western road, is also popular and slowly developing into a tourist hangout, but isn't nearly as charming as Puerto Colombia.

ORIENTATION

The park's highest point is Pico El Cenizo (2436m). From its east–west ridge, the cordillera rolls dramatically down north to the coast, and south to Maracay. Two roads, both paved, cross the park from north to south. Both originate in Maracay and go as far as the coast. The western road leads from Maracay to El Playón, then ends at the town of Cuyagua.

The eastern road heads from Maracay to Choroní, then 2km further on ends at Puerto Colombia. It's narrower, poorer and more twisting, but it climbs up to 1830m and is more spectacular. Both roads are about 55km long and are occasionally blocked by landslides in the rainy season. There's no road connection between the coastal ends of these roads; an expensive boat ride is the only way to get from one to the other.

The coast has rocky cliffs, interspersed with golden sandy bays filled with coconut groves – some almost totally virgin and undeveloped.

WALKING & HIKING

The area along the coast, where most of the towns and villages are located, offers the simplest and best options for walkers. Carrying water and shade protection is crucial, however, as these coastal paths are often unshaded.

It's possible to walk from Puerto Colombia a few hours west to Aroa or east to Chuao. Another trail begins 6km south on the road from Choroní, at the place known as 'El Mamón'; the walk from here to Chuao will take five to seven hours. The route is confusing in parts because of various side paths, so consider taking a local guide (see p122).

Further up the mountains, the trails are few and far between. The terrain is covered by

BIRD-WATCHING 101

Parque Nacional Henri Pittier is a true bird-watcher's paradise and one of the most important biological reserves in the country. The 580 avian species recorded here include 30 kinds of hummingbirds, 15 of warblers, 14 of hawks, nine of owls, seven of woodpeckers and four of kingfishers.

Estación Biológica Rancho Grande (p127), a decrepit old building that has seen much better days, is a key observation spot. It boasts a huge rooftop terrace with a feeder that attracts many birds – great for close-up shots. A nearby trail provides more natural access, and the station is strategically located close to Paso Portachuelo (1128m), the lowest pass in the mountain ridge and a natural migratory route for birds flying inland from the sea from such distant places as Argentina and Canada.

The best times for bird-spotting are early in the morning and late in the afternoon. December through to March is perhaps the best time for viewing migratory birds, though October and November are also good.

Endemic species to watch out for include the Groove-billed Toucanet, Buffy Hummingbird, Handsome Fruiteater, Helmeted Curassow, Blood-eared Parakeet, White-tipped Quetzal, Rufous-cheeked Tananger, Guttulated Foliage-gleaner, Venezuelan Flycatcher, Scalloped-breasted Antpitta, Black-throated Spinetail, Plain-flanked Rail, Tepui Swift, Green-tailed Emerald, Red Siskin, Fulvous-headed Tanager, Venezuelan Wood Quail, Violet-chested Hummingbird, Pale-headed Jacamar, Yellow-bellied Bristle-Tyrant and White-bearded Flycatcher.

Rare species include the Yellow-bellied Tyrannulet, Harpy Eagle, Black-backed Antshrike, Long-billed Starthroat, Sooty Grassquit, Euler's Flycatcher, Orchard Oriole, Crested Eagle, Hooded Warbler, Steely-vented Hummingbird, Maroon-faced Parakeet and Black-manibled Toucan.

For good Venezuelan birding guides seek out:

- *Birding in Venezuela* by Mary Lou Goodwin (2003)

- *Birds of Venezuela* by Steven L Steven L. Hilty (2002)

- *Birds of Venezuela: photographs, sounds and distributions,* Peter Boesman (1999, CD-ROM)

- *Venezuela, Paraíso de Aves* by Carlos Ferraro Russo & Miguel Lentino Armitano (1992, available in English, Spanish and German)

For more information look up:

- www.angel-ecotours.com/pdf/henripittier_birds.pdf (a list of all 580 species)

- www.audubonvenezuela.org (Venezuela's Audubon Society website)

- www.birdvenezuela.com/birding_henri_pittier.htm (good general information)

THE CENTRAL NORTH

A LITTLE HISTORY...

The park's coastline has been inhabited for centuries. Interestingly, all the old towns are set well back from the waterfront; Ocumare de la Costa, Cuyagua, Cata, Choroní and Chuao were all founded several kilometers inland from the sea to protect themselves against the pirates who roamed the coast. Puerto Colombia and El Playón are relatively recent settlements.

There was also a big African population in these older towns, and their legacy has been preserved in the sensual culture and music. Drums have long been an integral part of life, and today their pulsating beat immediately sparks dancing on weekend nights and holidays – particularly during the Fiesta de San Juan on June 23 and 24.

thick forest, and rainfall is high. The cordillera's northern slopes receive more rain than the southern ones, and the upper parts are pretty wet most of the year. The driest months are January to March.

The hike from Turmero (14km east of Maracay) to Chuao is one of the few trails that traverse the cordillera. It is reasonably easy to follow, though its upper reaches can get very wet and muddy in the rainy season. This hike can be done in two or three days, but officially you'll need a guide.

TOURS

Many posadas in the Puerto Colombia and El Playón areas offer tours. For something more personal ask around for guides who can take you on hikes in the area and give you more information and attention.

Casa Luna (☎ 951-5318, 0412-435-3056; jungletrip@choroni.net) The personable owners of the posada in Puerto Colombia (opposite), Claudia Beckmann and Emilio Espinoza, also act as guides. They do one- and two-day tours of the national park (US$20 to US$40), along with day trips to area beaches (US$32 to US$56). They can also organize diving trips and airport transfers. English and German are spoken.

Fernando Nocua (☎ 0416-0424670; www.expedicionesjaguar.com.ve) Fernando is a Venezuelan who works for Expediciones Jaguar and speaks English. He knows the El Playón area best and can guide tours there, including a five- to six-hour hiking trip to Cumboto (good for birding). He can also take you to beaches like La Cienaga, Cata/Catita and Cuyagua.

Reiner Wendorf (☎ 808-9393, 0416-345-8390) Reiner is a German and long-time resident of the area. He does day tours around the Choroní area that include hiking and visiting waterfalls and plantations (US$20 to US$25, minimum two people). Rainer knows the area's flora and fauna and might be able to organize multiday tours. He speaks English, Spanish and – of course – German.

Virgilio Espinal (☎ 991-1106, 0416-747-3833; www.cocuy.org.ve; senttovivi@hotmail.com) 'Vivi' is a good English-speaking guide for walks and casual bird-watching. Knowledgeable about the park, Vivi operates a rustic mountain refuge known as 'El Cocuy,' near the village of Uraca, which serves as a base for tours ranging from two hours to several days. Day rates range from US$15 to US$20.

GETTING THERE & AWAY

Most travelers get to the park via Maracay's bus terminal. Both the eastern and western roads are very curvy, so if you're very prone to motion sickness consider downing the proper pill. Also consider taking a bus rather than a por puesto; buses take longer but are slower on the curves.

Buses to Puerto Colombia and Choroní leave regularly from Anden 5 (platform 5) and run from 6:30am to 7pm (US$3, two hours). Por puestos to these destinations park just outside the southern gate of the terminal (US$6, 1½ hours).

Buses to El Playón (marked 'Ocumare de la Costa') leave regularly from Anden 6 and run from 6:30am to 7pm (US$3, two hours). Por puestos park just outside the southern gate of the terminal (US$6, 1½ hours).

Boats in both Puerto Colombia and El Playón can take you to any beach you wish. The charge is by boat, so the fare depends on the number of passengers (usually up to 10). Prices are negotiable and possibly inflated, so always try to bargain.

Approximate boat rates are given under each town's section. Boats between Puerto Colombia and El Playón cost around US$100 and take about one hour. Otherwise, to travel between the two areas you have to return to Maracay.

Note that transportation prices for buses, por puestos and boats may rise on weekends, when demand is high.

Puerto Colombia

This attractive and well-visited coastal town was once the area's local port. It has developed into one of Venezuela's most popular travelers' destinations, and attracts backpackers like bees to honey. Unlike sleepy and nostalgic Choroní further inland, Puerto Colombia is full of young crowds, posadas and restaurants. It's a great base for excursions to the national park and beaches, and has a laid-back vibe that can be positively addictive. Weekends are party times on the malecón (the coastal boulevard), with drumming circles revving up everyone's spirits.

The closest and most popular beach is **Playa Grande**, a 10-minute walk by road east of town – just head over the pedestrian bridge and you'll reach it. It's about half a kilometer long and shaded by coconut palms. Playa Grande is quite developed; many people camp here and there are a few restaurants (but no hotels). It also gets very busy (and littered) on weekends.

For something isolated, hike an hour to small and undeveloped **Playa El Diario**. You'll need to walk south out of town about 15 minutes on the main road, then cross a small yellow bridge. Take the side road to the right, Calle El Cementerio, which goes 500m to a small cemetery (you'll pass some fancy hotels). Follow the road for another 200m, then take a path branching off to the right. Walk about 15 minutes, then take another path to the right, which will lead you to the beach. Bring food, plenty of water and lots of sun protection (there's no shade).

For a good view and photo opportunity, climb to Cristo Mirador, east of town and up the hill about 20 minutes. You can go further for higher panoramas too. Before you set off, though, ask locals if it's safe: there's always some danger of robbery in isolated places.

INFORMATION

There are no banks in Puerto Colombia (or Choroní, for that matter) so stock up with cash in Maracay. There are a couple of internet places in town. **Coffe Mey** (9am-10pm), next to Posada Túcan, has a good connection. **Movistar** (7am-10pm) also offers telephone services.

A green open bus called 'El Trencito' shuttles between Puerto Colombia and Choroní every hour or so (US$0.50). Otherwise the walk is about 20 minutes.

At the time of writing a new bus terminal was due to be finished in Puerto Colombia in 2007, 1km from the malecón. It was currently being used only on busy weekends and in high season; until this situation changes buses stop in front of Hostal Colonial.

CASH IS WHERE IT'S AT

At research time there was still no bank nor official money changer in all of Parque Nacional Henri Pittier. Until this situation changes, remember to obtain *bolívares* in Maracay, the nearest city with banking services (you might be able to unofficially change US dollars in Puerto Colombia or El Playón). Also, keep in mind that few hotels and posadas take traveler's checks or credit cards.

SLEEPING

Puerto Colombia has plenty of places to stay – everything from budget to luxury – and the number keeps growing. You can camp on the beach or sling your hammock between the palms (both free), but don't leave your tent unattended. Showers are available for US$2.50.

Be warned: prices rise by a whopping 30% to 80% on weekends and for major holiday periods (Christmas to early January, Carnaval, Holy Week and all of August). The rates listed below are for midweek and off-peak times.

Budget

Casa Luna (951-5318; jungletrip@choroni.net; Calle Morillo; dm/d/tr US$7/12/19) Just five simple rooms are available at this small posada run by a friendly German-Venezuelan couple. All but one are shared bathroom, and there's a kitchen for guests. They have a rare dormitory – great for budget single travelers. A rooftop terrace is being built, and area tours are available. It's located right next to Hostal Colonial and a bit noisy, so bring earplugs.

Don Miguel (0414-446-1665; Calle Morillo; d with/without air-con US$38/14; P) A cheap and functional place with 15 simple fan rooms. Larger air-con room for up to five people are available (US$65). Located right next to the *guardia nacional* post.

Hostal Colonial (218-5012; www.choroni.net; Calle Morillo 37; d/tr/q/apt US$17/19/21/40) This classic backpacker pad, on the main street into town, comes with a variety of large but poorly lit rooms featuring saggy beds. There's a sociable common dining area, however, plus kitchen use and a small breakfast restaurant in back. Doubles with outside bathroom are US$12.

THE CENTRAL NORTH

Other choices:

Posada La Abuela (Calle Los Cocos; d/tr/q without bathroom US$14/21/26) Friendly family posada with basic but decent fan rooms, all with shared bathroom.

Posada Playa Grande (☎ 437-9767; Calle Los Cocos; s/d US$19/33) Good, small bright rooms; located close to the boat dock.

Doña Enriqueta (☎ 991-1158; Calle Color 3; d with fan/air-con US$19/33; ⬛) Small posada with dark boring rooms. Close to the malecón.

Midrange

Posada Tucán (☎ 991-1178; www.posadatucan.com; Calle Morillo; d with fan US$26-30; t/q with air-con US$45/54; ⓟ ⬛) Run by a German-Venezuelan couple is this casual place with eight good, no-frills rooms. There are two larger rooms with kitchen for up to six people. Area tours and airport transfers are available; it also rents body boards.

Montañita (☎ 281-0317; Calle Morillo; d with fan/air-con US$33/56) Just one block from the malecón, this 20-room posada has air-con rooms on the ground floor and fan rooms upstairs (where they catch a breeze). There's a shady courtyard with plants and mosaic accents, plus a restaurant. The rooftop patio gives views of the area.

Posada La Parchita (☎ 991-1233; posadalaparchita@ yahoo.com; Calle Trino Rangel; d US$38; ⓟ) This quiet, charming family-run posada is tucked away down a backstreet next to the river. It has a handful of simple, tidy rooms with fans set around a cute garden patio with hammocks. On weekends breakfast is included (and it'd want to be; prices almost double!).

Hostal Vista Mar (☎ 991-1250; Calle Colón; d/tr with fan US$38/42, with air-con US$60/70; ⓟ ⬛) Here's an older, no-frills hotel featuring clean, simple and darkish rooms with high ceilings and minimal furniture. It's located at the far end of the malecón and has a breezy, bamboo-shaded rooftop with hammocks, all overlooking the sea. Fan rooms are smaller and older than the air-con rooms.

La Posada de Choroní (☎ 991-1191; www.laposada dechoroni.3a2.com; Calle Morillo; d US$42) A good peaceful choice boasting a lovely courtyard with potted plants and lined with attractive hallways. Rooms are small but neat and comfortable and come with cute decor. Small Continental breakfast included.

Posada Riqui Riqui (☎ 991-1061; ulfjaeger@cantv.net; Calle Morillo; d with fan/air-con US$42/52; ⓟ ⬛ 🛠) This exceptional posada is set on lovely planted

grounds with a bit of a hacienda feel. Just seven lovely and simple rooms are offered, some sleeping five to 10 people (US$60 to US$140). Hammocks and a small pool offer relaxation. It's German-owned, but he might be around on weekends only.

Posada Pittier (☎ 991-1028; www.posadapittier.com; Calle Morillo; d/tr/q US$47/60/75; ⓟ ⬛) Small and pretty, this sweet posada has nine neat and comfy rooms with a bit of personality. They're set around a little grassy area with hammocks lining the open hallways. It's located next to Hostal Piapico, on the main road at the very entrance to town; look for the coral-colored outside wall.

Posada Tom Carel (☎ 991-1220; www.posadatomcarel .com; Calle Trino Rangel; d US$50; ⬛) This colorful family posada is a cozy little paradise with rustic stairs, plenty of plants and intricate tile-and-pebble mosaic floors. The 11 rooms are small but lovely, many with hammocks strung up over the beds. It's located not too far from Hostal Colonial.

Casa Pueblo (☎ 991-1006; posadacasapueblo@yahoo .com; Calle Trino Rangel 9; d with fan/air-con US$50/88; ⓟ ⬛) One of the nicer modern places in town is this beautiful posada with tile-and-mosaic touches in hallways. The 18 rooms are attractive and comfortable; the more expensive upstairs air-con ones have private balconies with hammocks. Fan rooms are downstairs and much simpler. There's a small fancy restaurant also.

Top End

Hostal Piapoco (☎ 991-1108; www.pipiaco.com; Calle Morillo; d incl breakfast US$60; ⓟ ⬛ 🛠) This is a modern place on the main road at the entrance to the town. It has neatly kept rooms (rooms 7 and 9 are the best) and a sunny patio around the pool, plus a few hammocks slung up by the restaurant. It's on the main road at the entrance to town, almost 1km from the malecón.

ourpick Posada La Casa de las García (☎ 991-1056, in Caracas 0212-662-2858; www.posadalasgarcia.com; Calle El Cementerio; s/d/tr/q incl breakfast US$50/65/80/100; ⓟ ⬛) This centuries-old family hacienda is well worth the walk out of town. Its grounds have pretty gardens, while the 13 charming, old-style rooms boast antique furniture along with modern touches like hairdryers. Hammock chairs hang in the open hallways. A newer extension at the back of the house has stylish, bright rooms with garden baths.

Mesón Xuchytlán (☎ 991-1234; Plaza Bolívar at Calle Morillo 22; d incl breakfast from US$70; 🟦) Right in the center of town, near Plaza Bolívar, is this attractive Mexican-style mansion. The 11 pleasant rooms are set around a nice courtyard with plants. Some rooms come with a Jacuzzi in their own small outdoor garden (US$112).

Posada Semeruco (☎ 991-1264; www.posadasemeruco.com; Calle Morillo 65; d/tr/q incl breakfast US$84/103/117; **P**) This elegant posada, situated near the *guardia nacional* post, is housed in a colonial-style building set around a sunny courtyard with hammock chairs. The 11 rooms have handsome old-style furniture and come with comforts like a fridge and a coffee-maker; doubles with fan are available for US$70. Its annex (same contact details) is not quite as large or nice, but is 25% cheaper and closer to the beach.

Posada Turpial (☎ 991-1123; Calle José Maitín 3; d incl breakfast & dinner US$90; 🟦 🖳) This pleasant posada is run by a German-Venezuelan couple and offers 11 colorful and tasteful rooms. There's a common area with hammocks and a shady patio with plants. It's located near Hostal Colonial.

Hacienda El Portete (☎ 991-1255; www.elportete.com; Calle El Cementerio; d/tr/q incl breakfast US$94/108/126; **P** 🟦 🖳 🐾) Just beyond La Casa de las Garcia is another part of what was once the same old hacienda complex. This colonial mansion isn't as endearing as its neighbor and the garden areas are a bit unkempt. Rooms are average and there are hammocks here and there, along with a large round pool and Jacuzzi. There's a restaurant, a bar and kids' play areas.

Hostal Casagrande (☎ 991-1251; www.hostalcasagrande.com; Calle Morillo 33; d/tr/q US$115/133/165; **P** 🟦 🐾) The 19 large, beautiful rooms in this stunning colonial-style hotel come with lovely artwork and rustic furniture. Even the halls are nice, and there's a shady courtyard with hammocks and a shallow birdbath-like pool for cooling off. There are spa services and an annex with more rooms. It's located opposite the church.

EATING

Restaurants are numerous and fried fish is the local staple. Budget eating is provided by a cluster of shack eateries on the way to Playa Grande (beware a lack of hygiene, however). There are midrange choices near the boat docks and at the beach itself.

Several posadas have their own restaurants. If you're vegetarian and willing to walk 20 minutes inland to Choroní, try the tiny restaurant in the Posada Colonial El Picure (p126), which has a few veggie dishes and a great intimate atmosphere.

Hostal Colonial (☎ 218-5012; Calle Morillo 37; mains US$3-4; 🕑 7:30am-11am) This small breakfast joint at the back of the Hostal Colonial serves breakfast only, and caters to backpackers' international tastes. It's a peaceful spot that cooks up Continental breakfasts along with *arepas*, plus some juices.

our pick Willy (☎ 951-5316; mains US$5-10; 🕑 Fri-Sun in low season, daily in high) Some consider this German-run enterprise the best restaurant in town. Ingredients are fresh, and selections include excellent fish and pasta. It's just over the pedestrian bridge on the way to Playa Grande, on the right side.

Brisas del Mar (☎ 991-1268; Calle Los Cocos; mains US$5-10; 🕑 8:30am-10:30pm) Good down-to-earth spot for pasta, seafood and meat dishes. Breezy open front area, though there's a narrow back balcony overlooking a canal. The bar has longer hours (and the restaurant has later hours in high season too).

Bar Restaurant Araguaneyes (☎ 991-1137; Calle Los Cocos 8; mains US$5-15; 🕑 8:30am-10:30pm) This lively restaurant offers good international and criollo food, and is also open for breakfast. There's a fair list of cocktails which are best enjoyed from the airy roof terrace.

Around Puerto Colombia

Beaches in the area are normally visited by boat, though some of them can also be reached on foot after a long, hard, sweaty hike. Negotiate with boat operators at the river's mouth in Puerto Colombia.

Playa Aroa (US$30 roundtrip per boat, 15 minutes one-way) is a lovely place with no services, though nearby **Playa Uricao** (US$35, 20 minutes) might have a weekend snack shack. There's good snorkeling but no shade at **Playa Valle Seco** (US$35, 20 minutes) while **Playa Cepe** (US$50, 45 minutes) is on a bay and has some services including a restaurant and midrange posada. Determine a pick-up time with the boat operator, and pay him when he picks you up. The trip may be quite rough if the waves are high, so be prepared to get wet.

Chuao, about 8km east of Choroní as the crow flies, is a small friendly village known for its cacao plantations and Diablos Danzantes celebrations (see p108). Villagers live in almost complete isolation here: the only road is a rough 4km trail to the sea. La Luzonera is a cheap posada on the plaza. Chuao also has a so-so beach, which you can reach by boat from Puerto Colombia (US$40, 30 minutes).

Choroní

An oasis of peace, charming Choroní is the place to escape the crowds of Puerto Colombia, which is about a 20-minute walk away. There's not much to do in this 385-year-old village other than greet the villagers as you wander the interesting narrow colonial streets, which are lined with fine pastel houses. The deeply shaded Plaza Bolívar has a lovely parish church, Iglesia de Santa Clara, with a finely decorated ceiling. The wall over the high altar has been painted to look like a carved retable.

Madre María de San José was born in Choroní in 1875 and dedicated her life to service for the poor. The house where she lived and worked is on the plaza. She later continued her work with the poor in Maracay, where she founded a religious congregation. She died at the respectable age of 92 and was beatified in 1995.

The feast of Santa Clara, the patron saint of the town, is celebrated in August.

SLEEPING & EATING

The town has two pleasant colonial hotels located on the main street (one with a restaurant), but eateries are few and far between.

Posada Colonial El Picure (☎ 991-1296; Calle Miranda 34; d US$28) Just four simple but clean rooms come with high ceilings at this pleasantly serene colonial building. They're set around a concrete courtyard with talking parrots and a tiny restaurant serving excellent home-cooked food, including vegetarian dishes (open 7am to 10pm, mains US$4 to US$8). There's an eight-room annex nearby.

Hostería Río Mar (☎ 991-1038, in Caracas 0212-941-1945; Calle Miranda; d/tr/q US$33/38/42; ☒) This attractive mustard-yellow house hides a good little hostel behind its heavy wooden door and wood-barred windows. It has nine small and simple but neat rooms with high ceilings. There's no common area, but a couple of hammocks hang in the dark hallway. It's just a few doors down (and across the street) from Posada Colonial El Picure.

Hotel Hacienda La Aljorra (☎ 0412-288-7624; laljorra@hotmail.com; Carrera Maracay-Choroní km 49; d US$38; P) This 18th-century cacao plantation has a renovated hacienda building 1.5km inland from Choroní, on the road to Maracay. The grounds have been neglected, but the building itself is a nice place with old tiled hallways with antique furniture and hammocks. The 10 high-ceilinged fan rooms are good sized but are dark and nothing special – room 9 is the best.

El Playón

Located at the end of the national park's western road, El Playón is the main town in this area and offers more than a dozen places to stay. It's much larger than Puerto Colombia but has none of its colonial charm, which makes it less attractive and less popular. There are also fewer tourist services. Boats leave from La Boca (the river mouth), toward the east end of town.

Good beaches abound in this area. The nearest one, **El Playón**, is right in town, and has a good surfing spot toward its west end. There are actually several small beaches here, the best of which is probably **Playa Malibú**, close to the malecón.

About 1½km to the west is **Playa Maya** (US$25, 10 minutes), a beautiful and isolated bay beach with no services. Just beyond is **La Cienaga** (US$28, 15 minutes) which has good snorkeling, diving and kayaking (the last two organized through Posada de la Costa Eco-Lodge, see opposite).

Five kilometers eastward is the area's most famous beach, **Playa Cata**. Girls hang on to your bikinis – there's an unexpectedly strong backwash! The beach is a postcard crescent of sand bordering Bahía de Cata, and marred only by two ugly apartment towers looming over the beach. There are plenty of shack restaurants. To get here take a bus from El Playón (US$0.50, 20 minutes) or hire a boat (US$28, 15 minutes).

Boats from Playa Cata take tourists to the smaller and quieter **Playa Catita**, on the eastern side of the same bay (US$25, 10 minutes). You can also walk there in an hour, but take water and sun protection. You'll pass interesting xerophytic vegetation (adapted for minimal water conditions) along the way.

Further east is the unspoiled and usually deserted **Playa Cuyagua**, which is good for surfers. You can get there by a 2.5km sand trail from the town of Cuyagua (bus to Cuyagua US$1.50, 45 minutes). You might also be able hire a boat from Playa Cata (US$35, 20 minutes).

Nearby towns to visit include **Ocumare de la Costa**, **Cata** and **Cuyagua**, noted for their Diablos Danzantes traditions – though the celebrations here are not as famous as those in Chuao. These towns are reached by bus.

SLEEPING & EATING

Many places to stay are within two blocks of the waterfront. Most posadas can arrange boat tours, including to see dolphins in the area. Prices rise about 20% on weekends and for major holiday periods (Christmas to early January, Carnaval, Holy Week and all of August). The rates listed below are for midweek and nonholiday times.

There are a few ramshackle restaurants in town and most posadas can serve food to their guests. Boconó, Acuario and Eco-Lodge have restaurants open to nonguests.

Doña Emma (☎ 993-1303; Calle California 11; d with fan/air-con US$17/28; P ⚋) This place is cheap but run-down and grungy, offering tiny hot rooms. Also try Posada Yolanda, nearby.

El Tesoro (☎ 0412-893-9118; Callejón La Boca; camping & hammocks per person US$2.50, s/d US$10/14) Funky as all get-out is this very *(very)* rustic and decrepit old shack looked over by the eccentric Herbert Matamoros. This is for hard-core backpackers only, and best for campers, who can stake a weedy hillside spot with views. Rooms are barely livable (your own linens are a good idea). It's located 100m from La Boca; find the rocky alley next to the empanada shop and look for an old yellow tin door.

Posada Los Helechos (☎ 993-1385; www.posada loshelechos.com; Calle Santander 63; d US$28; P ⚋) This decent posada offers seven small rooms with small bathrooms (one has a kitchen), but has a nice patio and hallways with lots of airy seating. There's a small restaurant and murky, greenish pool used at your own risk. It's six blocks inland from La Punta (at the west end of the beach).

Hotel La Paragua (☎ 993-1466; Calle Vargas 74; d/tr US$30/47; P ⚋ ⚋) A better deal than nearby Acuario is this hotel with good, basic, small rooms sporting tiny bathrooms. It has a pool and is one block further inland from Acuario.

Posada Boconó (☎ 993-1434; www.posadabocono .com; Calle Fuerzas Armadas 44; d/tr/q US$38/42/47;

P ⚋) Run by a Dutch-Venezuelan couple is this colorful posada next to the beach. The good-sized rooms are in two buildings, one of which is 80 years old and strewn with antique furniture. There are plenty of common spaces with chairs and hammocks, plus a good restaurant-bar area. Bike rental and transfers available; English, Italian and Dutch spoken.

Posada Loley (☎ 993-1252; loleyenlacosta@hotmail .com; Calle Fuerzas Armadas; d/tr incl breakfast US$56/61; ⚋ P ⚋) Near Eco-Lodge and one block back from the beach, this family posada has been completely remodeled into a pleasant place with 10 neat rooms. There's a patio with swimming pool and meals are available.

Posada de la Costa Eco-Lodge (☎ 993-1986; www .ecovenezuela.com; Calle California 23; s or d incl breakfast US$60-82, 6-person cabaña US$117; ⚋ ▯ ⚋) Set in a sunny garden, this premiere posada offers 26 simple but attractive and well-decorated rooms, some set around a small pool with falls. Larger rooms cost more but come with private balcony with hammock. There's a restaurant, bar, bike rental, wi-fi and plenty of relaxing patio areas. It also offers tours, including a kayaking and diving package at Playa La Cienaga. English is spoken.

Hotel Acuario (☎ 993-1956; www.hotelacuario.com .ve; Calle Vargas; d US$70; P ⚋ ⚋) This modern hotel seems a bit overpriced, but does feature clean, neat rooms with cable TV and fridge. There's a nice pool with bar area and two Jacuzzis, as well as a restaurant. The hotel is four blocks inland.

Estación Biológica Rancho Grande

Far away from the coastal towns and beaches, this dilapidated **biological station** (☎ 0243-550-7734; day-use fee US$2.50; ⚋ 8am-4pm) is just off the road to El Playón, a few hundred meters before Paso Portachuelo (a bird migratory route). Surrounded by cloud forest, this station sits at an altitude of 1100m; keep your eyes peeled for the sign.

The station is in a run-down, supposedly haunted old building that was originally commissioned by Juan Vicente Gómez to be a posh country hotel. The building was half completed when Gómez died and became deserted when workers heard of the dictator's death. Park founder Henri Pittier suggested establishing the new park's research station here; his proposal became a reality in the mid-1940s. The station is run by the Faculty of Agriculture of the Universidad Central de Venezuela, based at El Limón, the northwestern outer suburb of Maracay.

For serious bird-watchers, it's feasible to see hundreds of species on a week-long visit to the station. There's a small feeding station on the large rooftop terrace that attracts certain species. You may also see monkeys, agoutis, peccaries, snakes and butterflies in the area.

An ecological path known as the Sendero Andrew Field heads through the forest behind the station. The loop, which is easily walked in an hour, provides myriad opportunities to see the local flora and fauna, particularly birds. You officially need a permit for this short walk, but this requires a ridiculous amount of bureaucracy (finding the Inparques office in Maracay's zoo, then going to a bank to pay a fee). Some friendly banter with the station's guard (along with perhaps a small tip) should be enough for 'permission' to do this walk.

The biological station has very basic, dormitory-style accommodations on the top floor, providing about 45 beds. Though intended for visiting researchers, they're hardly ever all taken. Tourists are welcome to stay for US$5 per head (US$1.50 for students with an ISIC card). No camping is allowed and no food is provided, but you can use the kitchen facilities. Bring linens or a sleeping bag, all food and water, a flashlight and rain gear. If you want to stay more than three days, get permission from the University. Remember, these are very rustic facilities.

CARABOBO STATE

VALENCIA
☎ 0241 / pop 1,400,000
Founded in 1555, five years before Caracas, Valencia is the country's third-largest metropolis and one of the first Spanish settlements in Venezuela. The city played a crucial part in the fight for independence and its aftermath, and today it's a prosperous, bustling urban sprawl bordered by mountains and nestled in the north–south valley of the Río Cabriales.

Much like its Spanish namesake, the Valencia region is famous for its orange groves and bullfighting (the city's Plaza de Toros Monumental is the second largest in world). The city generates nearly a quarter of the country's national manufacturing production and is also the center of the most developed agricultural region.

Valencia is not a huge tourist draw, but does boast a few museums and surrounding attractions, and is an important air and land transportation hub. A new metro system – Venezuela's second – is currently being constructed), and will eventually link destinations along Avs Bolívar and Lara. The first trains should begin running in 2007.

Set at an altitude of around 500m, Valencia has an average temperature of about 77°F, with hot days ameliorated by the evening breeze that rolls down from the mountains.

History
Valencia has had a violent and tumultuous history. It had not yet reached its seventh birthday when Lope de Aguirre, the infamous adventurer obsessed with finding El Dorado, sacked the town and burned it to the ground. Twenty years later, the town, not yet fully recovered, was razed by Carib people. Then in 1667 the town was seized and destroyed again, this time by French pirates. The town's proximity to Lago de Valencia didn't help either. The disease-breeding marshes brought about smallpox epidemics that decimated the population and scared away many survivors. Then in 1812 a devastating earthquake shook the Andean shell, leaving Valencia in ruins yet again.

And as if all that wasn't enough – the war for independence came to Valencia. Just two years after the earthquake, the town was besieged by royalist troops under the command of José Tomás Boves (fittingly known as 'the Butcher'). The ensuing slaughter left 500 people dead. Over the next seven years no fewer than two dozen battles were fought around the town, only ceasing on June 24, 1821, when Bolívar's decisive victory at Carabobo secured Venezuela's independence.

The year 1826 saw Valencia become the first town to oppose Bolívar's sacred union, Gran Colombia. Its inhabitants called for Venezuelan sovereignty and, four years later, this demand became a reality. Congress decreed formal secession here and made Valencia the newborn country's capital, before switching it a year later to Caracas.

The town caught new economic wind in its sails after WWII, and today Valencia is Venezuela's most industrialized city.

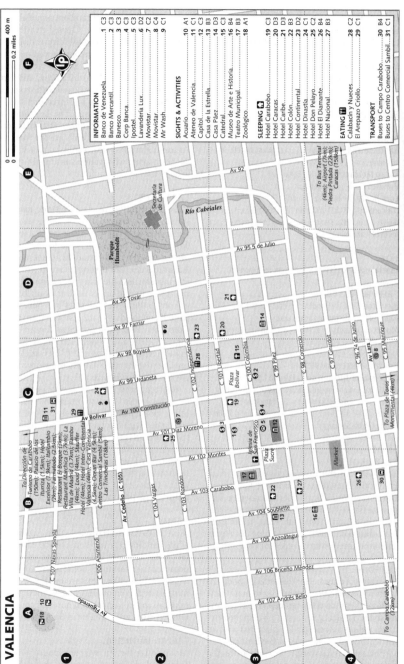

VALENCIA

0 400 m
0 0.2 miles

INFORMATION
Banco de Venezuela..............1	C3
Banco Mercantil....................2	C3
Banesco................................3	C3
Corp Banca...........................4	C3
Ipostel.................................5	C3
Lavandería Lux.....................6	D2
Movistar...............................7	C2
Movistar...............................8	C4
Mr Wash..............................9	C1

SIGHTS & ACTIVITIES
Acuario...............................10	A1
Ateneo de Valencia.............11	C1
Capitol...............................12	C3
Casa de la Estrella...............13	B3
Casa Páez...........................14	D3
Catedral.............................15	C3
Museo de Arte e Historia....16	B4
Teatro Municipal.................17	B3
Zoológico...........................18	A1

SLEEPING 🛏
Hotel Carabobo...................19	C3
Hotel Caracas.....................20	D3
Hotel Caribe.......................21	D3
Hotel Colón........................22	B3
Hotel Continental................23	D2
Hotel Dinastía.....................24	C1
Hotel Don Pelayo................25	C2
Hotel El Diamante...............26	B4
Hotel Nacional....................27	B3

EATING 🍴
Calabacín y Nueces.............28	C2
El Arepazo Criollo...............29	C1

TRANSPORT
Buses to Campo Carabobo.......30	B4
Buses to Centro Comercial Sambil...31	C1

Parque
Humboldt

Secretaría
de Cultura

Río Cabriales

To Bus Terminal
(4km); Aeropuerto
Piedra Pintada (22km);
Caracas (158km)

Av 92

Av 95 5 de Julio

Av 96 Tovar

Av 97 Farriar

Av 98 Boyacá

Av 99 Urdaneta

Av 100 Constitución

Av 101 Díaz Moreno

Av 102 Montes

Av 103 Carabobo

Av 104 Soublette

Av 105 Anzoátegui

Av 106 Briceño Méndez

Av 107 Andrés Bello

C 107 Navas Spínola

C 106 Aismendi

C 105

C 104 Vargas

C 103 Rondón

Av Cedeño (C 105)

C 102 Independencia

C 101 Libertad

C 100 Colombia

C 99 Páez

C 98 Comercio

C 97 Girardot

C 96 24 de Junio

C 95 Manrique

Plaza
Bolívar

Plaza
Sucre

Iglesia de
San Francisco

Market

Av Bolívar

Av Figueredo

To Dirección de
Turismo de Carabobo
(150m); Palacio de los
Iturriza (1.5km); Hotel
Excelsior (0.9km); Italcambio
(2km); Farmatodo (2.5km);
Restaurant El bosque (3km);
Restaurant Marbrisa (3.7km); La
Villa de Madrid (3.7km); Bambu
(4km); Loud (4km); Stauffer
Hotel (4km); Hotel Inter-Continental
Valencia (4km); Casa Valencia
(4.5km); Ocean Bar (4.5km);
Centro Comercial Sambil (4km);
Las Trincheras (18km)

To Plaza de Toros
Monumental (4km)

To Campo Carabobo
(32km)

Information

LAUNDRY
Lavandería Lux (☎ 858-5419; Calle 103 Rondón; 🕑 8am-noon & 1:30-5:30pm Mon-Fri, 8am-noon Sat)
Mr Wash (☎ 858-2904; Av Cedeño; 🕑 8am-1pm & 2-6pm Mon-Fri, 8am-6pm Sat)

MEDICAL SERVICES
Farmatodo (🕑 24hr) Located 2.5km north of center.

MONEY
Banco de Venezuela (Av 101 Díaz Moreno at Calle 101 Libertad)
Banco Mercantil (Calle 100 Colombia)
Banesco (Av 101 Díaz Moreno)
Corp Banca (Av 101 Díaz Moreno)
Italcambio (☎ 821-8173; No 12, Edificio Talía, Av Bolívar Norte, Urbanización Los Sauces) Located about 2km north of Plaza Bolívar.

POST
Ipostel (Calle 100 Colombia; 🕑 8am-5pm Mon-Fri)

TELEPHONE
Movistar (Calle 103 Rondón; 🕑 8am-5:30pm Mon-Fri, 9am-5:30pm Sat) Internet access also.
Movistar (Av Lara; 🕑 8:30am-6pm Mon-Sat) Internet access also.

TOURIST INFORMATION
Dirección de Turismo de Carabobo (☎ 8585-9506; www.carabobo.gov.ve; 3rd fl, Edificio Valenap, Av Bolívar Norte & Penalver; 🕑 8am-noon & 1-5pm Mon-Fri) Located above BOD bank, the tourist office is about 750m north of Plaza Bolívar.

Sights

PLAZA BOLÍVAR
The heart of the historic town, this plaza boasts the inevitable monument to Bolívar, though this one claims a certain novelty. The bronze figure, pointing toward Campo Carabobo, stands on a 10m-high white Italian marble column cut from a single block of stone. The monument was unveiled in 1889.

CATEDRAL
The colonial **cathedral** (Av 99 Urdaneta) is about 420 years old, but it's been altered by so many generations that today it's a hodgepodge of historical styles. The latest restoration was in the early 1950s, which saw the ceiling plastered with an intricate design resembling cake frosting.

The cathedral's most revered treasure, the figure of Nuestra Señora del Socorro, is kept in the chapel in the left transept on an elaborate red-and-gold stage. Carved in the late 16th century, the sorrowful Virgin in black has an expression of perpetual shock and sadness. She was the first statue in Venezuela to be crowned (in 1910) by Rome, and her original gold crown is encrusted with so many precious stones it has to be stored in a safe.

The two large paintings, *The Last Supper* and *The Entry into Jerusalem,* that hang on each of the chapel's side walls are the work of Antonio Herrera Toro, a well-known Valencia-born artist who painted murals in many local churches and buildings.

CASA PÁEZ
This beautifully preserved **historic mansion** (☎ 857-1272; Av 98 Boyacá at Calle 99 Páez; admission free; 🕑 9am-noon & 3-5.30pm Tue-Fri, 9am-2pm Sat & Sun Feb-Oct, 9am-4pm Tue-Sun Nov-Jan) is the former home of Venezuela's first president, General José Antonio Páez. He distinguished himself by forging a formidable army of *llaneros* (plainsmen) who fought under Bolívar, contributing greatly to the achievement of independence. In 1830, on the day Venezuela split from Gran Colombia, Páez took power as the first acting president and established his residence in the new capital. A year later he was elected president of the republic and moved with the government to Caracas.

Restored and furnished with period fittings, the house is today a museum. The walls of the cloister lining the lovely central patio are graced with fascinating murals depicting the nine battles the general fought. The work was done by Pedro Castillo and supposedly directed by Páez himself. Ask the attendant to show you the tiny prison and torture room at the back of the house. Wall paintings by unfortunate prisoners can still be seen here.

CAPITOL
Built in 1772 as a convent, this dazzlingly white building takes up half a block. The **Capitol** (☎ 857-1326; Calle 99 Páez; 🕑 9am-5pm Mon-Fri) became the government house a century later, when Guzmán Blanco pushed out the resident nuns – a bad habit of his, which he indulged at religious institutions throughout the country. Guided visits are available in Spanish.

TEATRO MUNICIPAL
Modeled on the Paris Opera House and inaugurated in 1894, the stunning chandeliered

ceiling of this 647-seat **theater** (☎ 857-4306; Calle 100 Colombia) was painted by Antonio Herrera Toro. It depicts famous folk of music and literature, including Goethe, Shakespeare and Beethoven. To see it during the day, enter through the back door (from Calle Libertad), which leads onto the stage; the guards should switch the lights on for you.

MUSEO DE ARTE E HISTORIA
This small local-history **museum** (Av 104 Soublette) is in the Casa de Los Celis, one of the most beautiful colonial mansions in the city, built in the 1760s and named after one of its owners. It was closed at research time but might be open during your visit.

CASA DE LA ESTRELLA
The sovereign state of Venezuela was born in this **historic house** (☎ 825-7005; Calle 100 Colombia at Av Soublette; admission free; ☺ 9am-5pm Tue-Fri, 10am-5pm Sat & Sun) on May 6, 1830, when Congress convened here and decreed secession from Gran Colombia. Erected as a hospital around 1710 (thus being the city's oldest existing house), the building was remodeled after independence as a college, which later became the Universidad de Valencia. Extensively restored over recent years, it's now a museum. The few exhibits on display include a brief history of Valencia's past posted on boards and a 12-minute video on the history of the house.

PALACIO DE LOS ITURRIZA
This curious orange-and-yellow-brick **museum** (☎ 824-1545; Av Miranda at Calle Rojas Queipo; admission free; ☺ 8am-noon, 1-5pm Mon-Fri) is in the 19th-century palace-like Quinta La Isabela, about 1.5km north of the center. The museum is dedicated to the city's history, though there's not much to see except for the fine interior of the palace. It's one block east off Av Bolívar; look for the Fiat dealership.

ACUARIO & ZOOLÓGICO
The favorite attractions for local inhabitants are undoubtedly the **aquarium** and **zoo** (☎ 857-4739; Av Fernando Figueredo; admission US$2.50, under 2yr free; ☺ 9am-4:30pm Tue-Fri, 10am-5:30pm Sat, Sun & holidays; ℗). The stars of the aquarium are the *toninas* (freshwater dolphins) kept in a large central pool. Shows are at 11am, 2pm and 4pm Tuesday to Friday, and 11am, 1pm, 3pm and 4:30pm weekends and holidays. Next to the pool is the aquarium-terrarium, which

showcases Venezuelan freshwater fish and snakes, including electric eels, piranhas and anacondas.

Beyond the aquarium is the small zoo, featuring Venezuela's most typical animal species, including jaguars, tapirs, Orinoco caimans, turtles and a variety of birds.

MUSEO DE BÉISBOL
This **museum** (☎ 841-1313; Centro Comercial Sambil, Mañongo; admission US$2.50; ☺ noon-8pm Mon-Sat, till 7pm Sun; ℗), in the popular Centro Comercial Sambil, 5km north of the city, is totally devoted to baseball fanaticism. It even has a pitching machine under the distinctive half-dome baseball roof of the shopping mall. Buses to Sambil run from the town center; taxis here are US$5.

Festivals & Events
The two major local events are **Semana de Valencia**, in late March, and the **Fiestas Patronales de Nuestra Señora del Socorro**, in mid-November. The former features cultural events, an agricultural fair, parades, bullfights etc. The latter is a religious feast in honor of the city's patron saint, in which the crowned Virgin is taken out of the church and paraded in a procession.

Every two years in October, the prestigious Salón Arturo Michelena opens in the **Ateneo de Valencia** (☎ 858-0046; www.ateneodevalencia.com; Av Bolívar) and goes on for five months until March. This is Venezuela's oldest visual-arts show, held every year since 1943. It presents a variety of styles and forms, including painting, photography, sculpture, performance, video and installations.

Sleeping
The cheapest accommodations are concentrated a few blocks around Plaza Bolívar, but these hotels are very basic and the area isn't the safest at night. They also tend to be dingy love hotels, with a check-in of 6pm or later (for overnight stays, that is).

BUDGET
The following budget choices are all part-time love hotels, which doesn't make them unsafe – just a bit seedy at times.

Hotel Continental (☎ 857-1004; Av 98 Boyacá No 101-70; d/tr US$10/19; ⚡) This colonial-style hotel is the cheapest budget option in the center. It has good security and service, along with decent rooms.

Hotel Caracas (☎ 857-1849; Av Boyacá No 100-84; d US$10) Located just behind the cathedral, this place is especially sleazy and falling apart at the seams. However, it has a cool, plant-filled courtyard retains a certain untouched 1920s charm.

Hotel Nacional (☎ 858-3676; Calle 99 Páez No 103-51; d with fan/air-con US$12/21; ⊠) This hotel is in an old building with an unpretentious *tasca*. The small patio out the back is surrounded by air-con rooms, which are better and brighter than the older fan rooms inside. Water pressure could be stronger.

Hotel Caribe (☎ 857-1157; Calle 100 Colombia No 96-68; d/tr US$14/17) The basic doubles at this hotel are set around a surprisingly nice, sunny courtyard in back, which comes with potted palms. The larger rooms are in the older and darker front area, however.

Hotel Carabobo (☎ 858-8860; Calle 101 Libertad No 100-37; d/tr US$17/26; ⊠) Ideally located just off Plaza Bolívar, this hotel still has one foot in the 1970s with some lurid plastic furniture remaining and poor maintenance in places. However, it's a step above many budget places in the center with secure, clean rooms and good beds.

MIDRANGE & TOP END

Hotel Colón (☎ 857-7105; Calle 100 Colombia No 103-37; d US$28; ⊠) Unmemorable hotel with hot-water bathrooms, TV and its own restaurant. The higher floors are brighter.

Hotel El Diamante (☎ 858-1595; Av 103 Carabobo; d with/without Jacuzzi US$52/42; P ⊠) This diamond of a hotel is by far the best central option in its price range. There's a professional atmosphere and the modern rooms are clean, spacious and comfortable; they also come with cable TV. There's a small *tasca* on the 2nd floor which does room service.

Hotel Excelsior (☎ 821-4055; Av Bolívar Norte 129-30; d/tr US$42/47; P ⊠) Stranded away north of the center, but in a safer area, is this reasonable hotel. It's a little worn around the edges but has modern, comfortable rooms with cable TV. There are suites with kitchen and fridge (US$52), but no restaurant.

Hotel Dinastía (☎ 858-8139; www.dinastiahotel.com; Av 99 Urdaneta at Av Cadeño; d/tr US$70/75; P ⊠) This smart three-star hotel offers around 100 large, comfortable rooms, half with close-up views of the next-door building. At least there's cable TV and fridges to distract. There's also a restaurant on the premises.

Hotel Don Pelayo (☎ 857-9378; Av 101 Díaz Moreno at Calle 103 Rondón; d incl breakfast US$70; P ⊠ ⊡) This large, 12-story hotel has an interesting curvy staircase and plain marble lobby at the entrance, but the hallways and rooms could use some paint, along with new carpets and furniture. At least there are plenty of services, including a restaurant, gym, room and laundry service and tour agency.

Stauffer Hotel (☎ 823-4022; www.staufferhotel.com.ve; Av Bolívar Norte; d incl breakfast US$126; P ⊠ ⊡) This tall, white, 18-story hotel, located about 4km north of town, is poorly signed and could use a paint job. The halls are a bit industrial and rooms aren't luxurious, but at least the top stories have good views and there's an attractive outdoor swimming pool on the 4th floor. Restaurant available.

Hotel Inter-Continental Valencia (☎ 813-3100; www.interconti.com; Calle Juan Uslar, Urbanización La Viña; d US$186-200; P ⊠ ⊡ ⊠) This five-star hotel, about 4km north of the city center, is the most luxurious place in town. Beautiful rooms and suites come with all the luxuries you'd expect. Other services include a gym, business center and great pool with nearby restaurant.

Eating

The center has plenty of cheap eateries in the backstreets, where set meals can be found for just a few bucks. However, the area is not renowned for quality dining. Restaurants here tend to close by 8pm except for the *tascas*, which by that time turn into drinking venues.

The city's upmarket restaurants are located north along Av Bolívar and especially in El Viñedo, which is about 2.5km north of the center. This trendy area lies on Av Monseñor Adams, which is just west off of Av Bolívar. A taxi here costs around US$6.

El Arepazo Criollo (☎ 857-9921; Av Bolívar; arepas US$2.50-6; ⊙ 24hr) This large, popular joint is strewn with wood tables and benches, and serves a long list of *arepas* at any time of day or night. No Spanish necessary – just point to your desired filling behind the glass case. Also on tap are other Venezuelan dishes, some sandwiches and plenty of juices.

Calabacín y Nueces (☎ 858-6550; Calle 102 Independencia at Av Urdaneta; 3-course menu US$4; ⊙ 11:45am-3pm Mon-Sat) For vegetarians and non-vegetarians alike, the best budget option in the center is this healthy spot. It serves up hearty meat-free set meals, delicious cakes, fresh juices and salads.

Restaurant El Bosque (☎ 823-5110; Av Bolívar Norte; mains US$5-10; ⏰ 11am-midnight Sun-Thu, till 1am Fri & Sat; P 🍴) Excellent large, modern spot for cheap grilled specialties. Some meats are served on a small charcoal BBQ left by your table. Also cooks up pizzas, lots of side dishes and drinks. Located 3km north of town, across from the PDV gas station; look for the squirrel atop their sign.

La Villa de Madrid (☎ 823-6654; Av Bolívar Norte No 152-75; mains US$6-16; ⏰ 11am-late; 🍴) Paella is a specialty at this classy old-style Spanish restaurant with dark wooden pillars and a huge rectangular bar hung with cured hams. Other traditional dishes include trout Navarre, rabbit in wine sauce and curried lamb. It's a popular place with large groups and can stay open as late as 4am. Look for the flags and glass lights outside a white, Spanish-style building.

Bambu (☎ 824-1177; Av Monseñor Adams 105; meals US$7-12; ⏰ dinner 6pm-11pm Mon-Sat) Located by the Plaza las Esculturas in El Viñedo is this slick and contemporary restaurant-bar-disco. You'll be sitting pretty in beanbag chairs on the terraced wood decks in front, with white tent roof overhead. The food is great – try the signature *chupe de mariscos* (seafood stew, served in bread bowl); it also has sushi, focaccia and pizza, with Nutella crêpes for dessert. It's a disco late at night.

Casa Valencia (☎ 823-4923; Av Bolívar Norte; mains US$13-20; ⏰ 11am-late) Boasting high ceilings, a large central grill and old hacienda feel, this elegant restaurant cooks up good meat and seafood dishes. Try the T-bone steak or filet mignon with mushroom sauce. There's pesto linguini and a salad bar for vegetarians. Service is attentive and there's a bar too.

Restaurant Marchica (☎ 825-3335; Av Bolívar Norte 152-210; ⏰ noon-11:30pm Mon-Sat, noon-9pm Sun; 🍴) At research time, this popular Spanish eatery was being remodeled into what appears to be a castle-themed building. It should be good (and perhaps the food too) so check it out.

Entertainment

Valencia's hippest venues are all north of the center, and many in either El Viñedo or near Centro Comercial Sambil. Taxis here are around US$6.

Bambu (☎ 824-1177; Av Monseñor Adams 105; ⏰ 11pm-3am Thu-Sat) This sophisticated venue is a restaurant for dinner, but turns into a hip nightclub after 11pm from Thursday to Saturday.

The music is loungy at the beginning of the evening (great for chilling out), but then the DJs and dance tunes stir up energy. If you don't want to rave, just bring your computer – they've got wi-fi as well.

Loud (Av Monseñor Adams; ⏰ 11pm-4am Thu-Sat) Located across Plaza las Esculturas from Bambu, this youthful disco is one of the most popular dancing venues at the moment. It plays techno-reggae and serves up decently priced drinks.

Ocean Bar (☎ 616-8200; Centro Comercial Vía Veneto, 2nd fl, Av Salvador Feo la Cruz; ⏰ 6pm-5am Thu-Sat) Located on the second floor (outside balcony) of a shopping center is this very trendy bar, which specializes in innovative, exotic cocktails. Go for a martini, cosmopolitan or the signature drink, the 'Ocean' – it'll knock you down. Live music and DJs play on weekends. It may extend the opening days to Monday to Saturday, so call first.

Getting There & Away

AIR

The airport is about 7km southeast of the city center (taxis US$10). It's served by all major Venezuelan airlines and a few international ones. Popular domestic destinations include Caracas, Barcelona, Maracaibo and Porlamar.

Dutch Antilles Express (www.flydae.com) has a direct flight to Curaçao four days per week, and at the time of writing **American Airlines** (www.aa.com) started a direct daily flight from Valencia to Miami, Florida.

BUS

The bus terminal is about 4km northeast of the city center, in the Disneyland-style Big Low Center, and is easily accessible by frequent local buses or taxi (US$5). The terminal is large and has many facilities, including restaurants, and telephone and internet services. Some shops will store luggage; look for 'Guarda Equipaje' signs.

Frequent destinations include Maracay (US$1.50, one hour), Puerto Cabello (US$2, one hour), Tucacas (US$4, two hours), Barquisimeto (US$5.50, 2½ hours), Caracas (US$5, 2½ hours), Chichiriviche (US$4.50, 2½ hours) and Coro (US$11, five hours).

Evening buses to faraway destinations include Maracaibo (US$20, nine hours), San Cristóbal (US$19, 10 hours), Mérida (US$24, 10 hours) and San Antonio del Táchira (US$18, 12 hours).

The most luxurious company is **Aeroexpresos Ejecutivos** (☎ 871-5558; www.aeroexpresos.com.ve) with services to Maracay (US$7), Caracas (US$10.50), Barquisimeto (US$12), Maracaibo (US$25), Puerto La Cruz (US$27) and Maturín (US$30).

There are half a dozen buses a day to San Fernando de Apure (US$15, eight hours), where you can change for the bus to Puerto Ayacucho.

CAMPO CARABOBO

For a taste of unadulterated Venezuelan patriotism, visit the **Carabobo Battlefield** (admission free; ⏲ 6am-6pm Tue-Sun), 32km southwest of Valencia. This is the site of the great battle fought on June 24, 1821, in which Bolívar's troops decisively defeated the Spanish royalist army with help from the lancers of General Páez and British legionnaires. A milestone in Latin American history, the victory effectively sealed Venezuela's independence. To commemorate the event, a complex of monuments has been erected on the battle ground.

Toward the end of the 1km entrance into the complex is a building on the right; inside is a diorama cubicle which screens historical films on the site. The end of the entrance road turns into the **Paseo de los Héroes**, a formal promenade lined with bronze busts of the battle heroes. Beyond is the large **Arco de Triunfo** (Triumphal Arch) and the **Tumba del Soldado Desconocido** (Tomb of the Unknown Soldier). Two unflinching, deadpan soldiers guard the tomb and its flaming torch; their shockingly red gala period uniforms seem more suitable for a Siberian winter than for the baking sun of Carabobo. Fortunately for them, the changing of the guard takes place every two hours (starting at 8am).

Just behind the arch is the impressive **Altar de la Patria**, a massive monument – the largest in Venezuela. Designed by Spanish sculptor Antonio Rodríguez del Villar and unveiled in 1930, the monument depicts the main heroes and allegorical figures, all fashioned in stone and bronze. On the top is an equestrian statue of Bolívar.

About 1km to the west is the **mirador**, a viewpoint from which Bolívar commanded the battle. It has a large model of the battlefield and a panoramic view over the whole site.

You can wander the site at will or find a guide hanging around the area; they give free tours (in Spanish) starting at about 8am or

9am. The park has plenty of grassy expanses for picnicking, and a few drinks and snacks are sold in a building near the Paseo de los Héroes.

Getting There & Away

Frequent suburban buses (marked 'Campo Carabobo') leave from Valencia's Av Lara to the battlefield (US$0.75, 45 minutes). They'll drop you off at the beginning of the entrance road. Take a hat and water, as it's a hot 15-minute walk up this long entrance road to the monuments. To avoid a long walk back, just head behind and to the left of the monuments to a side gate, carefully cross the highway to a bus stop and flag the local bus back to Valencia.

PARQUE ARQUEOLÓGICO PIEDRA PINTADA

Mysterious stone petroglyphs are scattered throughout Carabobo state, the largest group of which is at the site known as Cerro Pintado or **Piedra Pintada** (admission free; ⏲ 9am-4pm Tue-Fri, 10am-4pm Sat & Sun; Ⓟ), 22km northeast of Valencia near the village of Tronconero. An important ritual center for pre-Hispanic communities, the site is covered by a jumble of weathered rocks and slabs scattered over a grassy slope.

Many of these stones bear shallow engravings of intriguing designs and figures, from owls to women giving birth, shamans and what is believed to be a sacred plan of the region. The exact age of the carvings is still a matter of discussion. Further on up the slope, there's an impressive group of upright megalithic stones; bring water and sturdy shoes to visit these.

The 12-hectare site, which was made an archeological park in 1996, has helpful Spanish-speaking guides on standby and there's a small museum in the visitors center.

Getting There & Away

To get to the park from Valencia, take the Maracay bus from the terminal and get off at Guacara (US$1.50, 15 minutes), 13km east of Valencia (ask the driver to drop you at the Puente de Guacara, near the large Centro Comercial Guacara). Go down the bridge and wave down the buseta marked 'Hospital-Tronconero,' which will bring you close to the Parque Arqueológico (US$0.50, 20 minutes). Get off at the end of the line and walk for 10 minutes, following the signs.

LAS TRINCHERAS

☎ 0241

Located 18km north of Valencia, the thermal springs of Las Trincheras – with up to 198°F temperatures recorded – are the world's second-hottest (after some in Japan). The site has been known for centuries and attracted explorers and naturalists throughout history, including Alexander von Humboldt, who used the waters to boil eggs in four minutes. In 1889 thermal baths and a hotel were built. In 1980 the old hotel was restored, a new one constructed beside it, and the murky-looking pools were remodeled. There are now three pools with temperatures ranging from 97°F to 118°F, as well as fountains, a sauna and a sociable mud bath where everybody slaps warm gloopy *lodo* on each other and lets it cake in the sun.

The springs are renowned for their therapeutic properties and recommended for the treatment of a variety of ailments, including rheumatic, digestive, respiratory and allergic problems. They also freshen and smooth the skin, and help with general relaxation.

You can either choose a **day pass** (admission US$3.25; ☻ 7am-9pm Tue-Sun, 7am-4pm Mon, mud bath until 5pm) or stay in the on-site hotel, using the baths and other facilities at no extra cost. The hotel also has a pool exclusively for guests, plus a bewilderingly long list of health treatments on offer (try the fruit and chocolate wraps!).

Sleeping & Eating

Centro Termal Las Trincheras (☎ 808-1502, in Caracas 0212-661-2703; www.trincheras.com; s/d/tr/q US$20/26/30/39; P ☒ ☒) The pleasant on-site hotel offers around 100 light, comfortable rooms with hot water and cable TV. The price includes use of the baths, sauna and other facilities. The restaurant offers all-day service for hotel guests and day visitors. It's usually easy to get a room during the week, but on weekends the hotel is full to bursting and reservations are a must.

Opposite the entrance to the baths complex is **Manantial de Luz** (☎ 921-5052; d/tr US$14/19; P), marked 'Hotel Turistico Restaurant,' which has seven basic rooms with fans and runs a great little **vegetarian restaurant** (set menu US$5; ☻ 8am-9pm Sat & Sun). Another decent place is **Doña Elba** (☎ 0414-663-6511; d US$14-19; P ☒ ☒), halfway toward the springs on the main road. It's a casual, colorful and interesting building with restaurant and swimming pool.

For simple family rooms look around the town for signs that read 'Se Alquilan Habitaciones.'

Getting There & Away

From Valencia, take one of the frequent Puerto Cabello buses, which can drop you at the freeway bridge in Las Trincheras (US$2, 20 minutes). From here it's a 10-minute walk to the baths. Taxis from Valencia cost US$14.

PUERTO CABELLO

☎ 0242 / pop 180,000

This port city isn't a huge tourist magnet, but does boast a scenic, restored colonial town center, two old forts and a lively malecón that attracts strolling families and vendors, especially on weekends. There's a decent beach complete with restaurant shacks, and yachts and ships anchor offshore. You can also visit the attractive surroundings, including beaches to the east and lush forests to the south.

Puerto Cabello began life in the mid-16th century as a simple wharf built on the bank of a coastal lagoon. The site was a perfect natural anchorage, protected from wind and waves and connected to the open sea by a convenient strait. Indeed, there was hardly a better place for a port on the Venezuelan coast.

During the 17th century the Dutch-run port grew fat on its contraband trade with Curaçao. It wasn't until 1730 that the Spanish took over the port, after the Real Compañía Guipuzcoana moved in. This company built an array of forts, and by the 1770s Puerto Cabello was the most heavily fortified town on Venezuela's coast. Thus, during the War of Independence, it became an important royalist stronghold, and was the last place in Venezuela to be freed from Spanish rule.

Today, Puerto Cabello can be divided into two parts: the small and attractive colonial sector, to the north, and the uninspiring new center, to the south. Plaza Bolívar roughly marks the borderline between the two.

Information

Cybercafé (Calle Miranda; ☻ 9am-9pm Mon-Sat, till 6pm Sun) Near the Hotel Fortín.
Ipostel (☻ 8am-4:30pm Mon-Fri) Near the end of the malecón.
Tourist office (☎ 362-1732; Calle Puerto Cabello; ☻ 8am-5pm Mon-Fri) In the large ferry building near the end of the malecón.

THE CENTRAL NORTH

Local banks include **Banco de Venezuela** (Calle Colón), at the end of the malecón, and **Banco Mercantil** (Plaza Bolívar). There's a cluster of six banks near the intersection of Calle Municipio and JJ Flores, including Corp Banca.

Sights
SPANISH FORTS

North of the old town, and separated from it by the entrance channel to the harbor, is colonial Fortín San Felipe, later renamed **Castillo Libertador** (admission free; ☼ dawn-dusk). It's a fine-looking fort, though in a state of disrepair. It was constructed in the 1730s to protect the port and warehouses. During the War of Independence, the fort was for a time in the patriots' hands, but it was lost to the royalists in 1812. Francisco de Miranda was jailed here before the Spanish sent him to prison in Spain. The fort was recovered in 1823, and later served General Gómez as a jail, mostly for political prisoners. Upon Gómez' death in 1935, the prison closed down and no less than 14 tons of chains and leg irons were thrown into the sea.

The fort is within the naval base, which operates a free hourly *bongo* (boat) across the channel from just below Plaza Flores, at the northern end of Paseo Malecón. The blue-and-white *bongos*, some of which have 'base naval' printed on a tarpaulin, will leave you near the naval-base entrance, from where the fort is a 10-minute walk west. En route, you could stop at the **Naval Museum** (☎ 360-1137; admission free; ☼ 8am-noon & 1:30-4pm Tue-Fri) to get your fill of torpedoes and propellers.

On the 100m-high hill to the south of the city sits another fort, **Fortín Solano** (admission free; ☼ dawn-dusk), built in the 1760s to secure commercial operations. Reputedly the last colonial fort built in Venezuela, it commands excellent views of the city and the harbor. The road to the fort branches off from the road to San Esteban on the outskirts of Puerto Cabello. Hence, you can combine a visit to the fort with the trip to San Esteban. Even if you want to visit only the fort, take a San Esteban carrito to the turnoff to avoid walking through a shabby barrio.

OLD TOWN
The part of the old town to the west of Calle Comercio has been restored and some of the facades painted in bright colors. It's now a pleasant area to explore or watch the world go by from the open-air restaurants on the tree-shaded waterfront boulevard, Paseo Malecón.

Don't miss the two historic streets, Calle de los Lanceros and Calle Bolívar; they're both next to each other and off the plaza. Note the overhanging balconies and massive doorways, including the fair-sized **Museo de Historia** (Calle Bolívar; admission free). Built in 1790 as a residence, this building has a graceful internal patio and facades over both streets. The museum was being refurbished at the time of research.

At the northern end of Calle de los Lanceros is the **Iglesia del Rosario**, a handsome yellow church built in 1780. The bell tower is made of wood – unique in Venezuela. One block north of the church is the **Casa Guipuzcoana**, built in 1730 as the office for the Compañía Guipuzcoana. Today it's a public library.

The library faces a triangular square with the **Monumento del Águila** (Eagle Monument) in the middle. This monument, a tall column topped by a condor, was erected in 1896 in memory of North Americans who gave their lives for Venezuelan independence. Recruited by Francisco de Miranda, in 1806 they sailed from New York to Ocumare de la Costa, north of Maracay. Upon dropping anchor, however, two boats with Americans aboard were surprised and captured by Spanish guard boats. Ten officers were hanged, and the remaining 50-odd recruits sent to prison.

Plaza Bolívar, at the southern edge of the colonial sector, boasts yet another fine equestrian statue of Bolívar. The massive, somewhat ugly edifice built from coral rock and occupying the eastern side of the plaza is the **Catedral de San José**. It was begun in the mid-19th century and completed only some 100 years later.

The colorful **Teatro Municipal** (☎ 361-9411; Calle Bolívar; ☼ 8am-5pm Mon-Fri depending on events) dates from 1880 and is a replica of one in Havana, Cuba. It's a beautiful theater with 617 seats, two balconies and a huge 640kg chandelier. Ballerina Ana Pavlova, tango songbird Carlos Gardel and violinist Augusto Brandt have all once performed here. Free Spanish tours are given.

Sleeping
Budget accommodations in town tend to double as shady love hotels (this is a port, after all). If you'd prefer to sidestep the town, see Los Caneyes, p138, for alternative accommodations along the coast.

Hotel Venezia (☎ 361-4380; Av Santa Bárbara No 13-36; d with fan US$14, d/tr with air-con US$17/24) One of the cheapest places is this small, simple Italian-run hotel opposite a large medical clinic.

Hotel El Fortín (☎ 361-4356; Calle Miranda; d/tr US$30/35 Ⓟ 🐾) The clean and comfortable El Fortín is one of the better budget options in town. The uniform, spacious rooms have cable TV, hot water and telephone. Try to get one of their business cards, graced with porno girls.

Hotel Bahía Azul (☎ 361-4033; Av Santa Bárbara 11-93; d/tr US$33/42; Ⓟ 🐾) Bahía Azul has 15 large, good-value, spotless rooms with cable TV and great attention to detail (you've never seen such intricately folded, fan-shaped sheets!).

Hotel Isla Larga (☎ 361-3290; Calle Miranda; d/tr US$43/48; Ⓟ 🐾 🖭) Fronting some scruffy wasteland near the bus terminal, this large, grey, slightly spooky building hums with the constant noise of 120 air-conditioners. It has large neat rooms, most with faraway sea views, fridge and sofa. There's a great pool area on 2nd floor, and the hotel comes with its own restaurant.

our pick **Posada Santa Margarita** (☎ 361-7113; www.ptocabello.com; Calle Bolívar No 4-36; d with fan/air-con US$60/70; 🐾 🖭) Boasting more character than all the other hotels in town put together, this 270-year-old renovated house comes with wonderfully charming old-time atmosphere. The brightly painted rooms have high ceilings, creaky wood floors and comfortable furnishings. There are relaxed sitting areas and a tiny pool, and breakfast is included.

Hotel Suite Caribe (Map p138; ☎ 364-2286; www .hotelscaribe.com; Av Salom 21, Urb La Sorpresa; d/tr US$80/90; Ⓟ 🐾 ▯ 🖭) For another step up the luxury ladder, try this tall, blockish hotel 5km west of the city center (2km east of the airport). It has a great swimming pool and sunny patio, plus its own restaurant, gym and sauna.

Eating

The colonial sector has some good eateries on or just off Paseo Malecón. The bus terminal has cheap grub, but the beach restaurant shacks are much more atmospheric.

Restaurant La Fuente (☎ 491-4145; mains US$5-14; 🕑 8am-5pm Mon, 8am-8pm Tue-Fri, 9am-10pm Sat, 4-10pm Sun) The strength of this *tasca* is fish and seafood dishes – though its set meals are good value. The ground floor comes with air-con, while the top floor has high stone arches and a good bar.

Restaurant Los Lanceros (☎ 361-8471; Paseo Malecón; mains US$7-13; 🕑 11:30am-10pm) In an old colonial building with a sea view, this upmarket Spanish restaurant has terrace seating along with a small pleasant air-con bar area. On the menu are paella, seafood and meat dishes.

Pizzería da Franco (☎ 361-6161; Paseo Malecón; mains US$7-15; 🕑 11am-10pm) This seafront spot has a family atmosphere and decent pizzas, with terrace seating outside.

Getting There & Away

AIR

The airfield is 7km west of Puerto Cabello, next to the freeway, but there are no scheduled tourist flights.

BOAT

At the time of writing, a new **ferry building** (www .puertoturistico.com; Calle Puerto Cabello) was revving up passenger services from Puerto Cabello to Bonaire, Curaçao and Isla de Margarita. For up-to-date information, see the website or visit the tourist office.

BUS

The bus terminal is on Calle Urdaneta, about 800m west of Av Bolívar. Frequent carritos run between the terminal and the center, but you can walk it in 10 minutes.

Buses depart every 15 minutes to Valencia (US$2, one hour), which has frequent connections to Caracas. Other destinations include Tucacas (US$2, 1¼ hours), San Felipe (US$3, 1¾ hours), Chichiriviche (US$3, 1¾ hours) and Barquisimeto (US$5, three hours). For transportation to the nearby beaches see p138, and to San Esteban, see p139.

TRAIN

Puerto Cabello is the terminus of the railway line to Barquisimeto, but only handles freight transportation these days.

AROUND PUERTO CABELLO
Beaches

Several beaches lie to the east of Puerto Cabello, off the road to Patanemo. The closest one is **Balneario Quizandal**, about 7km by road from the city. This beach is quite developed, with a parking lot, showers and restaurants, though it is not the best beach. However, boats from here can take you to **Isla Larga**, a beautiful, sandy island popular with beach-goers, swimmers and snorkelers. There are

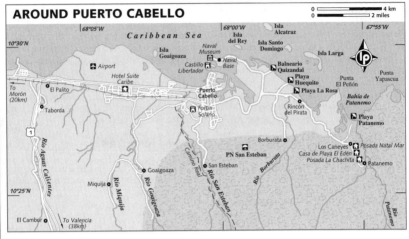

AROUND PUERTO CABELLO

THE CENTRAL NORTH

two wrecks near the island, a bonus attraction for snorkelers and divers. Several food stalls will be more than happy to stuff you with fish (open weekends and sometimes weekdays as well). Take good sun protection, as there is no shade. Many holidaymakers make the trip on weekends, so the two-way boat trip will cost US$4.50 per person, but during the week you'll have to pay the fare for the whole boat (negotiable).

The next exit off the Patanemo road, 1km beyond the one to Quizandal, leads to the small **Playa Huequito**. In the same place, another road branches off to the right and heads south to **Borburata**, the oldest town in Carabobo, founded in 1548. The town is widely known for its **Fiestas de San Juan** (June 23 and 24) and **San Pedro** (June 28) but is otherwise pretty sleepy and there's not much to do. If you want to stay here check out the seven basic rooms at the **Posada de Mi Tío** (☎ 361-2244; r US$21; ☒). Buses from Puerto Cabello's terminal cost US$0.75.

Back on the main road and continuing eastward from the junction, another road branches off to **Playa La Rosa** (admission per person/car US$1/2.50), one of the tidiest, best-maintained and safest beaches, as it lies next to a military area.

Further eastward about 7km is the 1.5km turnoff to **Playa Patanemo**. This is the best beach in the area, wide and shaded by coconut palms. It tends to swarm with beachgoers on weekends, but is fairly solitary on weekdays. It's lined with food outlets, including

churuata-style (thatched hut) restaurants. You can pitch your tent anywhere amid the palms, but it's safer to camp next to one of the restaurants. Be sure to bring repellent for mosquitoes.

Shortly beyond the Patanemo turnoff lies the village of **Los Caneyes**, which hosts several places to stay, including the colorful and friendly **Posada Natal Mar** (☎ 0412-536-7958; d/tr US$28/47; ☐ ☒), with five windowless, no-frills rooms. There's a good, bright and airy restaurant on the 2nd floor. Not too far away is **Casa de Playa El Edén** (☎ 0416-403-3292; d US$47; 8-person cabañas US$140; ☒ ☒), surely the pick of the bunch. It boasts a cool, open-air restaurant, small swimming pool and tropical gardens. The 11 rooms have high tropical ceilings and beautiful mosaic stone floors. Breakfast is included.

About 1.5km south of Los Caneyes is the village of **Patanemo**, noted for the Diablos Danzantes celebrations on Corpus Christi (60 days after Easter, in May or June) and for drumbeats on Fiesta de San Juan (June 23 and 24). **Posada La Chachita** (☎ 302-3062; d with fan/air-con US$19/24; ☐ ☒) is a family home with seven musty, no-frills rooms.

GETTING THERE & AWAY

Carritos run regularly between the Puerto Cabello bus terminal and Patanemo, and will put you down at any turnoff of your choice, within reasonable walking distance of the beach. The ride to Patanemo village takes half an hour and costs US$0.75.

San Esteban

Seven kilometers south of Puerto Cabello, the pleasant little village of San Esteban is surrounded by lush vegetation and is blessed with a cooler mountain climate. There are some wonderful swimming holes, small waterfalls and lounging rocks here at La Toma (where some buses terminate), which is very popular with families on hot weekends.

Nearby is a large rock called **Piedra del Indio**, which is covered with petroglyphs. There's another one 500m down the road near the blue pedestrian bridge and the 'Polar – Piedra del Indio' sign. Also close to La Toma is the starting point for a few hikes, including the Camino Real – an old Spanish trail leading south to Valencia (see right).

As you enter the village you'll likely notice the beautifully restored mansion housing the **Museo Villa Vicencio** (☎ 0414-415-6081; admission free; Y 9am-4pm Mon-Fri), which displays taxidermy animals and insects along with some local flora.

San Esteban was the birthplace of Bartolomé Salom, one of the heroes of the War of Independence, who accompanied Bolívar all the way to Ayacucho. The **house** (admission free; Y 9am-4pm) where he was born, located next to the yellow school, has been left half ruined. Inside the main room is a life-sized statue of the general with an intense expression, slightly diminished by its bizarre position sitting in a hammock with a vase of flowers near his feet.

About 300m up the main road from Salom's house lies **Posada Mi Jaragual** (☎ 302-2004; d/tr US$28/33; P ✕), alongside the river. Rooms here are dark with tiny bathrooms, but there's a nice restaurant on the premises and some great swimming holes nearby. The owner keeps a fascinating little collection of liquors and medicines, bottled with everything from snakes to beetles to a white bat; he even sells an 'aphrodisiac' potion.

GETTING THERE & AWAY

Carritos to San Esteban depart regularly from outside the bus terminal in Puerto Cabello (US$0.50, 25 minutes). Many buses travel straight up to El Pueblo, passing Posada Mi Jaragual, then turn back a few hundred meters, ford the river and head up the other side to La Toma, where most of the swimming holes are and the hiking trails begin. Some buses might finish at one of these destinations and not both, but they're both within easy walking distance of each other.

Parque Nacional San Esteban

This national park, adjacent to the western part of Parque Nacional Henri Pittier, stretches from San Esteban southward almost to Naguanagua, on the northern outskirts of Valencia. Like its eastern neighbor, the park protects a part of the Cordillera de la Costa, noted for its rich and diverse flora and fauna.

There's a popular trail in the park known as the **Camino Real**. In colonial times it was the main route linking Puerto Cabello with Valencia, along which goods were transported. The trail leads from north to south, passing over the ridge at an altitude of about 1400m. You can still see traces of the cobbled Spanish road and will even encounter the original Spanish bridge, the 1808 Puente de los Españoles. The trail is relatively easy, though side paths joining it can be confusing. Although the walking time between San Esteban and Naguanagua is about eight hours, count on two days to take it at a leisurely pace.

Many walkers departing from the northern end (San Esteban) make it just a one-day roundtrip by only going as far as the Spanish bridge. It's about a three-hour walk up and a two-hour walk back down.

There are other eight- to 10-hour hikes in the area, including to La Cumana and Guacara (which eventually links to Parque Nacional Henri Pittier).

Hiring a guide for all hikes is a wise idea. In San Esteban ask for guides at the Inparques kiosk (located above La Toma) or at the Museo Villa Vicencio. In Puerto Cabello contact Deysi Pulgar at the tourist office for good trail information.

The Northwest

If Venezuela were a restaurant, the northwest would be the chef's *menu de dégustation* – a chance to savor all the delicious morsels that make up the country. There's something for every taste – rainforests and deserts, coral islands and beaches, caves and waterfalls, and South America's largest lake.

Colorful Coro is one of the oldest settlements in the New World, and Venezuela's first capital. It's also a popular traveler's chill-out spot. Nearby are two strikingly different environs – the desert wildness of the Peninsula de Paraguaná, and the misty green forests of the Sierra de San Luis. The favorable winds off Adícora, on Paraguaná's east coast, have made it the top spot for budget kitesurfers in Venezuela.

The white-sand cays of Parque Nacional Morrocoy beckon beach-lovers with warm Caribbean waves and colorful reefs. Or escape the heat, if you prefer, and head for the hills – relax in the small colonial towns around Barquisimeto, sample Venezuela's finest wines in Carora, or indulge in an all-night, cigar-smoking séance with the faithful at the shrines of María Lionza.

THE NORTHWEST

HIGHLIGHTS

- Let the afternoon breeze gently rock your hammock in colorful, oh-so-groovy **Coro** (p142)

- Test your mettle against wind and wave going kitesurfing in **Adícora** (p151)

- Work on your tanlines on the white-sand beaches of the **Parque Nacional Morrocoy** (p155)

- Discover *gaita*, the music of **Maracaibo** (p171), during the Feria de la Chinita in November

- Marvel at the unique lightning phenomenon of **Catatumbo** (p181)

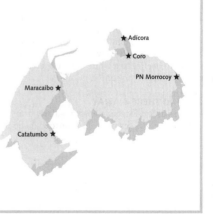

THE NORTHWEST

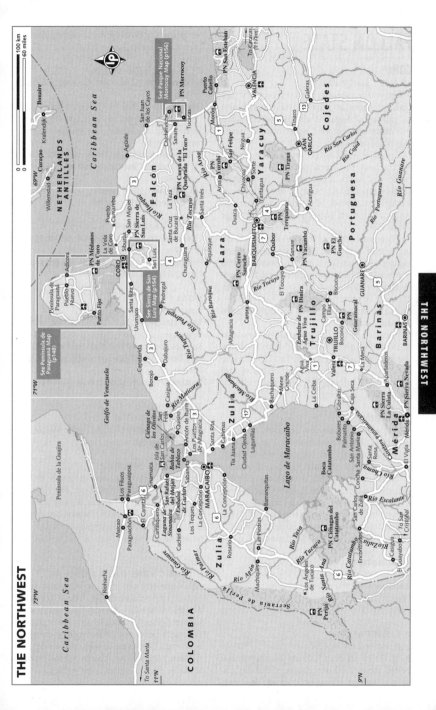

See Parque Nacional Morrocoy Map (p156)

See Península de Paraguaná Map (p148)

See Sierra de San Luís Map (p154)

FALCÓN STATE

CORO

☎ 0268 / pop 200,000

When you're swinging in your hammock on a Coro afternoon and that coastal breeze blows in, you can understand why the natives called this place *curiana*, the Caquetío word meaning 'place of winds.'

Travelers tend to get stuck here, enjoying the heat, the breeze and one of the best-preserved historic centers in the country. Cobblestoned Calle Zamora, in particular, is a bright patchwork of Caribbean flavor and was included on Unesco's World Heritage list in 1993.

Coro is an excellent base to explore a striking part of Venezuela. It boasts two interesting and completely different regions: the arid Península de Paraguaná (p147) and the lush, mountainous Sierra de San Luis (p153). They can each be toured in a day (see Tours, p145), or you can linger for a while and explore them on your own.

Founded in 1527, Coro is one of the oldest settlements in the New World, and became the first capital of Venezuela in 1528. It's also the capital of Falcón state, and boasts several universities, bringing a young and cultured air to the proceedings.

Orientation

Coro's center, where you are likely to spend just about all your time in town, is small, compact and pleasant for leisurely strolls about the streets. Conveniently, here are all but one of the important sights, a lion's share of hotels and restaurants, and, surprisingly, even the airport, just a five minute walk from the center. Probably your only trip away from the center (and a recommended one) will be a visit to Parque Nacional Médanos de Coro.

Information

EMERGENCY

Ambulance (☎ 171)
Fire (☎ 171)
Police (☎ 171)

INTERNET ACCESS

Internet access in Coro is cheap: US$0.70 to US$0.90 an hour. Several facilities listed below are in the historic center and close at 8pm or earlier. If you need to use the internet late in the evening, some of the following cybercafés, located away from the center, are open till late:

ATC Micro Suply (Calle 35 Falcón)
Falcontech (☎ 252-8413, cnr Calles Manaure & Zamora; ☯ 8am-9pm)
Ciudad Bitácora (cnr Calles 33 Zamora & Jansen; ☯ 7am-2am) The largest and fastest cybercafé in town, five blocks east of Av Manaure. Take a sweater – the air-con is set to arctic.
El Triángulo Azul (Castillo Don Leoncio; Av Manaure; ☯ 9am-midnight) Seven blocks south of Calle Falcón, near Banesco.
L&D Sistemas (Calle 33 Zamora)
P&P Connections (Plaza Falcón)

MEDICAL SERVICES

Clínica Nuestra Señora de Guadalupe (☎ 252-6011; Av Los Médanos)
Hospital Universitario Dr Alfredo van Grieken (☎ 252-5700; Av El Tenis)

MONEY

Banco de Venezuela (Paseo Talavera)
Banco Mercantil (Calle 35 Falcón) Two blocks east of Av Manaure.
Banesco (Av Manaure) Eight blocks south of Calle Falcón.
Corp Banca (Calle 33 Zamora) Three blocks east of Av Manaure.
Italcambio (airport) Changes cash and traveler's checks.

TELEPHONE

Movistar (Calle 35 Falcón)
CANTV (Av Los Medanos) Across the street from the bus terminal and also has internet.

TOURIST INFORMATION

CorFalTur (Corporación Falconiana de Turismo; ☎ 252-4198, 253-0260; corfaltur@hotmail.com, www.visitfalcon .com; Paseo Alameda; ☯ 8am-noon & 2-6pm Mon-Thu, 8am-4pm Fri) The office is on the central pedestrian mall just north of Plaza Bolívar. They publish an excellent, detailed bilingual tourist guide to Falcón state (US$12).

Sights

HISTORIC MANSIONS & MUSEUMS

All of the city's interesting museums are in restored colonial buildings. The **Museo de Arte de Coro** (☎ 808-3603; 251-5658; Paseo Talavera; admission free; ☯ 9am-12:30pm & 3-7:30pm Tue-Sat, 9am-4pm Sun), in a beautiful 18th-century mansion, is a branch of the Caracas Museo de Arte Contemporáneo and, like its parent, features thought-provoking and well-presented temporary exhibitions.

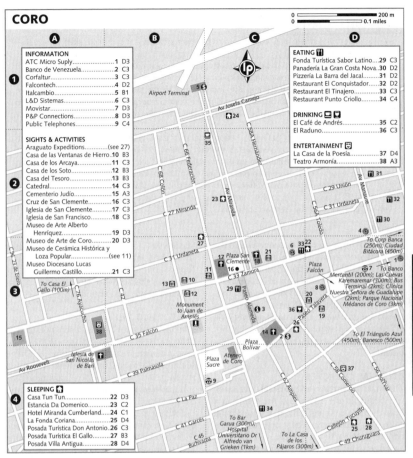

CORO

THE NORTHWEST

Diagonally opposite, in another great historic mansion, the **Museo de Arte Alberto Henríquez** (☎ 252-5299; Paseo Talavera; admission free; 9am-noon & 3-6pm Tue-Sat, 9am-noon Sun) also has modern art – shows change regularly but are always worth a visit. At the back of the mansion is an old synagogue, founded in 1853. This is the first synagogue in Venezuela, though the present furnishings are all replicas.

For an insight into the colonial past, go two blocks north to the **Museo Diocesano Lucas Guillermo Castillo** (☎ 251-1298; Calle 33 Zamora; admission US$0.90; 9am-noon & 3-6pm Tue-Sat, 9am-2pm Sun), named after a local bishop. Accommodated in 15 rooms of a 17th-century Franciscan convent, the museum boasts an extensive col-

lection of religious and secular art from the region and beyond, including Venezuela's oldest tempera painting and some extraordinary statues of Madonna carved in wood. It's one of the best collections of its kind in the country. All visits are guided (in Spanish only), and the tour takes about 45 minutes.

A short walk west is the **Casa de los Arcaya** (☎ 251-0023; Calle 33 Zamora) with its attractive, tile-roofed balconies. The mansion houses the **Museo de Cerámica Histórica y Loza Popular** (admission free; 9am-noon & 3-6pm Tue-Sat, 9am-1pm Sun), a small but interesting museum of antique pottery and ceramics from all over the world. There's also a beautiful garden.

The **Casa de las Ventanas de Hierro** (Calle 33 Zamora; admission US$1.20; 8am-6pm Mon-Sat) is noted for

---

VENEZUELA'S FIRST CAPITAL – ALMOST GERMAN?

Walking about the streets of Coro, it's hard to believe this town – and, indeed, all of Venezuela – was almost a German colony.

Coro was founded in 1527 by Juan de Ampiés, making it one of the oldest settlements in the New World, and the first capital of colonial Venezuela. But that same year King Carlos I of Spain was forced to lease the entire city and province to the Welsers of Germany to conquer, settle and exploit. The king was forced to sign the contract because he was heavily in debt to German banking firms for loans he had used to buy the title of Holy Roman Emperor Karl V (Charles V) in 1519.

The Germans were eager to find El Dorado – the mythical City of Gold – and Teutonic expeditions soon began landing on Venezuela's shores. For nearly 20 years Coro was the jumping-off point for these German conquistadores, but the only wealth Coro's streets ever saw was nothing more than a cornucopia of German oaths when no gold was found.

In 1546 the contract with the Welsers was cancelled and the administrative seat of the province moved to El Tocuyo, 200km to the south. (Caracas became the third, and final, capital in 1577.) Very little remains of the German presence.

---

a splendid 8m-high plaster doorway and the wrought-iron grilles (brought from Seville, Spain, in 1764) across the windows. It now shelters a private collection of historic objects collected by the family over generations. Nearby, the **Casa del Tesoro** (Calle 33 Zamora) houses an art gallery, while the **Casa de los Soto** (Calle 33 Zamora) is a private residence and cannot be visited but is worth looking at from the outside.

COLONIAL CHURCHES

The massive, fortress-like **catedral** (Plaza Bolívar) was begun in the 1580s and finished half a century later, making it the oldest surviving church in Venezuela. There are no remainders of its early history inside, but the 1790 baroque main retable is a good example of late-colonial art.

Two blocks north is the 18th-century **Iglesia de San Francisco** (Calle 33 Zamora). The cupola of the 1760s Capilla del Santísimo Sacramento, at the top of the right aisle, is a very fine piece of Mudejar art, showing the strong influence of Moorish style in medieval Spain.

Just a stone's throw to the west of San Francisco is another 18th-century church, the **Iglesia de San Clemente** (Calle 33 Zamora). It was laid out in a Latin cross-plan and is one of the very few examples of its kind in the country. Note the anchor hanging from the middle of the ceiling, which commemorates St Clement's martyrdom (he was drowned after being weighed down with an anchor).

In the barred pavilion on the plaza between the two churches is the **Cruz de San Clemente** (Plaza San Clemente). This is said to be the cross used in the first mass celebrated after the town's foundation. It's made from the wood of the *cují* tree, a slow-growing species of acacia that is found in this arid region.

CEMENTERIO JUDÍO

Established in the 1830s, Coro's **Cementerio Judío** (cnr Calles 33 Zamora & 23 de Enero) is the oldest Jewish cemetery still in use on the continent. It's normally locked and the keys are kept in the Museo de Arte Alberto Henríquez (p143). Inquire there for a guide to show you around the graveyard.

Jews came to Coro from Curaçao in the early 19th century, a period of intensive trade with the Dutch islands. In the course of time, they formed a small but influential commercial community, despite persecution by the post-independence caudillo governments. Today there are perhaps a dozen Jews still living in Coro.

The cemetery was founded by Joseph Curiel, a rich Jewish merchant who met Simón Bolívar in Angostura and offered him the help of the Venezuelan Jewish community in the cause of independence. Curiel's tomb is one of the most elaborate, while the grave of his 10-year-old daughter, dated 1832, is the oldest tomb in the cemetery.

PARQUE NACIONAL MÉDANOS DE CORO

Just northeast of the city is a spectacular desert landscape, dominated by sand dunes up to 30m high, giving an impression of being in the middle of the Sahara. The **Parque Nacional**

Médanos de Coro (www.losmedanos.com in Spanish; admission free; ☺ 9am-6pm) was created in 1974 to protect this unique environment on the isthmus of the Península de Paraguaná.

To get to the park from the city center, take the Carabobo bus from Calle Falcón and get off 300m past the large Monumento a la Federación. From here it is a 10-minute walk north along a wide avenue to another public sculpture, the Monumento a la Madre. A few paces north there is nothing but sand.

Be cautious – armed robbery of tourists in Los Médanos has been reported by many travelers. Go in the late afternoon, when the security presence is strongest, and take only what you need.

Tours

Budget full-day tours (per person US$30 to US$40) to Península de Paraguaná and the Sierra de San Luis are organized by the managers of the **Posada Turística El Gallo** (☎ 252-9481; posadaelgallo2001@hotmail.com; Calle 66 Federación No 26) and **La Casa de los Pájaros** (☎ 252-8215; rstiuv@gmail.com; Calle Monzón No 74).

Araguato Expeditions (☎ 0286-252-9481, 0416-469-1617; www.araguato.org; Calle 66 Federación No 26) also offers tours countrywide, including to Los Llanos. Their office is in Posada Turística El Gallo.

Sleeping

Casa Tun Tun (☎ 404-0347; casatuntun@hotmail.com; Calle 33 Zamora btwn Calles 56A Toledo & 58A Hernández; hammock/dm/s US$4/6/7, d without/with bath US$12/16) Tun Tun (Knock Knock) is the name of this friendly, Belgian-owned posada. Long-time travelers themselves, they've got room for 18 people in a mixture of dorms, hammocks, and private rooms. Facilities include a barbeque, laundry service, free coffee and a wicked old vinyl jukebox.

Posada Turística El Gallo (☎ 252-9481; posadaelgallo2001@hotmail.com; Calle 66 Federación No 26; hammock/dm/d/tr with shared bath US$5/7/12/14, d/tr with private bath US$14/16) What El Gallo lacks in luxury, the French owner makes up for with an encyclopedic knowledge of tourism in the region. The rooms in the posada are simple with no private facilities, but clean and to the point, plus there's laundry service and kitchen. For those wanting a little bit more comfort, their new Casa El Gallo around the corner offers an additional half a dozen rooms with private bath.

La Casa de los Pájaros (☎ 252-8215; www.casadelospajaros.com.ve; Calle Monzón No 74; hammock US$7, dm/d with fan US$7/23, dm/d with air-con US$9/28; ☒ ☐) The 'House of Birds' is owned and run by Venezuelan architect Roberto, who is constantly expanding and rebuilding this very unique home. There's five deliciously cool rooms (including air-con dorm beds), guests can use the kitchen and internet (30 minutes free access per day) and the owner organises local tours.

Posada Villa Antigua (☎ 0414-682-2924; Calle 58 Comercio No 46; d US$17-23; ☒) The Villa Antigua (Old-fashioned Village) has some suitably old-fashioned rooms arranged around an attractive patio. The rooms have bathrooms and some not-so-old-fashioned, quiet air-conditioners. Check out the inexpensive restaurant.

La Fonda Coriana (☎ Callejón Tucuyito; d US$18-22; ☒) Just around the corner from Villa Antigua, La Fonda is another likable six-room posada, which also has its own restaurant.

Posada Turística Don Antonio (☎ 253-9578; Paseo Talavera No 11; d/tr US$26/41; ☒ ☒) This acceptable posada has been rebuilt in a colonial style and you can't argue with its location – smack dab in the heart of Coro. It has nine comfy *matrimoniales* and three triples, all equipped with bathroom and air-conditioning.

our pick **Estancia Da Domenico** (☎ 252-7703, 0414-687-6874; da_domenico@yahoo.es; Av Miranda btwn Calles 27 Miranda & 31 Urdaneta; s/d/t/q/ste US$32/49/56/64/73; ☒ ☒) This newest of developments is a spic-and-span new B&B, with walls draped in artwork – the works are for sale – and all the usual luxuries you might want, including air-con, cable TV, laundry service and a yummy restaurant on the ground floor.

Hotel Miranda Cumberland (☎ 252-3344, 252-3022; www.hotelescumberland.com/falcon.htm; Av Josefa Camejo; s/d/tr/ste US$52/58/64/65; ☒ ☒ ☐ ☒) Diagonally opposite the airport terminal, Cumberland is the biggest place to stay in town, with spacious air-conditioned rooms and suites, all with safe boxes and internet connections. The hotel has its own restaurant, bar and a bean-shaped swimming pool surrounded by coconut palms. Room prices include buffet breakfast.

Eating

Panadería La Gran Costa Nova (☎ 252-6680; Av Manaure; meals US$3-5; ☺ 6am-9pm) This mammoth bakery packs them in at all times of the day, and no wonder – they crank out some yummy breakfasts, lunches and snacks.

Fonda Turística Sabor Latino (Paseo Alameda; breakfasts US$2.50, lunches US$3.50-4.50; ⏰ 8am-8pm) Nestled in the central pedestrian mall, this is a good spot for some of the cheapest meals in town (including 14 different set breakfasts) in a simple interior or at the shaded tables outside. The menu features staples of Venezuelan cuisine, including *arepas* (stuffed corn pancakes).

Restaurant El Tinajero (Calle 33 Zamora; mains US$3.50-6) El Tinajero is an enjoyable, inexpensive eatery serving popular Venezuelan fare on two tiny patios of a rustic historic house.

Restaurant Punto Criollo (☎ 252-2043; Calle 66 Federación; breakfasts US$2-3, lunches US$4.50-5.50; ⏰ 7am-3pm Mon-Sat) This simple eight-table place gets completely packed with patrons at lunchtime and deservedly so. It also offers filling breakfasts.

Las Cuevas Karemaremar (0416-686-272; Calle 35 Falcón; mains US$5-12, ⏰ 7am-11pm) When the owner greets you with a handshake and warm welcome, you know you're onto something good. This new kid on the block does a mean mixed grill, with fish, pasta, chicken, and some OK salads too.

Restaurant El Conquistador (☎ 252-6794; Calle 31 Urdaneta; mains US$6-15; ✎) Satisfactory food, prompt service and tastefully decorated interior make El Conquistador one of the best eateries in town. Go for *parrilla aire* (mixed grill), *mar y tierra* (surf and turf) or *paella valenciana*, which are among their specialties.

Pizzería La Barra del Jacal (☎ 252-7350; Calle 29 Unión; mains US$7-12) This attractive open-air restaurant offers more than just pizzas, and is a refreshing spot to sit with a beer, especially in the evening when a gentle breeze dissipates the heat of the day.

Drinking

Bar Garua (www.bargarua.com; cnr Calles Monzon & 68 Colón; ⏰ 7pm-late) This classic old-time bar has been here since 1943. Sit with a cold one and soak up the atmosphere, or chat to some of the friendly locals.

El Café de Andrés (☎ 253-0870, 0414-740-5065; Av 27 Miranda btwn Av Josefa Camejo & Calle Norte; mains US$8-14; ⏰ 6:30pm-late Wed-Sat) Just across the street from the Hotel Cumberland, this funky new bar-cum-restaurant has quickly become one of the hippest joints in town. Come early for the food, and linger late over drinks for the live music, which kicks in around midnight.

El Raduno (cnr Calle Hernández & Paseo Talavera; ⏰ 4pm-late Thu-Sat) This massive disco is the only party venue within walking distance from the center and it gets packed with students on the weekends. There's also a breezy rooftop terrace for a quiet beer in the late afternoon.

Entertainment

Cine en la Calle (Paseo Talavera) A free open-air cinema cast against the wall on buildings along Paseo Talavera every Tuesday at 7pm. It focuses on Venezuelan and Latin American films.

La Casa de la Poesía (☎ 252-8675; Calle 58 Comercio; ⏰ 7pm Wed) Groovy baby, poetry readings in Coro, and don't tell me you come here just for the poetry. Fliers advertise 'photography exhibits, conversation, poetry recitals, live music, and salsa-latin-jazz-chill-out.' Conversation…oh behave!

Teatro Armonía (Calle 35 Falcón) The city's main performing-arts venue. Free concerts by the local philharmonic orchestra (considered to be the best in the country) are held every Thursday at 7:30pm.

Getting There & Away

AIR

The **Aeropuerto Internacional José Leonardo Chirinos** (☎ 251-5290, 251-2065; Av Josefa Camejo) is just a five-minute walk north of the city center. Avior (☎ 253-1689) currently offers one daily flight to Caracas (US$90 to US$105), where you need to change for other destinations.

It may be cheaper or more convenient to fly from the airport in Punto Fijo (p150), which is better serviced by the major airlines. You'll need to go there if you want to fly direct to the Dutch Antilles.

BUS

The **Terminal de Pasajeros** (☎ 252-8070; Av Los Médanos) is about 2km east of the city center, and is accessible by frequent city transportation. There are ordinary buses to Punto Fijo (US$3.20, 1¼ hours, 90km), Maracaibo (US$9, four hours, 259km) and Valencia (US$9, five hours, 288km) leaving every half-hour until about 6pm. Most of the direct buses to Caracas (US$16 to US$20, seven hours, 446km) depart in the evening, but you can easily take one of the buses to Valencia and change.

Several direct buses go nightly to Mérida (US$19 to US$23, 12 hours, 782km) and to San Cristóbal (US$18 to US$23, 12 hours, 698km); all these buses depart in the evening and go via Maracaibo. If you're in a hurry, go to Barquisimeto (US$9, seven hours, 418km) and change there.

Within the region, there are buses to Adícora (US$2.20), on the eastern coast of Península de Paraguaná, as well as por puesto jeeps to Curimagua (US$3), in the Sierra de San Luis. Buses to Valencia can drop you off in Tucacas (4 hours, 203km), but for Chichiriviche (3¾ hours, 195km) you'll have to get off at the junction in Sanare (3¼ hours, 184km) and change; busetas pass frequently (20 minutes, US$0.90). You have to pay the full fare to Valencia for both destinations (US$9).

PENÍNSULA DE PARAGUANÁ

☎ 0269 / pop 273,000

You get the feeling Paraguaná wishes it were still an island – in geography and character, it has more in common with the nearby Dutch Antilles than the continent just a thin strip of sand away. Beautiful beaches, of course, lead the list of attractions and a favorable onshore wind has made Adícora the leading budget spot for windsurfing and kitesurfing in the country.

Flat as a pancake and dry as a parched mouth, the peninsula is punctuated only by the singular Cerro Santa Anta (830m), which rises abruptly from the middle of the plain, and can be seen from every angle. Only 40 scant days of rain per year water this arid landscape, which is covered in *cardón,* a columnar cactus tree, whose wood is used to make striking furniture.

If you've got room in your backpack for a new fridge or washer/dryer combo – or perhaps, say, a laptop – take advantage of Paraguaná's status as a *zona libre,* or duty-free zone. Punto Fijo is the peninsula's trading hub and the many Arab merchants there will gladly haggle with you all afternoon.

Paraguaná offers a striking contrast of desert and beach, wind and waves, colonial towns and nature reserves, pink flamingos and colorful salt mines. There's enough to keep you here for a while.

HISTORY

The original inhabitants of Paraguaná were the Amuay, Guaranao and Caquetío people, all belonging to the Arawak linguistic family, but today these people are extinct. Europeans first saw Paraguaná in 1499, when Alonso de Ojeda landed at Cabo de San Román, on the northern tip of the peninsula. Some 130 years later, the Dutch settled the nearby islands of Curaçao, Aruba and Bonaire, and since then there has been a steady mix of Spanish, Dutch and indigenous cultural influences.

The earliest colonial towns emerged not on the peninsular coast, but inland, close to Cerro Santa Ana, as it provided the only source of fresh water. Some of the towns' old urban fabric remains, including several churches.

Things began to change with the oil boom. In the 1920s an oil terminal was built in Punto Fijo to ship oil overseas from Lago de Maracaibo. Refineries were constructed in the 1940s, and Punto Fijo embarked on a boom that continues today, rapidly becoming the largest urban center on the peninsula. The area around the city is dominated by the oil industry and crisscrossed by multilane highways. The rest of the peninsula, however, hasn't rushed into progress and modernity. It's still dotted with small old towns and their tiny colonial churches.

ORIENTATION

There's an array of paved roads on the peninsula, except in the almost uninhabited northwest. Having an independent means of transportation is a great advantage here, because buses and por puestos are not frequent, but they do service most of the larger localities, including Punto Fijo, Santa Ana, Moruy, Pueblo Nuevo and Adícora.

The usual springboard for the peninsula is Coro, from where buses go to Adícora and Punto Fijo, the only places with a reasonable choice of accommodations and food. Punto Fijo is much better serviced by public transportation, but otherwise it's an unremarkable place. It's better to go to the more pleasant Adícora and use it as a base for further excursions, such as viewing flamingos at Laguna de Tiraya or hiking up Cerro Santa Ana. Day tours around the peninsula organized from Coro (p145) are worth considering if you want just a quick taste of Paraguaná.

Punto Fijo

Punto Fijo is the only city on the peninsula, and first appeared on maps in 1925, when an oil terminal was built serving Lago de Maracaibo. Its two refineries, in Amuay and Punta Cardón, are among the largest in the world, but don't expect a tour – even journalists get turned away.

THE NORTHWEST

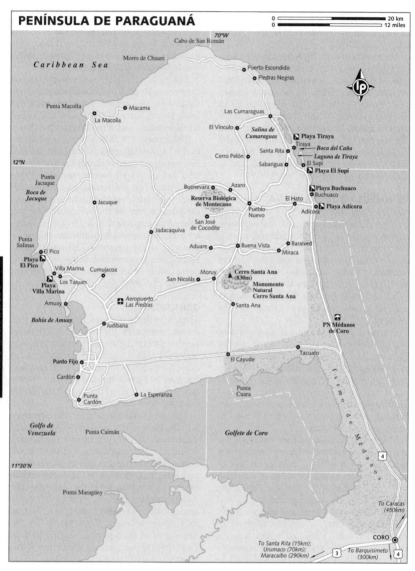

PENÍNSULA DE PARAGUANÁ

Today Punto Fijo is an industrial city of about 140,000 inhabitants, and the center of commerce on the peninsula. As such, it has a good range of hotels and restaurants – establishments that are scarce elsewhere on Paraguaná – but is otherwise of marginal interest, except perhaps to stay overnight en route to or from the Dutch Antilles.

ORIENTATION & INFORMATION

The downtown is based on two north–south streets, Av Bolívar and Av Colombia, along which many stores, hotels, restaurants and banks are located. Useful banks include **Banco de Venezuela** (cnr Av 21 Bolivia & Calle 78 Comercio), **Banco Mercantil** (cnr Av 17 Bolívar & Calle 86 Girardot) and **Corp Banca** (cnr Av 21 Bolivia & Calle 81 Falcón). **Cyber Café**

Manhattan (cnr Av 14 Perú & Calle 79 Arismendi) is one of several central internet facilities, also **Chat-Mania**@ (Calle 79 Arismendi btwn Avs 16 Brasil & 17 Bolívar), or you can use the internet at **CANTV** (cnr Av 22 Méjico & Calle 81 Falcón).

SLEEPING & EATING
Punto Fijo has a few places to stay and most have their own restaurants.

Hotel Presidente (☎ 245-8964, 245-5156; cnr Av 14 Perú & Calle 79 Arismendi; d US$21-23, tr US$33, ste US$35-44; ⊠) The rooms in this modern establishment are unimpeachable, as are the even better suites, furnished with deliciously charming Nixon-era hardwood desk acreage. Conspire the night away.

Hotel Bahía (☎ 245-5743; fax 245-8254; cnr Av 17 Bolívar & Calle 82 Mariño; d US$23-26, tr US$30; ⊠) Another cheap option in the center. Rooms are rather small and dim but otherwise acceptable.

Hotel El Cid (☎ 245-5743; cnr Av 17 Bolívar & Calle 78 Comercio; s/d/tr/ste US$26/30/36/53; P ⊠ 🖳) This amazing one-stop shop has everything you might need – a glitzy internet café, telephone *cabinas,* a groovy bar and restaurant, and even a disco. You wonder what kind of hotel they would have if they put as much effort into their rooms as they do the rest of the business.

Hotel La Península (☎ 245-9734, 245-9776; hotel peninsula@eldish.net; Calle Calatayud; d US$40-45, tr/ste US$55/70; P ⊠ 🖳) On Punto Fijo's southeastern outskirts, La Península is one of the city's top offerings, with well-maintained rooms, two restaurants, swimming pool, gym and pool tables.

Casa de las Tres Ventanas (☎ 277-0627; lastres ventanas@cantv.net; Calle Principal, Los Taques; d US$51-60, tr US$70, ste US$67-108; ⊠ P) This upmarket new posada offers B&B-style service, views of the sunset from their garden courtyard, Mediterranean meals to order and tourist excursions around Paraguaná. It's just five minutes from both airport and beach, and 10 minutes to the center of Punto Fijo.

Tasca-Restaurant Imperial (☎ 246-5987; bodegon imperial@msn.com; cnr Av 17 Bolívar & Calle 78 Comercio; mains US$4-11) This oasis of air-con and beer may be your salvation if you get stuck in Punto Fijo. Good solid food, especially the *chivo* (goat), and a big screen TV and bar to while away the hours.

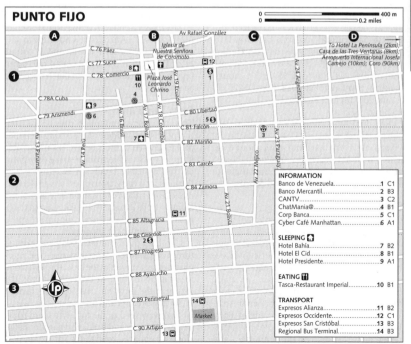

GETTING THERE & AWAY
There is no longer a ferry service running to the Antilles.

Air
Punto Fijo's airport, **Aeropuerto Internacional Josefa Camejo** (☎ 246-0278), is about 10km northeast of the city and is labeled in all the air schedules as 'Las Piedras,' not 'Punto Fijo.' There are no public buses to the airport; a taxi from the city center will cost US$7. There are daily flights to Caracas (US$85 to US$115) and Maracaibo (US$75 to US$90).

There are several departures a day to nearby Aruba, a 15-minute flight. Airlines come and go frequently on this particular route – particularly the many smaller charter carriers – so do check around before buying. **Santa Bárbara** (☎ 0212-204-4000) has a daily morning flight to Aruba (US$185 return), and **Tiara Air** (☎ 415-3488) has several flights a day (US$210 return), and also does charter flights.

Bus
Punto Fijo has not yet built a central bus terminal; bus companies have their own offices scattered throughout the city center. **Expresos Occidente** (cnr Calle 78 Comercio & Av 21 Bolivia), **Expresos Alianza** (cnr Calle 85 Altagracia & Av 18 Colombia) and **Expresos San Cristóbal** (cnr Calle 90 Artigas & Av 18 Colombia) service long-distance routes, including Caracas (US$18 to US$22, 8½ hours, 536km), Maracaibo (US$11 to US$13, 5½ hours, 349km), San Cristóbal (US$20 to US$25, 14 hours, 788km) and Mérida (US$21 to US$24, 15 hours, 872km).

Regional buses depart from the market square. Buses to Coro (US$3.20, 1¼ hours, 90km) run every half-hour until about 6pm. There are also hourly buses to Pueblo Nuevo via the freeway and Santa Ana, and busetas to Pueblo Nuevo via Judibana and Moruy.

Santa Ana
Originally a Caquetío settlement, Santa Ana was founded in the 1540s, although no-one is sure of the exact date. Once Paraguaná's major urban center, it's now a quiet little town, renowned mostly for its colonial church – one of the prettiest country churches in Venezuela. It's also a convenient starting point for a hike to the top of the dramatic Cerro Santa Ana.

The church, on the eastern side of Plaza Bolívar, was built in the 16th century – thus being the first church on the peninsula – and

was extended and remodeled at the end of the 17th century. The unusual bell tower was built around 1750, and at the same time the main retable was added – it's an amazing piece of popular art graced with naive elements. The church is often open during the day, but if you find it locked, go to the Casa Parroquial, on the northern side of Plaza Bolívar, and somebody may open it up for you.

Santa Ana has several basic places to eat, but nowhere to stay overnight. The Inparques office is one block north of the church. Buses between Pueblo Nuevo and Punto Fijo pass on the main road every hour or so.

Moruy
Moruy is most famous for its *silletas paraguaneras,* chairs made from the wood of the *cardón* cactus, which thickly covers most of the peninsula. You can buy them on the roadside stalls here, and also in the neighboring hamlet of San Nicolás.

A short 6km northwest of Santa Ana, Moruy's lovely colonial church also attracts visitors. Built between 1670 and 1683, it is modest in internal furnishing and decoration, but is beautifully proportioned and has a charming facade.

Moruy is a popular starting point for hikes up Cerro Santa Ana. There's nowhere to stay overnight in the village and only a couple of places for a meal. Busetas and buses run regularly to Punto Fijo, Pueblo Nuevo and Santa Ana.

Cerro Santa Ana
This unexpected mountain rises 830m from the plains, in sudden and striking defiance of the parched flatness below. It's impossible to miss – it's visible from nearly every point on the peninsula. It actually has three peaks; the highest is the westernmost and looks dramatic from almost every angle. The mountain, along with its environs (19 sq km altogether), has been decreed a natural monument and is under the control of Inparques.

Climbing the mountain, you pass through three totally different ecosystems – the xerophytic desert species at the base, through cloud forest at 500m, and, at the very summit, the plants of the semi-*páramo* (open highland), including orchids and bromeliads.

Two ways lead to the top. The main route begins at Moruy and heads eastward for 800m along an unpaved road to the Inparques post and a bivouac area. From here, a proper trail heads to the highest peak. It's about a three-hour walk up to the summit (two hours back down).

Another starting point is the town of Santa Ana, from where a rough road from the Inparques office heads north to another bivouac site (a 30-minute walk). The trail that begins here leads to the lowest, eastern peak, then continues up westward along the crest to the main peak. This route is not clear at some points, so you should be careful not to get lost.

Because of the extreme midday heat, Inparques only permits hikers to start uphill until about 9am. You should register before departure at the respective post, but there's no charge. Hikers need to return by 3pm and mark their return on the list.

The peak is always windy and frequently shrouded in cloud. Occasionally it rains in the upper reaches, especially during the wet months (between September and January). Take along a sweater, waterproof gear and proper shoes – the path near the top can be muddy.

Pueblo Nuevo

pop around 8000

Pueblo Nuevo is the largest town in the inland portion of Paraguaná. It became the capital of Paraguaná in 1829 until the oil boom stripped it of the title in favor of Punto Fijo.

Although it continues to maintain importance as an agricultural center, the economy now depends primarily on the arts and crafts industry – especially pottery, for which it is well known – making it a good place to go shopping. It still contains some fine colonial houses and a church dating from 1758, although the latter was remodeled in the 20th century.

SLEEPING & EATING

Posada de Luis (☎ 988-1072, 0414-6963019; Calle Falcón; d/tr US$33/38) This likeable, neat, 10-room posada, 300m west of Plaza Bolívar, is the main place to stay in the center of Pueblo Nuevo.

Casa de los Vientos (☎ 808-5000, 0416-564-4027; per person US$51) Near the small hamlet of Sacuragua, between Pueblo Nuevo and Buena Vista, sits this beautiful new posada. Stay in a room in the colonial house, or one of the new tree-shaded, self-contained cabins the owner built

himself. Price includes dinner and breakfast, and the owner can organize transportation around the peninsula.

Restaurant Popular (☎ 988-1133; Calle Falcón; mains US$2-5) It's indeed popular, serving straightforward, tasty meals at low prices. Try *chivo*, the local specialty.

GETTING THERE & AWAY

There are frequent buses, busetas and por puestos to Punto Fijo (via Moruy) and Adícora, and two busetas a day direct to Coro.

Reserva Biológica de Montecano

This small wooded area, only 16 sq km, is the only remaining lowland forest on the peninsula. Amazingly, it provides a habitat for 62% of the plant species of Falcón state and attracts a great variety of birds. The **Montecano biological reserve** (admission US$0.90; ◷ 9am-6pm) is about 7km west of Pueblo Nuevo. It is run by Infalcosta, a Coro-based institute established in 1995 for the development and conservation of Falcón's arid coastal areas.

The reserve's visitors center is on a narrow road leading to the village of San José de Cocodite, which branches off from the Pueblo Nuevo–Buena Vista road 2km south of Pueblo Nuevo. There's no public transportation on this side road; you can hitch or walk 5km from the turnoff. From the visitors center, a guide will take you on a trip along a looped path that winds up and down through the reserve. It's an easy 1½-hour walk through an unusual habitat full of amazing plants and birds, and you'll even find a small lake on the way. The best times to see the birds are early in the morning and late afternoon, and you avoid the burning heat of midday. The admission fee includes guide service.

Adícora

The small town of Adícora, on Paraguaná's eastern coast, is set at the tip of a narrow, eastern-pointing strip of land and has beaches on both sides, a scant five minutes' walk apart. It's most famous for its windsurfing and kitesurfing, but also boasts fine, colorful Caribbean streets and a reasonable choice of accommodations and restaurants. It's not uncommon to meet tourists in Adícora who've been there for a month or more.

Reputedly founded in the middle of the 16th century, it was once one of the most important ports in western Venezuela. Prosperity came in the 18th century when the Compañía Guipuzcoana built a trading base here. Strolling around the streets, you'll still find brightly colored Dutch-Caribbean houses characterized by barred windows on pedestals, topped with decorated caps.

ACTIVITIES

Adícora has gained international fame as a **kitesurfing** and **windsurfing** center, with some of the best wave and wind conditions on Venezuela's coast. The winds are strongest and most consistent from January to May, and the calmest from September to November, and the breeze is always onshore, ensuring you don't make an unplanned visit to the Dutch Antilles. It's a choice spot, virtually untouched by tourism, beautifully relaxed and informal, and not too expensive.

There are currently only two local operators – Archie and Pachi, German and Venezuelan respectively. Both can be found on the Playa Sur (South Beach), and offer similar windsurfing/kitesurfing courses, equipment rental and simple accommodations.

You'll pay around US$200 for a two-day kitesurfing class. You generally have to take the class before you're permitted to rent gear (around US$50 to US$80 per day) and go solo. Windsurfing is a bit cheaper (expect to pay around US$30 per day for equipment rental) and beginner's instruction goes for around US$30 extra per day. Both offer instruction in a variety of languages.

Windsurf Adícora (☎ 988-8224, 0416-769-6196; www.windsurfadicora.com) The biggest and most reliable facility, run by Venezuelan Pachi. It offers both windsurfing and kitesurfing, plus good accommodations. Rooms go for US$10 per person with fan, US$15 with air-con, plus there's complete apartments with two rooms for US$30-40, including private kitchen.

Archie's Kite & Windsurfing (☎ 988-8285, 415-7313; www.kitesurfing-venezuela.com) Archie offers instruction in multiple languages and rents simple rooms, including some that have air-conditioning. Long-term visitors in a dorm bed pay US$12, furnished apartments go for US$30, and bungalows for 4-6 people US$60. He also sometimes leads kitesurfing and BBQ excursions to more remote, 4WD-only accessible beaches.

SLEEPING & EATING

Adícora has a better choice of places to stay than most other towns on the peninsula. Prices are higher on weekends, when tourists arrive. Some locals rent out rooms in their homes,

which can make for some of the cheapest and safest forms of lodging – ask around. On the other hand, don't rent unattended cabañas or beach houses; these places are easy prey for robbers. There are restaurants in the buildings along the beach, though most of them are only open on weekends.

If you're coming to Adícora for the windsurfing or kitesurfing, or you're simply after a good budget bed, check out the windsurfing schools left.

Posada Casa Rosada (☎ 988-8004; Calle Malecón; d/tr/q US$28/37/47; 😤) This beautifully restored colonial building surrounds a lush garden courtyard and serves up German-influenced food in the peaceful front restaurant. One of the family-sized rooms comes self-contained with kitchen and fridge.

Posada Turística La Nova Carantoña (☎ 988-8173; carantona@cantv.net; Calle Comercio; d US$37; 😤) In a fine old house, one block back from the beach, this enjoyable place offers nine rustic, stylish rooms arranged around a sunny courtyard, plus a budget restaurant shaded by two palm trees.

Campamento Vacacional La Troja (☎ 988-8048, 415-5030; la_troja@hotmail.com; Calle Santa Ana; r per person US$45; P 😤) Occupying an entire block in the middle of town, this massive walled complex, built in the traditional style and set in a lush garden (quite unusual on the arid peninsula), provides comfortable and stylish accommodations and food. Spacious rooms have a fan and bathroom and the price includes both dinner and a hearty breakfast. There's a good-sized pool, too.

Hacienda La Pancha (☎ 511-1269, 0414-969-2649; www.venaventours.com/haciendalapancha; r per person US$56; P 😤 😠) Those with there own transportation may enjoy this luxurious über-posada, just five minutes west of Adícora in the hills. Brightly decorated and well run, La Pancha offers eight comfortable rooms, an excellent restaurant, and a lush garden with hammocks. The price is a package deal that includes dinner and breakfast.

Posada Guadalupana (☎ 988-8178; Calle Comercio; www.exploreadicora.com; self-contained apt/detached house US$60/70; P 😤) Self-contained apartments are the name of the game in this newly remodeled old colonial building. Each apartment has a well-furnished kitchen with stove, fridge and kitchen table, and they also rent a separate detached beach house.

Club Social la Estrella de Adícora (988-8015; Calle Comercio; mains US$3-8; 🕐 Mon-Thu 4-10pm, Fri & Sat

11:30am-1am) Dance under the stars in the "Star of Adícora." Drop by for a quiet drink during the week; the weekend is when the restaurant opens and the dancing begins.

GETTING THERE & AWAY
Adícora is linked to Coro (US$2.20, one hour, 50km) by half a dozen buses a day, the last departing at around 5pm. There are also por puestos to Pueblo Nuevo and busetas to Punto Fijo. Transportation varies heavily with the season – during peak tourist times, more buses and por puestsos ply this route.

Lagunas & Salinas
Flamingos feed at **Laguna de Tiraya,** about 6km north of Adícora. Peak season is November to January, but you can be pretty sure of finding some birds almost year-round. The lagoon is accessible by the paved road to Santa Rita (which skirts the western shore of the lagoon), but there is no public transportation on this road. You can walk or try to hitch (the traffic is mainly on weekends; at other times it's sporadic), or take a taxi from Adícora.

The flamingos may be quite close to the western shore or off in the distance, on the eastern side of the lagoon. As a rough rule, they come to the western shore in the afternoon after doing their morning fishing on the eastern side.

Further north, between Santa Rita and Las Cumaraguas, is the **Salina de Cumaraguas,** where salt is mined using rudimentary methods. The lagoon is noted for the amazingly beautiful color of its water, which ranges from milky pink to deep purple.

If you have your own transportation, you can explore the region further north as far as **Cabo de San Román,** which is the northernmost point in Venezuela, and from where, on a clear day, you can see as far as Aruba. If you're without a car, there are irregular por puestos (US$1.75) on a paved road from Las Cumaraguas to Pueblo Nuevo via El Vínculo. Be prepared for the heat: take sufficient water, sunscreen, sunglasses and a hat.

Beaches
The beaches on Paraguaná don't match those of Morrocoy or Henri Pittier and the dearth of coconut palms means that they usually lack shade. Like all other beaches in Venezuela, Paraguaná's beaches are quiet on weekdays and swamped on the weekends.

The beaches on the eastern coast stretch almost all the way from Adícora to Piedras Negras. **Adícora** is the most popular and well-kept beach resort; the beaches at **El Supí** and **Buchuaco** are often covered with litter. **Tiraya** is less popular with holidaymakers because it's harder to reach. On the western coast, the popular beaches include **Villa Marina** and **El Pico,** both serviced by local transportation from Punto Fijo.

SIERRA DE SAN LUIS
☎ 0268
For those seeking relief from the coastal heat, or a chance to do some hiking, the Sierra de San Luis offers green mountains chock-a-block with tiny colonial towns, waterfalls, 20 caves and a dozen *simas* – deep vertical holes in the earth. There's a good choice of walking paths and excellent bird-watching, and an array of hotels and restaurants to cater to most tastes.

The Sierra is a vital source of water for the whole coastal area, including the Península de Paraguaná. About 200 sq km of this rugged terrain was made into a national park in 1987. Elevations within the park range from 200m up to 1501m on Cerro Galicia, the park's highest point. Average temperatures range between 60°F and 75°F, according to altitude. Annual rainfall is moderate, not exceeding 1500mm, and the wettest months are October to December.

Orientation
Curimagau, San Luis, and Cabure are the major towns of the Sierra, all of which are accessible by public transportation from Coro. Curimagua is the closest to Coro (45km) and is the only one regularly serviced. Curimagua and its environs also have the best choice of accommodations and provide the most popular and convenient base for visiting the region. You can go there on your own and stay in a posada, from where you can explore the Sierra. Some of the posada owners will offer visitors excursions around area sights, or at least provide them with information on what to see and how to get there. The Swiss owner of **Finca El Monte** (☎ 404-0564; fincaelmonte@yahoo.com) is one of the few in the mountains who speaks English, and offers walking tours throughout the Sierra de San Luis.

You can also take a day tour to the Sierra from Coro (see Tours p145), which covers most of the sights listed below.

Sights

The most popular attraction in the mountains is the **Camino de los Españoles**, an old Spanish trail between Cabure and La Negrita; its best-preserved part is near Acarite, where there is a brick Spanish bridge dating from around 1790. You have to walk the trail to see the **Cueva de Zárraga** and the **Cueva del Nacimiento**, both spectacular local caves. It's about a three-hour walk to cover the whole trail. Be sure to wear stout shoes and bring water and insect repellent.

Midway between Curimagua and San Luis is the **Haitón de Guarataro**, an impressive local *sima*. It's 305m deep, but the mouth is only about 12m in diameter. Northeast of Cabure is the **Cataratas de Hueque**, the largest and the most spectacular of the region's waterfalls.

Of the three main towns, **San Luis** is possibly the most picturesque. Founded in 1590, it's the oldest Spanish settlement in the area and has preserved some of its colonial architecture, including a fine church.

You can also walk a loop up **Cerro Galicia**, to **Cerro Paraguariba**, and then back to Curimagua. The trail is hard to follow, so be sure to take a local guide – it's both easy and dangerous to get lost.

Sleeping & Eating

Accommodations in the Sierra range from small, family-run posadas to larger hotels, some with their own nightclubs. Many places come alive only on the weekend, when city holiday-makers can fill hotels to capacity.

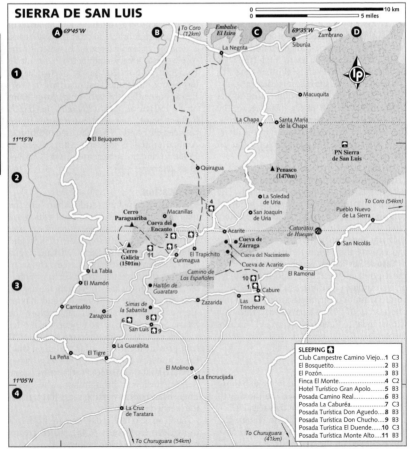

SIERRA DE SAN LUIS

0   10 km
0   5 miles

THE NORTHWEST

Unless otherwise noted, all places listed here are open during the week, have rooms with private bathrooms and provide meals.

CURIMAGUA & AROUND

ourpick **Finca El Monte** (☎ 404-0564; fincaelmonte@ yahoo.com; s/d/tr US$9/15/20; **P**) Friendly Swiss couple Ernesto and Ursula run this cozy family posada. They serve delicious meals (vegetarian on request), organize walking tours in the area, and are one of the few places in the mountains where English is spoken. They also roast, grind and serve organic coffee they grow themselves. Just 5km northeast of Curimagua, on the road to Coro, this is hands down the best traveler's option in the Sierras.

El Pozón (☎ 0416-428-6969; d US$18; **P**) Just down the road from Finca El Monte is this quiet family home, which offers comfortable rooms and a restaurant that serves up home-style creole cooking. They grow their own fruit and coffee, and have a special interest in traditional and herbal remedies, including – wait for it – whole, pickled snake, curled up in a jar of rum.

Posada Turística Monte Alto (☎ 416-0835; d US$18, cabañas US$30-35; **P**) About 2km west of Curimagua, this agreeable posada, stuck to a steep hillside, offers five matrimonial rooms, two cabañas (for four to five guests) providing great views, and a no-nonsense restaurant.

El Bosquetito (☎ 252-3602, 0414-682-0656; www .bosquetito.com; d US$21, cabins for 5 or 6 US$26-30; **P**) This charming rural posada – the name means "Tito's Forest" – surrounds a well-developed English-style garden on the slope of the hill. Usually open only on weekends, meals and drinks are all available, to be consumed in the shade of the white garden gazebo.

Hotel Turístico Gran Apolo (☎ 416-1202; hotelgranapolo@cantv.net; d/tr/q US$23/33/37; **P** **⌘**) This motel with hotel aspirations has just 15 rooms, but the excellent service, good-sized pool, restaurant, bar and rooftop terrace (for admiring them handsome mountain views) all contrive to make the masquerade seem real. Crucially, they are open all week long, not just for the weekend-trippers.

SAN LUIS

Posada Camino Real (☎ 404-2709; d/tr/q US$9/12/14; **P**) The owner of this posada built the place with his own two hands, and it shows. The rooms are simple, but comfortable, and there's a lovely garden with a hammock to while away

the afternoons. His wife prepares some of the best home-style creole cookin' to be found in these here mountains.

Posada Turística Don Aguedo (☎ 666-3073; Calle Principal; d/tr US$13/16; **P**) This charming place at the foot of the mountain has four perfectly acceptable rooms with bathroom and fan, and a rustic restaurant serving filling meals. It's an oasis of tranquility, except for early morning cockcrow.

Posada Turística Don Chucho (☎ 666-3053; d/tr US$16/20; **P** **⌘**) Set on a hilltop, the disco in this place boasts speakers big enough to fill the entire valley with *reggaetón* (fusion of music styles including hip hop and reggae). Open all week, but come on the weekend to party hearty with the crowds of *caraceños* who descend on the place.

CABURE

Posada Turística El Duende (☎ 809-9066, 661-1079; d/q US$19/33; **P**) Set 1.5km up a steep, recently-paved road from town, this oasis of tranquility has five cute, pink rooms and a flowering garden set around a 300-year-old ceiba tree. Rustic-style restaurant and bar, too.

Posada La Cabureña (☎ 661-1093; Calle Bolívar; d/tr US$23/30; **P** **⌘**) Next to the church, this six-room place provides neat, homely rooms with air-con, bathroom and hot water. The sheer number of pictures on the walls makes you feel as if you are in a provincial museum.

Club Campestre Camino Viejo (☎ 661-1016; d US$23-33, cabañas US$47-56; **P** **⌘** **⌘**) Next to the local cemetery, the Country Club is popular with Venezuelans for weekend getaways, and offers the most complete facilities, including cabins, chalets, restaurant, bar, swimming pool and disco on weekends. They sometimes organize horse tours, too.

Getting There & Away

The usual point of departure for the Sierra is Coro. Por puesto jeeps to Curimagua (via La Chapa) depart from 5am until midafternoon (US$3, 1½ hours, 45km). There are also infrequent por puestos to Cabure (via Pueblo Nuevo de la Sierra), some of which continue up to San Luis. Be sure to specify precisely where you want to go.

PARQUE NACIONAL MORROCOY

One of the most spectacular coastal environments in Venezuela, Parque Nacional Morrocoy comprises a strip of mainland and an offshore area dotted with islands, islets and cays. Some islands are skirted by white-sand beaches and surrounded by coral reefs. At the eastern edge of Falcón state, Morrocoy is one of the most popular parks with those looking for beaches and diving.

The park is also well known for its variety of waterbirds, including ibises, herons, cormorants, ducks, pelicans and flamingos. They permanently or seasonally inhabit some of the islands and coastal mangroves, especially the **Golfete de Cuare**, which is one of Venezuela's richest bird-breeding grounds and has been declared a wildlife refuge.

Venezuelan beachgoers come en masse on holidays and weekends and leave the islands

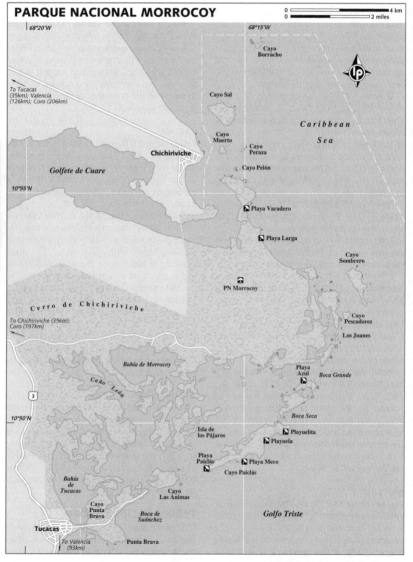

PARQUE NACIONAL MORROCOY

0 _____ 4 km
0 _____ 2 miles

68°20'W   68°15'W

Cayo Borracho

To Tucacas (35km); Valencia (126km); Coro (206km)

Cayo Sal

Caribbean Sea

Cayo Muerto

Cayo Peraza

Chichiriviche

Cayo Pelón

Golfete de Cuare

10°55'N

Playa Varadero

Playa Larga

Cayo Sombrero

PN Morrocoy

Cerro de Chichiriviche

To Chichiriviche (35km); Coro (197km)

Cayo Pescadores

Los Juanes

Bahía de Morrocoy

Caño León

Playa Azul   Boca Grande

3

10°50'N

Boca Seca

Isla de los Pájaros

Playuelita

Playuela

Playa Paiclás

Playa Mero

Cayo Paiclás

Bahía de Tucacas

Cayo Las Ánimas

Cayo Punta Brava

Boca de Suánchez

Golfo Triste

Tucacas

To Valencia (93km)   Punta Brava

littered. The fragile island environment is unfortunately beginning to suffer from human interference, though you can still enjoy deserted and apparently virgin beaches on weekdays. More significantly, some of the coral has died, especially the coral closest to the surface, purportedly the result of a chemical leak in the 1990s. Independent biologists claimed that up to half of the hard coral was dead. It has begun to rebound, but it's likely to take decades for the full recovery. Cayo Sombrero was the least touched by this tragedy and the best coral diving and snorkeling is to be found there.

Orientation

The park lies between the towns of Tucacas and Chichiriviche, which are its main gateways. Both have well-organized boat services to the islands, as well as an array of places to stay and eat. You can use them as a base for day trips to the islands, but if you have a tent or a hammock you can stay on the islands themselves.

The most popular island is Cayo Sombrero, which has fine coral reefs and some of the best beaches. It's more exposed to the open sea than most other islands, and the breeze means that it has fewer insects. Other places good for snorkeling include Playuela and Boca Seca.

Sleeping & Eating

Camping is officially permitted on four islands: Cayo Sal, Cayo Muerto, Cayo Sombrero and Cayo Paiclás. If you plan on staying in a hammock, make absolutely sure you take along a good mosquito net. All four of the islands have beach restaurants and/or food kiosks, but some of them may be closed on weekdays in the low season.

Before you go camping, you need to contact the Inparques office in Tucacas (see following) and shell out a camping fee of US$1 per person per night, payable at the Banesco in Tucacas.

When camping on the islands, take sufficient water, some food to save on predictably overpriced beach eateries, snorkeling gear, good sun protection and a reliable insect repellent. The insects here – small biting gnats known locally as *puri-puri* – are most annoying in windless months, usually November and December. They are particularly nasty early in the morning and late in the afternoon. You can use gas camping stoves, but no open fires are permitted.

Getting There & Away

Boats to the islands normally take up to seven or eight people and charge a flat rate per trip. Prices to all islands and beaches are posted next to the ticket office close to the loading dock in Tucacas. They are roundtrip fares per boat, not per person. The fare to the farthest islands, such as Cayo Sombrero or Cayo Pescadores, is around US$51. Closer destinations include Playa Paiclás (US$28), Playa Mero (US$30), Playuela (US$33) and Playa Azul (US$37). The boat will pick you up from the island in the afternoon or at a later date, depending on when you want to return. On weekdays during the off-season, you can usually bargain down the price.

Before you decide to go to one particular island or beach, check for excursions with stops on various islands, organized by some boat operators and hotel managers. Both the Caribana Hotel (p158) and Posada Amigos del Mar (p160) organize boat trips, expect to pay roughly US$10 to US$15 per person.

Chichiriviche has two piers: the Embarcadero Playa Norte, near the eastern end of Av Zamora; and the Embarcadero Playa Sur, about 1km southwest. Boat fares are the same at both piers. As in Tucacas, the boat takes a maximum of seven to eight passengers, and the fare given is per boat. Popular shorter trips include Cayo Muerto (US$14), Cayo Sal (US$16) and Cayo Pelón (US$19), whereas Cayo Sombrero (US$47) is the leading further destination. The return time is up to you, and haggling over the price is also possible.

CHICHIRIVICHE

☎ 0259 / pop 12,000

Chichiriviche is the northern gateway to Parque Nacional Morrocoy, providing access to half a dozen neighboring cays. Accommodations, food and boats are in good supply, and the recent paving of the roads has turned this once Miss Ugly into something that, well, you might actually want to kiss.

Access to the town is from the west, by the 12km road that runs along a causeway through mangrove swamps. The area lining this road is a favorite feeding ground for flamingos, which gather here mostly between August and January; however, a small community can remain up to March or even April, as long as there's sufficient water. November is usually the peak month, when up to 5000 birds are in the area.

Orientation

Upon entering the town proper, the access road divides. Its main branch, Av Zamora (also called Av Principal), continues straight ahead to the bus terminus and the town center, ending at the waterfront next to the northern pier. This area boasts a number of hotels, restaurants and other businesses. The southern branch, Vía Fábrica de Cemento (Cement Factory Rd), goes to the cement plant south of town, providing access to the southern pier on the way.

Information

In the absence of a tourist office you can ask hotel managers for local information. The **Banco Industrial de Venezuela** (Av Zamora) gives advances on Visa, but that's about all it can do for you; it doesn't accept MasterCard. Internet access is provided by several cyber-cafés, including **Bit Manía** (Paseo Bolívar), **Comunications City** (Av Zamora), near the bus stop, and **Morrocoy@Services** (Av Zamora). Chichiriviche has no diving schools.

Sleeping

Morena's Place (☎ 815-0936, 0412-709-4714; posadamorenas@hotmail.com; Sector Playa Norte; r per person US$7) This five-room posada offers the only dorm beds in town. It's in a fine old house near the waterfront, about 500m from where the bus drops you off. It's run by friendly English-speaking Carlos, who also offers a laundry service, budget meals and tours, and rents out two kayaks (US$12 a day).

Villa Gregoria (☎ 818-6359; aagustinm@yahoo.es; Calle Mariño; d with fan/air-con US$13/20; P) This Spanish-run and Spanish-looking posada, near the bus terminus, has good rooms with bathrooms. Choose a room on the upper floor – they are brighter and more attractive – and relax in a hammock or an armchair on the great terrace. The owner organizes car tours to Coro and Puerto Cabello, and boat tours to the islands.

Posada Milagro (☎ 815-0864; Av Zamora; d US$21) Just 50m back from the seashore, the Milagro has six simple *matrimoniales* with bathrooms, fans and sea views. Ask for a room in the Licorería Falcón and choose one on the top floor for better vistas.

Posada La Negra (☎ 815-0476; Calle Mariño No 32; d US$21-33;) This colorful old Carib building is named after its owner, a friendly old black lady, who will welcome you into her large family home and look after you personally.

You can even use her kitchen and fridge, if you like.

Caribana Hotel (☎ 815-1491; Paseo Bolívar; d US$33-42, tr US$48;) The refurbished Caribana offers neat rooms with fine tile work and comfortable beds, and organizes tours. It's just off Av Zamora.

Hotel La Garza (☎ 818-6711; hotellagarza@cantv.net; cnr Av Zamora & Vía Fábrica de Cemento; d US$30-40; P) At the entrance to the town, 1km back from the waterfront, La Garza has a long-standing tradition and maintains its reasonable standards and facilities, including its refreshing swimming pool and adjacent restaurant. Rooms vary in size and quality, so it's best to have a look before checking in.

Hotel Capri (☎ 818-6026; hotel_capri@cantv.net; Av Zamora; d US$30-47, self-contained apt US$70;) The Capri offers self-contained apartments with kitchen, fridge, microwave and all the goodies you might need just steps from the waterfront.

Coral Suites Hotel & Spa (☎ 815-1033; www.hotelcoralsuites.com; Vía Fábrica de Cemento; ste US$60-100; P) A big, modern five-star affair, this is a touch of Miami in Chichiriviche. Enjoy a vast swimming pool with water slides, plus tennis courts, two restaurants, a conference room for up to 1000 people and beds wide enough to sleep across.

Hotel Gabón (☎ 815-0055, 815-1023; www.hotelgabon.com; Calle Marina; s/d/ste US$85/106/148) This brand-spanking new hotel sits rights on the waterfront, with impeccable new rooms (some with sea views), airy rooftop bar and a pool under construction. You can't miss this one – check the waterfront skyline for the big blue dome.

Hotel Mario (☎ 818-6811; hotelmariovzla@cantv.net; Calle Zamora; s/d/tr/q US$237/349/493/633; P) The largest hotel with the most complete facilities in Chichiriviche, the Mario specializes in weekend package deals that include transportation from Caracas, plus breakfast, dinner and boat excursion.

Eating

Restaurant El Rincón de Arturo (Av Zamora; breakfasts US$3.25, set lunches US$3; closed dinner) Budget travelers are likely to appreciate the straightforward tasty meals in this tiny, rustic place.

Chatoguagua's (☎ 0416-433-8258; Av Zamora; breakfasts 3.50, mains US$4-9) For good ol' down-home creole cookin', look no further than this affordable restaurant. They even do a respectable paella to share, if you have the patience to wait for it.

Tasca Eridali (☎ 815-0813; Av Zamora; pizzas US$5-12, fish US$5-15) This yummy pizzeria also does good pasta and fresh fish, all served by a David Hasselhoff look-alike. Call him by his nickname – 'Baywatch' – and he'll show you his tattoo!

Ristorante Il Faro (☎ 416-0066; Calle La Marina; mains US$6-15; ☻ noon-10pm) Set in a beautiful colonial-style mansion, Il Faro has some of the best food in town and not only Italian, as its name would suggest. Take a table on the spacious upper-floor terrace with wide vistas over the sea and enjoy the *parrillada de mariscos* (seafood grill) or a lobster – both local specialties.

Restaurant Txalupa (☎ 818-6425; El Malecón; mains US$8-12; ☻ noon-10pm) This respectable Basque-run establishment does good fish and seafood at reasonable prices. It's on the 1st floor, providing views of the fishing boats on the shore and the islands on the horizon. Upstairs is a *tasca* (Spanish-style bar-restaurant) and disco with still better views. Try *crema de mero*, the local fish soup specialty.

Getting There & Away

Chichiriviche is about 22km off the main Morón–Coro highway and is serviced by half-hourly buses from Valencia (US$4.20, 2½ hours, 126km).

There are no direct buses to Chichiriviche from Caracas or Coro. To get there from Caracas, take any of the frequent buses to Valencia (US$4, 2½ hours, 158km) and change there for a Chichiriviche bus. From Coro, take any bus to Valencia, get off in Sanare (US$6.50, 3¼ hours, 184km) at the turnoff for Chichiriviche and catch one of the many busetas that pass by.

TUCACAS

☎ 0259 / pop 25,000

This ordinary, hot town on the Valencia–Coro road, has nothing to keep you for long. But with the Parque Nacional Morrocoy just a stone's throw away, the town has developed into a holiday center dotted with hotels and restaurants. Plenty of new developments are springing up toward the south of town, between the Morón road and the beach.

Orientation

The town's lifeline is Av Libertador, a 1km road stretching between the Morón–Coro road in the west and the bridge to an island in the east. Many hotels and restaurants are on or just off this street. Buses stop at the intersection of the two roads.

The island across the bridge, Cayo Punta Brava, is part of the national park. A 15-minute walk from the bridge along the paved road will bring you to the beach, which is shaded with coconut palms; more beaches lie further east on the same island, accessible by road. To visit other islands in the park, go to the *embarcadero* (landing dock) close to the bridge, which is packed with pleasure boats waiting for tourists.

Information

Tucacas has no reliable tourist office – try the staff at your hotel or scuba-diving operators. The office of **Inparques** (☎ 812-2176; Av Libertador; ☻ 8am-12:30pm & 2-5pm), which you need to contact if you want to camp on the islands, is close to the bridge. Pay your camping fee at **Banesco** (Av Libertador), which also gives cash advances on Visa and MasterCard (from the cashier, not the ATM). **Banco Provincial** (Carretera Coro-Morón) has a useful ATM, but it's 2km south of the center. The diving schools will all be happy to accept your cash dollars and may take your traveler's checks as well.

Tucacas has several internet facilities on the main drag (Av Libertador), including Inversiones New Time and CANTV.

Activities

There are three scuba diving operators in town. All offer diving courses and guided tours run by licensed instructors, and have shops selling diving and snorkeling gear, some of which can be rented. Expect to pay roughly US$300 for a four-day NAUI openwater course and US$60 to US$65 per day for a local diving trip. Equipment, prices and quality of instructors vary, so be sure to shop around.

Submatur (☎ 812-0082; fax 812-1051; morrocoysubmatur1@cantv.net; Calle Ayacucho No 6) is owned and managed by Mike Osborn from Guyana. With 40-odd years' experience, it is one of the oldest diving schools in the country. Two-day and longer diving trips in a sailing boat to Bonaire and Islas Las Aves can also be organized (US$130 per day).

Frogman Dive Center (☎ 812-4112; fax 0241-824-3879; www.frogmandive.com, collazo@telcel.net.ve; C.C. Bolívar – Local No 3, Plaza Bolívar) is a new dive shop just off Plaza Bolívar, run by Valencia native Manuel Collazo.

Amigos del Mar Divers (☎ 812-1754; amigos-del-mar@cantv.net; Calle Democracia No 1), near the *embarcadero*, is cheaper than the rest. It's owned by a Belgian, André Nahon, one of the former instructors of Submatur.

Sleeping

Posada Amigos del Mar (☎ 812-3962, 0414-484-7570; Calle Nueva; s/d/tr/q US$12/14/19/23; ℗) This rapidly crumbling posada would not be worth the ink, except that Belgian owner André is one of the few people in town who speaks English. The posada is just behind the Ambulatorio Urbano, a three-minute walk from the bus stop.

Posada de Carlos (☎ 812-1493; Av Libertador; s/d with fan US$14/19, d with air-con US$28; ✷) 'Sí Hay Habitación' – yes, there are rooms – reads the handmade sign outside. This best of the budget options has eight rooms with bathroom and fan, and you can use the kitchen.

Posada El Ancla (☎ 812-0253; posadaelancla@cantv.net; Calle Páez; d/q US$16/20; ℗ ✷) El Ancla is a friendly, family-run, four-room place, two blocks south of Av Libertador. Rooms don't have private facilities but there are four shared bathrooms, exactly one per room.

Posada d'Alexis (☎ 812-3390; posadaalexis@hotmail.com; Calle Falcón; d US$19-20, q US$28; ℗ ✷ ☎) Next door to Posada Náutica, this is another nice small guesthouse with its own restaurant. Rooms are arranged around a pool with a waterfall and amazing weeping willows.

Posada Venemar (☎ 812-2669; www.venemar.com; Av Libertador; d US$45-50, ste US$70; ✷) Near the bridge, Venemar offers good-quality *matrimoniales* and suites – all with sea views – plus a fine restaurant, which is one of the best places in town for a seafood dinner.

Posada Náutica (☎ 812-2559, 812-2685; Calle Falcón; r US$47; ✷ ☎) This is B&B Venezuelan-style. This pretty, three-story house shelters seven comfy rooms, there's a pleasant restaurant downstairs and a small pool. The prices include a yummy breakfast.

Aparto Posada del Mar (☎ 812-0524; www.apartoposadadelmar.com; Av Silva; d US$59-70, tr US$67-76, ste US$98; ℗ ✷ ☎) This spacious waterfront compound offers reasonable rooms (great suites with sea views), an adequate restaurant, a swimming pool, a kitchen for guests, a private dock with boat rental and a sauna, should you need to warm yourself in this steamy climate.

Posada Balijú (☎ 812-1580; www.posadabaliju.com.ve; Calle Libertad; r US$70; ℗ ✷) Right on the waterfront, this is one of the most charming places around, providing tranquility, stylish surroundings and a family atmosphere. It's available by package only, which includes bed, breakfast, lunch, dinner and boat excursions.

Eating

our pick **Panadería La Reina de Mar** (Av Libertador; breakfast US$2-3, mains US$2-4; ⏱ 8am-8pm) In a touristy town filled with typically over-priced restaurants, the 'Queen of the Sea' is the budget diner's salvation. This Italian-owned bakery-and-then-some does divine sandwiches, chicken, lasagna, yummy cakes and the best coffee. They're open for breakfast, lunch and dinner – so honestly, why eat anywhere else?

Lunchería La Entrada (☎ 812-4683; Av Libertador; meals US$2-4) This popular place serves up filling breakfasts, fresh juices and stuffed *arepas* until well into the afternoon.

Bodegón del Mar (☎ 812-1646; Av Libertador; mains US$8-16) This white-tablecloth angel is one of the best seafood altars in town. They're good at all sort of cocktails, too – rum punch or shrimp cocktail, anyone?

Restaurant El Timón (☎ 812-0783; Av Libertador; mains US$9-15; ✷) El Timón offers solid, satisfying food – particularly seafood – at good prices, and you can eat it inside or at the tables outside.

Getting There & Away

Tucacas sits on the Valencia–Coro road, so buses run frequently to both Valencia (US$3.80, 1½ hours, 91km) and Coro (US$9, 3¾ hours, 197km). Buses from Valencia pass through regularly on their way to Chichiriviche (US$0.90, 40 minutes, 35km).

LARA & YARACUY STATES

BARQUISIMETO

☎ 0251 / pop 820,000

'We Are Building the Model City of the Revolution' proclaim the signs, and indeed they are – massive public works projects are under way in this relaxed, incredibly livable city. Yup, Barquisimeto's got a prom date with Chávez and he's spending big. There's a new, modern trole bus line to whisk people from the gargantuan new intercity bus terminal (artist drawings suggest something akin to the Epcot Center) through the new, inner-city pedestrian-only boulevard, past the shiny new civic center and redeveloped botanical gardens, to the city's new crowning glory – literally – the Monumento al Sol Naciente, a circular sundial of massive stones on the scale of Stonehenge. Most of these projects are expected to be completed by late 2007 or early 2008.

Barquisimeto has a few (nonrevolutionary) attractions worth visiting as well and is the perfect jumping-off point for the surrounding region – a beautiful land of arid hills, Venezuela's best wine and the mysteries of María Lionza (see the boxed text p165).

Originally founded in 1552, Barquisimeto moved three times before eventually being established at its present-day location in 1563. Its growth was slow, as the indigenous tribes in the region were fierce in defending their territory. It wasn't until the 20th century that the city really developed to become a thriving commercial and industrial center and the capital of Lara state. Today, it's Venezuela's fourth-largest city, after Caracas, Maracaibo and Valencia.

Orientation

Barquisimeto's center, spreading to the north of Plaza Bolívar, has a regular grid pattern, which is easy to navigate. Its main commercial street, and new pedestrian boulevard, is Av 20, heavily packed with shopping centers and stores. A trole bus line is planned to run down Av 20, with connections to the suburbs and the bus terminal.

The area around Plaza Bolívar is quieter, but becomes a ghost town after dark, so don't plan on night walks there. More attractive and relaxing is the city's eastern sector, along Av Lara and Av Los Leones, about 3km east of the center. The area is dotted with spanking new shopping malls, well-appointed restaurants and trendy night spots – a destination for the city's beautiful people.

Information
EMERGENCY
Fire (☎ 171)
Police (☎ 171)
Ambulance (☎ 171)

INTERNET ACCESS
There's a ridiculous number of cybercafés in Barquisimeto, all fast and cheap (US$0.70 to US$1.00 an hour). The **Centro Comercial Capital Plaza** (cnr Av Vargas & Av 20) has around 10 cybercafés, and it's a good point to start if you are nearby. Other central places include the following:
D&G Website Internet (Centro Comercial BarquiCenter, Av 20 btwn Calles 22 & 23)
formula1.com (Calle 23 btwn Carreras 18 & 19)
Internet y Copias (cnr Carrera 19 & Calle 24)

MEDICAL SERVICES
Clínica Razetti (☎ 232-7111, 231-9011; Calle 27 btwn Carreras 21 & 22)
Hospital Central Universitario Dr Antonio María Pineda (☎ 251-3846; cnr Av Las Palmas & Av Vargas)
Policlínica de Barquisimeto (☎ 254-0044; cnr Av Los Leones & Av Madrid) Northeast of town.

MONEY
Banco de Venezuela (cnr Av 20 & Calle 31)
Banco Mercantil (cnr Carrera 19 & Calle 29)
Banco Provincial (cnr Av 20 & Calle 31)
Banesco (cnr Carrera 19 & Calle 27)
Corp Banca (cnr Av 20 & Av Vargas)
Italcambio Airport (☎ 443-1910; 🕓 7am-7pm); City (☎ 254-9790; Centro Empresarial Barquisimeto, Av Los Leones; 🕓 8:30am-4pm)

POST
Ipostel (Plaza Bolívar)

TELEPHONE
Both of these also have internet.
CANTV (Carrera 19 btwn Calles 25 & 26)
Movistar (Carrera 19 btwn Calles 24 & 25)

TOURIST INFORMATION
Cortulara (Corporación de Turismo del Estado de Lara; ☎ 255-7544, 255-6613; www.cortulara.gov.ve; Edificio Fundalara, Av Libertador; 🕓 8am-noon & 2-6pm Mon-Fri) It's over 2km northeast of the center, near the Complejo Ferial. To get there, take Ruta 12 bus from anywhere along Carrera 19 in the center. The office operates information desks in the bus terminal and at the airport. Their website is an excellent source of information on the region.
Cortubar (Corporación de Turismo Barquisimeto; ☎ 710-1802; Palacio Municipal, 3rd fl; 🕓 8am-noon & 2-6pm Mon-Fri) The city tourist office, in city hall.
Inparques (☎ 254-2933, 254-8118; Parque del Este; Av Libertador; 🕓 9am-noon & 2-5pm Mon-Fri) The office provides information about the national parks in the region, Yacambú and Terepaima, and books accommodations in the parks.

THE NORTHWEST

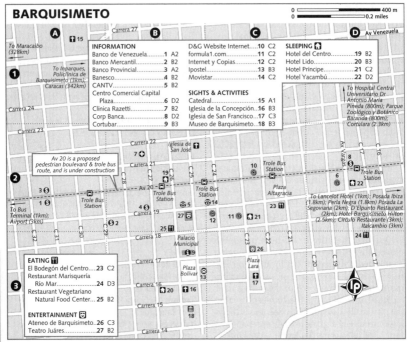

BARQUISIMETO

0   400 m
0   0.2 miles

INFORMATION	
Banco de Venezuela.............1	A2
Banco Mercantil...................2	B2
Banco Provincial..................3	A2
Banesco.............................4	D2
CANTV................................5	B2
Centro Comercial Capital	
Plaza..............................6	D2
Clinica Razetti....................7	B2
Corp Banca.........................8	D2
Cortubar.............................9	B3

D&G Website Internet.......10	C2
formula1.com....................11	C2
Internet y Copias..............12	C2
Ipostel.............................13	B3
Movistar...........................14	C2

SIGHTS & ACTIVITIES	
Catedral...........................15	A1
Iglesia de la Concepción..16	B3
Iglesia de San Francisco...17	C3
Museo de Barquisimeto..18	B3

SLEEPING	
Hotel del Centro.............19	B2
Hotel Lido.......................20	B3
Hotel Príncipe.................21	C2
Hotel Yacambú.................22	D2

EATING	
El Bodegón del Centro....23	C2
Restaurant Marisquería	
Río Mar......................24	D3
Restaurant Vegetariano	
Natural Food Center... 25	B3

ENTERTAINMENT	
Ateneo de Barquisimeto..26	C3
Teatro Juáres.................27	B2

Av 20 is a proposed pedestrian boulevard & trole bus route, and is under construction

To Maracaibo (328km)

To Inparques, Policlínica de Barquisimeto (3km); Caracas (342km)

To Bus Terminal (1km); Airport (3km)

To Hospital Central Universitario Dr Antonio María Pineda (800m); Parque Zoológico y Botánico Bararida (800m); Cottulara (2.3km)

To Lancelot Hotel (1km); Posada Ibiza (1.8km); Perla Negra (1.8km) Posada La Segoviana (2km); D'Elpunto Restaurant (2km); Hotel Barquisimeto Hilton (2.5km); Círculo Restaurante (3km); Italcambio (3km)

Sights

The lovely **Plaza Bolívar**, full of splendid tall palm trees, is the birthplace of the city. The pretty **Iglesia de la Concepción** (Plaza Bolívar), on the square's southern side, was Barquisimeto's first cathedral, but it was destroyed in the earthquake of 1812 and rebuilt 30 years later in a different style.

A few steps south of the church is the **Museo de Barquisimeto** (☎ 717-1022; Carrera 15 btwn Calles 25 & 26; admission US$0.50; 🕑 9am-5pm Tue-Fri, 10am-5pm Sat & Sun) in an imposing historical building with a rectangular courtyard centered on a chapel. It was built in the 1910s as a hospital and later used for other purposes, until authorities decided to demolish it to make way for modern buildings. Thanks to public protests, though, it was restored and turned into a museum. Its rooms house various temporary exhibitions, usually interesting and well displayed, and always a surprise.

The tiny **Plaza Lara**, two blocks east of Plaza Bolívar, is the city's only area with colonial character, thanks to the restored historic buildings lining the square. It's no doubt the finest historic plaza in town and is charm-

ingly shaded with old trees. On the northern side of the plaza is the **Ateneo de Barquisimeto** (☎ 232-4655; cnr Carrera 17 & Calle 23), a busy center for cultural activities. Go in and check what's on.

The handsome **Iglesia de San Francisco** (Plaza Lara), on the southern side of the plaza, was built in 1865 and carried the distinction of being Barquisimeto's second city cathedral, until the modern **Catedral de Barquisimeto** (cnr Avs Venezuela & Simón Rodríguez) was constructed in the 1960s. It's a bold, innovative design noted for its parabolic concrete roof and a centrally located high altar. The cathedral is open only for mass (normally at 6pm weekdays, with more services on Sunday), so plan accordingly.

Parque Zoológico y Botánico Bararida (☎ 252-4774; cnr Av Los Abogados & Calle 13; admission US$1; 🕑 9am-5pm), 1.5km northeast of the center, features the botanical and zoological gardens. It's a large, relaxing park with an artificial lake and cafés, and it's worth coming here to have a close look at some of Venezuela's typical animals, such as the tapir, jaguar and capybara.

Festivals & Events

The city's biggest annual event is the **Fiestas Patronales de la Divina Pastora**. The patron saint's day is January 14, and its central feature is a solemn procession parading the image of the Virgin Mary from the shrine in Santa Rosa village into the city. The celebrations go for several days before and after the saint's day, and include agricultural fairs, concerts and sports events held in the Complejo Ferial (fairgrounds).

Sleeping

Most visitors will want to stay in the city center for good accommodations that are close to the main sights. The eastern suburbs offer the city's best lodgings, but little in the way of budget accommodations. If you're in transit and looking for a place to crash for a night, you can choose from half a dozen basic hotels in an unattractive area on the northern side of the bus terminal. But do yourself a favor and check out a few before settling in – they differ significantly in standards and rates.

Hotel del Centro (☎ 808-0378; Av 20 btwn Calles 26 & 27; d/tr with fan US$14/16, d/tr/q with air-con US$18/20/23; 🖳) Hidden among dozens of shoe shops, the Hotel del Centro is really central and just about the cheapest acceptable option in the area. Rooms are basic, but surprisingly large, and all have private bathrooms and cable TV. Some of the rooms on the upper floors provide excellent bird's-eye views of the busy commerce on the street below.

Hotel Lido (☎ 231-5568; Carrera 16 btwn Calles 26 & 27; d US$23-28, tr US$37; 🅿 🖳) The bundles of towels and room keys on the reception desk – designed to facilitate a quick entry and exit – clue you in to the popularity of this central hotel. Just one block from the Plaza Bolívar, this small place is not a Sheraton, but all rooms have air-con and bathrooms, and it isn't expensive.

Hotel Yacambú (☎ 252-6746; fax 251-3229; hotelyacambu@gmail.com; Av Vargas btwn Av 20 & Carrera 19; d/tr/ste US$37/42/75; 🖳) Nestled on a busy avenue, Yacambú has already passed its years of glory, yet it still does a rife business. Grab one of the two suites – they are noticeably better than the ordinary rooms and have balconies. The hotel has an enjoyable, inexpensive restaurant.

Lancelot Hotel (☎ 252-2021; cnr Av 20 & Calle 2; s/d/tr US$47/56/65; 🅿 🖳 🖳) You can see the mighty ramparts of this castle-themed hotel from afar. It's a comfortable place to lay aside the chain mail underwear, especially in the Jacuzzi-equipped suites. Conveniently situated midway between the center and the restaurants along Av Vargas.

Hotel Príncipe (☎ 231-2111, 231-2544; fax 231-1731; Calle 23 btwn Carreras 18 & 19; d US$61, ste US$70-75; 🅿 🖳 🖳) This big hotel has 140-plus rooms, plus an outdoor pool, restaurant and bar. It has definitely seen better days, but if everything else is full, the 'Prince' is an acceptable, central option.

Posada La Segoviana (☎ 252-8669; posadalasegoviana@hotmail.com; Calle 7 btwn Carreras 2 & 3, Urbanización Nueva Segovia; d US$63-68, tr/q/ste US$81/88/107; 🅿 🖳) This was Barquisimeto's first posada, set in a quiet residential eastern suburb, about 2km from the city center. With just nine rooms, it provides personalized service and cozy ambience, but it's often full, so book well in advance.

Posada Ibiza (☎ 267-9221; Calle 3 No 1-71; d/ste US$72/81; 🅿 🖳) This minimalist-style posada is decorated in black, white and chrome, and still shimmers with newness. Very comfortable rooms offer air-con, hot water and cable TV. There's a popular new restaurant downstairs.

Hotel Barquisimeto Hilton (☎ 710-6111; www.barquisimeto.hilton.com; Urbanización Nueva Segovia, Carrera 5 btwn Calles 5 & 6; d US$215, ste US$425; 🅿 🖳 🖳 🖳) In the same suburb as La Segoviana, the five-star Hilton provides Barquisimeto's ultimate luxuries. All the rooms have floor-to-ceiling windows and most have high-speed internet access. Facilities include a gym, an outdoor pool and a ballroom.

Eating

The city center is packed with places to eat, particularly Av Vargas and its environs and, to a lesser extent, Av 20. The best restaurants, though, are in the eastern suburbs.

Restaurant Vegetariano Natural Food Center (cnr Carrera 18 & Calle 26; meals US$3-5; 🕙 11am-4pm Mon-Fri) This popular and central vegetarian spot serves straightforward set lunches and snacks.

El Bodegón del Centro (☎ 231-6556; cnr Carrera 19 & Calle 21; mains US$5-12; 🕙 11am-11pm Mon-Sat) This *tasca*-style restaurant with a large bar in the middle and dark-wood furniture does solid, stick-to-your-ribs food, but ignore the menu and ask for the special of the day instead.

Perla Negra (☎ 267-9221; Calle 3 No 1-71; mains US$8-17; 🕙 11am-11pm) Perla Negra is a hip new

'Restaurant and Pub' that has a good smell in the air and was packed out when we were there, just a few short months after opening. It serves up wicked portions of steak, pasta and fish, and the bar invites you to linger long after your meal.

Restaurant Marisquería Río Mar (☎ 252-2702; Calle 17 btwn Carreras 17 & 18; mains US$9-17; ⏲ 11:30am-9pm) Río Mar is one of the best seafood eateries in town. The interior looks pretty ordinary, but the food is first class and fresh. Try the *canoa de mariscos* (seafood with pineapple) or *paella marinera*.

Círculo Restaurante (☎ 254-0975; Urbanización El Parral, Centro Empresarial Proa; mains US$9-22; ⏲ noon-3pm & 7-11pm Mon-Sat) This smart restaurant, with a modern, scarcely decorated interior, offers creative and delicious dishes combining Italian and French cuisine, and has a sushi bar.

D'Elpunto Restaurant (☎ 254-8367; Urbanización Nueva Segovia, cnr Carrera 1 & Calle 4; mains US$10-17; ⏲ noon-3pm & 7-10:30pm Mon-Sat, noon-4:30pm Sun) D'Elpunto serves what they call *comida creativa* (creative food). The waiters will be happy to explain the intricacies, but if you still have doubts about what to choose, probably the best bet is to order the *menú de degustación* (US$14), which features samples of seven different creations by the chef.

Entertainment

Ateneo de Barquisimeto (☎ 232-4655; cnr Carrera 17 & Calle 23), on Plaza Lara, is a busy center of cultural activities, including musical works and changing art exhibitions.

Teatro Juáres (☎ 231-6743; cnr Carrera 19 & Calle 25) is the city's main theater center and it hosts other cultural events as well, including music performances.

Getting There & Away

AIR

The **Aeropuerto Jacinto Lara** (☎ 441-9940; Av Vicente Landaeta) is 4km southwest of the center. The Ruta 7 city bus runs between the bus terminal and the airport, or you can take a taxi (US$5). Flights to and from Barquisimeto are serviced by **Aeropostal** (☎ 231-1176, 442-4317) and **Santa Bárbara** (☎ 443-1224).

There are several departures a day to Caracas (US$95 to US$120), and Santa Bárbara has one direct flight daily to Maracaibo (US$140). To other destinations, you need to go via either Caracas or Maracaibo.

BUS

Barquisimeto straddles an important crossroads, with roads and buses leading in all directions. The large and busy **Terminal de Pasajeros** (☎ 442-2189; cnr Av Rómulo Gallegos & Carrera 24), 2km northwest of the center, is linked by frequent city buses to the center and other districts. At time of research a new bus terminal was being built, including a connection to the trole bus line that will run down Av 20.

Buses depart regularly throughout the day to Valencia (US$4 to US$5, three hours, 183km), Maracaibo (US$8.25, five hours, 328km), Barinas (US$6.75, 4½ hours, 258km), Guanare (US$5, 3½ hours, 173km), Valera (US$5.50, four hours, 243km) and Caracas (US$10 to US$13, 5½ hours, 341km). Half a dozen buses depart nightly to Mérida (US$14 to US$18, eight hours, 449km) and San Cristóbal (US$15 to US$19, nine hours, 521km). Buses to Coro (US$12, seven hours, 418km) go every two to three hours. Buses within the region (to Quíbor, El Tocuyo, Sanare and Chivacoa) run frequently.

CHIVACOA
☎ 0251 / pop 46,000

Chivacoa, 58km east of Barquisimeto on the road to Valencia, is the jumping-off point for Cerro de María Lionza, the holy mountain that is home to the cult of María Lionza (see the boxed text opposite). As such, Chivacoa boasts a number of *perfumerías* selling everything imaginable related to the cult. Don't miss browsing through these shops to get a taste of the phenomenon – it's a unique and striking experience! Note the huge amounts of cigars and candles – indispensable ritual accessories – and hundreds of strange essences, perfumes and lotions. Have a look at the books and brochures dealing with magic, witchcraft and foretelling, and get familiar with the cult's pantheon, as every *perfumería* has a complete stock of plaster figures of the deities in every size and color.

Sleeping & Eating

In Chivacoa there a few places to stay and most have their own restaurants.

Hotel Venezia (☎ 883-0544; Centro Comercial Venezia, cnr Calle 12 & Av 9; s/d/tr/q US$10/16/21/26; P ⌘) Marginally better – and cheaper – than the rest, all the rooms in this brightly colored hotel have private bath and air-con. The hotel surrounds a pleasant courtyard of small shops, including a yummy pizza restaurant and bar – a refreshing place to sit and relax in the evening, when a cooling breeze moderates the day's heat.

Hotel Abruzzese (☎ 883-0419; Av 9 btwn Calles 10 & 11; d with fan US$12, d with air-con US$16-18, tr with air-con US$23; P ⊠) A block from Plaza Bolívar, Abruzzese has neat rooms with private facilities. Ask the friendly staff for a room with a balcony.

Hotel El Lucitano (☎ 883-0366; cnr Calle 10 & Av 12; s/d/tr US$14/19/23 ⊠) Not the most central location, but still a cheap, acceptable option. All rooms have private bathrooms and air-con, and a reasonable *tasca*-style restaurant lurks downstairs.

Getting There & Away

Plenty of buses run between Barquisimeto and Valencia or San Felipe, all of which call in at the Chivacoa bus terminal. There are also direct buses from Barquisimeto to Chivacoa, marked 'Chivacoa Directo' (US$2.10, one hour, 58km), as well as por puestos (US$3.40, 45 minutes). To get into Chivacoa from the terminal take por puesto Ruta 4.

CERRO DE MARÍA LIONZA

The Cult of María Lionza counts an ever-growing number of devotees in not only Venezuela, but also Colombia, Puerto Rico and the Dominican Republic. Its most sacred area – and the focus for pilgrimages – is the mountain range referred to as the Cerro de María Lionza, south of Chivacoa. Devotees come here year-round, mostly on weekends, to practice their rites. The biggest celebrations are held on October 12 (Discovery of America) and during Semana Santa (Holy Week), when thousands of people cram themselves into this tiny place, where screaming in tongues and walking on fire and broken glass sometimes take place.

The cult first became famous in the 1950s when Venezuelan dictator General Jiménez was a worshipper, and when Panamanian salsa singer Ruben Blades wrote a song about her in the 1970s, she hit the international big time.

The followers have built several sanctuaries along the northern foothills of the mountains, where they flock before heading up the slopes. The most important of these are Sorte and Quiballo (or Quibayo). Both have their own altar mayor (high altar), where the initial celebrations are performed, before the group and its medium head off to the shrine of their choice – one of many that are scattered over the forested rugged land. It's at these shrines where the proper rites are performed, which may last the whole night or longer and usually include a trance séance.

Cerro de María Lionza is part of a much larger mountain formation known as the Macizo de Nirgua. Covered with thick rainforest, the range is rich in endemic species. In 1960, Inparques declared the 117-sq-km area as the Monumento Natural María Lionza, in an attempt to protect the region from overuse by

---

THAT VOODOO THAT YOU DO – CULT OF MARÍA LIONZA

A striking amalgam of native indigenous creeds, African voodoo and Christian practices, the cult of María Lionza involves magic, witchcraft, esoteric rites and trance rituals.

The cult is pantheistic and involves a constellation of deities, spirits and other personalities with very diverse origins. At the top of the hierarchy is María Lionza, a female deity usually portrayed as a beautiful woman riding a tapir. One story of her origin tells of a woman from a dark-skinned tribe who gave birth to a light-skinned, green-eyed girl of surpassing beauty. The girl grew up to be venerated by her tribe and, eventually, by the surrounding peoples. As the years passed, her life became the stuff of legends and ever since she has been revered by her devoted followers.

Often referred to as La Reina (Queen), María Lionza is followed by countless divinities – historical and legendary personages, saints and powers of nature – usually grouped into *cortes* (courts). The list of the most popular deities includes Cacique Guaicaipuro, the Virgen de Coromoto, Negro Felipe and Dr José Gregorio Hernández, and you'll even find Simón Bolívar.

Few serious studies of the cult have been conducted, so many of its aspects, such as its origins or doctrines, are still obscure. What is clear, however, is that the cult attracts more and more followers every year and spiritual centers proliferate in cities throughout the country. The 'guides,' or intermediaries, who run these centers claim to be able to communicate with deities and spirits, heal the sick, tell the future and the like.

the cult's followers. However, the religious significance of the place overshadows its natural wealth.

Quiballo

Not really much of a town, Quiballo is just a collection of several dozen shabby shacks that are either *perfumerías* or basic places to eat. The high altar – really, little more than a shack itself – sits on the riverbank, and shelters a bizarre collection of images – figures of Bolívar, various indigenous caciques, and numerous statues of María Lionza herself.

Come on the weekend, or during a holiday period, if you can, when you can join the faithful as they sit in front of the altar, smoke cigars and light candles.

Quiballo is far larger than Sorte, and has both the Inparques office and a Guarda Nacionál post, and seems to be more accustomed to casual visitors. However, it's not a tourist spot by any definition. Behave sensibly and modestly, and don't openly use your camera, which may arouse hostile reactions from cult believers.

Hiking Cerro de María Lionza

From the Quiballo altar, a path goes over the bridge to the opposite bank of the river (in which the faithful perform ritual ablutions) and then splits into a maze of paths that wind up the mountain, some climbing to the very top. All along the paths are *portales* (gates), shrines dedicated to particular deities or spirits. On the top are Las Tres Casitas (Three Little Houses) of María Lionza, Negro Felipe and Cacique Guaicaipuro. Technically, the trip to the top can be done in less than three hours. In practice, though, it may take far, far longer, for various reasons.

Followers of the cult point out that the trip is full of drawbacks and dangers. At each portal you have to ask the appropriate spirit for permission to pass. This is done by smoking cigars, lighting candles and presenting offerings. Permission may or may not be granted. Various devotees commented that they had tried on various occasions and hadn't succeeded. Those who continue on without permission may be punished by the spirits. Some, local stories claim, have never returned.

The Inparques staff members have a far more pragmatic standpoint. They don't recommend the trip to the top because of muddy paths, snakes and the possibility of getting lost.

An additional problem is that, like any other place with crowds of people, this one attracts thieves. Robberies have been reported by visitors. Try not to venture too far on your own and keep your wits about you. If you're desperate to go to the top, consider taking a guide, for both safety and orientation. Some locals in Quiballo may accompany you. The question of to what degree you comply with the spirits' wishes is up to you.

Wandering around, especially on weekends, you may come across a group of faithful practicing their rituals. Keep away unless you're invited or unless you are with a guide who will introduce you.

Sleeping & Eating

There are no hotels in either Sorte or Quiballo, but you can camp in a tent or sling a hammock on the river bank as the pilgrims do. If this is the case, never leave your tent and belongings unattended. It's much better to hang your hammock in a cabaña in Quiballo for a small fee. You won't starve at the shack restaurants, but their offerings are mostly basic.

Getting There & Away

Jeeps and vans to Quiballo (US$0.90, 20 minutes, 8km) depart when full from Chivacoa's Plaza Bolívar. They run regularly on weekends, but there may be only a few departures on weekdays. Jeeps to Sorte (US$1.40, 15 minutes, 6km) are even less frequent. The jeeps travel 4km south on a paved road to the María Lionza roadside altar, then turn right onto a rough road and continue through sugarcane plantations for another 4km to Quiballo. The road to Sorte branches off to the left 1km past the altar.

QUÍBOR

☎ 0253 / pop 42,000

This swiftly growing satellite town, 35km southwest of Barquisimeto, is a thriving folkart and craft center. It's also worth stopping here to have a look at the pre-Columbian indigenous heritage of the region.

Sights

The **Cementerio Indígena de Quíbor** (cnr Av 8 & Calle 12), just off the Plaza Florencio Jiménez, is a pre-Hispanic cemetery accidentally discovered in 1965. Numerous tombs and more than 26,000 pottery pieces have been excavated in what is thought to be a burial ground for tribal elders of an aboriginal community that lived here around the 3rd century AD. It's Venezuela's most important discovery of this kind.

Most of the finds from the graveyard are now on display in the **Museo Antropológico de Quíbor** (☎ 491-3781; cnr Calle 12 & Av 10; admission free; ⏰ 9am-4pm Tue-Sun), two blocks north of Plaza Bolívar. The collection includes indigenous tombs, funerary urns, mortuary offerings and a lot of pottery.

One of the oldest colonial relics, dating from the town's foundation in 1620, is the **Ermita de Nuestra Señora de Altagracia** (Calle 13 btwn Av 19 & Av 20), a fortress-like church on the northern edge of Quíbor. The large **Iglesia de Nuestra Señora de Altagracia** (Plaza Bolívar) is also named after the patron saint, but was only built in 1808 and was reconstructed after the earthquake of 1881.

The best place to see (and buy) crafts is the **Centro de Acopio Artesanal** (cnr Av Rotaria & Cubiro road; ⏰ 9am-5pm), a large craft center 1km southeast of Quíbor. The center stocks crafts made in Quíbor and in the nearby towns and villages, such as Tintorero, Guadalupe, Cubiro and Sanare.

Sleeping & Eating

Quíbor has two places to stay and one of them has its own restaurant.

Hotel El Gran Duque (☎ 491-0149; Av Florencio Jiménez; d with fan US$8-10, d with air-con US$12-14; ❄) Next to La Ceiba gas station, at the entrance to the town from Barquisimeto, this inexpensive hotel does not have a romantic location, but otherwise is OK, and all its 22 rooms have private facilities.

Hostería Valle de Quíbor (☎ 491-0601; cnr Av 5 & Calle 7; d US$32; Ⓟ ❄ 🏊) Four blocks southeast of Plaza Bolívar, this is the best place to stay in town. Occupying large grounds that give a feeling of a country location, the Hostería offers 33 comfortable rooms in a two-story hotel building and a further 40 rooms in bungalows. All rooms have private bathrooms, hot water and air-con, and you can have tasty, inexpensive meals at the hotel's prepossessing restaurant beside the pool.

Getting There & Away

Buses between Barquisimeto and Quíbor run frequently from 6am to 6pm (US$0.90, 45 minutes, 35km). There are also por puestos (US$1.50, 30 minutes). In Barquisimeto, they depart from the bus terminal; in Quíbor, they line up at the corner of Av 6 and Calle 12, one long block south of Plaza Bolívar. Buses to El Tocuyo run along Av 7, lining Plaza Bolívar.

EL TOCUYO

☎ 0253 / pop 54,000

The glorious days of El Tocuyo, 30km southwest of Quíbor, are still palpable in the ruins of colonial churches, in the museums and in the stories of old inhabitants. Referred to as the 'Mother City of Venezuela,' this was once a wealthy town and Venezuela's capital. Devastated by an earthquake in 1950, El Tocuyo is today not much more than an ordinary modern city, yet it's worth coming to see what's left of the past.

History

Founded in 1545 in a verdant valley of the Río Tocuyo, Nuestra Señora de la Pura y Limpia Concepción del Tocuyo swiftly developed into one of Venezuela's most important towns. It was established 200km back from the coast, but had access to the sea via a navigable river. Just two years after its foundation, the authorities moved the seat of government here from Coro, and the town became the province's capital for the next 30 years. Splendid colonial churches and mansions popped up and the city was a starting point for expeditions to explore and settle the colony. Barquisimeto and Caracas were founded from El Tocuyo.

In 1577 the capital was transferred to Caracas, but El Tocuyo continued to expand, taking advantage of its fertile soil that's ideal for growing sugarcane and a variety of vegetables. It was here that the Spanish first introduced sugarcane to the continent, and the crop could be harvested year-round thanks to favorable climatic conditions.

Unfortunately, a serious earthquake in 1950 ruined all seven colonial churches and a good number of opulent public buildings. The job was completed by Colonel Marcos Pérez Jiménez, Venezuela's dictator at the time. On his orders, most of the damaged structures were demolished and a new town was built on the site. El Tocuyo is now a modern town with just a handful of restored or reconstructed historic buildings.

Sights

The **Iglesia de Nuestra Señora de la Concepción** (Carrera 11 btwn Calles 17 & 18) is the town's most important monument. The church was badly

THE NORTHWEST

damaged in the 1950 earthquake and, like most other buildings, it was bulldozed – despite the fact that it could have been repaired. It was later reconstructed and its whitewashed exterior is noted for its unusual bell tower and fine facade. Inside, the extraordinary retable from the 1760s (which miraculously survived the earthquake) takes up the whole wall behind the high altar. Like almost all altarpieces of the period, it was carved entirely out of wood but, unusually, was not painted or gilded; it's the only one of its kind in the country. The church is open only for religious services, normally held at 6pm on weekdays, with more masses on Sunday. If you can't make it to the service, go to the Casa Parroquial beside the church, and someone is likely to let you in.

None of the other colonial churches were restored or reconstructed, but two were left in ruins, untouched from the day of the earthquake: the **Iglesia de Santo Domingo** (cnr Carrera 10 & Calle 19), and the **Iglesia de Belén** (Carrera 12 btwn Calles 15 & 17). One of the few buildings that somehow withstood the quake is the **Convento de San Francisco** (Plaza Bolívar), though the adjacent church didn't make it. Today the building is occupied by the Casa de la Cultura – go inside to see its spacious two-story arcaded courtyard.

El Tocuyo has two small museums, both related to the town's history. The **Museo Arqueológico JM Cruxent** (Plaza Bolívar; admission free; 8am-4pm Mon-Fri) has a small collection of pre-Hispanic pottery, photos depicting the damage by the 1950 earthquake, and regional crafts. Note the remains of a 30m-long steam riverboat from around 1850, proving that the Río Tocuyo was navigable for large vessels.

The **Museo Lisandro Alvarado** (Calle 17 btwn Carreras 10 & 11; admission free; 9am-noon & 2-5:30pm Mon-Fri), named after the locally born politician, doctor and anthropologist, features old maps, documents, paintings and etchings and a variety of historic objects. Watch out for an amazing old bell from the no-longer-existing San Francisco Church.

Sleeping & Eating

Posada Colonial (☎ 663-0025; Av Fraternidad btwn Calles 17 & 18; d/tr/q US$23/28/33; P X 🏊) The most enjoyable and central place to stay, a stone's throw from Plaza Bolívar, this colonial-style posada has 24 neat rooms and a pool in the garden surrounded by coconut palms. Ask for one of the rooms upstairs, which have balconies.

If the posada can't accommodate you for some reason, there are two marginally cheaper but less attractive options:

Hotel Venezia (☎ 663-1267; cnr Calle Comercio & Carrera 9)

Hotel Nazaret (☎ 663-2434; Av Fraternidad btwn Calles 7 & 8)

Getting There & Away

Buses between Barquisimeto and El Tocuyo (US$1.60, 1¼ hours, 65km) run at least every half-hour until about 6pm. There are also por puestos (US$2.10, one hour).

SANARE

☎ 0253 / pop 18,000

This refreshingly cool holiday spot sits high above the heat of the plains, and its curving, twisting mountain streets, awash in greenery and dotted with flowerpots, leave little doubt why the town bears the nickname the 'Garden of Lara.' Founded in 1620, it boasts some fine historic architecture and a handsome parish church, the three-nave Iglesia de Santa Ana. It's surrounded by forested hills and is the gateway to the Parque Nacional Yacambú.

Information

The **Instituto de Turismo de Municipio** (☎ 449-0139; Plaza Bolívar; 8:30am-3:30pm Mon-Fri) is in the *alcaldia* (town hall).

Sleeping & Eating

Sanare has at least half a dozen places to stay and most have their own restaurants.

Hotel Taburiente (☎ 449-0148; Av Miranda; d/tr/q US$19/28/37) Nestled right behind the church, this neat and very central 21-room hotel is a good deal and it, too, has its own restaurant.

Posada Turística El Cerrito (☎ 449-0016; Calle Providencia; d/tr/q US$28/30/37) About 500m south of Plaza Bolívar (take Calle 17 from the square), this is a charming and stylish place. Built in a colonial style, the posada has 14 rooms (with bathrooms) lining a patio, plus a budget restaurant.

Hotel La Fumarola (☎ 449-0754; Sector Palo Verde; tr US$51; P 🏊) Probably the most comfortable option, La Fumarola is 3km north of Sanare on the road to Quíbor. It has cabañas, a restaurant and a pool.

Getting There & Away

Minibuses run regularly between Barquisimeto and Sanare (US$1.70, 1¼ hours, 57km) until midafternoon.

PARQUE NACIONAL YACAMBÚ

At the northern end of the Andean massif, this park reaches elevations of up to 2200m and has Venezuela's only active volcano, locally called La Fumarola after the cloud of smoke that floats over it. This park protects a 270-sq-km chunk of the mountain range known as the Sierra de Portuguesa, southeast of Sanare.

Most of the area is covered with cloud forest with plant species typical of the Andes, many of which are endemic. About 60 species of orchid have been recorded. There haven't been any detailed studies of the fauna, but it is remarkably rich and includes rare, endangered mammals such as the *oso frontino* (spectacled bear) and jaguar. The park is particularly good for bird-watchers.

Yacambú is an important water resource for the region and there's a large reservoir, the Embalse Yacambú, formed by a dam built just south of the park. The rainy period is from April to November; in higher areas the mean annual rainfall reaches 3000mm.

Orientation

Access to the park is from Sanare by the 30km road that goes to the dam. This road crosses the park and passes near the Inparques administrative center at El Blanquito, about 20km from Sanare. The rangers here can give you information about the walks and sights, including *miradores* (lookout points), waterfalls and the Cañón de Angostura, the gorge formed by the Río Negro.

Sleeping

The park provides accommodations in four 12-bed cabins and a 70-bed house (normally used by large tour groups) in El Blanquito, but you need to pay for the whole cabin (US$17) or house (US$98), not just the beds you're going to use. You need to bring your own sheets and a sleeping bag is recommended. There is a simple kitchen, but no food is available in El Blanquito. Camping is allowed for US$2 per tent. You should book cabins several days in advance at the Inparques office (p161) in Barquisimeto. Payment for both cabins and camping has to be made at a bank before you go – Inparques will give you details.

Getting There & Away

There doesn't seem to be a regular form of public transportation to the park other than occasional por puestos from Sanare. Negotiate the ride with drivers in Sanare.

CARORA

☎ 0252 / pop 95,000

This colorful, slumbering colonial town was founded in 1569 and has preserved much of its colonial architecture, despite several serious floods, the last in 1973. The historic center has been restored and is a charming place, particularly Plaza Bolívar, which is one of Venezuela's most amazing plazas.

Carora's main claim to fame, however, is its wine – Venezuela's best – and you can visit the vineyards and wineries, and see the whole production process. Though commercial production only began in 1990, the wine has already won international medals.

Information

INTERNET ACCESS

Ciber El Rincón de la Amistad (Plaza Torres)
Zona Ciber (cnr Av Francisco de Miranda & Calle 22)

MONEY

Banco de Venezuela (cnr Av Francisco de Miranda & Calle 20)
Banco Provincial (cnr Av 14 de Febrero & Carrera Lara)
Banesco (cnr Carrera Lara & Calle Rivas)

TELEPHONE

CANTV (Av 14 de Febrero btwn Carreras Lara & Bolívar) Also has internet.

TOURIST INFORMATION

Centro de Información y Atención Turística (Av Francisco de Miranda; ⊙ 8am-noon & 2-5pm Mon-Fri, 8am-3pm Sat & Sun) It's in a kiosk in front of the bus terminal.

Sights

The historic quarter, centered on the postcardlike Plaza Bolívar and populated with elegant tall palm trees, is neat, well kept and colonial in style, even though not all the buildings date from that period. Have a look at the mid-17th-century **Casa Amarilla** (Plaza Bolívar), Carora's oldest surviving building, now a public library, and **El Balcón de los Álvarez** (Plaza Bolívar), a two-story 18th-century house where Simón Bolívar stayed in 1821. The **Casa de Juan Jacinto Lara** (cnr Calle San Juan &

Carrera Torres) is the birthplace of the hero of the War of Independence, who gave his name to the state.

The town has some fine colonial churches. The main one, the mid-17th-century **Iglesia de San Juan Bautista** (Plaza Bolívar) shelters an amazing, richly gilded main retable dating from 1760. The church is only open in the late afternoon, but if you turn up at any other reasonable time of the day, enquire in the Casa Parroquial, right behind the church, and someone is likely to open it for you.

The **Capilla San Dionisio** (cnr Carrera Torres & Calle Comercio) dates from 1743. It's used only for special ceremonies, such as funerals, and is closed at other times. About 300m northeast of San Dionisio, in the middle of arid woodland, is the striking ruin of the **Iglesia de la Purísima Concepción**, commonly referred to as the 'Portal de la Pastora.' You'll get a good view of the ruin from the dike at the end of Calle Comercio.

The **Capilla del Calvario** (cnr Carrera El Calvario & Calle Comercio) has a beautiful facade, a fine example of local baroque. Its simple interior features an interesting main retable, plus two side retables

on both walls. The chapel is often open in the morning, but if it's locked, the keys are kept in Casa Parroquial.

Sleeping

Hotel Parrilla Barí (☎ 421-6745; Av 14 de Febrero; d with fan/air-con US$12/$15, tr US$19; P 🞧) One of the cheapest central shelters, Barí is basic but acceptable and all of its 13 rooms have private facilities. Choose a room away from the busy road.

El Rincón del Bogavante (☎ 0416-652-0288; Plaza Torres; d/tr/ste US$16/21/24; 🞧) Bean bags in all the rooms send this new hotel's grooviness quotient through the roof. Comfortable and very central, they also offer a solid *tasca* downstairs, plus there's an internet café next door.

Hotel Irpinia (☎ 421-6362; cnr Carrera Lara & Av 14 de Febrero; d/tr/q US$22/26/29; P 🞧) Another convenient place in the center, Irpinia has 36 neat, spacious rooms with bathrooms and air-con; take one facing the inner courtyard – they are quieter.

Hotel Katuca (☎ 421-3310; Av Francisco de Miranda; d/tr/q/ste US$27/29/32/45; P 🞧) Just 300m from the bus terminal, Katuca is convenient for

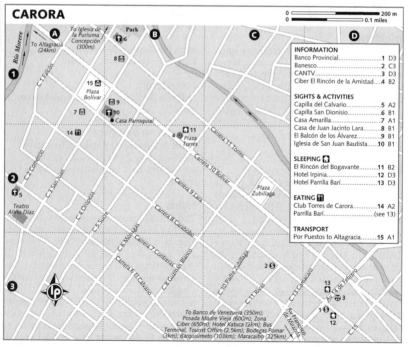

THE NORTHWEST

CARORA

0 —————— 200 m
0 —————— 0.1 miles

WHEN THE TROPICS MEAN WINE

Venezuela has almost no wine tradition, but this is slowly changing at **Bodegas Pomar** (☎ 421-2191, 421-2225; www.bodegaspomar.com.ve; Carretera Lara-Zulia), 3km south of Carora city center, where the country's best wine is produced. It comes in 17 varieties and is marketed under the Viña Altagracia label for distribution throughout the country.

Bodegas Pomar takes you through the whole production process, from sorting the grapes to packing the final product into cardboard boxes. Grapes come from the 125-hectare vineyard in the village of Altagracia (hence the wine's brand name), 24km northwest of Carora. Altagracia's climate is a harmonious blend of low humidity, good sunlight, warm days and fresh nights year-round, so the crop can be harvested twice a year (in March and September).

There's three weeks of festivities each harvest time and you can visit Bodegas Pomar then. They offer a variety of tours to suit all budgets (although commentary is in Spanish only). During harvest time, their basic facility tour and wine tasting starts at 9am (Monday to Friday) lasts two hours and costs US$15; they also offer a four-hour tour (Tuesday to Friday) for US$25.

For those wanting more frills, full-day tour packages, including lunch and a more expansive wine tasting, are available for US$80; US$105 gets you breakfast as well. They also offer two-day packages, including the Fiesta de la Vendimia or Wine Harvest Party, which gets you two days of wine tastings, meals prepared by guest chefs, harvest blessing, hot-air balloon flight (weather permitting) and the chance to turn your feet purple in the grape vats. Two-day visits range from US$150 to US$250 per person, transportation and accommodations not included.

The precise dates of the festivities vary each year, so contact them ahead of time. Anything but the most basic of tours should be booked and paid for in advance through the Caracas **office** (☎ 0212-202-8907, clubpomar@empresas-polar.com).

If you haven't got your own wheels, you can take a taxi there, or share one of the por puestos to Altagracia, which depart infrequently from Plaza Bolívar.

buses, but not much more. Otherwise, it's a pleasant place, with a large leafy garden, 34 decent rooms and its own restaurant.

Posada Madre Vieja (☎ 421-2590; Av Francisco de Miranda; d/tr/q US$33/38/47; P ☒) Set in spacious garden-like grounds, Madre Vieja offers 16 fair-sized rooms in a two-story building away from the noisy road and has an enjoyable restaurant in a palm-leaf thatched *churuata*.

Eating

Parrilla Barí (☎ 421-6745; Av 14 de Febrero; meals US$4-8) The restaurant of Hotel Parilla Barí looks extremely basic, yet the food is OK, portions are generous and none of its 40-plus dishes cost more than US$8.

Club Torres de Carora (☎ 421-3410; Calle San Juan btwn Carreras Carabobo & Lara; mains US$7-10; ☒ noon-3pm & 7pm-11 Wed-Mon) Most facilities (including a swimming pool) in this great rambling colonial mansion are for members only, but the restaurant is open to all and is excellent value.

Getting There & Away

Carora is located about 3km north off the Barquisimeto–Maracaibo freeway. The **Ter-minal de Pasajeros** (Av Francisco de Miranda) is on the southeastern outskirts of town, about 600m northwest off the freeway. The terminal is linked to the town's center by city mini-buses.

Carora has half-hourly buseta connections with Barquisimeto (US$3.20, 1½ hours, 103km), and there are also por puestos (US$5, 1¼ hours). It's an interesting trip on a good autopista (freeway) across arid, hilly countryside. Ordinary buses to Maracaibo (US$7.90, 3½ hours, 225km) come through from Barquisimeto every hour. To Caracas (US$12 to US$17, seven hours, 444km), buses come through from Maracaibo; it may be faster to go to Barquisimeto and change there.

ZULIA STATE

MARACAIBO

☎ 0261 / pop 2 million

Perhaps Maracaibo holds the key to understanding the puzzle that is Venezuela. This is where the oil comes from and the wealth that seems to touch on every aspect of national life. Here we find a once-colorful Caribbean village dunked in a sea of oil, coated in a vast sea of concrete, and somewhere, lurking beneath that painful skin of modernity, a fun-loving Caribbean soul, that maybe, just maybe, pangs for yesteryear and the uncomplicated life the oil took away.

Stroll about the old town, if you have a day or two, and sit in the shade of the leafy plazas, enjoying a fresh icy *coco frio*. Wander through Las Pulgas – the flea market – getting lost in the seemingly endless variety of hawkers and sellers and merchants of all sorts. But at night, stick to the new town, for safety's sake, and for the myriad restaurants to be found there, where Maracaibo's oases of pleasure cluster, as though seeking refuge from the littered, barren streets.

Maracaibo is also one of the few places in Venezuela where you might catch sight of the indigenous Guajiro people, some of the very few to have kept to their traditional dress and customs. Maracaibo is Venezuela's only city with any significant indigenous community.

Founded as a trading post in 1574, Maracaibo was a backwater on the shores of the vast Lago de Maracaibo, until 1914, when drillers struck oil. By the late 1920s Venezuela came to be the world's largest exporter of oil, the Saudi Arabia of South America, while Maracaibo developed into the country's oil capital, with two-thirds of the nation's output coming from beneath the lake. Today, it's the capital of Zulia, Venezuela's richest state, and an important port. The *maracuchos*, as local inhabitants are called, feel they are producing the money that the rest of the country is spending, and Zulia state (at the time of writing) was the only state without a pro-Chávez state government.

Maracaibo is a sweltering stop for travelers on the way to or from Colombia's Caribbean coast. Stay a day or two to visit some of the city's icons, including the old holy basilica and the brightly painted restored houses on Calle Carabobo.

With a few more days up your sleeve, it's well worth exploring the city environs noted for a colorful blend of tradition and modernity. In particular, be sure to make a detour to see the old *palafitos* on the shores of Laguna de Sinamaica. Five hundred years ago, Spanish sailors saw these over-water houses on stilts and named the place 'Little Venice' – Venezuela.

Orientation

Maracaibo is a big metropolis with vast suburbs, but the tourist focus is on the central districts. Generally speaking, these encompass the historic center to the south and the new center to the north. Getting between the two is easy and fast, so it doesn't really matter much where you stay. The new center, however, offers a far better choice of hotels, restaurants and other facilities, and it's safer at night. The old quarter boasts more sights, but they can all be visited on one or two leisurely daytime trips.

Information

EMERGENCY
Fire (☎ 171)
Police (☎ 171)

INTERNET ACCESS
Cyber Place (Map p177; Av 8 btwn Calles 72 & 73)
Cyber Zone (Map p173; Local PNC 17A, Centro Comercial Lago Mall, Av El Milagro)
en red cyber café (Map p177; Av 5 de Julio btwn Avs 3H & 3Y)
Postnet (Map p177; Av Bella Vista btwn Calles 69 & 70)

MEDICAL SERVICES
Hospital Central (Map p175; ☎ 722-6404; Av El Milagro btwn Calles 94 & 95)

MONEY
Major banks in Maracaibo have plenty of branches and the city also has a few *casas de cambio*.
Banco de Venezuela Historic Center (Map p175; cnr Av 5 & Calle 97); New Center (Map p177; cnr Av Bella Vista & Calle 74)
Banco Mercantil New Center (Map p177; cnr Av Bella Vista & Calle 67)
Banco Provincial Historic Center (Map p175; cnr Av El Milagro & Calle 97); New Center (Map p177; cnr Av Bella Vista & Calle 74)
Banesco New Center (Map p177; cnr Av Bella Vista & Calle 71)
Casa de Cambio Maracaibo New Center (Map p177; ☎ 797-2576; Av 9B btwn Calles 77 & 78); Av El Milagro (Map p173; ☎ 792-2174; Centro Comercial Lago Mall, Av El Milagro).
Corp Banca Historic Center (Map p175; cnr Av Libertador & Av 14); New Center (Map p177; cnr Av Bella Vista & Calle 67)
Italcambio Airport (☎ 736-2513); Av 20 (Map p173; ☎ 783-2040; Centro Comercial Montielco, cnr Av 20 & Calle 72); Av El Milagro (Map p173; ☎ 793-2983; Centro Comercial Lago Mall, Av El Milagro)

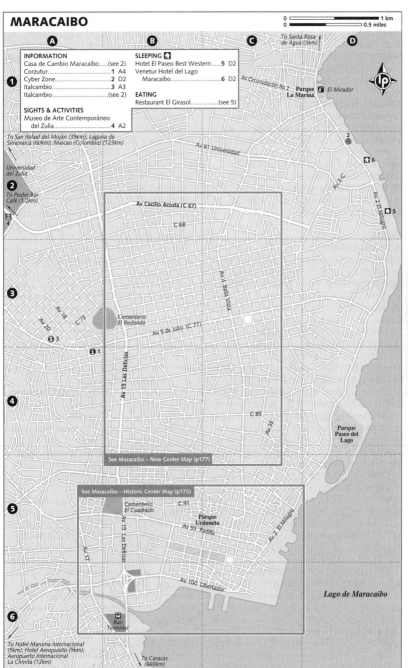

MARACAIBO

0 ——————— 1 km
0 ——————— 0.5 miles

INFORMATION
Casa de Cambio Maracaibo.....(see 2)
Corzutur..................................**1** A4
Cyber Zone.............................**2** D2
Italcambio...............................**3** A3
Italcambio...............................(see 2)

SIGHTS & ACTIVITIES
Museo de Arte Contemporáneo
   del Zulia..............................**4** A2

SLEEPING
Hotel El Paseo Best Western......**5** D2
Venetur Hotel del Lago
   Maracaibo...........................**6** D2

EATING
Restaurant El Girasol...............(see 5)

To Santa Rosa
de Agua (3km)

Av Circunvalación No 2

Parque
La Marina   El Mirador

To San Rafael del Moján (39km); Laguna de
Sinamaica (60km); Maicao (Colombia) (123km)

Av 61 Universidad

Universidad
del Zulia

Av 3 C

Av 2 El Milagro

To Poster Bar
Café (1.2km)

Av Cecilio Acosta (C 67)

C 68

Av 4 Bella Vista

Cementerio
El Redondo

Av 5 de Julio (C 71)

Av 18

C 73

Av 20

Av 15 Las Delicias

C 85

Av 3 E

See Maracaibo – New Center Map (p177)

See Maracaibo – Historic Center Map (p175)

Cementerio
El Cuadrado

C 91

Parque
Urdaneta

Av 15 Las Delicias

Av 93 Padilla

Av 2 El Milagro

Av 17

Av 100 Libertador

Parque
Paseo del
Lago

Lago de Maracaibo

Bus
Terminal

To Hotel Maruma Internacional
(5km); Hotel Aeropuerto (9km);
Aeropuerto Internacional
La Chinita (12km)

To Caracas
(669km)

THE NORTHWEST

lonelyplanet.com

TELEPHONE

CANTV (Map p175; Local 43, Centro Comercial Plaza Lago, Av Libertador)

Movistar Bus Terminal (Map p175; Av 17); Centro Comercial La Redoma (Map p175; Local 52-53, Av Libertador); Paseo Ciencias (Map p175; Calle 96 No 10K-29)

TOURIST INFORMATION

Corpozulia (Corporación de Desarrollo de la Región Zuliana; Map p177; ☎ 794-9424; www.corpozulia.gov .ve; Edificio Corpozulia, Av Bella Vista btwn Calles 83 & 84; ☑ 8am-4pm Mon-Fri) Located 2km north of the historic center, accessible by the Bella Vista por puestos.

Corzutur (Corporación Zuliana de Turismo; Map p173; ☎ 783-4928; www.zuliaturistica.com; Edificio Lieja, cnr Av 18 & Calle 78; ☑ 8am-4pm Mon-Fri) Located 2km northwest of the historic center.

Sights

HISTORIC CENTER

The historic center boasts most of the tourist sights, a short walk from each other. The axis of this sector is the **Paseo de las Ciencias**, a seven-block-long greenbelt laid out after the demolition of the colonial buildings that formed the core of Maracaibo's oldest quarter, El Saladillo. This controversial plan, executed in 1973, effectively cut the very heart out of the old town. The only structure not pulled down was the blue-colored neo-Gothic **Iglesia de Santa Bárbara** (Map p175; cnr Av 8 & Calle 95).

At the western end of the Paseo is the **Basílica de Chiquinquirá** (p175), which features opulent interior decor. In the high altar is the venerated image of the Virgin of Chiquinquirá, affectionately referred to as La Chinita. Legend has it that the image of the Virgin, painted on a small wooden board, was found in 1709 by a humble campesina) on the shore of Lago de Maracaibo. Upon being brought to her home, the image began to glow. It was then taken to the church and miracles started to happen. In 1942 the Virgin was crowned as the patron saint of Zulia. Pilgrims gather here year-round, but the major celebrations (p176) are held in November.

The eastern end of the Paseo de las Ciencias is bordered by the **Plaza Bolívar** and the 19th-century **catedral** (Map p175; cnr Av 4 & Calle 95). The most revered image in the cathedral is the Cristo Negro or Cristo de Gibraltar, as it was called originally in the church of Gibraltar, a town on the southern shore of Lago de Maracaibo. The town was overrun and burned by Indians in 1600, but the crucifix miraculously

survived, even though the cross to which the statue was nailed was incinerated. The image is in the chapel to the left of the high altar.

The arcaded mid-19th-century **Palacio de Gobierno** (Map p175; Plaza Bolívar) is also called the Palacio de las Águilas (Palace of the Eagles) for the two condors placed on its roof. Next door is the late 18th-century Casa Morales, better known as **Casa de la Capitulación** (☎ 725-1194; Plaza Bolívar; admission free; ☑ 8am-noon & 1-6pm Mon-Fri), for it was here that the Spaniards who were defeated in the naval battle of Lago de Maracaibo signed the act of capitulation on August 3, 1823, sealing the independence of Gran Colombia. This is the only residential colonial building left in the city. It has been restored, fitted with period furniture and decorated with paintings of heroes of the War of Independence.

Across the street from the casa is the mighty, art deco **Teatro Baralt** (p179), which you can tour.

A short walk north from the center is **Museo Urdaneta** (Map p175; Calle 91A No 7-70; admission free; ☑ 8:30am-3pm Mon-Fri), which is dedicated to Maracaibo-born General Rafael Urdaneta, the city's greatest independence hero. Built on the site of Urdaneta's birth, it features a collection of objects, documents, paintings and other memorabilia related to the general and the events of the period.

Calle 94, better known as **Calle Carabobo**, has been partly restored to its former appearance, and is notable for its brightly colored facades and grilled windows. The most spectacular part of the street is between Avs 6 and 8. Also worth visiting is the **Mercado Artesanal San Sebastián** (Map p175; cnr Av El Milagro & Calle 96), a colorful Guajiro craft market full of beautiful hammocks and other crafts.

South of the Paseo de las Ciencias lies **Las Pulgas** – the flea market. Streets are crammed with stalls selling everything from fresh fish to pirate DVDs. Here also is **Plaza Baralt**, the historic trading district from Maracaibo's earliest days, and the imposing old market-building, which operated as the Mercado Principal from 1931 to 1973. It has been wholly remodeled and refurbished, and opened as the **Centro de Arte de Maracaibo Lía Bermúdez** (p179).

NORTHERN SUBURBS

The lakeshore **Parque La Marina** (Map p173; cnr Av El Milagro & Av Bella Vista), 5km north of the center,

THE NORTHWEST

MARACAIBO – HISTORIC CENTER

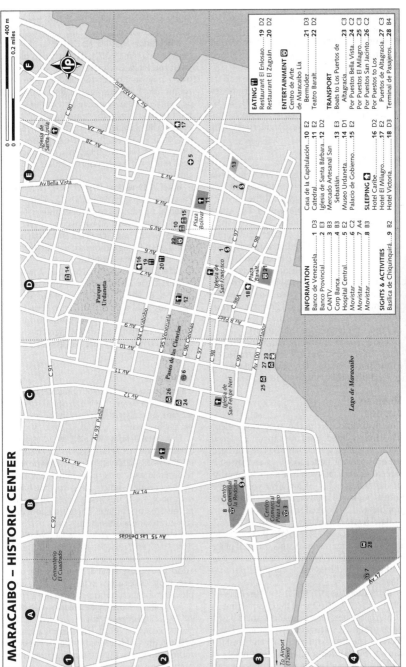

features **El Mirador**, a lookout on the top of a 50m-high tower, which provides a good view over the city and the lake. Restoration is going slowly – the lookout has been closed for repairs since 2002.

Northwest of the city center, on the university's grounds, the strikingly modern **Museo de Arte Contemporáneo del Zulia** (Map p173, ☎ 759-4866; Av Universidad; admission free; ☉ 9am-5pm Tue-Sun) stages temporary displays of modern art in its huge exhibition halls.

Festivals & Events

Maracaibo's major annual event is the **Feria de la Chinita**, which springs to life around November 10 and continues until the coronation of the Virgin on November 18. Apart from religious celebrations, the week-long festival includes various cultural and popular events such as bullfights, *toros coleados* (rodeo with bulls), street parades and, obviously, music – above all the *gaita* (see the boxed text p179), the typical local genre. The best time to listen to the *gaita* is on the eve of November 18, when musical groups gather in front of the basilica to play the *Serenata para la Virgen* (Serenade for the Virgin).

The Feria de la Chinita marks the beginning of the Christmas celebrations, reflected in the illumination of Av Bella Vista and a general Christmas atmosphere.

Sleeping
BUDGET

The historic center is the most convenient place to stay, but doesn't offer anything special in the way of accommodations. The northern suburbs provide better lodgings and are a bit safer after dark, but you'll be away from most of the major sights. Whichever you use, be sure to book well in advance – even the budget options can be booked solid.

Hotel Nuevo Montevideo (Map p177; ☎ 722-2762, 722-7299; Calle 86A No 4-96; d US$12; P 🖭) Set in an old rambling mansion, this tranquil place has 13 large rooms with high ceilings, air-con and private facilities. Also a popular *por rato* (love motel).

Hotel Astor (Map p177; ☎ 791-4510, Plaza República; s US$12, d US$13-14; 🖭) One of the cheapest hotels at one of the best locations, the Astor is basic, yet passable. It's attractively positioned in a hip and safe area, with a dozen trendy restaurants within a 200m radius. Unfortunately, it had just been sold at the time of our research

and it is not clear what the future holds. Be sure to call ahead.

Hotel Caribe (Map p175; ☎ 722-5986; Av 7 No 93-51; s with fan US$12 d/tr US$21/24; 🖭) Just two blocks from the Plaza Bolívar, the 60-room Caribe has a new section at the back. These new rooms have noiseless, central air-con that can be pretty efficient, but there's no way to switch it off or to graduate the temperature.

Nuevo Hotel Unión (Map p177; ☎ 793-3278; Calle 84 No 4-60; d US$14-16; 🖭) Just a few steps from the Corpozulia tourist office, this small budget spot offers six basic rooms with air-con and cable TV.

Hotel Victoria (Map p175; ☎ 322-6159, 721-2654; Plaza Baralt; s/d/tr/q US$19/23/28/32; 🖭) This white colonial building is your best budget bet in the old town, with 32 rooms and a pleasant common area to sit for a chat at the end of the day. Try and snag a room with a balcony view over the busy market plaza.

Hotel El Milagro (Map p175; ☎ 722-8934; Av El Milagro No 93-45; d in old section US$33-42, d/tr in new section US$56-84; P 🖭) The corridors of the Miracle Hotel are clad almost entirely in eerie white tile, with spick-and-span rooms to match. Recently refurbished, the Milagro has gone upmarket, just make sure you ask for a room in the new section.

MIDRANGE

There are no midpriced or upmarket hotels in the old city center; they've all opted for more elegant, new districts, mainly in the northern part of the city.

Gran Hotel Delicias (Map p177; ☎ 797-0983; www .hoteldelicias.com; cnr Av Las Delicias & Calle 70; s/d/tr/ste US$38/44/49/58; 🖭 🖭 🖭) The Delicias provides reasonable standards and facilities, and is one of the cheapest hotels in town that has its own pool – a bonus you'll surely appreciate in this steamy climate. There's a good-value restaurant and a disco, too.

Hotel Aeropuerto (☎ 787-5578, fax 787-5445; Calle 100 No 49A-62; s/d/t/q US$40/42/47/51) The Hilton-like lobby and refined, polite service make a great effort to disguise what are really pretty ordinary motel-like rooms in this sprawling complex, the cheapest option close to the airport.

Apart Hotel Suite Golden Monky (Map p1770; ☎ 797-3285; goldenmonky@hotmail.com; Calle 78 No 10-30; d/tr/ste US$43/60/74; P 🖭 🖭) Central and convenient, the Golden Monky offers a variety of rooms and suites; the restaurant downstairs is pretty good value too.

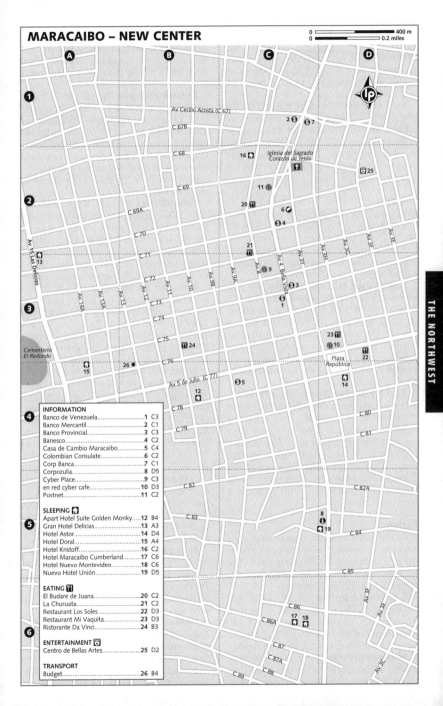

MARACAIBO – NEW CENTER

0 ━━━━━ 400 m
0 ━━━━━ 0.2 miles

THE NORTHWEST

Hotel Doral (Map p177; ☎ 797-8385; cnr Av 14A & Calle 75; d US$40-45, tr/q US$47/61; ✹) This small 22-room hotel isn't anything particularly memorable, yet it has quiet, acceptable air-con rooms and the room rate includes breakfast in the adjacent restaurant.

Hotel Maracaibo Cumberland (Map p177; ☎ 722-2944; www.hotelescumberland.com/maracaibo.htm; Calle 86A No 4-150; s/d/ste US$49/58/75; P ✹) Roughly midway between the old and new centers, this five-floor 88-room hotel is a good compromise between quality and price, and has a breezy rooftop terrace.

TOP END

Hotel Kristoff (Map p177; ☎ 200-4000; www.hotelkristoff.com; Av 8 No 68-48; s US$127, d US$138-170, ste US$397-451; P ✹ 🖵 ☎) Smaller than many hotels, the Kristoff has a wide range of facilities, including a restaurant and gym, and a deliciously palm-fringed pool with outdoor bar.

Venetur Hotel del Lago Maracaibo (Map p173; ☎ 794-4222; fax 793-0392; www.venetur.gob.ve; Av El Milagro; s US$130-190, d US$135-195, ste US$250-560; P ✹ 🖵 ☎) Opened in 1953, this large lakeside five-star hotel is Maracaibo's institution. It offers 368 rooms, two restaurants, a sizeable swimming pool, sauna and its own beach, though you are advised not to bathe because the water in the lake is polluted.

Hotel El Paseo Best Western (Map p173; ☎ 792-4422; www.hotelelpaseo.com.ve; cnr Av 1B & Calle 74; s/d/ste US$140/160/180; P ✹ 🖵 ☎) This attractive waterfront high-rise hotel may now sport the Best Western logo, but its 70 unusually large rooms all have private bathrooms, hot water, silent air-con, cable TV and a fridge. Downstairs is a business center with internet access and a small pool. Be sure to ask for a room with lake views.

Eating

Most upmarket restaurants are nestled in the northern sector of the city, in particular in the new center around Plaza República. The historic center hosts a lot of cheap eateries, but nothing really posh or classy.

El Budare de Juana (Map p177; ☎ 798-3219; cnr Av 8 & Calle 70; arepas US$3.50, juices US$1.80; ☺ 7am-11pm) This clean and efficient *arepera* offers 25 different kinds of delicious *arepas* and a dozen freshly made juices to wash the food down.

Restaurant El Enlosao (Map p175; Calle 94; mains US$4-6) Set in a charming historic mansion, the Casa de los Artesanos, El Enlosao serves unpretentious but tasty Venezuelan food at low prices. The *parrilla* (grill) is so copious that you may struggle to finish it, but if you're after something small, ask for the *sopa del día* (soup of the day) for just US$2.50.

Restaurant El Zaguán (Map p175; ☎ 717-2398; cnr Calle 94 & Av 6; mains US$5-10) A few paces away from El Enlosao, the white tablecloths and leatherbound menus of El Zaguán greet you with the air-con set to arctic – surely a plus in the midday heat. They serve quality local and international food, and in the evenings you can eat outside in the shade of two beautiful old ceiba trees.

Poster Bar Café (☎ 783-2105; Av 22 & Calle 67; mains US$7-15) This classy new spot is one of the few places in Venezuela where you can get a good cup of loose-leaf tea. They serve a quality selection of meat, fish and pasta, and the wine comes in proper balloon glassware. There's wi-fi too, so bring the laptop and stay awhile.

Restaurant Los Soles (Map p177; ☎ 793-3966; Av 5 de Julio No 3G-09; mains US$8-14) Run by a Mexican family, this bright, airy new spot brings some authentic Mexican flavor to town. You can have your tacos and enchiladas outside, if you want, but the colorful interior offers deliciously cool air-conditioning.

Restaurant El Girasol (Map p173; ☎ 792-4422; Hotel El Paseo Best Western, cnr Av 1B & Calle 74; mains US$9-17; ☺ noon-3pm & 7pm-midnight) This is the only revolving restaurant in the country – an entire circle takes about two hours and 20 minutes and the floor-to-ceiling windows all around provide for great views. It offers international cuisine, including a fair choice of pasta, fish and seafood.

La Churuata (Map p177; ☎ 798-9685; cnr Calle 72 & Av 8; mains US$10-18; ☺ noon-midnight) Far from the palm-thatched jungle hut the name suggests, this trendy steak house combines delicious food with enjoyable decor. There's also an adjacent bar.

Ristorante Da Vinci (Map p177; ☎ 798-8934; Av 11 btwn Calles 75 & 76; mains US$10-19) With a mock Renaissance fountain in front of the restaurant, Da Vinci is, predictably, an Italian affair and is consistently popular with locals for its fine food and relaxed atmosphere.

Restaurant Mi Vaquita (Map p177; ☎ 791-1990; Av 3H No 76-22; mains US$11-20; ☺ noon-11pm) Founded in the early 1960s, Mi Vaquita is arguably the best-known steak house in town and it does a great job. It has a warm timber-decked interior and a lively bar to the side.

THE NORTHWEST

GAITA – THE MUSIC OF MARACAIBO

The *gaita* is Maracaibo's musical identity – what tango is to Buenos Aires. It's a lively percussion- and voice-based sound, performed by a small band, with lyrics often improvised on religious or political themes. A classical *gaita* ensemble includes the *cuatro* (a small, four-stringed guitar), *tambora* (large wooden drum) and *furruco* (another drum-based instrument). Ricardo Aguirre (1939-69), nicknamed 'El Monumental,' is considered one of the greatest *gaita* singers.

Gaita is most popular from October to January, peaking during the Christmas season, when it can be heard everywhere – in bars and buses, on the street and on the beach. Plenty of restaurants and bars across town stage live *gaita* music in that period.

Most musicologists agree that *gaita* has Spanish origins, but it evolved in Maracaibo's central quarter of El Saladillo, part of which was razed for the Paseo de las Ciencias. *Gaita* hasn't been overshadowed by the nationwide *joropo;* on the contrary, it has made its way well outside Zulia to become the second most popular national beat.

Entertainment

Have a look in *Panorama,* Maracaibo's major daily paper, for what's going on in the city.

Centro de Arte de Maracaibo Lía Bermúdez (Map p175; ☎ 723-1355, 723-0166; Av Libertador btwn Avs 5 & 6) The center has an auditorium where it hosts musical events, theater and arthouse films. It also stages temporary exhibitions.

Centro de Bellas Artes (Map p177; ☎ 791-2950; Av 3F No 67-217) Bellas Artes has a multipurpose auditorium used for concerts, arthouse films and theater performances. It's also home to the Orquesta Sinfónica de Maracaibo and the Danza Contemporánea de Maracaibo.

Teatro Baralt (Map p175; ☎ 722-3878; cnr Calle 95 & Av 5) Inaugurated in 1932, this is the main central venue for theater performances, but it also stages other events. Half-hour guided tours are run 9am to noon weekdays, if there are no other activities in the theater.

Getting There & Away
TO/FROM COLOMBIA

Three bus companies – **Bus Ven** (☎ 723-9084), **Expresos Amerlujo** (☎ 787-7872), and **Expreso Brasilia** (01800 051 8001) – run air-conditioned buses to Cartagena via Maicao, Santa Marta and Barranquilla (all in Colombia). All three have early morning departures daily from Maracaibo's bus terminal, although the Expreso Brasilia service originates in Caracas. Expect to pay roughly US$37 to US$53 for Santa Marta and US$51 to US$58 for Cartagena. The buses cross the border at Paraguachón (you actually change buses there) and continue through Maicao, the first Colombian town.

It's cheaper to go by por puesto to Maicao (US$10, 2½ hours, 123km) and change there. It's also your only option if you miss the early morning buses. Por puestos depart regularly from about 5am to 3pm and go as far as Maicao's bus terminal. From there, several Colombian bus companies operate buses to Santa Marta (US$13, four hours, 251km) and further on; buses depart regularly until late afternoon.

All passport formalities are done in Paraguachón on the border. Venezuelan immigration charges a US$16 *impuesto de salida* (departure tax), paid in cash by *bolívares* by all tourists leaving Venezuela.

You can change *bolívares* into Colombian pesos at the Maracaibo terminal or in Paraguachón or Maicao, but don't take them further into Colombia: they're difficult to change beyond Maicao. Wind your watch back one hour when crossing from Venezuela to Colombia.

Ask for 90 days when entering Colombia.

AIR

The **Aeropuerto Internacional La Chinita** (☎ 735-8094; Av El Aeropuerto), about 12km southwest of the city center, is not linked by city buses; take a taxi (US$9). Maracaibo is serviced by most major airlines, including **Aeropostal** (☎ 735-1490), **Aserca** (☎ 735-3607), **Avior** (☎ 735-1910) and **Santa Bárbara** (☎ 783-5158).

There are more than a dozen flights daily to Caracas (US$65 to US$105), serviced by all the listed airlines. Aeropostal and Santa Bárbara fly direct to San Antonio del Táchira (US$70 to US$100), and Avior and Santa Bárbara go direct to Mérida (US$80 to US$100). Avior flies to Valencia (US$115 to US$125), and Curaçao (US$112 to 159), and Santa Bárbara has one flight daily to Barquisimeto (US$140). For other destinations you usually have to change planes in Caracas.

THE NORTHWEST

BUS

The large and busy **Terminal de Pasajeros** (Map p175; ☎ 722-1443; Av 15) is about 1km southwest of Maracaibo's historic center. City buses link the terminal to the center and to other districts.

Ordinary buses to Coro (US$9, four hours, 259km) and Valera (US$7, four hours, 238km) run every half-hour. Buses to Barquisimeto (US$8.80, five hours, 328km) depart every hour and stop en route in Carora (US$7.50, 3½ hours, 225km). There are regular departures to Caracas (US$18 to US$26, 10½ hours, 669km), though most buses depart in the evening. Four or five buses depart nightly for San Cristóbal (US$14 to US$18, eight hours, 439km) and five to six buses go to Mérida (US$14 to US$18, nine hours, 523km).

CAR & MOTORCYCLE

Maracaibo has all the major car rental companies. Most have desks at the airport, but some also maintain offices in the city.

Aco Rent a Car (☎ 735-3610; Airport)

Budget Airport (☎ 735-1256); City (Map p177; ☎ 798-3107; Calle 76 No 13-08)

Hertz Airport (☎ 735-0832); City (☎ 736-2357; Hotel Maruma Internacional, Av Circunvalación 2)

Thrifty (☎ 735-1631; Airport)

Getting Around

City transportation is serviced by buses and por puesto cars. You are most likely to need them to get between the historic center and the northern suburbs, which are linked to each other by three main roads: Av El Milagro, Av Bella Vista and Av Las Delicias. El Milagro por puestos depart from Av Libertador (Map p175). The Bella Vista por puestos leave from the corner of Av 12 and Calle 96 (Map p175). From the same corner depart San Jacinto por puestos, which run north along Av Las Delicias.

It can sometimes be difficult to hail a regular cab in the street. Two radio taxi companies you might try are **Unión Taxi 976** (☎ 793-9151) and **Radio la 13** (☎ 736-5273).

AROUND MARACAIBO
Laguna de Sinamaica

The most popular tourist sight around Maracaibo, Laguna de Sinamaica, is noted for the *palafitos* – houses built on piles along the lakeshore. Reputedly it was here that the Spanish explorers Alonso de Ojeda and

Amerigo Vespucci saw native people living in *palafitos* in 1499, and gave Venezuela its name (see p23).

Today, pleasure boats take tourists for trips around the lagoon and its side water channels to see the famous *palafitos*. Some houses are still traditionally built of *estera,* a sort of mat made from a papyrus-like reed that grows in the shallows. If you ignore the TV antennas sticking out from the roof of almost every house, they probably don't look much different from their predecessors 500 years ago. Many houses, though, are now built from modern materials, including timber, brick and tin.

Laguna de Sinamaica is 60km north of Maracaibo and makes for an easy day trip from the city. Take a bus heading to Guana or Los Filuos from the Maracaibo bus terminal and get off in the town of Sinamaica (US$2.40, two hours, 60km). From there, por puestos do a short run on a side road to Puerto Cuervito (US$0.50, 10 minutes, 5km), on the edge of the lagoon.

In Puerto Cuervito, a fleet of pleasure boats waits all day long to take tourists around the lagoon. A boat takes up to six passengers and charges US$16 per boat. Since there are very few tourists coming these days, it usually takes a lot of time to collect six passengers. Come on the weekend, when more visitors turn up, but even then be prepared for a long wait. You could try to bargain down the fare for an earlier departure too. The standard tour takes about an hour, but you can go for a longer trip for a small extra charge. There's a restaurant in Puerto Cuervito.

Los Puertos de Altagracia

Called either Los Puertos or Altagracia for short, this town faces Maracaibo from the opposite side of the strait. It has preserved some of its old architecture, particularly the charming, typical houses painted in bright colors. The most interesting area is around Plaza Miranda, the square just one short block up from the lakefront. A stroll about the town, together with the boat trip from Maracaibo, justifies a half-day tour.

Boats from Maracaibo to Altagracia (US$1.60, 40 minutes) depart every two hours until about 6pm from the wharf off Av Libertador (Map p175). In Altagracia, the boats anchor at the pier 100m southwest of Plaza Miranda.

There are also por puestos that leave when full from next to the wharf in Maracaibo and arrive at Altagracia's bus terminal (US$1.90, 40 minutes). The ride is via the Rafael Urdaneta Bridge. Boats are the more pleasant means of transportation, but sometimes break down, leaving por puestos as the only option.

Ciénaga de los Olivitos

Lovely pink flamingos live year-round at Ciénaga de los Olivitos, about 20km northeast of Altagracia, the only place in Venezuela where they have built nests. The mangroves are home to many other bird species as well – about 110 species have been recorded in the region. The 260-sq-km area covering the lagoon and its environs was decreed a wildlife reserve in 1986 and is administered by Profauna. Before you set off to the marshes, contact the office of Profauna (☎ 761-4959, 761-4547) in Maracaibo for information.

The Ciénaga de los Olivitos is not easy to get to, as it is inaccessible by road. Take a bus or por puesto from Altagracia to Quisiro, get off in the village of Ancón de Iturre and talk to the local fishers. Better still, negotiate a taxi in Altagracia to take you to the Profauna post.

Isla de San Carlos

San Carlos Island is famed for its impressive, massive fort, the **Castillo de San Carlos**, which was built in the 1670s to guard the lake entrance from pirates. Even though the mouth was largely protected by a sandbar, many marauders were eager to cross over and sack Maracaibo. The fort was in Spanish hands until the 1823 battle of Lago de Maracaibo and after their defeat it passed to the republicans.

In 1903 the fort was bombarded by a fleet of warships sent by Germany, Italy and Great Britain to blockade Venezuelan ports after the country failed to pay its foreign debts. During the dictatorship of Juan Vicente Gómez, the fort served as a jail for political prisoners, after which it was used as an arms depot. Finally decreed a national monument, it was extensively restored in the late 1980s to become a tourist attraction.

Castillo de San Carlos is built on a four-pointed-star plan, with circular watchtowers at each corner and a square courtyard in the middle. San Carlos Island is about 45km north of Maracaibo, and with its fine white-sand beaches and the castle, it makes a great day trip.

GETTING THERE & AWAY

The fort is accessible by boats from the town of San Rafael del Moján. San Rafael, 39km north of Maracaibo, is serviced by a number of buses and por puestos from the city's bus terminal.

Parque Nacional Ciénagas del Catatumbo

The (literally) striking feature of this area is the lightning (see the boxed text below) which continues almost uninterrupted without any claps of thunder. The phenomenon, referred to as Relámpago de Catatumbo (Catatumbo Lightning) or Faro de Maracaibo (Maracaibo Beacon), can be observed at night all over the region, weather permitting, from as far away

---

CATATUMBO LIGHTNING – WHO TURNED OFF THE THUNDER?

The 1937 tourist brochure *Venezuela Turística* includes the Catatumbo Lightning as one of the country's unique tourist attractions. It says that the natural phenomenon is found nowhere else on earth and that its cause is unknown. Both of these statements remain true today.

Centered on the mouth of the Río Catatumbo at Lago de Maracaibo, the phenomenon consists of frequent flashes of lightning with no accompanying thunder, which gives an eerie sensation. Even though the luminosity and frequency of the lightning have diminished over recent decades and it can stop for some days, on clear dry nights you are in for an unbelievable and shocking experience. You will even be able to read this guidebook by the light of the lightning!

Various hypotheses have been put forth to explain the lightning, but so far none have been fully proven. The theory that stands out is based on the topography of the region, characterized by the proximity of 5000m-high mountains (the Andes) and a vast sea-level lake (Lago de Maracaibo) – a dramatic configuration found nowhere else in the world. The clash of the cold winds descending from the freezing highlands with the hot, humid air evaporating from the lake is thought to produce the ionization of air particles responsible for the lightning.

as Maracaibo and San Cristóbal. Traveling by night on the Maracaibo–San Cristóbal or San Cristóbal–Valera roads, you'll get a glimpse of it, but the closer you get, the more impressive the spectacle becomes. Tours organized from Mérida (p192) are the best way to see the Catatumbo Lightning close up. The national park also features the rich vegetation and wildlife of the vast wetlands bordering Lago de Maracaibo to the north of the Río Catatumbo.

The Andes

Like a thin sliver of delight, the snowy violence of the Andes surges northward and makes one last gasp before it dies, the Patagonian chill struggling for the very Caribbean itself. It's here the mountains met defeat, as though a sudden army of beaches rose up in defiance of this so alien terrain.

This long-forgotten war leaves behind a striking contrast, a mountainous travelers' playground of craggy vistas and cool mountain air, and world-class mountaineering through the granite statues of those primeval generals. One imagines Pico Bolívar (5007m), like its namesake, leading the charge, with Pico Humboldt (4942m) and Pico Espejo (4765m) riding on his flanks.

Mérida, sweet Mérida, is the heart of it all, and the adrenaline rush of a lifetime. Them thar mountains mean climbing and trekking, sure, but canyoning and rafting, too, and the paragliding – well, what can we say but eat your heart out, Wilbur Wright.

Off the beaten track, but well worth the effort, are the neighboring states of Trujillo, with its green mountains and colonial towns where time seems to stand still, and Táchira, toward Colombia, where the national parks offer wilderness too infrequently visited.

HIGHLIGHTS

- Elevate yourself on Mérida's famous **teleférico** (cable car; p190)
- Find mountain hospitality in the remote mountain village of **Los Nevados** (p200)
- Careen down waterfalls on a **canyoning trip** (p190), organized from Mérida
- Go mountain trekking to **Pico Bolívar** (p198) and **Pico Humboldt** (p199), Venezuela's highest peaks
- Watch the mysterious Good Friday Passion play in **Tostós** (p211)

THE ANDES

THE ANDES

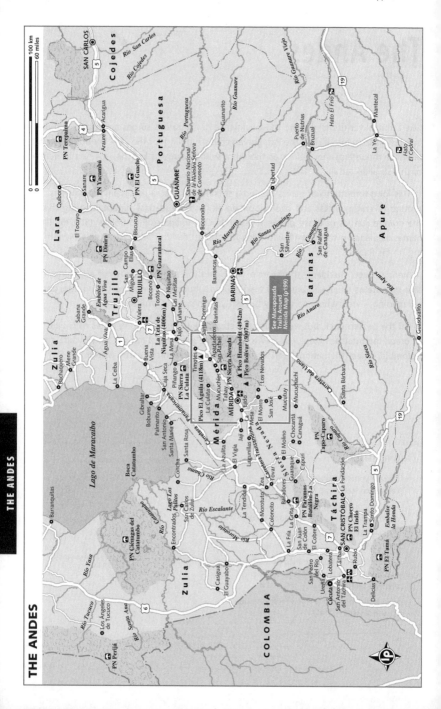

MÉRIDA STATE

MÉRIDA

☎ 0274 / pop 310,000

An adventure-sports playground, Mérida is the sort of place people come to intending to stay a couple of days and end up spending a couple of weeks. With a just-right climate, great restaurants and nightlife, and the mountains towering snowy oh-so-near, Mérida makes a lovely short holiday, but an even better base camp for extended adventures throughout the region.

With gargantuan mountain views looming over the city in every direction, it's no surprise that mountain trips are a main attraction – Pico Bolívar (5007m) is just 12km away, and there are numerous mountaineering and hiking opportunities for every fitness level. There's a handy shortcut to the peaks – Mérida's famous *teleférico*, the world's highest and longest cable-car system. It makes a great day trip, or you can get off at the top with your crampons and ice axe and go climbing. You can also trek down to the quaint colonial town of Los Nevados.

Adrenaline junkies will find a huge range of adventure sports to indulge in, from paragliding to whitewater rafting to mountain biking, and the newest craze, canyoning. Additionally, most wildlife safaris to Los Llanos leave from Mérida, a highly recommended trip.

Mérida is a student town – more than 50,000 students from several universities flood the city every year – giving the city a young face and a bohemian, cultured air. It also means you'll find some of the best nightlife in Venezuela, and the only gay scene outside of Caracas. Foodies will also be delighted to discover a wide selection of excellent, reasonably priced restaurants serving a variety of cuisine.

History

Founded deep in the heart of the Andes and separated by the high mountains from both Colombia and Venezuela, nothing much happened in the tiny town of Mérida during its 250 years under Spanish domination. In 1812 an earthquake devastated the center, further hindering its development.

After Venezuela's independence, the isolation that had retarded Mérida's progress

---

MÉRIDA'S ILLEGITIMATE BIRTH

Why did he do it? What personal or political drama lurks behind the historical facts? Because the guy who founded Mérida – well, he really wasn't supposed to.

His name was Captain Juan Rodríguez Suárez, and in 1558 he led an expedition from Pamplona (just across the present-day border, in Colombia) into the Sierra Nevada of what is now Venezuela. Upon entering a deep, long valley bordered by two towering mountain ranges he founded a town and named it Mérida, after his birthplace in Spain.

At that time Pamplona was an important political and religious center in the Spanish viceroyalty of Nueva Granada (present-day Colombia), and a number of official expeditions had set out from there to explore the region and found new settlements (including San Cristóbal and Barinas). But this expedition was different because Rodríguez Suárez was in search of gold and was not authorized to found new cities, which could only be done by a royal decree from the Spanish Crown.

This really pissed off the governor of Pamplona, who sent out an expedition to track down Rodríguez Suárez. He was caught, arrested for 'usurpation of Royal prerogative,' and found guilty. His sentence was to be dragged from the tail of his horse around the streets of Bogotá until he was dead, and his body to be 'quartered' and left to rot, unburied.

But Rodríguez Suárez managed to save the horse from that indignity. With the help of a few old friends, including the local bishop, he escaped from jail – presumably on horseback – and fled to Trujillo (Venezuela), where he was granted political asylum, becoming the first political refugee in the New World. In a petty revenge of the colonial bureaucracy, a certain Juan de Maldonado was sent out again from Pamplona, with all his paperwork in order, and re-founded Mérida in 1560, legally. Posterity, however, has judged in favor of the adventurer, and Rodríguez Suárez is recognized as the founder of the city, and 1558 as the year of Mérida's true, if illegitimate, birth.

THE ANDES

suddenly proved to be its ally. During the federation wars in the mid-19th century, when Venezuela was plunged into full-blown civil war, the city's solitude attracted refugees fleeing the bloodshed, and the population began to grow. It was not, however, until the 1920s that access roads were constructed and later paved, which smoothed the way for Mérida's

subsequent development. Its transition from a town into a city really took place only over the past few decades.

Orientation

You can never get lost in Mérida – just remember that uphill is always north and west, and downhill south and east. Bounded on either side

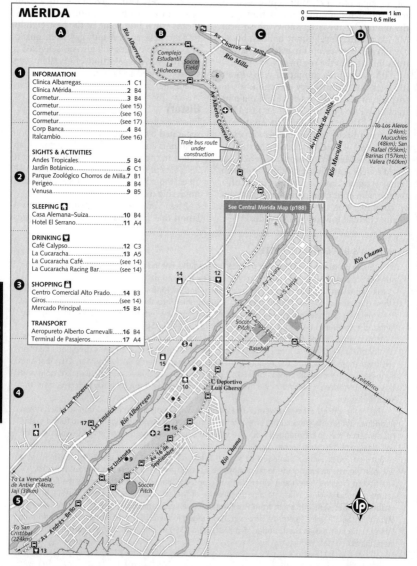

MÉRIDA

0 _____ 1 km
0 _____ 0.5 miles

INFORMATION
Clínica Albarregas...........................1 C1
Clínica Mérida................................2 B4
Cormetur.......................................3 B4
Cormetur..................................(see 15)
Cormetur..................................(see 16)
Cormetur..................................(see 17)
Corp Banca....................................4 B4
Italcambio.................................(see 16)

SIGHTS & ACTIVITIES
Andes Tropicales.............................5 B4
Jardín Botánico...............................6 C1
Parque Zoológico Chorros de Milla.7 B1
Perigeo...8 B4
Venusa...9 B5

SLEEPING
Casa Alemana–Suiza.......................10 B4
Hotel El Serrano.............................11 A4

DRINKING
Café Calypso.................................12 C3
La Cucaracha.................................13 A5
La Cucaracha Café......................(see 14)
La Cucaracha Racing Bar.............(see 14)

SHOPPING
Centro Comercial Alto Prado........14 B3
Giros.......................................(see 14)
Mercado Principal..........................15 B4

TRANSPORT
Aeropureto Alberto Carnevalli......16 B4
Terminal de Pasajeros....................17 A4

Complejo Estudantil La Hichecera

Soccer Field

Trole bus route under construction

See Central Mérida Map (p188)

C Deportivo Luis Ghersy

Soccer Pitch

Baseball

To Los Aleros (24km); Mucuchíes (48km); San Rafael (55km); Barinas (157km); Valera (160km)

Teleférico

Soccer Pitch

To La Venezuela de Antier (14km); Jají (38km)

To San Cristóbal (224km)

Río Albarregas
Río Milla
Río Mucujún
Río Chama
Av Chorros de Milla
Av Alberto Carnevali
Av Hoyada de Milla
Av 2 Lora
Av 5 Zerpa
26 Campo Elias
Av Los Próceres
Av Las Américas
Av Urdaneta
Av 16 de septiembre
Av Andrés Bello

THE ANDES

by two parallel rivers, the town sits on a sloping *meseta* (alluvial terrace) and stretches 12km from the colonial center in the north toward Ejido, its working-class suburb, in the south.

The airport is just 2km southwest of the center, while the bus terminal is a little further west. Both are linked to downtown by frequent city buses.

Information

EMERGENCY
Fire (☎ 171)
Police (☎ 171)

INTERNET ACCESS
Mérida has plenty of internet facilities and they are probably the cheapest in Venezuela, at US$0.70 to US$0.90 per hour. Following are some central locations:
Ceyco (Map p188; Plaza Milla) Linux-friendly. On the east side of the plaza.
Ciber Café El Russo (Map p188; Av 4 Simón Bolívar No 17-74)
Conection Center (Map p188; Av 2 Lora No 17-40)
Cyber Nevada Palace (Map p188; Calle 24 Rangel btwn Avs 5 Zerpa & 6 Rodríguez Suárez) Skype-friendly.
Cyber Sp@ce (Map p188; Calle 21 Lazo btwn Avs 2 Lora & 3 Independencia)
La Abadía (Map p188; Av 3 Independencia No 17-45) There's water in the restaurant of the same name.
Ponte's Punto (Map p188; Calle 23 Vargas btwn Avs 6 Rodríguez Suárez & 7 Maldonado)

LAUNDRY
Some posadas offer laundry service; if yours doesn't, there are many central facilities.
Lavandería Andina (Map p188; Av 7 Maldonado No 22-45)
Lavandería Ecológica (Map p188; cnr Av 4 Simón Bolívar & Calle 16 Araure)
Lavandería La Especial (Map p188; cnr Av 4 Simón Bolívar & Calle 15 Piñango)
Lavandería Marbet (Map p188; Calle 25 Ayacucho No 8-35)
Lavandería Yibe (Map p188; Av 6 Rodríguez Suárez No 19-25)

MEDICAL SERVICES
Clinica Albarregas (Map p186; ☎ 244-8101, 244-7283; Calle Tovar 1-26)
Clinica Mérida (Map p186; ☎ 263-0652, 263-6395; Av Urdaneta 45-145)

MONEY
Banco de Venezuela (Map p188; Av 4 Simón Bolívar btwn Calles 23 Vargas & 24 Rangel)

Banco Mercantil (Map p188; cnr Av 5 Zerpa & Calle 18 Fernández Peña)
Banesco (Map p188; Calle 24 Rangel btwn Avs 4 Simón Bolívar & 5 Zerpa)
BBVA (Map p188; Av 4 Simón Bolívar at Calle 14 Ricaurte)
Corp Banca (Map p186; Av Las Américas)
Italcambio (Map p186; ☎ 263-2977; Aeropuerto Alberto Carnevalli, Av Urdaneta)

POST
Ipostel (Map p188; Calle 21 Lazo btwn Avs 4 Simón Bolívar & 5 Zerpa)

TELEPHONE
CANTV (Map p188; cnr Calle 26 Campo Elías & Av 3 Independencia) Also has internet.
Movistar (Map p188; Calle 20 Federación No 4-64) Also has internet.

TOURIST INFORMATION
Cormetur (Corporación Merideña de Turismo; ☎ 0800-637-4300; cormeturpromocion@hotmail.com) Main tourist office (Map p186; ☎ 262-1603, 263-4701; cnr Av Urdaneta & Calle 45; ⊙ 8am-noon & 2-6pm Mon-Fri); Airport (Map p186; ☎ 263-9330; Av Urdaneta; ⊙ 7am-6pm); Bus terminal (Map p186; ☎ 263-3952; Av Las Américas; ⊙ 7am-7pm); Mercado Principal (Map p186; ☎ 262-1570; Av Las Américas; ⊙ 7am-7pm Mon & Wed-Sat, 7am-2pm Tue & Sun); Teleférico (Map p188; ☎ 252-1997; Parque Las Heroínas; ⊙ 7am-6pm Wed-Sun)
Inparques (Map p188; ☎ 262-1356, 262-1529; http://sierranevada.andigena.org in Spanish; Teleférico, Parque Las Heroínas) Permits for Parque Nacional Sierra Nevada and Parque Nacional Sierra La Culata.

Sights
Mérida is a delightful place for a leisurely stroll. Marvel at the bustle in the central **Plaza Bolívar** (Map p188) near the city's business heart; or, at the north end of town, sit yourself down in a leafy spot in the redeveloped **Plaza Milla** (Map p188), a shady spot for a delicious picnic.

Check out the monumental **Catedral de Mérida** (Map p188). Begun in 1803, based on the plans of the 17th-century cathedral of Toledo in Spain, it was not completed until 1960, and probably only then because things were sped up to meet the 400th anniversary of the city's founding.

Next to the cathedral, the **Museo Arquidiocesano** (Map p188; ☎ 252-1238; Plaza Bolívar; admission US$1.40; ⊙ 9am-5pm Mon-Sat, 9am-1pm Sun) features a fine collection of religious art. Note the Ave

THE ANDES

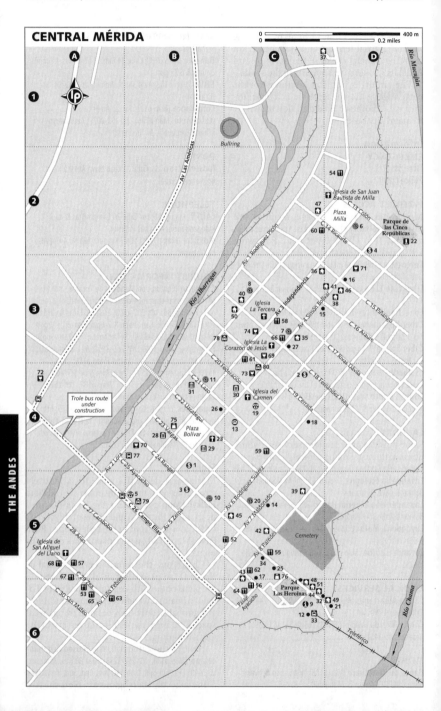

CENTRAL MÉRIDA

Bullring

Iglesia de San Juan Bautista de Milla

Plaza Milla

Parque de las Cinco Repúblicas

Iglesia La Tercera

Iglesia La Corazón de Jesús

Iglesia del Carmen

Plaza Bolívar

Trole bus route under construction

Iglesia de San Miguel del Llano

Cemetery

Parque Las Heroínas

Río Mucujún

Río Albarregas

Río Chama

Teleférico

THE ANDES

María bell cast in AD 909, thought to be the world's second-oldest surviving bell. It must have been brought from Spain by the missionaries and somehow ended up in the church of Jajó. By the early 20th century, though, it was unused and intended to be melted for reuse. Luckily, a priest from Valera sent it to Mérida for a closer inspection, thus saving it from destruction.

Across the plaza is the **Casa de la Cultura Juan Félix Sánchez** (Map p188; ☎ 808-3255; Plaza Bolívar; admission free; ⏲ 9am-8pm Mon-Fri, 9am-5pm Sat). Rooms on the upper floor are used for temporary exhibitions of work by local artists and craftspeople. On the ground level there's a craft shop (see p197).

The building of the Universidad de los Andes, just off the plaza, houses the **Museo Arqueológico** (Map p188; ☎ 240-2344; cnr Av 3 Independencia & Calle 23 Vargas; admission US$0.45; ⏲ 8-11:30am & 2-5pm Tue-Fri, 11am-6:30pm Sat & Sun), which has a pottery collection dating from 25,000 BC to 50,000 BC.

The large, modern Centro Cultural Tulio Febres Cordero shelters the **Museo de Arte Moderno Juan Astorga Anta** (Map p188; ☎ 252-4380; Calle 21 Lazo btwn Avs 2 Lora & 3 Independencia; admission free; ⏲ 9am-4pm Tue-Fri, 10am-2pm Sat & Sun). It stages changing exhibitions of modern art by Venezuelan artists, and sometimes concerts.

Set in a beautiful 300-year-old mansion with a courtyard, the **Museo de Arte Colonial** (Map p188; ☎ 252-7860; cnr Av 4 Simón Bolívar & Calle 20 Federación; admission US$0.50; ⏲ 9am-4pm Tue-Fri, 10am-2pm Sat & Sun) has a small but carefully assembled collection of sacred art, dating mostly from the 18th century.

The small Parque de las Cinco Repúblicas boasts Venezuela's oldest **Bolívar monument** (Map p188; Calle 13 Colón btwn Avs 4 Simón Bolívar & 5 Zerpa), dating from 1842. The small bust sitting atop a high, massive column looks totally out of proportion.

Visit the **Parque Zoológico Chorros de Milla** (Map p186; ☎ 244-3864; Av Chorros de Milla; admission US$1.40; ⏲ 8am-5pm Tue-Sun) on the northern outskirts of the city, 4km from the center. Set on a mountain slope along the Río Milla and named after the waterfalls in the park, the small, scenic zoo features a selection of local fauna, including jaguars, condors, anacondas, capybaras, tapirs and capuchin and spider monkeys. Don't

THE ANDES

miss walking uphill along the creek to see the waterfalls.

Not far from the zoo is the **Jardín Botánico** (Map p186; ☎ 416-0642; Av Alberto Carnevali; admission US$0.90; ☺ 8am-5pm Tue-Sun). Inaugurated in 2000, the botanical garden is still young, and only a small portion of the total 44 hectares is open to the public. It's worth coming anyway, particularly on Saturday or Sunday, when an unusual 'aerial path' is open for visitors. You 'walk' using ropes between platforms built atop four tall trees. The 'trip' takes 1½ hours and costs US$7.

Activities

Mérida is the adventure-sports capital of Venezuela, and offers excellent conditions for activities as diverse as canyoning, paragliding, rock-climbing, rafting, mountaineering, bird-watching and horseback riding. There are heaps of local tour operators – see p192 for details.

TELEFÉRICO DE MÉRIDA

An essential experience of any visit to Mérida is the **teleférico** (Map p188; ☎ 252-1997, 252-5080; www.telefericodemerida.com in Spanish; Parque Las Heroínas), the world's highest and longest cable-car system. It was constructed in 1958 by a French company and runs 12.5km from the bottom station of Barinitas (1577m) in Mérida to the top of Pico Espejo (4765m), covering the ascent in four stages. The three intermediate stations are La Montaña (2436m), La Aguada (3452m) and Loma Redonda (4045m).

The ascent to Pico Espejo takes close to two hours if you go straight through. It's best to go up as early as possible, as clouds usually obscure views later in the day. You can then take some short walks around Pico Espejo and/or Loma Redonda before going back. Don't forget to take warm clothes and sunblock.

Apart from splendid views during the trip itself, the cable car provides easy access for high-mountain hiking, saving you a day or two of puffing uphill. Bear in mind, however, that acclimatization problems can easily occur by quickly reaching high altitudes.

The cable car has, in the past, gone through sporadic periods of brokenness. When it is operating, however, it's open Wednesday to Sunday, and during Venezuelan holiday periods it runs daily. The first trip up is at 8am and the last at 11:30am (7:30am and noon, respectively, in peak season). The last trip down is at about 2pm (4pm in peak season). The roundtrip ticket from Mérida to Pico Espejo costs US$26; children 12 and under pay US$18, seniors US$15; no student discounts are available.

HIKING & TREKKING

There are excellent hiking and trekking opportunities in the trails linking the many remote villages in the mountains around Mérida (see the boxed text p198) and in the Parques Nacionales Sierra Nevada (p198) and Sierra La Culata (p201).

PARAGLIDING

Of Mérida's wide array of adventure sports, paragliding is easily the most iconic – there's even pictures of paragliders on the side of the city's garbage trucks. Most visitors glide on tandem gliders with a skilled pilot, so no previous experience is necessary. The usual starting point for flights is Las González, an hour-long jeep ride from Mérida, from where you glide for 20 to 30 minutes down 850 vertical meters. The cost of the flight (US$60 to US$70) includes jeep transportation.

You can also take a paragliding course that lasts approximately one week, covering theory (available in English) and practice (including solo flights); the cost is US$400 to US$500. The course allows you to fly solo, but you'll still have to rent a paraglider (US$50 per flight, US$200 per week, plus the cost of transportation).

X-treme Adventours (p193) is the main paragliding operator, although the sport is offered by most all-around Mérida tour companies, which will either have their own pilots or will contract one for you.

CANYONING & RAFTING

Canyoning is quickly becoming Mérida's latest iconic, 'must-do' adventure sport. Not for the faint of heart, it consists of climbing, rappelling and hiking down a river canyon, and through its waterfalls. It's been described by travelers as 'awesome, terrifying, beautiful, insane but amazing' and 'quite possibly the maddest thing you can do without getting killed.' Full-day, all-inclusive canyoning tours go for around US$50 to US$80.

There's also whitewater rafting organized on some rivers on the Andes' southern and western slopes. It can be included in a tour to Los Llanos or done separately as a two- to four-

THE ANDES

CLIMATE & WEATHER IN THE MOUNTAINS

As a general guide, the Venezuelan Andes enjoy a dry season from December to April. May and June is a period of changeable weather, with a lot of sunshine, but also frequent rain (or snow at high altitudes). It is usually followed by a short, relatively dry period from late June to late July before a long, really wet season begins. August to October are the wettest months, during which hiking can be miserable. The snowy period – June to October – may be dangerous for mountaineers.

The weather changes frequently and rapidly, even in the dry season. Rain (or snow, at upper reaches) can occur any time, and visibility can drop dramatically within an hour, leaving you trapped high up in the mountains for quite a while. Be careful and hike properly equipped, with good rain gear and warm clothing, as well as some extra food and water. Particular care should be taken on remote trails, where you may not meet anyone for days. Also keep in mind the risk of altitude sickness.

---

day rafting tour (US$45 to US$70 per person per day). It's normally a wet-season activity, but some rivers allow for year-round rafting. Arassari Trek (p192) offers some of the most adventurous canyoning and rafting tours.

MOUNTAIN BIKING

Several tour companies organize bike trips and rent bikes. Shop around, as bicycle quality and rental prices may differ substantially between the companies. One of the more popular bike tours is the loop around the remote mountain villages south of Mérida known as Pueblos del Sur. For a more challenging ride, try a trip up and back to El Refugio in Parque Nacional Sierra la Culata. The downhill through the high grasslands really gets the adrenaline pumping. Bike rental varies substantially, between US$10 to US$40 a day, depending on quality.

WILDLIFE-WATCHING

A recommended excursion out of Mérida is a wildlife safari to Los Llanos (p220), the immense plain savanna south of the Andes that offers some of Venezuela's best wildlife-watching. Most tour companies in Mérida offer this trip, usually as a four-day tour for US$180 to US$250.

There is excellent bird-watching in the Sierra Nevada around Mérida. The most popular destination is the Humboldt Trail, which winds its way from the Inparques office at La Mucuy to the summit of Pico Humboldt (p199). It's normally walked as an overnight or multiday hike, but also makes a great birding day trip, where you are likely to see scores of bird species and the occasional *oso frontino* (spectacled bear).

FISHING

Anglers may be interested in trout fishing. The most popular places to fish are Laguna Mucubají and the nearby Laguna La Victoria, and, to a lesser extent, Laguna Negra and Laguna Los Patos (see p201 for details on how to get there). The fishing season runs from mid-March to the end of September. You need a permit from **Inapesca** (☎ 262-3842) in Mérida. The permit costs US$16 and allows angling in Mérida state's national parks. Bring your own fishing equipment. You can buy some gear in Mérida, but don't rely on renting the stuff from tour companies or anywhere else.

Courses

Mérida is a very good place to study and practice Spanish. In the Andes, Spanish is spoken more slowly than in other parts of the country, so you are likely to find it easier to understand. The city has several language schools and the prices of language courses tend to be lower here than just about anywhere else in the country.

There are also plenty of students and tutors offering private lessons – inquire at popular traveler hotels and tour companies.

The major institutions offering Spanish courses include the following:

Instituto Latino Americano de Idiomas (Map p188; ☎ 262-0990; www.latinomérida.com; Edificio Don Atilio, cnr Av 4 Simón Bolívar & Calle 21 Lazo)

Iowa Institute (Map p188; ☎ 252-6404; www.iowainstitute.com; cnr Av 4 Simón Bolívar & Calle 18 Fernández Peña)

Venusa (Map p186; ☎ 263-8855, 263-7631; www.venusacollege.org; Edificio Tibisay, Av Urdaneta 49-49)

THE ANDES

MÉRIDA – A LAND OF FIESTAS

There's always an excuse for a party, and in no place is this more so than Mérida. The biggest annual bash is unquestionably the **Feria del Sol**, held in the week before Ash Wednesday. There's music, dancing, sports events, bullfights and – of course – a beauty pageant.

The mountain towns around Mérida are also rich in festivities, most of which have religious roots and are linked to the religious calendar. You can take it for granted that every village will be holding a celebratory feast on the day of its patron saint. There are frequent local buses to all the following destinations; inquire at the tourist office for details.

January – Paradura del Niño Game in which villagers 'steal' the infant Jesus from his crib, then search for him and celebrate his 'finding'; it's popular throughout the region for the entire month.

January 6 – Los Reyes Magos (Epiphany) Particularly solemn carol-singing ceremony in the town of Santo Domingo.

February 2 – Los Vasallos de la Candelaria Ritual dances in La Parroquia, Mucuchíes, Bailadores and La Venta.

Easter – Semana Santa (Holy Week, leading up to Easter) Observed in many towns and villages, including particularly La Parroquia, Lagunillas, Santo Domingo, Chiguará and La Azulita.

May 15 – Fiesta de San Isidro Labrador A type of agrarian rite in honor of the patron saint of farmers, celebrated with processions featuring domestic animals and crops; it's most elaborate in Apartaderos, Mucuchíes, Tabay, Bailadores and La Azulita.

July 25 – Fiesta de Santo Apóstol Held in Lagunillas, Ejido and Jají.

September 30 – Los Negros de San Gerónimo Celebrated in Santo Domingo.

October 24 – Fiesta de San Rafael Patron saint's day feast in San Rafael.

December 8 – Fiesta de la Inmaculada Concepción Spectacular display of some 20,000 candles, which are lit in the evening in the main plaza of Mucurubá.

December 29 – Fiesta de San Benito Event held in honor of Venezuela's only black saint, in which the locals take to the streets in red-and-black costumes and sometimes black-colored faces, and spend the day dancing to the rhythm of drums and parading from door to door; observed in Timotes, La Venta, Apartaderos and Mucuchíes.

December 31 – Despedida del Año Viejo (Farewell to the Old Year) Midnight burning of life-size human puppets, often stuffed with fireworks, which have been prepared weeks before and placed in front of the houses; celebrated regionally.

Tours

Mérida is chock-a-block with tour companies, and the competition helps keep prices reasonable. Mountain trips figure prominently in most agencies' offerings; for treks to nearby Pico Bolívar and Pico Humboldt, expect to pay US$55 to US$70 per person per day.

Trekking to the mountain village of Los Nevados is another popular mountain trip. Most companies offer trips there, but you can easily do it on your own. It's a two- to three-day trip.

If you've got a hankering for some off-the-beaten-track hiking, check out the *mucuposadas* (see the boxed text, p198). Tours organized by **Andes Tropicales** (Map p186; ☎ 263-8633; www.andestropicales.org; cnr Av 2 Lora & Calle 41), the travel-agency wing of the not-for-profit development company, is especially recommended. (It can also organize domestic/international airline tickets, and transfers to and from the trail heads.)

Special-interest tours readily available in Mérida focus on paragliding, canyoning, wildlife watching, mountain biking, rafting, rock climbing, fishing and horseback riding. Some companies handle rental of mountaineering equipment, camping gear and bikes; if you just need equipment, not a guide or a tour, check **Cumbre Azul** (Map p188; ☎ 251-0455; Calle 24 Rangel No 8-153), which specializes in rental.

As elsewhere in the country, Mérida's tour companies will normally accept cash payment for their services in US dollars. Most will accept traveler's checks, but not credit cards. Following are the best-established and most reliable local tour companies:

Arassari Trek (Map p188; ☎ /fax 252-5879; www.arassari.com; Calle 24 Rangel No 8-301) This Swiss-owned outfit pioneered many of the most popular tours in Mérida, including trips to Los Llanos and to Catatumbo. It employs some of the best guides, many of whom are respected naturalists, including Alan Highton (wildlife and bird-watching) and Roger Manrique (bird-watching). It offers a full range of some of the most creative rafting, canyoning, biking, trekking and mountaineering tours, and also sells domestic and international airline tickets.

Guamanchi Expeditions (Map p188; ☎ 252-2080; www.guamanchi.com; Calle 24 Rangel No 8-86) This hands-on tour company, one of the longest-operating in Mérida, is owned and run by John Peña, a long-time mountain guide. It offers a selection of well-prepared tours up the mountains and down to Los Llanos, and also runs rafting and canyoning trips. It has bicycles for rent, and staff are happy to provide information on do-it-yourself biking and walking trips. Check out its posada in Los Nevados.

Natoura Adventure Tours (Map p188; ☎ 252-4216; www.natoura.com; Calle 24 Rangel No 8-237) Managed by José Luis Troconis, this heavyweight travel agency specializes in custom-tailored travel and adventure tourism, and will happily organize your trip for you from overseas. It uses good gear and conducts tours in small groups, with quality guides. It also sells domestic/international airline tickets.

X-treme Adventours (Map p188; ☎ 252-7241; www.xatours.com; Calle 24 Rangel No 8-45) The main place in town for paragliding, this young, adventurous Venezuelan-owned agency offers hiking, mountain biking, ATV and bridge-jumping as well as a full array of hotel, tour and flight booking.

There are plenty of other tour operators in town, many of which nestle around Parque Las Heroínas and along Calle 24 Rangel. They may be reliable and will cost much the same or even less than those listed. Shop around, talk to other travelers and check things thoroughly before deciding.

Sleeping

Mérida has heaps of places to stay all across the center. Most of these are posadas, which are usually small, inexpensive family-run guesthouses with a friendly atmosphere. Nearly all have hot water and provide laundry facilities, and some allow guests to use the kitchen.

The line between hotel and posada, though, is increasingly blurring, as several of the newer posadas easily outstrip hotels in luxury and service. Should you prefer a conventional hotel, however, there are several reasonable midrange to high-end places to lay your head for the night.

BUDGET

Posada Patty (Map p188; ☎ 251-1052; Calle 24 Rangel No 8-265; r without bathroom per person US$6) Friendly Colombian Patty offers some of the cheapest beds in town. They're on the spartan side, with shared bathrooms, but the price is unbeatable. You can use the kitchen and fridge, and Patty also offers some of the cheapest laundry services around, and not just for the guests.

Posada Jama Chía (Map p188; ☎ 252-5767; Calle 24 Rangel No 8-223; dm/d US$7/14) This grandmotherly posada offers the best – not to mention some of the only – dorm beds in town. The rooms are clean, mattresses comfy, and guests can use the kitchen.

Yesenia (Map p188; ☎ 252-7766; Calle 24 Rangel No 8-321; d without bathroom US$11, high-season surcharge US$7) This newest addition to Mérida's 'Budget Row' offers five new, comfortable rooms surrounding a colorful patio. The bathrooms are shared, but there's plenty of hot water. At the time of research, the friendly Bolivian owner was building two self-contained apartments in the basement.

Posada El Floridita (Map p188; ☎ 251-0452; Calle 25 Ayacucho No 8-44; s/d US$12/14) This Cuban-run, nine-room guesthouse is one of the cheapest options with private facilities, but it's nothing special. Take a room on the upper floor – they are brighter.

Posada Alemania (Map p188; ☎ 252-4067; Av 2 Lora No 17-76; s/d/tr US$14/21/26, without bathroom US$12/16/21) Owned by a German lad once upon a time, this now Venezuelan-run posada is a popular one. Rooms surround a central garden courtyard, and there's a good kitchen guests can use. The owner runs a tour agency from the posada.

Posada Suiza (Map p188; ☎ 252-4961; cnr Av 2 Lora & Calle 18 Fernández Peña; s/d/tr/q US$14/19/24/29, s/d without bathroom US$14/19) The Suiza shares the same owner and style as the Alemania, and is just that titchy bit nicer. It offers 10 rooms set around a colonial-style courtyard, and has a quiet terrace with hammocks at the back, with views of the mountains. The buffet breakfast at US$4 is one of the best in Mérida.

ourpick Posada Guamanchi (Map p188; ☎ 252-2080; www.guamanchi.com; Calle 24 Rangel No 8-86; d/tr/q US$20/30/40, without bathroom US$14/21/28; P) This rambling posada with four floors, a terrace and two kitchens is the sort of place where rough-stubbled, fleece-wearing, sun-reddened mountain climbers stumble into the lounge room with cries of 'dude, wicked cool!' Grab a double at the back, if you can; they have great views of the *teleférico*.

THE ANDES

Posada Mara (Map p188; ☎ 252-5507; Calle 24 Rangel No 8-215; d/tr/q US$15/21/28) This flashback to the '70s offers 10 small, clean rooms on two floors. It's a bit soulless, but still good value.

Posada La Montaña (Map p188; ☎ 252-5977; posadalamontana@intercable.net.ve; Calle 24 Rangel No 6-47; s/d/tr/q US$23/35/47/58) This classic, well-run posada is a perennial favorite for its location, well-kept rooms and helpful staff. Rooms have private bathrooms and safety deposit boxes, there's wi-fi available, and a new terrace tempts, with hammocks and gorgeous mountain views. The restaurant downstairs serves up high-quality meals, including solid breakfasts.

Posada Los Bucares (Map p188; ☎ 252-2841, 251-0566; www.losbucares.com, info@losbucares.com; Av 4 Simón Bolívar No 15-5; s US$23-28, d US$28-34, tr US$30-36; P) This historic mansion has been partly refurbished in simple, comfortable style. The cozy, rustic rooms are set around a small patio, and a tiny *cafetín* serves up good morning coffee.

Posada Casa Vieja (Map p200; ☎ 417-1489, 0414-374-8334; www.casa-vieja-mérida.com; Transandina, Tabay; d/tr/q US$23/30/47; P) For those looking for a quiet retreat, this cheerful posada offers quality lodgings in relaxed country surrounds, a short 11km outside Mérida. Bird-lovers especially will delight in the garden – full of heliconias – designed to attract the local hummingbirds. The German owner runs a travel agency from the posada.

Posada Luz Caraballo (Map p188; ☎ 252-5441; fax 252-0177; Av 2 Lora No 13-80; s/d/tr/q US$23/31/37/42; P) Facing the tree-filled Plaza Milla, the Luz offers 42 rooms spread over three floors. Popular with tour groups and serving basic meals downstairs, this well-maintained posada can't quite shake that just-a-motel feeling.

La Casona de Margot (Map p188; ☎ 252-3312; www.lacasonademargot.com; Av 4 Simón Bolívar No 15-17; d/tr/q US$28/33/37, 6-/8-bed r US$56/84, high-season surcharge US$10) The stylish rooms in this old colonial building boast such high ceilings that some rooms have been lofted, creating rooms perfect for a large family. Free coffee, fluffy white towels and a small garden patio add to the allure.

Posada El Escalador (Map p188; ☎ 252-2411; www.elescalador.com; Calle 23 Vargas No 7-70; d/tr/q US$28/35/47) The 'Mountain Climber' is a good place to begin or end a mountain adventure. It's just around the corner from most of the agencies, and the posada rents rain jackets, too.

Casa Alemana–Suiza (Map p186; ☎ 263-6503; cnr Av 2 Lora & Calle 38 No 130; www.casa-alemana.com; d/tr/q US$33/37/44) In the south end of town, this posada has a different feel from the more touristy center. The rooms are spacious and quiet. The roof deck has great views of the mountains and Alemana–Suiza can also organize tours all over the country.

MIDRANGE & TOP END

Hotel El Tisure (Map p188; ☎ 252-6072; www.tisure.com; Av 4 Simón Bolívar No 17-47; s/d/tr/ste US$28/46/56/70; P) Owned by a Frenchwoman from Martinique, this delightfully cozy hotel will appeal to those with European tastes, and is exceptional value for the price. Good location, and a quality bar and restaurant downstairs.

ourpick Posada Casa Sol (Map p188; ☎ 252-4164; www.posadacasasol.com; Av 4 Simón Bolívar btwn Calles 15 Piñango & 16 Araure; s/d/ste US$37/42/49; 💻) This exquisite guesthouse challenges the definition of a posada, with a sense of luxury and service normally expected from a fine hotel. Walls dripping with cast-iron sculpture, high-thread-count sheets, multilingual staff and breakfast under an ancient avocado tree all add up to a very memorable experience.

Hotel Prado Río (Map p188; ☎ 252-0633; www.hotelpradorio.com.ve; Av 1 Rodríguez Picón; d US$51-65, tr US$84; P 💻 🐕) Set in vast, walled-in grounds, the Prado Río offers all the luxuries you might expect, just a short walk from the center. Besides the 13 spacious rooms in the main hotel building, there's a colony of 66 cabañas arranged in the form of a Mediterranean town with a further 84 rooms. The complex is well maintained and adorned with flowers, and has its own restaurant and bar and a large swimming pool.

Hotel Mistafí (Map p188; ☎ 251-0729; hotelmistafi@cantv.net; cnr Av 3 & Calle 15; d/tr US$56/70; P 🐕 💻) Chuck on the sunnies, mate, and massage the ol' liver; bright colors and Chivas Regal in the honeymoon suite are what Venezuelans want when it comes to luxury, and this place delivers. For comfort in ostentatious style, the brass tack–shiny Mistafí cannot be beat. For a touch of tranquility with your Scotch, ask for a room at the back – they have mountain views.

Hotel El Serrano (Map p186; ☎ 266-7447; hotel serrano@movistar.net.ve; Av Los Próceres 48-110; s/d/tr/q/ste US$65/70/84/98/112, US$10 pool fee; P 🐕 💻 🐕) Never leave the building is what this oh-so-Venezuelan resort is all about, and with a restaurant, conference room, wi-fi access, expansive rooms, downstairs dance club and a swimming pool surrounded by flowering plants and shady trees, why bother going anywhere?

Mérida Suites (Map p188; ☎ 251-2459; fax 251-2650; Av 8 Parades btwn Calles 21 Lazo & 22 Uzcategui; d US$77; P ⊕) This swish new hotel offers five fully self-contained apartments with kitchen, pots and pans, stove, fridge, computer with broadband and washer/dryer combo. It's set in a central yet tranquil spot, just opposite the cemetery. Discounts are available for stays longer than a week.

Eating

ourpick Heladería Coromoto (Map p188; ☎ 252-3525; Av 3 Independencia No 28-75; ice-cream US$1.50-3.50; ⏲ 2:15pm-9pm Tue-Sun) The most famous ice-cream parlor in South America, Coromoto holds the *Guinness Book of Records* title for most number of ice-cream flavors. Eat your heart out, Baskin-Robbins, this place has more than 900 for you to taste (although not all are available on the average day). Create your own combinations, like a Mexican sundae – black bean, beef, chili, onion, and tomato. *¡Olé!*

La Nota (Map p188; ☎ 252-9697; cnr Calle 25 Ayacucho & Av 8 Parades; snacks US$2-3, mains US$3-5) With three floors of big, Big, BIG burgers, La Nota's monster whoppers are big enough to feed two. There's eight sauces to flavor your burger, including one that's – blue???

Restaurant Vegetariano El Tinajero (Map p188; Calle 29 Zea No 3-54; set meal US$2-3; ⏲ 11am-7pm) This peaceful vegetarian spot serves up quality veggie soups, hot mains and natural juices. Delicious, light portions, and exceptional wholemeal bread.

Estragón Café (Map p188; ☎ 0414-080-6339; www.estragoncafé.com; cnr Av 8 Parades & Calle 24 Rangel; breakfast US$2-3, meals US$4-6) The name of this cozy little restaurant is not a reference to *Waiting For Godot*, but rather to the amazing vinegars and sauces it makes from tarragon (*estragón* in French). It serves delicious, affordable gourmet food – crepes, steaks with sauces, yummy desserts, and don't miss the *ensalada estragón*.

Casa Andina (Map p188; ☎ 252-4811; Av 2 Lora No 12-30; set meal US$2.50, mains US$3-5) Budget eaters, rejoice – with the best, cheapest set meals in town, this historic restaurant-cum-museum is worth the short walk to the edge of town. Tables surround a lovely garden patio, and

a few front rooms house a collection of pre-Hispanic stone and pottery pieces.

Buona Pizza (Map p188; ☎ 252-7639; Av 7 Maldonado No 24-46; pizza US$3-5) Convenient, central and open till late, this is a recommended budget pizza outlet; takeaway is available.

T'Café (Map p188; cnr Av 3 Independencia & Calle 29 Zea; mains US$3-6; ⏲ 10am-late) Choose from breakfasts, sandwiches, pizza and delicious Venezuelan dishes at this hip open-air café-restaurant. The café is blessed with wi-fi, and is a good place for a coffee by day or a beer by night. Check out the paraglider hanging from the ceiling.

Federico's Pizzas (Map p188; ☎ 416-3963; Pasaje Ayacucho; pizza & pasta US$4-7, mains US$7-10) This cozy two-level spot with pastel-colored walls, tasteful decoration and quiet background music is very romantic. It serves some of the best pasta in town, great crispy-crust pizza and an assortment of meat and fish dishes.

Café Mogambo (Map p188; ☎ 252-5643; cnr Calle 29 Zea & Av 4 Simón Bolívar; breakfast US$4-7, light meals US$5-10) With its prominent 1920s-style bar, art deco plasterwork, soft lighting and antique ceiling fans, mood is the name of the game in this trendy bistro, a haven for wine buffs. Food is served all day, including some of the only decent Mexican food in town, and on weekend nights you'll find live jazz or salsa music mellowing away in the corner.

Restaurant Vegetariano El Sano Glotón (Map p188; Av 4 Simón Bolívar No 17-84; mains US$4.50-5.50; ⏲ 11am-4pm) This salad-lover's delight is a welcome refuge from the usual Venezuelan deep-fried yumminess. Wholemeal (baked) empanadas, natural juices, and good bread, too.

La Astilla (Map p188; ☎ 251-0832; Calle 14 Ricaurte btwn Avs 2 Lora & 3 Independencia; pizzas & mains US$5-9; ⏲ breakfast, lunch & dinner) Pizza is the flagship of this restaurant on Plaza Milla, but it also does respectable trout, meat and pasta dishes. Popular with locals, this place is fantastic value.

La Abadía (Map p188; ☎ 251-0933; www.grupoabadia.com; Av 3 Independencia No 17-45; mains US$5-12; ⏲ noon-11pm) This meticulously reconstructed former monastery is a Mérida institution, and serves good-quality salads, meat and pasta, plus you get 30 minutes free internet before or after your meal.

ourpick La Abadía Del Angel (Map p188; ☎ 252-8013; www.grupoabadia.com; Calle 21 Lazo btwn Avs 5 Zerpa & 6 Rodríguez Suárez; mains US$5-12; ⏲ noon-1am) Brought to you by the same people who gave you La Abadía, this groovy restaurant-cum-bar serves up some of the best steak, salads and pasta in town, and of course you get 30 minutes free internet before or after your meal. It's got three floors of funky Arabic decoration, and you can even rent a hookah pipe by the hour. The bar serves up mean cocktails, and is a good place to meet people.

La Mamma & Sushi-Bar (Map p188; ☎ 252-3628; Av 3 Independencia btwn Calles 19 Cerrada & 20 Federación; mains US$7-12, sushi US$9-14; ⏰ noon-1am) This wicked new hotspot has grown well beyond its Italian roots, and serves up great grub till late. Live music on weekend nights, and check out the cocktail list – a chocolate-vodka 'Chocolatov,' anyone?

La Trattoria da Lino (Map p188; ☎ 252-9555; Pasaje Ayacucho; mains US$7-11) If you are after a fine Italian dinner, you won't do wrong coming to this well-appointed restaurant with a delicate Mediterranean touch and savory, authentic home-cooked Italian food.

Restaurant Miramelindo (Map p188; ☎ 252-9437; Calle 29 Zea btwn Avs 4 Simón Bolívar & 5 Zerpa; mains US$8-15) One of the best restaurants in the center, Miramelindo serves international fare, including some Basque dishes, and has a sushi bar.

La Sevillana (Map p188; ☎ 252-9628; cnr Av 5 Zerpa & Calle 29 Zea; mains US$8-19) Wine racks line the walls of this classic Spanish seafood restaurant, where the specialty is fish, fish and more fish, just about any which way you like it – there's even German and Chilean dishes on the menu.

Drinking & Entertainment

Party nights in Merida are, of course, Thursday, Friday and Saturday. Things don't normally get popping until 10pm or 11pm, and all of the following close at 1am, unless otherwise stated.

Alfredo's Bar (Map p188; cnr Av 4 Simón Bolívar & Calle 19 Cerrada) This bar competes to have the cheapest beer in Venezuela, and at prices like these (about US$0.25 per bottle, US$0.50 on weekends after 7pm) on weekend nights it can be impossible to get in, let alone sit or dance. The large outdoor area at the back pumps the *reggaetón* (fusion of music styles including hip-hop and reggae) to the stars, and a smaller front lounge swings with salsa and merengue.

Birosca Carioca (Map p188; ☎ 252-3804; www.birosca carioca.com; Calle 24 Rangel No 2-04; ⏰ until 3am) Like the sign over the bar says, 'Alliance for a Venezuela without *reggaetón*.' It plays just about

everything else, though, and occasionally hosts live music events. The student crowd forgoes glassware in favor of bright-blue plastic sand-castle buckets – try not to lose track of which straw is yours.

Café Calypso (Map p186; Centro Comercial Viaducto; ⏰ 9am-late Mon-Sat) This mild-mannered shopping center café has a secret identity. By day, it's a tranquil coffee bar. Come back at night, though, and Mr Hyde emerges, when international DJs freak it up with the techno, and the barman serves up some of the tastiest caipirinhas and mojitos in town. Open till 3am, and sometimes later, the Calypso rarely fills up before midnight.

Clover Rock Bar (Map p188; ☎ 416-5570; Av 4 Simón Bolívar btwn Calles 14 Ricaurte & 15 Piñango) This intimate, smoky bar plays loud rock and salsa and sometimes has live music. It's frequented by students and young folks and is a good place to meet people.

El Bodegón de Pancho (Map p188; ☎ 244-9819; Centro Comercial Mamayera, Av Las Américas) Within walking distance from the center, El Bodegón is one of the oldest discos in town, and it continues to draw crowds. The timber-decked ground-level hall has the charm of an old tavern and vibrates with Latin rhythms, with bands usually playing on Friday. Upstairs is a large dance floor, which blasts out hip-hop, trance and the like.

El Hoyo del Queque (Map p188; ☎ 252-4306; cnr Av 4 Simón Bolívar & Calle 19 Cerrada) Some say this is the best bar in Mérida. Others disagree. No, they say, it's the best bar in Venezuela. Still others argue it's the best in the world. Hyperbole? Most certainly, but whatever side you take, this rocking bar with the nonsense name packs 'em out every night, often spilling into the street, until the French owner tries – often in vain – to close things down around 1am.

Gurten Café Poco Loco (Map p188; ☎ 251-2379; Av 3 Independencia btwn Calles 18 Fernández Peña & 19 Cerrada) Are the bright-red walls a reference to Venezuelan politics, or an attempt to spark *amor*? We're not entirely sure, but this new Swiss-owned sports bar packs them in till late with a mixture of rap, *reggaetón* and salsa. The owner is also refurbishing a hotel upstairs…in case, perhaps, those red walls have the desired effect?

La Cucaracha (Map p186; Centro Comercial Las Tapias, Av Andrés Bello) The biggest and loudest disco in town, with capacity for over 1000 people, this place has two dance floors, one with techno,

THE ANDES

the other Latin-Caribbean. Popular with local teenage couples.

La Cucaracha Café (Map p186; Centro Comercial Alto Prado, Av Los Próceres) This vast modern nightclub has two large bars and live Latin music at the weekend. This is upmarket territory, where rich young things mingle the night away. There's a hefty cover charge to keep the riff-raff out.

La Cucaracha Racing Bar (Map p186; Centro Comercial Alto Prado, Av Los Próceres) Upstairs from the café is the Racing Bar, and the most impressive of the Cucaracha family. Racing is the theme here; there are life-sized racing boats and bikes and a Porsche hanging from the ceiling, and two reputedly original Formula One crates – a red Ferrari and a blue Williams – sitting atop the bars.

Shopping

Mérida is a good place to buy local crafts.

Casa de la Cultura Juan Félix Sánchez (Map p188; ☎ 808-3255; Plaza Bolívar; ☾ 9am-noon & 3-6pm Mon-Sat) The large, well-stocked craft shop on the ground level offers a wide variety of authentic, locally made handicrafts.

Mercado Artesanal (Map p188; Parque Las Heroínas; ☾ 9am-6pm) This small arty crafts market sits just opposite the Parque Las Heroínas, near the *teleférico*, and is home to a dozen stalls selling arts and crafts.

Mercado Principal (Map p186; ☎ 262-1570, 262-0437; Av Las Américas; ☾ 7am-4pm) This vast, busy and colorful main city market has dozens of stalls selling arts and crafts. Some of the city's best traditional Venezuelan food is also to be found here, on the 2nd floor. Try dishes such as *pechuga rellena a la merideña* (chicken breast stuffed with ham and cheese, breaded, deep-fried, and slathered in mushroom sauce). On the ground floor, hit the bull's-eye with a *super batido*, a milkshake reputed to enhance virility, made of half a dozen fruits, vegetables, raw quail eggs, raisin wine and the special ingredient – two raw bulls' eyes, slit open and squeezed into the blender.

Giros (Map p186; ☎ 244-1313; Centro Comercial Alto Prado, Av Los Próceres; ☾ 10am-9pm Mon-Sat, 3-9pm Sun) The best CD shop in town. Run by friendly Argentinean and Uruguayan staff, it has a wide choice of Latin rhythms, Venezuelan *gaita* and *joropo*, jazz and classics, and you can listen to it while sipping delicious coffee from a small café at the back.

Getting There & Away

AIR

The **Aeropuerto Alberto Carnevalli** (Map p186; ☎ 263-9330, 263-4352; Av Urdaneta) is right inside the city, 2km southwest of Plaza Bolívar, accessible by buses from the corner of Calle 25 and Av 2. **Avior** (☎ 244-2454) and **Santa Bárbara** (☎ 263-4170) fly daily to and from Caracas (US$120 to US$150). There are also direct flights to Maracaibo (US$80 to US$100), Valera (US$60 to US$80), Valencia (US$90 to US$120), Barquisimeto (US$80 to US$110) and San Antonio del Táchira (US$60 to US$70).

BUS

The **Terminal de Pasajeros** (Bus Terminal; Map p186; ☎ 263-3952; Av Las Américas) is 3km southwest of the city center; it's linked by frequent public buses, which depart from the corner of Calle 25 Ayacucho and Av 2 Lora.

Sixteen buses run daily to Caracas (US$16 to US$23, 13 hours, 790km) and half a dozen to Maracaibo (US$14 to US$18, eight hours, 523km). Small buses to San Cristóbal depart every 1½ hours from 5:30am to 7pm (US$8.50, six hours, 224km) – all go via El Vigía and La Fría, not via the Carretera Transandina route.

Four buses daily run to Valera (US$8, five hours, 160km) via the Carretera Transandina, five go to Barinas (US$6.75, four hours, 157km), and five go to Barquisimeto (US$13, six hours, 418kms) via the Carretera Panamericana. Both roads are spectacular. Two night buses now run daily to Coro (US$19 to US$23, 12 hours, 782km) and go via Maracaibo; if you're in a hurry, go to Barquisimeto, and change.

Regional destinations, including Apartaderos and Jají, are serviced regularly throughout the day.

CAR & MOTORCYCLE

Three car-rental companies have their desks at the airport, but two will only rent a car to travel within the region. One tour agency also offers car rental as part of a larger tour package. A small car rented by the local companies will cost around US$65 to US$75 daily, including insurance and unlimited mileage.

Alquil-Auto (☎ 263-1440) Travel restricted to Mérida state.

Budget (☎ 262-2728) No restrictions, but much more expensive than the other two local companies.

Dávila Tours (☎ 263-4510) Restricted to Mérida and Barinas states.

Natoura Adventure Tours (p193) Offers Venezuela-wide self-drive tours to those with sufficient Spanish.

Getting Around

The city is well serviced by small buses and minibuses, but they stop running around 8pm to 9pm, leaving taxis as the only alternative. Taxis are cheap, so you may prefer to move around by taxi anyway. They are particularly convenient for trips to and from the bus terminal and airport, when you're carrying all your bags with you. The taxi trip between the city center and the bus terminal or airport will cost about US$2.50 each way. At the time of research, a trole bus line connecting Mérida to Ejido, its densely packed working-class suburb 12km to the south, was under construction, and was expected to open in late 2007.

Línea Tele-Cars (☎ 263-9589, 263-8834) is a reliable taxi company with radio service. Apart from services within the city, the company organizes taxi trips around the region, including Jají, El Águila, Mucuchíes and San Rafael and the theme parks.

AROUND MÉRIDA

The region that surrounds Mérida offers plenty of attractions, both natural and cultural. Many sights are accessible by road, so you can get around by public transportation. This is particularly true of the towns and villages on the Carretera Transandina and surrounding mountain slopes and valleys. Many of them have preserved their historic architecture and old-time atmosphere.

Exploring the region is quite easy, as transportation and accommodations along the Carretera Panamericana are in good supply. Virtually every sizable village on the road has at least one posada or hotel, and there are plenty of roadside restaurants.

Parque Nacional Sierra Nevada

The most popular high-mountain trekking area is the Parque Nacional Sierra Nevada, east of Mérida, which has all of Venezuela's highest peaks, including Pico Bolívar, Pico Humboldt and Pico Bonpland (4883m). Climbing these peaks shouldn't be attempted without a guide unless you have climbing experience. Guided trips are offered by most of Mérida's tour operators (p192).

Pico Bolívar, Venezuela's highest peak (5007m), is one of the most popular peaks to climb. Given the country's mania for Bolívar monuments, it's no surprise that a bust of the hero has been placed on the summit. The climb requires a rope, and ice and snow equipment in the rainy season, which will be provided by your guide. What you can do without a guide is hike along the trail leading up to Pico Bolívar. It roughly follows the cable-car line, but be careful walking from Loma Redonda to Pico Espejo – the trail is not clear and it's easy to get lost.

MUCUPOSADAS – ANCIENT TRAILS, HOT WATER

A spider's web of ancient trails links the many remote villages in the mountains around Mérida, in the Sierra Nevada and Sierra de la Culata. Until recently it has been difficult to explore this area – there was little in the way of accommodations, services or guides.

This is slowly changing, due largely to the efforts of Andes Tropicales (p192), a European Union microfinancing project whose goal is to promote rural tourism in the region. Since the mid-1990s it's been offering small, easily repaid loans to indigenous mountain villages to help them create the services necessary to attract visitors.

The result? A unique network of trails, with *mucuposadas* – 'mucu' means 'place of' in the local dialect – each spaced a day's travel apart, permitting comfortable and relaxed four- to five-day treks, with hot showers and home-cooked food to look forward to every night. So remote, in fact, are some of these villages that a local guide or a GPS device are necessary, to prevent getting lost. You can even download the GPS data for free from the Andes Tropicales website.

The *mucuposada* trails follow more or less the existing ancient pathways through the mountains, and trek through cloud forest, pastureland, the glacial landscapes of the *páramo* (open highland), and even coffee and cacao plantations. In most cases the *mucuposadas* are the only places to stay in very remote, very beautiful locations.

This is sustainable, rural ecotourism at a budget price – the *mucuposadas* charge roughly US$15 to US$20 per night, including dinner and breakfast; tours organized by Andes Tropicales currently run around US$40 to US$50 per day, local guide and mules included.

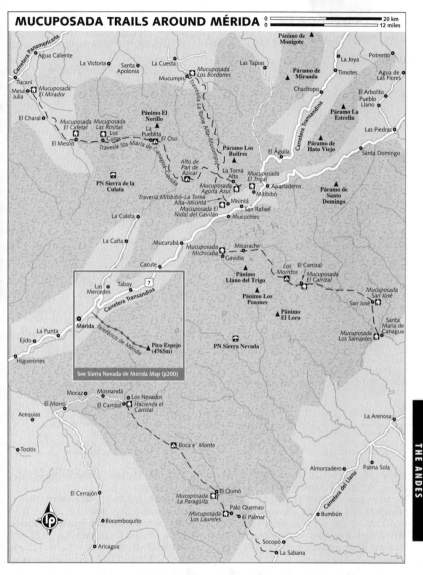

MUCUPOSADA TRAILS AROUND MÉRIDA

0   20 km
0   12 miles

See Sierra Nevada de Mérida Map (p200)

THE ANDES

Venezuela's second-highest summit, **Pico Humboldt** (4942m), is also popular with high-mountain trekkers. There's not much here in the way of mountaineering, but the hike itself is marvelous. The starting point for the trek is La Mucuy, accessible by road from Mérida. A four- to six-hour walk from La Mucuy will take you up to the small **Laguna La Coromoto** (3200m), where trekkers normally camp the first night. The next day, it's a four-hour walk to reach **Laguna Verde** (4000m), one of the largest lakes in the area. Some hikers stay here the second night, or you can walk for another hour to **Laguna El Suero** (4200m), a tiny lake almost at the foot of the glacier. It gets freezing at night, so have plenty of warm

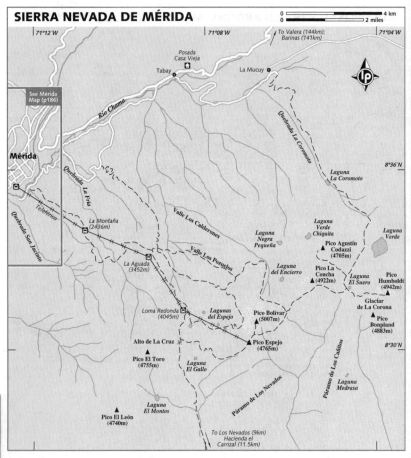

SIERRA NEVADA DE MÉRIDA

THE ANDES

clothes. Pico Humboldt is a two- to four-hour ascent, depending on the weather. You reach the snow line at about 4850m. Further up, crampons and an ice axe are recommended, and keep an eye out for crevasses. Again, this climb is best done with an experienced local guide, particularly in the rainy (snowy) season.

Back at Laguna El Suero, you can return the same way to La Mucuy or continue along the route known as **La Travesía** to the cable-car top station at Pico Espejo (4765m). After an initial 500m ascent from the lake, the trail to Pico Espejo (four to six hours) goes for most of the way at roughly the same altitude of nearly 4700m. You can then climb Pico Bolívar before returning to Mérida by foot

or *teleférico*. The whole loop normally takes four to six days.

An easier destination is **Los Nevados**, a charming mountain village nestled at 2440m. Simple accommodations and food are available, including Posada Guamanchi (see p193) and **Posada Bella Vista** (☎ 0415-212-0410); both charge around US$14 to US$18 per person for lodging, including dinner and breakfast the next morning (there are no restaurants in the village). The trip is normally done as a two-day loop that includes rides by cable car, mule and jeep. The usual way is to go by cable car up to Pico Espejo, have a look around and go down (also by cable car) to Loma Redonda. Then walk (five to six hours) or ride a mule (US$7, four to five hours) to Los Nevados for the night. The next day, you take a jeep to Mérida (US$50 for up to five people, four to five hours, 63km) along a breathtaking, cliffside-hugging track.

Rather than stay in Los Nevados itself, you can also walk an extra hour past the village to the 200-year-old **Hacienda el Carrizal** (☎ 263-8633; per person incl dinner & breakfast US$16), part of the *mucuposada* network. It's a working farm that produces maize, wheat and potatoes, and you can either walk back to Los Nevados the next day, or use it to begin the five-day, four-night trans-Andean trek to El Quinó and La Sabana.

Parque Nacional Sierra La Culata

The Parque Nacional Sierra La Culata, to the north of Mérida, also offers some amazing hiking territory, and is particularly noted for its desertlike highland landscapes. Take a por puesto to La Culata (departing from the corner of Calle 19 Cerrada and Av 2 Lora), from where it's a three- to four-hour hike uphill to a primitive shelter known as El Refugio, at about 3700m. Continue the next day for about three hours to the top of **Pico Pan de Azúcar** (4660m). Be sure to return before 4pm, the time the last por puesto tends to depart back to Mérida.

Some guided tours don't return the same way, but instead descend southeast through an arid moonscape-like terrain to a chain of mountain lakes and on down to Mucuchíes via natural hot springs. Trails are faint on this route, and it's easy to get lost if you don't know the way; don't wander too far unless you're an experienced trekker.

Another interesting area for hiking is further east, near **Pico El Águila** (4118m). Take a morning bus to Valera and get off at Venezuela's highest road pass, **Paso del Cóndor** (4007m), about 60km from Mérida. Bolívar marched this way on one of his campaigns, and a statue

of a condor was built here in his honor (hence the name of the pass).

There's a roadside restaurant where you can have a hot chocolate before setting off. Take the side road up to Pico El Águila (a 20-minute walk), crowned with a communications mast, to reach a beautiful *páramo* (open highland) filled with *frailejones* (espeletia) and great panoramic views.

Back at the pass, walk 5km south to **Laguna Mucubají** (3540m). The path leads through another splendid *páramo,* before descending to the Barinas road and the lake, one of the largest in the region. There is an Inparques post here that will provide information about the area. From here it's an hour's walk through reforested pine woods to **Laguna Negra**, a small, beautiful mountain lake with amazingly dark water. A 45-minute walk further uphill will bring you to another fine lake, **Laguna Los Patos**.

A trail from Laguna Mucubají leads 7km south up to the top of **Pico Mucuñuque** (4672m), the highest peak in this range, which is known as the Serranía de Santo Domingo. The roundtrip will take the good part of a day. It's a rather difficult hike, as the trail is not clear in the upper reaches and you have to ascend over 1100m from the lagoon. Ask for detailed instructions at the Inparques post by Laguna Mucubají.

Jají & Around

The best known of the mountain villages is Jají (*ha-hee*). It was extensively reconstructed in the late 1960s to become a manicured, typical *pueblo andino* (Andean town), and its delightful Plaza Bolívar is surrounded by a whitewashed church and old balconied houses that now host craft shops. Jají has a few posadas and restaurants, should you like to linger longer. You can also visit an old coffee hacienda on the town's outskirts.

THE ANDES

NATIONAL PARK PERMITS

Some of Mérida's tour operators can provide information about the tours discussed in this chapter, as well as other do-it-yourself tours. Don't ignore their comments about safety measures. If you are going to stay overnight in either the Parque Nacional Sierra Nevada or La Culata, you need a permit from Inparques. Permits cost US$0.90 per person per night and are issued on the spot by Inparques outlets at the park's entry points, including one next to the cable-car station (see p187), one in La Mucuy and another one by Laguna Mucabají. Bring your passport, as most rangers will ask to see your identification before granting a permit. Don't forget to return the permit after completing your hike – this is to make sure nobody is left wandering lost in the mountains.

The town is about 38km west of Mérida, easily accessible by buses from the bus terminal (US$0.90, 50 minutes). A bonus attraction is the spectacular access road from Mérida, which winds through lush cloud forest.

About 8km before Jají, beside the road, is the **Chorrera de las González**, a series of five waterfalls. You can stop here to bathe in the falls' ponds, or just to have a look. Instead of returning by bus straight back to Mérida, you can walk 1.5km along the road (toward Mérida) to a junction, take a right turn and walk another 7km to La Mesa, a fine old town. Por puestos from La Mesa will take you to the larger town of Ejido, where you change for Mérida. It's a great day trip out of Mérida.

Mucuchíes & Around

For something a little less touristy, check out Mucuchíes, a 400-year-old *pueblo andino* which is especially proud of its beautiful parish church on Plaza Bolívar. Stroll about the adjacent streets to see the lovely little houses; some of them are craft shops, offering attractive handmade textiles, particularly ponchos woven on archaic looms. You may need to buy a poncho if you stay for a while – it gets a bit chilly at night. The town has plenty of accommodations, just take your pick.

About 7km further up the road is the village of San Rafael, noted for its amazing, small stone chapel built by local artist Juan Félix Sánchez, who died in 1997 and is buried inside. This is his second chapel; the first, in similar style, was built two decades ago in the remote hamlet of El Tisure, inaccessible by road. You can walk there in five to six hours or rent a mule.

Any bus to Valera, Barinas or Apartaderos will drop you at Mucuchíes or San Rafael. Alternatively, inquire at Mérida's tour operators or tourist offices about transportation to Mucuchíes.

CIDA Astronomical Observatory

North of San Rafael, at an altitude of about 3600m, is the **Centro de Investigaciones de Astronomía** (CIDA; ☎ 0274-245-1450; www.cida.ve in Spanish), an astronomical observatory with four telescopes and a museum of astronomy. It's normally open to the public only on weekends, but in peak holiday seasons (Christmas, Carnaval, Easter, August) it's open daily. CIDA is off the main road, and there is no public transportation on the access road to the observatory, but tours are organized from Mérida by **Perigeo** (Map p186; ☎ 0274-263-8805, 0414-565-9744; Centro Comercial Glorias Patrias, cnr Av Urdaneta & Calle 37). Tours (US$21 per person) depart on Saturday at 2pm (daily in high season) from Parque Las Heroínas and return around midnight.

Theme Parks

An enterprising Mérida businessman with an aching for the past has opened three theme parks in the area, all dedicated to nostalgia. They have become favorite attractions for Venezuelan tourists, though they may look somewhat tacky to foreign travelers. Put aside at least three hours to visit each park and go on weekends or during holiday periods to experience a touch of Venezuelan popular culture. Don't go if it's raining, because much of the action takes place outdoors.

Los Aleros (☎ 245-0053; www.losaleros.net in Spanish; admission US$18; ☉ 9am-6pm, ticket office closes 4pm), on the road to Mucuchíes, 24km from Mérida, was opened in 1984. It's a re-creation of a typical Andean village from the 1930s, complete with its Plaza Bolívar, church, school, post office, cinema, shops, bakery, restaurant and a working radio station. It's brought to life with period events, music, crafts and food, and a few extra surprises. Everything really looks and feels as it did 70 years ago, except for the prices. Por puestos from the corner of Calle 19 Cerrada and Av 4 Simón Bolívar in Mérida will take you there (US$1.45, frequent departure).

La Venezuela de Antier (☎ 245-0033; www.lavenezueladeantier.net in Spanish; admission US$21; ☉ 9am-7:30pm, ticket office closes 3pm) opened in 1991. It's a sort of Venezuela in a capsule, reproducing the country's landmarks, costumes and traditions. You'll find replicas of the bullring of Maracay, the Urdaneta bridge of Maracaibo and Mérida's oldest monument to Bolívar. You'll see Amazonian Indians in their palm-leaf thatched *churuatas* (traditional huts), Guajiro women dressed in their traditional *mantas*, and General Juan Vicente Gómez will show up in full uniform. Dancing devils from San Francisco de Yare will dance in their monstrous masks, and cockfights are held at the weekend. There's also an impressive collection of vintage cars. The park is 14km from Mérida on the Jají road; take a por puesto from Calle 26 Campo Elías between Av 3 Independencia and Av 4 Simón Bolívar.

THE ANDES

La Montaña de los Sueños (☎ 245-0033; www.montanadelossuenos.com; admission US$15; ◷ 4pm-midnight, ticket office closes 8pm), 52km west of Mérida, was opened in 2002. This is a Venezuelan Hollywood, revolving around the movie theme, featuring film- and cinema-related paraphernalia, plenty of archaic cine cameras, movie studios and two cinemas screening old films. You can even act out old movie scripts on re-created movie lots, and take home the videos. You'll also find a lot of vintage cars and an unbelievable collection of amazing old jukeboxes – no doubt South America's record. And, of course, there's a good supply of bars and restaurants to eat and drink in till late. To get to La Montaña, take the Chiguará bus from Mérida's bus terminal. For a late return, the park's attendants can call a taxi for you (US$18).

TRUJILLO STATE

VALERA
☎ 0271 / pop 93,000
Valera has been nicknamed the 'Gateway to the Andes,' and from here you can practically smell the cooler mountain weather, just a short, greenery-clad bus journey into the hills. It's a pleasant town at the base of the mountains, and worth looking around for a day. Conveniently, Valera is an important transportation hub, with regular bus connections within the mountains and beyond, and has the state's only airport.

Founded in 1820, Valera began to grow rapidly after the construction of the Carretera Transandina was completed in the 1920s. Today it's the largest and most important urban center in Trujillo state and the state's only real city – far larger and more populous than the state capital, Trujillo.

Information
INTERNET ACCESS
Expect to pay US$0.80 to US$1.10 per hour for internet access in Valera.
Cybermax (cnr Av Bolívar & Calle 8)
Cybertek (Centro Comercial Edivica, Av Bolívar btwn Calles 8 & 9)
motorway.net (Centro Comercial Iglio, cnr Av Bolívar & Calle 7)

MEDICAL SERVICES
Hospital Central de Valera (☎ 225-8976; Final Calle 6)

MONEY
Banco de Venezuela (Plaza Bolívar)
Banco Provincial (cnr Av Bolívar & Calle 9)
Banesco (cnr Av Bolívar & Calle 6)
Corp Banca (cnr Av Bolívar & Calle 5)
Delsur (Plaza Bolívar)

POST
Ipostel (cnr Av 11 & Calle 7)

TELEPHONE
CANTV (Centro Comercial Edivica, Av Bolívar btwn Calles 8 & 9)
Movistar (Calle 9 btwn Avs 9 & 10)

TOURIST INFORMATION
Centro de Información Turística (☎ 221-2747; Av Bolívar btwn Calles 10 & 11; ◷ 8am-noon & 1:30-5pm Mon-Fri)

Sights
Erected in 1925, the neo-Gothic **Iglesia de San Juan Bautista** (Plaza Bolívar) takes pride in being the tallest church in the Venezuelan Andes, and it is truly majestic. Its twin towers rise to 44m, and the interior is illuminated through large, colorful stained-glass windows commissioned in Germany.

The **Museo Tulene Bertoni** (cnr Av 13 & Calle 6; admission free; ◷ 8am-5:30pm Mon-Fri) has a varied collection related to the history of the city and the region, including pre-Hispanic pottery, religious paintings from the colonial era, and old weapons and furniture. Note the fossils of mollusks dating back to the period when the region was a seabed, about 80 million years ago.

Sleeping
Hotel Aurora (☎ 231-5675; Av Bolívar btwn Calles 9 & 10; s/d/tr US$9/14/19, d with balcony US$16; ℗ ✷) This funky hotel is built around an airy central atrium that rises three floors to the roof. Rooms are painted drab olive, but the mattresses are comfy and the place is clean. It's set right smack dab on Av Bolívar, in the center of things, and it's worth the extra couple of bucks for a balcony to watch the world go by.

ourpick La Posada del Guerrero (☎ 231-2062; Calle 9 No 5-38; d with fan US$14-16, with air-con US$16-18; ✷) Set on a quiet street just steps from the center, this cozy spot is the only posada in town, and your best bet in any price bracket. Friendly staff, a fish tank in the reception desk, and lovely fake roses and dried plants contribute

THE ANDES

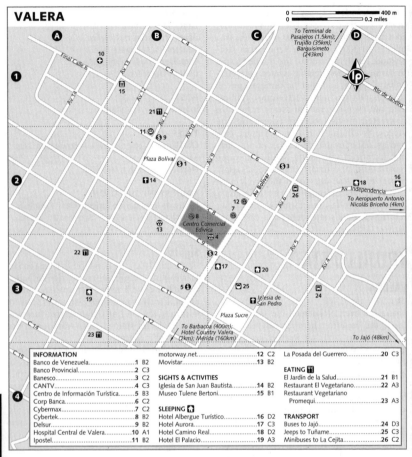

to the family feel. Rooms are comfortable, and while most have air-con, it's borderline whether you actually need it.

Hotel Albergue Turístico (☎ 225-5016; hotelalbergueturistico@hotmail.com; Av Independencia; s/d/tr/q US$28/30/35/40; P X) This motel-style offering is just a short walk from town, and has 20 spacious rooms, excellent bathrooms with lots of hot water, and a small restaurant. Check the rooms first – some of the mountain views have been blocked by construction across the street.

Hotel El Palacio (☎ 225-2923; Av 10 Centro Comercial Miami Center; s/d/tr/ste US$30/42/61/65; P X) The NASA-sized satellite dish on the roof suggests more space center than palace, but these 50 reasonable rooms are well kept, and the suites

have Jacuzzis. There's a Greek restaurant on the third floor, too.

Hotel Camino Real (☎ 225-2815, 221-4817; Av Independencia; s/d/tr/q US$40/42/44/46; P X) For those wanting a proper hotel, this 60-room, 10-floor high rise is the best – and only – option in town. Rooms are well kept, have good hot water, and sport lazy-boy-type recliners in front of the TV. The rooftop bar and restaurant is worth the price of the room – the food's a good deal, the beer is ice-cold, there's still more comfy armchairs, and did we mention the views? They go on forever.

Hotel Country Valera (☎ 231-5612, 231-0377; Av Bolívar; d US$42-47, tr/ste US$51/56; P X) Two kilometers southwest of the center you'll find the Country Valera, a comfortable 55-room modern hotel, and a good choice if you don't mind staying away from the downtown. It has its own restaurant.

Eating

The city center is full of functional, if forgettable, places to eat. Ironically, the newest, best place to eat in town is opposite the town's only McDonalds.

our pick **Barbacoa** (☎ 231-4314; Av Bolívar; mains US$7-12) Who would expect to find such a talented and creative chef in this small mountain town? It's not just grilled meat done to perfection – he adds freshly cut wedges of pineapple. Mango and chicken salad? Oh, you get a yummy baked apple with that, too. Beautiful salads for the veggie-eaters, and at US$9 for the mixed grill, you carnivores are getting a Venezuelan bargain.

There's also a good choice of vegetarian restaurants serving set meals at lunchtime:

El Jardín de la Salud (Av 11 No 6-24; set menu US$3-4; ☽ lunch Mon-Fri)

Restaurant El Vegetariano (Calle 11 No 11-21; set menu US$3-4; ☽ lunch Mon-Fri)

Restaurant Vegetariano Promequi (Calle 13 No 8-77; set menu US$3-4; ☽ lunch Mon-Fri)

Getting There & Away

AIR

The **Aeropuerto Antonio Nicolás Briceño** (☎ 244-1378) is about 4km northeast of the city center. A taxi will cost about US$5, or you can take a La Cejita minibus from the corner of Av 6 and Calle 6.

Avior (☎ 244-0055) has four flights daily to Caracas (US$110 to US$120), and five to Mérida (US$60 to US$80).

BUS

The **Terminal de Pasajeros** (☎ 225-5009; Av México) is about 1.5km northeast of the center. To get there, take the northbound city bus marked 'Terminal' from Av Bolívar.

There are a dozen buses a day to Caracas (US$14 to US$20, 9½ hours, 584km); most depart in the evening, and all go via Barquisimeto, Valencia and Maracay. Ordinary buses to Barquisimeto (US$4.50, four hours, 243km) run every one to two hours. Expresos Valera has half-hourly departures to Maracaibo (US$8.50, four hours, 238km).

Transporte Barinas has four buses daily to Mérida (US$8, five hours, 160km) along the spectacular Carretera Transandina. The road winds almost 3500m up to Paso del Cóndor (at 4007m it is the highest road pass in Venezuela), before dropping 2400m down to Mérida. There are also por puesto taxis to Mérida (US$12, four hours).

Por puesto minibuses to Trujillo (US$1.30, 40 minutes, 35km) depart every 10 to 20 minutes from the bus terminal, and to Boconó (US$4, 2¼ hours, 106km) every 30 minutes.

Buses to Jajó (US$1.50, 1½ hours, 48km) depart from the corner of Calle 8 and Av 4 (locally known as Punto de Mérida) every 40 minutes from 7am to 5pm.

Two or three jeeps a day to Tuñame (US$2.20, two hours, 74km) depart from Av 6 between Calles 9 and 10.

TRUJILLO

☎ 0272 / pop 38,000

Browsing Trujillo's markets, elbow-to-elbow with the locals in these crowded mountain streets, you need only look up for a soul change – green vistas surround the town in every direction. A flicker of a place set high up in the Andes, where time seems almost to stand still, there is something here for everybody – the city-dweller on a mountain getaway, the lover of native handicrafts, and the bargain-hunter will all find reasons to smile.

Trujillo is the capital of Trujillo state, despite the certain grumblings of much larger Valera, just 35km to the southwest. At 450 years and counting, Trujillo boasts some fine colonial architecture, and her trump card is the world's largest statue of the Virgin Mary – from her eyes at the top some say you can see as far as Lago de Maracaibo on a clear day.

Trujillo was the first town to be founded in the Venezuelan Andes (in 1557), but the continuous hostility of the local Cuica indigenous group caused it to be moved several times. It was called the 'portable city' because seven different locations were tried before the town was permanently established at its present site in 1570.

Located in a long narrow valley, El Valle de los Cedros, Trujillo has an unusual layout – it's only two blocks wide but extends more than 2km up the mountain gorge. Despite new suburbs at the foot of the historic sector, Trujillo remains a small and provincial place, in both appearance and spirit.

THE ANDES

Information

INTERNET ACCESS
Ciber Café Los Balcones (Plaza Bolívar)
DMT Sistemas (Edificio Almendrón, cnr Av 2 Bolívar &
Calle 1 Candelaria)

MONEY
Banco de Venezuela (cnr Av 3 Colón & Calle 2 Comercio)
Banco Provincial (Av 2 Bolívar btwn Calles 2 Comercio
& 3 Miranda)
Banesco (Av 19 de Abril)

TELEPHONE
CANTV (cnr Av 2 Bolívar & Calle 5 Carrillo)
Movistar (cnr Av 1 Independencia & Calle 5 Carrillo)

TOURIST INFORMATION
Cortrutur (Corporación Trujillana de Turismo; ☎ 236-
1455, 236-1277; ⏱ 8am-5pm Mon-Fri) The office is in La
Plazuela, 3km north of Trujillo.

Sights

OLD TOWN
Trujillo's historic quarter stretches along two
parallel east–west streets, Av 1 Independencia
and Av 2 Bolívar. In the eastern part of the

sector is the leafy **Plaza Bolívar**, the town's historical heart and still the nucleus of the city's
life today. The mighty **catedral** (Plaza Bolívar),
completed in 1662, has a lovely whitewashed
facade and some charming old altarpieces
inside.

There are some graceful historic buildings
around the plaza, including the **Convento Regina Angelorum** (cnr Av 1 Independencia & Calle 3 Miranda).
Built in the early 17th century as a convent,
it's now the public library. Do go inside to
see its splendid courtyard. You'll find more
surviving colonial houses west of the plaza,
on Av 1 Independencia and Av 2 Bolívar. The
best approach to sightseeing is to take either of
the two streets uphill and return down by the
other one. They merge 10 blocks further up to
become Av Carmona, but the best architecture
is within a few blocks of the plaza.

The **Casa de la Guerra a Muerte** (☎ 236-6879; Av 1
Independencia No 5-29; admission free; ⏱ 8am-6pm Mon-Fri,
8:30am-1pm Sat & Sun), also known as the Centro
de Historia, houses an interesting history
museum. Exhibits include old maps, armor,
period furniture, pre-Columbian pottery and
even a fully equipped kitchen with a historic

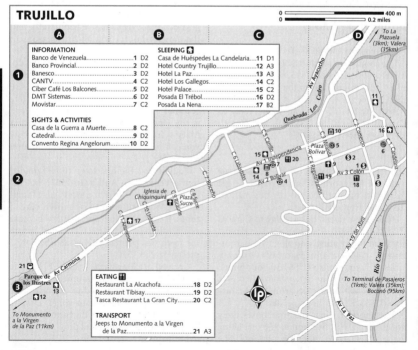

TRUJILLO

0 _____ 400 m
0 _____ 0.2 miles

INFORMATION	
Banco de Venezuela	1 D2
Banco Provincial	2 D2
Banesco	3 D2
CANTV	4 C2
Ciber Café Los Balcones	5 D2
DMT Sistemas	6 D2
Movistar	7 C2

SIGHTS & ACTIVITIES	
Casa de la Guerra a Muerte	8 C2
Catedral	9 D2
Convento Regina Angelorum	10 D2

SLEEPING 🛏	
Casa de Huéspedes La Candelaria	11 D1
Hotel Country Trujillo	12 A3
Hotel La Paz	13 A3
Hotel Los Gallegos	14 C2
Hotel Palace	15 C2
Posada El Trébol	16 D2
Posada La Nena	17 B2

EATING 🍴	
Restaurant La Alcachofa	18 D2
Restaurant Tibisay	19 D2
Tasca Restaurant La Gran City	20 C2

TRANSPORT	
Jeeps to Monumento a la Virgen	
de la Paz	21 A3

To La
Plazuela
(3km); Valera
(35km)

Quebrada Los Cedro

Plaza
Bolívar

Iglesia de
Chiquinquirá

Plaza
Sucre

Parque de
los Ilustres

To Monumento
a la Virgen
de la Paz (11km)

Av Carmona

Río Castán

Av 19 de Abril

Av La Paz

To Terminal de Pasajeros
(1km); Valera (35km);
Boconó (95km)

stove. It was in this house on June 15, 1813, that Bolívar signed the controversial Decreto de Guerra a Muerte (Decree of War to the Death), under which all captured royalists were to be summarily executed. The table on which the proclamation was signed and the bed in which Bolívar slept are part of the exhibition.

MONUMENTO A LA VIRGEN DE LA PAZ

This gigantic, 47m-high monument is said to be the world's tallest **statue of the Virgin Mary** (admission US$0.75; ☺ 9am-5pm). Inaugurated in 1983, the massive, concrete statue stands on a 1700m-high mountaintop overlooking Trujillo, 11km southwest of the town. The internal elevator and staircase provide access to five *miradores* (lookout points), the highest of which peeks out through the Virgin's eyes. You can enjoy views over much of Trujillo state, and on a clear day you can even see the peaks of the Sierra Nevada de Mérida and a part of Lago de Maracaibo.

Jeeps to the monument leave from next to the Parque de los Ilustres in Trujillo. They depart upon collecting at least five passengers and charge US$0.90 per head one-way for a 20-minute trip. On weekdays the wait may be quite long, but you can pay for five seats and have the jeep to yourself. It's best to start early, as later in the day the Virgin is often shrouded by clouds, even in the dry season. If you feel like some exercise, the monument is a two- to three-hour walk uphill from town.

Sleeping

Hotel Palace (☎ 236-6936; cnr Av 1 Independencia & Calle 5 Carrillo; s/tr US$6/9, d US$7-8) The daily washing adorns the central garden courtyard of this hyperbolically named cheapie. But what it lacks in comfort – no air-con or TV, for instance – it more than makes up for with good ceiling fans and great prices.

Hotel Los Gallegos (☎ 236-3193; Av 1 Independencia No 5-65; s/d/tr/q with fan US$12/21/27/33, d with air-con US$21; **P** ⊗) A luscious if eclectic selection of Edwardian and wicker furniture adorns this neat, well-run posada. Hot water, cable TV and friendly staff make this 32-room hotel a reasonable choice.

Posada El Trébol (☎ 236-6078; Calle 1 Candelaria No 1-53; d with fan US$12, with air-con US$14, with air-con & king-size bed US$16, q US$19; **P** ⊗) A sense of luxury pervades this brand spanking new option, with 16 bright rooms offering both tranquil-

ity and a very central location, just steps from Plaza Bolívar and the center of town.

Posada La Nena (☎ 236-7009; Calle 11 Arismendi; tr US$16; ⊗) Being refurbished at the time of our research, La Nena is owned and managed by a friendly naive-style painter, and has five neat rooms that are specifically nonsmoking. All the rooms should be re-opened by the time you get there.

Hotel La Paz (☎ 236-4864, 236-5157; cnr Calle 15 & Av Carmona; d/tr/q US$16/30/33; **P** ⊗) This seven-story edifice, a bit out of proportion for this site, offers 28 spacious suites, though they are rather on the basic side and pretty worn out.

Casa de Huéspedes La Candelaria (Calle 1 Candelaria; d US$16-18; **P** ⊗) Two blocks downhill from Plaza Bolívar, this inviting, 15-room new hotel is excellent value. Rooms are spotless and quiet and have fridge and private bathrooms with hot water.

ourpick **Hotel Country Trujillo** (☎ 236-3942, 236-3646; Av Carmona; d US$21-27, tr US$33; **P** ⊗ ⊛) The Country is definitely the best place in town, offering spacious, air-conditioned rooms that have wide, comfortable beds, fridges and stylish furniture. It has a fair-sized swimming pool (which can be used by nonguests for US$4), and a relaxed restaurant by the pool that serves both local and international cuisine.

Eating

Restaurant Tibisay (cnr Calle 4 Regularización & Av 3 Colón; mains US$3.50-4.50) Mind your matches, the local firemen eat here. You can see why – it serves solid, stick-to-your-ribs food in an unpretentious cafeteria atmosphere, and with prices to match.

Restaurant La Alcachofa (Av 3 Colón btwn Calles 2 Comercio & 3 Miranda; set meal US$4; ☺ lunch) Simple and modest, this is the only vegetarian spot in town, serving a filling *menú ejecutivo* (set meal) at lunch only.

Tasca Restaurant La Gran City (☎ 236-5254; Av 1 Independencia; set meal US$4, mains US$6-9) Perhaps nothing particularly special by Caracas standards, but here it's one of the best eateries in town, and it also offers a solid *menú ejecutivo* for US$4, something that is hard to get in Caracas for this price.

Getting There & Away

The **Terminal de Pasajeros** (Av La Paz) is 1km north-east of the town's center, beyond Río Castán, and is accessible by urban minibuses. The terminal is rather quiet, and the only really frequent connection is with Valera (US$1.10, 40 minutes, 35km). A few night buses go to Caracas (US$14 to US$19, 9½ hours, 589km). Transportation to Boconó (US$3.50, two hours, 95km) is infrequent and thins out in the late morning. You may need to go to Valera, from where minibuses to Boconó depart regularly until about 5pm.

BOCONÓ

☎ 0272 / pop 48,000

Simón Bolívar called Boconó the 'Garden of Venezuela,' and it's easy to see why. The region is famed for its lush natural vegetation, and for the cultivation of vegetables, coffee and orchids. In fact, it's said that Boconó produces a majority of Venezuela's vegetable crops (though whether this is testimony to the fertility of the local soil, or to the perennial unpopularity of vegetables on the Venezuelan table, is a matter of debate).

Boconó itself is a peaceful town nestled on the banks of the Río Boconó, and surrounded by the greenest of green hills. The town is 95km southeast of Trujillo, and the journey there, via a winding mountain road, is a spectacular attraction in itself. The mountain air will come as a welcome respite for lovers of cooler climes – the average temperature is just 68°F.

Boconó is an important regional craft center, known particularly for its weaving, basketry and pottery, and there are plenty of home workshops and craft shops in town. The surrounding region is dotted with pretty little towns such as San Miguel, Tostós and Niquitao, for which Boconó is a convenient jumping-off point.

Boconó was founded in 1560 on one of the sites chosen for Trujillo, but when the state capital made one of its several moves, some of the inhabitants decided to stay on. Isolated for centuries from the outside world, Boconó grew slowly and remained largely self-sufficient. It wasn't until the 1930s that the Trujillo–Boconó road was built, linking the town to the state capital and the rest of the country, although a sense of isolation is still palpable around the place.

Information

INTERNET ACCESS

The below all charge around US$0.80 to US$1.10 per hour for internet access.

Café Cibertzion (Centro Comercial Doña Blanca, Calle 4 Vargas)

Inversiones Osnapa (Av 3 Miranda btwn Calles 4 Vargas & 5 Bolivar)

MEDICAL SERVICES

Hospital Rafael Rangel (☎ 652-2513; Av Rotaria)

MONEY

Banco de Venezuela (Av 2 Sucre btwn Calles 5 Bolívar & 6 Jáuregui)

Banco Provincial (cnr Av 4 Independencia & Calle 4 Vargas)

Banesco (cnr Av 4 Independencia & Calle 4 Vargas)

POST

Ipostel (cnr Calle 5 Bolívar & Av 2 Sucre)

TELEPHONE

CANTV (Plaza Bolívar)

Movistar (cnr Calle 4 Vargas & Av 4 Independencia)

Sights

The **Museo Trapiche de los Clavo** (☎ 652-3655; Av Rotaria; admission free; ☯ 8am-5pm Tue-Sun) occupies the walled-in compound of a 19th-century sugarcane hacienda. The core of the museum is the original *trapiche* (sugarcane mill) and exhibits related to traditional sugar production, but there's more to see here. One of the buildings features temporary exhibitions, while another shelters several craft shops. In the southwestern corner is a pleasant open-air restaurant, whereas in the northern end are craft workshops – look for the textile workshop, where you can see artisans weaving rags and blankets on their archaic rustic looms.

The **Ateneo de Boconó** (☎ 652-1131; Calle 3 Páez) is another place where you can see local weavers at work in their textile workshop on the upper floor. The Ateneo runs arts-and-crafts exhibitions from time to time. Down the road from the Ateneo is the **Paseo Artesanal Fabricio Ojeda** (cnr Calle 3 Páez & Av Cuatricentenario), a craft market featuring a collection of craft stands.

The small **Museo Campesino Tiscachic** (☎ 652-3313; Calle Tiscachic; admission free; ☯ 9am-3pm Mon-Fri) has quite an interesting exhibition of crafts – mostly woodcarving, pottery and basketry – fashioned by local artisans. It's in the Centro de Servicios Campesinos Tiscachic, 150m northeast of town past the bridge and off the road to Valera. The center hosts a lively food market on Saturday.

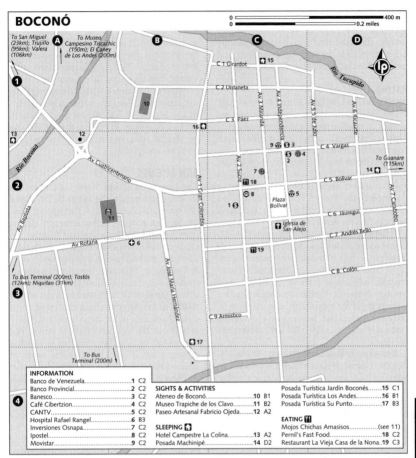

BOCONÓ

Sleeping

Posada Turística Los Andes (☎ 652-1100; Calle 3 Páez No 1-08; s without bathroom US$10, d/tr with bathroom US$12/16) This basic posada surrounds a pleasant courtyard with flowering red plants. Some rooms lack both windows and private facilities, but there's hot water, and it's cheap.

Posada Turística Jardín Boconés (☎ 652-0171; Calle 1 Girardot No 3-05; d/tr/q US$14/19/23, high-season surcharge US$5) This romantic, 100-year-old house has a leafy central garden shaded by two old mango trees. It has eight cheerful, tranquil rooms, all with private bathroom and hot water. Meals are available on request, or you can use the kitchen.

Posada Turística Su Punto (☎ 652-1047; Av José María Hernández; d/tr/q US$16/21/23; P) This groovy

posada, decorated throughout with antiques and crafts, has six spotless rooms in three bungalows, and a good restaurant that serves *pollo de canasta*, the local specialty.

Hotel Campestre La Colina (☎ 652-2695; www .hotel_lacolina.com.ve; Vía Las Guayabitas; d US$28; P) Set on a slope next to the river, this relaxing place with a countryside feel has a colony of chalets scattered over its spacious grounds, a hotel building overlooking the river, and its own restaurant. It's an ideal place for motorists, but will also perfectly suit travelers without their own wheels.

Posada Machinipé (☎ 652-1506; eliztp@gmail.com; Calle 5 Bolívar No 6-49; d/tr/q US$28/37/47; P) This cozy posada feels so much like home, you might not want to leave. And what's the hurry? The

Machinipé is a deliciously relaxing holiday spot, the seven rooms are all super-duper comfy, and the friendly owners will happily organize tours to the regional attractions, and are excellent sources of local information.

Eating

Pernil's Fast Food (cnr Calle 5 Bolívar & Av 2 Sucre; snacks US$2-4) This smart, modern new corner spot has already conquered local stomachs thanks to its tasty sandwiches, hamburgers, stuffed *arepas* (corn pancakes) and Arab shawarmas.

Mojos Chichas Amasisos (Museo Trapiche de los Clavo, Av Rotaria; breakfast US$3, lunch US$4-7; ☺ 8am-3pm) This small outdoor nook is tucked away in the grounds of the Museo Trapiche, and offers creole breakfasts as well as pasta, fish, beef and chicken for lunch.

El Caney de los Andes (Calle Tiscachic; mains US$4.50-8) Come to eat, drink and maybe dance in this huge rustic hut thatched with palm leaves, right behind the Museo Campesino Tiscachic. It has become popular for its delicious *carne en barra* (beef grilled on a stick), but it's equally good for a drinking session, particularly at the weekend, when there's live music (*joropo, gaita,* mariachi) till late, sometimes till dawn.

Restaurant La Vieja Casa de la Nona (☎ 0416-414-9056; Calle 7 Andrés Bello btwn Avs 2 Sucre & 3 Miranda No 4-29; mains US$5-9) Dining on home-style creole tucker in 'Gramma's Old House,' you can't help but smile. The place is full of antiques – there's an old piano in one of its four cozy rooms – and did we mention the food? It doesn't get much more down-home than this.

Getting There & Away

All transportation options arrive and leave from the new bus terminal just south of town.

Minibuses heading to Valera (US$4, 2¼ hours, 106km) depart when full until about 5pm. Minibuses to Trujillo (US$3.50, two hours, 95km) cost about the same, but stop running in the late morning.

There are a few nightly buses to Caracas (US$13 to US$18, 10 hours, 542km), operated by two companies, Transporte Las Delicias and Expresos Los Andes. They all go via Guanare. If your aim is Guanare (US$5.60, 3½ hours, 115km) and you miss the last mid-afternoon bus, catch a Caracas-bound bus. There are minibuses to San Miguel (US$1.40, 40 minutes, 27km) every hour or so.

Jeeps to Niquitao (US$1.60, 50 minutes, 31km) depart from Av Sucre about every 30 minutes until 5pm or 6pm on weekdays. At the weekend, they leave when full (every one to two hours). The Niquitao jeeps don't enter Tostós, but there are direct jeeps to Tostós (US$0.90, 20 minutes, 12km) departing from the same stop. Also from this stop are jeeps to Las Mesitas (US$3.20, 1½ hours, 44km), beyond Niquitao. In theory, three jeeps run per day, at 1pm, 3pm and 5pm, but only the first two are reliable.

SAN MIGUEL

The tiny town of San Miguel is famous for its colonial church, the **Iglesia de San Miguel** (☺ 9am-noon & 2-5pm Mon-Fri, 9:30am-noon Sat, 11am-2pm Sun), an austere, squat structure dating from around 1760. Its unusual features include roofed external corridors on both sides and a Latin-cross layout, a design rarely used in Venezuela. However, the church's star attraction is its extraordinary 18th-century retable in the high altar. Painted with decorative motifs in bright colors in a charming naive style, this is one of the most beautiful, folksy retables in the country. Even if you're not a great fan of churches, this one is worth a detour – San Miguel is just 27km north of Boconó through bucolic countryside.

There's more to see in the church, including two side retables in the transept, made in the same style as the main one, though a bit more modest. And don't miss the statue of the blind Santa Lucía holding her eyes on a plate, on the left side of the arch leading to the chancel. It's a singularly impressive sight. Use the opening hours as guidelines only and ask around for the priest if you find the church locked.

The town's main event is the **Romería de los Pastores y los Reyes Magos** (Pilgrimage of the Shepherds and Magi), celebrated annually from January 4 to 7.

Sleeping & Eating

Hostería San Miguel (☎ 0416-772-8398; Plaza Bolívar; d US$10-12, tr US$14) Opposite the church, this is the only place to stay in town. It's pretty modest, but comfortable and not without charm. All its eight rooms have bathrooms with hot water, and the rooms upstairs also have balconies. Meals may be available by prior arrangement, though probably only in the high season.

Getting There & Away

San Miguel lies 4km off the Boconó- Trujillo road. The narrow, paved side road to the town branches off 23km from Boconó. Minibuses to Boconó (US$1.40, 40 minutes, 27km) run every hour or so.

TOSTÓS

During Holy Week, diminutive Tostós is the focus of nationwide attention for its celebrations of **Vía Crucis Viviente**, a stunning Passion play re-enacting the last days of Christ's life. This blend of religious ceremony and popular theater, performed by locals who play the parts of Jesus, the apostles and Roman soldiers, is held on Good Friday. On that day the town fills up, and the crowd's emotions become almost hysterical when Christ is crucified. The rest of the year, Tostós is as it has been for more than 380 years: a sleepy town picturesquely tucked into the hillside.

The town is 12km southwest of Boconó and can be easily reached by regular por puesto jeeps (US$0.90, 20 minutes).

NIQUITAO

☎ 0271 / pop 5000

Niquitao is another pretty colonial town, spectacularly set in a long valley surrounded by mighty mountains. Founded in 1625, it still has much of its historic fabric in place, particularly around Plaza Bolívar. Niquitao is famous for its fruit wines, including blackberry and strawberry wine, and for its *sanjonero* (the strong, locally distilled bathtub gin).

The town sits at an altitude of nearly 2000m and has a typical mountain climate, with warm days and chilly nights – come prepared. It's a good base for excursions (see right).

Sleeping & Eating

Niquitao has a few posadas to stay in and most can provide meals.

Posada Mamá Chepy (☎ 885-2173; Calle Páez; d US$12) Well Mamá Chepy ain't as cheap as she used to be, but she's still a bargain-basement steal in this tiny mountain town. Set about 400m uphill from the Plaza Bolívar, she offers six rustic rooms, and serves home-cooked meals from her kitchen, if you ask nicely.

Posada Turística Guirigay (☎ 885-2149; Av Bolívar; d US$12, tr US$16-18; P) This quaint, family-run posada is just one block south of the plaza, and offers five comfortable rooms set around a central patio. All the rooms have bathrooms and hot water, and are excellent value for money. The hard-working kitchen in the restaurant serves up breakfasts, soups, stuffed *arepas* and *asados* (grills) well into the afternoon.

Posada Turística Niquitao (☎ 885-2042; www .ptn.ciberexpo.com; Plaza Bolívar; s/d/tr/q US$28/47/56/75; P) Set in a meticulously restored colonial mansion, reputedly almost 400 years old, the Niquitao is the most stylish and elegant lodging option. Its rooms are comfortable and spotless, and its own restaurant specializes in local cuisine.

Getting There & Away

Jeeps (taking up to 12 passengers) service Niquitao from Boconó (US$1.60, 50 minutes, 31km) every 30 minutes on weekdays and every one to two hours at the weekend.

From Niquitao there is a 13km road (partly paved but in bad shape) winding uphill to Las Mesitas. Jeeps service this route from Boconó. Beyond Las Mesitas, a rough road leads to the town of Tuñame (transportation is scarce on this stretch), from where a better road continues downhill to Jajó. Tuñame has a couple of basic posadas and a jeep link to Valera.

AROUND NIQUITAO

Niquitao is a convenient base for trips to the surrounding mountains, including Trujillo state's highest peak, **La Teta de Niquitao** (4006m). You can walk there from Niquitao, but it will take two days roundtrip, so be prepared for camping. You can also go by jeep; the day trip to the top will include a two- to three-hour jeep ride uphill via Las Mesitas to the Llano de la Teta, followed by an hour's walk to the summit.

Another possibility is to climb **Pico Guirigay** (3870m). It's also a long, hard hike, or an easy day trip by jeep plus an hour's walk to the top. Jeep excursions can be arranged through hotel managers in Niquitao, who can also suggest other interesting destinations in the region. A jeep taking up to 10 people will cost US$210 to US$250 for a full-day trip (check tour prices offered by Posada Machinipé in Boconó). Horse-riding trips can also be arranged in Niquitao.

For shorter excursions around Niquitao you won't need a jeep or a guide. One good day trip is to **Viaducto Agrícola**, a spectacular old iron bridge over the lush Quebrada El Molino. You can go down to the stream of El Molino, 80m below the bridge, and take a refreshing bath. The bridge is on the Niquitao–Las Mesitas road, a 30-minute walk from Niquitao.

In the same area, a bit further up the road, is the site of the **Batalla de Niquitao**, which took place on July 2, 1813, and was one of the important battles of the War of Independence. The battlefield is a memorial site, with busts of the battle heroes.

Another easy trip out of Niquitao is to **Las Pailas**, scenic waterfalls in the Quebrada Tiguaní that are a leisurely walk uphill from the town. You can bathe here too, though the water is pretty cold.

JAJÓ

☎ 0271 / pop 4000

Set amid gorgeous green mountains, Jajó is one of the finest small colonial towns in Trujillo state. Established in 1611, the town has preserved much of its old architecture and atmosphere – its prettiest part lies just north of Plaza Bolívar.

Sleeping & Eating

There are a few places to stay in Jajó and they either have their own restaurants or are willing to provide meals.

Posada de Jajó (☎ 225-2977, 414-4558; Plaza Bolívar; tr/q US$14/17; **P**) Set in a colonial building on the plaza (recognizable by its balcony), this six-room place is on the basic side but has much Old World charm. Señora Amparo, who runs the posada, can provide home-cooked meals, but let her know in advance.

Hotel Turístico Jajó (☎ 225-2977; Plaza Bolívar; d US$14-16, tr US$19) The only modern building on the square, this three-story, 17-room hotel spoils the appearance of the plaza but is otherwise OK, and provides good vistas over the square from its front rooms – be sure to ask for one of them. It has its own restaurant, which serves good trout.

Posada Pueblo Escondido (☎ 0416-174-6738, 0414-734-5559; Plaza Bolívar; r US$16) This two-story colonial building, next to the church, has four simple rooms with bathroom, to sleep up to four people. The friendly owners can provide information about the region and will be happy to cook for you if you wish.

Posada Marysabel (☎ 0416-871-3233, 0414-734-9466; Calle Páez; d/tr/q US$23/33/37; **P**) Two short blocks north of Plaza Bolívar, the eight-room Marysabel offers reasonable standards, though some rooms don't have windows – have a look

around the place and choose the room. The *tasca* has a pool table, and is conveniently open for breakfast. The owners are good sources of information on the region.

Mi Refugio (☎ 231-2428, 0414-729-0122; Plaza Bolívar; q US$23, 12-bed apt US$47; **P**) This basic refuge offers two pleasant, self-contained apartments, each with a small kitchenette, fridge, cooking utensils and private facilities. Downstairs is a *matrimonial* with individual beds, and upstairs is an apartment with four rooms – a mixture of double, twin and single rooms – but the catch is you have to rent the whole floor. Owned by a local doctor, the place is clean, basic and friendly.

Getting There & Away

The usual point of departure for Jajó is Valera (US$1.50, 1½ hours, 48km). Buses run every 40 minutes till about 5pm in both directions.

Jajó is linked by an interesting but rough mountain road to Boconó (via Tuñame, Las Mesitas and Niquitao) that climbs almost to 3800m. There are jeeps to Tuñame from Valera, but no regular transportation further on to Las Mesitas.

TÁCHIRA STATE

Most travelers who find their way to Táchira are in transit to Colombia, and don't stay for long. The national parks here, though, easily hold their own with their cousins elsewhere in the country, and there are growing facilities to accommodate travelers. Several tour agencies in Mérida have recently begun to offer tours.

SAN CRISTÓBAL

☎ 0276 / pop 247,000

This bustling, commercial city feeds off trade with Colombia, and spreads its business across a green-as-green mountain slope, down steep streets, past old men playing chess in the leafy plazas, and across the footpath. Called 'La Ciudad de la Cordialidad' (the Friendly City), perhaps this is because everyone has a smile, and something they want to sell you. Flip-flop lovers, beware – wear shoes on these busy commercial streets, or your toes will be trod on.

Set at a pleasant 800m, San Cristóbal is surrounded by misty green hills, scattered with the dotted beginnings of its growing suburbs. It's a good base to explore the local national parks, or stop in town for a day or two and have a quick look around. January is especially lively, when the city goes mad for two weeks celebrating its Feria de San Sebastián.

Founded in 1561 by Juan de Maldonado, the town was ruled from Nueva Granada (present-day Colombia) for more than 200 years, but didn't grow any bigger than an obscure hamlet. In 1777 it came under Venezuelan administration, but remained small and linked to Colombia because of the lack of roads to anywhere in Venezuela. A trip to Caracas was at least a two-week boat expedition by river down to Lago de Maracaibo and then by sea along the coast. It wasn't until 1925 that

the winding Carretera Transandina reached San Cristóbal from Mérida, and it was only in the 1950s that the Carretera Panamericana was completed, providing the city with a fast, lowland link to the center of the country.

Today San Cristóbal is the capital of Táchira state and a thriving commercial center fueled by the proximity of Colombia, just 40km away. It's an important transit point on the Carretera Panamericana between Venezuela and Colombia; you'll pass through if you are traveling to or from anywhere in Colombia except the Caribbean coast.

Orientation

San Cristóbal's historic quarter is centered on a triangle of three squares – Plaza Maldonado,

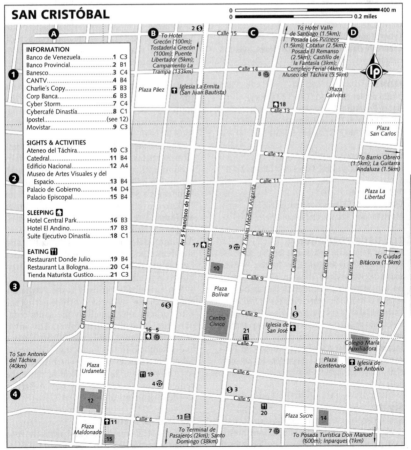

Plaza Bolívar and Plaza Sucre – but the city has expanded in all directions far beyond its downtown area. The focus of the new development has moved to the east and north, with the ironically named Barrio Obrero (literally, 'Working Class Suburb') 1.5km northeast of the center, where you'll find the cream of city's restaurants and nightclubs. The tourist office, Cotatur, is 1km further to the northeast.

Information

INTERNET ACCESS

There are quite a few cybercafés in the center, including several in the Centro Civico. Expect to pay around US$1 per hour.

Charlie's Copy (Calle 7 btwn Carrera 4 & Av 5 Francisco de Hevia)

Ciudad Bitácora (Calle 11 btwn Carreras 21 & 22, Barrio Obrero; ☻ 9am-2am) Open late near the bars of Barrio Obrero. Careful – don't drink and type!

Cyber Storm (Calle 4 btwn Carreras 8 & 9)

Cybercafé Dinastía (cnr Av 7 Isaias Medina Angarita & Calle 14)

MONEY

Banco de Venezuela (cnr Calle 8 & Carrera 9)

Banco Provincial (cnr Av 5 Francisco de Hevia & Calle 15)

Banesco (cnr Av 7 Isaias Medina Angarita & Calle 5)

Corp Banca (cnr Av 5 Francisco de Hevia & Calle 8)

POST

Ipostel (Edificio Nacional, Calle 4 btwn Carreras 2 & 3)

TELEPHONE

CANTV (cnr Av 5 Francisco de Hevia & Calle 5)

Movistar (Av 7 Isaias Medina Angarita No 9-97)

TOURIST INFORMATION

Cotatur (Corporación Tachirense de Turismo; ☎ 357-9655, 357-9578; cnr Av España & Av Carabobo; ☻ 8am-noon & 2-5:30pm Mon-Fri) The tourist office is 2.5km northeast of the city center, accessible from the bus terminal or from buses in the center; look for the Línea Intercomunal white bus with green stripes. Cotatur has desks at the airport terminals of Santo Domingo and San Antonio, open during flight times only.

Inparques (☎ 347-8347; Parque Metropolitano, Av 19 de Abril; ☻ 8am-12:30pm & 2-6pm Mon-Fri) Just south of town, Inparques provides information about the national parks in the region.

Sights

San Cristóbal began its life around what is now Plaza Maldonado. The monumental, twin-towered **catedral** was completed in the early 20th century, after the previous church had been wrecked by an earthquake. It houses the venerated statue of San Sebastián, the city's patron saint. Next door to the cathedral is the fine, neocolonial **Palacio Episcopal**. On the northern side of the plaza is the massive, late-19th-century **Edificio Nacional**, the city's largest historic building, today home to public offices, courts of law and the post office.

Plaza Bolívar is not a colonial square either. The oldest building here is the stylish **Ateneo del Táchira** (☎ 342-0536), built in 1907 as the Sociedad Salón de Lectura. Today it hosts a cultural center with its own art gallery and an auditorium staging theater performances and screening art-house movies. Do go inside to see what's on.

There are more historic buildings on and around Plaza Sucre, including the large **Palacio de Gobierno**. Also known as the Palacio de los Leones, because of the stone lions on its roof, this palace-like edifice was built in the 1910s as a government house.

Another turn-of-the-century mansion houses the **Museo de Artes Visuales y del Espacio** (☎ 343-3102; cnr Carrera 6 & Calle 4; admission free; ☻ 9am-1pm & 3-7pm Tue-Sat). Its 14 rooms feature changing exhibitions of painting and sculpture by local artists.

The **Complejo Ferial** (cnr Av España & Av Universidad), 4km northeast of the center, is a large fairground and sports complex, complete with exhibition halls, a stadium, a velodrome and Venezuela's second-largest bullring. About 1.5km north of the complex is the **Museo del Táchira** (☎ 353-0543; Final Av Universidad; admission free; ☻ 8am-5:30pm Tue-Fri, 10am-6pm Sat & Sun). Accommodated in a spacious old coffee and sugarcane hacienda, the museum features interesting exhibitions on the archaeology, history and ethnography of the region.

San Cristóbal's curiosity is the **Puente Libertador**, an old suspension bridge across the Río Torbes, constructed by the same company that built the Eiffel Tower. This intricate iron structure was brought from Europe and assembled in the 1920s, and has carried vehicular traffic ever since. The bridge is off Av Antonio José de Sucre, 5km north of the center; to get there, take any bus to Táriba, Cordero or Palmira.

Festivals & Events

San Cristóbal's major annual bash is the **Feria de San Sebastián**, held in the second half of

January. It includes agricultural and industrial fairs, bullfights, bicycle races and other sports events, a crafts fair, popular music, dances and parades, plus a lot of food and drink. Many events take place at the Complejo Ferial.

Sleeping

For upmarket accommodations, head to the northeastern suburbs, beyond Barrio Obrero. The city center has a good choice of inexpensive lodging but nothing really upscale.

Hotel El Andino (☎ 343-4906; Carrera 6 btwn Calles 9 & 10; s/d/tr US$14/19/24) Just half a block from the Plaza Bolívar, this is the most acceptable cheapie in town, secure and family run, although also popular as a *por rato* (love motel).

Posada Turística Don Manuel (☎ 347-8082; Carrera 10 No 1-63; s/d/tr US$16/21/28; P) This cozy, small family home offers four simple rooms, and guests can use the kitchen and fridge. It's a bit tricky to find the place, and it's often full, so do call ahead.

Hotel Grecón (☎ 343-6017; Av 5 Francisco de Hevia btwn Calles 15 & 16; d US$23-32; P X) The cheapest option you'll find for air-con and cable TV in town, the Grecón is a small hotel offering 20 spotless rooms, and it's just a short walk north of the center.

Hotel Central Park (☎ 341-9077; cnr Calle 7 & Carrera 4; s/d/tr with fan US$28/31/42, with air-con US$23/33/44; X) Renamed and being refurbished when we were there, this is one of the best overall values in town. All rooms have hot water, and some have air-con (but cost a wee bit extra).

Suite Ejecutivo Dinastía (☎ 343-9530; cnr Calle 13 & Av 7 Isaias Medina Angarita; s/d/tr US$43/48/58; P X) An offspring of the more expensive Hotel Dinastía, one block to the north, this small place provides comfortable and quiet rooms (not suites as its name would suggest). It was closed for remodeling when we visited, but should be reopened by the time you get there.

Posada El Remanso (☎ 342-1587; Av Principal de Pueblo Nuevo, Los Naranjos; d/tr/q US$74/104/120, ste US$90-112; X) This small, ambitious posada is growing by leaps and bounds. It now offers 14 comfortable rooms in a quiet residential suburb close to the tourist office. Room rates include breakfast, and it can provide lunch and dinner on request.

Posada Los Pirineos (☎ 355-6528; posadapirineos@ cantv.net; btwn Calle 15 & the prolongacíon of Av Carabobo; d US$63; X P) Los Pirineos offers 15 plush rooms, each in a different color scheme and style. With fresh flowers, a terrace with mountain views, and just steps from Barrio Obrero, this is easily San Cristóbal's best posada. Meals available on request.

our pick **Castillo de la Fantasía** (☎ 353-0848, 353-0848; castillodelafantasiahotel@yahoo.es; Av España, Pueblo Nuevo; d US$101, ste US$108-118; P X Q) The 'Fantasy Castle' is an opulent eclectic mansion with much character and style. Built only in 1988, it will take you back in time a century or more with its 18 old-fashioned rooms (each different and individually named), stylish furniture and ancient statues. Yet it has most of the modern amenities, including noiseless air-conditioning and Jacuzzi. Breakfast is included in the room rates.

Hotel Valle de Santiago (☎ 342-5090; www.hotel-valledesantiago.com; Av Las Pilas, Santa Inés; s/d US$106/116, ste US$133-159; P X X Q) This is one of the city's best hotels, set in a stylish brick building 1.5km northeast of the center. Modern, small (25 rooms) and comfortable, it provides most facilities you'd wish for, including a well-appointed restaurant, lobby bar, gym, internet access and nonsmoking rooms. Room rates include breakfast.

Eating

The city's main dining quarter is Barrio Obrero, which has loads of restaurants, including some of the best in town. A good place to start is Carrera 20, sarcastically nicknamed by the locals the 'Calle del Hambre' (Street of Starvation). The center also has lots of restaurants, though mostly budget ones, including numerous greasy spoons serving set lunches for US$2.50 to US$4.

Restaurant Donde Julio (Carrera 4 No 5-34; breakfast US$2, lunch US$3) This large, brightly lit restaurant does delicious creole set meals of roast chicken and steak. It's not gourmet, but it's some of the best value in the center.

Tienda Naturista Gustico (☎ 0416-579-0609; Calle 7 btwn Av 7 Isaias Medina Angarita & Carrera 8; snacks US$2-3) This lunchtime veggie place cranks out the homemade yogurt, wholemeal bread, wholemeal empanadas and other yummy snacks well into the afternoon.

Tostadería Grecón (☎ 343-6017; Av 5 Francisco de Hevia btwn Calles 15 & 16; arepas US$2.75-4; dinner only) Come here for some of the best *arepas* in town, and with a huge choice of fillings, too.

Restaurant La Bologna (☎ 343-4450; Calle 5 No 8-54; mains US$3-5) The sign says 'international food,' and it is – if you're not from Venezuela. It serves up hearty, economical Venezuelan food, and is popular with locals and tourists alike. The large potted plants and tasteful decor bring a little bit of elegance to the center.

La Guitarra Andaluza (☎ 356-0573; Pasaje Acueducto btwn Carreras 20 & 21; mains US$8-12; ✆ noon-4pm & 6-10:30pm) This classic Spanish restaurant sits in the heart of Barrio Obrero, and offers a good mixture of steak, chicken and pasta dishes, and a good wine list. Some weekend nights there's live salsa.

Getting There & Away

AIR

San Cristóbal's airport, **Aeropuerto Base Buenaventura Vivas** (☎ 234-7013), is in Santo Domingo, about 38km southeast of the city, but not much air traffic goes through there. The airport in San Antonio del Táchira is far busier and just about the same distance from San Cristóbal.

BUS

The vast and busy **Terminal de Pasajeros** (☎ 346-1140; Av Manuel Felipe Rugeles, La Concordia) is 2km south of the city center and linked by frequent city bus services.

More than a dozen buses daily go to Caracas (US$17 to US$22, 13 hours, 825km). Most depart in the late afternoon or evening for an overnight trip via El Llano highway. Ordinary buses to Barinas (US$9, five hours, 313km) run every hour or so between 5am and 6:30pm.

Buses to Mérida (US$8.50, five hours, 224km) go every 1½ hours from 5:30am to 7pm, but they may depart before their scheduled departure time if all seats are taken. The 7pm bus is unreliable if fewer than 10 passengers show up. Five buses depart nightly for Maracaibo (US$14 to US$17, eight hours, 439km).

Busetas to San Antonio del Táchira (US$2.10, 1¼ hours, 40km), on the Colombian border, run every 10 or 15 minutes; it's a spectacular but busy road. If you're in a hurry, consider sharing a por puesto, or take a taxi.

CAMPAMENTO LA TRAMPA

Four hours east of San Cristóbal lies Embalse la Honda, a man-made lake. The hydroelectric power produced by the dam supplies much of western Venezuela and parts of eastern Colombia with electricity. It's famous for one of its most striking, photographed points – the steeple of the submerged church in **Potosí**, the now-underwater town, which still pokes up from beneath the surface, and can be visited by boat tour.

our pick **Campamento La Trampa** (☎ 0276-341-6591, in San Cristóbal 0276-347-4428, 0276-347-4663; www .latrampa.org.ve in Spanish; s/d/ste US$16/19/37, cabins US$25-121; **P** 🖳 🖳), originally a small workers' village built to feed and house the many foreign engineers and local workers who built the dam, was redeveloped by the government into this ecotourist resort after it was abandoned at completion of the project in the early 1990s. Set on a green point jutting out into the lake, the camp is a great spot for exploring some of the less frequently visited national parks in Táchira state. Popular activities include white-water rafting, mountain-biking, free climbing, trekking, and the not-to-be-missed boat tour to the lake's drowning steeple. There's also some small, pre-Columbian ruins nearby you can check out.

Accommodations are in a choice of the hotel, cabins and *módulos* (a dormitory-style arrangement, popular with the many school groups that come to visit). There are 70 cabins in all, housing between four and 12 each, and all are self-contained, including private bathroom, kitchen and a small garden.

The camp sprawls over 30 hectares, and continues to be under rapid redevelopment. It boasts capacity for up to 600 guests – including three dining rooms that can each feed 200 people simultaneously – plus a 230-seat auditorium, a bar, a disco, a pool hall, an outdoor beach volleyball court, a restaurant, barbeque areas, saunas, a vast outdoor pool, a church, a heliport and even a taxidermy museum.

Several tour companies in Mérida offer trips that include a visit to La Trampa, but it's easy to get there on your own. From San Cristóbal, look for transportation to Pregonero (US$4.50, four hours, 133km). **Expreso Barinas** (☎ 346-5383) runs around eight por puestos daily that leave when full. Get off in Siberia (US$3.80, 3½ hours, 105km), where camp guards at the *vigilancia* post can give you a lift to La Trampa. If for some reason they aren't there, ring the camp and someone will come pick you up.

SAN PEDRO DEL RÍO

☎ 0277 / pop 5000

The tiny town of San Pedro del Río is Táchira's little architectural gem. With its narrow cobblestone streets lined with red-tile-roofed,

THE ANDES

single-story whitewashed houses, it looks like a typical old Spanish town straight out of a picture postcard. It has been extensively restored and is well cared for and clean. Particularly lovely is Calle Real, the town's central nerve, along which most craft shops and restaurants have nestled.

San Pedro has become a popular weekend haunt for Venezuelans from the region, mostly from San Cristóbal, 40km away. On these days, food and craft stalls open and the town blossoms. During the rest of the week, by contrast, San Pedro is an oasis of peace and solitude.

Sleeping

Posada Turística Mi Vieja Escuela (☎ 291-3720; cnr Calle Real & Carrera Calanzancio; s US$23-27, tr/q US$32/35; P ⊠) Located in an old school, Escuela will learn you a thing or two about hospitality. It's got eight neat rooms, some with air-con, and a lovely central patio to soak up the afternoon sun. It does a filling breakfast on request for US$4, and organizes walks and excursions in the local area.

Posada Turística Paseo La Chiriri (☎ 291-0157; Calle Los Morales 1-27; d/tr/q US$23/33/38) One block west of Plaza Bolívar, La Chiriri doesn't have the yesteryear's air of the Escuela, but has equally clean rooms, a barbeque area and a craft shop. Some rooms come with nice, big balconies – grab one if you can.

Eating

Dining spots have mushroomed since tourists began to come, but most of them open only on weekends. Local specialties include *gallina* (boiled and roasted hen) served with yucca, rice and salad, which can be found on the menu of most restaurants. The whole bird with accompaniments (US$20) will feed four to six people.

La Casona de los Abuelos (☎ 291-4830; cnr Calle Real & Carrera General Márquez; mains US$4.40-8) Open more regularly than most other restaurants, this is a large, colonial-style mansion that serves typical local fare, including *gallina*.

Other restaurants worth trying (on weekends only) include **Río de las Casas** (Calle Real), **El Balcón** (Calle Real) and **El Refugio de San Pedro** (Plaza Bolívar).

Getting There & Away

From San Cristóbal, take the half-hourly Línea Colón bus to San Juan de Colón and ask the driver to let you off at the turnoff to San Pedro (US$2.20, 1¼ hours, 40km), from where it's a 10-minute walk to the town. To return from San Pedro to San Cristóbal, take the Expresos Ayacucho bus to San Juan de Colón (US$0.65, 20 minutes, 9km) and change for the Línea Colón bus to San Cristóbal (US$2.20, 1½ hours, 49km). There may be one or two direct buses a day from San Pedro to San Cristóbal.

If you are coming from the north (eg from Mérida or Maracaibo), get off at the turnoff to San Pedro, about 9km past San Juan de Colón (the driver will know where to let you off). Going to Mérida from San Pedro involves a few changes. Take the Expresos Ayacucho bus to San Juan de Colón and change for one of the frequent buses to La Fría (US$1.40, 50 minutes), where you get a bus to El Vigía, and change again there for a Mérida bus.

SAN ANTONIO DEL TÁCHIRA

☎ 0276 / pop 33,000

San Antonio is a Venezuelan border town, sitting on a busy San Cristóbal–Cúcuta road and living off trade with neighboring Colombia. It's a pleasant enough place, but there's not much reason to visit, and the budget-conscious will find better and cheaper facilities across the border in Cúcuta, a much larger town. Wind your watch back one hour when crossing from Venezuela to Colombia.

Information
IMMIGRATION

DIEX (Carrera 9 btwn Calles 6 & 7; ☺ 6am-10pm) This office puts exit or entry stamps in passports. All tourists leaving Venezuela are charged a US$16 *impuesto de salida* (departure tax). You need to buy stamps for this amount in a shop (open till 5pm only) across the road from DIEX. Nationals of most Western countries don't need a visa for Colombia, but all travelers must get an entry stamp from DAS (Colombian immigration). The DAS office is just past the bridge over the Río Táchira (the actual border), on the right.

INTERNET ACCESS

CompuNet Cyber Café (Calle 6 No 8-28)
Infoplanet Cybercafé (Calle 4 No 3-45)

MONEY

While there are plenty of *casas de cambio* (money exchange offices) in the center, particularly on Av Venezuela and around the DIEX office, you will get significantly better

SAN ANTONIO DEL TÁCHIRA

rates for all currency transactions on the opposite side of the bridge – a five-minute walk – or in Cúcuta. None of the money exchanges will touch your traveler's checks. There are a few banks around Plaza Bolívar:

Banco de Venezuela (cnr Calle 3 & Carrera 9)
Banco Sofitasa (Carrera 8 btwn Calle 5 & 6)

POST
Ipostel (cnr Carrera 10 & Calle 2)

TELEPHONE
CANTV (cnr Calle 4 & Carrera 13)
CANTV (Av Venezuela btwn Calle 4 & 5) Also has internet.
Movistar (cnr Av Venezuela & Calle 4)

TOURIST INFORMATION
Tourist information desk (Aeropuerto Juan Vicente Gómez) Open only during flight times; 2km northeast of town.

TRAVEL AGENCIES
Turismo Internacional (☎ 771-5555; Av Venezuela 4-04)
Turismo Turvinter (☎ 771-0311; Av Venezuela 6-40)
Turismo Uribante (☎ 771-1779; Av Venezuela 5-59)

Sleeping & Eating
San Antonio del Táchira has a number of decent places to stay and each has it its own restaurant.

Hotel Residencial Colonial (☎ 771-2679; Carrera 11 No 2-55; s/d/tr/q with fan US$7/9/14/21, d with air-con US$14; 🍴) Chattering parakeets and two caged peacocks greet you at the Colonial, where the mattresses may well date from the colonial era. Rooms are basic but have private facilities, and are easily the cheapest in town.

Hotel Terepaima (☎ 808-8653; Carrera 8 No 1-37; d/tr with fan US$14/16, with air-con US$16/19; P 🍴) This grandmotherly place has 10 rooms, but only a few with air-con. Service is a bit arthritic, but it's on a quiet, tranquil street, and the rustic restaurant below serves good set meals.

Hotel Don Jorge (☎ 771-1932; hoteldongjorge@hotmail .com; cnr Calle 5 & Carrera 9; s/d/tr/q/ste US$19/26/29/35/37; P 🍴) Clean, neat and to-the-point, the Don Jorge has had more than 20 years to get it right, and continues to deliver well-maintained, good-value rooms. Arguably the best-value accommodations in town.

Hotel Adriático (☎ 771-5757; cnr Calle 6 & Carrera 6; s/d/tr/q US$26/35/38/45; P 🍴) You can't go wrong with the Adriático, which offers 45 fair-sized rooms with new, silent air-conditioners. Some rooms have balconies, if you want to watch the world go by. The hotel restaurant is reasonable and not expensive.

Getting There & Away
TO/FROM COLOMBIA
Buses (US$0.70) and por puestos (US$0.90) run frequently to Cúcuta in Colombia (12km). You can catch both on Av Venezuela, or save yourself some time by walking across the bridge, getting your Colombian entry stamp from the DAS office (on your right), and looking for a shared taxi on the other side. Ask for 90 days when entering Colombia.

Buses go as far as the Cúcuta bus terminal. Most, but not all, pass through the center – be sure to ask if you're planning on stopping for a while. You can pay in *bolívares* or pesos.

The Cúcuta terminal is dirty, busy and unsafe – one of the poorest in Colombia – so watch your belongings closely. You may be approached by well-dressed, English-speaking characters who will offer help in buying your bus ticket. Ignore them – they are con artists. Buy your ticket directly from the bus office.

From Cúcuta there are frequent buses to Bucaramanga (US$12, six hours, 201km) and two dozen buses daily to Bogotá (US$34, 16 hours, 630km).

AIR
The **Aeropuerto Juan Vicente Gómez** (☎ 771-2692), 2km northeast of town, can be reached by Ureña buses. They depart from Plaza Miranda, but if you don't want to go that far,

you can catch them on the corner of Calle 6 and Av Venezuela.

Aeropostal, Santa Barbara and Rutaca have daily flights to Caracas (US$80 to US$110). Aeropostal and Santa Bárbara fly direct to Maracaibo (US$70 to US$100). Santa Bárbara also flies to Mérida (US$50 to US$70). Airlines have their desks at the airport, but you can book and buy tickets at the central travel agencies. Shop around – their prices differ.

There are no direct flights to Colombia from San Antonio; go to Cúcuta across the border, from where you can fly to Bogotá, Medellin and other major Colombian cities (for a much better price than you'd get for a flight to those cities from Maracaibo or Caracas).

BUS
The bus terminal is midway to the airport. Half a dozen bus companies operate buses to Caracas (US$26 to US$32, 14 hours, 865km), with a total of seven buses daily. All depart between 4pm and 7pm and use the El Llano route. Most of these bus companies also have offices in the town center: **Expresos Los Llanos** (☎ 771-2690; Calle 5 No 4-26), **Expresos Mérida** (☎ 771-4053; Av Venezuela 6-17), **Expresos Occidente** (☎ 771-4730; cnr Carrera 6 & Calle 6) and **Expresos San Cristóbal** (☎ 771-4301; Av Venezuela 3-20). They all sell tickets, but then you have to go to the terminal anyway to board the bus.

No direct buses run to Mérida; go to San Cristóbal and change there. Por puestos to San Cristóbal leave frequently from the corner of Av Venezuela and Carrera 10 (US$2.10, 1¼ hours, 40km).

THE ANDES

220

Los Llanos

Like the Wild West of yore, Los Llanos is the mythological heart of Venezuela. The tough-guy cowboys living rough off and riding the plains are the fierce *llanero* warriors of song and story, praised by Simon Bolívar himself as the best soldiers he ever had.

Sandwiched between the soul-stirring sky and the endless plains is where you'll find the real star of any visit – the jaw-dropping diversity of bird and animal life. Look out into the night and you may find a bowlful of caiman eyes looking back at you from the lagoon. Chuckle also at the enormous herds of capybara, the world's largest rodent, as they live their lives in the marshy undergrowth. Come the dry season, a thousand scarlet ibises rise in a cloud of feathered pink from a shrinking oasis, prepared for their annual migration.

Los Llanos is also home to Venezuela's patron saint, the Virgen de Coromoto, who miraculously appeared more than 350 years ago. An astonishing cathedral has been built in the middle of the plains in homage to the Virgin and is now a landmark that draws pilgrims from every corner of the country.

This is the land that inspired two national obsessions – *joropo,* the hypnotic fast finger-picking of the harp-playing *llaneros,* and *coleo,* the local version of rodeo, where instead of lassos, the bull is pulled to the ground by the tail. It is here in Los Llanos that you can enjoy both of these activities first-hand, in authentic and spontaneous settings.

HIGHLIGHTS

- Venture out on a wildlife safari amid caimans, dolphins and birds, organized from the **hatos** (p222)
- Join the pilgrims at the astonishing **Santuario Nacional de Nuestra Señora de Coromoto** (p232)
- Learn to dance to the pulsating rhythms of **joropo music** (p230)
- Cheer on the cowboys as they compete in **coleo** (p234), the local version of rodeo
- Explore the spiritual capital of **Guanare** (p230)

Geography & Climate

Sometimes called the Serengeti of South America, the Los Llanos ecosystem stretches across 300,000 sq km in Venezuela (plus another 250,000 sq km in Colombia). It's mostly covered by grass, with ribbons of gallery forest along the rivers and islands of woodland scattered around.

Rivers are numerous and, in the wet season, voluminous. The main ones are the Apure, Meta, Arauca and Capanaparo, all of which are left-bank (south) tributaries of the Orinoco.

The climate is extreme in both wet and dry seasons, resulting in either floods or droughts. The wet period lasts from May to November and brings frequent and intense rains. The rivers overflow, turning much of the land into lagoons. In the dry season, December to April, the sun beats down upon the parched soil and winds blow the dust around.

Getting Around

You can fly into either end of Los Llanos, Barinas in the west or San Fernando de Apure in the east, but you'll have to rely on land transportation to take you into the heart of the savanna. San Fernando de Apure is accessible by paved roads from Maracay/Caracas in the north and Barinas/Guanare in the northwest. There's also a paved road from San Fernando southward to Puerto Páez, on the Colombian border.

TOURING LOS LLANOS
Budget Tours

While it is possible to visit Los Llanos independently, the enormity of the plains, the travel time involved and the scarcity of rural accommodations make tours the best option for wildlife viewing, especially for those on a budget. The majority of budget tour companies leading safaris to Los Llanos are based in Mérida, but a few are cropping up in the coastal towns. Expect to pay between US$180 and US$250 for a four-day, three-night excursion; remember, as always, you tend to get what you pay for.

A typical budget tour includes off-road safaris in a jeep (sitting on the roof is recommended, but strictly optional), a boat tour (in season), horseback riding, piranha fishing and usually bird-watching in the morning or evening. Most guides will try to catch an anaconda or river turtle for you. Some may also offer whitewater rafting to break up the

lengthy trip to and from Mérida. All tours include the services of a bilingual guide.

Accommodations are in one of the four basic *campamentos* outside Mantecal, except for Arassari Trek, who own their own *campamento* closer to Barinas. Sleeping is in hammocks, with shared bathrooms and cold water. Food is simple and filling, but nothing special.

There are many tour agencies offering trips to Los Llanos and there is no shortage of quality, bilingual guides. Some of the most reputable include:

Araguato Expeditions (p145) Based in Coro, this outfit is a small tour company that offers expeditions Venezuela-wide, including to Los Llanos.

Arassari Trek (p192) Pioneered budget tours to Los Llanos, and continues to be one of the best in the business. Most of their guides are respected naturalists, including Alan Highton and Roger Manrique.

Guamanchi Expeditions (p193) Offers tours to Los Llanos, led by a variety of well-prepared guides.

Tony Martin (☎ 0293-642-5541, 0414-831-3026; extremexpeditions@hotmail.com) Martin is a biologist and ornithologist who offers very hands-on wildlife tours. Nominally based from his posada, Hotel Cochaima (p263), in Santa Fe, he can also arrange to pick you up from Mantecal.

Campamentos

Budget tours from Mérida stay in one of four budget *campamentos* near Mantecal. Only one of these – Campamento Turístico Rancho Grande – can be visited independently. There's also a *campamento* inside the Parque Nacional Cinaruco-Capanaparo.

Campamento Turístico Rancho Grando (☎ 0416-873-1192; www.aventurasranchogrande.com; Vecindario El Palmar) First developed in the mid-1980s, Rancho Grande is the oldest *campamento* in the Mantecal area. It sits right on a river, where there are excellent wildlife-viewing opportunities. The owner, Ramón, offers a budget package of three days, two nights (for a total of four safaris) for US$100, including meals and transportation to and from Mantecal. Accommodations are a choice between bed or hammock – you might find the hammocks more comfortable – and guides are Spanish-language only.

Las Churuatas del Capanaparo (☎ 0212-235-1287, 239-2019; fmatas@trolk.com.ve; Margen sur del Capanaparo, La Macanilla) This remote camp sees few foreign tourists and is situated on the southern bank of the Río Capanaparo, 110km south of San Fernando de Apure. It's just inside the

LOS LLANOS

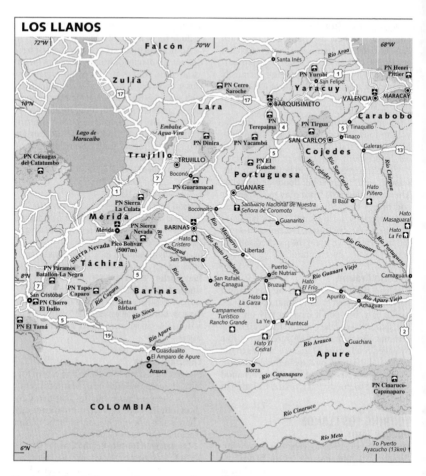

Parque Nacional Cinaruco-Capanaparo, the only national park in Los Llanos. The owner charges US$40 per day for very basic accommodations in one of the *churuatas* – palm-thatched huts with beds for four people, plus hammocks, private bath and electricity. The price includes breakfast, lunch and dinner, but safaris are extra, and go for US$35 to US$50, depending on your choice of: walks, boat trips, horseback riding or fishing. There are also indigenous settlements nearby that you can visit. The camp is not far from the San Fernando–Puerto Páez highway, near the ferry crossing on the Río Capanaparo. Call in advance and they can arrange to pick you up. In the rainy season be sure to bring insect repellent.

Hatos

The *hatos* are large cattle ranches that also offer accommodations and ecotourism safaris. Unlike in the rainforests of the Amazon, cattle production has done minimal damage to the ecosystems of these vast, grassy wetlands, and the poor level of nutrients in the soil makes it difficult to fatten livestock for market. So it comes as no surprise that many of the *hatos* have turned to ecotourism, and most have strict conservation measures in place to maintain this abundant natural resource – the plentiful wildlife.

Excursions are basically photo safaris in a jeep or boat. There's usually one trip in the morning and another in the afternoon – the best times to observe the wildlife and to avoid

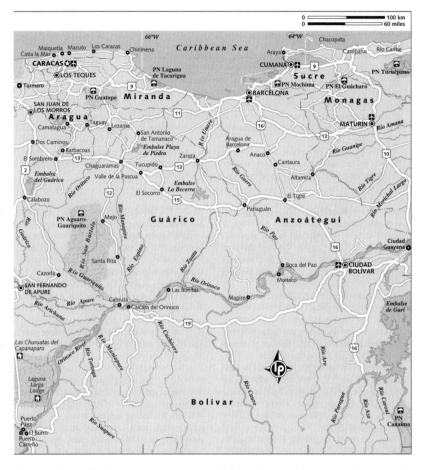

the unbearable midday heat. Boat trips are more common in the rainy period, while jeep rides prevail in the dry season. Visitors are taken deep into wilderness areas where animals, and especially birds, are plentiful and easy to see. Among the mammals and reptiles, capybaras and caimans are particularly common (see the boxed text p227). Fishing for piranhas is also an activity offered by all the *hatos*. Ask to eat what you catch; they are tasty.

Visits to some *hatos* are available only as an all-inclusive package, which has to be booked and paid beforehand, usually in Caracas. Packages are normally three-day, two-night visits that include full board and one or two excursions each day. Other *hatos* are more flexible, allowing visitors to come without paying beforehand, stay a day or two and pay accordingly. Expect to pay between US$130 and US$180 per person per day, which adds up to some US$400 to US$600 for a three-day tour.

Bilingual guides can vary from place to place and are not always on duty. Be sure to ask in advance if a guide who speaks your language will be there during your stay.

HATO EL FRÍO

The Spanish-run **Hato El Frío** (Map pp222-3; ☎ 0240-808-1004, 416-540-9420; www.elfrioeb.com, elfriolosllanos@cantv.net; P 🖳 🕿) occupies about 80,000 hectares on both sides of the Mantecal–San Fernando road, in what is known as Llano Bajo (Lower Plain). It's home to 45,000 head of cattle, an estimated 10,000 capybaras and

---

WHEN TO GO ON A WILDLIFE SAFARI IN LOS LLANOS

Wildlife is abundant in both rainy and dry seasons. The main difference is that in the dry season most animals flock to scarce sources of water, which makes them easy to watch. In the wet season, on the other hand, when most of the land is half-flooded, animals are virtually everywhere, but are harder to spot because they are not concentrated in certain areas.

The dry season is considered the high season. This is a good time to come, as you can expect good weather and more trip options because more land is accessible. The closer to the end of the dry season you come, the better. In late March or early April, just before the first rains, the crowds of caimans or capybaras can be unbelievable! In most *hatos*, the high season also means higher prices.

If you go in the dry season, take a hat, sunglasses and sunblock. They may also be useful in the wet season, when you'll need wet-weather gear as well. Whenever you come, don't forget a flashlight, mosquito repellent, good binoculars and a camera.

15,000 spectacled caimans. The *campamento*, 2km north of the road, also houses a biological research station, where visiting scientists do field research. Caimans, turtles and the rare Orinoco crocodile are bred here and there is a retraining program for ocelots and jaguars that have been illegally captured.

Accommodations are in a choice of 10 comfortable rooms; doubles, twins and triples are available. For those who can't live without it, the charmingly rustic dining room has recently seen the anachronistic addition of that Los Llanos rarity, a TV (note the satellite dish).

For those who prefer their animals in person instead of on TV, there are boat and jeep tours available for four-hour excursions in the morning and the afternoon. There's a choice of several different excursions in both the dry and wet seasons.

When there are vacancies, El Frío accepts individual travelers turning up without bookings, but an advance call is recommended. The price is US$120 per person per day in the high season (November 15 to April 30) and US$100 the rest of the year, with a US$30 supplement for single occupancy.

The entrance to El Frío is 187km west of San Fernando (42km east of Mantecal) and is easily accessible by public transportation. The San Fernando–Barinas buses will drop you off at the main gate and the *hato* road guard will call for someone will come pick you up. They can also arrange pickup from the San Fernando airport (about two hours by car) for up to four people (US$120).

HATO PIÑERO

The best-known ranch in the Llano Alto (Upper Plain), **Hato Piñero** (Map pp222-3; in Caracas

☎ 0212-991-1135, 0212-992-4413; biotours_gbs@hotmail .com, www.hatopinero.com; Biotur Hato Piñero, 6th fl, Edificio General de Seguros, No 6-B, Av La Estancia, Chuao, Caracas) is in Cojedes state, close to the town of El Baúl. It's accessible by road from the central states. If you are coming from Caracas, head to Valencia, from there it's about 220km south.

Given its location, Piñero has a somewhat different spectrum of wildlife from that of the ranches in the Llano Bajo. Set on the northern edge of the plains, this 75,000-hectare ranch also has plateau and gallery forest on the rolling hills, and is surrounded by four rivers. The wet season comes later (in late May or early June) and ends earlier (in September). Although capybaras and caimans are not ubiquitous here, there is a large variety of other animals, including ocelots, monkeys, anteaters, agoutis, foxes, tapirs and iguanas. This is largely the effect of hunting and logging bans, which were introduced as early as the 1950s.

Scientific research takes place at the *hato's* biological station, where many significant discoveries have been made about the unique Llanos ecosystem. Their private herbarium, where the potential medicinal properties of the indigenous plant life are investigated, is one of a kind.

The delightful colonial guesthouse can accommodate 25 visitors in rooms with private bathrooms. Packages can be booked in Caracas; they include full board and excursions, and cost US$160 per day in the low season (May to November) and US$180 from December to April. The ranch can provide transportation to and from Caracas (US$280 roundtrip for up to four people).

Since 2004 Hato Piñero has legally been confiscated by the government, although the ecotourism part of the business continues to run normally (see the boxed text below).

HATO EL CEDRAL

About 65km southwest of El Frío is **Hato El Cedral** (Map pp222-3; in Caracas ☎ 0212-781-8995; www .hatocedral.com; 5th fl, Edificio Pancho, No 33, Av La Salle, Los Caobos, Caracas; Ⓟ ☒ ⓢ). El Cedral is the most heavily marketed of the *hatos*, and one of the oldest, and is popular with wealthy Venezuelans as a holiday spot.

The ranch itself covers 53,000 hectares and has around 15,000 head of cattle. More than 300 bird species have been recorded on the ranch, as well as 20,000 capybaras and numerous other species. The *campamento*, 7km west off the road, provides comfortable lodging in 25 air-conditioned double rooms, all equipped with private bathrooms with hot water, and there is also a tiny pool. The dining room serves typical Creole food and there is a small *joropo* group that plays every night before dinner. Several different excursions are offered, by boat or specially prepared minibus, and there are sometimes optional night walks available (for a small extra fee).

El Cedral stringently requires advance booking in Caracas. The price in the high season (December 1 to April 30) is US$190 per person a day in a double room. In the off-season,

---

FUTURE OF THE HATOS

Venezuela has a well-developed system of national parks but only one, Cinaruco-Capanaparo, protects some of the unique Llanos environment. The rest of this fragile ecosystem depends primarily on the sage management of the *hatos* for protection from misuse through hunting or overdevelopment.

The *hatos*, however, are currently under threat from the current Chávez government, which looks askance at these large, private landholdings. The promise of land reform helped bring Chávez to power in 1999 – the land was not productive, he charged, and should be redistributed.

One large landholder who was targeted was the Branger family, who own Hato Piñero (opposite). Located in the upper Llanos, a short six hours by car from Caracas, the *hato* was a high-profile landholding, made more so by the presence of the ecotourism lodge. Pressure was put on the Brangers to 'join the revolution.'

According to Jaime Branger, the president of the corporation that owns Hato Piñero, in 2004 the governor of Cojedes state issued a decree confiscating Hato Piñero and Hato Paraima (a 53,000-hectare ranch he also owns). Branger contends that this move was illegal under Venezuelan law. One by one, he says, he countered the government's arguments.

'What does it mean to be 'productive'?' he asks. 'If I chop down the forest on my land to make a quick buck, is that productive? What happens then? There's no more forest. We can all go home.' The large-scale development of the land – 60% to 70% of which is under water for six months of the year – would destroy the environment, he contends. 'Traditional methods of measuring production do not apply. It's a question of sustainability.'

He received support from an array of environmental groups, and from the many universities that conduct research at the Piñero biological station. Eventually, he says, the government ordered the Interior Ministry to negotiate with him. He has been forced to sell more than half of Hato Paraima – 30,000 hectares. The price, he says, was reasonable enough under the circumstances, but he would have preferred to have kept the property.

As far as Hato Piñero goes, he has proposed to put 50,000 hectares into a private nature reserve, so that neither he nor any future owner may develop the land. The government has yet to officially sign off on the deal.

Branger is not alone. Owners of most of the major *hatos* have been forced to enter negotiations with the government to sell or give away portions of their landholdings. Some, such as Hato Cedral, have tried to sell the least ecologically sensitive portions of their land. Others, such as Hato El Frío, are seeking Unesco recognition to prevent confiscation.

The 2006 re-election of Chávez bodes ill for the future of the Los Llanos environment. The seizure of the national telephone company (at the time of writing) leaves little doubt that he intends to fulfill his campaign promises to nationalize and re-distribute Venezuela's wealth. The consequences to this unique ecosystem could be damaging and permanent.

it's US$160. The ranch is accessible by infrequent San Fernando–Elorza buses, but if you prefer, the *hato* can provide a car from Barinas (US$180 roundtrip for up to four people).

HATO LA GARZA

For those seeking luxury in exclusive surroundings, look no further than **Hato La Garza** (Map pp222-3; ☎ 0273-414-1176, www.hatogarza.com, info@hatogarza.com; P ⚌ 🖳 ⛴), about halfway between Bruzual and Mantecal. La Garza is a water buffalo and cattle ranch of 6500 hectares, and has been a nature reserve since the mid-1990s. Three main rivers cut across the property and a quarter of the land is gallery forest, making it a good spot for wildlife watching.

La Garza offers excursions in jeep or by boat depending on the season, and are one of the few *hatos* to offer safaris on horseback. Accommodations are in one of three large suites or two twin rooms, all with private terraces, king-size beds, cable TV and hot water. Most of the food served is organically grown on site and they can cater for dietary restrictions. There's also a richly decorated bar and a pool area with a view of both the savanna and the forest.

Booking and payment in advance are stringently required. The price year-round is US$170 per person. They can organize pickup from Barinas (2 hours, US$100 return) or Mantecal (half an hour, US$30). The Mantecal–Barinas bus passes the *hato* – just ask the driver to let you off at La Garza.

There is also a small landing strip that can accommodate light planes. There is currently no charter service available.

HATO LA FE

One of the smallest, cheapest and most accessible *hatos* is **Hato La Fe** (Map pp222-3; ☎ 514-6263, 0414-468-8749, 0414-325-4188; www.posadahatolafe.com, soreliafranco@yahoo.es; P ⚌ ⛴) It's in Guárico state, in what is called the Llano Medio (Middle Plain), about 74km north of San Fernando de Apure. It covers just 1070 hectares, so understandably there are fewer animals here than at the large ranches. There are not many capybaras, but you'll find spectacled caimans, anteaters, capuchin monkeys, iguanas and plenty of birds. Excursions are organized both inside and outside the ranch, including one to the neighboring Hato Masaguaral, which has a biological station that breeds Orinoco caimans.

A beautiful colonial-style mansion, next to the road, provides the base for excursions. It has seven rooms (three with and four without bathrooms) and a charming restaurant, plus a 14-meter pool at the back. The prices are US$100 per day in the high season (November 1 to March 30) and US$85 the rest of the year, all-inclusive except for long trips outside the ranch. You can lower the cost if you camp in your tent or sling your own hammock. The ranch is friendly to casual visitors, but call ahead to check the availability of rooms – if you're just passing through, a B&B service will set you back US$35, with no excursions or extras.

For those looking for extreme relaxation, the *hato* now offers a complete spa service, including massage, foot reflexology, body exfoliation and moisturizing, mud-therapies and neurosedatives. Expect to pay roughly US$20 per hour.

La Fe is roughly midway between San Fernando de Apure and Calabozo: buses run every half-hour (US$2.20, 1½ hours). Get off at *alcabala* (road check post), which is next to the ranch's gate.

HATO CRISTERO

A short 28km south of Barinas lies **Hato Cristero** (Map pp222-3; ☎ 0273-552-2695, 0414-454-4193, 0414-567-0201; hatocristero@yahoo.es, www.hatocristero .net; P ⚌ ⛴). Converted into an ecotourist resort in the mid-1990s, this 1100-hectare ranch sits on the edge of the Upper Llanos and is one of the smaller hatos. It offers good wildlife viewing, in particular bird-watching, although you won't find nearly as many capybaras, caimans or anacondas as you would in the Lower Llanos.

Hato Cristero is the closest ecotourist resort to both Barinas and Mérida, and thus makes an especially good option if you are short on time or don't want to make the long trek necessary to reach the heart of the Lower Llanos.

They offer a variety of safaris (by jeep, by boat and on horseback) and there's usually an optional night-time excursion available. Lodging is in air-conditioned cabins with large private bath and hot water, TV, fridge and safety-deposit box. There are currently seven rooms, including five triples, one double and one single (four more are under construction), plus a swimming pool. Much of the food they serve is grown or produced on the farm, including a cheese they make themselves.

THE WILDLIFE OF LOS LLANOS

Apart from the legendary anacondas and piranhas, Los Llanos is most famous for the myriad birds that gather seasonally to breed and feed, or live permanently on the grassy plains and wetlands. About 360 bird species have been recorded in the region, which accounts for a quarter of all the bird species found in Venezuela. Waterbirds and wading birds predominate, and the list includes ibises, herons, cormorants, egrets, jaçanas, gallinules and darters. The *corocoro*, or scarlet ibis *(Eudocimus ruber)*, noted for its bright red plumage, appears in large colonies in the dry season. Three-quarters of the world's *corocoro* population lives in Venezuela.

As for mammals, the most common local species (apart from the omnipresent cattle, of course) is the *chigüire*, or capybara *(Hydrochoerus hydrochaeris)*. This is the world's largest rodent, growing up to about 60kg, and has a face like a guinea pig and a coat like a bear's. It's equally at home on land and in the water, feeding mainly on aquatic plants. Other local mammals include armadillos, peccaries, opossums, anteaters, tapirs, ocelots and the occasional jaguar. Two interesting aquatic mammals are the *tonina*, or freshwater dolphin *(Inia geoffrensis)*, and the *manatí*, or manatee *(Trichechus manatus)*, which inhabit the large tributaries of the Orinoco. Both are endangered species, and numbers of the latter are dangerously low.

Also threatened with extinction is the largest American crocodile, the Caimán del Orinoco *(Crocodylus intermedius)*. These huge reptiles once lived in large numbers and grew up to 8m from head to tail but the population was decimated by ranchers, who killed them for their skins. Far more numerous is the *baba*, or the spectacled caiman *(Caiman crocodylus)*, the smallest of the family of local caimans, growing up to 3m in length.

The price year-round is US$150 a day. They can pick up groups of up to five people from the Barinas airport or bus terminal (US$40), or you can grab any bus heading to San Silvestre, Canaguá, Santa Lucia or Santa Inés, and get off at the main gate.

Laguna Larga Lodge

Situated just inside the southern boundary of the Parque Nacional Cinaruco-Capanaparo, Laguna Larga offers fishing trips on the Río Cinaruco and nearby lagoons. The lodge has four twin-share rooms with fan, and packages include three meals a day, domestic liquor and as much fishing as you can handle in two-seater boats for US$280 a day per person, US$350 if you're solo. They offer big discounts on week-long stays – US$2790 (double-occupancy) will get you a ten-day package, including six full- and two half-days' fishing, charter flights to and from Caracas, and two nights' accommodations in the capital.

The fishing in the rivers of the Lower Llanos boasts enormous *pavón* (peacock bass), the fang-toothed *payara* (vampire fish), plus *bagre* (catfish) that grow up to 60kg. All sport fishing is catch-and-release only. The fishing season runs 15 November to 15 April, but a lack of rain can extend the season to the end of April.

Visit is by reservation only, through their Caracas representative Alpitour (p356). If you're not coming from overseas or from Caracas, pick-up can be arranged from San Fernando de Apure (US$100) or Puerto Ayacucho (US$150), or you can take the bus to the ferry crossing at the Río Cinaruco, where they can pick you up by boat.

BARINAS

☎ 0273 / pop 295,000

Barinas is the biggest city in Los Llanos. It's the capital of a vast agricultural and ranching region, and the discovery of oil has given an edge of prosperity to the town. It's also an important transportation hub, and an ideal jumping-off point for adventures in Los Llanos.

The city has had a turbulent past, the relics of which can still be seen today. It's a likeable place, and the humid, muggy climate takes the edge off the small-town hustle and bustle. The center is compact and walkable, and is surrounded by large, leafy suburbs.

History

Barinas' long and checkered history began in 1577 when it was founded by Spanish conquerors from Pamplona in Nueva Granada (now Colombia). At the beginning of the 17th century, tobacco gave the town an economic base and overseas fame, as Barinas was the only region in the colony that the Spanish Crown allowed to grow tobacco. Other crops, including sugarcane, bananas and cacao, were subsequently introduced to the region, as was raising cattle. By the end of the 18th century, Barinas was Venezuela's largest and wealthiest town after Caracas.

The civil wars that plagued Venezuela during the 19th century affected the development of the town and the state, but afterwards a steady revival began. Agriculture and the cattle industry were joined by a short-lived timber industry, which took advantage of the extensive tropical forest in the region, chopping it down rapidly and indiscriminately. Meanwhile, oil was discovered in the region south of Barinas and is today pipelined to the coast near Morón.

Information

INTERNET ACCESS

Centro de Navegaciónes Barinas (Calle 4 Arzobispo Méndez btwn Avs 5 Libertad & 4 Montilla) Open late.

Password Conection (Av 6 Medina Jiménez btwn Calles 6 Plaza & 5 de Julio)

You Ciber.com (cnr Av 9 Briceño Méndez & Calle 7 Cedeño)

MONEY

Banco de Venezuela (cnr Av 7 Marqués del Pumar & Calle 6 Plaza)

Banco Mercantil (cnr Av 7 Marqués del Pumar & Calle 3 Bolívar)

Banco Provincial (cnr Av 7 Marqués del Pumar & Calle 9 Carvajal)

Banesco (cnr Av 7 Marqués del Pumar & Calle 11 Cruz Paredes)

Corp Banca (cnr Av 5 Libertad & Calle 10 Camejo)

POST

Ipostel (Calle 9 Carvajal btwn Avs 4 Montilla & 5 Libertad)

TELEPHONE

Movistar (cnr Av 7 Marqués del Pumar & Calle 4 Arzobispo Méndez)

TOURIST INFORMATION

Corbatur (Corporación Barinesa de Turismo; ☎ 552-7091; Palacio del Marqués, Plaza Bolívar; ✆ 8am-noon & 2-6pm Mon-Fri)

Sights

The unusual, two-block-long Plaza Bolívar still boasts buildings dating from the city's fat

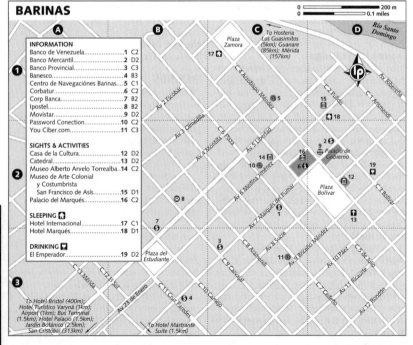

BARINAS

0   200 m
0   0.1 miles

To Hostería
Los Guasimitos
(5km); Guanare
(85km); Mérida
(157km)

Río Santo
Domingo

INFORMATION
Banco de Venezuela.................1 C2
Banco Mercantil........................2 D2
Banco Provincial........................3 C3
Banesco.....................................4 B3
Centro de Navegaciónes Barinas...5 C1
Corbatur.....................................6 C2
Corp Banca................................7 B2
Ipostel.......................................8 B2
Movistar.....................................9 D2
Password Conection................10 C2
You Ciber.com.........................11 C3

SIGHTS & ACTIVITIES
Casa de la Cultura...................12 D2
Catedral...................................13 D2
Museo Alberto Arvelo Torrealba..14 C2
Museo de Arte Colonial
  y Costumbrista
  San Francisco de Asís...........15 D1
Palacio del Marqués................16 C2

SLEEPING
Hotel Internacional..................17 C1
Hotel Marqués.........................18 D1

DRINKING
El Emperador...........................19 D2

Plaza
Zamora

Plaza del
Estudiante

To Hotel Bristol (400m);
Hotel Turístico Varyná (1km);
Airport (1km); Bus Terminal
(1.5km); Hotel Palacio (1.5km);
Jardín Botánico (2.5km);
San Cristóbal (313km)

To Hotel Mastrante
Suite (1.5km)

Plaza
Bolívar

Palacio de
Gobierno

LOS LLANOS

days. The pastel-colored, graceful **catedral** was built in the 1770s, except for the bell tower, which was added in 1936.

Across the plaza is the imposing **Palacio del Marqués**, occupying one entire side of the square. Commissioned by the Marqués de las Riberas de Boconó y Masparro as his private residence and constructed in the 1780s, the palace reflected the owner's wealth and Barinas' prosperity at the time. It was partly ruined during the Wars of Federation in the mid-19th century, but was later restored. It now houses governmental offices, including the tourist office.

Also set on the plaza is the colonial-style **Casa de la Cultura** (☎ 552-3643), built in the 1780s as the town hall and jail. José Antonio Páez, a republican hero, was imprisoned here but managed to escape, liberating 115 of his fellow prisoners in the process. The building was the town jail until 1966, but today it houses a cultural center and auditorium, staging art exhibitions and various cultural events.

Named after a local poet, the **Museo Alberto Arvelo Torrealba** (☎ 532-4984; cnr Calle 5 de Julio & Av 6 Medina Jiménez; admission free; ☼ 8am-noon & 3-5pm Tue-Sun) is set in a splendid 200-year-old mansion with a charming patio and a tree-shaded garden. It features an exhibition related to the history of the city and the region.

The **Museo de Arte Colonial y Costumbrista San Francisco de Asís** (☎ 533-4641; Av 6 Medina Jiménez btwn Calles 2 Pulido & 3 Bolívar; admission free; ☼ 2-5pm Mon, 8:30-11:30am & 2-5pm Tue-Fri) has a bizarre 30,000-piece private collection of old objects, including kerosene lamps, hospital beds, jukeboxes, crucifixes, chamber pots, fire extinguishers, wedding dresses, surgical instruments, turtle shells – you name it. It's stunning. The friendly attendants, accompanied by the owner's six dogs, will show you around and have stories about every single exhibit. Note the first street gas lamps from Plaza Bolívar.

In the vast grounds of the Universidad Nacional Experimental de los Llanos Ezequiel Zamora (Unellez), 3km southwest of the center, the **Jardín Botánico** (☎ 546-4555; Av Alberto Torrealba; admission free; ☼ 8am-3pm Mon-Fri) has many beautiful trees, a plant nursery and a small zoo featuring local species.

Sleeping & Eating

There's a variety of accommodation choices and half a dozen cheap hotels around the bus terminal.

Hotel Palacio (☎ 552-6947; opposite bus terminal; s/d/tr US$12/16/20) Well it ain't no palace, but it's 50m from the bus station, reasonably clean and has air-con and cable TV. The rooms are priced for romance – don't be surprised to see couples come and go.

Hotel Marqués (☎ 552-6576; Calle 3 Bolívar No 2-88; d US$16-21, tr/q US$23/27; P ⊠) The only real budget option in the center, the Marqués offers 50 spotless, freshly painted bright blue rooms, all with air-con and cable TV. A block away from the Plaza Bolívar and close to everywhere you might want to go in the center.

Hotel Internacional (☎ 552-2343, 552-3303; Calle 4 Arzobispo Méndez; d US$26-30, tr/q US$35/40; P ⊠) The 48-room, three-star Internacional is the oldest hotel in town and great value. Built in the early 1950s (when there was still no reliable road connection with Caracas), it has large rooms, high ceilings, spacious common areas and a no-nonsense restaurant serving copious meals. Ask for a room overlooking the lovely courtyard with a fountain.

Hostería Los Guasimitos (☎ 546-1546; guasimitos@cantv.net; d US$33-42, tr US$44; P ⊠ 🖳 ⊠) Travelers with their own transportation may be interested in this country-style motel off the road to Guanare, about 5km northwest of the city center. The complex features 100 spacious rooms with fridge, bathroom and hot water. There is also a gym, internet café, large swimming pool, bar and a restaurant serving typical regional food.

Hotel Turístico Varyná (☎ 533-3984; hotelvarinat@cantv.net; Av 23 de Enero; d US$37-42, tr US$47; P ⊠) This motel-style place, set on a busy thoroughfare, still manages to provide a surprising amount of tranquility in a colony of 10 single-story cabins, each of which has four rooms with a bathroom and hot water.

Hotel Bristol (☎ 532-1425; hotelbristol@cantv.net; Av 23 de Enero; s/d US$64/69, ste US$90-117; P ⊠) Popular with business travelers, the decor in the Bristol hasn't changed for a couple of decades, but it has all the amenities, plus a convention hall, beauty salon and barber shop, all in the same building.

Hotel Mastranto Suite (☎ 541-41126, fax 532-1876; www.mastrantosuite.com; Av Cuatricentenaria; s/d US$125/137, ste US$365-485; P ⊠) It doesn't get much more luxurious than this almost faultlessly beautiful hotel. Hallways are hung with tasteful paintings, rooms feature king-size beds and the bathrooms will make your jaw drop.

Drinking

Packed on weekends, **El Emperador** (☎ 533-4938; Calle 3 Bolívar btwn Avs 8 Sucre & 9 Briceño Méndez) is the biggest party in the center. It also offers a peaceful, wood-paneled side bar for a quiet drink, and *parrilla* at lunchtime during the week.

Getting There & Away

AIR

The **Aeropuerto Nacional de Barinas** (☎ 533-2063; Av Codazzi) is 1.5km southwest of Plaza Bolívar. **Avior** (☎ 532-1203) has several flights per week to Caracas (US$89 to US$172), and **Conviasa** (☎ 247-341-3178) offers a thrice-weekly service to San Fernando de Apure (US$33-50).

BUS

The **Terminal de Pasajeros** (Av Cuatricentenaria) is 2km west of Plaza Bolívar and is serviced by local buses. Barinas has regular buses southwest to San Cristóbal (US$8.50, five hours, 313km) and northeast to Caracas (US$18 to US$22, 8½ hours, 512km). Buses to Guanare (US$2.25, 1¼ hours, 85km) run every half-hour from 4am to 6pm.

There are frequent departures to Mérida (157km). The smaller *por puesto* vans (US$9, four hours) are faster than the full-size buses (US$5.50, six hours). The road, which winds up the mountain slopes, is spectacular; sit on the right for some dramatic views.

Several companies, including Expresos Los Llanos and Expresos Zamora, operate buses southeast into Los Llanos, with half a dozen departures daily to San Fernando de Apure (US$12 to US$15, nine hours, 469km). It's a hypnotic (some would say monotonous) way to travel right across the best part of Los Llanos.

GUANARE

☎ 0257 / pop 114,000

Since its founding nearly four hundred years ago, Guanare has been famous as a spiritual center. You can hardly throw a stone in Guanare without hitting a church or other religious monument (although you probably shouldn't do that).

Guanare is famed above all for its Virgen de Coromoto (or Nuestra Señora de Coromoto),

---

JOROPO – MUSICAL PULSE OF LOS LLANOS

The first time you hear *joropo*, you'll probably wonder where the security guard was when the cowboys snuck into the orchestra pit and stole the harp.

This is the music of the *coleo*-loving, hard-riding, beef-eating Los Llanos cowboy. One imagines them fighting dueling harps after a long day in the saddle; indeed, these fast-paced rhythms with their dexterous finger-picking, and high-pitched twangy vocals may well conjure up the image of a Venezuelan cousin to Appalachian bluegrass.

New media laws specify that 50% of all broadcast music in Venezuela must be by Venezuelan artists, so you'll hear these foot-stomping, harp-led rhythms long before you reach Los Llanos. You'll need to come here, though, to see the phenomenon firsthand – every second inhabitant of the plains sings or plays one of the *joropo* instruments, and every village has at least one *joropo* ensemble. You can love it or hate it, but you can't escape it. In any case, it is likely to be a new musical experience, since *joropo* is almost unknown outside Venezuela and Colombia.

Also known as the *música llanera* (Llanos music), the *joropo* is believed to have its origins in the Spanish flamenco, but it has changed considerably over the centuries in its new home. It's usually sung and accompanied by a small band that normally includes the *arpa llanera* (a local harp), a *cuatro* (four-string small guitar) and maracas (gourd rattles). There's a dance form of *joropo* as well.

The harp came over from Spain during the colonial period, but it was not until the 20th century that it made its way into *joropo* music. By that time, it had evolved into quite a different instrument, smaller and less elaborate than its European parent. Normally associated with lyrical salon music, the harp has found a totally new form of expression in *joropo*. Presumably reflecting the hard life of the *llaneros* (inhabitants of Los Llanos), it sounds clear and sharp, often even wild.

The harp is sometimes replaced by the *bandola*, another European offspring; it's a mandolin derivative, with a pear-shaped body and four nylon strings. The *cuatro* accompanies the melody played by the harp or the *bandola*. The *cuatro* is also of European origin and has gradually changed in the New World.

the country's patron saint. It was around here in 1652 that the Virgin miraculously appeared before an Indian chief and left him an image of herself (see the boxed text p233). The site became a destination for pilgrims from around the region. The canonization in 1942 of the Virgin as the patron saint of Venezuela contributed to even larger floods of the faithful; today it's Venezuela's major pilgrimage center, attracting half a million visitors a year.

The focus of pilgrimages has moved to the exact place of the Virgin's apparition, 25km south of Guanare, where a huge sanctuary has been built, yet Guanare continues to pull in pilgrims as the Virgin's traditional home and the only city in the area.

Information

INTERNET ACCESS
Invermega (Carrera 6 btwn Calles 17 & 18)
Sistemas Integrales (Carrera 5 btwn Calles 13 & 14)

MONEY
Banco de Venezuela (cnr Carrera 6 & Calle 15)
Banco Mercantil (cnr Carrera 5 & Calle 6)
Banco Provincial (cnr Carrera 5 & Calle 20)
Banesco (cnr Carrera 6 & Calle 16)

TELEPHONE
Both of these also have internet:
CANTV (Carrera 6 btwn Calles 16 & 17)
Movistar (Carrera 5 btwn Calles 10 & 11)

TOURIST INFORMATION
Corpotur (Corporacíon Portugueseña de Turismo; ☎ 251-0324; Pabellón de Exposiciones, Av IND; 🕑 8am-noon & 1-4pm Mon-Fri) The office is opposite the Instituto Nacional de Deporte, 1.5km southwest of the center.

Sights

The most important religious monument is the **Basílica Catedral de Nuestra Señora de Coromoto** (Plaza Bolívar; 🕑 6:30am-noon & 2-7pm Mon-Fri, 6:30am-7:30pm Sat & Sun). It was constructed in 1710–42, but the 1782 earthquake almost completely destroyed it. The holy image of the Virgin, which had been kept inside, was saved and returned to the reconstructed church. It resided here until 1999, when it was taken to the new *santuario* (p232).

Once inside the church, your eyes will immediately be caught by a three-tier main retable, an excellent piece of colonial baroque art made in 1739. It later took 16 months to gild. In front of the retable stands the elabo-

rate 3.4m-high *sagrario* (tabernacle), made entirely of silver in 1756. A painting on the dome over the high altar depicts the legend of the Virgen de Coromoto. The colorful stained-glass windows were commissioned in Munich, Germany.

The mid-18th-century **Convento de San Francisco** (☎ 251-6483; cnr Carrera 3 & Calle 17) no longer serves its original purpose as a convent. In 1825, Venezuela's first college was opened here. Today, the building accommodates the offices of the Universidad Nacional Experimental de los Llanos. You can enter its spacious courtyard, which has retained much of its old style and charm. The adjacent church is now used for university meetings and symposiums.

Opposite the church is a splendid two-story colonial mansion, one of the few buildings remaining from the Spanish period. It's now home to the **Museo de la Ciudad de Guanare** (☎ 253-0832; cnr Carrera 3 & Calle 17; admission US$0.50; 🕑 8am-4pm Tue-Fri, 8am-2pm Sat), and features exhibits related to the town's history. Don't miss visiting the rooms on the upper floor, which shelter a small but fine collection of historic religious art.

Two blocks north is **Parque Los Samanes** (cnr Carrera 1 & Calle 16; admission US$0.20; 🕑 8:30am-5pm Tue-Sun), named after the species of spreading tree that grows in the park. You'll find an impressive specimen in front of the entrance. Bolívar's troops reputedly camped here in 1813.

There are several monuments dedicated to the Virgen de Coromoto in the town center, including the 1928 statue on **Plaza Coromoto**, seven blocks east of Plaza Bolívar along Carrera 5. On the same square you'll find a charming sculptured scene depicting the miraculous appearance of the Virgin to the Indian cacique and his family.

Outside the center, just 500m west of the tourist office, is the **Museo de los Llanos** (☎ 253-0102; Complejo Ferial José Antonio Páez; admission free; 🕑 8:30am-12:30pm & 2:30-5:30pm Tue-Sun), which has an archeological collection from the region.

Festivals & Events

As might be expected, Guanare's annual celebrations revolve around the Virgen de Coromoto. Most pilgrims flock to the city in time for the **Fiesta de la Virgen de Coromoto** on September 8, the anniversary of the Virgin's appearance.

Guanare is also noted for its **mascarada**, a three-day-long celebration that culminates in a parade of *carrozas* (floats) and a very realistic re-enactment of the Christ's crucifixion during Semana Santa.

Sleeping

Posada del Reo (☎ 808-0373; cnr Calle 16 & Carrera 3; d US$9, s/d/t/q with air-con US$12/14/16/18; ✗) Plastic handcuffs make the key rings of this most economical (and comfortable) of options, the former jail. Don't be surprised to meet heavily armed guards on the stairs, either, as the ground floor continues to house municipal offices. At prices like these, it's recommended to book ahead.

Hotel Italia (☎ 253-1213, 251-4277; Calle 20 btwn Carreras 4 & 5; d US$12-14, tr US$14-16; P ✗) This rambling budget option sprawls over four floors and pouts with an air of glory days gone by. The 87 rooms have been revamped and all have air-con, cable TV and hot water (although in this climate, we have to wonder – why?).

Hotel del Este (☎ 251-7165; Calle 12 & Av Unda; s/d/tr/q US$14/16/20/25) This otherwise unremarkable offering is not far from the bus station. More importantly, it's just across the street from a busy commercial center that's open late, making it safe to wander a short ways for a late-night bite.

Motel La Góndola (☎ 251-2802, 253-1480; cnr Carrera 5 & Calle 3; d US$22-24, tr US$33; P ✗) The central La Góndola, 400m west of Plaza Coromoto, is quiet, enjoyable and good value. Its 42 fair-sized rooms are arranged around two spacious courtyards, while the cozy restaurant serves palatable food at economic prices.

Hotel Mirador (☎ 253-4520, 253-5320; cnr Avs Circunvalación & IND; s/d/tr US$29/31/33; P ✗ ✑) The Mirador is the largest hotel in town, although the views are mostly of the gigantic car park and the concrete skeleton of an abandoned extension across the street. Rooms have hot water and a fridge, and are comfortable enough, but don't expect first-class service.

ourpick **Posada del Cabrestero** (☎ 253-0102; Calle la Manga de Coleo; d US$33; ✗) This delicious posada is easily the best option in town. Fifteen rooms surround a delightful garden courtyard and have central air-con, fridge and cable TV; some have their own patio with hammock, to laze away the hot afternoons.

Eating

Papa Boris Restaurant (☎ 253-3035; cnr Carrera 6 & Calle 13; set menu US$4, mains US$5-10; ✑ 11am-9:30pm; ✗) Papa Boris gives you an option to eat

inside or out – both are cool and lovely. As for food, you have quite a choice, but go for the specialty – *batea* – which is a *parrilla*-type dish served on a wooden board. The *batea mixta* comes with pork, chicken, beef and all the accompaniments – it feeds two people, unless you are very hungry.

El Bodegón de Pedro Miguel (☎ 251-4358; cnr Calle 15 & Carrera 8; mains US$6-8) A long-standing *tasca*-style restaurant, with a long menu, moderate prices and a dim interior. It serves good seafood, too.

Los Toldos (☎ 0414-792-8929; Av Simon Bolívar; mains US$6-10) It hasn't got a menu, it hasn't got air-con – heck, it doesn't even have four walls – but this massively popular spot cranks out the *asado*, fresh off the grill. They do monster, heart-clogging *arepas con queso* (corn pancakes filled with cheese), and some mighty fine juices, too.

Getting There & Away

BUS

The **Terminal de Pasajeros** (Av UNDA) is 2km southeast of the city center, and is serviced regularly by local transportation. To get there from the center, take the eastbound busetas No 12 or 24 from Carrera 5.

Guanare sits on El Llanos highway, so there is a fair bit of traffic heading southwest to San Cristóbal (US$11 to US$15, 6½ hours, 398km) and northeast to Caracas (US$12 to US$16, seven hours, 427km). There are hourly buses to Barquisimeto (US$5, 3½ hours, 173km) and several departures a day to Boconó (US$4.50, 3½ hours, 115km). Buses to Barinas (US$2.25, 1¼ hours, 85km) run frequently until 6pm. If you are heading to Mérida, go to Barinas and change.

SANTUARIO NACIONAL DE NUESTRA SEÑORA DE COROMOTO

☎ 0257

The **Santuario Nacional** (☎ 251-5071, 251-5427; ✑ 8am-6pm) marks the holy site where the Virgen de Coromoto (see the boxed text, opposite) allegedly appeared in 1652. A cross was placed here after the event, and was later replaced with a chapel, but the site was isolated and rarely visited. Instead, the pilgrims flocked to Guanare's church, which for centuries boasted the holy image and effectively acted as the Virgin's shrine.

In 1980 the construction of a huge church at the actual site of the apparition commenced

A VENEZUELAN MIRACLE

One sunny day in 1652, as Indian Chief Coromoto and his wife were crossing a stream near their hut, a radiant lady of incredible beauty appeared and walked over the water toward them. While they stared at the divine creature, she started talking to them in their own language. She urged the chief to go with his tribe to the white men to have holy water poured over their heads so that they could go to heaven.

Astonished and confused, the chief promised to comply. He told the story to the Spaniard who owned a nearby plantation and with his permission the whole tribe soon moved onto the settler's land and built their huts. They were put to work on the plantation and given religious instructions.

As months passed, though, the chief was increasingly unhappy with the indoctrination and wanted to return to his native pastures. One day he refused to assist in religious acts and went back to his hut. While he tried to rest and calm his anger, the beautiful lady suddenly appeared again, radiating with rays of light more dazzling than the midday sun.

This time the chief was not in a peaceful mood. He grabbed his bow and arrows, but the shining vision moved quickly around. He then tried to catch her in his hands but the dazzling creature vanished. When he opened his hand all he found was a small image of the divine lady.

Angry and irritated, he threw the image down and ran into the dark night. While he was madly running through the woods, he was bitten by a venomous snake. Only then, moments before his death, did he ask to be baptized, and he told his tribe to do likewise.

The radiant lady, named after the Indian chief the Virgen de Coromoto, is today the patron saint of Venezuela, while the tiny image he found in his hand is the object of devotion by millions of Venezuelans.

and was completed for the papal visit in February 1996, when 300,000 faithful attended a mass. The holy image of the Virgin has been brought to the site from Guanare.

From the outside, this all-concrete cathedral looks something like a cross between an aging rustbelt sports stadium and a Spielberg spaceship; from the inside, it looks like – and has the acoustics of – a rock concert hall. Alone in the church, the overwhelming sound is of twittering birdsong, echoed and amplified by the vast acres of concrete curvature.

One can't help but wonder if Venezuelan architect Erasmo Calvani got his start building multistory car parks, as the irregular structure and rapidly moldering concrete finish bring to mind peak hour traffic more than the Venezuela's most famous virgin. Some saving grace is to found, however, in the marvelous stained-glass windows on the wall behind the high altar, which depict the history of the apparition, as depicted by another Venezuelan artist, Guillermo Márquez.

The high altar is believed to be at the exact location where the Virgin appeared. The holy image is in an elaborate reliquary right behind the altar. You can get close and see the image through the magnifying glass. It's an oval painting measuring 22mm by 27mm. Today its colors are almost totally washed out and the picture is pretty faint and indistinct.

You can go up to a 36m viewing platform, built between the two towers (76m and 68m) and providing vast panoramic views; it's accessible by elevator for a nominal fee. A museum in the basement of the church features religious paraphernalia related to the Virgin and a collection of votive offerings.

At time of research a basic hotel and restaurant were being built directly adjacent to the cathedral, but no contact details were yet available.

Getting There & Away

The Santuario is 25km south of Guanare – 10km by the main road toward Barinas, and then a further 15km by the paved side road branching off to the south. Small buses, operated by Línea Los Cospes, depart every 15 minutes from the corner of Carrera 9 and Calle 20 in Guanare, and will deposit you right at the church's entrance (US$0.60, 40 minutes).

MANTECAL

☎ 0240 / pop 5000

Cowboy hats and cowboy boots remind you pretty quick straight this is a cow town, where the bovine is king. Mantecal is authentic

Los Llanos, where the favored after-dark pastime is rumored to be cattle-rustling.

Four of the independent budget *campamentos* lie within an hour's drive of Mantecal, as do Hatos El Frío, El Cedral, and La Garza, and you are likely to pass through town if visiting any of them.

Mantecal is also a good place to watch *coleo* (see the boxed text below). The annual *fería* runs 25 to 30 January and the 1st of May sees the *gran concurso del coleo*, when some of the best at the sport come to compete.

There are also quality locally made leather goods to be found in Mantecal at bargain prices. Almost every other shop sells leather gear – and not just the touristy stuff either. The street vendors cluster along the Calle de Coleo.

Information

Banco de Venezuela (Av Libertador)

CANTV (Av Libertador) Internet service is planned.

Inversiones Interplazas (☎ 994-0255; Carrera 1) Internet service. Opposite Plaza Bolívar.

Sleeping & Eating

Hotel Punto Fresco (☎ 808-3228; Av Libertador; d US$16-21, tr US$26; P ♨) The 'Fresh Point' is conveniently set just at the entrance to town and faces the highway. The rooms are not as fresh as they once were, but all have cable TV and air-con, and there's a budget restaurant downstairs.

Hotel Imperio (☎ 994-0253; Carrera 1; d US$16-21, tr US$26; P ♨) Don't let the ugly orange reception desk fool you – the Imperio harbors surprisingly quiet, well-maintained rooms, and the bar and restaurant downstairs is excellent.

Hotel Don Guido (☎ 808-3465; Calle Guido Cianfrocca No 41; d US$21-28, sextuple US$47; P ♨) 'Sleep in Comfort in the Italian Style' proclaims their business card and we can't argue with that. This bright blue building in the center of town is impossible to miss, the interior is tastefully decorated and the rooms are the best in town.

La Nueva Era Panadería (☎ 0416-248-9774; Av Principal; ☯ 7am-4pm) This central meeting point, just steps from the intercity bus stop, does good juices and sandwiches for breakfast and lunch, and snacks throughout the day. Air-con makes it a convenient pick-up, drop-off and where-the-hell-is-my-bus spot.

Getting There & Away

Situated on the main San Fernando–Barinas highway, Mantecal has good transportation options to both those destinations. Buses to Barinas (US$5, 240km, 4½ hours) depart roughly half-hourly, those for San Fernando de Apure (US$7, 229km, 3hrs) depart hourly. Service begins around 5:30am and runs until around 8pm. There is no intercity bus station in Mantecal. All buses run down Av Principal and stop in the center of town.

COLEO – GO ON, PULL MY BULL

A sport by cowboys for cowboys, *coleo* is the Venezuelan version of rodeo – except the aim is to pull a bull to the ground, by the tail. It is a game of skill, acrobatic daring and above all, consummate horsemanship.

First, a narrow corral is set up – the *mancha de coleo,* or sleeve. A bull is let loose through the *mancha* and four cowboys give chase. Participants are awarded points for their performance and get extra points if they can roll the animal over with its legs in the air – this also tends to be a real crowd-pleaser. After a while the bull can be reluctant to stand again after being yanked to the ground, so some contestants will resort to biting the bull's tail with their teeth – or, failing that, the use of electric cattle prods.

These are not the dangerous, spirited animals used in the bullfights more popular in Spain and in neighboring Colombia, but rather the white Zebu from India, bred for their docility and resistance to harsh climes. Although injuries to participants are rare, *coleo* can be dangerous to both cows and cowboys alike. Broken cowboy bones mend, and injured bulls are taken off to the slaughterhouse for that day's *parrilla*.

Predictably, all this outrages animal rights activists, who have called for a ban on the sport. Enthusiasts counter that *coleo*, along with baseball and *joropo*, is a part of the national identity and have petitioned President Chávez to officially protect it. Whatever you might think, *coleo* is an indelible part of the Los Llanos way of life, and worth a look.

SAN FERNANDO DE APURE

☎ 0247 / pop 79,000

The capital of Apure state, San Fernando, is an old river port hundreds of miles away from any sizable urban center. The remoteness, the river and the lazy pace of life give the city a certain charm, but most visitors come to San Fernando on their way to the *hatos* (p222) in the surrounding region, which boast some of the best wildlife-watching Los Llanos has to offer.

San Fernando started as a missionary outpost at the end of the colonial era. Sitting on the bank of the large Río Apure, in the very heart of Los Llanos, the town developed into an important trading center, growing rich on the trade in heron and egret feathers, and caiman skins. By the early 20th century, it was Venezuela's second largest river port, after Ciudad Bolívar. Today, cattle raising is the major activity in the region, followed by crop farming. Crops and livestock are funneled through San Fernando and trucked north to Caracas and the central states of Aragua, Carabobo and Miranda.

Information

INTERNET ACCESS

Cominser (cnr Carrera 6 Páez & Calle 11 24 de Julio)
Cybernazareth (cnr Carrera 6 Páez & Paseo Libertador)

MONEY

Banco Mercantil (Paseo Libertador btwn Carreras 8 Aramendi & 9 Colombia)
Banco Provincial (Plaza Páez)
Banesco (cnr Paseo Libertador & Av 1 de Mayo)
Corp Banca (cnr Av Miranda & Calle 14)

TELEPHONE

CANTV (cnr Calle 18 Piar & Carrera 4) Also has internet.
Movistar (Bus Terminal)

TOURIST INFORMATION

Coratur (Corporacion Apureña de Turismo) City Main Office (☎ 342-9963; Calle Rodríguez Rincones; ☷ 8am-noon & 2-6pm Mon-Fri); Airport (☎ 0414-377-8833; ☷ 8am-noon & 2-6pm Mon-Fri)

TRAVEL AGENCIES

Doña Bárbara (☎ 341-2235, 0416-248-9030, fax 341-3463, cbestrada_864@hotmail.com; Calrrera 4 Bolívar No 28, btwn Calle 8 Queseras del Medio & Calle Urdaneta) Once part of the now-closed Hato Doña Bárbara, this travel agency remains a good source of information about travel to the *hatos*, including La Fé, El Frío and El Cedral.

Sights

Walk along Paseo Libertador, the city's main thoroughfare. At its northern end is a circular plaza, its large **fountain** adorned with six charmingly kitsch concrete caimans. Beside the fountain is the **Monumento a Pedro Camejo**, a bronze equestrian statue of one of the bravest lancers to have fought in Bolívar's army. Camejo, who died in the battle of Carabobo, is known as Negro Primero, as he was the first black person to distinguish himself in the War of Independence.

Just east of the fountain is the ornate, two-story **Palacio Barbarito**, built by the Italian Barbarito brothers at the turn of the 19th century. At that time the Río Apure used to pass by just a few meters from the palace pier, and boats came directly from Europe up the Orinoco and Apure. The brothers made a fortune on heron and egret feathers during the 1910s bonanza, but later on, when the business deteriorated, they sold the palace and left. It then passed through the hands of various owners who divided and subdivided it repeatedly, so much of the original internal design has been lost.

About 600m south along Paseo Libertador is the **Monumento a Los Llaneros**, dedicated to the tough *llanero* soldiers who made up the backbone of Bolívar's army. Another 600m down the Paseo is the huge **Monumento a San Fernando**, an allegorical monument to the city presented by the city itself.

The Plaza Bolívar, six blocks west of Paseo Libertador, boasts a modern tent-like **catedral** and an old **masonic lodge**, and is pleasantly shaded with trees.

Sleeping

Hotel La Torraca (☎ 342-2777, 342-2676; Paseo Libertador; d US$15-17, tr/ste US$19/22; ℗ ☒) The reception desk doesn't look very promising, but don't worry – the 48 rooms, distributed over three floors, are airy, bright and good value. Most of them look at the back and are quiet, but if you want some action, take a front room with a balcony and watch the world go by on the busy Paseo Libertador.

Hotel Trinacria (☎ 342-3578, 342-3778; Av Miranda; d US$19-21, tr/q US$30/40; ℗ ☒) Comfort seems to be the guiding light here, with newish mattresses, quiet air-con and well-kept rooms. Taking the edge off the spartan finish (everything is painted white) are the red faux-velvet drapes and Louis XIV coats-of-arms above the beds.

LOS LLANOS

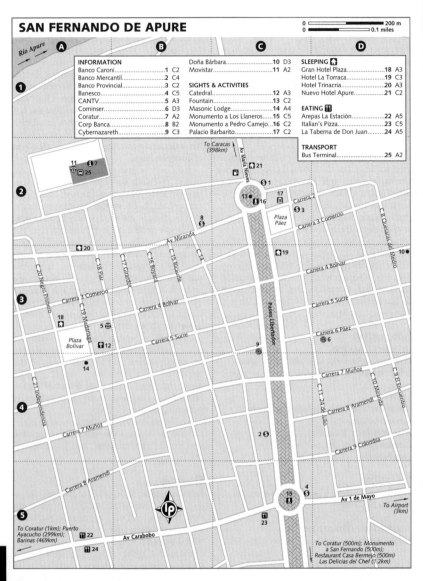

SAN FERNANDO DE APURE

0	200 m
0	0.1 miles

INFORMATION
Banco Caroni..........................1 C2
Banco Mercantil.....................2 C4
Banco Provincial.....................3 C2
Banesco...................................4 C5
CANTV....................................5 A3
Cominser................................6 D3
Coratur..................................7 A2
Corp Banca............................8 B2
Cybernazareth.......................9 C3

Doña Bárbara.......................10 D3
Movistar...............................11 A2

SIGHTS & ACTIVITIES
Catedral...............................12 A3
Fountain...............................13 C2
Masonic Lodge.....................14 A4
Monumento a Los Llaneros....15 C5
Monumento a Pedro Camejo...16 C2
Palacio Barbarito..................17 C2

SLEEPING 🏠
Gran Hotel Plaza.................18 A3
Hotel La Torraca.................19 C3
Hotel Trinacria...................20 A3
Nuevo Hotel Apure.............21 C2

EATING 🍴
Arepas La Estación..............22 A5
Italian's Pizza.....................23 C5
La Taberna de Don Juan......24 A5

TRANSPORT
Bus Terminal......................25 A2

Nuevo Hotel Apure (☎ 341-0119, 341-2646; Av María Nieves; s/d US$40/42; 🅿 ❄) This motel-style 29-room establishment offers comfy, quiet accommodations and a good, inexpensive restaurant. There's a mixture of older rooms and new ones, so check out a few first – the new generation has king-size beds for no extra charge. Even if you aren't driving, this is one of the best bets in town, and at a reasonably central location.

Gran Hotel Plaza (☎ 342-1504, 342-1255; Plaza Bolívar; s/d/tr US$53/53/65; 🅿 ❄) This is possibly San Fernando's top place to stay, though don't expect any Sheraton-like luxuries. It has 42 fairly reasonable rooms with views over the peaceful and leafy plaza, and is just about the only hotel in town that has hot water, if you really need it in this steamy, sticky climate.

Eating

Arepas La Estación (Av Carabobo; arepas $1.50; 🕑 5:30pm-3:30am) This is a food kiosk, serving great *arepas* (stuffed corn pancakes) with 20 different fillings till late.

Italian's Pizza (Av Carabobo; 🕑 4:30-7:30pm Wed-Mon; pizzas US$5-15) This new, two-level pizza parlor pumps out the best, and quite possibly only, pizzas in town. Shatter those pizza-and-beer dreams, though; this family joint prefers not to serve the frothy stuff. Their ice cream, however, is a delicious consolation.

Restaurant Casa Bermejo (☎ 342-7613; Paseo Libertador; mains US$7-15) Set at the foot of the giant Monumento a San Fernando, this stylish spot sports waiters in vests and brightly colored tablecloths. It serves up good pasta, steak, and seafood, especially the *bagre* or *dorado,* a yummy river fish that is not often seen on local menus. Backpackers, beware – shorts and flip-flops will get you an evil stare.

Las Delicias del Chef (Av Intercomunal Los Centauros; mains US$9-18; 🕑 11:30-11 Tue-Sun) This wine-lover's delight, set just outside of town in the grounds of the Italian-Venezuelan club, serves up some of the best pasta in town, not to mention a mean steak. Friday night and Sunday brunch boast live, soft jazz music – good for the digestion, insists the manager.

La Taberna de Don Juan (☎ 342-6259; Av Carabobo; mains US$12-18) Don Juan is a respectable, slightly upmarket restaurant, hosting discos and sometimes live music – including *joropo* –

on weekend nights. They serve up quality international fare, including *paella valenciana,* one of their specialties

Getting There & Away

AIR

The little-used **Aeropuerto Nacional Las Flecheras** (☎ 341-1012; Av 1 de Mayo), just 3km east of the city center, recently began seeing air traffic again. **Avior** (☎ 532-1203) now flies six times weekly to Caracas (US$83 to US$104) and **Conviasa** (☎ 341-3178) offers a thrice-weekly service to Barinas (US$33-50).

BUS

The bus terminal is on the northern outskirts of the city, near the river. You can either walk there (five minutes from Plaza Bolívar) or take a taxi (US$1.40).

There are several departures a day to Caracas (US$13 to US$16, eight hours, 398km), or you can go by any of the half-hourly buses to Maracay (US$12, seven hours, 319km) and change there. Half a dozen buses a day travel to Barinas (US$13 to US$15, nine hours, 469km) on a remote road across the heart of the plains. Keep a look out for animals.

Six buses a day (all in the morning) set off for another interesting ride, south to Puerto Ayacucho (US$14, seven hours, 299km) via Puerto Páez. The road is now paved all the way and traversable year-round, but the bridges over the Capanaparo and Cinaruco are incomplete, so the trip includes *chalana* (ferry) crossings across these two rivers and, obviously, across the Orinoco between Puerto Páez and El Burro. It's a very enjoyable trip.

The Northeast

Venezuela's northeast holds a wealth of natural beauty to explore. Its coastline is ringed with sun-drenched islands and golden Caribbean beaches, while surrounding waters harbor rich coral reefs and pods of playful dolphins. This area is a popular destination for Venezuelans on beach holidays, but quite a few foreign travelers pass through as well.

Large and developed Isla de Margarita is one of the most well-known island destinations in the Caribbean, attracting more international holidaymakers than anywhere else in Venezuela. But the mainland features much more idyllic stretches, including the dazzling islands and beaches of Parque Nacional Mochima, as well as the off-the-beaten-path sandy coves hidden away in remote stretches of the coastline beyond Río Caribe.

The northeast isn't just about its pretty beaches, however. Inland there are lush mountains and verdant valleys to explore. This region also boasts Venezuela's most famous cave, and is home to fascinating wildlife, rugged peninsulas, obscure hiking trails and a scattering of historical forts, towns and churches where the Spanish conquered and settled. Plus there are quirky destinations, including salt pans, cacao plantations, hot springs and water-buffalo ranches. It also lays claim to the only spot where Columbus came ashore in South America.

Apart from Isla de Margarita, the northeast is not Venezuela's most well-known region to visit, but the hidden treasures you'll come across here and there make a trip worthwhile – and its relative remoteness is an invitation to some enchanting adventures.

HIGHLIGHTS

- Find an unknown beach on **Isla de Margarita** (p240)
- Explore the picturesque islands of **Parque Nacional Mochima** (p260)
- Skinny dip at the secluded beaches east of **Río Caribe** (p277)
- Be amazed by the nocturnal, whiskered birds of **Cueva del Guácharo** (p285)
- Worship the remote tropical beaches of **Isla La Tortuga** (p266)

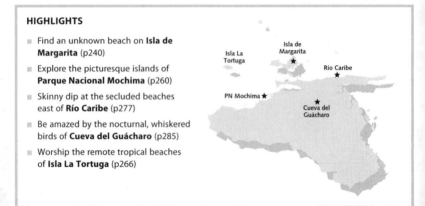

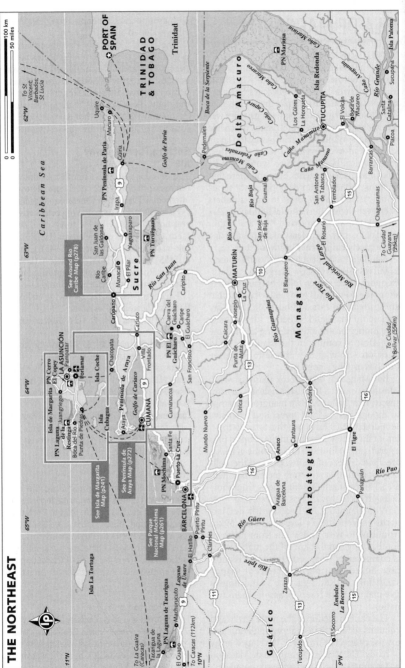

THE NORTHEAST

0   100 km
0   50 miles

Caribbean Sea

To St
Vincent;
Barbados;
St Lucia

PORT OF
SPAIN

TRINIDAD
& TOBAGO

Trinidad

Isla Paloma

Sucupana

Rio Grande

Santa
Catalina

Placoa

Boca de
Macareo

Barrancas

El Volcán

TUCUPITA

Isla Redonda

PN Marissa

Los Güires
La Horqueta

Caño Macareo

Caño Mariusa

Caño Macareo

Delta Amacuro

Uquire
Macuro

Güiria

PN Peninsula de Paria

Pedernales

Caño Pedernales

Caño Manamo

Caño Manamito

Caño Manamo

San Antonio
de Tabasca

Temblador

Chaguaramas

To Ciudad
Guayana
(295km)

Boca de la Serpiente

Golfo de Paria

Irapa

Yaguaraparo

San Juan de
las Galdonas

Río
Caribe

Manacal

El Pilar

Sucre

San José
de Buja

Río Buja

Guamal

Caño Mánamo

Río Amana

PN Turuépano

See Around Río
Caribe Map (p278)

Carúpano

Cariaco

Chacopata

Caripito

Caripe

MATURÍN

La Cruz

El Blanquero

Río Guanipa

Monagas

El Rosario

Río Morichal

To Ciudad
Bolívar (55km)

Isla de Margarita
See Isla de Margarita
Map (p241)

PN Cerro
El Copey
Pampatar
PN Laguna
de la
Juangriego
Restinga
Boca del Río
Punta de Piedras

LA ASUNCIÓN

Porlamar

Isla Coche

Isla
Cubagua

Peninsula de Araya

Golfo de Cariaco

Villa
Frontado

Cueva del
Guácharo
PN El
Guácharo
El Guácharo

San Francisco

Cumanacoa

Urica

Punta de
Mata

Caicara

Aragua de
Barcelona

Anaco

Cantaura

San Andrés

El Tigre

Río Pao

Río Güere

Anzoátegui

Araya

CUMANÁ

See Peninsula de
Araya Map (p272)

Santa Fe

PN Mochima
See Parque
Nacional Mochima
Map (p261)

Puerto La Cruz

BARCELONA

Puerto Píritu
Píritu

Clarines

El Hatillo

Mundo Nuevo

San
Francisco

Pariaguán

Zaraza

El Socorro

Embalse
La Becerra

Río Ipire

Río Unare

Laguna
de Unare

Tucupido

Guárico

Isla La Tortuga

To La Guaira
(Caracas)

Tacarigua de
la Laguna

Laguna de Tacarigua

Machurucuto

El Guapo

To Caracas (112km)

ISLA DE MARGARITA

☎ 0295 / pop 385,000

One of the country's top holiday destinations – just ask your nearest Venezuelan – is Isla de Margarita, with its beautiful beaches. Sunseekers flock here en masse to pay their respects to the island's warm sands, bathe in its azure waters and stuff themselves at its many beachside restaurants. While Margarita is way too large, scruffy and overdeveloped to be described as a 'tropical beach paradise,' you might be able to find a few beaches here and there that are more isolated than its popular hot spots. But the island mainly caters to large numbers of charter-flight international holidaymakers looking for white sand and blue sea within reach of a comfy bed, plenty of shops and bars, and a nicely chilled margarita cocktail.

Another reason people come to this comely island is to spend money. Margarita is a duty-free port, and it's often full of bargain hunters shopping themselves into loads of goods that are stuffed into cars and boats on their way back to the mainland. Whether they actually save money or not after exerting all the time and effort of coming to the island is a good question – though any excuse to go to the beach is usually a good one.

But Margarita offers more than just sand, sun and spending. It boasts a rich and colorful spectrum of habitats, from mangrove swamps to mountainous cloud forest and extensive semidesert. It features two fine Spanish forts, one of the oldest churches in the country plus a sprinkling of little old towns, some of which are vivid centers of craftwork. And the well-developed tourist structure means that there are all kinds of activities on offer – from snorkeling trips to world-class windsurfing.

With an area of 1071 sq km, Isla de Margarita is Venezuela's largest island, 69km from east to west and 35km from north to south. Lying some 40km off the mainland, it is composed of what were once two islands, now linked by a narrow, crescent-shaped sandbank, La Restinga. The island houses five major nature reserves, among them two national parks.

The eastern section is the more fertile and contains 95% of the island's population and towns, connected by a well-developed array of roads. The western Península de Macanao is, by contrast, arid and sparsely populated, with around 25,000 people living in a dozen villages dotted along the coast.

The island's typically Caribbean climate is glorious year-round: temperatures are between 75°F and 85°F, mitigated by evening breezes. The rainy period lasts from November to January, with rain falling mostly during the night. Peak seasons include Christmas, Easter and the August holiday period. May, June and October are the quietest months.

Getting There & Away

AIR

The island is a lucrative market, so almost all the major national airlines fly into **Aeropuerto Internacional del Caribe General Santiago Mariño** (☎ 0295-269-1027). The following prices are general fares and very prone to change, so use them as guidelines only: Caracas (US$85); Barcelona (US$60); Carúpano (US$45); Cumaná (US$55); Valencia (US$70); Maturín (US$55); and Los Roques (US$160). Roundtrip fares to Port of Spain, Trinidad, are around US$245.

Except for Aserca, the following airline offices are located in Porlamar:

Aereotuy (LTA; Map p244; ☎ 415-5778; Av Santiago Mariño)

Aeropostal (Map p244; ☎ 263-9374; www.aeropostal.com; Centro Comercial Galerías, Av 4 de Mayo)

Aserca (☎ 269-1460; www.asercaairlines.com; Centro Comercial Sambil local MN-14, Av Jóvito Villalba, Pampatar)

Avior (Map p244; ☎ 263-8615; www.aviorairlines.com; Av 4 de Mayo)

Conviasa (Map p244; ☎ 263-9646; www.conviasa.com; Centro Comercial Galerías local 27, Av 4 de Mayo)

Laser (Map p244; ☎ 263-9195; www.laser.com.ve in Spanish; Calle Maneiro)

BOAT

Puerto La Cruz and Cumaná are the main jumping-off points to Margarita; ferries arrive at Punta de Piedras (29km west of Porlamar). Frequent small buses (US$0.80, 35 minutes) run between Punta de Piedras and Porlamar; taxis charge US$15. There are also small boats to the island from the dock of Chacopata, on the Península de Araya; these go directly to Porlamar.

From Puerto La Cruz

This route is served by **Conferry** (Map p244; ☎ 261-6780; www.conferry.com in Spanish; Calle Marcano, Porlamar; ◷ 8am-noon & 2-5pm Mon-Fri, 8am-noon Sat), which has several departures daily. Check the website for exact times and dates.

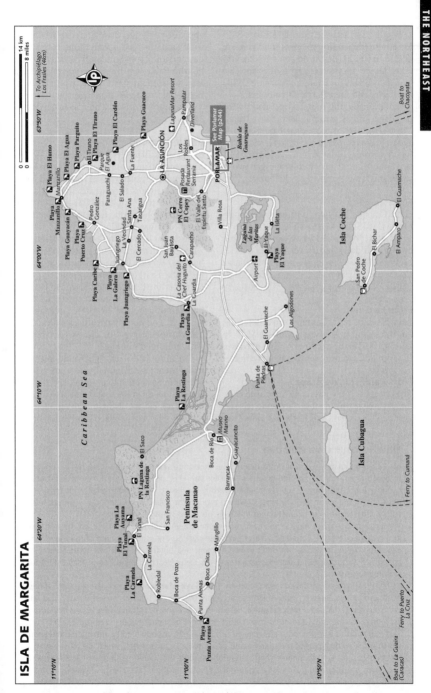

ISLA DE MARGARITA

Regular ferries cost from US$8 to US$11 for adults (depending on class) and cars are US$18 to US$23 (depending on size); the trip takes about 4½ hours. Express ferries cost US$20 to US$29 for adults and cars are US$33 to US$46, and the trip takes two hours.

Additionally, the route is operated by the passenger-only hydrofoil, **Gran Cacique Express** (☎ 264-2945; www.grancacique.com.ve; Edificio Blue Sky, Av Mariño; ☷ 8am-noon & 2-6pm Mon-Fri, 8am-2pm Sat), with two departures per day at 7am and 4pm (US$19, two hours). On all ferries, children aged two to seven and seniors over 65 pay half price.

From Cumaná

Gran Cacique has two to three daily departures (US$18 to US$20, two hours).

Naviarca (☎ 239-8439; www.grancacique.com.ve) has one to two daily departures (adults US$13, cars US$22 to US$28; 3½ hours). Naviarca tickets are only available at Punta de Piedras (☎ 239-8439).

From La Guaira

In high season only, Conferry runs boats from La Guaira, near Caracas (adults US$40 to US$54, cars US$82 to US$117). Kids aged two to seven and seniors over 65 pay half price.

From Peninsula de Araya

The cheapest route to Isla de Margarita is on the passenger-only boat service which ferries between Chacopata and Porlamar. Boats run approximately every two hours, or when full, from 8am until about 4pm Monday to Saturday and until 2pm Sunday. The schedule can be unreliable – if there are few passengers around, some departures may be canceled. Boats hold up to 70 passengers and are not for the queasy at sea. The trip takes one to 1½ hours (US$5).

Getting Around

Margarita's airport is in the southern part of the island, 20km southwest of Porlamar. There is no public transportation that can take you from the airport to your destination; you'll have to spring for a taxi (US$12). Going to the airport, however, there are por puestos from Porlamar (US$3).

Porlamar is the island's transportation hub, where frequent small buses (called micros or busetas) service towns and beaches around the eastern part of the island. Public transportation on the Península de Macanao is poor.

There are about a dozen car-rental companies opposite the airport's international terminal, and many have offices in Porlamar. The cheapest cars go for about US$50 per day with unlimited mileage.

For more laid-back sightseeing, plenty of travel agencies will happily show you around. They offer general-interest tours, specific trips (eg Laguna de la Restinga) and activities (eg horseback riding, fishing, snorkeling, scuba diving). The Archipiélago Los Frailes, north-

---

FINDING YOUR OWN PARADISE

Isla de Margarita has 167km of world-famous coastline endowed with some 50 beaches big enough to bear names, not to mention countless smaller stretches of sandy coast. Many beaches have become highly developed tourist magnets with swish hotels, beachside restaurants, bars, and deck chairs and sunshades for rent. However, though the island is no longer a virgin paradise, with a little legwork you can still find relatively deserted strips of sand too.

Margarita's beaches have little shade, and some are virtually barren. Those on the northern and eastern coasts are generally better than those skirting the southern shore of the island. You can camp on the beaches, but don't leave your tent unattended, as theft can occur. Swimmers should be aware of the dangerous undertows on some beaches, including at Playas El Agua and Puerto Cruz.

Top destinations include **Playa Guacuco** and **Playa Manzanillo**. One of Margarita's finest beaches is **Playa Puerto Cruz**, which has arguably the widest, whitest stretch of sand and still isn't too overdeveloped. **Playa Parguito**, next to Playa El Agua, has strong waves good for surfing, and **Playa Caribe** is a 1.5km-long gem with a few open restaurants but no posadas – yet.

If you want to escape from people, head for the largely unpopulated **Península de Macanao**, which is the wildest part of the island – and so are some of its beaches, which are mostly shade-less and deserted. A reasonable road skirts right around the barren peninsula so travelers with their own transportation can easily explore the whole coastline. Take plenty of water.

ISLAND TOP PICKS

Once you've tanned your bottom on those sandy beaches and are looking for something different, consider the following:

- Dive or snorkel around the **Archipiélago Los Frailes** (p250)

- Try your hand at windsurfing or kitesurfing off **Playa El Yaque** (p253)

- Escape the crowds to remote **Península de Macanao** (opposite)

- Drift the mangrove tunnels of **Parque Nacional Laguna de la Restinga** (p253)

- Catch the sunset with an ice-cold beer at **Juangriego** (p251)

- Pay your respects to her holiness the Virgen del Valle in her pilgrimage site in **El Valle del Espíritu Santo** (p249)

---

east of Margarita, is a popular destination for snorkeling.

Conferry runs a ferry service one to two times daily between Punta de Piedras and Isla de Coche (adults US$1.50, cars US$5; one hour). Kids aged two to seven and seniors over 65 pay half price.

PORLAMAR

pop 125,000

The largest and busiest urban center on the island, Porlamar is likely to be your first stop when you arrive from the mainland. It's a bustling city full of shops, hotels and restaurants, but isn't overly interesting or attractive. It does have a beach, however, and has been a duty-free port since 1973. East of the center are the fanciest shopping centers, casinos and nightlife destinations. In fact, new suburbs and tourist facilities are being built all the way along the coast as far as Pampatar.

Porlamar has come a long way since 1536, when it was originally founded. Less than 40 years later, Christopher Columbus sailed past the island on his way to the mainland. You can glimpse some of the city's past in the older part of town; tree-shaded Plaza Bolívar is the historic center.

Information

EMERGENCY

Police (☎ 264-1494; Centro Comercial Bella Vista, cnr Calle San Rafael & Av Terrenova)

IMMIGRATION

DIEX (☎ 263-4766; Calle Arismendi No 7-85; ☯ 7am-noon & 1-4:30pm Mon-Fri) Get your visa extended here (though it may take weeks).

INTERNET ACCESS

Most internet places charge under US$1 per hour.

Centro de Conexiones (Calle Velázquez; ☯ 8am-8pm Mon-Thu, till midnight Fri & Sat, till noon Sun)

Digicom (Calle Fermín; ☯ 8am-8pm Mon-Sat)

Movistar (Calle Marcano; ☯ 9am-7pm)

LAUNDRY

Lavandería Divino Niño (☎ 0416-807-0828; Calle Cedeño; per 5kg US$3; ☯ 8:30am-6:30pm Mon-Fri, till 2:30pm Sat)

Lavandería Edikö's (Calle Fermín; per 5kg US$3.50; ☯ 8am-7pm Mon-Sat, 8:30am-1pm Sun)

Lavandería La Burbuja (☎ 263-2115; Calle Maneiro; per 3kg US$3.50; ☯ 7am-7pm Mon-Sat) There is also another branch at Calle Fajardo.

MEDICAL SERVICES

Many clinics and pharmacies are clustered on and around Av 4 de Mayo, near the hospital.

Clínica La Fe (☎ 262-2711; Av Jóvito Villalba, Los Robles) A good clinic outside the center.

Hospital Central Dr Luis Ortega (☎ 261-1101, 261-6508; Av 4 de Mayo) The most convenient central clinic.

MONEY

Most stores accept cash dollars for payment using the official exchange rate, though some will give you the black-market rate (negotiate). Credit cards are widely accepted in shops, upmarket hotels and restaurants.

Banco de Venezuela (Blvd Guevara)

Banco Mercantil (Calle San Nicolás)

Banesco (Av 4 de Mayo)

Corp Banca (Centro Comercial Galerías, Av 4 de Mayo) There's another branch on Calle Velázquez.

There are *casas de cambio* (money-exchange offices) in the airport as well as in the city.

Cambios Cussco (☎ 261-3379; Calle Velázquez)

Italcambio (☎ 265-9392; Ciudad Comercial Jumbo, Nivel Ciudad)

Triple Casa de Cambio (☎ 261-0458; Edificio Tiffany Palace, Av 4 de Mayo)

POST

DHL (☎ 263-5321; Calle Maneiro; ☯ 8am-6pm Mon-Fri)

Ipostel (☎ 416-3583; Calle Maneiro; ☯ 8am-noon & 1-4:30pm Mon-Fri)

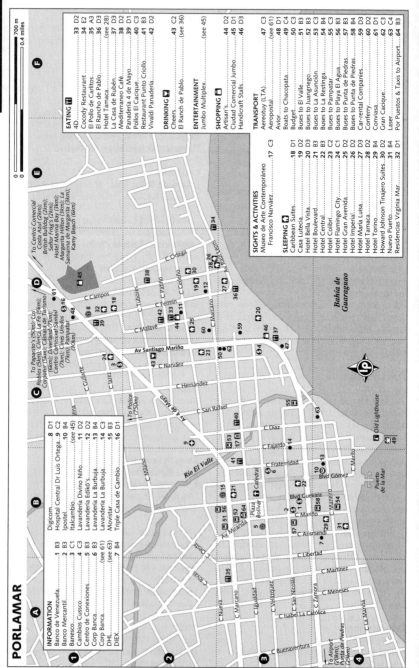

TOURIST INFORMATION

Cámara de Turismo (☎ 262-0683; caturmar@cantv
.net; Quinta 6, Av Virgen del Valle, Urbanización Jorge
Coll; ☺ 8:30am-12:30pm & 2-5pm Mon-Fri) This private
tourist-information corporation is in a residential district
beyond Corpotur.

Corpotur (☎ 262-2322; Centro Artesanal Gilberto Men-
chini, Av Jóvito Villalba, Los Robles; ☺ 8:30am-12:30pm
& 1:30-5:30pm Mon-Fri) This government-run tourist office
is midway between Porlamar and Pampatar.

Sights & Activities

One of Porlamar's few tourist sights is **Museo
de Arte Contemporáneo Francisco Narváez** (☎ 261-
8668; cnr Calles Igualdad & Díaz; ☺ 9am-5pm Mon-Fri), in a
large, modern building in the town center. On
the ground floor is a large collection of sculptures and paintings by the Margarita-born artist Narváez (1905–82), while the upper floor
is used for temporary exhibitions.

Sleeping

Porlamar has something for every budget.
Cheapies are mostly located in the older town
center, west of Av Santiago Mariño, while
standards are generally better at hotels to the
east. Three kilometers out of town in Urbanización Costa Azul you'll find the four- to
five-star hotels.

Prices given are for the low season. Expect
to pay around 30% or more when visiting
around vacation or holiday times (August,
December, Semana Santa and Carnaval).

BUDGET

Nuevo Puerto (☎ 263-8888; Calle La Marina; d US$14)
Truly run-down, this ragged joint is only for
serious penny-pinchers who seek only a roof
over their head. The basic, decrepit rooms have
tilted floors, but some do look out to sea – and
a tiny bit of quirky old charm does exist.

Hotel Torino (☎ 261-7186; Calle Mariño No 7-33; s/d
US$17/19; ✣) Here's a good budget choice that's
quiet inside despite being on a busy commercial street. Rooms are basic but decent, there's
a common area in which to hang, and it's
friendly enough. Check out the odd painting
of a knocked-over tree by room 18.

Residencias Virginia Mar (☎ 261-2373; Calle Fermín; d/tr with fan US$17/19, with air-con US$26/33; ✣)
Another large, basic hotel with sizable but
boring budget rooms, some quite dark. Top-
floor doubles, facing a covered balcony over
the street, are the best choices. Staff can be
rather gruff.

Hotel Tamaca (☎ 261-1602; tamaca@unete.com.ve; Av
Raúl Leoni; s/d with fan US$18/25, s/d with air-con US$21/30;
✣) Porlamar's main backpacker hang-out has
rooms and halls which are rather bleak and
come with spotty plumbing and old air-con.
But the front courtyard is a little haven, complete with leafy restaurant seating, open bar
area and dozens of caged, chirping parakeets.

Hotel Central (☎ 264-7162; Blvd Gómez; d/tr US$21;
✣) Located on bustling Blvd Gómez, this
cheap option has basic rooms and kitschy halls
with tacky paintings and odd lighting. Rooms
are dark and simple. The best part is the large
balcony overlooking the pedestrian street.

MIDRANGE

Hotel Boulevard (☎ 261-0522; hotelboulevard@cantv
.net; Calle Marcano; d/tr/q US$31/37; ℗ ✣ ▣) Not a
luxurious choice, but it does have 48 clean,
comfy rooms with big windows (those facing
north have a view of mountains around an
ugly building). There's a restaurant on the
premises.

Hotel Flamingo City (☎ 264-5564; Av 4 de Mayo; s/d
US$33/35; ✣) Strategically placed on the main
shopping street, Flamingo City has uniform,
carpeted rooms with a fridge and a safe. It's
recognizable by the bright-blue paint job, and
its position in the shadow of an enormous
bank building next door.

Hotel María Luisa (☎ 261-0564; www.hotelmarialuisa
.com.ve; Av Raúl Leoni; s/d US$36/40; ℗ ✣ ▣) Water-
front hotel with bright, white-tiled rooms
sporting big windows (some with sea views)
and cable TV. The small swimming pool has
a pleasant-enough patio-bar area. The hotel
is good value for money, and within strolling
distance of seafront restaurants.

our pick **Casa Lutecia** (☎ 263-8526; Calle Campos;
d/ste incl breakfast US$42/52; ✣) One of the most
pleasant stays in Porlamar, this pretty little
Mediterranean-like spot is strewn with flowers, hanging vines and palm trees, which gives
it a tropical feel and relaxed atmosphere. The
highlight is an excellent rooftop pool boasting
a sunny bar-terrace. Rooms are pleasant and
comfortable, and come with cable TV.

Hotel Colibrí (☎ 261-6346; hotelcolibri@hotmail.com;
Av Santiago Mariño; d US$42; ℗ ✣) This pleasant,
upmarket hotel has 70 sparklingly clean, modern rooms with flowery bedspreads and cable
TV. Corridors are decorated with mosaics,
art and pastel-pink paint, and hotel services
include a restaurant and car-rental office in
the lobby.

Caribbean Suites (☎ 264-2120; carsuites@hotmail .com; Calle Fermín; ste US$52; P 🛏) This four-story option has comfortable, modern family-oriented suites, all boasting kitchenettes.

Howard Johnson Tinajero Suites (☎ 263-8380; www.hotelhowardjohnson.com in Spanish; Calle Campos; s/d incl breakfast US$52/60; P 🛏 🖥 🍴) This 10-story apartment hotel has a comfortable collection of spacious, family-friendly suites. They all feature a kitchenette with fridge, microwave and coffeemaker, but there's also a restaurant if you don't want to start up the pan.

Other midrange choices:

Hotel Gran Avenida (☎ 261-7457; Calle Cedeño; d US$33; 🛏) Boring rooms with fridge and TV, and most lack natural light (get a room in front with windows).

Hotel Imperial (☎ 261-6420; Av Raúl Leoni; d US$35; P 🛏) A large white hotel with good, but plain and outdated, rooms. Higher-up rooms come with balcony and sea views.

TOP END

Most of Porlamar's upmarket hotels and nightclubs are located 3km east of the city in a large area called Urbanización Costa Azul. These destinations, some located at the beach, tend to be spread out from each other and the area still has some large, ugly bare patches, so it's not great place in which to stroll around. Taxis are the main means of getting around.

Hotel Bella Vista (☎ 261-7222; www.hbellavista.com; Av Santiago Mariño; d incl breakfast US$76-85; P 🛏 🍴) This hotel, the best in central Porlamar, is hardly a luxurious stay – service isn't up to par and the gardens and overall decor could be spiffed up a bit. Plus an ugly fence separates the hotel from the beach, though the pool area is nice. Sea-view rooms cost more.

Hotel Marina Bay (☎ 262-5211; www.hotelmarinabay .com; Calle Abancay, Costa Azul; s/d incl breakfast US$80/112; P 🍴 🛏 🖥 🍴) Good choice by the sea and close to Porlamar's nightlife. It comes with almost 200 comfortable and fully equipped rooms with balcony, most looking down over the central swimming pool. There are several restaurants and bars, along with a casino.

Margarita Hilton (☎ 260-1700; www.hilton.com; Calle Los Uveros, Costa Azul; d incl breakfast US$80; P 🍴 🛏 🖥 🍴) The beachside Hilton has been setting the standard in Porlamar for 11 years, and still can't be beaten for luxury. It boasts good service, the glitziest casino in town and a garden-filled complex that's packed with boutiques, bars and restaurants.

A highlight is the pool area, which boasts waterfalls, islands, volleyball and fountains.

La Samanna de Margarita (☎ 262-2222; www .lasamannademargarita.com; Av Francisco Esteban Gómez; d incl breakfast US$250; P 🍴 🛏 🖥 🍴) This Mediterranean-style hotel offers airy rooms with balconies (get a sea view) and romantic four-poster beds draped in curtains. Bathrooms have quirky fish accents and give you the choice to bathe in either (filtered) salt or fresh water – very unique. Plus there's an on-site spa which offers facials, massages, reflexology and mud baths, along with a large Jacuzzi pool – a very pampering experience indeed.

Eating

Porlamar has quite a few restaurants catering for every price range. Most of the restaurants pitched at tourists are east of Av Santiago Mariño in the eastern sector of the city.

RESTAURANTS

Restaurant Punto Criollo (☎ 263-6745; Calle Igualdad 19; mains US$5-14; ☯ 11am-midnight; 🛏) Deservedly popular with locals for its solid food and great prices, this busy and efficient restaurant has homey, comfortable atmosphere and a wealth of menu choices. Try the *churrasco a la llanera* (grilled steak), garlic shrimp, veggie pizza or spaghetti *alfredo*. Portions are large.

El Rancho de Pablo (☎ 263-1121; Av Raúl Leoni; mains US$10-14; ☯ 9am-1am Wed-Mon) The biggest and best of a clutch of beachfront restaurants in the area, this shady spot sees all manner of folk enjoying seafood, pastas, meats and salads while peeking at the beachgoers going by.

Hotel Tamaca (☎ 261-1602; Av Raúl Leoni; mains US$10-14) If you're a backpacker and not staying here, you should at least drop in for a meal or drink. The leafy patio restaurant is a pleasant little paradise from the city's concrete, and the large cages nearby are filled with parakeets. There's also an airy bar that's an excellent place to hook up with fellow travelers. A pool table provides extra entertainment.

La Casa de Rubén (☎ 264-5969; Av Santiago Mariño; mains US$10-16; ☯ noon-10pm Mon-Sat) Somewhat hidden from the road in a windowless building, this family restaurant specializes in excellent seafood dishes. Try some fish soup, tasty shrimp (cooked nine ways) and seasonal lobster. There's also rabbit for the adventurous.

ourpick Cocody Restaurant (☎ 261-8431; Av Raúl Leoni; mains US$13-19; ☯ 6pm-11:30pm Thu-Tue; 🛏) Run by a friendly French family, this romantic beachfront restaurant offers well-prepared, excellent European cuisine. Choose from seafood crepes, beef kebabs or fettuccine with salmon and asparagus. There are French wines to sip, or even (expensive) Perrier. The three-course menu costs US$23.

Mediterraneo Café (☎ 264-0503; Calle Campos; mains US$13-19; ⏰ 11am-3pm & 6:30-11pm Tue-Sat; 🛇) This smart Italian restaurant serves delicious local and Mediterranean dishes on an outdoor terrace and in an air-con interior. Check out the tagliatelle with lobster or the linguini with asparagus; there are meat dishes too.

Another dining option is Cheers (right).

CAFÉS & QUICK EATS

Panadería 4 de Mayo (Calle Fermín at 4 de Mayo; sandwiches US$2-4.50; ⏰ 7am-11pm) Of several bustling *panaderías* (bakeries) in the vicinity, this invariably popular spot comes up trumps. It also has beautiful pastries, sandwiches and cakes, and its terrace is one of Porlamar's top people-watching spots.

Vivaldi Panadería (☎ 263-3150; Calle Patiño at Calle Malavé; sandwiches US$3.50-6; ⏰ 7am-10pm Mon-Sat, till 2pm Sun; 🛇) A tranquil spot for frothy cappuccinos, excellent pastries and a morning newspaper, Vivaldi's bakery has a pleasant little terrace or air-con interior from which to choose.

4D (☎ 261-5805; Calle Malavé; ice cream US$2-5; ⏰ 11:30am-midnight) Opposite Vivaldi is this popular ice-cream parlor with a large, shaded terrace. Grab some friends and go for the bucket-sized tubs of ice cream in 27 flavors from strawberries-and-cream to tiramisu (US$7).

El Pollo de Carlitos (Calle Marcano; mains under US$5; ⏰ noon-1am Mon-Sat) This rustic restaurant does great grilled chicken and meats and has an airy front patio, but it's located in an unattractive area. Try the half chicken with *hallaca* (chopped meat and vegetables in corn dough, steamed in banana leaves) and salad.

Pollos El Cacique (☎ 261-7219; Calle Igualdad; mains under US$5; ⏰ 10am-10pm) A reasonably good-value chicken affair, this time in a popular and modern fast-food environment with identically uniformed staff. There are just a couple of side dishes and some juices, otherwise it's only *pollo*.

Drinking & Clubbing

Bars and nightclubs appear and disappear at lightning speed on Isla de Margarita, so ask your nearest hipster for the latest hotspots. Most of the trendy nightclubs and bars are beyond Porlamar center, and some (like the popular club Nikki Beach) are open in high season only. There's always a collection of rustic shacks, well stocked with cold beers, on the beach.

British Bulldog (☎ 267-1527; Centro Comercial Costa Azul, Av Bolívar; ⏰ 9pm-late Thu-Sat, Tue-Sat in high season; 🛇) Margarita's first and only British-style pub, with live rock music on weekends. It was being remodeled at research time, but promised good things to come, so check it out if you need a drink.

Cheers (☎ 261-0957; Av Santiago Mariño; ⏰ noon-11pm Mon-Sat; mains US$13-18; 🛇) Ripping off the US sitcom's logo and identity is this surprisingly pleasant restaurant-bar with a dark pub atmosphere, good food and a great U-shaped bar. There are tasteful wood and brick accents, along with sports on the TV. It's on the 2nd floor.

El Rancho de Pablo (☎ 263-1121; Av Raúl Leoni; ⏰ 9am-11pm Wed-Mon) Lulled by the sound of waves and with the sea breeze in your hair, it's hard not to slip into a mellow holiday mood at this beachside bar and restaurant. There are several smaller huts and bars nearby.

La Terraza (⏰ 0414-794-5513; Centro Comercial Redoma, Av Jóvito Villalba; ⏰ 10pm-4am Thu-Sat, nightly in high season) Located 8km from Porlamar in Los Robles, this is the current hot spot. It's in a large building on the 4th floor, and has a breezy open terrace overlooking the nearby commercial area. There are white lounges and high tables, plus four bars and disco lights. Be like the cool crowd and come after midnight.

Kamy Beach (⏰ 808-6066; Av Aldonza Marique, Playa Varadera; ⏰ 11pm-4am Thu-Sat, nightly in high season) This slick, beachside nightclub has a distinct tropical feel, with swaying palms, thatched-roofed bars and square beds (with romantic curtains) on the sand. White lounge sofas and airy terraces overlook the beach – great for chilling out and listening to the waves. Live bands and DJs also.

Señor Frog's (☎ 262-0451; Centro Comercial Costa Azul, Av Bolívar; ⏰ 6pm-4am Tue-Sun, nightly in high season; 🛇) One of Porlamar's most popular party destinations is this brightly colored building accented with cartoon figures inside and out. It's a restaurant until 11:30pm, then a thumping Latin-pop-orientated *discoteca* (disco) by night. Opah – another nightspot – and British Bulldog are in the same building.

Entertainment

Movie lovers can head to the screens at **Cines Unidos** (☎ 262-1568; Centro Comercial Sambil, Los Robles) or **Jumbo Multiplex** (☎ 264-6665; www.cinex.com.ve in Spanish; Ciudad Comercial Jumbo).

Gamblers will want to try their luck at the casinos, which are located in the upmarket hotels in Urbanización Costa Azul, 3km east of the city. Try the Hilton.

Shopping

Venezuelans are crazy for shopping on Isla de Margarita, and they'll all agree that Porlamar is a great place to buy up the goods. Several sparkling malls dot Porlamar and Pampatar, packed with imported duty-free goods from clothes and jewelry to electrical knick-knacks. Prices are less than on the mainland, but whether the difference is worth the energy and expense for a trip to the island is questionable. Look for sales and pluck up the nerve to ask for '*su mejor precio*' (your best price), even in boutiques.

The most elegant and expensive shopping areas are on and around Avs Santiago Mariño and 4 de Mayo. Here you'll find jewelry, imported spirits, fashionable clothing, computers etc. Right in town is the huge six-level **Ciudad Comercial Jumbo** (Av 4 de Mayo at Calle Campos; P ⊠). Or catch a bus out to **Centro Comercial Sambil** (Av Bolívar; ⌚ 10am-9pm Mon-Sat, noon-8pm Sun; P ⊠), which is one of the shiniest of the island's shopping malls.

The old center has some of the cheapest shops and is more of a fun local experience. The streets south of Plaza Bolívar bustle all day long, especially the two central pedestrian malls, Blvd Guevara and Blvd Gómez.

For local crafts, one of the few outlets is **Artisan's** (☎ 261-9626; Calle Malavé; ⌚ 9am-4pm Mon-Fri, 9am-1pm Sat), but most of the stuff is pretty kitschy. Check out the voluptuous ceramic figurines. In the afternoon, handicraft stalls open along the southern part of Av Santiago Mariño, selling their wares until 9pm or 10pm.

Getting There & Around

Porlamar is the main base for international and national routes to Isla de Margarita; see p240 for details.

Frequent buses link Porlamar to the rest of the island, including Pampatar, La Asunción and Juangriego. They leave from different points in the city center; see the Porlamar map (p244) for bus stops.

There are several car-rental companies in front of the Hotel Bella Vista, but you'll find other places in town. **Budget** (☎ 264-7539; Calle Marcano) has cars from around US$50 per day with unlimited mileage.

PAMPATAR
pop 50,000

Much less built-up than its neighbor Porlamar, which lies 10km to the southwest, is this unpretentious beachside city. The small colonial center shelters some historic buildings that nostalgically hint at bygone days (though most of the city is more modern). A nearby beach features calm waters and fishing boats with roosting pelicans, and also provides views of islets in the distance. Founded in the 1530s, Pampatar was one of the earliest settlements on Margarita, and within 50 years it grew into the largest shipping center in what is now Venezuela.

If you decide to swim at the beach, ask about water quality – pollution has been a problem in the past.

Sights

Pampatar's fort, the **Castillo de San Carlos Borromeo** (⌚ 8am-6pm), is in the center of town, on the waterfront. It was built from 1663 to 1684 on the site of a previous stronghold that was destroyed by European pirates. It's the best-preserved fort on the island, and a classic example of Spanish military architecture. Check out the 800kg front door (a reproduction). Admission is free but donations are appreciated.

Opposite the fort is the **parish church**, a sober, whitewashed construction from 1748. Go inside to see the crucifix, Cristo del Buen Viaje, over the high altar. Legend has it that the ship that carried the crucifix from Spain to Santo Domingo called en route at Pampatar, but despite repeated efforts it couldn't depart until the Christ image had been unloaded. It has remained in Pampatar since. To the right of the church is the **Casa de la Cultura** (admission free), in the old customs house, worth a peek for its occasional art exhibits.

The beach extends for 1km east of the fort, and exudes old-world charm, with rustic boats anchored in the bay and fishermen repairing nets on the beach. The cape at the far eastern end of the bay is topped by another fort, the ruined **Fortín de la Caranta** (built 1586–1626). It provides sweeping views of the area.

The theme park **Diverland** (☎ 262-0813; www
.parquediverland.com in Spanish; Av Jóvito Villalba, Pampatar;
adults/child under 10 yr US$5/3; ☺ 6pm-midnight Fri-Sun),
3km west of Pampatar center, has a modest collection of rollercoasters and other attractions.
One of the biggest draws within this complex is
the separately run **Waterland** (☎ 262-5545), which –
by reservation only – lets you swim with dolphins and seals in the attached swimming pool.
A basic video, briefing and 30 minutes with the
dolphins costs around US$50.

Courses

Centro de Lingüística Aplicada (CELA; ☎ 262-8198; www
.cela-ve.com; Calle Corocoro, Quinta Cela, Urbanización Playa El
Ángel) offers intensive Spanish-language courses
at different levels (two weeks about US$400).
Excursions and cultural activities liven things
up, and family stays are available.

Sleeping & Eating

Aparthotel Don Juan (☎ 262-3609; Calle Almirante Brión
10; d US$19; ☼) This is a very run-down, basic
and depressing cheapie – at least prices don't
rise in high season. Ask for a window for some
light. Kitchenettes are available for a few more
bolívares. Located about a 15-minute walk east
of the *castillo* and a bit hard to find; take a taxi
or keep asking for directions.

   Posada La Bufonera (☎ 262-9977; Calle Almirante Brión;
d/tr US$28/33; P ☼) Across the street from Don
Juan, this coral-colored place has 20 no-frills
rooms with small baths and very rustic kitchenettes. It's right on the beach; unfortunately the
rooms are separated from the sands by ugly security walls and fences. Call ahead to reserve.

   La Posada de Aleja (☎ 0416-695-5355; lapos
adadealeja@hotmail.com; Calle Nueva Cadiz; r US$36; ☼)
This colorful, family-run posada has an odd
mishmash facade. There is nice tiling in the
common area and a grassy patio out back,
next to the beach. Rooms for up to 14 people
are available. It's a hard place to find: near the
town's entrance, look for the nine-story Bahia
Azul building (near the Circulo Militar) and
follow the road in front one block, then turn
right and go 20m.

   Hotel Flamingo Beach (☎ 262-4822; flamingo@
enlared.net; Calle el Cristo; d US$70-108; P ☼ ☎)
About a 30-minute walk past Pampatar's
center and up a hill is this decent three-star
choice. Rooms are good and come with fridge;
try to get one with a sea view. There are two
glass elevators, a nice outdoor pool, a tennis
court and a small private beach.

LagunaMar Resort (Map p241; ☎ 400-4000; www
.lagunamar.com.ve; Sector Apostadero; s/d incl 3 meals
US$107/152, kids under 12 yr half-price; P ☼ ☐ ☎)
This enormous beachside resort is 5km north
of Pampatar and boasts an impressive list of
facilities, including a casino, tennis courts, a
kids' club, nine swimming pools (one with
wave machine, another with waterslides) and
a private lagoon for water sports including
kayaking and waterskiing. A day pass (US$30)
includes use of the facilities, drinks and lunch.
It's best to taxi here, as it's down a 2km road
from the highway.

   When your tummy grumbles head for the
line of palm-thatched shacks on the beach,
each with a powerful sound system and good
supply of cold beer and fried fish. For something fancier, try the **Guayoyo Café** (☎ 262-4514;
6pm-1am Mon-Sat). It's across the street from the
Hotel Flamingo Beach (a 30-minute walk),
but boasts awesome views over the water.

Getting There & Away

There are very frequent buses to Porlamar
(US$0.35, 20 minutes); they run north along
Av 4 de Mayo. Taxis cost US$5 to Porlamar
and US$14 to the airport.

EL VALLE DEL ESPÍRITU SANTO
pop 15,000

Commonly called 'El Valle,' this small town
is Margarita's spiritual capital and home to
the island's patroness, the miraculous Virgen
del Valle. Her image, kept in the mock-Gothic
church on the plaza, draws pilgrims from
all around eastern Venezuela year-round –
but especially on September 8, the Virgin's
day. The whole week afterward sees the village packed with revelers camped out on the
streets. El Valle is the first Marian religious
sanctuary in the Americas.

   The fanciful, gingerbread house–like **Basílica
de Nuestra Señora del Valle**, standing out in its
twin-peaked glory on the central plaza, was
built from 1894 to 1906 and is the current
home of the Virgin. According to local history, the image of the Virgin was brought to
the town around 1510. Her statue is to the
right of the high altar, usually surrounded by
a huddle of devotees. You can buy rosaries,
amulets and crafts – along with a few hundred images of the Virgin – from a crowd
of religious stalls next to the church. Shops
around the main plaza are also good places
to buy crafts.

The **Museo Diocesano** (admission US$1; ⏰ 9am-noon & 2-5pm Tue-Sat, 9am-1pm Sun), behind the church, has objects related to the Virgin plus various offerings from the faithful asking for favors.

In a different vein, diagonally opposite the church is the **Casa Museo Santiago Mariño** (admission US$0.25; ⏰ 8am-5pm), the house where its namesake hero of the War of Independence was born in 1788. The sizable country mansion has been painstakingly reconstructed and fitted with vintage furniture and well-displayed period memorabilia. Look for the effeminate painting of Generalissimo Francisco de Miranda, posing suggestively on a bed.

Buses between Porlamar and El Valle shuttle frequently (US$0.30, 15 minutes).

LA ASUNCIÓN

pop 25,000

Although Porlamar is by far the largest urban center on the island, the small, sleepy town of La Asunción is the state capital of Nueva Esparta. This tranquil spot is set in a fertile, verdant valley.

Built in the second half of the 16th century is the **catedral**, located on the attractive, tree-shaded Plaza Bolívar. It's one of the oldest surviving colonial churches in the country and widely thought to be the second-oldest after Coro's cathedral. Note the unusual bell tower and a portal with a delicate Renaissance facade.

On the northern side of the plaza is the **Museo Nueva Cádiz** (☎ 416-8492; Plaza Bolívar; ⏰ 9am-4pm Mon-Fri, till 1pm Sat & Sun), named after the first Spanish town in South America, which was established around 1500 on Isla Cubagua, south of Margarita. An earthquake in 1541 completely destroyed the town. The museum displays a small collection of exhibits related to the region's history and culture. Admission is free, but donations are always appreciated.

Just outside town, a 10-minute walk southward up the hill, is the **Castillo de Santa Rosa** (admission free; ⏰ 9am-5pm), one of seven forts built on the island to protect it from pirate attacks. It provides great views and has some old armor on display.

Buses from Porlamar will let you off on Plaza Bolívar (US$0.50, 25 minutes).

PARQUE NACIONAL CERRO EL COPEY

If you have your own wheels (or are willing to hire a taxi) and want to leave the crowds behind, head up into this fresh, hilly **national park** (☎ 242-0306), southwest of La Asunción. The old road climbs up through cool, scented woodland, and near the top a side road branches off to the west and up toward some radio towers. There's potential bird-watching (look for the yellow-shouldered parrot) and hiking in the area.

You can stop for a meal (or the night) at the idyllic **Posada Restaurant Serrania** (☎ 242-3864; Carrera La Asunción-El Valle; d/f US$38/47, mains US$7-17; ⏰ 9am-7pm Tue-Sun, daily in high season; 🅿), 3km from La Asunción. This restaurant has great views and offers seafood and traditional Venezuelan dishes. There's also a posada, which offers five good, little rooms with bathroom, fridge and TV, or there's a family room. But it's the view over treetops and down to the sea that you'll remember.

PLAYA EL AGUA

This pleasant 3km-long stretch of white sand has become Margarita's trendiest beach, attracting both elite Venezuelan tourists and lobster-colored gringos by the score. During short holiday peaks, bathing here can prove to be a sardine-can experience; if you're looking for more peace come here in the slower times, when it's a more welcoming and wonderfully laid-back spot.

The shoreline is shaded with coconut groves and densely dotted with thatched-roof restaurants and bars that offer a good selection of food, cocktails and music. Souvenir sellers stroll the beach, hoping to make a few sales. The northern, less developed part of the beach tends to have fewer crowds.

Nightlife is slim as are shopping choices and services. There's no bank, but **Cambios Cussco** (⏰ 9am-5:30pm Mon-Sat, till 3pm Sun), on the beach road, can change money.

A few roads head inland from the beach road, and after about 1km meet the main highway to Porlamar.

Activities

Travel agencies along the beach offer trips to **Los Frailes**, a small archipelago of coral islands northeast of Margarita. It's a great place for **scuba diving** (2 dives US$80) or **snorkeling** (US$38). Various other water sports are available, and in high-season there's sometimes **bungee-jumping** nearby Playa El Agua.

Parque El Agua (☎ 234-8559; www.parqueelagua.com in Spanish; Av 31 de Julio; adult/child US$17/12; ⏰ 10am-Wed-Sun, Tue-Sun high season), near Playa El Cardón, is a large family-friendly water park with chutes and a large outdoor Jacuzzi. The park is a short taxi ride south of Playa El Agua.

Sleeping

Across the street from the beach is a swath of mostly midrange to luxury, top-end hotels and holiday homes. Backpackers should head to Juangriego (right) instead. The following prices are for low season: expect tariffs to rise 25% or more in high season, unless otherwise stated.

Posada Nathalie (☎ 249-1973; www.posadanathalie .com; Calle Camino Real; d US$28; ⚙ 🖭) One of Playa El Agua's most pleasant stays is this intimate, 12-room posada run by a friendly Dutch family. It's a simple, well-run place featuring clean, tidy rooms with fridge. There's an outdoor common area with a barbecue and a small nearby swimming pool. Look for the posada up the dirt road at the entrance to the beach, in the souvenir stalls' parking lot. Prices don't rise in high season.

Hotel Miramar Village (☎ 249-1797; Calle Miragua; s/d US$52/80; ⚙ 🖭) Popular with French, Germans and Dutch, this all-inclusive, Mediterranean-like hotel features 35 good, spacious rooms – some with walk-in closets. Wood bridges connect the two-story buildings, and despite the resort atmosphere there's also an intimate feel of sorts. The restaurant is airy and there's a triangular pool area beyond. It's about a one-minute walk to the beach. Minimum stay is two nights.

Chalets de Belén (☎ 249-1707; Calle Miragua; d US$56-70, 6-person casa US$117; P ⚙) This rustic, intimate place is run by a Venezuelan woman named Belén and her three small poodles. Belén has just four clean, comfortable and small rooms with homey touches; they come with shared patios. There's one 'casa' (two-bedroom apartment) with kitchenette. They're all in an overgrown garden, and it's a short walk to the beach. Minimum stay is three nights (five for the casa). Prices are negotiable in low season.

Hotel Cocoparaiso (☎ 249-0117; d incl breakfast US$75; P ⚙ 🖭) A very pleasant stay, this spot is just across the street from the beach. Twenty-six comfortable, spacious rooms are on tap, some with a large front patio complete with a hammock; others might have private back patios off their bathrooms. There is also a small pool and palm-shaded grounds.

Hotel Costa Linda Beach (☎ 249-1303; www.hotel costalinda.com; Calle Miragua; d incl breakfast buffet US$85; P ⚙ 🖭) This attractive blue-and-orange hotel is about a five-minute walk inland from the beach. There's a breezy restaurant-bar, a relaxing pool area and rooftop terraces. Rooms are simple but tasteful; the best ones (higher up) boast small balconies, hammocks and sea views. Tropical plants are everywhere and there's even a tiny gym and kids' playroom. Cash earns a 10% discount; prices vary highly depending on the month.

Eating

The whole beach is lined with snack shacks and fancy restaurants, so you'll have a good selection when all that sand time makes you hungry.

Margarita's Café (mains US$7-12; ⏱ 7am-9pm) For no-nonsense, reasonably priced eating try this busy joint on the beach road, which cooks up 'international' breakfasts and other casual dishes. It's across from the beach near Cambio Cussco and has a shady front sidewalk area.

Thai Chi (☎ 249-0527; Calle Miragua; mains US$10-12; ⏱ 6-11pm Thu-Tue) If you're looking for something exotic, walk about 10 minutes inland to this fine Thai restaurant. On the menu are dishes like stir-fried rice with chicken and vegetables, curry fish, and beef in coconut sauce.

La Isla Restaurant (☎ 249-0035; mains US$10-19; ⏱ 9am-11pm) This is a good, thatched-roof restaurant right on the beach. Seafood is big here – try the jumbo shrimp, crab linguini or lobster with cognac. Those not fond of shellfish can go for the pizza, pasta or paella.

Another worthy restaurant is Pacífico, an excellent French eatery nearby.

Getting There & Away

The beach has regular bus transportation from Porlamar (US$0.80, 45 minutes), so you can easily come for the day if you can't afford to stay overnight. Taxis from the airport cost US$17; they're US$12 from Porlamar.

JUANGRIEGO

pop 45,000

Some of Margarita's most fabulous sunsets are seen from this humble city, which is set along the edge of a fine bay in the northern part of Margarita. Juangriego also has a pleasant beach harboring rustic fishing boats and resting pelicans, and far away on the horizon the peaks of Macanao are visible – and spectacular when the sun sets behind them.

The city has a few banks and internet cafés, along with two discos, some bars and various tourist-oriented restaurants. It's a good backpacker destination, as accommodations are more affordable than in places like Playa El Agua and it's less congested than Porlamar. Nearby, Playa Caribe, about a 10-minute taxi ride away, is one of the island's best beaches – relatively pristine, but with a few services for comfort.

Crowning the hill just north of town is the **Fortín de la Galera** (admission free; ☉ dawn-dusk). These days little remains of the colonial fort (destroyed by the Spanish royalist army in 1817) other than some stone walls with a terrace and a refreshment stand, but it sees a steady trail of love-struck couples arriving in the late afternoon for a sweeping view of the sunset.

If you're coming from La Asunción, consider stopping off in Santa Ana to see its church, which is similar to the La Asunción cathedral but two centuries younger. In the nearby village of El Cercado, typical Venezuelan pottery is made.

Sleeping

Juangriego is increasingly catering to tourism. Prices for hotels can rise about 25% in high season.

Hotel Río Avia (☎ 253-1630; Calle La Marina; d US$17-19; P 🞮) A Spanish-run place offering nine dark, very basic rooms with disturbingly caged doors and colored glass windows. At least it's breezy and there's a small communal table at which to sit. Located just up the street from Hotel Patrick.

Hotel Gran Sol (☎ 253-3216; Calle La Marina; d/t/q US$17/19/21; 🞮) Strangely located at the back of the small Centro Comercial Juangriego, and just back from the beach, is this uninspiring but cheap hotel. The 19 rooms are plain, old and dark.

El Caney (☎ 253-5059; Calle Guevara 17; d/tr US$19/24; 🞮) Behind a gated front is this colorful little Peruvian-run posada. There's a sweet stone patio in front, complete with thatched roof, plus a small palm garden out back. The 11 rooms are rustic and dark but comfortable, and a tiny basic kitchen is open to guests. Look for it half a block from the main street and a block from the beach.

ourpick Hotel Patrick (☎ 253-6218; www.hotel patrick.com in Dutch; Calle El Fuerte; d with fan/air-con US$24/28; 🞮 🖳) Not far from the beach is this Dutch-run spot that caters to backpackers. There are nine simple and attractive rooms, plus a good hangout area with tables, sofas, hammocks and a bar nearby. It serves breakfast, does tours and organizes occasional weekend barbecues and beach parties. To top it off, there's wi-fi.

Eating & Drinking

Club La Playya (☎ 0414-789-3537; mains US$12-21; ☉ 8am-11pm) Grab a taxi, head to Playa Caribe (about 10 minutes' drive) and plant yourself here. Run by the gregarious Argentine, Carlos, this completely open restaurant has tables overlooking the beach and lounges on the sand. Good food and great music make for a relaxing afternoon, and full-moon parties are always a possibility. Hours are longer in high season.

Restaurants and bars dot the beachfront, all perfectly positioned to keep sunset watchers fed and watered with romantic suppers and cold beer. One of the best is **Brisas Marinas** (☎ 253-0791; mains US$7-14; Calle La Marina; ☉ 10am-9pm), with a shady patio overlooking the beach. You can also try the good but expensive **El Viejo Muelle** (☎ 253-2962; Calle La Marina; mains US$10-20; ☉ 10am-11pm) with seating on the sand. Hotel Patrick serves breakfasts and has a bar open to nonguests.

Getting There & Away

Frequent buses run between Porlamar and Juangriego (US$0.80, 45 minutes) via La Asunción. Taxis from Porlamar and the airport both cost around US$10.

CARAPACHO

Carapacho is just another small, sleepy village away from the island's coast, but travelers looking for a very local experience and some peaceful, nonbeach solitude might enjoy a stay here. Behind high walls is **La Casona del Chef Huguito** (☎ 259-0040; Calle Miranda 134; s/d US$42/48; P 🞮 🖳), a minihacienda with a little patio courtyard and a tiny pool. Eleven mostly windowless rooms are dark but charmingly rustic, with comfortable amenities like fridge and TV. Some have a kitchenette, and one boasts its own private plunge pool. The posada is located in a white, orange and green triangular building across from the local church; there's no sign, so it's best to call ahead and tell them you're coming. Taxis from Porlamar should cost around US$12.

PARQUE NACIONAL LAGUNA DE LA RESTINGA

This **national park** (8am-4:30pm) covers the lagoon and a large mass of mangroves riddled with narrow, labyrinthine channels at its western end. This is a habitat for a variety of birds, including pelicans, cormorants and scarlet ibises.

Buses from Porlamar go regularly to La Restinga (US$1, 45 minutes) and will deposit you at the entrance to the embarkation pier (taxis from Porlamar cost US$15). From there, five-seat motorboats will take you on a **boat trip** (half-hr/hr per boat US$14/24) drifting along the interconnecting *caños* (channels) that cut through the mangroves. Note the romantic *caño* names like Mi Dulce Amor (My Sweet Love) and Túnel de los Enamorados (Tunnel of Lovers).

The boats end up at a fine shell beach, where you can grab fresh fried fish in an open-air restaurant shack before returning back to the embarkation pier at your leisure. In the low season, be prepared for long waits, or pay for the empty seats.

MUSEO MARINO

This good **Marine Museum** (291-3231; Blvd El Paseo, Boca del Río; adult/child US$3.50/1.75; 9am-4:30pm, till 5:30pm in high season) is worth the trip across the island, especially for families. It has a shallow pool of safe-to-handle starfish, snails and other underwater fauna that will thrill the kids. But don't stick your hands in the outdoor turtle pool as there are a couple of small sharks in the water. The museum also has a small aquarium of other colorful marine life and large exhibitions of coral, shell and photography.

PLAYA EL YAQUE

pop 1500

One of the world's best places for windsurfing and kitesurfing is this pleasant and well-developed beach, located just a few kilometers south of Margarita's airport. Tranquil, shallow waters and steady winds have given El Yaque an international reputation, and it's become a hang-out for these windsport communities. A couple of important national and international competitions take place here every year, attracting big sports stars and their hangers-on.

Several professional outfits on the beachfront have **windsurfing rental** (per hr/day/2 days US$26/63/120). They also offer lessons at US$38 per hour, or US$235 for an advanced course of 10 hours. There is also **kitesurfing** (half-/full-day rental US$52/77, 2-hr lesson US$90).

There are no banks in El Yaque, but a few *cambios* will change your cash or traveler's checks.

Sleeping

As elsewhere on the island, expect prices to jump in the high season.

El Yaque Motion (263-9742; www.elyaquemotion.com; Calle Principal; d US$26-390, apt US$52;) The absolute best deal in town is this German-run posada near the entrance into town (a 10-minute walk to the main beach). It's a well-run place offering clean, neat rooms with good furniture. Three apartments are available for families, and there's a rooftop kitchen and terrace for everyone to use. The owner also helps those interested in renting houses for large groups of up to 10 people. Airport pickup is available.

Windsurf Paradise (263-8890; www.windsurf-paradise.com; Calle Principal; d incl buffet breakfast US$60-90;) This pleasant miniresort boasts a restaurant with a great deck overlooking the beach. The pool area, with its wood and stone walks, also has a relaxing feel. Standard rooms are attractive and feature hammocks outside, but also line the hotel's entrance – go for superior rooms if you want higher ceilings, private balconies, more space and possible poolside location.

Surfhotel Jump'n Jibe (263-8396; www.jumpnjibe.com; Calle Principal; d incl buffet breakfast US$95;) Of several midrange hotels fronting onto El Yaque beachfront, this cool, relaxed choice is one of the best. It has 17 sparkling rooms (including one apartment), a palm-filled garden and terrific sea views (even better if you can afford a private balcony). A small terrace overlooks the beach area.

Windsurfer's Oasis (263-9216; www.windsurfersoasis.com; Calle Principal; d incl buffet breakfast US$130;) This three-story white hotel is one of the most prominent buildings in town. It's right on the beach but you can also hang out in the pool, surrounding patio and Jacuzzi. Rooms are modern and simple and come with cable TV and fridge; most have balconies and

THE NORTHEAST

sea views. The hotel has its own restaurant/bar over the beach.

Getting There & Away
Several buses per day run between Porlamar and El Yaque (US$0.75, 30 minutes). Taxis from Porlamar cost US$14; from the airport it's US$10.

ANZOÁTEGUI STATE

BARCELONA
☎ 0281 / pop 425,000

A feeling of yesteryear still lingers within the heart of the old town of Barcelona, a large coastal city and capital of the Anzoátegui state. The colorful colonial center is a pleasant place, with leafy plazas and a mishmash of historic architecture. The city was founded in 1671 by a group of Catalan colonists and it hasn't rushed into modernity at quite the frenetic pace of its more youthful neighboring city, Puerto La Cruz, with which Barcelona is gradually merging into a single urban sprawl.

Information
Banco de Venezuela (Plaza Boyacá)
Banesco (Carrera 9 Paéz)
CANTV (☘ 7:30am-7:30pm Mon-Fri, 8am-6:30 Sat) Internet and telephone services.
Corp Banca (Plaza Bolívar)
Corporación de Turismo del Estado Anzoátegui
(Coranztur; ☎ 275-0474; www.coranztur.com in Spanish; Av 5 de Julio; ☘ 8am-noon & 2-5pm Mon-Fri) Barcelona's main tourist office, located on the ground floor of the Gobernación building.
Dirección de Turismo (☎ 277-8388; Carrera 13 Bolívar; ☘ 8am-noon & 2-5:30pm Mon-Fri) On the 2nd floor of the Centro Commercial Pasaje Colonial, this place is a joke compared to Coranztur.
Ipostel (☎ 275-6209; Carrera 13 Bolívar; ☘ 8am-noon & 1-5pm Mon-Fri)
Italcambio (☎ 275-3882; ☘ 8:30am-5pm Mon-Fri, 9am-2pm Sat) At the airport.

Sights
The city's historic center is Plaza Boyacá, which boasts a statue of General José Antonio Anzoátegui, the Barcelona-born hero of the War of Independence after whom the state is named. On the western side of this tree-shaded plaza stands the **catedral**, built a century after the town's founding. The most

venerated object in the cathedral is the glass reliquary in a chapel off the left aisle, where the embalmed remains of Italian martyr San Celestino are kept. The richly gilded main retable dates from 1744.

On the southern side of the plaza is the fascinating little **Museo de Anzoátegui** (☎ 416-1941; admission free; ☘ 8am-5pm Mon-Fri, 9am-1pm Sat & Sun), housed in the oldest surviving building in town (built in 1671). The museum features a variety of objects related to Barcelona's history. The highlight is the surreal collection of puppetlike religious statues brought over by the Spanish and equipped with movable limbs. Only their faces, hands and feet have been properly finished as they were originally dressed in robes.

An annex to the museum is housed in the **Ateneo de Barcelona** (☎ 419-0226; cnr Calle 1 San Félix & Carrera 12 Juncal; admission free; ☘ 8am-noon & 2-5pm Mon-Fri), two blocks east. On the 2nd floor of this colonial-style building is a 44-piece collection of art (most of which dates from the 1940s and 1960s) by prominent modern Venezuelan artists.

Plaza Rolando is flanked by the **Iglesia del Carmen** and the **Teatro Cajigal**, both dating from the 1890s. The latter is an enchanting, small theater still used for stage performances and concerts.

Further to the northwest, Plaza Bolívar is occupied by the **Casa Fuerte**, which was once a Franciscan hospice, but was destroyed by the Spanish royalist army in a heavy attack in 1817. Over 1500 people who took refuge here, defenders and civilians alike, lost their lives in the massacre that followed. The surviving parts of the walls have been left in ruins as a memorial.

Sleeping & Eating
Barcelona has nothing upmarket – for this you need to go to Puerto La Cruz.

Hotel Neverí (☎ 277-2376; cnr Avs Fuerzas Armadas & Miranda; s/d US$17/21; ☒) Marked by the vivid mural of tropical flowers and birds, this place has a deceptively grand staircase and large no-frills rooms with firm beds. It can be very noisy – get a room away from the busy intersection.

ourpick Posada Copacabana (☎ 277-3473; Carrera 12 Juncal; s/d/tr US$19/21/30; ☒) The best place in town and a great deal, with 16 simple but lovely rooms and a great location near the church.

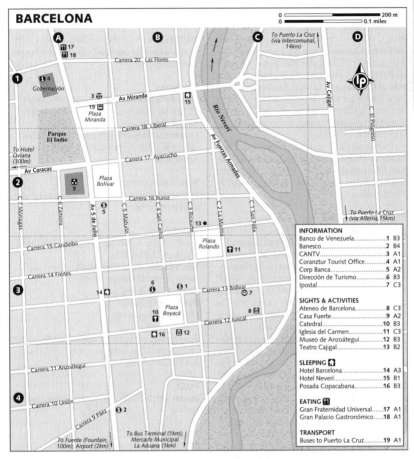

BARCELONA

INFORMATION	
Banco de Venezuela	1 B3
Banesco	2 B4
CANTV	3 A1
Coranztur Tourist Office	4 A1
Corp Banca	5 A2
Dirección de Turismo	6 B3
Ipostal	7 C3

SIGHTS & ACTIVITIES	
Ateneo de Barcelona	8 C3
Casa Fuerte	9 A2
Catedral	10 B3
Iglesia del Carmen	11 C3
Museo de Anzoátegui	12 B3
Teatro Cajigal	13 B2

SLEEPING	
Hotel Barcelona	14 A3
Hotel Neverí	15 B1
Posada Copacabana	16 B3

EATING	
Gran Fraternidad Universal	17 A1
Gran Palacio Gastronómico	18 A1

TRANSPORT	
Buses to Puerto La Cruz	19 A1

Hotel Oviana (☎ 276-4147; Av Caracas; d US$33; P ⊠) One of Barcelona's better options, though some five blocks west of Plaza Bolívar. Rooms are clean and simple, and have good hot-water bathrooms and cable TV. Front ones are noisy.

Hotel Barcelona (☎ 277-1076; Av 5 de Julio; d US$38; ⊠) This high-rise hotel has a good position overlooking a pedestrian boulevard. Halls are painted an awful lime green, but the good rooms are well furnished and come with cable TV.

Gran Fraternidad Universal (☎ 277-5045; Av 5 de Julio; set meal US$3; ⊠ 8am-6pm Mon-Fri) This cheap vegetarian restaurant has simple breakfasts and good, generous set lunches. It also has a tiny natural-products shop and offers yoga and tai-chi classes.

Gran Palacio Gastronómico (☎ 276-2920; Av 5 de Julio; mains US$3.25-6; ⊠ 6:30am-10pm) Down-to-earth cafeteria serving a basic menu of chicken, pasta, burgers and hotdogs. Also sandwiches, sides and – for the brave – banana splits.

The *mercado municipal* (municipal market) next to the bus terminal has the city's cheapest eateries.

Getting There & Away
AIR
The airport is 2km south of the city center. Buses leave from the *fuente* (fountain), about 500m south of Plaza Bolívar, and pass within 300m of the airport (US$0.35). Airlines providing regional services include **Avior** (☎ 274-9545), **Aserca** (☎ 274-1240) and **Rutaca** (☎ 276-8914).

BUS

The bus terminal is 1.5km southeast of the plaza, next to the market. Take a bus going south on Av Fuerzas Armadas or walk 15 minutes.

Practically all long-distance buses originate in Puerto La Cruz, but some buses on their way to Caracas and Ciudad Bolívar may stop here. There are four daily buses to Altagracia de Orituco (US$6, 4½ hours). Local destinations include hourly buses to Píritu (US$1.50) and Clarines (US$1).

To Puerto La Cruz, catch a bus from Plaza Miranda (US$0.50, 45 minutes). Faster por puesto minibuses (US$1, 30 minutes) depart from near the *fuente*, about 500m south of Plaza Bolívar.

PUERTO LA CRUZ

☎ 0281 / pop 227,000

This busy city is the main gateway to Venezuela's favorite holiday destination, Isla de Margarita (p240), as well as a springboard to the beautiful Parque Nacional Mochima (p260), which stretches just north and east of the city. Taking advantage of its position, it has grown into the nation's major water-sports center, boasting half a dozen marinas and yacht clubs.

Up until the 1930s Puerto La Cruz was no more than an obscure village. It boomed after rich oil deposits were discovered to the south, and port facilities were built just east of town to serve as a main terminal to ship oil overseas. Nowadays, this city is a youthful, dynamic and quickly expanding place.

The city itself is not noted for its beauty, though it features a lively 10-block-long waterfront boulevard, Paseo Colón, packed with hotels, restaurants, shops and tourist services. This seafront area, which borders a decent beach, comes to life in the late afternoon and evening, when kitschy craft stalls open and a gentle breeze sweeps away the heat of the day. It's a good place to just sit under a palm tree gazing at the sun setting beside offshore islands and at the occasional dolphin pod frolicking in the distance.

Information

EMERGENCY

Policia Estado Anzoátegui (☎ 266-1414; Calle Los Cocos)

INTERNET ACCESS

Centro Commercial Cristoforo Colombo (☎ 268-6010; upper fl, Paseo Colón; ◷ 9am-9pm Mon-Fri,

11am-9pm Sat) Pick your internet café among the cluster on the 2nd floor.

Internet Café (Av 5 de Julio; ◷ 8am-7pm Mon-Fri, till noon Sun) Above the Centro de Conexiones; take the stone steps on the right.

LAUNDRY

Lavandería Libertad (☎ 265-5204; Calle Libertad 100; per 3kg US$3; ◷ 8am-noon & 2-7:30pm Mon-Fri, 8am-8pm Sat)

Lavandería Margarita (☎ 265-1980; Calle Bolívar 160; per 3kg US$3; ◷ 7am-noon & 2-7pm Mon-Fri, 7am-7pm Sat)

MEDICAL SERVICES

Farmatodo (Plaza Colón; ◷ 24hr) Modern and bright, douches and diazepam.

MONEY

Most major banks are within a few blocks south of Plaza Colón.

Banco de Venezuela (Calle Miranda)

Banco Mercantil (Calle Arismendi)

Banesco (Calle Freites)

BBVA (Calle Carabobo)

Corp Banca (Av 5 de Julio)

For traveler's checks try **Italcambio** (☎ 265-3993; Centro Comercial Paseo del Mar, Paseo Colón; ◷ 8:30am-5pm Mon-Fri, 9am-1pm Sat).

POST

Ipostel (☎ 268-5355; Calle Freites; ◷ 8am-noon & 1-5pm Mon-Fri)

TELEPHONE

CANTV (Paseo Colón; ◷ 7:30am-10pm)

Tours

Travel agencies can be found on Paseo Colón and offer tours around Parque Nacional Mochima as well as further afield. Full-day boat tours include snorkeling, lunch and drinks, and cost up to US$40. Note that tours organized from Santa Fe (p263) and Mochima (p264) are cheaper. Some of the most popular destinations are Playa El Saco and Playa Puinare (both on Isla Chimana Grande), as well as Playa El Faro (on Isla Chimana Segunda), which all have nice beaches and food facilities. Playa El Faro also has curious iguanas and the best snorkeling grounds.

These destinations all have boat services that run to and fro (per person US$6 to US$10), so you don't need to take a formal

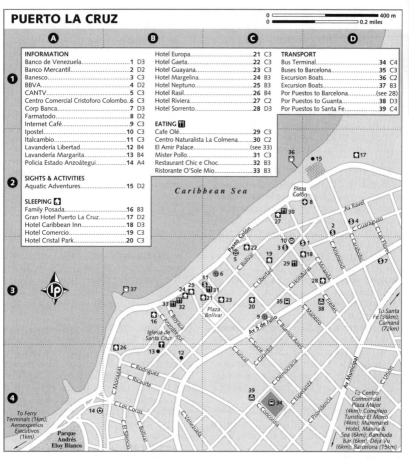

PUERTO LA CRUZ

0 — 400 m
0 — 0.2 miles

INFORMATION
Banco de Venezuela..........................1 D3
Banco Mercantil................................2 D2
Banesco..3 C3
BBVA...4 D2
CANTV...5 C3
Centro Comercial Cristoforo Colombo..6 C3
Corp Banca..7 D3
Farmatodo...8 D2
Internet Café.....................................9 C3
Ipostel..10 C3
Italcambio.......................................11 C3
Lavandería Libertad.........................12 B4
Lavandería Margarita.......................13 B4
Policía Estado Anzoátegui................14 A4

SIGHTS & ACTIVITIES
Aquatic Adventures.........................15 D2

SLEEPING
Family Posada..................................16 B3
Gran Hotel Puerto La Cruz...............17 D2
Hotel Caribbean Inn.........................18 D3
Hotel Comercio................................19 C3
Hotel Cristal Park.............................20 C3

Hotel Europa...................................21 C3
Hotel Gaeta.....................................22 C3
Hotel Guayana................................23 C3
Hotel Margelina...............................24 B3
Hotel Neptuno.................................25 B3
Hotel Rasil.......................................26 B4
Hotel Riviera....................................27 C2
Hotel Sorrento.................................28 D3

EATING
Cafe Olé...29 C3
Centro Naturalista La Colmena........30 C2
El Amir Palace.............................(see 33)
Mister Pollo.....................................31 C3
Restaurant Chic e Choc....................32 B3
Ristorante O'Sole Mio......................33 B3

TRANSPORT
Bus Terminal....................................34 C4
Buses to Barcelona..........................35 C3
Excursion Boats...............................36 C2
Excursion Boats...............................37 B3
Por Puestos to Barcelona.............(see 28)
Por Puestos to Guanta.....................38 D3
Por Puestos to Santa Fe...................39 C4

Caribbean Sea

Plaza Colón

Av Ravel

Paseo Colón

Plaza Bolívar

Av 5 de Julio

Iglesia de Santa Cruz

C Boyacá

C Anzoátegui

C Monagas

C Ricaurte

C Rodriguez

C Los Cocos

El Silencio

C Bolívar

C Libertad

C Honduras

C Miranda

C Arismendi

C Carabobo

C Las Flores

C Maneiro

C Freites

C Juncal

C Girardot

C Sucre

C Buenos Aires

C Democracia

C Esperanza

C Bolívar

C Venezuela

C Concordia

C Providencia

Av Municipal

C Unión

To Santa Fe (36km); Cumaná (72km)

To Centro Commercial Plaza Major (4km); Complejo Turístico El Morro (4km); Maremares Hotel, Marina & Spa (6km); Bambuda Bar (6km); Déjà Vu (6km); Barcelona (15km)

To Ferry Terminals (1km); Aeroexpresos Ejecutivos (1km)

Parque Andrés Eloy Blanco

tour. Excursions depart from piers on either end of Plaza Colón, leaving around 8am and returning in the afternoon. Inexpensive camping is possible on the islands; negotiate with boat operators for a later pickup date.

Aquatic Adventures (☎ 0414-806-3744), located at the marina and run by an American woman, organizes diving courses and tours. Two dives with equipment included costs about US$65; a full-day introductory session is US$75. Openwater SSI courses are US$300, and snorkeling equipment rents for US$10 to US$15.

Also consider **Diving & Safari** (☎ 808-0453; excalibur_excursion@hotmail.com), run by an Italian based in Playa Colorada, which does local diving trips, along with fishing excursions; see p262.

Boat-lovers looking for guidance can contact **Allen McLay** (☎ 0416-893-2886; www.yachting -venezuela.com) who does custom boat tours in the area and beyond (see p262).

Sleeping

Puerto La Cruz is an expensive place to stay by Venezuelan standards, and hotels fill up fast in the high season. Many hotels are on Paseo Colón and the adjoining streets, and this is the most lively and safe area to stay. Be careful walking the inland blocks at night – use taxis.

BUDGET

Hotel Guayana (☎ 265-2175; Plaza Bolívar; d/tr US$14/17; ☒) A cheap stay with eight rooms, located on Plaza Bolívar.

Family Posada (☎ 265-3953; Calle Anzoátegui; d US$14; ☒) Inexpensive, small and intimate family posada with good security and basic rooms.

MIDRANGE

The following accommodations all have cable TV and hot water.

Hotel Margelina (☎ 268-7545; Paseo Colón; d/tr US$21/26; ☒) Great location, but grungy depressing rooms with open showers. There are slightly interesting, but gloomy, checkerboard hallways.

Hotel Europa (☎ 268-8157; Plaza Bolívar; s/d/tr US$21/24/28; P ☒) Pass through the car park entrance to reach the entrance to this sparsely adorned hotel, where the only extravagance is a neon-lit image of the Virgin Mary at the top of the stairs. It has clean, spacious rooms; try for a balcony over the plaza.

Hotel Neptuno (☎ 265-3261; fax 265-5790; Paseo Colón at Calle Juncal; s/d US$24/28; ☒) The popular Neptuno offers good-value rooms. Get one facing the street: they are brighter and more spacious. An open-sided restaurant near the top floor boasts sweeping views out to sea.

Hotel Sorrento (☎ 268-6745; hotelsorrento@cantv .net; Av 5 de Julio No 60; d US$24-31, 4-6 person ste US$43-63; P ☒) The cheapest rooms in this five-story, orange-brick hotel are really small – pay more for more space. Get an outside room with street view for more light. Family suites have fridges.

Hotel Comercio (☎ 265-1429; Calle Maneiro 9-D; d/tr US$28/33; ☒) Small, old and rather boring rooms. They do have good security, however.

Hotel Cristal Park (☎ 267-0744; fax 265-3105; Calle Libertad at Calle Buenos Aires; d US$35; P ☒) Attractive halls but small unmemorable rooms. Family suites offer more breathing space.

Hotel Gaeta (☎ 265-0411; Paseo Colón at Calle Maneiro; d incl breakfast US$36-56; P ☒) Smack in the middle of the seafront boulevard, this hotel has four floors of good, clean rooms with colorful bedspreads and wicker furniture. Sea-view rooms cost more, but are also bigger and better. Breakfast included.

TOP END

Hotel Riviera (☎ 265-3247; hotel-riviera@cantv.net; Paseo Colón 33; d with city/sea view US$56/59; P ☒ ▯) Located right on the seafront, this eight-story hotel features a big ugly marble lobby and small, average rooms; for more space it's

---

COMPLEJO TURÍSTICO EL MORRO

This large and modern complex on the waterfront, 4km west of the city center, is one of the most ambitious urban projects ever to be carried out in the country. Set on a coastal stretch of land, roughly in the form of a 1.5km x 2km rectangle, the complex is a model residential retreat for stressed-out urbanites, designed and built entirely from scratch. The complex is crisscrossed by a maze of canals, on the banks of which a whole city of apartment blocks and houses has sprung up. The area boasts shopping centers, hotels, nightspots, parks and golf courses.

---

worth snagging a balcony room with sea views.

Hotel Caribbean Inn (☎ 267-4292; hotelcaribbean@ cantv.net; Calle Freites; d US$58, ste US$58-70; P ☒ ☎) This impersonal 12-story hotel has decent and ample rooms with older furniture, some boasting views over the area. Suites are also available.

Hotel Rasil (☎ 262-3000; www.hotelrasil.com.ve in Spanish; Calle Monagas at Paseo Colón 6; d with city/sea view US$75/80; P ☒ ☎) Despite a remodeling, standard rooms at this 25-floor hotel remain unimaginative, but at least they're better value than the suites (unless it's the presidential suite, of course). Some have balconies from which to enjoy the panoramic sea views, only slightly marred by an unattractive patch of wasteland.

Gran Hotel Puerto La Cruz (☎ 500-3611; www.hoteles premier.com; Paseo Colón; d incl breakfast from US$133; P ☒ ▯ ☎) This ship-shaped, five-star option is located just beyond the marina. Almost all rooms have beautiful sea views (with balcony and see-through shower). Other services include a casino, a spa, a business center and good wheelchair accessibility, not to forget the swimming pools and the private beach.

Maremares Hotel, Marina & Spa (☎ 281-1011; www.maremares.com; d incl breakfast from US$195; P ☒ ▯ ☎) The newest and classiest hotels are mostly in the Complejo Turístico El Morro (above), including this vast five-star complex with its own spa, tennis courts, sauna, marina and a positively gigantic 3000-sq-m swimming pool (complete with wave machine). And only a short putt away is a new nine-hole golf course.

Eating

The cream of the city's restaurants are along Paseo Colón. This area stays alive well into the evening, when fresh breezes alleviate the heat and people gather in the establishments overlooking the boardwalk. It's mostly an upmarket area, but it also shelters some inexpensive Middle Eastern fast-food eateries serving set lunches. Cheap food carts open at night near Plaza Colón.

Centro Naturalista La Colmena (☎ 265-2751; Paseo Colón 27; 3-course menu US$4; ☒ 11:45am-2pm Mon-Fri) This lunch-only vegetarian café and natural-products shop has flowery tables and a tiny covered terrace looking out across the boulevard to the sea. It serves good and healthy set lunches.

Hotel Neptuno (☎ 265-3261; Paseo Colón at Calle Juncal; mains US$4.50-8; ☒ 8am-10pm Mon-Sat) This restaurant, toward the top of the Hotel Neptuno, offers filling meat, pasta and seafood dishes, but the principal attraction is the wide-ranging view out to sea (great for sunsets).

Ristaurant O'Sole Mio (☎ 265-2623; Paseo Colón; mains US$5-10; ☒ 11am-10pm) A good, reasonably priced Italian restaurant serving vegetarian pizza, shrimp salad and pesto on your pasta. Venezuelan specialties also available.

El Amir Palace (☎ 282-0209; Paseo Colón 123; mains US$6-14; ☒ noon-midnight Tue-Sun) Efficient service and Arabian specialties highlight this modern place on Paseo Colón. It cooks up fish, pasta and meat dishes, along with some salads and good kebabs.

Restaurant Chic e Choc (☎ 265-2551; Paseo Colón; mains US$8-17; ☒ 11:30am-2:30pm & 7-11pm Mon-Sat; ☒) Characterized by the shiny chrome tubing outside and low curvy booths in a low-lit setting inside, this restaurant is recommended for its French cuisine: everything from duck *à l'orange* to jumbo shrimps flambéed *'à la pirate.'*

The **Centro Comercial Plaza Mayor** (☎ 281-6820; www.ccplazamayor.com in Spanish) has a food court serving fast food from sushi to coconut ice cream and there are also restaurants overlooking a lagoon.

Bambuda Bar (☎ 281-6986; Av Américo Vespucio; ☒ dinner only) and **Déja Vu** (☎ 282-2734; Av Américo Vespucio; ☒ 6-11pm) are two very hip eateries that serve sushi and Asian fusion and turn into discos after dinner.

You could also try the following:

Cafe Olé (☎ 268-6244; Calle Frietes 24; snacks US$3; ☒ 6:30am-7pm Mon-Sat) Small, modern café with good pastries and coffee.

Mister Pollo (Calle Sucre off Paseo Colón; mains US$2.50-4; ☒ 11:30am-10pm) Tasty chicken at low prices.

Shopping

Located in the Complejo Turístico El Morro (see the boxed text opposite), **Centro Comercial Plaza Major** (☎ 281-6820; www.ccplazamayor.com in Spanish) is the city's largest and most popular shopping mall. It's a modern, colorful, indoor/outdoor place with lots of fancy shops, restaurants, kids' attractions and cinemas. Locals love to hang out here, check out the canals nearby and just stroll around; for the traveler it's an interesting place to analyze middle-class Venezuelan consumerism (or just shop and eat). Taxis from Puerto La Cruz' center cost around US$7; you can also take a Barcelona por puesto (which run until 6pm) for US$1. They go right by the shopping mall.

Entertainment

Taxis to the following places in the Complejo Turístico El Morro cost about US$7 (more later at night).

Bambuda Bar (☎ 281-6986; Av Américo Vespucio; ☒ 11pm-5am Wed-Sat) This trendy spot, next to the Maremares Hotel, is a current favorite. It's an airy and tropical restaurant for dinner, but at 11pm turns into the city's most popular nightclub. There are several lounge-dance areas with either DJs or good live music. Wednesday is ladies night – free drinks for women until midnight.

Déja Vu (☎ 282-2734; Av Américo Vespucio; ☒ 11pm-5am Thu-Sat) A popular place, not too far away from Bambuda Bar, Déja Vu is also a restaurant earlier in the evening before transforming itself into a happenin' disco. There is a large outdoor terrace overlooking the water (some 'exclusive' people arrive by boat), while live music energizes the weekend crowds.

Getting There & Away

The nearest airport is in Barcelona (see p255).

BOAT

Puerto La Cruz is the major departure point for Isla de Margarita, with services offered by **Conferry** (☎ 267-7847; www.conferry.com; Sector Los Cocos) and **Gran Cacique Express** (☎ 267-7286; www.grancacique.com.ve; Sector Los Cocos). Smaller excursion boats leave from the small piers in town. See p240 for fare details and travel times.

The ferry terminals are accessible by por puesto from the center (taxis US$2.50). Go in the daytime – it's a spectacular journey between the islands of Parque Nacional Mochima.

BUS

The busy bus terminal is four blocks from the beach. Bus destinations include Caracas (US$15, five hours), Carúpano (US$7, 4½ hours), Ciudad Bolívar (US$14, four hours), Cumaná (US$4, 1½ hours) and Maturín (US$7, three hours). Sit on the left for views in the trips to Carúpano and Cumaná.

Por puesto destinations include Caracas (US$21, four hours), Carúpano (US$12, four hours), Ciudad Bolívar (US$17, 3½ hours), Cumaná (US$6, 1¼ hours), Guanta (US$0.40, 10 minutes), Los Altos de Sucre (US$1, 40 minutes), Maturín (US$12, two hours) and Santa Fe (US$1, 45 minutes).

To Barcelona, take a city bus from Av 5 de Julio (US$0.50, 45 minutes to one hour). Por puestos leave from the same area (US$1, 30 minutes).

Aeroexpresos Ejecutivos (☎ 267-8855) has one of the best services to Caracas (US$17 to US$19, five departures daily), leaving from the ferry terminal west of town.

CLARINES & PÍRITU

The small towns of Clarines and Píritu, both by the Caracas–Barcelona highway, have two of the best-restored and most interesting small-town colonial churches in the region.

Founded in 1694, **Clarines** is an old colonial town about 1km south of the highway. Its church, **Iglesia de San Antonio** (☉ 9:30-11:30am & 3-6pm), is at the upper end of the historic town. Built in the 1750s, the church is a massive, squat construction laid out in a Latin-cross floor plan, and is one of only a few examples of its kind in Venezuela. Twin square towers border the austere facade. The most unusual features of the structure are the two external arcades running between the towers and the transepts on both sides of the church. The single-nave interior is topped with a wooden cupola and is refreshingly well balanced in proportion. Over the high altar is a three-tier main retable dating from around 1760. It is placed against the wall, which still bears its original painting depicting a curtain.

Píritu, 16km east of Clarines, lies just north of the highway (but the access road branches off from the highway 2km before the town

and rejoins it 2km beyond). The town was founded in 1656, and about half a century later, the fortresslike **Iglesia de Nuestra Señora de la Concepción** (admission free; ☉ 8am-11am & 5-6:30pm) was built. This three-nave church has quite a number of remarkable colonial altarpieces. The main retable and the two side retables date from about 1745 and are richly gilded.

Scattered around each town center are small local restaurants serving cheap set meals.

Getting There & Away

Clarines and Píritu are usually visited as a daytrip from Barcelona or Puerto La Cruz. As both towns are just off the Caracas–Barcelona highway, access is easy. Apart from the long-distance buses running between these two cities, there are hourly buses from Barcelona to both Píritu (US$1.50) and Clarines (US$1).

PARQUE NACIONAL MOCHIMA
☎ 0293

About three dozen arid islands dot the clear, warm waters of Mochima, a 950-sq-km national park covering the offshore belt of the Caribbean coast between Puerto La Cruz and Cumaná. Most of the islands are barren and rocky in parts, and strewn with brush and cacti, but some also have fine beaches for soaking up the tropical sun. Coral reefs, which offer good snorkeling and diving opportunities, surround a few of the islands; Isla Venado is an especially good destination. Pods of dolphins are a common sight in the area's waters.

Roughly bisected by the border of Anzoátegui and Sucre states, the park also includes a strip of mountainous hinterland lined with appealing bays and beaches. The area offers year-round warmth and the waters are usually calm, abounding with marine life. Tranquility seekers will be happy midweek, when only a handful of beachgoers are to be found on the more far-flung islands.

Be warned that deserted beaches can be unsafe, particularly at night. There have been reports from campers of robberies on island and mainland beaches, but ask a local for the current situation.

Also, note that there are no banks in the area: bring money from Puerto La Cruz or Cumaná. Only Santa Fe has a (slow) internet café.

See under individual towns for transportation information.

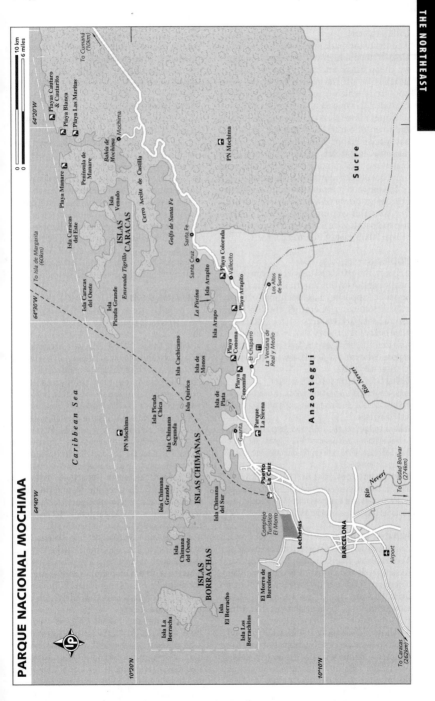

PARQUE NACIONAL MOCHIMA

0   10 km
0   6 miles

64°20'W

To Cumaná
(10km)

Playas Cautaro & Cautarito
Playa Blanca
Playa Las Maritas
Mochima
Bahía de Mochima

Playa Manare

Península de Manare

PN Mochima

Isla Caracas del Este

Isla Venado

Cerro Aceite de Castilla

ISLAS CARACAS

Golfo de Santa Fe

Isla Caracas del Oeste

Santa Fe

To Isla de Margarita (60km)

64°30'W

Isla Picuda Grande

Ensenada Tigrillo

Santa Cruz

Playa Colorada

Isla Arapito

Vallecito

Isla Arapo

Playa Arapito

La Picina

Caribbean Sea

Isla Cachicamo

Los Altos de Sucre

Sucre

Isla de Monos

Playa Conoma

El Chaparro

La Ventana de Real y Medio

Isla Picuda Chica

Isla Quirica

Isla de Plata

Playa Conomita

Anzoátegui

Isla Chimana Segunda

PN Mochima

Guanta

Parque La Sirena

Río Neverí

ISLAS CHIMANAS

Isla Chimana Grande

Isla Chimana del Sur

Puerto La Cruz

To Ciudad Bolívar (274km)

Isla Chimana del Oeste

Complejo Turístico El Morro

Río Neverí

ISLAS BORRACHAS

Isla La Borracha

Isla El Borracho

El Morro de Barcelona

Lecherías

BARCELONA

Airport

Isla Los Borrachitos

To Caracas (262km)

10°20'N

64°40'W

10°10'N

ORIENTATION

The mainland park lies along the Puerto La Cruz–Cumaná highway, serviced frequently by cheap buses and por puestos. A dozen beaches lie off the road, one of the most popular of which is the palm-studded Playa Colorada, 27km east of Puerto La Cruz.

About 8km east of Playa Colorada is the town of Santa Fe, which has become a backpacker haunt with fair tourist facilities and a decent stretch of sand. Another 15km east along the Cumaná highway a side road branches off 4km downhill to the small village of Mochima, a jumping-off point for nearby beaches (it doesn't have a beach of its own). For something completely different take a trip to Los Altos de Sucre (p265), a mountain village 30km east of Puerto La Cruz.

TOURS

Trips to the park's islands are organized by boat operators from Puerto La Cruz (p259), Santa Fe (opposite) and Mochima (p264).

The following operators conduct tours around the park's waters:

Allen McLay (☎ 0416-893-2886; www.yachting-venezuela.com) A Scotsman based in Playa Colorada, McLay can organize customized boat tours to anywhere in Venezuela for sailors and yachties.

Diving & Safari (☎ 808-0453; excalibur_excursion@hotmail.com) Franco Podda, an Italian based in Playa Colorada, does boat tours, along with local diving and fishing trips.

Jakera Lodge (☎ 808-7057; www.jakera.com) Run by some Englishmen and based in Playa Colorada, this outfit does boat tours along with kayaking/snorkeling trips to nearby destinations.

Tony Martin (☎ 642-5541, 0414-831-3026; www.hosteltrail.com/extremexpeditions) Based out of Santa Fe, Martin does area boat tours (though he specializes in hands-on Los Llanos adventure trips).

Isla de Plata

This is one of the most popular islands among Venezuelans, thanks to the beach and coral reefs, as well as its proximity to the mainland. There are food and drink stalls here but no drinking water. It also has a startling, surreal view of the huge cement plant nearby, which mars the tropical beach experience a bit.

Isla de Plata is about 10km east of Puerto La Cruz and is accessible by frequent boats from the pier at Pamatacualito, the eastern suburb of Guanta. This suburb is serviced by regular por puestos from Puerto La Cruz (US$0.40,

10 minutes). Boats run regularly, especially during weekends, taking 10 minutes to get to the island (roundtrip US$3). Excursion boats from Puerto La Cruz are more expensive and less regular.

Playa Colorada

This pleasant beach has fine orange sand shaded with coconut groves. One of the top coastal destinations for locals, it has been populated with a colony of souvenir kiosks and a line of rustic restaurants. The main village consists of only a few streets and lies across the highway and up the hill from the beach.

On weekends, it swarms with a young crowd looking to party and enjoy the spectacular sunset. You may also find boats willing to take you out to La Piscina, a snorkeling destination between the two nearby islands of Arapo and Arapito. Otherwise, Jakera Lodge does area boat tours and you could join in on these.

SLEEPING & EATING

All posadas are across the highway, up the hilly streets of the village. Prices may rise in high season.

Jakera Lodge (☎ 808-7057; www.jakera.com; dm/hammock without/with breakfast & dinner US$7/15) Heaven for rustic backpackers, this laid-back place has a screened hammock room, small open dorms and a communal vibe (think barbecue parties). Salsa classes, Spanish lessons and volunteer opportunities are available. Jakera also offers airport/city transfers, kayaking/snorkeling trips and adventure expeditions around Venezuela. It's close to the bus stop on the highway; ring at the large metal door.

Posada Edgar Lemus (☎ 0416-795-0574; s/d/tr US$10/19/24; 🗷) Just beyond Jakera, this basic family place has five spacious, clean rooms hidden behind a wild garden. Enter from the highway via a gate and cement wall.

Quinta Jaly (☎ 808-3246; Calle Marchán; s/d/tr US$14/17/21; 🅿 🗷) Opposite Posada Nirvana, this posada is run by a French-Canadian. There are five dark, simple rooms and the sprawling grounds are dotted with tropical plants. Kitchen access is available, as is an optional breakfast (US$3.25).

Posada Nirvana (☎ 808-7844; Calle Marchán; d US$15, apt US$25; 🅿 🗷) Swiss-run guesthouse with pleasant garden and outdoor common area with hammocks and kitchen. Fabulous breakfasts are available for US$4. One room has shared bath (US$10), and only one room has air-con. Located 500m uphill from the main road.

Posada Christina (☎ 808-0453; excalibur_excursion@ hotmail.com; s/d/tr US$20/25/30) Just three lovely rooms with fan are on offer at this intimate Italian family posada. There's a peaceful patio with hammocks and vocal parrots out back. Well-made meals are available for extra. Franco also does diving, fishing, local boat tours and trips around Venezuela.

Café Las Carmitas (☎ 0416-912-4266; mains US$5-10; ☟ noon-9pm) This casual Portuguese-run place offers good pizza, pasta, burgers and fish dishes. Serves breakfast in high season only. It's one block up the main road from the highway and to the left.

Santa Cruz

There's not much in this plain, hilly village for the tourist – exactly how some folks like their vacation. It does have a small beach next to the National Guard, which keeps it clean and safe. The one posada in town is **Villa La Encantada** (☎ 0416-781-0430; christian@insightsvenezuela .com; d US$20; ☀), offering 12 good fan rooms spilling down a hillside. There's even a pool to splash around in, and an outside kitchen BBQ area. It's 500m down the main street from the highway; any bus or por puesto can let you off here.

Santa Fe

This fishing town is popular with the international backpacker crowd for its tourist services, along with its proximity to the islands of Parque Nacional Mochima. Despite the fact that most seaside posadas are esconced behind high fences topped with barbed wire – making them look like security compounds – there is still a laid-back atmosphere amid the locals' day-to-day bustle. Travelers spend their days touring the nearby islands and their nights drinking beer or *merengadas* (fruity milkshakes) on the beach – all without breaking the budget.

Santa Fe's tourism came about thanks to the grassroots initiative of some residents, inspired by journalist and writer José Vivas, to make the place a traveler's destination. There are now a dozen posadas along the kilometerlong beach, many owned and managed by foreigners. The beach itself is nothing special, but it's regularly cleaned and the water is clear and sheltered. Dolphin pods are often spotted from shore.

There's one **internet café** (☟ 8am-9pm) with slow connection in town, right behind Club Nautico restaurant and inside the mini-*lunchería* (cheap restaurant serving staple food and snacks), also offering telephone services. And remember, there are no banks in town – get your cash in Puerto La Cruz or Cumaná. Bring insect repellant.

TOURS

Most posada and hotel managers organize tours and excursions. A standard full-day boat trip (US$12 to US$17) will normally feature La Piscina and the Islas Caracas, calling at two or three beaches and stopping for snorkeling (equipment provided). The Posada Café del Mar offers some of the cheapest boat trips – about US$10 per person, with a minimum of four people.

Tony Martin (☎ 642-5541, 0414-831-3026; www .hosteltrail.com/extremexpeditions), an energetic and feisty Venezuelan based out of Extremexpeditions House, speaks fluent English and can organize area boat tours. His specialty is Los Llanos (p220), however, and he also does expeditions to the Canaima region (p312) from Santa Fe.

SLEEPING

Most of the places listed here are along the beach, just a stone's throw from each other.

Quinta La Jaiba (☎ 231-0027; d with shared bathroom US$10, with private bathroom US$14-19) A no-nonsense place offering five basic rooms with fan. Located just beyond Café del Mar.

Hotel Cochaima (☎ 416-6368; s/d/tr US$12/14/19; ☀) This sizable but basic hotel has 20-odd rooms (three have air-con) with small, barred windows and a heavy industrial feel. There's a cheap restaurant on the second floor.

Posada Café del Mar (☎ 231-0009; d/tr US$14/19) Entering the beach, this is the first posada. Its glass-fronted rooms are dark because you need to draw the curtains for privacy. Hammock space is US$5 and there's a good restaurant downstairs. This is a busy place; lock up your valuables.

Posada Los Siete Delfines (☎ 416-7449; lossieted elfinessantafe@hotmail.com; d with fan/air-con US$17/21; ☀) This strange, no-frills place is painted a bright blue inside (too blue actually) and the metal doors give it a prisonlike feel. Rooms and open baths are tiny, like cells. Only two come with air-con. Better are the rooftop pool table and terrace.

Extremexpeditions House (☎ 642-5541; d/tr US$17/21) This relatively new posada has eight good, simple rooms with fan and cable TV. There's a second-floor balcony with sea views, while down below is a shady tiled area with relaxing hammocks. In front is a concrete patio, with a gate securing the posada from the beach. Use of a rustic, open kitchen is included.

Santa Fe Resort & Dive Center (☎ 0414-773-3777; www.santaferesort.com; d with shared bathroom US$17, seafront d/tr with bathroom US$42; **P**) This pleasant 'resort' is simply a nice posada with vine-shaded gardens and highly varied rooms, including spacious seafront options that are deliciously light and breezy. It also has a two-bedroom apartment (US$56) and an on-site dive center.

Bahía del Mar (☎ 231-0073; bahiadelmar_8@hotmail.com; d US$19; **P** ☒) Decent budget rooms are available at this 11-room posada run by a French Canadian. There's a grassy back area with hammocks and outdoor kitchen with barbecue. Top-floor rooms have sea views.

La Sierra Inn (☎ 231-0042; cooperativasantafedemis amores@hotmail.com; s/d US$21/26, 4-person apt US$56; **P** ☒ ▣) Just beyond is this hotel managed by José Vivas himself. It has dark, basic rooms, most located on the ground floor under sea level. The best is the suite on the second floor (US$28) with hammock and view. Common terraces offer beach views from inside the barbed-wired compound.

Posada La Belina (☎ 416-6796; dido2413@yahoo.com; s/d with fan US$24/38, d with air-con US$47-56; **P** ☒) Run by an Italian-Venezuelan couple is this seven-room posada at the far end of the beach. Rooms are small, clean and modern and come with cable TV. There's also a restaurant (for guests only) on the premises.

Le Petit Jardin (☎ 416-6611; lepetit.jardin@yahoo.com; d US$28-38; **P** ☒) Located one block inland is this beautiful new French-run posada. On offer are seven small, but lovely and colorful, rooms with thoughtful details and firm beds. There's an excellent pool in the grassy garden and plenty of patios in which to relax. Complimentary coffee and pastry greet you in the mornings.

EATING & DRINKING
The market has cheap eateries with counter seating, but only for breakfast and early lunch.

Los Molina (mains US$3.25-19; ☻ 8:30am-9pm) Small and casual beach shack near Posada

Los Siete Delfines, serving breakfast, seafood and pasta.

Posada Café del Mar (☎ 231-0009; mains US$6-18; ☻ 8:30am-9pm Tue-Sun, daily in high season) The most popular backpacker's hang-out spot, with tables on the sand and tasty food off the grill. Offers breakfast and is a good place to drink in the evenings, but service can be bad.

Club Nautico Restaurant (☎ 231-0026; mains US$7-20; ☻ 11am-9pm Wed-Mon) The largest and smartest restaurant in town, this beachside spot has seafood, meats, pasta and salads on the menu. Try the *pabellón criollo* – a Venezuelan specialty of shredded meat, rice, beans and plantain.

Tasca El Birrazo (chicken dinners US$10; ☻ 5:30-10pm) Hang out with the locals at this interesting, modern restaurant that turns into a disco at night. It's on the main road out of town.

Oceanic Café (Calle La Boca; ☻ weekends in low season, nightly in high season) Not really a café at all, but rather the town's only nightclub and a popular hang-out spot for the locals. Good for cheap booze and alcoholic concoctions served in coconuts.

GETTING THERE & AWAY
Buses and por puestos from Puerto La Cruz and Cumaná should drive all the way down the town's 1km entrance road (to the market) and not just stop at the highway. A new bus terminal at the highway, however, might change this.

Mochima
The peaceful village of Mochima is a small community where everyone knows everyone else. It has no beach of its own, but it is a jumping-off point to half a dozen isolated mainland beaches inaccessible by road. The beaches are beautiful, though shadeless, and are solitary except during major holiday peaks. Only the more built-up Playas Blanca and Las Maritas have food facilities open daily year-round, so if you're going to more isolated beaches remember to take snacks and water.

TOURS
Transportation to the beaches is provided from the wharf in the village's center, where boats anchor and *lancheros* (boatmen) sit on the shore and wait for tourists. They can take you to any beach, among them Playas Las Maritas (US$17), Blanca (US$17), Manare

(US$21) and Playas Cautaro and Cautarito (US$54). The listed figures are roundtrip fares per boat, and you can be picked up whenever you want. Don't hesitate to bargain!

A three-hour tour, which includes snorkeling, costs around US$14 per person for six to 10 people. Longer tours, which can include cruises to Islas Caracas, La Piscina and Playa Colorada, plus snorkeling, are also available. Some hotels can organize boat tours for their guests.

Mochima has two small scuba-diving operators: **Aquatics Diving Center** (☎ 430-1649, 0414-777-0196; info@scubavenezuela.com) and **La Posada de los Buzos** (☎ 416-0856, in Caracas 0212-961-2531, 0414-242-6143; faverola@cantv.net). Both organize diving courses, dives and excursions, and handle snorkel rental; the latter also runs rafting trips on the Río Neverí.

SLEEPING

Posada Villa Vicenta (☎ 416-0916; d with fan/air-con US$14/19; 🍴) Located one block back from the wharf, this posada has four levels stepping their way up the hillside, each with a small rustic terrace boasting fine bay views (better on the higher floors). The 12 rustic, stone-walled rooms have fans and open, cold-water showers.

Posada El Mochimero (☎ 0414-773-8782; d with fan/air-con US$14/19; 🍴) This hostel, opposite the restaurant of the same name, has 17 basic, colorful rooms with cold-water bathrooms. Those upstairs are much lighter and better tiled.

Posada Doña Cruz (☎ 416-6114; d US$19; 🍴) This colorful, though impersonal, little posada has four nice, colorful rooms with cable TV and painted designs. A six-person apartment is also available. Ask for the owners to the right of the wharf, under the blue-and-white water tower.

Posada El Pozo (☎ 0414-773-7643; s/d/tr US$19/2428; 🍴) This great new family-run place, located near the basketball court, has just four clean rooms with pretty tiles, pastel colors and cable TV. More rooms might be built upstairs.

Posada Girasol (☎ 416-0535; d US$22; 🍴) Run by Brigitte and Roger, a Swiss woman and her Venezuelan husband, this small posada has only three comfortable rooms with cable TV. There's a tiny patio out back and sun-flower decor on the walls. They're working on constructing two apartments upstairs. Good breakfasts are available.

Posada Gaby (☎ 0414-773-1104; d with fan US$24, d/tr with air-con US$28/33; 🍴) This blue house, on the sea brink at the far end of the village, has 22 spacious rooms with solid built-in furniture; the upstairs ones are better. They also have a restaurant with sea views and a dock.

EATING

El Rancho de Compa (arepas US$2; 🕑 7am-1pm, plus dinner in high season) Located near the wharf, this place has some of the best *arepas* (filled corn pancakes) in Venezuela. Say *'hola'* to José, the chef.

Puerto Viejo (☎ 416-0810; mains US$5-10; 🕑 4-9pm Mon, Wed & Fri, 11am-9pm Sat & Sun, 11am-9pm daily in high season) Right near the wharf, this good, colorful restaurant offers typical seafood and meat dishes along with a fun fish theme. Try the excellent piña colada (US$2.50).

El Mochimero (☎ 0414-774-9133; Calle La Marina; mains US$7-24; 🕑 11am-9pm) Sitting on a platform over the sea, this Spanish-run restaurant has excellent and well-prepared dishes (try the grilled steak, or *lomito a la plancha*). There's also good fish, paella and salads, but service can be iffy.

GETTING THERE & AWAY

Buses from Cumaná cost US$1 and take 40 minutes. To Santa Fe or Puerto La Cruz, first take a bus to the *crucero* (highway crossroad), then flag down the proper bus.

Los Altos de Sucre

This mountain hamlet sits at an altitude of about 900m and has a fresh climate that's wonderfully cool compared to the coast. It's a typical one-street village, snaking up and down the rugged terrain for almost 5km without any pronounced center. The surrounding highlands are verdant and sprinkled with coffee and cacao haciendas.

Although Los Altos de Sucre is only 4km back from the coast as the crow flies, it doesn't provide many panoramic views of the coast and the islands beyond. The best vistas are from the winding access road as you approach the village. Once you enter it, about 7km from the turnoff at the coastal highway, the road gradually descends inland. Jeeps continue for about 5km to their terminus on the opposite end of the village.

Los Altos de Sucre is serviced regularly throughout the day by jeeps from Puerto La Cruz (US$1, 40 minutes).

THE NORTHEAST

SLEEPING & EATING

Prices rise during the holidays. Campers can find a few places offering sites for about US$4 per person.

Posada del Payez (☎ 0416-818-0633; d US$24; P) Offers 15 simple fan rooms on a hillside spot with great views from its restaurant terrace. Try to get room 16, which has its own private balcony.

Posada & Restaurant Vista Montaña (☎ 0293-431-2541; www.posadavistamontana.com; s/d Mon-Fri US$35/48, s/d Sat-Sun US$43/64; P) Ten beautiful rooms come tastefully decorated here, sporting hammocks and 320-count bed sheets. There's an awesome rooftop terrace with jungle views, a breezy TV lounge and a restaurant that cooks up tasty food. For the kids there's a play area and a small zoo (!) nearby; for the adults there are spa services and yoga and tai-chi sessions. Area tours are available. Breakfast is included in the room cost.

Neblina Posada & Restaurant (☎ 0293-433-1057; neblinalosaltos@hotmail.com; d/tr incl breakfast & dinner US$84/112; P ⚎) This friendly and peaceful spot is 500m down a very rough dirt road. It has just seven rustic and lovely rooms with artsy touches and balconies boasting fabulous mountain views. A small waterfall pond surrounded by plants is nearby. Prices can be cheaper without meals, but there aren't many restaurants in town. Call for pickup from the main road.

Restaurant Chepina (☎ 0293-433-2133; mains US$5-12; ⏲ 10am-4pm) For amazing views of Mochima, stop at this hilltop café, which serves typical dishes like *mondongo* (seasoned cow's stomach in bouillon with vegetables) and *pabellón criollo*, along with a great chicken soup.

La Ventana de Real y Medio (Map p261; ☎ 431-4620; mains $6-15; ⏲ 9am-late) This awesome spot is just 1.5km from the coastal highway and boasts a terrace restaurant serving *comida criolla* (typical Venezuelan cuisine) with spectacular views. It's just changed ownership, so call to make sure it's open.

ISLA LA TORTUGA

This desolate paradise lies about 85km from the mainland and has yet to be discovered by mass tourism. It's composed of an arid, flat island (Venezuela's second largest at 160 sq km) and three smaller islets, and harbors rich reefs teeming with colorful corals and many varieties of fish. There are almost no

services on the island and not much to do other than swim, snorkel and enjoy the beautiful sunsets.

La Tortuga was first discovered in 1499 by Alonso de Ojeda, a Spanish explorer and an old sailing buddy of Christopher Columbus. In the 17th century the area became a pirate hideout, even sheltering the infamous raider Henry Morgan. The island was also used by Dutch profiteers for salt harvesting until 1631, when they were ousted by the governor of Cumaná.

Today, La Tortuga is even more virgin that Los Roques and practically uninhabited – a few fishermen hang around in lobster season and one posada has recently claimed ground. There are few buildings, mostly fishermen's huts. One of these huts might have rooms to rent, but you'll need to bring you own sheets. In fact, unless you're staying at the posada, you'll need to be completely self-sufficient. Bring a swimsuit, towel, snorkeling equipment, sun protection (there's little shade on the island), toilet paper, medications, insect repellant and all food and water you'll need – and remember to take it all away with you again.

The one posada on the island is **Rancho Yemaya** (☎ 0414-339-5574, in Caracas 0212-753-7855; www .ranchoyemaya.com; per person incl all meals US$155). It's a simple one-story place with seven rooms and outside hammocks. There's a generator for electricity and drinking water is available. Reserve in advance.

You can always camp, but remember there's no water or electricity. Seafood might be available from fishermen who can cook it for you, but otherwise you'll need to bring all your own food and water (and money).

Getting There & Away

Getting to La Tortuga is not easy, which is why it's still a paradise. If you don't own a private yacht or small plane you'll have to rely on the little public transportation to the island, and all of it is expensive. It takes about six to seven hours in a small motor boat and 10 to 12 hours in a sailboat or yacht to reach the island.

Several private individuals and companies offer transportation, and include the following:

Allen McLay (☎ 0416-893-2886; www.yachting-vene zuela.com) Based out of Playa Colorada, can organize sail and yacht rentals with crew.

Crasqui (☎ 0414-247-3498; geocities.com/guayolos roques) A Los Roques operator that does transportation and packages to La Tortuga from Huguerote, a port east of Caracas.

Explore Yachts (in Caracas ☎ 0212-287-0517; www .explore-yachts.com/charter/tortuga.htm) Operates sailboats, cruises and flights to La Tortuga; there are diving options also.

Tony Martin (☎ 642-5541, 0414-831-3026; www .hosteltrail.com/extremexpeditions) Based out of Santa Fe, might be able to fix you up with a cheaper private boat.

If you're short on time and would rather fly, contact **Jean-Luc Tersin** (☎ 0281-263-5181; jeanluctersin@hotmail.com), a Frenchman based out of Puerto La Cruz. He does flights to La Tortuga that leave at 9am and return at 5pm (US$400 return for four to five people, 30 minutes). You can stay and return another day (one way US$350), but remember there are few overnight services on the island.

SUCRE STATE

CUMANÁ
☎ 0293 / pop 290,000

Founded by the Spanish in 1521, Cumaná has the interesting distinction of being the oldest existing town on the South American mainland. Although several devastating earthquakes in the past have destroyed much of the city's historic architecture, there are still a number of streets that retain their colonial charm. There is also a large fort crowning a hillock above the town center. Today the city is both the capital of Sucre state and an important port for sardine fishing and canning.

Cumaná has some beaches nearby, the closest being Playa San Luis, southwest of the city. More beaches, like Santa Fe and Playa Colorada, are in the Parque Nacional Mochima, a little further down the coast. The city is also one of the jumping-off points to Isla de Margarita and a convenient gateway to the nearby Península de Araya. Much further inland but a possible daytrip away is the Cueva del Guácharo.

Information
INTERNET ACCESS
Internet Café (Calle Sucre; ☺ 8:30am-6pm Mon-Fri, till noon Sat)

MONEY
Most major banks are on Calle Mariño and Av Bermúdez, including:
Banco de Venezuela (Calle Mariño at Calle Rojas)
Banco Mercantil (Av Bermúdez at Calle Gutierrez)
Banesco (Calle Mariño at Calle Carabobo)

POST
Ipostel (☎ 432-2616; Calle Paraíso; ☺ 8am-noon & 2-6pm)

TELEPHONE
CANTV (Calle Montes; ☺ 7am-9pm)

TOURIST INFORMATION
Dirección de Turismo (☎ 808-7769; Calle Sucre; ☺ 8am-noon & 2:30-5:30pm Mon-Fri) There's also a tourist stand at the airport open 7am to 6pm.

Sights
The grandest and best-restored colonial structure in town is the coral-rock **Castillo de San Antonio de la Eminencia** (admission free; ☺ 7am-7pm), with good views over the city and coastline from a hill just southeast of the center. Constructed in 1659 on a four-pointed-star plan, it has survived repeated pirate attacks and destructive earthquakes.

There were originally four such forts in the area, and the remains of nearby **Castillo de Santa María** (built in 1669) are within the grounds of Santa Inés church – sweet-talk the priest and he may let you through to have a peek at what remains.

Next to Castillo de San Antonio is the small, concrete **Museo de Arte Contemporáneo de Cumaná** (☎ 416-4363; admission free; ☺ 9am-noon & 3-6pm Tue-Fri, 9am-2pm Sat & Sun). It stages changing exhibits of modern art, and is only open on weekends if there are events.

The streets around the **Iglesia de Santa Inés** have retained their colonial appearance. The church itself dates from 1929 and has few objects from earlier times inside, apart from the 16th-century statues of *El Nazareno* (Christ with the Cross) and the patron saint, Santa Inés – both are in the chapels in the right-hand aisle. The **catedral**, on Plaza Blanco, is also relatively young and has a hodgepodge of altarpieces in its largely timbered interior.

The city has more museums, though they are pretty modest. The **Casa Natal de Andrés Eloy Blanco** (☎ 0414-777-8555; Plaza Bolívar; admission free; ☺ 9am-noon & 3-6pm Mon-Fri) is a historic house where one of Venezuela's most extraordinary

CENTRAL CUMANÁ

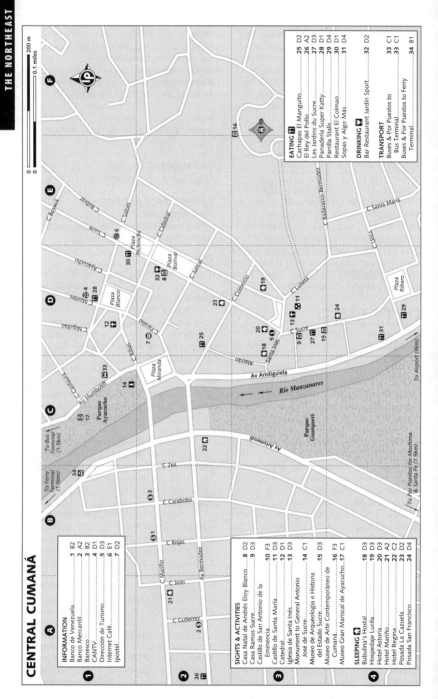

poets was born in 1896 (see p38). **Casa Ramos Sucre** (☎ 431-3777; Calle Sucre No 29; admission free; ⊗ 8am-noon & 2-6pm Mon-Fri) is dedicated to another local poet, José Antonio Ramos Sucre, born here in 1890. Sucre's poetry was well ahead of his time, and it was only in the 1960s that his verses attracted the attention of scholars, publishers and finally readers. Long before that, he committed suicide at the age of 40. The well-preserved house is stuffed with beautiful period furniture.

Next door to the Casa Ramos Sucre, the **Museo de Arqueología e Historia del Estado Sucre** (Calle Sucre; admission free; ⊗ 8:30am-noon & 2:30-5:30pm Mon-Fri) has a small archaeological collection, though it was closed for renovations at the time of writing.

The **Museo Gran Mariscal de Ayacucho** (☎ 432-1896; Av Humboldt; admission free; ⊗ 9am-noon & 3-6pm Tue-Fri, 3-7pm Sat & Sun) is dedicated to the Cumaná-born hero of the War of Independence, General Antonio José de Sucre (1795–1830), who liberated Peru and Bolivia. His statue is nearby in the park.

Sleeping

Hotel Astoria (☎ 433-2708; hotelastoria_7@hotmail. com; Calle Sucre 51; s/d/tr US$12/19/28; P ⊠) Good for penny-pinchers, this no-frills place has 23 decent-sized and windowless but well-lit rooms with cable TV and air-con. It's the best choice among the cluster of cheapies here.

Hospedaje Lucila (☎ 431-2044; Calle Bolívar; d without/with air-con US$14/17; ⊠) This basic little homestay is almost cute, with 21 small rooms around a courtyard strewn with family washing. Rooms are basic and dark, and mattresses saggy, but there's cable TV.

Posada La Cazuela (☎ 432-1401; Calle Sucre 63; d US$24; ⊠) This small, homey family posada has just four simple rooms (though they might add a few more) with cable TV and bamboo ceilings.

Hotel Mariño (☎ 432-0751; jjruiz34@hotmail.com; Calle Mariño; d US$24; P ⊠) High-rise offering sizable rooms with old furniture and dank bathrooms, but at least the views are good.

Hotel Regina (☎ 432-2581; Av Arismendi; d US$28; P ⊠) This plain and outdated place has a good location near the river. Choose an east-facing room on the top floor to get away from street noise and for views over the city center, including its two churches and the fort. There's a restaurant and a little bar on the premises.

Bubulina's Hostal (☎ 431-4025; Callejón Santa Inés; d from US$33; ⊠) A great choice in the center in this intimate, one-story historical building down a narrow colonial street. There's a bright indoor plant hallway with 12 comfortable rooms around it; all have flowery decorations and curvy ironwork furniture. There's also a little restaurant for guests only. German is spoken.

ourpick Posada San Francisco (☎ 431-3926; posada sanfrancisco@hotmail.com; Calle Sucre 16; s/d $26/38; ⊠) This beautiful posada located in a renovated old *casona* (large house) has nine spacious rooms with tall cane ceilings. They're all arranged around a tranquil, palm-filled patio with traditional-style tiles. There's an attractive bar and a good restaurant too.

Eating & Drinking

The city center has few upper-range restaurants; most are budget eateries. The cheapest (and grungiest) grills are the *parrilla* stalls near Plaza Ribero (open 12:30pm to 11pm).

Panadería Super Katty (☎ 431-2955; Plaza Blanco; ⊗ 6am-10pm) A small bakery with good pastries and enough frosted cakes to cater for a dozen weddings. Good coffee, but you'll sip it standing up.

Sopas y Algo Más (☎ 0414-189-6876; Av Aristiguieta; mains US$3-8; ⊗ 7am-3pm) Just three soups, three main dishes and four desserts are available at this small but hopping restaurant set in a shady concrete patio. The menu is on the wall, the service is quick and the food is cheap and delicious. Look for the green garage door.

El Rey del Pollo (☎ 433-1822; Av Bermúdez; ½ chicken $4.50; ⊗ noon-8pm Mon-Sat) Cheeep chicken at this casual, popular and bustling fowl eatery.

Posada San Francisco (☎ 431-3926; Calle Sucre; mains US$5-14; ⊗ 7am-3pm, 6-11pm) The peaceful open-air patio restaurant at this colonial posada makes for an intimate atmosphere in the evening, when lights are left low and the stars are visible above. On the menu are meats, seafood, pasta and cocktails – the four most important food groups.

ourpick Les Jardins de Sucre (☎ 431-3689; Calle Sucre 27; mains US$7-14; ⊗ 6-10pm Mon, noon-3pm & 6-10pm Tue-Thu, till 11pm Sat & Sun) One of Cumaná's best restaurants is this French place with shady patio, small water garden and attentive service. Dishes like pork in four spices and smoked-salmon salad will liven up taste buds, as will the French and Chilean wines. Daily specials like duck and rabbit are available.

Restaurant El Colmao (☎ 432-2005; Calle Sucre at Plaza Pichincha; mains US$9-12; 🕑 noon-2am Mon-Sat; 🅿) This windowless Spanish restaurant serves up the usual specialties like shellfish stew, grilled prawns and squash Provençal. The second dining room comes with a stage for live music; otherwise there's just soccer on the TV.

Bar Restaurant Jardín Sport (Plaza Bolívar; beer US$0.60; 🕑 6am-midnight) The locals' favorite for chatting the day away is this informal open-air bar in a courtyard off Plaza Bolívar. It has a few pool tables in back and serves inexpensive snacks, but it's the cheap beer that keeps punters returning for more.

Getting There & Away

AIR
The airport is about 4km southeast of the city center. Airlines providing services include **Avior** (☎ 467-2340; www.avior.com.ve) and **Santa Bárbara** (☎ 467-2933; www.santabarbaraairlines.com).

BOAT
Naviarca (☎ 431-5577; www.grancacique.com.ve) runs ferries to Isla de Margarita's dock at Punta de Piedras; see p242 for details. Naviarca also operates a ferry to Araya on the Península de Araya, although it's much easier to go by small boats called *tapaditos* (see p272).

To get to the ferry docks in Cumaná snag a bus or por puesto (US$0.30) from just north of the bridge, or take a taxi (US$2.50).

BUS
The bus terminal is 1.5km northwest of the city center and is linked by frequent buses and por puestos (both US$0.30) along Av Humboldt; go outside the terminal and take them going right (south).

Bus destinations include Caracas (US$18, seven hours), Carúpano (US$4.50, 2½ hours), Ciudad Bolívar (US$12, seven hours) and Puerto La Cruz (US$5, 1½ hours).

Por puesto destinations include Carúpano (US$7, two hours) and Puerto La Cruz (US$6, 1½ hours). The por puesto to Caripe (US$8, three hours) departs daily around 3pm to 3:30pm; look for grey vans with racks (it passes the Cueva del Guácharo just before Caripe). Por Puestos to Santa Fe (US$1, 45 minutes) and Mochima (US$1, 40 minutes) depart from just south of town, near the Redoma El Indio (buses to here cost US$0.30; taxis are US$3).

PENÍNSULA DE ARAYA
☎ 0293

Lying just across the deep and intensely blue Gulf of Cariaco from Cumaná, the Península de Araya comprises a 70km-long and 10km-wide finger of strikingly barren land characterized by arid red sands and scrubby dunes. Punta Arenas, on the peninsula's end, is just 5km northwest of Cumaná as the crow flies, but it's some 180km by road. The peninsula's sparse population is scattered through a handful of coastal villages on the northern coast, along which the solitary and rather rough road runs. The town of Araya is the largest settlement here and easy to get to by boat or ferry from Cumaná.

The peninsula's two major attractions – a huge colonial fort, the Castillo de Santiago, and the vast Salinas de Araya – are both near the town of Araya, at the western end of the peninsula.

Araya
Araya sits on the Bahía de Araya, with its pier in the middle. The Castillo de Santiago is 750m to the south, while the *salinas* (salt pans) spread outward to the north.

There's a decent beach between the town and the fort, but it doesn't come with a lot of shade. Most places to stay are located near this beach.

SIGHTS
Salinas de Araya
This sprawling salt-extraction site is run by **Sacosal** (☎ 437-1123) and includes three areas: the *salinas naturales* (natural salt lagoon; referred to as Unidad 1), *salinas artificiales* (artificial salt pans; Unidad 2) and the main complex near the pier (not open to the public), where salt is sorted, packed and stored.

The *salinas naturales,* about 1km east of town, consist of a pink-hued salt lagoon, from which the salt is dragged to the shore by specially constructed boats, cleaned and then left to dry in enormous glistening heaps. Walk five minutes behind town to the blue-and-white 'Unidad Laguna Madre' building, which is down the hill and near the green-and-yellow chapel. If you're lucky someone will have time to explain the process to you (in Spanish); they're less busy on weekends.

The *salinas artificiales,* a few kilometers north of the town, are a colorful array of rectangular pools filled with salt water. The intense strength

A PINCH OF SALT

For such a lifeless stretch of land, Araya has a compelling history. The Spaniards first claimed the peninsula in 1499. After the discovery of fabulous pearl fisheries offshore, they sailed down to the western tip of the peninsula to find another, quite different treasure – extensive *salinas* (salt pans).

Salt, an essential means of preserving food, was an increasingly valuable commodity in Europe. However, it was the Dutch who took advantage, and rather cheekily set about extracting the salt from under the Spaniards' noses in the mid-16th century. The Spanish, on the other hand, blindly concentrated on their pearl harvesting and it wasn't until the pearl beds were wiped out in the late 16th century that they realized their mistake. By that time, the *salinas* were being furtively exploited not only by the Dutch but also by the opportunistic English, and there wasn't a lot the Spanish could do about it. Various battles were fought, but plundering of the salt continued.

In exasperation, the Spanish Crown set about constructing a mighty fortress in 1618. However, it took almost 50 years to be completed thanks to pirate raids, storms and heat so fierce that the men mostly worked during the night. The fortress became the most costly Spanish project to be realized in the New World to that time, but once equipped with 45 cannons and defended by a 250-man garrison, La Real Fortaleza de Santiago de León de Araya repelled all who attempted to take it.

However, the fort's fortunes changed again in 1726 when a wild hurricane threw up a tide that broke over the salt lagoon, flooding it and turning it into a gulf. With the salt reserves lost, the Spanish abandoned the peninsula. Before leaving, they set about blowing up the fort to prevent it from falling into foreign hands. Although they ignited all the available gunpowder, however, the sturdy bulwarks resisted. Damaged but not destroyed, the mighty bulwarks still proudly crown the waterfront cliff.

Meanwhile, the *salinas* slowly returned to their previous state, and mining was gradually re-introduced. Today they are Venezuela's largest *salinas* and produce about half a million metric tons of salt per year.

of the sun evaporates this water, leaving behind pure salt, which is then harvested; the pool is then refilled and the process begun again. Numerous pools in different stages of evaporation create a variety of color tones, from rich creamy pinks to deep purple. The water coloration has a lot to do with *artemia*, a microscopic saltwater shrimp found in the water.

A poorly maintained old *mirador* (lookout) is on the hill to the east of the *salinas*, providing a good view over this chessboard of pools. It's on the road to Punta de Araya, 2km north of Araya. Hard-core salt aficionados can hire a taxi for a look around; just be prepared for baking heat and don't forget to take plenty of water, sunscreen, sunglasses and a hat.

Castillo de Santiago

This, the biggest and oldest colonial fort in the country (see the boxed text above), is commonly referred to as El Castillo (The Castle). The four-pointed structure stands on the waterfront cliff at the southern end of the bay, a hot 20-minute walk from town. Although

damaged, the gargantuan coral-rock walls are an awesome sight and give a good impression of how the fort must have once looked. You can wander freely around the site, as there's no gate.

SLEEPING & EATING

Posada Helen (☎ 437-1101; Calle El Castillo; d with fan/air-con US$17/19; ✗) Close to the Araya Wind is this homely posada, which has some good, comfortable and slightly frilly rooms with tiled floors and cable TV. For entertainment there's a large cage with a talking parrot and many parakeets.

Posada Araya Wind (☎ 437-1132; Calle El Castillo; d/tr US$19/21; ✗) The most stylish posada in town, the neatly decorated Araya Wind offers up 15 good rooms with cane roofing. The attractive hallways harbor a scattering of antique-style wooden chairs.

Restaurant Araya Mar. (☎ 437-1382; set menu US$5, r US$19; ☽ 7:30am-9pm) This airy, modern restaurant has an open front that catches the breeze. It also offers seven clean, air-con rooms with cable TV.

THE NORTHEAST

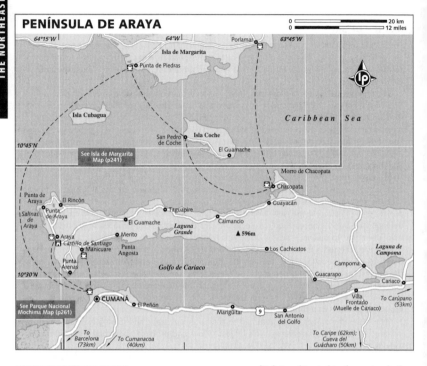

PENÍNSULA DE ARAYA

GETTING THERE & AWAY

Naviarca (in Cumaná ☎ 431-5577; www.grancacique.com
.ve) runs several ferries daily between Cumaná
and Araya (US$2, one hour); schedules aren't
dependable, however. A better bet is the small
tapadito boats, which offer frequent, faster and
more reliable service. They go between Cumaná and Manicuare (US$1, 20 minutes) every
20 to 30 minutes from 6am to 5pm, and the
remaining Manicuare–Araya leg is covered by
frequent por puestos (US$0.50, 10 minutes).

Although there's a paved road between Araya
and Cariaco (95km), there's little traffic traveling
along it. There are occasional por puestos from
Araya to Cariaco, but you can't rely on them.
Traffic dies completely after 3pm.

There's a boat service between Chacopata
and Porlamar, on Isla de Margarita (see
p242). There are direct por puestos between
Chacopata and Carúpano (US$6, 1½ hours).

CARÚPANO

☎ 0294 / pop 145,000
Not particularly interesting in itself, Carúpano
is the last city of any size on Venezuela's eastern Caribbean coast. It's an active port for

cacao, which is cultivated in the region before
being shipped overseas.

For the traveler, Carúpano provides a convenient stepping-stone to the lovely beaches
lining the Península de Paria. There are also
inland attractions around the area. And if you
happen to be here in late February or early
March, you'll be treated to one of Venezuela's biggest and liveliest Carnavals – a giant
party which attracts thousands of people and
lasts for four boisterous days (see the boxed
text p275).

Information
INTERNET ACCESS
Internet Hernandez (Av 4 Juncal; ⏱ 8am-9pm Mon-
Fri, 10am-9pm Sat & Sun)

MEDICAL SERVICES
Farmacia SAAS (⏱ 24hr) Toiletries galore.

MONEY
The following banks all have ATMS:
Banco de Venezuela (Av 3 Independencia)
Banesco (Plaza Colón)
Corp Banca (Plaza Colón)

POST

Ipostel (☎ 332-2924; Av 2 Carabobo; ☼ 8am-noon & 2-5pm Mon-Fri)

TELEPHONE

CANTV (☎ 331-9555; Av 4 Juncal; ☼ 8am-7pm Mon-Fri, 8am-6pm Sat) Telephones and good internet access.

TOURIST INFORMATION

Corpomedina (☎ 331-5241; playamedina@cantv.net; Carúpano Airport) Provides information and booking for its cabañas at Playa Medina (p278) and Playa Pui Puy (p279).

Dirección de Turismo (Edificio Rental Fundabermudez, 1st fl, Av 3 Independencia No 8; ☼ 8am-noon & 12:30-5:30pm Mon-Fri) Information on Sucre state.

Fundación Thomas Merle (☎ 331-3370; www.fundacionthomasmerle.com in Spanish; Plaza de Santa Rosa de Lima) Local organization that does social work in education and conservation. Volunteer opportunities are available for fluent German speakers. It also books accommodations at Hato Río de Agua (p280) and Hacienda Aguasana (p280). It might be able to organize walking excursions with botanical emphasis. Information is also available at Posada La Colina.

Municipal Tourist Office (Av 4 Juncal at Av Perimetral; 8am-noon & 2-5pm Mon-Fri) This city tourist office was planning to open in a new location at research time.

Sights

Despite its regular chessboard layout, a reminder of the town's colonial origins in 1647, the town has no outstanding historic monuments. However, you might want to visit the two main churches, **Iglesia de Santa Catalina** (Plaza Colón) and **Iglesia de Santa Rosa de Lima** (Plaza de Santa Rosa de Lima); the modest **Museo Histórico de Carúpano** (Plaza de Santa Rosa de Lima; admission free; ☼ 8:30am-noon & 2:30-6pm Mon-Fri); and the unusually large Mercado Municipal.

Festivals & Events

Carúpano springs to life for the four days (Saturday to Tuesday) before Ash Wednesday (late February to early March), when Carnaval is held and there are dances, drumming, parades and lots of rum (see the boxed text p275). Thousands of people flood the town, so don't expect to find a room – but you'll be staying up all night anyway.

Sleeping

IN CARÚPANO

Pensión Venezuela (☎ 511-1466; Calle Cantaura No 49; d with shared bathroom US$8) Cheapest bet around the bus terminal. Look for plants outside and a sign that says 'pension.'

Hotel Maria Victoria (☎ 416-9653; Av Perimetral; s/d US$14/17) Cheap family posada with dark, depressing rooms and saggy beds.

Hotel San Francisco (☎ 331-1074; Av 4 Juncal 87A; d/tr US$24/28; P ✕) Plain Jane rooms can be noisy, but the hotel's location is busy and good. There's cable TV, but no hot water.

Hotel Victoria (☎ 331-1554; fax 331-1776; Av Perimetral; s/d US$28/38; P ✕ ✻) This large hotel, a 10-minute walk east of the bus terminal on the seafront boulevard, has decent rooms with tile baths, cable TV and some art on the walls. It's clean and has firm beds, but can be noisy if there's a weekend party downstairs. Air-con has two controls: nonexistent or deep freeze.

Hotel Lilma (☎ 331-1361; Av 3 Independencia No 161; d/tr US$31/33; P ✕) Characterless Lilma offers hot-water bathrooms but no cable TV. Halls are retro-ugly. There's a decent restaurant and a smoky bar.

our pick Posada La Colina (☎ 332-2915; merle@telcel.net.ve; Av Rómulo Gallegos 33; s/d incl breakfast $47/59; P ✕ ✻) Far and away the most special hotel in town, Posada La Colina is in a renovated old mansion and offers comfortable but not luxurious rooms with bamboo furniture, hot-water bathrooms and cable TV. There's an awesome pool area with good open-air restaurant boasting views over town.

Hotel Euro-Caribe Internacional (☎ 331-3911; www.hoteleurocaribe.com.ve; Av Perimetral; d incl breakfast US$72; P ✕ ✻ ▭ ✻) This high-rise hotel peers down on the seafront. The lobby is outdated and rooms average, but the list of amenities includes king-size beds, an internet café, a gym, a bar, a restaurant, a pool and even a bingo casino.

AROUND CARÚPANO

There are some good posadas on breezy Playa Copey, about 6km west of the city (taxi US$4).

Posada Nena (☎ 331-7297; www.posadanena.com; Calle Principal, Playa Copey; d from $19; P ✕ ▭ ✻) Not an upscale place but just one block from the beach, Posada Nena has 11 decent rooms, a small pool, a restaurant and lounging areas with old furniture. The sandy garden is dotted with palms and hammocks. Fan and air-con rooms are available; the three-room annex next to a grubby lot is nearer to the beach.

Posada Casa Blanca (☎ 331-6896; Calle Principal, Playa Copey; d US$28; P ✕) With a prisonlike back gate leading directly onto the beach, this family house has six quirky rooms with hippie fabrics lining the ceiling. It's a funky mishmash of textiles, fake flowers and patterned wallpaper. There's a small concrete restaurant-bar area that peeks to the water.

Eating

There are plenty of small eateries scattered throughout the city.

Mercado Municipal (Calle El Mercadito) If you're pinching pennies, this marketplace is one of the best options for unsophisticated local dishes (breakfast and lunch only).

Panadería La Mansión del Pan (Av Juncal; 6am-9pm Mon-Sat;) People flock here for breakfast and daytime snacks: join them for the *pasteles* (pastries), *cachitos* (hot filled croissant) and a thimble-sized cup of coffee.

Panadería La Bolivariana (Av Independencia; 6am-8pm Mon-Sat) Another modern, attractive bakery with good deli sandwiches, pastries and drinks.

Mama Pancha Arepera (arepas US$2-3; 24hr) How can you lose with a name like this? Outside street eating with a neon sign.

Lunchería El Oasis (331-0144; Plaza Bolívar; mains US$2.50-7; 5:30pm-10pm) This tiny but busy Middle Eastern cubbyhole fronts leafy Plaza Bolívar. It's popular for excellent falafels, kebabs and cabbage rolls. Toss it all down with the very tasty and healthy yogurt drinks.

El Fogón de la Petaca (331-2555; Av Perimetral 1; mains US$8-13; noon-10pm Mon-Thu, till 11pm Fri & Sat, till 9pm Sun;) This smart joint on the seafront boulevard serves a variety of meats, seafood

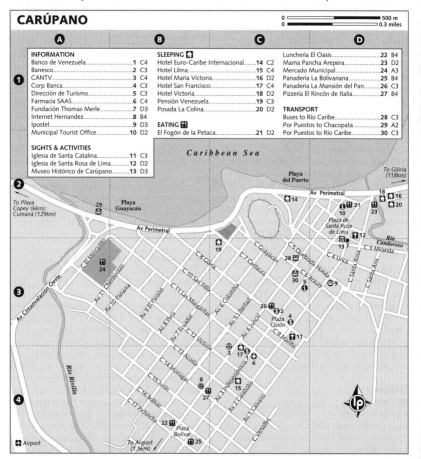

CARÚPANO

INFORMATION		SLEEPING		Lunchería El Oasis..........................22 B4
Banco de Venezuela.........................1 C4		Hotel Euro-Caribe Internacional......14 C2		Mama Pancha Arepera....................23 D2
Banesco...2 C3		Hotel Lilma....................................15 C4		Mercado Municipal.........................24 A3
CANTV...3 C4		Hotel Maria Victoria.......................16 D2		Panadería La Bolivariana..................25 B4
Corp Banca......................................4 C3		Hotel San Francisco.......................17 C4		Panadería La Mansión del Pan.........26 C3
Dirección de Turismo.......................5 C3		Hotel Victoria................................18 D2		Pizzería El Rincón de Italia..............27 B4
Farmacia SAAS.................................6 C4		Pensión Venezuela.........................19 C3		
Fundación Thomas Merle..................7 D3		Posada La Colina............................20 D2		TRANSPORT
Internet Hernandez..........................8 B4				Buses to Río Caribe........................28 C3
Ipostel...9 D3		EATING		Por Puestos to Chacopata...............29 A2
Municipal Tourist Office..................10 D2		El Fogón de la Petaca.....................21 D2		Por Puestos to Río Caribe...............30 C3

SIGHTS & ACTIVITIES	
Iglesia de Santa Catalina.................11 C3	
Iglesia de Santa Rosa de Lima.........12 D2	
Museo Histórico de Carúpano.........13 D3	

Caribbean Sea

PARTY TIME IN CARÚPANO

If you find yourself in Carúpano at the right time in February (or perhaps early March), there's one bash you won't want to miss – colorful **Carnaval**, quite possibly the most lively, boisterous and crazy rave you'll ever experience. Carúpano's celebration is the largest of its kind in Venezuela, and encompasses four full days of heavy drinking, steamy dancing and general nonstop, blowout partying. It's had some influences from rowdy neighbor Trinidad, which probably explains much of the riotous atmosphere.

Thousands upon thousands of revelers arrive from all over the country to take part in these fanatical celebrations. They'll don extravagant papier-mâché masks and dress up in dazzling costumes of animals, monsters, Spanish conquistadores and even well-known celebrities. Parades with dressed-up floats set the stage for skimpily clad performers gyrating to sexy music rhythms and heady drum beats – try to spot the trannies, who'll often have the best (ie skimpiest) outfits and rowdiest attitudes. Marching bands also tramp down the streets, adding to the din by making as much noise as they can.

The best action is often down in the crowds, however, as partiers sing along with the music while pounding on home-made drums and feverishly shaking their booty (sometimes on top of cars) without inhibition. Merengue, salsa, Caribbean beats and even rap – it's all good enough to get the fires going. All the while, everyone keeps pounding gallons of beer, rum and anything else they can get their paws on, keeping the drunken revelry at its peak.

Carnaval is craziest on its last two days, always Monday and Tuesday (the latter of which is Mardi Gras and the last day of Carnaval). The floats become more elaborate and a glorious Queen is paraded about, trailed by huge papier-mâché caricatures. There are masquerade balls, impromptu bands, people throwing water balloons and food stalls selling their wares to hungry partiers. There are also a few sly foxes slinking around picking pockets, so watch your belongings.

Carnaval falls on the four days before Ash Wednesday, which is 46 days before Easter Sunday. The following list has Carnaval dates for the coming years, so you'll have plenty of time to prepare – and find that perfect skimpy feathered dress.

■ 2008: February 2–5

■ 2009: February 21–24

■ 2010: February 13–16

■ 2011: March 5–8

■ 2012: February 18–21

---

and pastas, with exceptional service and a decent wine list. There are separate smoking and nonsmoking rooms: a rarity in Venezuela.

Pizzería El Rincón de Italia (☎ 331-3459; Av Juncal; mains US$9-17; ⏲ 11:30am-10pm) For Italian food like pizzas, pastas, meats and salads, hit this decent restaurant located in a pretty open-air courtyard studded with potted plants.

Getting There & Away

AIR

The airport is 1.5km west of the city center and provides services to Porlamar, on Isla de Margarita, and Caracas. You can also rent cars here for about US$70 per day.

BUS

The bus terminal is a short walk from the center on Av Perimetral. Destinations include Caracas (US$19, nine hours), Ciudad Guayana (US$17, seven hours), Cumaná (US$5, 2½ hours), Güiria (US$7, 2½ hours), Maturín (US$8, 3½ hours) and Puerto La Cruz (US$7, 4½ hours).

Buses to Río Caribe leave from the corner of Calle 5 Quebrada Honda and Av 4 Juncal (US$0.80, 45 minutes). Por puestos leave nearby, from Calle 6 Araure and Av 4 Juncal (US$1.25, 30 minutes).

Other por puesto destinations include Cumaná (US$7, two hours), Güiria (US$9, two hours), Maturín (US$10, three hours) and Puerto La Cruz (US$11, four hours).

For Isla de Margarita, the shortest and cheapest way is via Chacopata. Direct por puestos depart from Av Perimetral near the market (US$6.50, 1½ hours); from Chacopata you take a boat to Porlamar (US$5, one to 1½ hours); see p242 for more details.

THE NORTHEAST

RÍO CARIBE

☎ 0294 / pop 12,000

Río Caribe is a pleasant and peaceful seaside town 25km east of Carúpano. It's popular with holidaymakers, and provides a useful springboard to the beautiful beaches further east, as well as to some inland attractions. If you come, visit the 18th-century church on Plaza Bolívar.

The town is an old port that grew fat on cacao exports, and the air of the former splendor is still palpable in the wide, tree-shaded Av Bermúdez with its once resplendent, now mostly decadent mansions. A boardwalk and pier are slated to be built, as is a bus terminal, which would bring more tourism to the area.

There are a few internet places in town; fight the video kids for a computer at **Karibea@n.com** (Calle Zea; ⏲ 9am-10pm). There's also a Banfoandes bank, but the ATM is iffy – bring cash from elsewhere.

Tours

So far there's little tourist infrastructure in town, which makes for a laid-back feel. Area tours are organized by most mid- to upper-range posadas; shop around, as routes, services and prices may vary. Day tours include a boat trip to a few beaches, the buffalo ranch and hot springs, Playa Uva and the Bukare cocoa plantation and various combinations of the above (for descriptions of these places see Around Río Caribe, opposite).

Sleeping

The town has a good range of accommodations, including several posadas.

Posada San Miguel (☎ 416-6344; soxfrite@hotmail.com; Calle Zea 83; s/d US$9/18; 🞬) Fifteen clean, simple and tiled rooms with small baths available at this new and rather antiseptic place (though homey touches might come in time). Get an outside window for light. Dark kitchen available and there's a rooftop terrace with possible bar being built.

Posada Don Chilo (☎ 646-1212; Calle Mariño No 27; d/tr US$10/14) A family place with seven cheap, no-frills (but decent), fan rooms and a terrace to hang out on.

Pensión Papagayos (☎ 646-1868; cricas@web.de; Calle 14 de Febrero; s/d US$10/14; 🞬) This tiny family home rents out just three good, well-kept rooms sharing two bathrooms, and you can use the kitchen and fridge. There's a tiny gar-

den and pleasant common dining area. Only one room has air-con (US$19).

Posada Kakao (☎ 646-1229; Calle 14 de Febrero; d US$12-17) Offering just three simple fan rooms (one with outside bath) is this old place with a bit of charm. There's a (limited) kitchen and bar area that guests can use, plus a small scruffy garden. It's run by a chocolate-maker.

La Posada de Arlet (☎ 646-1290; Calle 24 de Julio 22; s/d/tr/q US$14/24/33/42) Owned and managed by a polyglot Swiss woman, this place is a modest but homely option with eight nice budget fan rooms and hallways with lounging areas. Good area advice is given and there's bike rental. Breakfast available.

ourpick Posada Shalimar (☎ 646-1135; www.posada-shalimar.com; Calle Bermúdez 54; s/d/tr/suite US$24/33/38/70; 🞬 🖳 🞬) Easily the most relaxing posada in town, this lovely Danish-run Moorish paradise has 13 attractive, pastel-colored rooms decorated with tasteful art and gorgeous tilework. Best of all is the gorgeous centerpiece pool. There's a pretty restaurant-bar in front and area tours are available.

Villa Antillana (☎ 646-1413; www.proyectoparia.com/antillana; Calle Rivero 32; s/d/tr/q incl breakfast US$24/35/42/59) Set in a restored 19th-century mansion, quiet Villa Antillana has just six attractive, rustic fan rooms around a pretty tiled courtyard with hammocks. There's a relaxing lounge area too. Services include bike rental and area trips; in season you can take a tour to set baby turtles free.

Posada Caribana (☎ 646-1242; www.caribana.com.ve; Av Bermúdez 25; d incl breakfast US$52; P 🞬) This upmarket and overpriced posada is located in a *casona* from the 19th century. It has 11 good-sized, tidy and plain rooms that line a traditional-style patio. The lounge area is decorated with rattan furniture, and there's a garden and a restaurant out back (where the best rooms are).

Eating

Posada Shalimar's restaurant and bar are open to the public from 3pm onward.

Tasca Mi Cocina (☎ 808-3088; Calle Juncal; mains US$4-7; ⏲ 11:30am-10pm; 🞬) This dark but popular and friendly hideaway has good food at good prices. The atmosphere is a bit industrial and stuffy; look for the green garage door and enter on the left side.

Restaurant Doña Eva (☎ 646-1678; Calle Girardot at Plaza Miranda; mains US$4.50-12; ⏲ 11am-11pm) Another down-to-earth choice, Doña Eva serves hearty pasta, chicken and seafood dishes. Set back from the road on a simple terrace, this is where locals relax with a cold beer. There's no sign; look for the green-and-yellow house.

Da More (☎ 646-1622; Av Bermúdez; dishes US$5-8; ☒ 6-11pm) This place cooks up great pizzas and pastas – try the spinach-stuffed tortellini with Roquefort cheese. And say 'hi' to Roberto, the Argentine who runs it.

Restaurant Casa Blanca (☎ 646-1162; Av Gallegos; mains US$7-8; ☒ noon-10pm) Located in the old schoolhouse near the entrance to town is this good restaurant. It offers well-made food like fish soup, curry chicken, garlic calamari and fried fish. Occasionally it serves *pastel de chucho* (shredded ray with plantain and cheese). Try the *negro en camisa* (a chocolate concoction) for dessert.

Pariana Café (☎ 494-2756; Av Bermúdez) This café, popular for its creative cuisine (think fusion) and a hip, casual atmosphere, was closed at research time, but hopefully it'll reopen.

Getting There & Away

Río Caribe currently has no bus terminal (though this may change in the future). For now, transportation departs from Plaza Bolívar.

To Carúpano there are frequent por puestos (US$1, 30 minutes) and buses (US$0.80); taxis cost US$12. Cruces Oriente has one daily bus to Puerto La Cruz and Caracas.

For details on transportation to the beaches around Río Caribe, see right.

AROUND RÍO CARIBE
☎ 0294

The coast east of Río Caribe has some of the country's loveliest beaches, many of which are nesting sites for green turtles. There are perhaps two dozen separate sandy stretches on the 50km coastal stretch between Río Caribe and San Juan de Unare, the last seaside village accessible by road. The most famous is Playa Medina, closely followed by Playa Pui Puy, but there are plenty of other lesser-known patches of paradise – all it takes is an adventurous spirit to find them.

The hinterland behind the beaches features a picturesque coastal mountain range rolling down into the vast plains that stretch to the south. The mountains and the plains shelter hot springs, buffalo ranches and cacao haciendas. There are over a dozen posadas scattered across the region, but roads are few and can be in bad shape, and transportation is infrequent.

On the one hand this makes getting around tricky, but on the other, it means that the region is, in general, blissfully free of tourists. Just be aware that in high season (August, December, Semana Santa and Carnaval) prices for accommodations rise.

GETTING THERE & AWAY

You can explore the region on your own or take advantage of a wealth of tours on offer. Tours are organized mostly by hotels and posadas in Río Caribe (opposite).

Infrequent por puesto pickup trucks, which get you close to the beaches, depart from the southeastern end of Río Caribe, opposite the PDV gas station. Destinations include the villages of Medina (US$0.75, 30 minutes), Pui Puy (US$2, two hours) and San Juan de las Galdonas (US$2, 1½ hours). They don't get as far as the beaches of Medina and Pui Puy: you need to walk the rest of the way, about a half-hour trip in either case. Since traffic thins in the early afternoon, this doesn't leave you much time for the beach; it's better to stay overnight.

It's much easier to get to the beaches by boat, but also much more expensive; renting a boat for the day costs around US$47. Negotiate a roundtrip price to your particular destination. Taxis are another expensive possibility.

Playa Loero & Playa de Uva

The first beaches worth visiting east of Río Caribe are side-by-side Playa Loero and Playa de Uva. They lie 6km from Río Caribe by the road to Bohordal, then another 6km by a paved side road that branches off to the left. At the end of this road, which goes up and over some tight curves and hills, is the tiny Playa de Uva and its idyllic **Campamento Playa de Uva** (☎ 416-6284; www.caribana.com.ve; s/d incl breakfast & dinner US$122/196; P ☒) in a grassy, palm-shaded cove. This little paradise has 12 airy, bright and comfortable rooms with screen walls and patios. There's a pretty swimming-pool area plus a palm-thatched restaurant. The beach itself is small but serene. Booking is via Posada Caribana (opposite) in Río Caribe.

Just to the west of Playa de Uva, Playa Loero is another pleasant, though less memorable, beach. It has no facilities, but you can string your hammock under the roof of the *churuata* (traditional palm-thatched, large circular hut).

There are several other cheaper posadas back in the village of Guayabero before the turnoff to the beach. Try **Posada La Ruta del Cacao** (☎ 0414-820-1355; oticampos@gmail.com; Via Playa Medina; r per person incl breakfast US$14; **P**), which has 10 large fan cabañas with minimal furniture and high bamboo ceilings. The grounds are grassy and there's a large bar area with hammocks, all under a thatched roof.

Hacienda Bukare

Near the small village of Chacaracual, 14km from Río Caribe, this old **cacao hacienda** (☎ 511-2739; www.bukare.com; s/d/tr incl breakfast US$17/24/28; **⊠**) is still in operation. Hour-long tours are given from 10am to noon and 3pm to 5pm Monday to Saturday, and 10am to noon Sunday (US$9 per person). They include a demonstration of processing cacao and, more importantly, a tasting.

The handsome historic house offers four simple and rustic rooms with fan and small balconies, along with a sunny, grassy garden

with Jacuzzi-like plunge pool. Other services include cozy on-site restaurant and area tours. Price includes airport transfers and transportation to a beach.

Playa Medina

Proceeding east, a paved road branches off 4km beyond Hacienda Bukare and goes 5km to the village of Medina then northward for 1km to a fork. The left branch goes for 2km to the picture-postcard crescent-shaped Playa Medina. This 400m-long stretch of paradise appears on more postcards in Venezuela than any other beach. It is indeed picture-perfect, set in a glorious deep bay fronted by a gentle arc of golden sand shaded with a forest of swaying coconut palms. And despite the soft sand, cleanliness and sheltered location, the isolated Playa Medina rarely gets overrun by beachgoers.

Amid the palms are stylish reservation-only cabañas and a restaurant, all operated by **Corpomedina** (☎ 0294-331-5241; playamedina@cantv.net; Carúpano Airport). The gorgeous, rustic cabañas with breakfast and dinner cost around US$54 per adult, depending on the season. There are

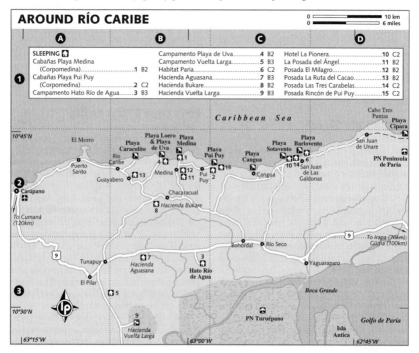

AROUND RÍO CARIBE

0 — 10 km
0 — 6 miles

SLEEPING 🛏		Campamento Playa de Uva............4 B2	Hotel La Pionera.....................10 C2
Cabañas Playa Medina		Campamento Vuelta Larga...........5 B3	La Posada del Ángel.................11 B2
(Corpomedina)...................1 B2		Habitat Paria........................6 C2	Posada El Milagro....................12 B2
Cabañas Playa Pui Puy		Hacienda Aguasana..................7 B3	Posada La Ruta del Cacao..........13 B2
(Corpomedina)...................2 C2		Hacienda Bukare.....................8 B2	Posada Las Tres Carabelas..........14 C2
Campamento Hato Río de Agua.......3 B3		Hacienda Vuelta Larga..............9 B3	Posada Rincón de Pui Puy............15 C2

eight cabañas, each housing up to six people; reserve in advance.

The beach can be used by anybody, though camping is not allowed. Señoras from the surrounding hamlets come and serve basic meals and snacks (such as fried fish and empanadas) for day-trippers.

Some budget accommodations options lie within walking distance of the beach. The family-run **Posada El Milagro** (☎ 0416-794-5291; r per person incl breakfast & dinner US$21), 2km up the hilly dirt road from the beach, offers basic fan rooms with bunk beds and cane ceilings.

One kilometer further inland (3km from the beach), in the middle of the village of Medina, is the colorful 20-room **La Posada del Ángel** (☎ 0416-794-7477; aserranoe@cantv.net; r per person US$14, with breakfast & dinner US$33; 🖳 🖳). It has a large, pleasant restaurant and bar area with hammocks and thatched roof. Only five of the rooms have air-con.

Playa Pui Puy

Taking the right branch of the fork 1km beyond the village of Medina, a 6km potholed road leads to the village of Pui Puy and continues for 2km to the beautiful Playa Pui Puy. One of the best beaches around, Pui Puy is a 1.3km-long arc of fine white sand lined with coconut groves. The sea is less sheltered here, and waves can get big enough for bodysurfers – especially from November to January. It also has a colony of 18 holiday cabañas and a restaurant operated by **Corpomedina** (☎ 0294-331-5241; playamedina@cantv .net; Carúpano Airport; r per person incl breakfast & dinner US$35). All cabañas are simple, two-room deals with fan and hammocks; reserve in advance. The restaurant serves average budget meals.

A cheaper option is **Posada Rincón de Pui Puy** (☎ 0416-894-1488; d US$24-38), sitting on the brink of the sea at the far end of the beach, with a panoramic view of the bay from its patio. The 17 colorful rooms range from tiny to large; the cheapest have showers outside.

Camping on this beach is permitted for a small fee. If you come with your own hammock, you might be able to sling it under the roof for a small fee also. Mosquitoes and sand flies appear in the mornings and evenings, particularly during the rainy season, so come prepared.

San Juan de las Galdonas

Few travelers venture further east than Playa Pui Puy, though beaches dot the coast as far as the eye can see. The seaside village of San Juan de las Galdonas has especially fine beaches. Its main access road is a paved 23km stretch that branches off the Río Caribe–Bohordal road 6.5km beyond the turnoff to Medina. Another access is by a badly potholed 22km road that connects to Río Seco, but you'll need a 4WD. Both roads wind spectacularly up and down over the mountain range.

Tiny San Juan is an authentic old port of about 1700 inhabitants that continues living its own sleepy little life. It's a good spot for travelers to hang out – there is a choice (albeit small) of accommodations and food, and there's more transportation to here than to anywhere else in the area. And you won't miss out on beaches, either – relatively nearby are several gorgeous, isolated stretches of sand. One boat operator is **Botuto** (☎ 511-1680, 0416-794-6424).

Local tour operators can also take you further into both Parque Nacional Península de Paria (p282) and Parque Nacional Turuépano (p280).

SLEEPING & EATING

Posada de Lalo (☎ 0416-815-5857; claudiadevivo@hotmail .com; dm US$15, 2-bedroom apt per person incl breakfast & dinner US$26) At the far eastern end of the village is this posada, located in a jungly area not far from the beach. There is one large two-bedroom apartment, along with an airy dormitory on the top floor. Both have huge balconies. Meals are at the Casa Galdona restaurant, a short walk away. Lalo, the owner, knows Parque Nacional Península de Paria well and can do hikes there in the slow season.

Posada Las Tres Carabelas (☎ 511-2729; d incl breakfast & dinner US$20) Beyond the hotel a few hundred meters is this Spanish owned and managed posada. It's a basic and rustic spot that sits spectacularly on top of a cliff high above the beach, providing gorgeous views over the sea. There are 13 good budget rooms with fans; room 5 is the best, with its kitchen and great views. Other perks include common areas with hammocks and a casual restaurant. Area tours are available, along with three-day trips to Parque Nacional Turuépano (see p280).

Hotel La Pionera (☎ 331-4500; www.hotellapionera .com; s/d US$24/29; 🖳 🖳) As you're coming into town, the first hotel you'll see is this atypical, four-story structure, which looms over the beach and offers more luxuries than anything else around. The 30 rooms are simple but spacious and comfortable. There is a good-sized swimming pool below and a breezy open restaurant-bar above; the top floor has awesome views. Area tours are available.

Habitat Paria (☎ 0416-483-7514; www.habitatparia .vzla.org; d/tr/q US$24/33/40;) Next to Posada de Lalo is this place, which has a gate onto the beautiful Playa Barlovento. It's an older option with 12 simple, dark, fan rooms. There are plenty of bare terraces where you can hear but not see the ocean. Services include a res-taurant and area tours. There's also an old pool and a sand volleyball court.

The best traveler's hangout is **Restaurant Casa Galdona** (☎ 0416-815-5857; mains US$5-10; ☺ 7am-4pm & 6-10pm), a small and cozy eatery that serves a mix of food like *arepas,* seafood soup, gin-ger chicken, paella and grilled fish. There's granola and yogurt for breakfast, and *te de cacao* (a kind of hot chocolate) for dessert.

Beyond San Juan de las Galdonas

From San Juan de las Galdonas, a dirt road (serviced by sporadic transportation) goes for 20km to the village of **San Juan de Unare**. An hour's walk east by a rough road brings you to **Playa Cipara**, one of the longest beaches in the area and an important turtle-laying grounds. From just east of here, the Parque Nacional Península de Paria (p282) stretches 100km along the coast to the eastern tip of the peninsula. A path to the park's nearest village, Santa Isabel, runs from Playa Cipara.

Hacienda Aguasana

Heading inland from Río Caribe to Tun-apuy, Hacienda Aguasana is a further 5km east on the Tunapuy–Bohordal road. This hacienda has a long trail of mineral-rich **aguas termales** (hot springs; ☎ 0414-304-5687; day-use fee US$5; ☺ 8:30am-6pm). There are 17 ponds of various sizes and with water of different tempera-tures scattered around the hacienda's grassy lands and linked by paths. Some ponds are natural, while others have been shaped. There are also bubbling hot-mud pools for you to achieve that instant elephantine look. Bring your bathing suit, though nudity is OK too (towels available).

Other services, such as acupressure and mud massage (half hour US$10), are avail-able. The hacienda also has four simple double rooms to rent for US$45, including breakfast and dinner at the on-site restaurant. Bookings

can be done through Posada La Colina (p273) in Carúpano.

Hato Río de Agua

A further 8km east beyond Hacienda Agua-sana, you'll find the entrance to Hato Río de Agua. This buffalo ranch, which occupies a 1000-hectare chunk of marshland to the south of the Tunapuy–Bohordal road, has 380 water buffalo as well as caimans and abundant bird life. The ranch's usual occupation has been the production of buffalo meat and cheese, but it has also turned to tourism. An attractive **campamento** (☎ 331-3847; d incl breakfast US$50), con-sisting of five conical cabañas and a thatched restaurant, sits 2km off the road. Packages can be booked by Posada La Colina (p273) in Carúpano.

Day visits (without accommodations and meals) are also possible between 7am and 6pm daily; they cost US$2.50 per person. The visit includes a brief look around the ranch, a short trip in a dugout canoe, the chance to sit on top of a water buffalo, a soft drink or fruit juice and a piece of the distinctively tangy buffalo cheese.

Hacienda Vuelta Larga

Heading west from the town of Tunapuy, after about 2.5km a paved side road branches off to the south and goes for 1km to Campamento Hacienda Vuelta Larga. The road runs an-other 7km to the hacienda proper.

Operated by Klaus Müller, **Hacienda Vuelta Larga** (☎ 666-9052; vueltalarga@cantv.net) is a 10-sq-km ecological ranch with water buffalo and about 230 bird species. The **campamento** (d per person incl breakfast & dinner US$49) provides lodging and hearty traditional food. Birding trips are conducted by Klaus' son, Daniel, who is an experienced bird-watcher (per person US$24).

Parque Nacional Turuépano

East of Hacienda Vuelta Larga stretches the wilderness of 726-sq-km Turuépano national park. It's a rarely visited marshland criss-crossed by a maze of natural water channels and populated by a wealth of wildlife, mainly birds and fish. The habitat is similar to that of the Delta del Orinoco, characterized by high temperature and humidity, along with a significant tide that gives rise to a peculiar type of vegetation. The park lacks any real tourist facilities.

To arrive, get to the village of El Pilar in the early morning, then catch a por puesto to Guariquén, where boats leave to explore the wetlands. For more information you can ask Billy of Hacienda Bukare (p278), who knows the area. Posada Las Tres Carabellas (in San Juan de las Galdonas, p279) does multiday tours to the park but can also give advice for independent travel. Hacienda Vuelta Larga (opposite) offers day tours (US$89).

GÜIRIA
☎ 0294 / pop 33,000

This ordinary town marks the easternmost point on Venezuela's coast reachable by road, 275km from Cumaná. It's the largest town on the Península de Paria, an important fishing port and a springboard to Trinidad.

Banco Mercantil (cnr Calles Bolívar & Juncal) and **Banesco** (Calle Bolívar) both have ATMs. For email there's an **internet café** (Calle Valdez; ⏰ 9am-8pm Mon-Fri, 10am-6pm Sat).

Sleeping & Eating
Hotel Miramar (☎ 982-0732; Calle Turipiari; d US$12; 🅿) This primitive little place offers up seven large, dark and decrepit rooms with ancient air-con. Look for the green-trim house with sea mural in front.

Hotel Plaza (☎ 982-0022; Calle Vigirima at Plaza Bolívar 18; d US$12-19; 🅿) Popular with travelers, this cheap hotel has a dark restaurant downstairs but good, somewhat modern rooms upstairs.

La Posada de Chuchú (☎ 511-2234; Calle Bideau 35; d US$24-28; 🅿) Close to the bus stops, this posada has large beige-colored rooms with cable TV, fridge and hot water. Try to get room 101, which sports a balcony facing the street.

Hotel Orly (☎ 982-1830; Av Paría; d US$30; 🅿) Here's the fanciest hotel in town, complete with cheap marble lobby and tacky decor. The modern rooms have cable TV and hot-water bathrooms, and some come with fridge. Look for the white stone lions outside.

Panadería (sandwiches US$1.25; ⏰ 6am-9pm; 🅿) Close to the bus stops, this modern bakery has sandwiches, pastries, breads and juices.

El Caney de la Carne (☎ 0414-784-1776; Calle Pegallos; set meals US$3.75; ⏰ 11am-midnight) On Sunday evenings, this little grill restaurant offers up beer and live music. The food menu runs the

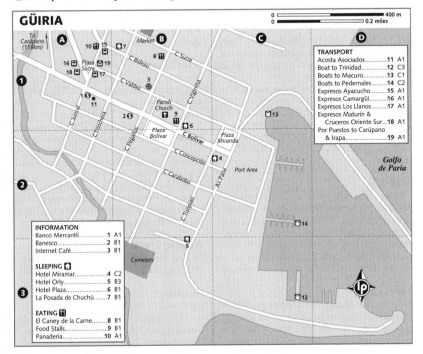

GÜIRIA

0 — 400 m
0 — 0.2 miles

TRANSPORT
Acosta Asociados............11 A1
Boat to Trinidad.............12 C3
Boats to Macuro.............13 C1
Boats to Pedernales........14 C2
Expresos Ayacucho.........15 A1
Expresos Camargüí.........16 A1
Expresos Los Llanos.......17 A1
Expresos Maturín &
  Cruceros Oriente Sur...18 A1
Por Puestos a Carúpano
  & Irapa.....................19 A1

Golfo de Paria

INFORMATION
Banco Mercantil...............1 A1
Banesco...........................2 B1
Internet Café....................3 B1

SLEEPING
Hotel Miramar..................4 C2
Hotel Orly........................5 B3
Hotel Plaza.......................6 B1
La Posada de Chuchú.......7 B1

EATING
El Caney de la Carne........8 B1
Food Stalls......................9 B1
Panadería.......................10 A1

regular gamut of cheap meat, fish and local dishes.

You'll find more eating outlets around the central streets, including cheap and filling food stalls alongside the church (open evenings only).

Getting There & Away
BOAT
Acosta Asociados (☎ 982-1556; grupoacosta@cantv.net; Calle Bolívar 31; ⌚ 9am-noon & 3-5pm Mon-Fri) operates a comfortable, air-conditioned passenger boat between Güiria and Chaguaramas (near Port of Spain, Trinidad). It arrives on Wednesday at around 12:30pm and leaves at around 3:30pm, but is often late. The trip takes three hours and costs US$104 one way (US$187 roundtrip). Be in the office in the early morning to reserve a spot.

Peñeros (fishing boats) leave from the northern end of Güiria's port to Macuro. Irregular fishing and cargo boats (a few per week) go to Pedernales, at the mouth of the Delta del Orinoco. The trip takes four to five hours and the fare is negotiable – usually around US$10 per person. From Pedernales, riverboats go south to Tucupita.

BUS
Several bus companies servicing Güiria have their offices close to each other around the triangular Plaza Sucre, where the Carúpano highway enters the town.

There are six buses a day to Caracas (US$20, 12 hours); they all go via Cumaná (US$10, five hours) and Puerto La Cruz (US$12, 6½ hours). There are buses (US$6, 2½ hours) and por puestos (US$9, two hours) to Carúpano and por puestos run to Irapa (US$2.50, 40 minutes).

MACURO
☎ 0294 / pop 2800
Macuro is a remote fishing village near the eastern tip of the Península de Paria. Its claim to fame is that Columbus reputedly landed somewhere around here in August 1498 – no records state the exact landing site. What is known is that this was the only place on South America's mainland where Columbus came ashore.

Although Macuro is a poor place, it's friendly and has some character. If you decide to come, visit the little history museum and consider a hike to Uquire (see opposite).

There are several very basic posadas, including **Posada Beatriz** (Calle Mariño; d US$14).

Boats from Güiria depart daily except Sunday, somewhere between 11am and noon (US$4.75, 1½ to two hours). Boats depart Macuro for Güiria early in the morning, around 5am. At the time of writing there was a very rough road from Güiria, but the condition of this road is unreliable.

PARQUE NACIONAL PENÍNSULA DE PARIA
This 375-sq-km park stretches for 100km along the northern coast of the peninsula, right up to its eastern tip. It encompasses a coastal mountain range, which looms up almost right from the sea and reaches its maximum elevation point at Cerro Humo (1257m). The coast is graced with many coves, in which tiny fishing villages have nestled.

The mountain is largely covered with forest, and the higher you go, the wetter it is. The upper reaches of the outcrop (roughly above 800m) form a typical cloud-forest habitat that's largely unexplored and intact, with rich and diverse wildlife. The southern foothills are being increasingly cleared by local farmers. An additional threat is the discovery of offshore oil, the exploitation of which may alter this remote bucolic peninsula completely.

Orientation
The park has no tourist facilities and access is not straightforward. The villages on the northern coast are best (or only) accessed by boat, the closest points of departure being Macuro and San Juan de Unare. However, boat trips are irregular and expensive. Access from the south is via the Carúpano–Güiria highway, but there are few gateways here leading into the park.

A few trails cross the park north to south, and these are the best way to get deeper into the wilderness. Ideally you should hire a guide, as the trails are not always easy to follow.

Walking Trails
One of the trails goes between the villages of Manacal and Santa Isabel, in the western end of the park. The rough road to Manacal branches off the Carúpano–Güiria highway 20km east of Yaguaraparo and winds up to the village at 750m. There are few vehicles along this road, so you may need to walk (three hours). There are no hotels in Manacal,

but informal accommodations can usually be arranged. If you have a hammock, you may be allowed to sling it under somebody's roof.

The trail from Manacal winds to the hamlet of Roma and then uphill to the 1000m crest, before descending to Santa Isabel, on the coast. Guides can be found in Manacal, and the hike will take about six hours. Stuck to the hillside high above the bay and dotted with rocky islets, Santa Isabel is a tiny fishing village. It shelters the rustic **Posada de Cucha** (d incl breakfast & dinner US$28), which offers beds and meals and a marvelous view over the rugged coast from its balcony.

There are no roads from the village, but a path goes westward to Boca del Río Cumaná (four hours), then along the shore to Playa Cipara (1½ hours) and onward to San Juan de Unare (one hour). The first part of the trail is faint, so a guide is recommended (available in Santa Isabel). Otherwise, negotiate for a boat to San Juan de Unare, then continue to San Juan de las Galdonas.

On the opposite, eastern end of the park is a path from Macuro to Uquire on the northern coast (four hours). Uquire has a good beach, and you may be able to arrange a room or hammock for the night. You can either walk back or hunt for a boat to return you to Macuro around the peninsula's tip.

If you don't fancy walking, hire a boat in Macuro to take you to Uquire and other nearby places, such as Don Pedro and San Francisco. Tours along the coast are organized from San Juan de las Galdonas (see p279).

MONAGAS STATE

MATURÍN

☎ **0291 / pop 410,000**

Founded in 1760 as a Capuchin mission, the bustling commercial city of Maturín has grown into a regional center for the agroindustrial sector. Large deposits of oil exploited in the region have added to the city's coffers. Maturín is also a busy regional transportation hub, connecting routes from the northeastern coast to the Delta del Orinoco and the Gran Sabana. It's not an overly interesting place and most travelers pass through quickly.

Information

The tourist office **Corporacion Monaguense de Turismo** (Cormotur; ☎ 643-0798; www.monagas.gov

.ve in Spanish; Hacienda Sarrapial, Av Alirio Ugarte Pelayo; ☼ 8am-noon & 2-6pm Mon-Fri) is 5km north of the city center in a colonial-style hacienda dating from 1823. To get there, take the Ruta 4 carrito (por puesto) from the center.

Most major banks and services are on Av Bolívar. Corp Banca is on the traffic circle (near the cathedral) on Av Bolívar at Calle 8. For changing traveler's checks there's the nearby **Italcambio** (☎ 642-2901; No 34, Centro Comercial Porto Fino, Av Bolívar at Carrera 8; ☼ 8am-12:30pm & 2:30-6pm). There are several internet places on Av Bolívar.

Sleeping

Budget hotels around central Plaza Ayacucho are easily accessible from the bus terminal by frequent city buses; get off at the intersection of Avs Juncal and Bolívar, two blocks from the plaza. Taxis to the center cost about US$3.

Hotel Ayacucho Plaza (☎ 641-3080; Plaza Ayacucho; d from US$12; ▨) This hotel is tucked away behind several layers of security bars. It has plain rooms with little *cucarachas* (cockroaches) to keep you company. Cable TV is extra. There's a similar hotel next door.

Hotel Puerto España (☎ 642-2476; Calle Cantaura 11; d from US$14; ▨) Decent budget rooms with cable TV, one block from Plaza Ayacucho. One of the area's better bets.

Hotel La Trinidad (☎ 642-9356; Calle 18 No 6; s/d US$14/22; ▨) Most of the tiled rooms at this hotel have cable TV and hot water, though they can be a bit gloomy. It's located a half block from the plaza and has another similar branch around the corner.

Hotel Monagas Internacional (☎ 651-8811; fax 651-8727; Av Libertador at Orinoco; d US$56; ▣ ▨ ▣) This formerly top-end hotel comes in very handy thanks to its position by the bus station. It's a high-rise affair with spacious, bright rooms; the top floors have good area views.

Stauffer (☎ 643-1111; www.staufferhotel.com.ve; Av Alirio Ugarte Pelayo; d US$185; ▣ ▨ ▤ ▣) On tropical grounds, this hotel has all the comforts of your typical five-star hotel and is located 3km north of town.

Getting There & Away

AIR

The airport is 2km east of the city center; eastbound buses 1 and 5 from Av Bolívar will let you off near the terminal. Local airlines include **Aeropostal** (☎ 643-8470), **Rutaca** (☎ 642-1635), **Conviasa** (☎ 641-1011) and **Ascerca** (☎ 641-2611).

BUS

The bus terminal is on Av Libertador, 2km southwest of the city center. There are plenty of buses to the center – cross Av Libertador to pick one up heading the right way. Taxis cost US$3.

Several buses run to Caracas daily, mostly in the evening (US$18, 8½ hours). Other destinations include Ciudad Guayana (US$8, 3½ hours), Tucupita (US$6, four hours) and Caripe (US$3.75, three hours). These regional routes are also serviced by faster por puestos for nearly double the bus fare.

The most luxurious service to Caracas costs US$18 with **Aeroexpresos Ejecutivos** (☎ 651-9411; Av Libertador), which has a terminal 0.5km from the main bus station.

RÍO MORICHAL LARGO

The lower course of the Río Morichal Largo, southeast of Maturín near the Delta del Orinoco, has beautiful lush vegetation, rich wildlife and Warao settlements. The tourist infrastructure includes a pleasure-boat service down the river. The embarkation point is on the highway to Ciudad Guayana, about 90km southeast of Maturín, where excursion boats wait for tourists.

The boat trips give a taste of the wildlife and the indigenous communities typical of the Delta del Orinoco; they're a shorter alternative to the delta tours out of Tucupita. You can go direct to the embarkation point and negotiate a trip with the boat operators, but be prepared to wait or pay for the empty seats. If you need one, the tourist office in Maturín can help you find a tour organizer.

The village of San José de Buja, 85km southeast of Maturín, is another springboard for a deltalike experience down along the Río Buja.

CARIPE

☎ 0292 / pop 17,500

Nestled in a verdant mountain valley halfway between Maturín and the Caribbean coast, Caripe is a pleasant, easygoing town renowned for its agreeable temperatures, coffee and orange plantations, and its proximity to Cueva del Guácharo, Venezuela's most visited and famous cave.

Caripe's cool climate makes an inviting weekend escape for Venezuelans from the steamy lowlands, and will often fill up during its elaborate Easter celebrations. The village itself is little more than two parallel streets, on which most activities and services are centered.

If you need cash, **Banesco** (Av Guzmán Blanco) has an ATM. For internet and telephone there's a **Movistar** (☽ 7:30am-9:30pm Mon-Sat, 7:30am-2pm Sun) one block up from Hotel Saman.

Sights & Activities

Caripe's number-one attraction is the Cueva del Guácharo (opposite), 12km from the town.

Save for a beautiful colonial high altar in the modern **parish church**, there's not much to see in town, but the rugged surroundings are ripe for **hiking**. If you want to explore and need an escort, try asking the guides at the Cueva del Guácharo, as they're often open to other work. Or drop in at the *ferretería* (hardware store) next to the Hotel Saman; if he's not busy, the effusive Oscar Gregori might have a lead on someone who can help with area tours.

El Mirador (1100m), to the north of the town, commands sweeping views over the Valle de Caripe; taxis here cost US$4. Among the other sights are two beautiful waterfalls: the 30m-high **Salto La Payla**, near the Cueva del Guácharo, and the 80m-high **Salto El Chorrerón**, an hour's walk from the village of Sabana de Piedra. Further away are the **Puertas de Miraflores**, a spectacular river canyon, and the **Mata de Mango**, which features 22 caves, including the impressive Cueva Grande and Cueva Clara.

Sleeping & Eating

Caripe has a few central hotels and there are plenty of upmarket chalets scattered around the surrounding countryside. Prices may rise on weekends.

IN CARIPE

Hotel San Francisco (☎ 414-2656; Av Chaumer; d US$14) Eighteen good, brightly painted rooms with cable TV and fan are available at this humble hotel, located right across from the church.

Hotel La Perla (☎ 0414-763-1130; Av Chaumer; d/tr US$17/19) A decent, basic hotel featuring spacious rooms with minimal furnishings and pretty tile floors. Comes with a restaurant below.

Mini Hotel Nicola (☎ 545-1489; Av Gusmán Blanco; d US$24; P) This intimate family house rents out a few clean, modern rooms with hot-water bathrooms. Look for the small 'hotel' sign and black gate in front.

Hotel Samán (☎ 545-1183; www.hotelsaman.com in Spanish; Av Chaumer No 29; d US$25) This long-running hotel is still the best in town. It has colorful, comfortable rooms (the best ones are upstairs) with firm beds and fans, and a pleasant court-yard packed with plants.

Trattoria da Stefano (☎ 414-6107; Calle Cabello; mains US$5-12; ☯ 11am-6pm Mon-Wed, 11am-10pm Thu-Sun) This pleasant place serves great pasta like ravioli with mushroom sauce and spaghetti with mussels, and has a comfortable dining area. It also features meats and fish on the menu, along with pizzas.

Restaurant Mogambo (☎ 545-1021; Av Chaumer; mains US$5-15; ☯ 7am-10pm; P) Across from Hotel La Perla is this eatery set in a pink chalet-style building. It cooks up basic but tasty grub (in-cluding hamburgers), and offers breakfast too. Closed Tuesdays in low season.

AROUND CARIPE

There are more places to stay outside town, particularly along the road between Caripe and the village of El Guácharo. Some have cabañas good for large groups. Reserve ahead for weekend stays.

Cabañas La Floresta (☎ 414-8878; Sector La Peña; d/tr/q US$28/31/35; P) Down a flowery lane and across a stream lies this peaceful place set on a grassy hillside. The simple cabañas (which sleep up to seven) are fitted with cable TV, well-equipped kitchens and outdoor barbe-cues. It's 2km from town on the road to Ma-turín (taxis US$3).

Pueblo Pequeño Vacation Villas (☎ 545-1843; pueblopequeno1@cantv.net; Sector Amanita off Via Cocollar; d/tr US$42/46; P ☒) Good rooms, some with kitchen and little front patios, are available at this sunny complex in the foothills. Most come with cable TV and fridge and can sleep up to six. There's a restaurant, a children's playground and a swimming pool. Taxis here cost US$3.

Cabañas Bellerman (☎ 414-8968; s/d US$52/62, 6-8 person cabañas US$85; P) On a forested moun-taintop above town is this liquor-producing complex with seven semicute, faux-German cabañas, all simply furnished but boasting kitchens and their own patios. Some have loft bedrooms. Caripe town is a 10-minute taxi ride away (US$5).

El Rincón de Walter (☎ 545-1797; ☯ 8am-9pm) Just outside town, on the road to Maturín, is this small joint dishing out tasty cups of strawberries and cream. It's worth the 20-minute walk from center, and has a restaurant nearby.

Getting There & Away

The bus terminal is at the northeastern end of the town, behind the market. Other than Maturín and Cumaná, there aren't many di-rect bus destinations linking Caripe to the outside world.

Frequent buses run to Maturín (US$4, three hours). Two minivans head to Cumaná at 6am daily (US$8, three hours) but you have to reserve a seat the day before at the Centro de Conexiones near the terminal. Alternatively, you can take a carrito to Santa Monica and connect from there to Cumaná.

CUEVA DEL GUÁCHARO

Venezuela's longest, largest and most mag-nificent cave, the **Guácharo Cave** (admission US$2.50; ☯ 8am-4pm Tue-Sun; P), is 12km from Caripe on the road toward the coast. It was declared Venezuela's first natural monument in 1949,

---

THE GUÁCHARO

The eerie shrieking and flapping that echoes in the high galleries of the Cueva del Guácharo is made by a curious, reddish-brown species of bird that is the only one of its kind in the world. The *guácharo*, or oilbird *(Steatornis caripensis)*, is a nocturnal, fruit-eating bird that inhabits caves in various tropical parts of the Americas, living in total darkness and leaving the cave only at night for food. It has a radar-location system (similar to bats) that enables it to navigate. It has a curved beak and enormous whiskers, and grows to about 60cm long, with a wingspan of a meter.

This colony is by far the biggest in Venezuela. From August to December, the population in this single cave is estimated at 10,000 birds, and occasionally up to 15,000. In the dry season the colony diminishes, but at least 8000 birds remain in March and April. The birds inhabit only the first chamber of the cave, 750m-long Humboldt's Hall. And the name of the first chamber following this area, *El Silencio* (Silence), echoes the relief felt by explorers to leave the birds' unsettling screeches behind.

and a 627-sq-km area around the cave was decreed the Parque Nacional El Guácharo in 1975. Alexander von Humboldt, the eminent scientist, penetrated 472m into the grotto in September 1799, and it was he who first classified its namesake inhabitant, the *guácharo,* or oilbird (see the boxed text p285).

Apart from this unique bird, the cave houses fish, crabs, spiders, ants, centipedes and bats. You'll likely see rodents scampering boldly along the ground. The cave also shelters a maze of stalactites and stalagmites that shine with calcium crystals. And if you finish the full tour, you'll be treated to a peek at the well-rounded rock formations in the Sala de los Senos (Room of the Breasts). If you get one of the cheekier guides, expect more x-rated interpretations of rock formations when the kids aren't listening.

All visits are by guided tours in groups of up to 20 people; tours take one to 1½ hours. A 1200m portion of the total 10.2km length of the cave is normally visited, though occasionally water rises in August and/or September,

limiting sightseeing to half a kilometer. Bring nonslippery shoes for tramping over the mud and *guano* (droppings). The reception building also has a small museum and cafeteria. Large bags must be left by the ticket office. Cameras with flash can be used only beyond the *guácharos* gallery, so as not to blind the birds.

If you enjoyed your tour, leaving your guide a tip is a decent gesture. English-speaking guides are sometimes available.

You can camp at the entrance to the cave after closing time; it costs US$1.50 per tent and the bathroom is open 24 hours. If you do camp, watch the hundreds of birds pouring out of the cave mouth at around 6:30pm and returning at about 4am. You can also take a short trip to the waterfall of Salto La Payla, a 25-minute walk from the cave.

Getting There & Away

A roundtrip taxi from Caripe to the cave costs US$7. Buses linking Cumaná and Caripe pass by the cave and can drop you at the entrance, which is 12km north of Caripe.

Guayana

Saturated by powerful rivers and traversed by few roads, Guayana feels wild and endless. This is Venezuela's natural wonderland, a great green expanse of steamy rainforest, rolling highland savanna and soaring table mountains. It's also home to many of Venezuela's greatest outdoor attractions, including the world's highest waterfall, Angel Falls.

Guayana extends throughout the whole of Venezuela's southeast, encompassing the states of Delta Amacuro, Bolívar and Amazonas. A sparsely populated region, it comprises half of the country's land, but is home to only 6% of Venezuela's population. A majority of the country's indigenous peoples live and thrive here, including the Warao, Pemón, Yekuana and Yanomami, and these groups account for 10% of the region's total population.

A singular brew of waterfalls, rivers and soaring mountains creates spectacular vistas and tantalizes outdoor adventurers. The forest canopy of the Delta del Orinoco teems with exotic birds and monkeys, while the Angel Falls (Salto Ángel) nose-dives into the thick jungle of the Parque Nacional Canaima. The undeveloped reaches of Amazonas shelter pristine wilderness parks and traditional indigenous settlements. Curious tepuis dot the wide open plains of the Gran Sabana, and Roraima's mysterious moonscape invites slow and careful exploration.

And for a look at the country's colorful independence history, Ciudad Bolívar dresses up with postcard-perfect streets.

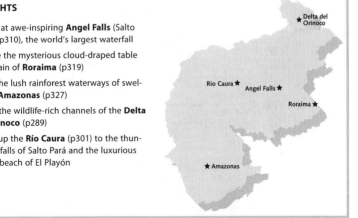

HIGHLIGHTS

- Marvel at awe-inspiring **Angel Falls** (Salto Ángel; p310), the world's largest waterfall
- Explore the mysterious cloud-draped table mountain of **Roraima** (p319)
- Trace the lush rainforest waterways of sweltering **Amazonas** (p327)
- Cruise the wildlife-rich channels of the **Delta del Orinoco** (p289)
- Travel up the **Río Caura** (p301) to the thundering falls of Salto Pará and the luxurious jungle beach of El Playón

★ Delta del Orinoco

Río Caura ★ Angel Falls ★

Roraima ★

★ Amazonas

GUAYANA

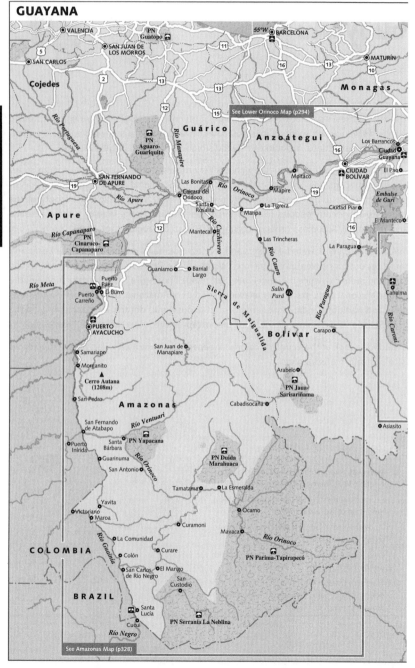

See Lower Orinoco Map (p294)

See Amazonas Map (p328)

DELTA DEL ORINOCO

Roaring howler monkeys welcome the dawn. Piranhas clamp onto anything that bleeds. Screaming clouds of parrots gather at dusk, and weaving bats gobble insects under the blush of a million stars. For wildlife-viewing on the water's edge, it's hard to outshine the Delta del Orinoco.

A deep green labyrinth of islands, channels and mangrove swamps engulfing nearly 30,000 sq km – the size of Belgium – this is one of the world's great river deltas and a mesmerizing region to explore. Mixed forest blankets most of the land, which includes a variety of palms. Of these, the *moriche* palm is the most typical and important, as it is the traditional staple food for the delta's inhabitants, the Warao people, and provides material for their dwellings, crafts, tools, household implements and wine.

The Río Orinoco reaches a width of 20km in its lower course before splitting into about 40 major channels (and perhaps 250 smaller ones), which flow out along 360km of Atlantic coast. The southernmost channel, Río Grande, is the main one and is used by ocean-going vessels sailing upriver to Ciudad Guayana.

The climate of the delta is hot and humid, with an average temperature of around 81°F throughout the year, though nights can be quite cool. Annual rainfall varies from 1500mm to 2500mm, and the closer you get to the coast the more it rains. The driest period is from January to March. The water level is usually at its lowest in March and highest from August to September, when many parts of the delta become marshy or flooded.

The best time to see the wildlife in the delta is in the dry season, when wide, orange, sandy beaches emerge along the shores of the channels. In the rainy months, when rivers are full, boat travel is easier, but the wildlife disperses and is more difficult to see.

Curiously enough, the state that encompasses the delta is not named after the Orinoco; rather it's named after the Amacuro, a small river that runs along part of the Guyana border and empties into the Boca Grande, the Orinoco's main mouth. Tucupita is the state capital and a base for Delta del Orinoco adventures.

GUAYANA

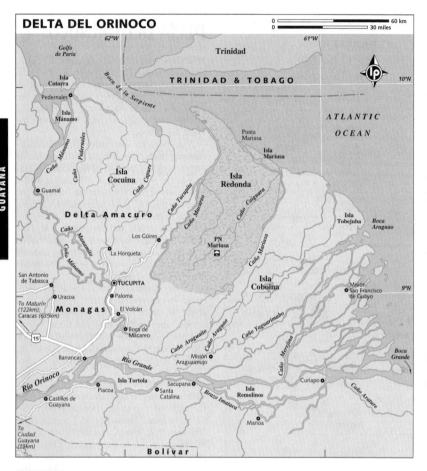

DELTA DEL ORINOCO

TUCUPITA

☎ 0287 / pop 55,000

Visits to Tucupita generally bookend a delta trip, and rarely do travelers come here otherwise. The capital of the Delta Amacuro state is a hot, steamy river port and the only sizable town in the Delta del Orinoco, but there is very little to hold you here. Still, the Plaza Bolívar is wide and shady and there are nice strolls along the Paseo Mánamo riverbank esplanade.

Tucupita sits beside the westernmost channel of the Delta del Orinoco, Caño Mánamo, which flows northward for 110km and empties into the Golfo de Paria near the town of Pedernales. Caño Mánamo has been blocked by a dike 22km south of Tucupita, erected in the 1960s as part of a flood-control program aiming to make land in the northern delta usable for farming. The road that runs atop the dike is Tucupita's only overland link with the rest of the country.

Tucupita evolved in the 1920s as one of a chain of Catholic Capuchin missions founded in the delta to convert the indigenous peoples. The missions established social programs that focused on providing education and health services; they opened up the region for both governmental activities and criollo colonists and, ultimately, for tourism.

Information

EMERGENCY

Emergency Center (☎ 171)

INTERNET ACCESS

Rates average around US$1 per hour.

Biblos (Calle Centurión) Fast connections.

Compucenter.com (Centro Comercial Delta Center, Plaza Bolívar)

Inversiones La Efectiva (Calle Pativilca) Phones as well.

LAUNDRY

Lavandería Génesis (Calle Delta)

MONEY

Banco de Venezuela (Calle Mánamo)

Banesco (Calle Petión)

Mi Casa (Plaza Bolívar)

POST

Ipostel (Calle Pativilca; ⏰ 8am-noon & 1-4:30pm Mon-Fri)

TOURIST INFORMATION

Servicio Autónomo Fondo de Turismo del Estado Amacuro (Av Arismendi; ⏰ 8am-3pm Mon-Fri)

Sights

The oldest building in town is the **Iglesia de San José de Tucupita** (Calle Mánamo), the Capuchin mission church constructed in 1930. It functioned as a parish church until the huge **Catedral de la Divina Pastora** (Av Arismendi) was completed in 1982, after almost 30 years of construction.

Tours

Trips to the delta drive the regional tourism economy, and there are plenty of local tour operators ready to set you up with a journey to match your wallet and comfort level. Tours usually consist of all-inclusive two- to four-day excursions and you can expect to pay between about US$60 and US$100 per person per day, depending on the company, the routes and conditions, and particularly on the number of people in the group. Activities tend to incorporate a jungle walk/slog – made possible with borrowed Wellington boots – a visit to a local Warao community, a trip in a typical wooden canoe and a stab at piranha fishing.

Tucupita doesn't draw a lot of tourists, so it may take a while for local tour agencies to fill a group. If you're pressed for time, book in advance, or you can pay more to go in a smaller group. Some travelers buy delta tours in Ciudad Bolívar, which may not be much more expensive and will save you time and money in the long run. Also consider Sacoroco River

Tours (p305) in Ciudad Guayana, which organizes reasonably priced trips to the southern delta. Some of Ciudad Bolívar's tour agencies use Sacoroco services, but are likely to charge more than you'd pay by booking directly. In any case it may be a good idea to check various options and contact agents before rushing to Tucupita.

Independent guides, known as *piratas*, will approach you on the street to ask if you want to buy a delta tour. Keep in mind that although these offers may be inexpensive, you do not have the same protections as you would from a licensed storefront business, and no recourse if they take the money and run. Check the state of a boat and safety equipment and the level of camp amenities before you hand over any cash.

All of the following tour companies have *campamentos* (camps) that serve as a base for trips around the area. With the exception of Cooperativa Osibu XIV, they all offer tours to the northern part of the delta toward Pedernales.

Aventura Turística Delta (☎ 0416-897-2285; a_t_d_1973@hotmail.com; Calle Centurión) One of the cheaper tours and more popular agencies, with a three-day option for US$60 per person if you have a minimum of five people.

Campamento Mis Palafitos (☎ 721-1733; www.deltaorinocomispalafitos.com; Centro Comercial Delta Center, Plaza Bolívar) One of the more expensive companies, it has boats leaving almost daily for its comfortable camp with 56 thatch-roofed cabins and private bathrooms. It accommodates a number of visitors that arrive via charter planes from Margarita.

Cooperativa Osibu XIV (☎ 721-3840; cnr Calles Mariño & Pativilca) The oldest local tour company in town, this family-owned business conduct tours to the far eastern part of the delta. It's a five-hour boat ride to their 10-cabaña camp with beds and bathrooms.

Tucupita Expeditions (☎ 721-0801; www.orinocodelta.com; Calle Las Acacias) Another more expensive agency, it runs the upscale Orinoco Delta Lodge, with 37 cabins and an attractive main lodge by the riverside. It primarily works with groups and also supports an indigenous school in the delta.

Sleeping

Pequeño Hotel (☎ 721-0523; Calle La Paz; s/d with fan US$6/9, d with air-con US$12; 🅿) With a quiet series of family-friendly rooms, it was in the midst of a new paint job at the time of research. The señora has been running this inexpensive hotel for over 40 years, and she doesn't put up with loud drunks or guests coming in past her 9:30pm bedtime.

Residencias San Cristóbal (☎ 721-4529; Calle San Cristóbal; d with fan US$14, d with air-con US$16-19, tr with air-con US$21; P ⊠) A signless 37-room establishment with small and slightly dingy split-color rooms, San Cristóbal is one of the cheapest places in town. The rooms upstairs are brighter.

Hotel Amacuro (☎ 721-0404; Calle Bolívar; d/tr with fan US$19/26, d with air-con US$23-30, tr with air-con US$37; ⊠) A pleasant option with sunny, good-sized rooms – a few dazzle with shiny turquoise walls – just off Plaza Bolívar. The front door isn't always well guarded.

Hotel Residencial (☎ 721-6128; Calle Pativilca; d US$23-33; ⊠) The many mirrored surfaces make no secret of its 'love hotel' identity, but rooms are cheerful and clean, and there are fridges, bedside lamps and fluffy towels. Rooms on the upper floor have the best light.

Hotel Saxxi (☎ 721-2112; Zona Paloma; d US$28-37, tr US$42; P ⊠ ⊠) Set back from the river and blessed by cool breezes, this large complex south of town has a restaurant, a bar and comfortable rooms with hot water. Although this is as upscale as it gets in these parts, the pool is murky and the disco on weekend nights can be loud. Catch a bus from the Mini Terminal, or take a taxi (US$3).

Eating

In the evening, food stalls open along Paseo Mánamo, turning it into a lively spot where locals gather to meet friends, eat, drink and have fun.

El Tasco (☎ 721-7017; Calle Dalla Costa; pastries US$2; ◷ 6am-7pm) Elbow your way to the frantic counter at this popular *panadería* (bakery), a central place to grab a breakfast of espresso coffee and flaky *pastelitos* (little pastries) or *enrollados* (rolls filled with meat or cheese). It has no tables, so duck across the street and people-watch in the plaza.

Restaurant Cen China Tonw (☎ 721-5077; Calle Petión; mains US$3-6; ◷ 11am-10pm) The wall texture resembles a sandbagged bunker, but the portions of Chinese food are heaping and inexpensive.

Mi Tasca (☎ 721-0428; Calle Dalla Costa; mains US$4-10; ◷ 11am-10:30pm) Ask anybody where to go for a lunch or dinner, and most locals will point

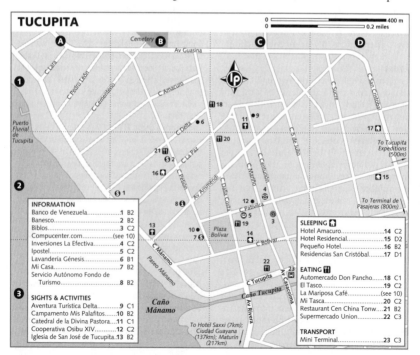

TUCUPITA

0 ___ 400 m
0 ___ 0.2 miles

THE CANOE PEOPLE OF DELTA DEL ORINOCO

The Delta del Orinoco is inhabited by the Warao (or Guarao) peoples, who have lived here from time immemorial. Today numbering about 25,000, they are Venezuela's largest indigenous group after the Guajiro of Zulia. Two-thirds of the Waraos live in the eastern part of the delta, between the Caño Mariusa and the Río Grande, where they are distributed across about 250 tiny communities.

The Waraos dwell along the small channels, constructing their open-sided, wooden huts on stilts on riverbanks and living mostly off fishing. Water is pivotal in their lives, as indicated by the tribe's name; in the local language *wa* means 'canoe' and *arao* means 'people.' They are excellent boat builders, making their dugout canoes from logs of large trees, using fire and simple axes.

Only half the Waraos speak Spanish. Most of the indigenous community still use their native language, officially classified as 'independent' because it doesn't belong to any of the major linguistic families. Linguists have not yet determined the origins of the language.

The Waraos are skillful craftspeople, renowned for their basketry and woodcarvings, especially animal figures carved from balsa wood. Their *chinchorros* (hammocks), made from the fiber of the *moriche* palm, are widely known and sought after for their quality and durability, and are sold at markets and craft shops across the country.

---

you to Mi Tasca. One of Tucupita's best eateries, with a varied menu, good prices, generous portions and quick service. Try the *lau lau* (catfish) – it's delicious.

ourpick La Mariposa Café (☎ 721-3810; Centro Comercial Delta Center; mains US$6-10; ⏰ 7am-10:30pm Mon-Sat, 7am-9pm Sun) A new and welcoming culinary oasis, its *comidas internacionales* include a variety of cuisines, from stroganoff to steak tartar, Greek salad to pollo 'Gordon Blue.' It also serves vegetarian pastas and soups and makes fresh juices to order.

To stock up on food for a delta trip:
Automercado Don Pancho (☎ 721-1612; Calle Dalla Costa; ⏰ 8am-12:30pm & 3-7:30pm Mon-Sat, 8am-noon Sun)
Supermercado Unión (☎ 721-1861; Calle Tucupita; ⏰ 8am-6:30pm)

Getting There & Away
Tucupita has a small airport served by charter flights only.

The **Terminal de Pasajeros** (cnr Carrera 6 & Calle 10) is 1km southeast of the center; walk or take a taxi (US$1). The **Mini Terminal** (Calle Tucupita) runs frequent local and suburban buses.

About half a dozen buses go to Caracas (US$16 to US$19, 11 hours, 730km) via Maturín, mostly in the evening. Some continue on to Maracay (US$19 to US$20) and Valencia (US$21 to US$22).

Expresos La Guayanesa has two daily buses to Puerto La Cruz (US$8) and to Ciudad Guayana (US$5, 3½ hours, 137km). Por puestos to Ciudad Guayana (US$9, 2½ hours)

are faster and easy to arrange. For Caripe and Cueva del Guácharo, take a bus to Maturín (US$4 to US$7, four hours, 217km), or a por puesto (US$8, three hours), and change.

LOWER ORINOCO

The industrial engine of the Guayana region, the Lower Orinoco comprises the region's main population and commercial centers. Massive hydroelectric projects such as the Represa de Guri take advantage of powerful rivers, generating a huge part of the country's electricity.

Ciudad Bolívar and Ciudad Guayana are the major cities, and together they account for almost 90% of the population of Bolívar, the country's largest state. Both cities sit on the south bank of the Río Orinoco, and each now has its own bridge. Ciudad Bolívar is a charming colonial city with well-preserved architecture, while Ciudad Guayana is a more modern urban sprawl. Located in the middle of the area's limited road network, they are busy transit hubs for jumping off to the rest of the region.

Other regional highlights include the fantastical Carnaval celebration of El Callao, and the low-key beaches of the Río Caura.

CIUDAD BOLÍVAR
☎ 0285 / pop 350,000
Decked out in a haughty splash of rainbow colors, Ciudad Bolívar knows it looks good. With a meticulously restored historical district

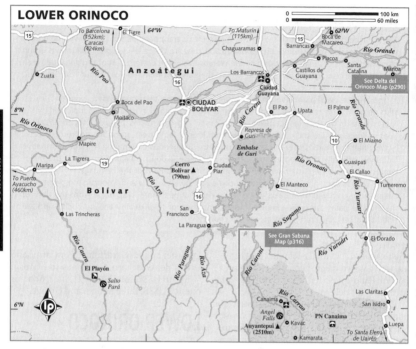

of colonial houses primped in candy colors, the city takes obvious and deserved pride in its appearance.

Most travelers venture to the city on the way to Angel Falls (Salto Ángel) and are smitten by the gorgeous architecture of the hilly historic center and its dazzling Río Orinoco views. This is just one section of the city, but the one that never fails to enthrall. Besides these notable buildings, this landmark city of Venezuelan independence has interesting parks and museums, as well as excellent infrastructure for visitors.

History

Founded in 1764 on a rocky elevation at the river's narrowest point, the town was named Santo Tomás de la Guayana de Angostura – *angostura* means 'narrows.' It grew as a lonely beacon on a great river, hundreds of miles away from any major cities, and within 50 years was already a thriving port and trade center. Then, suddenly and unexpectedly, Angostura became the spot where much of the country's (and the continent's) history was forged.

Libertador Simón Bolívar came here in 1817, soon after the town had been liberated from Spanish control, and set up the base for the military operations that led to the final stage of the War of Independence. The town was made the provisional capital of the yet-to-be-liberated country. It was in Angostura that the British Legionnaires joined Bolívar before they all set off for the battle of Boyacá in the Andes, which secured the independence of Colombia. The Angostura Congress convened here in 1819 and gave birth to Gran Colombia, a unified republic comprising Venezuela, Colombia and Ecuador. The town was renamed 'Ciudad Bolívar' in 1846, in honor of the hero of the independence struggle. Today it's the capital of Bolívar state, Venezuela's largest, occupying over a quarter of the country's territory.

Orientation

Located on the Río Orinoco approximately 420km upstream from the Atlantic, the city's northern boundary is the mighty Orinoco itself. The wide Paseo Orinoco boulevard lines the riverbank, buzzing with shopping centers.

To the south the spiffed-up historic quarter spreads over a gentle hillside, with houses coated in a vibrant painter's palette. Modern suburbs surround the historic center, with the bus terminal to the southwest and the airport at the southern end of Av Táchira.

There are a number of excellent accommodations in the historic center, but unfortunately the neighborhood closes up in the early evening. It becomes a very attractive colonial ghost town: few restaurants are open, foot and car traffic peters out and some streets are not well lit.

Information
EMERGENCY
Emergency Center (☎ 171)

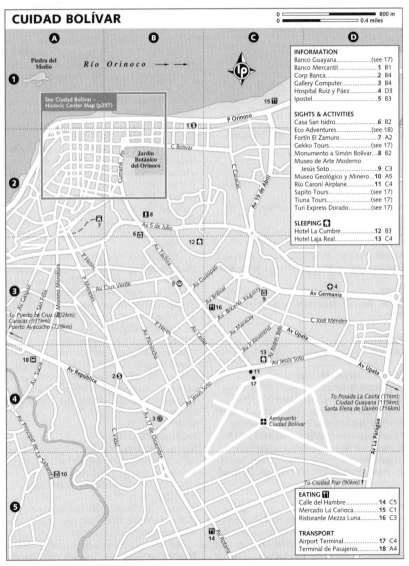

CUIDAD BOLÍVAR

0   800 m
0   0.4 miles

Piedra del Medio

Río Orinoco →

See Ciudad Bolívar – Historic Center Map (p297)

Jardín Botánico del Orinoco

P Orinoco

C Bolívar

Cumaná

C Caracas

Av 19 de Abril

Av 5 de Julio

Av Táchira

P Heres

P Mentes

Av Cruz Verde

Moreno Mendoza

San Felix

Av Gaspar

To Puerto La Cruz (502km);
Caracas (591km);
Puerto Ayacucho (728km)

Av Guasipati

Av Bolívar

Av Briceño Yragorri

Av Germania

C José Méndez

Av Maracay

P Heres

Av Cedeño

Av P Reverend

Av Andrés Bello

Av Upata

Av Jesús Soto

Av Sucre

Av República

Av Jesús Soto

C Vidal

AV 17 de Diciembre

Aeropuerto Ciudad Bolívar

To Posada La Casita (11km);
Ciudad Guayana (115km);
Santa Elena de Uairén (716km)

Av Upata

Av La Paragua

To Ciudad Piar (90km) ↑

Av Pichincha

Av Principal de la sabana

Av Rotaria

INFORMATION
Banco Guayana...................(see 17)
Banco Mercantil.....................**1** B1
Corp Banca.............................**2** B4
Gallery Computer....................**3** B4
Hospital Ruiz y Páez................**4** D3
Ipostel....................................**5** B3

SIGHTS & ACTIVITIES
Casa San Isidro.......................**6** B2
Eco Adventures..................(see 18)
Fortín El Zamuro....................**7** A2
Gekko Tours.......................(see 17)
Monumento a Simón Bolívar...**8** B2
Museo de Arte Moderno
    Jesús Soto..........................**9** C3
Museo Geológico y Minero...**10** A5
Río Caroní Airplane...............**11** C4
Sapito Tours.......................(see 17)
Tiuna Tours........................(see 17)
Turi Express Dorado............(see 17)

SLEEPING 🏠
Hotel La Cumbre...................**12** B3
Hotel Laja Real.....................**13** C4

EATING 🍴
Calle del Hambre..................**14** C5
Mercado La Carioca.............**15** C1
Ristorante Mezza Luna.........**16** C3

TRANSPORT
Airport Terminal....................**17** C4
Terminal de Pasajeros............**18** A4

GUAYANA

INTERNET ACCESS
Internet connections are generally fast and cheap (US$0.80 to US$1 per hour).
Chat Café Boulevard (Map p297; cnr Calles Bolívar & Igualdad)
Ciber Play (Map p297; Paseo Orinoco btwn Calles Igualdad & Libertad)
Galaxia.com (Map p297; Centro Comercial Abboud Center, Paseo Orinoco btwn Calles Piar & Roscio) Slow connection but convenient location.
Gallery Computer (Map p295; cnr Avs República & Jesús Soto; ☼ 24hr)
V@l Web (Map p297; Calle Venezuela)

LAUNDRY
Lavandería Woo Lee & Co (Map p297; ☎ 632-3014; Calle Zea btwn Calles Piar & Roscio)

MEDICAL SERVICES
Hospital Ruiz y Páez (Map p295; ☎ 632-4146; Av Germania)

MONEY
Banco de Venezuela (Map p297; cnr Paseo Orinoco & Calle Piar)
Banco Guayana (Map p295; airport terminal, Av Jesús Soto)
Banco Mercantil (Map p295; cnr Paseo Orinoco & Calle Zaraza)
Banesco (Map p297; cnr Calles Dalla Costa & Venezuela)
Corp Banca (Map p295; cnr Paseo Meneses & Calle Vidal)

POST
Ipostel (Map p295; Av Táchira btwn Avs Cruz Verde & Guasipati)

TELEPHONE
CANTV (Map p297; cnr Paseo Orinoco & Calle Dalla Costa)

TOURIST INFORMATION
Corporación de Turismo (Map p297; ☎ 0800-265-4837; www.turismobolivar.gob.ve; Paseo Orinoco btwn Calles Constitución & Igualdad; ☼ 8am-noon & 2-5:30pm Mon-Fri) In addition to the office on the Paseo Orinoco, the very helpful Bolívar state tourism office runs a toll-free information line (8am to 8pm Monday to Saturday), with operators who speak English, German and Italian. The easy-to-navigate website has loads of useful information as well.

Sights
PASEO ORINOCO
A pulsing waterfront boulevard shaded by arcaded houses, the Paseo Orinoco is the border between the Colonial Quarter and the broad shore of the Río Orinoco. During the day boisterous street vendors pack the sidewalks hawking an A to Z of household goods and tasty nibbles. Before dusk residents take their evening *paseo* (promenade) along the side closest to the river; the sunset views are fantastic.

In the middle of the Paseo is the **Mirador Angostura viewpoint** (Map p297), a rocky headland that protrudes into the narrowest point of the river. In the month of August the river level peaks and the water laps just below your feet. In March, by contrast, the water level can be as much as 15m lower. Just west is the **Piedra del Medio islet** (Map p295), and you can easily see the graceful span of the **Puente de Angostura** 5km upstream. As the only bridge across the entire 2140km length of the Orinoco for almost 30 years, it was a source of local pride. However, a second bridge opened at Ciudad Guayana in late 2006.

Across the street from the lookout is the **Antigua Cárcel** (Map p297; cnr Calle Igualdad & Paseo Orinoco; admission free; ☼ 9am-5pm Tue-Sun), a restored 18th-century prison building that functioned as a jail until 1952 and now contains the Bolívar state culture offices. There's a gallery space for revolving art shows, though unfortunately the exhibits aren't related to the building's history.

Three blocks west on the Paseo, another example of impressive colonial architecture is the Casa del Correo del Orinoco, which houses the **Museo de Ciudad Bolívar** (Map p297; ☎ 632-4121; Paseo Orinoco; admission US$1.50; ☼ 9am-noon & 2-5pm Mon-Fri), a hodgepodge of modern art and historic objects. The most interesting artifact is the original printing press of the *Correo del Orinoco,* the new republic's first newspaper, published from 1818 to 1821. Fascinating old city maps decorate the walls around it. Also of interest is a pre-Colombian petroglyph unearthed near the Represa de Guri.

HISTORIC CENTER
The Casco Historico (Historic Center), or colonial quarter, is where you want to roam around. A compact and hilly section of the city, it has grand old homes splashed in bright, beautiful colors. Most of the tourism infrastructure is situated here but, frustratingly, all commerce halts at dusk and at night the streets become quite deserted.

The district's center is the slightly recessed **Plaza Bolívar** (Map p297), which contains the requisite statue of El Libertador as well as five allegorical statues personifying the five countries Bolívar liberated. On the east side of the plaza rises the enormous **catedral** (Map p297), begun right after the town's founding and completed 80 years later.

The brash pink **Casa del Congreso de Angostura** (Map p297; admission free; 9am-5pm Tue-Sun) dominates the western side of the plaza. Built in the 1770s, in 1819 it was home to lengthy debates by the Angostura Congress. You can still sense the air of those days while strolling about the formal rooms, wide corridors and elegant courtyards.

On the northern side of the plaza is the **Casa Piar** (Map p297; admission free; 9am-5pm Tue-Sun), where General Manuel Piar was kept prisoner in October 1817 before being positioned against the cathedral wall and executed by firing squad. Piar liberated the city from Spanish control, but rejected Bolívar's authority and was sentenced to death in a controversial and much criticized trial. The plaque on the cathedral's wall marks the spot where he was shot dead, while Bolívar watched the execution from the Casa del Congreso de Angostura.

The 18th-century **Casa de los Gobernadores** and **Casa Parroquial** (both Map p297), next to each other on the upper side of Plaza Bolívar, are other fine historic buildings, but are not open to the public. The presence of all the state politicos contributes to the high number of security personnel and sedan cars in the immediate vicinity.

One block south is the **Alcaldía de Heres** (Map p297; cnr Calles Igualdad & Concordia), a pair of fine old buildings on both sides of the street, connected by the graceful arch of an aerial walkway.

Don't miss visiting **Parque El Zanjón** (Map p297), an unusual city park strewn with massive *lajas* (boulders). The red-tile-roofed **Casa de Tejas** (Map p297), a former 19th-century home constructed on one of the boulders, now holds a small art gallery.

On the southern edge of the colonial sector is the delightfully tree-shaded **Plaza Miranda** (Map p297). Positioned at the halfway point between the cathedral and the cemetery, it was once known as the Plaza Descanso (rest), because funeral pallbearers would stop to break here along the way to burials. A sizable build-

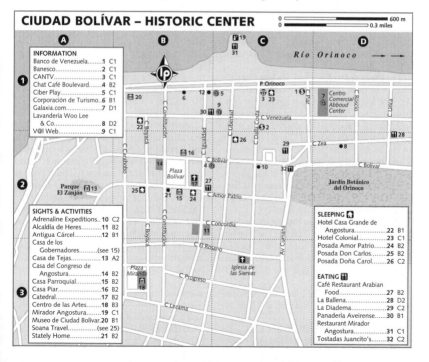

ing on its eastern side was constructed in 1870 as a hospital, but it never served that purpose. It has had a bizarre list of tenants instead, having been used as a prefecture, theatre, army barracks and police station. Eventually, after extensive refurbishing, it opened in 1992 as the **Centro de las Artes** (Map p297; ☎ 632-9735, 0414-895-9717; admission free; ☒ 9am-5pm Tue-Sun) and stages temporary exhibitions of modern art.

OUTSIDE THE HISTORIC CENTER

The **Fortín El Zamuro** (Map p295; admission free; ☒ 9am-5pm Tue-Sun) is a small fort built in the late 18th century atop the highest hill in the city, just south of the colonial quarter. It provides fine views over the old town. The entrance is from Paseo Heres.

The **Casa San Isidro** (Map p295; Av Táchira; admission free; ☒ 9am-5pm Tue-Sun) is a lovely colonial mansion set in a coffee hacienda that once reached all the way to the airport. Bolívar stayed here for a few months, during which he reputedly composed his vehement speeches for the Angostura Congress. The house's interior is maintained in the style of Bolívar's era.

Kitty-corner from San Isidro is the gigantic **Monumento a Simón Bolívar** (Map p295; cnr Avs Cumaná & 5 de Julio). Erected in 1999, this 10m-high bronze statue is by far the tallest monument to the hero ever built in Venezuela. The message comes through loud and clear: don't mess with El Libertador.

The **Museo de Arte Moderno Jesús Soto** (Map p295; ☎ 632-0518; cnr Avs Germania & Briceño Iragorry; admission free; ☒ 9:30am-5:30pm Tue-Fri, 10am-5pm Sat & Sun) contains an extensive collection of work by Jesús Soto, an internationally renowned contemporary artist who was born in Ciudad Bolívar in 1923 and died in 2005. The English-language tours are particularly good, and you can actually go inside some of the kinetic sculptures. On Saturday the museum screens two **films** (child/adult US$1/2), one for children and one for adults; it holds concerts on Sundays.

Don't miss the **Río Caroní airplane** (Av Jesús Soto), conveniently parked in front of the airport. An adventurous American pilot, Jimmie Angel, crash-landed this small plane on top of Auyantepui in 1937 (see the boxed text, p310) as he sought to prove the existence of an enormous waterfall. The plane was removed from the tepui in 1970, restored in Maracay, and brought here.

In the southwestern suburb of La Sabanita the **Museo Geológico y Minero** (Map p295; ☎ 651-4665; Universidad de Oriente, Av Principal de la Sabanita; admission free; ☒ 8am-noon & 2-5pm Mon-Fri) gets to the heart of the region's wealth with exhibitions on Guayana's mines, mining techniques and machinery.

Tours

ANGEL FALLS (SALTO ÁNGEL)

Ciudad Bolívar is the main gateway to Angel Falls, and tours to the falls are the staple of virtually all the tour operators in the city. One of the most popular tours, offered mainly in the dry season, is a one-day package that includes a roundtrip flight to Canaima, a flight over Angel Falls, lunch, a short boat excursion in Canaima and a walk to other nearby falls. Tours depart from Ciudad Bolívar between 7am and 8am and return between 4pm and 5pm, costing about US$280 to US$325 per person.

Another popular offering is a three-day package that includes a boat trip to the foot of Angel Falls instead of a flight over it (US$280 to US$370). These trips are normally run in the rainy season only, but depending on weather patterns they can sometimes operate longer. Trips generally wind down between January and April.

Some agents offer tours to Angel Falls via La Paragua, a small town midway to Canaima, accessible by road from Ciudad Bolívar. Instead of flying all the way from Ciudad Bolívar to Canaima (70 minutes), tourists are driven to La Paragua, from where they take a 25-minute flight to Canaima. This cuts down the flight's cost and ultimately the tour price by up to US$50.

Most agents will offer a variety of other tours that include Angel Falls (eg Angel Falls and Kavac), and may tailor tours to suit your particular requirements. For example, if you don't want to come back to Ciudad Bolívar but would rather continue to Santa Elena de Uairén, the tour operators can replace the Canaima–Ciudad Bolívar return portion with the Canaima–Santa Elena ticket, charging the difference in airfares.

Tour companies use the services of small local airlines, all of which are based at Aeropuerto Ciudad Bolívar. The planes are generally five-seater Cessnas with a luggage allowance limit of 10kg. These airlines can fly you to Canaima (US$70 to US$90 one-way), and can include a pass over Angel Falls for another US$70. You can buy tickets directly from the airlines or from tour operators.

OTHER TOURS

All the tour companies offer a range of other tours. Trips to the Gran Sabana are possibly the most popular – though they will cost less if bought in Santa Elena de Uairén. These tours are usually offered as four-day jeep trips for about US$280 to US$370 all-inclusive.

Another tour appearing on the itinerary of various operators is Río Caura, normally scheduled as a five-day trip costing US$280 to US$395. Also popular is the trek to the top of Roraima, which costs roughly US$256 to US$465 for a six- to seven-day tour. It's cheaper to go by bus to Santa Elena de Uairén and buy this tour there. Some agencies also sell Delta del Orinoco tours (US$60 to US$100 per day for three- to four-day tours). These prices are estimates: rates fluctuate widely based on group size and the amenities and lodging type provided.

TOUR COMPANIES

A tourism hub, Ciudad Bolívar has a huge number of operators, and many of them work together. Shop around before booking a tour, as prices and the inclusion of items like transfers can vary. Most tour offices are in the airport terminal or the historic quarter. Cash, either in *bolívares* or US dollars, provides the best tour rates, and a few operators have European bank accounts that let you pay by credit card without a surcharge.

Recommended operators:

Adrenaline Expeditions (Map p297; ☎ 632-4804, 0414-886-7209; adrenalinexptours@hotmail.com; cnr Calles Bolívar & Dalla Costa) A helpful agency that offers one of the cheapest tour packages to Angel Falls, via La Paragua. Ricardo, a free spirit in a 4WD, leads the endorphin-pumping journeys of the Gran Sabana, leaving no waterfall unseen and no swimming spot unswum.

Eco Adventures (Map p295; ☎ 651-9546, 0414-893-1318; ecoadventurebess@hotmail.com; bus terminal, cnr Avs República & Sucre) Friendly agency hidden in a passageway at the bus terminal.

Gekko Tours (Map p295; ☎ 632-3223, 0414-854-5146; www.gekkotours-venezuela.de; airport terminal, Av Jesús Soto) Run by the seemingly untiring Pieter Rothfuss of Posada La Casita, Gekko offers a wide range of good-quality tours. It also has its own planes.

Sapito Tours (Map p295; ☎ 0414-854-8234, 0414-854-8562; www.sapitotours.com; airport terminal, Av Jesús Soto) Representative of Bernal Tours from Canaima.

Soana Travel (Map p297; ☎ 632-6017, 0414-854-6616; soanatravel@gmx.de; Posada Don Carlos, cnr Calles Boyacá & Amor Patrio) Based at the posada and run by its German owner, Martin Haars, Soana specializes in Río Caura tours.

Tiuna Tours (Map p295; ☎ 632-8697, 0414-893-3003; tiunatours@hotmail.com; airport terminal, Av Jesús Soto) Ciudad Bolívar's office of the major Canaima operator.

Turi Express Dorado (Map p295; ☎ 632-7086, 0414-893-9576; www.turiexpressdorado.com; airport terminal, Av Jesús Soto) A reliable company offering both local and regional trips at good prices.

Festivals & Events

August is prime time for celebrations here, and the city's largest yearly party, the **Feria del Orinoco**, takes place late in the month to coincide with the river's peak *sapoara* (or *zapoara*) season. Brace yourself for *sapoara* fishing competitions, tons of delicious *sapoara* on the local menus, aquatic sports, an agriculture fair, and a range of cultural and other popular events. This is also the time to watch fishermen cast their *atarrayas* (circular fishing nets). On August 5 the city honors its patron saint in the **Fiesta de Nuestra Señora de las Nieves** – though it's doubtful the city has ever experienced snow.

Sleeping

Posada Amor Patrio (Map p297; ☎ 632-4485, 0414-854-4925; plazabolivar@hotmail.com; Calle Amor Patrio; d/tr US$16/21) A popular backpacker's haunt in a 265-year-old colonial building, this centrally located posada has five playfully themed rooms with shared bathrooms. Guests can lounge in the airy Salon de Ritmo, a homage to Cuban jazz, cook in the kitchen, quaff cold beer from the honor bar or book a tour. Hammocks (US$6) are also available on the rooftop terrace.

our pick **Posada Don Carlos** (Map p297; ☎ 632-6017, 0414-854-6616; www.hosteltrail.com/posadadoncarlos; Calle Boyacá; d with fan US$16-21, d/q with air-con US$28/37; P 🔀 🖳) An atmospheric colonial mansion surrounding a lush garden courtyard. Rooms have soaring ceilings, sections of exposed adobe and enormous wooden doors, and the common spaces have gorgeous old-world furniture, including an antique bar. If the visuals weren't enough, it also has free high-speed internet, meals upon request, a kitchen, and drinks to peruse in the honor bar. Swing to sleep in a hammock (US$7) if the rooms are booked full.

Posada Doña Carol (Map p297; ☎ 511-6171, 0416-129-8186; www.hosteltrail.com/posadadonacarol; Calle Libertad; d with fan US$19, d/tr/q with air-con US$23/28/33; 🔀) A

GUAYANA

homey new posada with five clean rooms and kitchen access. A few rooms have no exterior windows, but upstairs rooms have breezy terraces.

Posada La Casita (☎ 623-3223, 0414-854-5146; www .gekkotours-venezuela.de; Urbanización 24 de Julio; s/d/tr/ q with fan US$19/23/30/35, with air-con US$25/29/36/41; P ✖ 🖳 🕭) A rural retreat 11km east of the city center, La Casita is a gorgeous green estate with a variety of sleeping options, good meals upon request and a dreamy sky-blue pool. Keep your eyes peeled for the monkeys, birds and turtles roaming the property. The owner, who also operates Gekko Tours, provides a free 24-hour pickup service when you arrive, and runs scheduled transfers to and from the city. If you're trying to stay on budget, you can pitch a tent for US$4 per person, or stay in a hammock for US$8.

Hotel Colonial (Map p297; ☎ 632-4402; Paseo Orinoco; d/tr/q US$21/26/30; ✖) This large hotel has seen better days, but the faded corridors lead to clean, good-sized rooms with high ceilings and TVs. Ask for an upper-floor room facing the Orinoco.

Hotel Laja Real (Map p295; ☎ 617-0100; www.lajareal .com; cnr Avs Andrés Bello & Jesús Soto; s/d/tr US$40/44/53; P ✖ 🕭) One of the most upscale hotels in town and conveniently situated just across the street from the airport, the Laja Real has 73 modern, minimalist rooms with fridges and hot water. An incredibly kid-friendly setup, it has a small companion pool and a mini-playground. Nonguests can splash in the full-sized outdoor pool for US$5.

Hotel La Cumbre (Map p295; ☎ 632-7709, 0414-385-1330; lacumbre@cantv.net; Av 5 de Julio; d/q/ste US$53/92/153; P ✖ 🖳 🕭) A panoramic oasis within the city limits, this spacious hotel sits on its own hill. Each of the 24 beautiful green- and blue-hued rooms have dynamite river views, hot water and private hammocks. Multiple terraces encircle an open swimming pool, and there's a restaurant with Pemón specialties and a sushi bar to boot.

Hotel Casa Grande de Angostura (Map p297; ☎ 632-4639; angostura@cacaotravel.com; cnr Calles Venezuela & Boyacá; s/d/tr/ste incl breakfast US$90/105/127/150; ✖ 🕭) The newest colonial-era posada in town is a sumptuous boutique hotel. Pop up to the rooftop terrace for a dip in the pool, or just soak up a spectacular sunset. A bubbling fountain graces an airy sky-lighted courtyard, and the rooms are tall, modern and oh so very peaceful.

Eating

Panadería Aveirense (Map p297; ☎ 622-3032; cnr Calles Venezuela & Igualdad; empanadas US$0.70; ✖ 7am-1pm & 3-8pm Mon-Sat) A typical bakery counter with good eye-prying coffee and the standard assortment of empanadas and pastries.

Café Restaurant Arabian Food (Map p297; ☎ 632-7208; cnr Calles Amor Patrio & Igualdad; mains US$2-5; ✖ 7am 8:30pm) Vegetarians take heart, you have not been forsaken. This small family-run café ramps up at noon with hearty lentil soup chock-full of greens and filling falafels, while omnivores can chow down on shawarma and kebabs.

Tostadas Juancito's (Map p297; ☎ 632-6173; cnr Av Cumaná & Calle Bolívar; set meal US$3-6, arepas US$2-3; ✖ 7am-6pm Mon-Sat, 7am-1pm Sun) A bright yellow wedge of an *arepera*, with outdoor seating on a busy bend across from the botanical garden. Relax with a newspaper and munch on *arepas* with a choice of over two dozen different fillings.

Restaurant Mirador Angostura (Map p297; ☎ 511-4843; Paseo Orinoco; mains US$3-5; ✖ 7am-7pm) A traditional *churuata* (palm-thatched hut) nestled right next to the Orinoco, with live criollo and *folklórico* music on the weekends and some of the cheapest meals (and beer) in town. The open circular structure looks like it should house a merry-go-round.

La Ballena (Map p297; ☎ 632-0231; cnr Calles Urica & Zea; mains US$4-9; ✖ 11am-10pm) La Bellena is a somewhat dim and slightly seedy bar, with a restaurant serving seafood and steaks at decent prices.

Ristorante Mezza Luna (Map p295; ☎ 632-0524; cnr Avs Táchira & Bolívar; pasta & pizza US$7-8, mains US$10-19) Fancy yet filling Italian meals served indoors or out. Polish off your pasta on the veranda or in a constellation of dining rooms set around a relaxing Spanish-tiled courtyard.

If you want a raft of options, try the **Mercado La Carioca** (Map p295; Paseo Orinoco; mains US$5-7; ✖ lunch), known as 'La Sapoara,' a riverside market with a few rustic eateries serving reasonably priced meals. And when the historic center shuts tight for the evening, grab a taxi to the **Calle del Hambre** (Estacionamiento del Estadio Heres, Av Rotaria; ✖ dinner), a block-long carnival of bright lights and a few dozen fast-food stalls that buzzes and sizzles until the wee hours of the morning.

La Diadema (Map p297; Calle Zea; ✖ 8:30am-6:30pm Mon-Sat, 8am-noon Sun) is a handy supermarket for self-catering; lots of natural granolas.

Shopping

Ciudad Bolívar is an important center for the gold trade, and it may be worth checking local jewelers if you plan on buying gold. Many of the gold shops nestle in two passageways in the historic center – Pasaje Bolívar and Pasaje Trivigno-Guayana. Both are in the block between Paseo Orinoco and Calle Venezuela, and between Calle Dalla Costa and Calle Piar.

Getting There & Around

AIR

The **Aeropuerto Ciudad Bolívar** (Map p295; ☎ 632-4803; Av Jesús Soto) is 2km southeast of the riverfront and is linked to the city center by local transportation. A number of tour agencies operate charter flights to Canaima. Flights depart for Caracas (US$80 to US$130) every day except Saturday. Rutaca also flies weekly to Porlamar (US$100) and has daily Cessna service to Santa Elena (US$160), often stopping at Canaima.

BUS

The **Terminal de Pasajeros** (Map p295; cnr Avs República & Sucre) is 1.5km south of the center. From Paseo Orinoco until 6pm, take the westbound buseta marked 'Terminal.' There is a small departure tax (US$0.25).

Plenty of buses go to Caracas (US$20, nine hours, 591km), the majority in the evening. Tall passengers looking for more legroom might consider Cruceros Oriente's sofa-bed coaches (US$26).

There are also direct buses to Maracay (US$20, 9½ hours, 627km) and to Valencia (US$19, 10½ hours, 676km), which don't go through Caracas, but via the shorter Los Llanos route. These are the buses to take if you want to go to Venezuela's northwest or the Andes and avoid connections in Caracas.

About a dozen smaller buses service Puerto Ayacucho (US$13 to US$15, 11 to 12 hours, 728km), some with air conditioning and some without. Buses depart every 15 to 30 minutes to Ciudad Guayana (US$2 to US$3, 1½ hours, 115km); from the parking lot, faster por puestos go to San Félix for US$5.

Buses for Puerto La Cruz (US$14 to US$19, four hours, 302km) leave every hour or two, and Expresos del Mar has two buses that stop at the popular Playa Colorada and Mochima beaches. Go to the front of the terminal for carritos to Puerto La Cruz (US$16), and if you pay a bit more they will drop you off directly at the Isla Margarita ferry.

A number of buses head south to Santa Elena de Uairén (US$14 to US$19, 12 hours, 716km), mostly in the evening. Note that there are at least five military checkpoints along the way where you need to show ID and sometimes disembark for random baggage rummaging. Don't take the night bus if you want a solid night's sleep.

RÍO CAURA

The picturesque Río Caura offers a variety of natural and cultural experiences few other rivers can match. The thick jungle setting resembles what you might find around Canaima, but unlike Angel Falls it is a year-round boat destination that's not seriously affected by the dry season. The birding is excellent, and tour groups are smaller and more personalized.

A right-bank (south) tributary of the Río Orinoco, the Caura joins the Orinoco about 200km southwest of Ciudad Bolívar. It's graced with islands, beaches and huge granite boulders, and cut by rapids and waterfalls. The most spectacular is Salto Pará. At the end of the lower Caura, two rapids form a huge lagoon and the long sandy beach of El Playón.

For a good part of its course, the Caura flows through wildlife-rich rainforest, with riverbanks inhabited by indigenous communities. The major groups here are the Yekuana, particularly renowned for their fine basketry, and the Sanema, who are descended from the Yanomami.

It's also one of Venezuela's least-polluted rivers, as yet unaffected by gold mining, though prospectors have been combing the region for a while. Finally, the Caura is a 'black river' (see the boxed text p304), so mosquitoes are scarce.

Tours

Various travel operators in Caracas (eg Akanán Tours), Ciudad Bolívar and other cities offer Río Caura tours. These are most often a five-day all-inclusive package costing US$60 to US$80 per day, with simple accommodations in hammocks.

Río Caura tours usually start in Ciudad Bolívar. From there, you venture west for 205km along the Puerto Ayacucho road, then along a small side road branching off to the south and running for about 50km to Las

Trincheras. There are several *campamentos* in the area, where tours stay the first and last nights. On the second day, boats go 130km upriver (a five- to six-hour ride) to the vast sandbank of El Playón, where you spend the night. The following day, there's a two-hour walk uphill to the amazing Salto Pará, consisting of five 50m-high falls.

The following are recommended trips and operators (also see p356 for more):

Estación Ecolóiga de Kakara (☎ Spanish 0285-632-4802, English 0285-632-4804) Fundación Cuyujani, a local NGO, runs a five-day ecotourism trip emphasizing Yekuana cultural practices and environmental sustainability. In additional to visiting Río Caura highlights, participants journey to a Yekuana-run biological research station, which is partially funded by the trips.

Jonás Tours (☎ 0285-651-3445, 0414-385-0948; jonastours54@hotmail.com) The pioneer of Río Caura tours, Jonás Camejo has over 15 years' experience in the Caura region. He leads four- to five-day trips, as well as custom trips. He also does a nine-day nature trip (US$800 to US$1000) with river transportation and trekking that incorporates six rivers; visitors stay in indigenous villages and animal sightings are often quite good.

Soana Travel (☎ 0285-632-6017, 0414-854- 6616; soanatravel@gmx.de; Posada Don Carlos, cnr Calles Boyacá & Amor Patrio) Based in Ciudad Bolívar.

CIUDAD GUAYANA

☎ 0286 / pop 750,000

A convenient and comfortable staging point for trips to the Delta del Orinoco and the Gran Sabana, Ciudad Guayana is a schizophrenic metropolis encompassing the unlikely twin cities of Puerto Ordaz and San Félix. The iron-ore port of Puerto Ordaz is a wealthy and modern prefab city, with a large middle-class population and a smorgasbord of restaurant and entertainment options that exist nowhere else in the region. Late-model cars cruise wide boulevards, wending through clusters of air-conditioned malls and gleaming office blocks. Although the streets are remarkably clean, the city feels a bit soulless. Colonial San Félix is a working-class city with a historical center, but it is rather frantic and grimy, with little tourist infrastructure and a reputation for being unsafe.

Officially 'founded' in 1961 to serve as an industrial center for the region, Ciudad Guayana embraced into its metropolitan boundaries these two very distinct urban components. At the time of its founding, the total population of both areas was 40,000.

Today the two parts have merged into a 20km urban sprawl that is home to 750,000 people. It's Venezuela's fastest-growing city and is likely to remain so until the population reaches the government's target of one million people.

All listings are in Puerto Ordaz unless otherwise noted.

Orientation

Located at the confluence of the Río Orinoco and the Río Caroní, Ciudad Guyana's two sibling cities of Puerto Ordaz and San Félix are linked by the east–west boulevard of Av Guayana. On the east bank of the Caroní, San Félix contains a busy bus terminal that is the central departure and arrival point for Ciudad Guayana. San Félix's Plaza Bolívar is approximately 1km north of the terminal, near the bank of the Orinoco.

On the west bank of the Caroní, Puerto Ordaz is dressed to impress, with leisurely cafés, upmarket hotels, endless choices of restaurants and internet spots galore. The city center hugs up against the Río Caroní. About 2km southwest, the Alta Vista district is centered on the Ciudad Comercial Alta Vista, a huge shopping mall. The airport is another 2km southwest, and a bit further west, the second bridge across the Orinoco opened in late 2006, the latest jewel in the city's shiny crown.

Perhaps because of the city's affluence, taxi drivers are prone to overcharging. Negotiate fares in advance; even cross-town rides shouldn't cost more than US$5.

Information

EMERGENCY

Emergency Center (☎ 171

IMMIGRATION

Brazilian Consulate (Map p303; ☎ 961-2995, 961-9233; Edificio Eli-Alti, Oficina 04, Carrera Tocoma, Alta Vista Norte; ☽ 9am-noon & 2-6pm Mon-Fri)

INTERNET ACCESS

Internet connections are generally fast and cheap (US$0.80 to US$1 per hour).

Ciudad Comercial Alta Vista (Map p303; Av Guayana, Alta Vista) There are dozens of cybercafés here.

Cyber Café Latin World (Map p305; Av Principal de Castillito)

Info Ware House (Map p305; Centro Comercial Topacio, Carrera Upata)

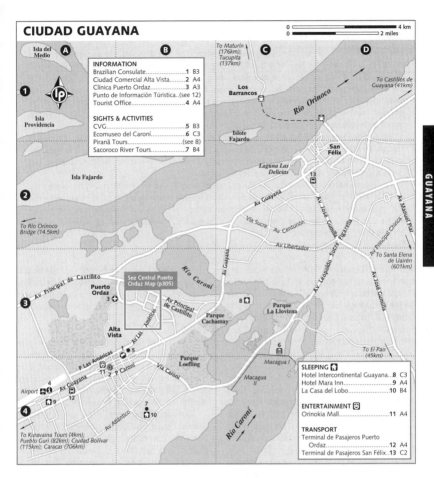

CIUDAD GUAYANA

Sala Web La Red.com (Map p305; Calle San Cristóbal)
Web Celular (Map p305; Torre Loreto II, Av Las Américas)
Phones too.

MEDICAL SERVICES
Clínica Puerto Ordaz (Map p303; ☎ 923-9630; Vía
Venezuela)

MONEY
Banco de Venezuela (Map p305; cnr Avs Las Américas &
Monseñor Zabaleta)
Banco Mercantil (Map p305; cnr Av Ciudad Bolívar &
Vía Venezuela)
Banco Provincial (Map p305; cnr Av Ciudad Bolívar &
Carrera Upata)
Banesco (Map p305; Vía Caracas btwn Calle Guasipati &
Av Las Américas)

Corp Banca (Map p305; cnr Calle Urbana & Carrera
Ciudad Piar)

TELEPHONE
CANTV (Map p305; Carrera Padre Palacios)

TOURIST INFORMATION
Punto de Información Turística (Map p303;
☎ 717-5733; Puerto Ordaz bus terminal, Av Guayana;
🕑 7am-9pm)
Tourist office (Map p303; airport terminal, Av Guayana;
🕑 7am-7pm Mon-Fri, 8am-noon & 2-6pm Sat, 10am-
6pm Sun) Very helpful.

Sights
Situated along the Río Caroní, Ciudad Guyana's three stunning parks (all open 5:30am

GUAYANA

BLACK RIVER, WHITE RIVER

› The color of rivers ranges from light grey or yellow (the so-called *ríos blancos,* literally 'white rivers') to dark coffee or even inky black (*ríos negros,* literally 'black rivers'). The color is a result of a number of factors, including the flora along the banks and the chemical components of the rock and soil of the riverbed. Generally speaking, a dark color results from a low organic decomposition, usually caused by poor nutrient levels in the soils (such as in the case of the Amazon rainforest). Black rivers are almost free of mosquitoes and other insects, and caimans are virtually unknown. In contrast, all these creatures abound in white rivers.

Most of the right-bank (southern) tributaries of the Orinoco, including the Caroní, Caura and Sipapo, are dark rivers, while most of the rivers of Los Llanos, such as the Apure and Arauca, are white rivers. The color of Río Orinoco itself largely depends on the colors of its tributaries, but generally, the lower its course, the lighter the color.

The most interesting place to see the color differences is at the confluence of a black river and a white river. The waters of the tributary don't usually mix with the main river immediately, but tend to form two parallel flows of different colors. This is clearly visible at the confluence of the Caroní and Orinoco at Ciudad Guayana, where dark- and light-colored waters flow side by side for more than 10km.

---

to 5:30pm Tuesday to Sunday) are a calming respite from urbanity, and all have free entry. Escape the heat with a stroll in the 52-hectare **Parque Cachamay** (Map p303; Av Guayana), a shady canopy of tropical trees dotted with blue morpho butterflies and scampering lizards. Then drink in the spectacular view of the river's 200m-wide waterfalls. Pushy monkeys enliven the adjoining **Parque Loefling** (Map p303; Av Guayana), which has roaming animals like capybaras and tapirs and a small zoo of native wildlife. Taxis (US$2) can take you to both parks. The 160-hectare **Parque La Llovizna** (Map p303; Av Leopoldo Sucre Figarella) is on the other (eastern) side of the Río Caroní. It has 26 wooded islands carved by thin water channels and linked by 36 footbridges. The 20m-high Salto La Llovizna kicks up the namesake *llovizna* (drizzle) of the park and waterfall. Enter the park from Av Leopoldo Sucre Figarella. Taxis from the center shouldn't cost more than US$4.

Nearby Parque La Llovizna and the enormous Macagua dam, the **Ecomuseo del Caroní** (Map p303; ☎ 964-7656; www.edelca.com.ve/ecomuseo; Av Leopoldo Sucre Figarella; admission free; ☼ 9am-9pm) contains an interesting art gallery with a photographic history of the dam and samples of pre-Hispanic ceramics unearthed during construction. A balcony looks out over the huge turbine room.

One of the most fascinating sights in San Félix is the confluence of the Ríos Orinoco and Caroní. At the bank of the Río Orinoco, just off the Plaza Bolívar, you can see the dark waters of the Caroní swirling into the much lighter Orinoco current (see the boxed text above). **Paso a Nado Internacional de los Ríos Orinoco-Caroní**, a massive swim competition across the two rivers, takes place in April.

Tours

Infrastructure junkies can tour some of the city's huge industrial establishments, including the steel mill and aluminum plant. For information on tours, contact the headquarters of **CVG** (Corporación Venezolana de Guayana; Map p303; ☎ 966-1530; Edificio CVG, Av Cuchivero, Alta Vista Norte).

Most local tour operators are located in Puerto Ordaz and they can organize expeditions to Guayana's highlights such as Angel Falls, Gran Sabana and Delta del Orinoco. They're often a bit more expensive than tours originating in Ciudad Bolívar, but convenient if you're already in town. Some companies will do half-day trips to the Castillos de Guayana and to Represa de Guri.

Recommended tour companies:

Ivarkarima Expediciones (☎ 923-1750, 0414-386-4913; ivarka@movistar.net.ve) A small company offering tours to regional highlights at reasonable prices. Frequent trips to the Gran Sabana and Angel Falls.

Kuravaina Tours (☎ 717-4463, 0414-872-3623; kuravaina@telcel.net.ve; Centro Industrial Sierra Parima Transversal 'C' Galpón No 6 Sector 321) Sells all the regional tours, as well as packages to Los Roques and Margarita; will pick you up from anywhere in the city.

Piraña Tours (Map p303; ☎ 922-77448; www.pirana tours.com; Hotel Intercontinental Guayana, Av Guayana) Offers relaxed local boat tours of the Ríos Caroní and Orinoco as well as regional trips.

Sacoroco River Tours (Map p303; ☎ 0414-868-2121, 0287-400-2649; sacoroco@yahoo.com; Calle Gahna No 19, Villa Africana, Manzana 32) Runs trips in the Río Grande area (southern) of the Delta del Orinoco, staying at its Campamento Oridelta in Piacoa. The owner, Roger Ruffenach, speaks English, German and French, and personally guides all the trips, which never have more than 10 guests. Prices are about US$70 per day.

Sleeping

La Casa del Lobo (Map p303; ☎ 961-6286; lobo_travel@yahoo.de; Calle Zambia No 2, Villa Africana, Manzana 39; r US$19; 🖳) Something of a backpacker institution in these parts – especially for German speakers. The German owner, Wolf, has five fan-cooled rooms with private bathrooms and offers free pickup from the Puerto Ordaz bus

terminal. There's a well-stocked bar on the patio, and meals upon request.

Posada San Miguel (Map p305; ☎ 924-9385; Calle Moitaco; d US$30-40, tr US$70; 🗷 🖳) A centrally located option with nifty perks like free morning coffee and internet access. The rooms are clean and tastefully decorated, although only the upstairs rooms have exterior windows.

Posada Turística Kaori (Map p305; ☎ 923-4038; kaoriposada@cantv.net; Calle Argentina, Campo B; d/tr/q US$37/46/56; 🅿 🗷 🖳) The smallish rooms resemble dorms, with unpainted wooden nightstands and bed platforms. All 20 rooms have cable TV, hot water and good mattresses.

Residencia Ambato 19 (Map p305; ☎ 923-2072; Calle Ambato No 19; d US$37; 🅿 🗷) A family-run, friendly lodging with seven spotless rooms,

GUAYANA

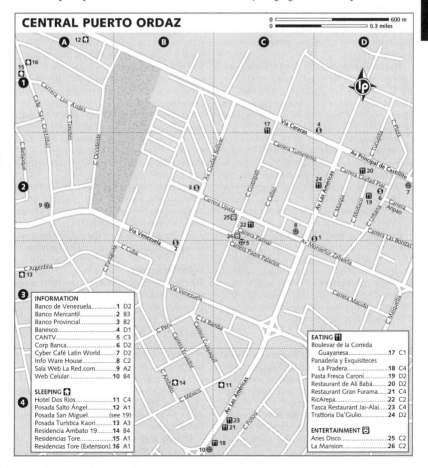

CENTRAL PUERTO ORDAZ

0   600 m
0   0.3 miles

located in a quiet residential neighborhood. Shaded outdoor rocking chairs encourage idle reading.

Hotel Dos Ríos (Map p305; ☎ 922-9188; hoteldos rios@telcel.net.ve; Calle México; s US$37-56, d US$46-70, tr US$60; P X R) A 70-room hotel popular with business travelers, with a relaxing outdoor pool and a handy poolside grill in a breezeway ringed by mature trees and lovely red flowers. The *habitaciones remodeladas* (renovated rooms) cost a bit more but are much nicer, and some of the south-facing rooms have views of the Represa Macagua.

Residencias Tore (Map p305; ☎ 923-0679; tore@cantv .net; cnr Calle San Cristóbal & Carrera Los Andes, Campo A-2; d/tr US$46/53; P X R) This posada encompasses two buildings across the street from each other, and every room exudes feistiness. Note the leopard-print shower curtains and wooden animal carvings – someone had fun decorating here. A sunny restaurant offers midpriced meals.

Posada Salto Ángel (Map p305; ☎ 922-6516; posada saltoangel@cantv.net; Vía Caracas, Campo A-2; d/tr US$50/71; X R) Spartan yet cheerful posada with 14 clean rooms, some with fridges. It has free coffee and internet, as well as a restaurant open for breakfast and lunch.

Hotel Mara Inn (Map p303; ☎ 953-0111; www.hotel marainn.com; Calle Neverí; s incl breakfast US$170-200, d incl breakfast US$183-250; P X R) An upscale modern hotel barely a suitcase toss from the airport, the place screams 'executive traveler on an expense account.' There's wi-fi access and a stylish restaurant, and the rooms have safes and ample bathrooms.

Hotel Intercontinental Guayana (Map p303; ☎ 713-1000; www.ichotelsgroup.com; Av Guayana; d US$190-230; P X R) A bit isolated unto itself, this luxury riverside hotel complex boasts marbled bathrooms, free internet services and fall-out-of-your-chair views of La Llovizna falls. Rates vary quite a bit, and often include breakfast. The website has the best rates.

Eating

Panadería y Exquisiteces La Pradera (Map p305; ☎ 923-5641; Torre Loreto II, Av Las Américas; pastries US$1; 6am-10pm) Pastries and strong coffee in a gleaming bakery-café. A hearty lunch *menú* (US$5) draws a midday crowd.

RicArepa (Map p305; ☎ 923-1483; Carrera Upata; arepas US$3-4; 24hr) Choose from almost two dozen types of fillings in this buzzing *arepera* that never closes.

Pasta Fresca Caroní (Map p305; ☎ 922-1587; Calle Moitaco; pasta US$4-6; 11:30am-3pm) Mix and match with a dozen types of fresh pasta and 15 yummy sauces. The dining room is spare, with plastic chairs, red-and-white tablecloths and florescent lighting.

Restaurant Gran Furama (Map p305; ☎ 922-3097; Av Las Américas; mains US$4-7; 11am-11pm) A popular place for Chinese takeout – perhaps because the staff seem somewhat disinterested. Even so, it's worth eating in to watch the flamboyant *platos calientes* send fireballs leaping to the chandeliers. A lot of seafood dishes to choose from and a few platters to keep vegetarians happy too.

Boulevar de la Comida Guayanesa (Map p305; Calle Guasipati; meals US$5-7; breakfast & lunch) A dozen covered food stalls vie for your business with typical food like empanadas, *arepas*, soups and fresh juices.

Tasca Restaurant Jai-Alai (Map p305; ☎ 717-3072; Edificio Amazonas, Av Las Américas; mains US$5-9; noon-3pm & 6-11pm Mon-Fri, noon-3:30pm & 6:30-11pm Sat) A bustling outpost of Spanish cuisine. Specialties include *pulpo a la gallega* (Galician-style octopus) and a mouth-watering *brocheta de mero* (seafood skewers).

Trattoria Da'Giulio (Map p305; ☎ 923-5698; Av Las Américas; mains US$6-8; 11:30am-2:30pm & 7-9:30pm) Italian comfort food that hits the spot, with warm and attentive waiters fussing over you like an honored guest. Pizzas (US$4) not available until dinnertime.

Restaurant de Alí Babá (Map p305; ☎ 922-4051; Carrera Ciudad Piar; mains US$6-9; 11am-8pm) Copper kettles adorn the walls of this intimate Middle Eastern eatery. Feast on falafels and stuffed grape leaves, or ask for the *plato mini típico variado* and sample a little bit of everything.

Entertainment

Aries Disco (Map p305; ☎ 0414-858-3639; Centro Comercial Trébol III, Sotano, Carrera Upata) Bust a move as the DJ mixes up blaring salsa, electronica and *reggaetón*. Play pool in the back room until 11pm, when things heat up on the spacious black-and-white checkered dance floor.

La Mansion (Map p305; ☎ 922-3855; Carrera Palmar) A family-friendly seafood restaurant by day, but live Latin music has hips swiveling between the tables after the sun goes down. Bands play from 8pm to 1am on the weekdays, and don't wind down till 5am or so on Friday and Saturday.

Orinokia Mall (Map p303; www.orinokiamall.com; Av Guayana, Sector Alta Vista) Kick up your heels at the bowling alley or catch a flick at the multiplex movie theater in South America's largest mall.

Getting There & Around

Don't look for 'Ciudad Guayana' in air and bus schedules, because there's no such destination – the airport and the bus terminals appear under the name of the sector where they are located.

AIR

The **Aeropuerto Puerto Ordaz** (Map p303; Av Guayana) sits at the western section of Puerto Ordaz on the road to Ciudad Bolívar. From the airport terminal, taxis to the city center are US$3 to US$5, but price gouging is common. The tourist office can help secure a reasonably priced onward taxi. Local buses into town run along the Paseo Caroní, but it's not the closest walk with heavy luggage, and you have to cross two busy highways as well. Note that the airport appears in all schedules as 'Puerto Ordaz.'

Puerto Ordaz is the major air hub of eastern Venezuela, with service by most major domestic airlines. Some popular direct flights include: Caracas (US$50 to US$140), Porlamar (US$90 to US$170), Barcelona (US$100 to US$180), Maracaibo (US$170 to US$210), Mérida (US$120) and Valencia (US$130 to US$140). Departure tax is US$0.50.

BUS

Ciudad Guayana has two bus terminals. The **Terminal de Pasajeros San Félix** (Map p303; Av José Gumilla) is the city's main transit stop. It can be unsafe here after dark, with local buses stopping service around 9pm. Taxis are recommended. The **Terminal de Pasajeros Puerto Ordaz** (Map p303; Av Guayana) is 1km east of the airport and the less utilized of the two stations. It's smaller, and safer, but has fewer connections than the San Félix station, and not all buses pass through here. However, the 2006 opening of the second bridge over the Orinoco, just west of the city, now makes it faster to take northbound por puestos and buses from this terminal.

From the San Félix terminal, departures to Caracas (US$19 to US$26, 10½ hours, 706km) start in the morning, but there are many more at night. The majority of them go to the Puerto Ordaz terminal. Originating in Ciudad Bolívar, nine daily buses stop on their way to Santa Elena de Uairén (US$14 to US$19, nine to 11 hours, 601km); all call at San Félix, but not all stop in Puerto Ordaz.

Also from San Félix, Expresos La Guayanesa has two buses a day to Tucupita (US$5, 3½ hours, 137km); por puestos (US$7, 2½ hours) run on demand and leave when full. Expresos Maturín goes to Maturín every hour or two (US$7 to US$8, 3½ hours, 176km); there are also por puestos (US$12 to US$13, two to three hours). Por puestos leave frequently for El Callao (US$9, 2½ hours).

From both terminals, buses leave for Ciudad Bolívar every half-hour or so (US$2 to US$3, 1½ hours, 115km); faster por puestos are US$4 to US$5. There are two morning departures to Puerto La Cruz (US$16, six hours) and a bus to Puerto Ayacucho (US$19, 12 hours). Direct buses to Maracay (US$19, 11 hours, 742km) and Valencia (US$19 to US$22, 12 hours, 791km) don't pass through Caracas, taking a shorter route via Los Llanos, and are convenient if you're going to Venezuela's northwest or the Andes.

CASTILLOS DE GUAYANA

Downstream from Ciudad Guayana, two old forts sit on the hilly right (south) bank of the Orinoco, overlooking the river. They were built to protect Santo Tomás, the first Spanish settlement founded on the riverbank in 1595. The older fort, **Castillo de San Francisco** (admission free; 8am-1pm & 2-5pm Tue-Sun), dates from the 1670s and was named after the monastery of San Francisco de Asís that had previously stood on the site. As pirate raids continued unabated, a second fort, the **Castillo de San Diego de Alcalá** (admission free; 8am-1pm & 2-5pm Tue-Sun), went up in 1747 on a nearby higher hill. However, it couldn't provide adequate protection for the town either.

Santo Tomás was eventually moved upriver and re-founded in 1764 as Santo Tomás de la Guayana de Angostura (present-day Ciudad Bolívar), and the forts were abandoned. At the end of the 19th century, the forts were remodeled and used to control river traffic until 1943. In the 1970s they were restored to their original condition and opened as a tourist attraction. Extensively refurbished again in 2003, they look even more impressive now. The higher fort commands long views over the Orinoco.

Getting There & Away

The forts are accessible by road from Ciudad Guayana's San Félix (US$2, 1¼ hours, 41km).

GUAYANA

Buses depart a few times a day from the place known as 'El Mirador,' in an eastern suburb of San Félix, which can be reached by city buses. Alternatively, take a tour – some travel agencies in Puerto Ordaz organize half-day tours to the forts.

REPRESA DE GURI

Guayana contains the world's second-largest hydroelectric project (the largest is Itaipú, on the border of Brazil and Paraguay; but when completed, China's massive Three Gorges Dam will take first place). Located south of Ciudad Guayana, it was built between 1963 and 1986 on the lower course of the Río Caroní, about 100km upstream from the Orinoco. With an electric potential of 10 million kilowatts, the complex satisfies over half of the country's electricity demand.

Officially named the Represa Raúl Leoni, but commonly referred to as the Represa de Guri, the mammoth dam is 1304m long and 162m high at its highest point. Eight million cubic meters of concrete were used to build it. **Embalse de Guri**, the 4250-sq-km reservoir created by the dam, is Venezuela's largest body of water after Lago de Maracaibo. The dam and some of the installations can be visited on a tour.

The state company that operates the dam, **Edelca** (☎ 0286-965-8448), runs free daily tours at 9am, 10:30am, 2pm and 3:30pm. From the visitors center (called Asuntos Públicos), you are taken by bus for a one-hour trip around the complex. Although you don't see much of the installations, you get a feeling for the enormous scale of the project.

The tour includes a stop at a lookout, from where you get a good general view of the dam and of the Torre Solar, a 50m-high kinetic sculpture by Alejandro Otero. You see one of the units of the powerhouse, embellished with a geometrical piece of art by another first-rank Venezuelan artist, Carlos Cruz Díez. Next you go to Plaza del Sol y la Luna, noted for a huge sundial showing months, hours and minutes. Finally, you go up to the dam's crest for panoramic views.

Getting There & Away

The Represa de Guri is about 85km by road from Puerto Ordaz and easy to reach. From Ciudad Guayana's Puerto Ordaz bus terminal, there are three daily buses to Pueblo Guri (US$2, 1½ hours), and one on Sunday; faster and more frequent por puestos (US$4, one hour) run there as well. Pueblo Guri is a village that was built close to the dam for the victims of the 1999 natural disaster in the Vargas state. Violent mudslides devastated a 100km stretch of the Caribbean coast, claiming up to 50,000 lives (see p96). A taxi from the village will take you to the visitors center (US$1, 4km). To return, go by taxi to Pueblo Guri (the staff in the visitors center will call a taxi for you) and change for a bus. Note that the last bus to Puerto Ordaz departs from Pueblo Guri at 3pm. You can do the whole trip by taxi (about US$40 roundtrip from Puerto Ordaz).

EL CALLAO

☎ 0288 / pop 12,000

An old-time mining settlement with a spectacular Carnaval celebration, El Callao is sited in Venezuela's richest gold region. In 1840 a frantic gold rush hit Guayana and made Venezuela the world's largest gold producer (see the boxed text opposite). The riverside town erupted dramatically during that period, and the flavor of its Carnaval festivities reflects the influx of Caribbean prospectors during that heady period.

Today El Callao is a quiet town, and the gold-shopping mecca of the region. It boasts a huge number of gold jewelers – as many as 25 on Plaza Bolívar alone – and many more down nearby side streets. The jewelry is not renowned for its artistic quality, but it's the cheapest gold in the country.

Even if you are not on a gold-shopping spree, it's worth visiting some of the many small workshops where the jewelry is produced using rudimentary manual techniques. Just walk around the central streets and look for 'Taller de Oro' signs. Buying gold on the street is not recommended; it's likely you'll be sold questionable goods.

There are plenty of gold mines around the town, of which the Mina Colombia is the largest. Operated by Minerven, the state mining company, it's the deepest gold mine in Venezuela, with galleries spread over seven levels, from 130m to 479m below the surface. It produces about three tons of gold per year. The mine is 3km south of El Calla and serviced by por puestos and taxis. It's occasionally open to tourists for free visits, organized in advance by written request. Contact the mine's **Departamento de Relaciones Públicas** (☎ 762-0210, 762-0216; www.cvgminerven.com) for more details.

GUAYANA

THE SEARCH FOR EL DORADO

As soon as the first conquistadores arrived in Venezuela, the search for gold took off – the quest for the fabled golden city of El Dorado. Guayana was one of the regions where the Spaniards thought El Dorado might be hidden. In 1531, in the first serious attempt to explore the interior, Diego de Ordaz sailed up the Río Orinoco as far as Raudales de Atures, near what is now Puerto Ayacucho, yet he found nothing. Many other attempts followed, including the 1595 expedition led by Sir Walter Raleigh, but El Dorado didn't show up. In fact, 300 years of the colonial period turned up virtually no gold at all.

The Spaniards did, however, have the right presentiment – in 1849 prospectors found exceptionally rich lodes on the Río Yuruarí near the present-day town of El Callao in Guayana, and the gold rush took off. Fortune seekers from all corners of Venezuela, as well as Trinidad, British Guiana (present-day Guyana) and beyond, flooded in to join what became one of the greatest gold rushes in modern history. By the 1880s the region was producing 15 tons of gold per year and Venezuela had become the world's biggest gold producer. El Dorado did finally materialize.

Larger gold deposits were later found in South Africa and elsewhere, and Venezuela is no longer the world's leader, yet it remains an important producer. Guayana's gold-rich basin spreads from El Callao southward up to the edge of the Gran Sabana, and is dotted with hundreds of gold mines. The total gold reserves of Guayana are estimated at about 10,000 metric tons, roughly 10% of the world's known reserves.

In an effort to stem environmental damage, the Chávez administration has recently taken off the gloves with illegal miners, imposing permit controls in traditional mining areas. Although the government has promised to help miners relocate or transition into other occupations, this assistance has not come fast enough for many workers living a hand-to-mouth existence. In 2005 the military clashed with small-scale miners blockading the Brazil-bound highway near Las Claritas, and in 2006, soldiers killed six in La Paragua.

In addition to Mina Colombia, there are a dozen large private mines and perhaps a hundred smaller ones within a 20km radius of El Callao. They are not tourist sights, but some may be visited by arrangement – ask at the jewelry shops and hotels in town.

Festivals & Events

Besides its mining industry, the town is renowned for its spectacular Trinidad-influenced Carnaval, a tangible legacy of the influx of people from the Antilles during the gold rush. The streets become a riot of color and sound, with calypso rhythms, steel bands and floats, and marchers wearing elaborate costumes. Creepy *diablos* sport masks sprouting multiple horns and faces. They carry a trident in one hand and crack a whip in the other. Women known as *madamas* wear vibrant dresses and Caribbean headscarves.

One of the most interesting Carnaval personas is the *mediopinto*. These revelers paint their faces and bodies black and roam the crowd, asking for donations and threatening to spread the goopy face-paint-love if you don't comply. A *medio* is a denomination of change, so the name comes from their demands of '*Medio o te pinto*' ('a coin or I'll paint you').

Carnaval celebrations last much longer here than in the rest of the country. Festivities start a week before Ash Wednesday (which can be in either February or March).

Sleeping & Eating

Book far in advance if you're coming for Carnaval.

Hotel Italia (☎ 762-0770, 762-0719; Calle Ricaurte; d US$19-21, tr US$23; 🅿) Two blocks northwest of Plaza Bolívar, the recently remodeled Italia has 28 rooms with bathrooms and an inexpensive restaurant.

Hotel New Millenium (☎ 762-0448; Plaza Bolívar; d US$19-28, tr US$33; 🅿 🅿) Conveniently situated right on the plaza, this hotel has 50 good-sized rooms with hot water and pleasant views.

Hotel El Arte Dorado (☎ 762-0535; Calle Roscio; d US$21-26, tr & q US$30; 🅿 🅿) Another good option about 300m south of the plaza, the 'Golden Art' has tidy rooms and a criollo restaurant.

Getting There & Away

El Callao is 1km off the highway running between Ciudad Guayana and Santa Elena, but many long-distance buses enter the town and stop near the bridge. Buses to Ciudad Guayana's San Félix (US$7, three hours, 177km) come through every hour or two, and por puestos (US$9, 2½ hours) frequently depart from the corner of Calle Heres and Calle Bolívar, one block north of the plaza. A few buses a day pass through en route to Santa Elena (US$10 to US$15, six to eight hours, 424km).

ANGEL FALLS & AROUND

Until bush pilot Jimmie Angel crash-landed his plane on top of Auyantepui in 1937, only the Pemón knew about the existence of Angel Falls. With a total height of 979m and a continuous drop of 807m, Angel Falls (Salto Ángel) is the world's highest waterfall. Leaping from the heart-shaped table mountain of Auyantepui ('Mountain of the God of Evil' in the local Pemón language) and funneling into the moody rock skyscrapers of the Cañón del Diablo (Devil's Canyon), the flume is 16 times the height of Niagara Falls. Buried in a remote and roadless area of river-etched jungle, the thundering cascade is Venezuela's top tourist destination.

Orientation

The outside world didn't learn about Angel Falls until the 1930s, and for good reason – the huge waterfall resides in a distant wilderness with no road access. About 50km northwest, the town of Canaima is the primary jumping-off point for trips to Angel Falls. Canaima doesn't have any overland link to the rest of the country, but it does have an airport.

Another less-used access point is Kavac, a small Pemón town at the southeastern tip of Auyantepui, but it's far less popular than Canaima and is used infrequently by organized tours. It's also isolated, but has its own airstrip.

A visit to Angel Falls is normally undertaken in two stages, with Canaima as the stepping-stone. Most tourists fly into Canaima, where they take a light plane or boat to the falls. No walking trails go all the way from Canaima (or Kavac) to the falls.

There are other attractions in the Canaima area, mostly waterfalls, of which the most popular is Salto El Sapo. Around Kavac the most frequently visited sight is the Cueva de Kavac (see p315).

Angel Falls, Auyantepui, Canaima and the surrounding area lie within the boundaries of the 30,000-sq-km **Parque Nacional Canaima**, Venezuela's second-largest national park, and the country's only park appearing on the Unesco World Natural Heritage list. Approximately 30 tepuis are within the park limits. It stretches eastward and southward almost to the borders with Brazil and Guyana and encompasses most of the Gran Sabana. All visitors to Canaima must pay a US$4 national park entrance fee at the airport.

Planning
WHEN TO GO
In the dry season (typically January through May) the volume of the falls lessens and fiz-

---

AN ANGEL FALLS TO EARTH

Angel Falls (Salto Ángel) is not named, as one might expect, after a divine creature, but after an American bush pilot, Jimmie Angel. Returning from a remote expedition, he claimed to have seen a motherlode of gold capping a gargantuan jungle waterfall.

But alas, Angel was a chronic teller of tall tales, and no-one believed his starry-eyed story of gold nuggets and mammoth waterfalls. So in 1937, to prove them wrong, a determined Angel loaded his wife and two friends into his four-seater airplane and went to look for his mythic falls. On this trip he managed to locate Auyantepui, the site of his previous discovery, but the plane stuck fast in the marshy surface and Angel couldn't take off again. Without food or supplies, the dazed gold-diggers trekked through rough, virgin terrain to the edge of the plateau, then descended a steep cliff, returning to civilization after an 11-day odyssey.

His larger-than-life claim was verified in 1949 and Angel was finally given his due, and the awe-inspiring cataract now bears his name. The plane was later removed from the top of the tepui by the air force, restored and placed in front of the airport terminal in Ciudad Bolívar, where it now resides.

ANGEL FALLS & AROUND

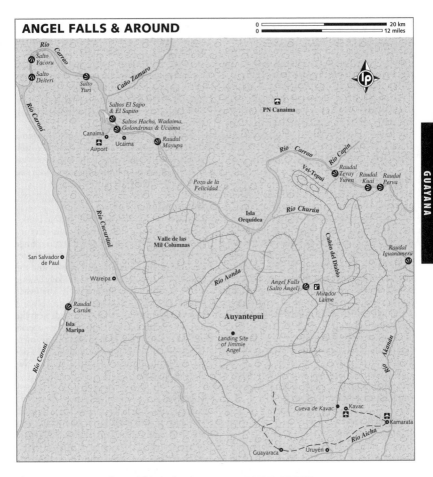

0   20 km
0   12 miles

Río Carrao
Salto Yacoru
Salto Deiteri
Salto Yuri
Caño Zamuro
Saltos El Sapo & El Sapito
Saltos Hacha, Wadaima, Golondrinas & Ucaima
Canaima
Airport
Ucaima
Raudal Mayupa
Río Caroni
PN Canaima
Río Carrao
Río Capín
Raudal Tevay
Vei-Tepui
Raudal Yuren
Raudal Kuai
Raudal Perva
Pozo de la Felicidad
Isla Orquídea
Río Churún
Río Cucurital
Valle de las Mil Columnas
San Salvador de Paul
Cañón del Diablo
Raudal Iguanamerú
Wareipa
Río Aonda
Angel Falls (Salto Ángel)
Mirador Laime
Raudal Cartán
Isla Maripa
Auyantepui
Landing Site of Jimmie Angel
Río Caroni
Río Akanán
Cueva de Kavac
Kavac
Kamarata
Río Aicha
Guayaraca
Uruyén

GUAYANA

zles out to mist as it drops. This is the time of year with the best chance of actually seeing it in a plane. Boat trips are slowly phased out during this period because the waterways are too shallow to navigate. If you go by boat at the beginning or the end of the dry season, expect a longer travel time because of the need to portage. In the rainy season, especially in August and September, the flow turns to a gushing shower. However, this is also when Angel Falls is frequently covered by a veil of mist and clouds. However, climate patterns are variable and unseasonable droughts and deluges can greatly effect the falls.

Shutterbugs should note that Angel Falls faces east, and is in direct sunlight from sunrise until midday.

WHAT KIND OF TRIP

Day trips leave from Ciudad Bolívar year-round, though the view depends on the season and the weather. Expect to pay US$280 to US$325 for a round-trip flight over the falls, with lunch in Canaima and a lagoon trip.

A more in-depth option is a three-day package from Ciudad Bolívar, with a one- or two-day motorized canoe trip to the falls and a stay in a rustic *campamento* along the way. If you have the time, these trips are lots of fun, and let you get a better sense of the jungle surroundings. And the relaxed build-up to seeing the falls lets you appreciate their grandeur and remoteness. Those on a tight budget can opt for a flight from the town of La Paragua, a three-hour drive from Ciudad Bolívar.

Packages run from US$280 to US$370, with the La Paragua option at the lowest end of the scale. Some tour companies will let you delay your return flight without cost so you can spend extra time in Canaima.

You can also fly to Canaima and arrange your own boat or plane trip to Angel Falls. Tour operators (right) wait at the airport, and you can buy a trip from them. It is usually more expensive than buying a package in Ciudad Bolívar, but you have more flexibility if you want to spend time in Canaima.

WHAT TO BRING

At the very least, pack a bathing suit, sun protection and good insect repellent. If you're taking a boat trip, you'll want a rain jacket or poncho and plastic bags for your camera and gear. Good walking shoes are recommended for the hour-long hike to the pool at the base of the falls, and it's convenient to have a small water bottle you can fill up at breakfast and carry with you. At night in the jungle, the temperature drops after dark; pants and a light jacket ward off chills. Blankets in the hammocks often need a washing, so a lightweight sleep sheet isn't a bad idea. And camps don't have electricity, which makes a flashlight useful.

If you bring your own tent (or a hammock and mosquito net) and cooking supplies, you'll save a bundle in Canaima.

CANAIMA

☎ 0286 / pop 1500

The closest population center to Angel Falls, Canaima is a remote indigenous village that hosts and dispatches a huge number of tourists. Although it is used as a base to reach Venezuela's number-one natural attraction, Canaima is a gorgeous place as well. The Laguna de Canaima sits at the heart of everything, a broad blue expanse framed by a palm-tree beach and a dramatic series of seven picture-postcard cascades, with a backdrop of anvil-like tepuis. Make sure to hike behind one of the falls and get the backstage experience of the hammering curtains of water. Their color is a curious pink, caused by the high level of tannins from decomposed plants and trees.

The rambling Campamento Canaima is on the west of the lagoon, with the best beach for swimming and taking photos. When swimming, stay close to the main beach – a

number of drownings have occurred close to the hydroelectric plant and the falls. From the airport there is a cluster of posadas about 15 minutes' walk to the north, and another few on the north end of the water. The southern end is the residential area for about 150 Pemón families. A few less-expensive posadas are here, although new construction appears to be in the works.

Between the Pemón village and the lagoon, there's an interesting thatched church. And if you spend the night and want a taste of local life, wander over to the mini soccer pitch and watch a spirited game after dinner.

Information

Canaima has no tourist office and no banks. Tour operators are the primary source of information and the larger posadas can change US dollars. The tour companies generally accept payment in dollars or *bolívares*, and the few who accept credit cards will likely charge a 10% surcharge for the privilege. The **Tienda Canaima** (☎ 962-0443, 0414-884-0940), a grocery and knickknack outpost at the crossroads near the airport, changes dollars and traveler's checks at a lousy rate. If you plan to explore the town, it sells useful double-sided maps (US$2) depicting both the town and the Parque Nacional Canaima.

Tours

Angel Falls is reached either by plane or boat, and all Canaima-based tour companies run boat trips and can arrange flights. Flights are in five-seater Cessna *avionetas*, most of which originate in Ciudad Bolívar. During the 40-minute round-trip ride from Canaima, the pilot will fly over the falls a few times, circle the top of Auyantepui and then return. From Canaima the flights are US$70 to US$90; US$90 to US$100 from Ciudad Bolívar. These trips can be arranged directly with the pilots at the airport or with local tour operators. For those opting for a flyover of Angel Falls, most operators also run day trips on the lagoon to see the nearby waterfalls.

Boat tours are arguably more fascinating than flights – they allow you to see the waterfall from a different perspective and, more importantly, enjoy it at a leisurely pace. The boat trip itself is a blast and the scenery is spectacular, particularly in the Cañón del Diablo.

Motorized canoes depart from Ucaima, above the Canaima waterfalls, and go up the

Ríos Carrao and Churún to Isla Ratoncito, at the foot of Angel Falls. From there, an hour's walk will take you uphill to Mirador Laime, the outcrop right in front of the falls.

Boats operate when the water level is sufficiently high, usually nine to 10 months a year, with some breaks between January and April. Tours are normally two- or three-day packages, with the nights spent in rustic *campamentos* (in hammocks).

The all-inclusive boat package costs US$175 to US$250 per person, and normally includes a trip to Salto El Sapo, the most popular waterfall in the Canaima area. It's a 10-minute boat trip from Canaima plus a short walk. Salto El Sapo is beautiful and unusual in that you can walk under it. Be prepared to get drenched by the waterfall in the rainy season – wear a swimsuit and protect your camera.

Reputable local tour operators:

Bernal Tours (☎ 632-7989, 0414-854-8234; www .bernaltours.com) Small family-run company based on an island in Laguna de Canaima, where participants stay and eat before and after the tour. Bernal Tours has its well-placed *campamento* on Isla Ratoncito, opposite Angel Falls.

Canaima Tours (☎ 962-5560; www.canaimatours .com) Based at its upmarket Wakü Lodge, this is by far the most expensive operator and its tours should be bought in advance in Ciudad Guayana. It also does tours to Kavac.

Excursiones Kavac (☎ 0414-853-2338, 0414-899-3475; www.excursioneskavac.com) Agency managed by the indigenous Pemón community. Marginally cheaper than Bernal Tours, it too has its *campamento* in front of Angel Falls. Trips originate in either Ciudad Bolívar or Canaima. It also does longer boat trips within the park and to Kavac.

Kaikarwa Tours (☎ 0414-865-9308; kaikarwa tours@hotmail.com) A Pemón-owned agency in business for a decade; it usually has a representative at the airport.

Tiuna Tours (☎ 962-4255, 0414-884-0502; tiunatours@hotmail.com) The largest and cheapest local company, with a large *campamento* in Canaima and a jungle camp up the Río Carrao at the Aonda.

Representatives from most tour operators can be found at the airport, playing cards with the Cessna pilots on standby and hustling up business from morning until midafternoon. Prices can be negotiated to some extent. Tiuna and Bernal have outlets at Ciudad Bolívar's airport. See p298 for tours organized from Ciudad Bolívar, which are likely to work out to be cheaper and more convenient than coming to Canaima and buying a tour.

When choosing between the tour companies, an important factor to consider (apart from price) is the location of their camps. Bernal and Kavac are more attractive because their camps face Angel Falls and you'll be able to see the waterfall for most of the day (including in the spectacular sunrise light), whereas Tiuna visits the falls from its Aonda camp for just a few hours.

Sleeping & Eating

Canaima has a dozen or so *campamentos* and posadas, and they tend to be geared toward tour groups. Separate accommodations prices start to look painful when not discreetly folded into Angel Falls packages, because rates are per person instead of per room. Most places also serve meals, but all supplies are flown in, so food prices aren't cheap either.

Because all food is imported, the few shops selling groceries mark them up to cover the costs. If you plan to cook your own food, try to bring it, but pack light: there's a 10kg luggage-allowance limit on Cessna flights.

With a tent, you can camp for free on the beach, the Laguna de Canaima lapping at your zippered nylon door. Pick up a free permit from the Inparques officer at the airport or from the Guardia Nacional post right behind Campamento Canaima. You can pitch your tent next to the post and ask the guards to mind your things when you are away.

Campamento Churúm (Kavac) (☎ 0414-899-3475, 0414-850-2686; ssmbelk@hotmail.com; hammocks/r per person US$7/12, breakfast US$9, lunch US$12, dinner US$12) Inside the Pemón village, in the southern area of town, the Excursiones Kavac *campamento* has five well-kept rooms (doubles, triples and quads) and a long and shady *churuata comedor* (a traditionally thatched, open-sided dining room) granting respite from the diabolical jungle sun. The best value in town, with big meals and vegetarian courses upon request.

Campamento Tiuna (☎ 962-4255, 0414-884-0502; hammocks/r per person US$10/25, breakfast US$5, lunch US$9, dinner US$9) The no-frills *campamento* of Tiuna Tours, located in the northern part of the village just off the lagoon. Free hammock lodging on the terrace if you take your meals here.

Posada Kaikusé (☎ 0414-230-0560; r per person US$16) Rooms are basic and a bit musty, with the odd lizard perched possessively on the wall, but it's the cheapest option in the more remote northern area. No restaurant, though airport transfers are included.

Posada Wey Tupü (☎ 0414-895-4333, 0414-884-0585; r per person US$23, breakfast US$7, lunch US$12, dinner US$12) A popular posada often booked out with groups, it offers 12 simple and clean fan-cooled rooms in the southern end of town near the school. Rooms sleep two to four people.

Posada Kusary (☎ 962-0443, 0414-884-0940; r per person US$24, r per person incl all meals US$116, breakfast US$9, lunch US$16, dinner US$16) Run by the owners of the Tienda Canaima, this posada exists somewhere between its two neighbors. Its 14 rooms are a step up from Kaikusé in over-all facilities, and a step down in price from Parakaupa. It also rents out a few basic and overpriced rooms behind the Tienda.

Posada Restaurant Morichal (☎ 877-4016; campamentomorichal@yahoo.com; r per person with fan/air-con US$37/70, incl all meals US$84/116, breakfast US$12, lunch US$16, dinner US$16; 🐾) A new five-room posada with lush landscaping, just a stroll across the road from the airport. A family-run place with doubles and triples, and two larger rooms with wood floors and the indulgence of air-conditioning.

Campamento Canaima (☎ 961-3071; www.hoturvensa.com.ve; r per person incl all meals low/high season US$177/195, breakfast US$20, lunch US$23, dinner US$23) Even if you don't stay here, you're likely to spend time nearby. The largest lodging in Canaima, with 107 rooms, it has lovely palm-thatched duplex cabañas that front the prettiest section of the lagoon beach. High-season prices reign from June through September, and most guests are visiting as part of Angel Falls tour packages. A large open *churuata* picks up the breeze at the pricey buffet restaurant, and there's a bar and a *fuente de soda* (snack bar).

Campamento Parakaupa (☎ 961-4963; campamentoparakaupa@hotmail.com; s incl all meals US$190, d/ste per person incl all meals US$146/163) In the northern part of town, ground-floor rooms have small hammock areas out front, and two gorgeous 2nd-floor suites have spacious floor plans and inspiring views of the surrounding tepuis. All rooms have hot water and fans; transfers from the airport are included.

Wakü Lodge (☎ 962-5560; www.wakulodge.com; 🐾 🖳) Buffering the north side of the lagoon, the Wakü is the best and most expensive game in Canaima. A lush and flowering estate, the grounds have prime views of the waterfalls and patrons have the choice of two upscale restaurants. All 15 rooms have both air-conditioning and a fan, tasteful furnishings, bathroom condiments galore and patios with hammocks. Overstuffed chairs invite lingering in the stylish lounges. Contact the office for prices.

Restaurant Imawary (set meal US$14, pasta US$5) The only (semi) regular restaurant in Canaima not attached to a posada; Los Simons (the proprietors) fires up the stove for lunch when there's sufficient demand. It serves fish, chicken, pasta, soups and fresh juices, and the bakery sets out hot fresh bread around midday.

Getting There & Away

Avior shuttles between Caracas and Canaima (US$180) twice a week, but only during the May to September high season. Flights between Canaima and Ciudad Bolívar are the most common, with a number of regional carriers flying in daily or as charters (US$70 to US$90). Flights to Kavac can also be chartered in Canaima. Various small airlines, including LTA and Rutaca, go to and from Porlamar (US$140); LTA is usually the cheapest carrier. Serami runs flights from Puerto Ordaz (US$120), and Rutaca has daily flights between Canaima and Santa Elena de Uairén (US$150). Six-seater Cessnas with a 10kg luggage allowance are used for flights to Ciudad Bolívar and Santa Elena; those prone to air queasiness might want to have motion-sickness pills and plastic bags on hand.

KAMARATA

Kamarata is an old Pemón village on the Río Akanán, at the southeastern foot of Auyantepui. Some decades ago it was discovered as an alternative access point for Angel Falls, and since then it has been attracting adventurous travelers. There are a few simple places to stay and eat in town, and an airstrip serviced irregularly by air taxis and charter flights on light planes.

In order to attract tourists, the locals built the village of Kavac, which has since taken over most of Kamarata's tourist traffic – that is, the little there is. Kavac is a hot two-hour walk from Kamarata, or a short drive on a dirt road.

KAVAC

The touristy offspring of Kamarata, Kavac consists of 20-odd 'new' *churuatas* built in the traditional style, resembling a manicured

Pemón settlement. Quiet and almost devoid of people, it sits on the savanna just southeast of Auyantepui.

The majority of tourists coming to Kavac are part of package groups put together by tour companies, mostly from Ciudad Bolívar. Independent travelers are rare guests here so beware being overcharged for tours, accommodations and food.

The area's major attraction is the **Cueva de Kavac**, which, despite its name, is not a cave but a deep gorge with a waterfall plunging into it. There's a natural pool at the foot of the waterfall, which you reach by swimming upstream in the canyon; be sure to bring your swimsuit with you. It's a pretty straightforward half-hour walk from Kavac to the gorge; you don't need a guide to get there.

Tours

Kavac plays host to three small tour/hotel operators that organize tours in the region – Asociación Civil Kamarata Kavac (the best), Makunaima Tours and Excursiones Pemón.

Boat trips to Angel Falls can be organized in the rainy season. The boats depart from Kamarata down the Akanán and Carrao Rivers, then up the Churún to Isla Ratoncito. Following a walk to the Mirador Laime, the boats then sail down the Ríos Churún and Carrao to Canaima, where the tours conclude. This is normally a four-day tour from Ciudad Bolívar and costs US$560 to US$750 per person, with a minimum of about four persons.

Kavac and Kamarata are starting points for a fascinating trip to the top of Auyantepui. Guides for this long and adventurous hike (of a week or more) can be contracted in either of the villages. The trail leads from Kavac via Uruyén to Guayaraca, from where it approaches the foot of the tepui before snaking uphill, following roughly the same route Jimmie Angel used for his descent in 1937 (see the boxed text p310). In three days (from Kavac), you'll reach a place called El Libertador, named after Bolívar, whose bust is placed here. You need another week or so to get to the point from where Angel Falls plunges. Count on roughly US$35 a day per guide for the group, plus another US$25 per porter.

The tour to Cueva de Kavac is a 2½ hour roundtrip from Kavac (tour US$21, with lunch US$37).

Sleeping

Any of the three tour operators will put you up for the night in a bed (US$28) or a hammock (US$19).

Getting There & Away

Kavac has an airstrip where light planes land several times a week from Ciudad Bolívar (US$145). Flights to/from Canaima are mostly on a charter basis.

GRAN SABANA

A wide open grassland that seems suspended from endless sky, the Gran Sabana (Great Savanna) invites poetic description. Scores of waterfalls appear at every turn, and its trademark tepuis sweep across the horizon, their mesas both haunting and majestic. More than 100 of these plateaus dot the vast region from the Colombian border in the west to Guyana and Brazil in the east, but most of them are here in the Gran Sabana. One of the tepuis, Roraima, can be climbed, and this trip is an extraordinary natural adventure.

Throw in a few sheep or cows, and in some places the undulating green landscape could be mistaken for lush Irish fields. But the prickly grasses of the Gran Sabana are not suitable for grazing or farming, and many Pemón families travel a considerable distance to tend small plots called *conucos*. Plumes of smoke are a common sight, as the Pemón burn patches of earth to clear land of brush and dangerous snakes, and also as a traditional form of celebration.

In geographical terms the Gran Sabana is the southeastern highland lying in the basin of the upper Río Caroní, at an elevation of over 800m. Its area is some 35,000 sq km, and much of it lies within the boundaries of Parque Nacional Canaima. Strictly speaking, the Gran Sabana doesn't include either the Valle de Kamarata or the savannas of Urimán and Canaima. The only sizeable town in the region is Santa Elena de Uairén, close to the Brazilian frontier. The remainder of the sparsely populated region is inhabited mostly by the 15,000 indigenous Pemón people, who live in some 270 scattered villages and hamlets.

Getting Around

The Gran Sabana was virtually inaccessible by land for many years. It wasn't until 1973 that a

GUAYANA

road between El Dorado and Santa Elena was completed, and the last stretch of this road was finally paved in 1992. Today it's one of the best highways in the country, and one of the most spectacular. If you're on a daytime bus, make sure you nab a window seat. The road is signposted with kilometer marks from the El Dorado fork (km 0) southward to Santa Elena (km 316) – a great help in orientation.

Although the El Dorado–Santa Elena de Uairén highway provides access to this fascinating land, public transportation on this road is infrequent (and often runs at night), making independent sightseeing inconvenient and time-consuming. Traveling away from the highway (eg to Kavanayén or Salto Aponguao) is still more difficult, as there are

no buses on these secondary roads and traffic is sporadic. An easy solution is a tour from Ciudad Bolívar or Santa Elena de Uairén.

If you're driving, keep one eye on the road markers. Between km 88 and Santa Elena (km 316), there is only one reliable place to refuel – km 172. Because of the lively gas-smuggling trade along the border, you can't bring extra tanks of gas, and if found, they may be confiscated. Don't let that filling station pass you by!

However you choose to explore the region, bring plenty of good insect repellent. The Gran Sabana is infested by small gnats known as *jejenes,* commonly (and justifiably) called *la plaga* (the plague). They are ubiquitous and voracious in the morning and late afternoon,

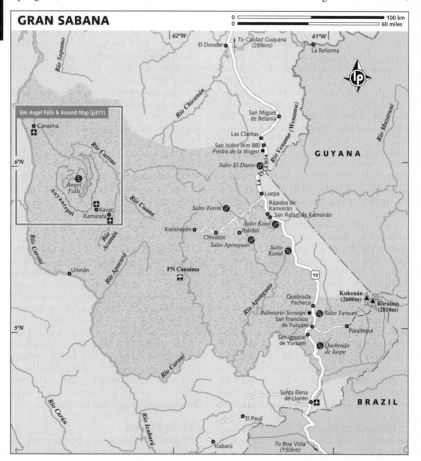

GUAYANA

THE MYSTERIOUS WORLD OF THE TEPUIS

Tepuis are flat-topped, cliff-edged sandstone mountains typical of southern Venezuela. Tepui (also spelled 'tepuy') is a Pemón word for 'mountain,' and it has been adopted internationally as the term to identify this specific type of table mountain. Curiously, the term 'tepui' is used only in the Pemón linguistic area – in the Gran Sabana and its environs. Elsewhere, the table mountains are called either *cerros* or *montes*.

Geologically, these massive tablelands are the remnants of a thick layer of Precambrian sediment laid down some two billion years ago when South America, Africa and Australia were joined together as part of the supercontinent Gondwana. Warping of the continental plates created fissures and fractures in the sandstone plain, which gradually eroded, leaving behind only the most resistant rock 'islands' – present-day tepuis.

Effectively isolated for millions of years from each other and from the eroded lower level, the tops of tepuis allowed the independent evolution of fauna and flora. Developing in such a specific environment, many species have preserved features of their remote ancestors, and no longer exist away from the table tops except as fossilized remains.

Botanical research has found roughly 2000 plant species on top of the tepuis, half of which are endemic – that is, they grow nowhere else. This is almost the highest percentage of endemic flora found anywhere in the world.

and their bites itch horribly for days. Even worse, you can't feel the little gremlins until it's too late.

EL DORADO TO SANTA ELENA

Heading southward from El Dorado, you pass a laundry list of tiny population outposts and undeveloped waterfalls. At km 85 is **Las Claritas**, a particularly dirty and busy ramshackle town, and 3km further south is **San Isidro** (often simply called 'km 88'), another unstable gathering of DIY shacks. Both settlements have developed as gold-mining supply centers for what is today one of Venezuela's major gold-rush areas. These localities rekindle memories of the old American gold outposts you see in the movies, with prospectors much in evidence and noisy bars crammed with tipsy miners. Neither town seems to be the safest spot on earth, but for those who wish to poke around for a while, both towns offer a choice of accommodations.

Proceeding south, at km 95 the road begins to wind up the so-called **La Escalera** (the Stairway). This portion of road, snaking through lush rainforest and ascending about 800m over 40km, is reputed to be one of the best bird-watching roads on the continent. One can see more than 15 species of parrots and six species of toucans on an average morning.

At km 98 you pass a huge sandstone boulder, **Piedra de la Virgen**, and 5km further on is the entrance to Parque Nacional Canaima. A board signals the start of the park; you don't

need a permit to enter. At km 119 is a pretty 35m-high waterfall called **Salto El Danto**. It's not visible from the road, but is very close to it.

The road continues to wind uphill to km 135, where the rainforest suddenly ends and you enter a vast, rolling grassland. This is the beginning of the Gran Sabana, which stretches south for nearly 200km. You are now at an altitude of about 1200m, which means more moderate temperatures – particularly during cloudy days – and chilly nights.

At km 141 is the Inparques office, and 2km further on you'll pass through a military checkpoint at Luepa. There's a gas station here, but it opens only during high-season periods. At km 147 a side road branches west for 70km to the village of Kavanayén (p318). Midway down this road, a dust trail departs south to the indigenous hamlet of Iboribó, from where you can walk to the marvelous Salto Aponguao (p318).

The main road continues south to **Rápidos de Kamoirán** (km 172). Besides the hotel and restaurant here, it also has the only year-round gas station before Santa Elena, so top off here if you're driving. There are some small rapids behind the complex. At km 195 is **Salto Kawí**, two small but exquisite cascades spilling onto red jasper rock, and at km 202 you'll find the spectacular and frequently visited Salto Kamá (p319).

The Quebrada Pacheco (p319), noted for yet another waterfall, is at km 237, and **Balneario Soruapé**, 1km off the road at km 244, is a popular place to bathe in natural pools and play slip-and-slide on the slick red rock bed. Just 3km further south you'll find the amazing curtain of Salto Yuruaní (opposite) before reaching the village of San Francisco de Yuruaní (p322) at km 250. Here a side road runs east to the indigenous village of Paraitepui (p322), the gateway town for a hike to the top of spectacular Roraima (opposite).

The highway proceeds south to the impressive Quebrada de Jaspe (p322), at km 273, one of the most popular falls in the region. About 5km down the highway, a rough jeep road branches off to the east and runs for 3km to two picturesque waterfalls, **Salto Agua Fría** and **Salto Puerta del Cielo**.

At km 316 you finally reach Santa Elena de Uairén (p322), the region's only town to speak of. The highway heads south to the Brazilian border (km 331) and continues to Boa Vista, 223km beyond the border.

There's a (mostly) unpaved road heading west from Santa Elena to the mining settlement of **Icabarú**, 115km away. Tours around this part of Gran Sabana are available from Santa Elena, and usually go as far as the friendly village of El Paují (p326), 73km from Santa Elena.

SALTO APONGUAO

One of the blockbuster waterfalls of the Gran Sabana, Salto Aponguao doesn't disappoint. It is about 105m high, and in the wet season it can be a wall of water nearly 80m wide. At its most robust, it looks like a multistory building exploding, but even in the dry season it's spectacular. The waterfall is also known by its indigenous name of Chinak-Merú (*merú* means 'waterfall' in the Pemón language).

Getting to the falls takes some work – it's off the highway, 32km along an unpaved road toward Kavanayén, plus another 11km south to the indigenous hamlet of Iboribó (public transportation would be nice, but no such luck). Villagers in Iboribó offer rustic lodging and serve simple meals.

Locals will take you in a *curiara* (dugout canoe) to the opposite side of the Río Aponguao and provide a mandatory guide for a trip to the waterfall – a 40-minute walk along a well-defined path. The fee for the boat ride and the guide is US$4 per person roundtrip. Locals also offer a boat service all the way from Iboribó to the falls, which takes 25 minutes each way and costs US$5 per person roundtrip, with a minimum of five passengers.

There's a well-marked path leading downhill to the foot of the falls, where you can bathe in natural pools. For a perfect sun-lit photo, come between midmorning and very early afternoon.

KAVANAYÉN

Spectacularly situated on the top of a small plateau, Kavanayén is a small indigenous village in the middle of the Gran Sabana. The village is about 70km west of the highway, and accessible by dirt road. It's surrounded by tepuis, with views of at least half a dozen of these table mountains, including the unique cone-shaped Wei Tepui (Mountain of the Sun).

Kavanayén developed around the Capuchin mission established here half a century ago. The missionaries erected a massive stone building for themselves and apparently assumed that the indigenous peoples wanted to live in a similar dwelling. Almost all the houses in the village are of heavy stone construction, a striking contrast to the thatched adobe *churuatas* you'll see elsewhere in the region.

A rough jeep trail leads from Kavanayén to the **Karuai-Merú**, a fine waterfall at the base of Ptari Tepui, 20km away. The road is bad and the trip may take up to 1½ hours, but the scenery is fabulous. You can walk, but it's a 10-hour roundtrip.

Tours

Mérida-based **Andes Tropicales** (☎ 0274-263-8633; www.andestropicales.org) promotes Gran Sabana trips run by a local Pemón cooperative. It offers adventurous one- to seven-day trekking and boating excursions from Kavanayén, visiting small Pemón villages and areas of natural and cultural interest.

A few Santa Elena tour companies, including **Backpacker Tours** (☎ 995-1524, 0414-886-7227; www.backpacker-tours.com; Calle Urdaneta) and **New Frontiers Adventure Tours** (☎ 416-0864, 0416-599-3585; www.newfrontiersadventures.com; Calle Urdaneta), can organize trips on an adventurous trail going between Karuai to Kamarata, but it takes at least a week to complete.

Sleeping & Eating

La Misión (☎ 0286-962-5100, 0286-960-3763; dm US$7) You'll find hot showers and very clean dormitory rooms in this place, located in the heart of town.

Hotel Kavanaduren (☎ 0286-962-0800; d US$14-19) Located at the entrance to the village, this hotel provides simple but acceptable rooms.

Campamento Mantopai (d US$23, per person with breakfast & dinner US$30) Provides meals and accommodations 8km north of Kavanayén, with 12 cabañas.

Restaurant de la Señora Guadalupe (mains US$6-12) Straightforward, home-cooked meals.

Getting There & Away
Kavanayén doesn't get a lot of traffic, and it's a three-hour drive from the highway; hitchhiking isn't the most reliable option. A better bet is a tour, though most of the standard Gran Sabana tours don't come this far. The last stretch of the road to Kavanayén is in poor shape, especially in the wet season, and a 4WD is recommended.

SALTO KAMÁ
Salto Kamá (Kamá-Merú) is a powerful 50m-high waterfall, 200m west of km 202. There are paths descending on opposite sides of the falls, so you can size it up from a number of different angles. The locals can take you on a boat trip (US$2) around the waterfall's pool and behind its water curtain; be prepared to get doused. Sunlight strikes the falls from late morning to late afternoon. To go swimming, you must pay a local guide (US$2) to accompany you.

Sleeping & Eating
Posada El Kamá (dm & r per person without bathroom US$5, r per person with bathroom US$7, breakfast US$6, lunch/dinner US$7) A small posada with six basic rooms and airy dorms with skylights. Located close to the falls, it has a gorgeous new criollo restaurant and a small store selling snacks and drinks. A few solar panels keep the lights on.

Campamento Kuranao (r with/without bathroom US$21/14) The basic rooms feel a bit musty; it also has an inexpensive restaurant. Inquire here for local guides to the falls.

Campamento Rápidos de Kamoirán (☎ 0289-808-1505, 0414-870-0568; d/tr/q US$16/19/19, mains US$2-10) A very popular and convenient place with 38 rooms (all with bathroom) and a reasonably priced restaurant. Virtually all motorists stop here because of the crucial km 172 gas station. Like any good highway rest stop, there's also a shop and some public phones.

Around Salto Kawí there are a number of basic cabañas (US$19) where you can sling your hammock or pitch a tent (US$2).

Getting There & Away
If you're traveling on your own, just stay on the road and flag down anything heading in the same direction. Keep an eye out for parked cars belonging to tourists visiting the falls; they may give you a ride when they leave.

QUEBRADA PACHECO
Also known as Arapán-Merú, this is a handsome multistep cascade just 100m east of the road at km 237. It looks all right from the road, but it gets better up close. The best light for photos is in the afternoon. There are six cabañas (US$21 to US$28) out front where you can hang your own hammock, or pitch a tent (US$2). Guests can use barbeque grills on the grounds, though the owners will cook meals if there are at least a few people. From here it's a 20-minute walk to the gorgeous Pozo Azul (Blue Well) swimming hole.

SALTO YURUANÍ
This wall of water is about 6m high and 60m wide, with amazing beer-colored water. It's at km 247, where you cross a bridge over the Río Yuruaní. From the bridge you'll see the waterfall, about 1km to the east, with the Yuruaní tepui in the background. The way to the falls is along both the southern and northern banks of the river. With a guide you can explore behind the water curtain – a thrilling walk, swim and crawl – but only during low-water periods. There's a place for camping next to the falls, but bring a lot of insect repellent as this waterfall is notorious for *jejenes*. The best sunlight strikes the falls in the late afternoon.

RORAIMA
A stately tepui towering into churning clouds, Roraima lures hikers and nature-lovers looking for Venezuela at its natural and rugged best. Unexplored until 1884, and studied extensively by botanists ever since, the stark landscape contains strange rock formations and graceful arches, ribbon waterfalls, glittering quartz deposits and carnivorous plants. Frequent mist only accentuates the otherworldly feel.

Tropical rainforest clings to the walls of the tepui, but the area was once heavily wooded on a scale unimaginable today. In 1925 one legendary Pemón fire reached such magnitude that it scorched the upper reaches of Roraima, decimating forests that once blanketed its

---

THE MOTHER OF ALL WATERS

Sitting on the three-way border between Venezuela, Guyana and Brazil, the 34-sq-km Roraima is the highest of all the tepuis – its plateau is at about 2700m and the tallest peak at 2810m. The indigenous Pemón people call it the 'Mother of all Waters,' presumably because Roraima is the source of rivers that feed all three of the surrounding great river basins – the Orinoco, the Essequibo and the Amazon.

Like most other tepuis in the region, Roraima has a rocky barren surface, swept by rain and wind, and few living organisms have adapted to these inhospitable conditions. Those that have include curious endemic species such as a little black frog *(Oreophrynella)* that crawls instead of jumps, and the *heliamphora (Sarraceniaceae)*, a carnivorous plant that traps unwary insects in beautiful, bucket-shaped, red flowers filled with rainwater.

German explorer Robert Schomburgk was the first European to reach the base of Roraima, in 1838, yet he considered the summit inaccessible. Various expeditions then failed to climb the plateau, until British botanists Everald Im Thum and Harry Perkins made it to the top in 1884 in a two-month-long expedition and discovered its unique plant and animal life.

The news fired the imagination of Sir Arthur Conan Doyle, the creator of Sherlock Holmes. Inspired by the fabulous stories of the explorers, he wrote his famous adventure tale, *The Lost World,* in which dinosaurs were still living on a remote plateau in the Amazon basin – giving Roraima an aura of mystery and romance.

---

slopes. Local elders can remember this dense landscape, and guides can point out charred roots that remain.

Although it's one of the easier tepuis to climb and no technical skills are required, the trek is long and demanding. However, anyone who's reasonably fit and determined can reach the top. Be prepared for wet weather, nasty *jejenes* and frigid nights at the summit. And give yourself at least five days roundtrip so you have sufficient time to explore the vast plateau of the tepui.

Orientation

Roraima lords over the eastern border of Venezuela and straddles small sections of Brazil and Guyana. The base of the mountain is approximately 47km east of San Francisco de Yuruaní and the El Dorado–Santa Elena highway, and 22km northeast of Paraitepui. The smaller Kukenán tepui sits just to the west. Maps highlighting Roraima's landmarks and hiking distances are widely available throughout the region.

Planning
WHEN TO GO

The dry season lasts from about December through April, but the top of the tepui receives rain throughout the year. The weather is highly temperamental, with intense sun giving way to rainy deluges in a matter of minutes. Peak holiday periods (see p14) should also

be considered, when the tepui can become crowded with vacationing Venezuelans.

WHAT KIND OF TRIP

Visitors cannot hike here independently. There are two ways to climb Roraima: join a tour-company group or go solo with a local guide. How you do the trip is a matter of preference, price and ability. On the one hand, tour companies arrange all your gear and food, and carry most of it. They are more expensive, but take care of all the transfers, food shopping and other logistics. Groups generally have a minimum number of participants, and if you haven't booked in advance, you may need to wait a few days or pay more if there aren't enough people. Alternatively, you can bring your own equipment and food, hire a guide, and backpack on your own schedule for a lot less money. Camping gear is also available to rent locally, though the cumulative costs can add up.

A number of experienced tours operators have offices in Santa Elena (see p324) and their rates (US$256 to US$420 per person) are better than those elsewhere in the country. There's also the advantage of checking out the quality of their tents and sleeping bags before buying a tour.

Guides (US$74 per day for a group of up to six people) can be arranged in either San Francisco or Paraitepui, as well as porters (US$37 per day), who are able to carry up to about 15kg. For a group of people hiking at different speeds, consider the addition of a porter to shepherd the stragglers.

WHAT TO BRING
Think hot, cold and wet. The top of the tepui generates its own microclimate, with rain and fog making multiple or constant daily passes over the eerie landscape. Temperatures hover toward freezing after dark, and soggy clothes may never dry. On the open savanna below, hot and humid conditions rule the day. So in addition to the usual camping gear, make sure you have a waterproof tent with fly, a warm sleeping bag, a ground pad, full rain gear, extra pairs of socks and some flip-flops or lightweight camp shoes to wear while hiking shoes recover from puddle plunges.

Toward the end of the trip, an extra camera battery will come in handy for digital cameras. Stash enough plastic bags for packing out all your garbage and waste, and bring extra food in case you choose to extend your stay – or the weather decides for you. Buy any food in Santa Elena de Uairén, Ciudad Guyana or Ciudad Bolívar. Paraitepui has few shopping options and San Francisco is only slightly better. And although you won't need insect repellent on Roraima itself, the bugs bite something fierce along the way, so pack some for the journey there and back.

Climbing Roraima
Once you have a guide or have joined a tour, you must sign in with the Inparques officer in Paraitepui and pay a US$2 entrance fee before setting out. Departures from Paraitepui are permitted only between 7:30am and 2pm to guarantee enough time to reach the first campsite at Río Tök (four hours from Paraitepui). The top can be reached in two days (total net walking time is about 12 hours up and 10 hours down), but most tour companies stretch it out over three days. There are several established campsites along the way with water sources for drinking and bathing. The next campsite is at the Río Kukenán (30 minutes past the Río Tök). A majority of groups spend the second night at the so-called *campamento base* (base camp) just before the mountain (three hours uphill from the Río Kukenán).

The Río Kukenán can throw a snag in your plans, as the water level rises sharply with rainfall and the resulting runoff from the Kukenán and Roraima tepuis. The river can quickly become furious and impassable, and you may need to cool your heels for several hours, or even a day, until the level drops. Generally, the water level is lower in the evening than in the morning. Sometimes local villagers will haul in a rubber raft (and charge) for the crossing, but don't count on it. When camping next to the river here, do not pitch tents on the shore side of the painted white rocks – they signify the river's high-tide mark.

From the base camp it's about four grueling hours to the top and the most demanding part of the hike. The trail leaves open savanna and

---

WHAT GOES UP MUST COME DOWN

Roraima's beauty is derived from its isolation, and the arrival of humans has taxed its fragile ecosystem. Past garbage-collection drives have reaped huge trash deposits, and every so often the government threatens to close the tepui to tourists, or at least impose severe daily quotas. Do more than your share by not just packing out all your trash, but picking up and bringing down other litter you see as well. On the mountaintop, use small amounts of biodegradable soap and don't wash hair with shampoo. Avoid stepping on flora, and do not succumb to the temptation of collecting souvenir quartz crystals – besides being illegal, Inparques often conducts searches at the trailhead.

In addition, all human waste and toilet paper must be packed off the tepui top. Most tour companies bring up portable toilet buckets, but if they are not provided, you must poop in a plastic bag, add *cal* (quicklime) as a drying agent, and carry down your mementos.

Roraima may be a once-in-a-lifetime experience for you, but keep things in perspective. Guides may make this strenuous journey a few times a month. Porters might slog up and down several times a week, lugging eggs, bottles of wine and other ridiculously heavy foodstuffs, all for the enjoyment of tourists. Be sure to share food and beverages, tip if you can, and don't haggle for sport. If you speak Spanish, you can hire a guide to organize everything in San Francisco, and your money will go directly to the local Pemón community without an intermediary taking a cut.

enters thick steamy rainforest, and the path becomes a continuous scramble up a steep slope. When the clouds part and you can see the valley below, the views are magnificent.

Once you arrive at the top of the tepui, your guide will lead you to one of several 'hotels' to set up camp. The hotels are sandy areas protected by cliffs or ridges of eroded rock, where you'll appreciate the cover when rain lashes the mesa.

It appears desolate, but life thrives here. Roots dart from crevices and thirsty bromeliads inhabit the boughs of sinuous trees. Strips of pink sand meander between soaring boulders and chilly pools of clear water. Vaulting rock to rock over rain deposits, you see tiny black frogs, curious sparrows and tiny blooming flowers.

Getting lost here is easy, so your guide will lead the way to the mountain's natural highlights. On a sunny day, **La Ventana** (Window) has some of the best and most vertiginous views. Three hours to the north, you'll pass through the lush riverbed of the **Valle Arabopo** on the way to the **El Foso** (Pit), a round deep sinkhole with interior arches. Just past this pool are **Valle de los Cristales**, **Laberinto**, **El Abismo** (Abyss) and the meeting point of Venezuela, Guyana and Brazil, **Punto Triple**. In the southwestern sector closer to most of the hotels, you can dunk into freezing quartz-lined ponds called **Jacuzzis**.

SAN FRANCISCO DE YURUANÍ

An industrious indigenous village on the highway 66km north of Santa Elena de Uairén, San Francisco is a convenient staging area for Roraima trips, and the main place to hire local guides. Modern market stalls line the roadside, catering to Venezuelans who visit the Gran Sabana in peak holiday periods, when local accommodations pump up their prices. There are a few basic posadas along the main road near the bus stop, including **Hospedaje Minina** (☎ 0289-808-2513, 0414-886-6771; low season r US$16-23, high season per person incl breakfast & dinner US$19), and in the high season, **Posada El Caney de Yuruaní** (☎ 0414-886-6707; per person US$5-7). You can also ask permission to pitch a tent on someone's land. A number of food stalls and basic eateries stay open year-round.

Almost a dozen buses a day run in each direction along the Ciudad Guayana–Santa Elena highway, stopping in San Francisco.

Taxis from Santa Elena to San Francisco cost US$20 per car and take about 35 minutes.

PARAITEPUI

A small and impoverished Pemón village 26km east of San Francisco, Paraitepui's economy is almost entirely dependent on tourism. The Inparques office can round up available guides and porters, or direct you to the *cooperativa* that rents out tents and sleeping bags. A few shops in the village sell basic packaged foods at inflated prices.

At the time of research, the town was close to completing its first lodging, 19 comfortable duplex cabañas with full bathrooms and stunning tepui views. For a convenient trailside start, another option is to camp near the Inparques office (and its spiffy new bathrooms); sometimes the ranger requests a fee.

The rutted road requires a high-clearance vehicle, and you can organize one in San Francisco. They carry up to six people (US$50, regardless of the number of passengers). There is very little traffic here, so hitching is not a solid bet. Jeeps are usually full, and on this rough road they are likely to ask for payment anyway. You could walk to Paraitepui, but it's seven hours of heat and hills.

QUEBRADA DE JASPE

One of the most unusual and popular waterfalls in the Gran Sabana, Quebrada de Jaspe (Jasper Creek) isn't known for a dramatic plunge but for the brilliant orange and red jasper rock beneath its waters. Kako Paru, its Pemón name, means 'fire creek,' and the design carved by the current creates a slick surface resembling stripes on a tiger. It's located at km 273 between San Francisco and Santa Elena, 300m to the east of the highway, hidden in a stretch of woodland.

SANTA ELENA DE UAIRÉN
☎ 0289 / pop 17,000

Bordering Brazil, Santa Elena de Uairén is a 4WD frontier town with rugged habits and a lilting Portuguese accent. It's the main transit point for overland sojourns to the south and the base for travelers exploring the waterfalls and tepuis of the Gran Sabana. The streets feel safe and Brazilian influence runs high, as many residents speak Portuguese as a first language.

Santa Elena was settled as a mining outpost in 1924, and it grew slowly until diamonds were discovered in the 1930s in the Icabarú region, 115km to the west. But the lack of a good road kept the town in a state of suspended development until the highway from El Dorado was completed in 1992. This is the only road link between Venezuela and Brazil, so you'll be passing through Santa Elena if you travel overland between them.

The city is a brazen black-market and smuggling hub. Gasoline prices in Brazil are almost 30 times higher than those in Venezuela (where gas is cheaper than water), which means there's serious money to be made. Until mid-2006 Brazilians could fill up in Santa Elena, and lines could stretch 1km down the road. But now well-armed military personnel guard the town's two gas stations – that Brazilians can no longer use – and locals are rationed. Residents can only fuel up on alternate days, upon presentation of cards monitoring their consumption. There's a thriving trade in gas sold from private homes, and sellers have acquired the unfortunate moniker of 'talibanes.'

To dampen down the black market, Venezuela opened a new gas station near the border, where Brazilians can purchase the gas they crave at intermediate prices, and there's often a queue of trucks. If you go to the Brazilian side of the border, look for the impound lot of cars, trucks and passenger buses caught sneaking over with multiple tanks of black gold.

Information
EMERGENCY
Emergency Center (☎ 171)

GUAYANA

SANTA ELENA DE UAIRÉN

0 ———————— 400 m
0 ———————— 0.2 miles

INFORMATION	
Banco Guayana	1 A2
Banco Industrial de Venezuela	2 A2
Brazilian Consulate	3 C1
CANTV	4 B3
Carmelo.net	5 C1
detodo.com	6 B3
DIEX	7 C1
Hospital Rosario Vera Zurita	8 B4
Ipostel	9 A2
Iruk Café	10 A2
Lavandería Amazonas	11 C1
Lavandería Cristal	12 B2
Moneychangers	13 A2
Mundo Cyber	14 B2

SIGHTS & ACTIVITIES	
Adventure Tours	(see 15)
Arima Tours	(see 24)
Backpacker Tours	15 B2
Kamadac	16 C2
Mystic Tours	17 B2
New Frontiers Adventure Tours	18 B2
Ruta Salvaje Tours	19 C1

SLEEPING 🛏	
Hotel Augusta	20 A2
Hotel Lucrecia	21 C2
Hotel San Marcos Rodríguez	22 B3
Moron Katok	23 B2
Posada Backpacker Tours	24 C2
Posada Michelle	(see 24)

EATING 🍴	
Alfredo's Restaurant	25 C2
Cachapa stand	26 B3
Inversiones Lakshmy	27 B3
Kamadac	(see 16)
Restaurant Michelle	(see 24)
Restaurant Nova Opção	28 A2
Restaurant Nova Opção Sucursal I	29 A2

ENTERTAINMENT 🎭	
Victoria Video	30 A3

TRANSPORT	
Por Puestos to El Pauji	31 B3
Por Puestos to La Línea	32 B3

To Bus Terminal (1.5km);
Representaciones y Servicios
Turísticos Alvarez (1.5km);
Ciudad Guayana (601km);
Ciudad Bolívar (716km)

To Éco Inn Anaconda (1km);
Raúl Helicópteros (3km);
Airport (7km); La Línea/Pacaraima
(Brazil, 15km); Boa Vista
(Brazil, 238km)

To Peace Villages
Foundation
(1.7km)

IMMIGRATION

Brazilian Consulate (☎ 995-1256, 995-1277; Av Antonio José de Sucre; ☾ 8am-noon Mon-Fri) The consulate building is set back from the road, across from the gas station. If you want to play it safe, get your visa beforehand – the nearest Brazilian consulate before Santa Elena is in Ciudad Guayana. A yellow-fever vaccination certificate is likely to be required before issuing a visa (see p363).

DIEX (☎ 995-1958, 885 1858; Av Mariscal Sucre, Sector entrada de Acurima; ☾ 8am-noon & 2-5pm Mon-Fri) Issues permits to visit the El Paují area.

INTERNET ACCESS

Internet connections are tremendously slow and notoriously erratic, and cost about US$1 per hour.

Carmelo.net (Av Mariscal Sucre)
detodo.com (Calle Lucas Fernández Peña)
Mundo Cyber (Calle Urdaneta)
Iruk Café (Calle Bolívar)

LAUNDRY

Lavandería Amazonas (Av Perimetral)
Lavandería Cristal (Calle Urdaneta)

MEDICAL SERVICES

Hospital Rosario Vera Zurita (Calle Icabarú) No phone; linked to ☎ 171 emergency services via radio.

MONEY

Scores of freelance moneychangers populate the intersection of Calle Bolívar and Calle Ur-

---

---

daneta, popularly known as Cuatro Esquinas. Expect to be collared by men flashing cash every day except Sunday afternoon. However, it's not a pressured or sketchy scene, and they offer some of the best exchange rates in the country for US dollars. It's also a good place to sell your *bolívares* and buy Brazilian currency if you're crossing the border. There are some *casas de cambio* on the same corner, and they may cash traveler's checks, but at a poor rate.

Banco Guayana (Plaza Bolívar)
Banco Industrial de Venezuela (Calle Bolívar)

POST

Ipostel (Calle Urdaneta btwn Calles Bolívar & Roscio) Closed for renovation at time of research, but expected to reopen. Mailbox located in bus terminal.

TELEPHONE

CANTV (Calle Zea btwn Calles Roscio & Lucas Fernández Peña)

Tours

Santa Elena has about a dozen tour agencies and they all do some type of day or multiday jeep trips around the Gran Sabana, mostly touring the area's spectacular waterfalls and far-flung swimming holes. The companies organize all-inclusive trips with food and basic lodging, but some let you pay for just transportation and a guide, a good budget option if you have your own camping gear. For an all-inclusive tour of three days, plan on spending between US$60 to US$80 daily per person for a group of at least four.

Tours to Roraima are the other best-sellers, with six-day all-inclusive treks running from US$256 to US$419 per person. Some agencies rent out camping equipment to backpackers, and can provide transportation to Paraitepui, the starting point for the Roraima trek. Jeeps are US$60 to US$80 per jeep each way for up to six people.

Another local tour option is the remote town of El Paují (p326), an interesting combination of natural attractions and counterculture community. It's a long drive, so overnight trips are recommended, and prices and conditions are similar to those for Gran Sabana tours.

Recommended local tour companies:
Adventure Tours (☎ 0414-853-7903; www.adventuretours.com.ve; Calle Urdaneta) Photography tours are a specialty.
Arima Tours (☎ 0416-0743, 0414-886-0243; www.arima-tours.net; Calle Urdaneta) Richard and Andrea Mata

specialize in horseback tours in the Gran Sabana. Office in the Posada Backpacker Tours.

Backpacker Tours (☎ 995-1524, 0414-886-7227; www.backpacker-tours.com; Calle Urdaneta) An attentive and responsible German-run company with comfortable Roraima treks and some of the best camping equipment.

Jaime Rodriguez (☎ 808-8470, 0414-778-5234; germanjaimerodriguez@yahoo.com) An experienced local guide fluent in English, Spanish and Pemón, he leads excellent Roraima tours emphasizing local culture and customs. A vivid and engaging storyteller who breathes life into the landscape and chilly tepui-top evenings, he is in the process of developing a Pemón guide cooperative.

Kamadac (☎ 995-1408, 0414-886-6526; www.aben teuer-venezuela.de; Calle Urdaneta) A German- and Venezuelan-owned agency, it offers staples (Gran Sabana, Roraima) as well as some more adventurous tours (Auy-antepui, Akopán Tepui).

Mystic Tours (☎ 416-0558, 0414-886-1055; Calle Urdaneta) This agency has some of the lowest prices for Roraima treks. It also does tours to El Pauji and Gran Sabana trips incorporating a more spiritual flavor.

New Frontiers Adventure Tours (☎ 416-0864, 0416-599-3585; www.newfrontiersadventures.com; Calle Urdaneta) A competent local outfit with experienced guides, it organizes all types of trekking tours, primarily from its website.

Ruta Salvaje Tours (☎ 995-1134, 0414-889-4164; www.rutasalvaje.com; Av Mariscal Sucre) A reliable company specializing in rafting trips. It also has the usual range of tours, including the Gran Sabana and Roraima.

Representaciones y Servicios Turísticos Alvarez (☎ 0414-385-2846, 0414-854-2940; www.roraimarsta .com; Bus Terminal, Av Perimetral) A personable and helpful presence in the bus terminal, Francisco Alvarez organizes regional tours and rents camping equipment as well.

If you have money to burn and no time to spare, **Raúl Helicópteros** (☎ 995-1711, 0414-886-7174; www.raulhelicopteros.com; Hotel Gran Sabana, Vía Brasil) will get you there in its fleet of light planes and helicopters. It will fly almost anywhere, including Kavac, Canaima and the top of Roraima (US$1400 roundtrip for four people).

Festivals & Events

Santa Elena's Carnaval, in February or March, underscores its proximity to Brazil, incorporating samba rhythms and a gaudy parade of *carrozas* (floats). The town celebrates the feast of its patron saint in mid-August.

Sleeping

Posada Michelle (☎ 416-0792; hotelmichelle@cantv .net; Calle Urdaneta; s/d/tr US$7/9/13) The undisputed backpacker headquarters, and the best place to fill out a tour group. A clean and surprisingly quiet posada with 25 rooms with fans, hot water and a basic kitchen downstairs. Half-day shower-and-rest rates (r per person US$7) and a shower-only option (per person US$2) are great for cleaning up after a Roraima trek or grabbing a nap before the night bus to Ciudad Bolívar. Bulletin boards on the front patio announce upcoming trips.

Moron Katok (☎ 995-5018; andrehina@hotmail.com; Calle Urdaneta; tr US$12, 5-person chalet US$19) Formerly called La Casa de Gladys, the new name of this longtime travelers' haunt means 'place of rest' in Pemón. Good value for groups, there's a handful of small triples, two fun chalets with lofts and hot water, and a large sit-down kitchen.

Posada Backpacker Tours (☎ 995-1524, 0414-886-7227; www.backpacker-tours.com; Calle Urdaneta; s incl breakfast US$14, d & tr & q per person incl breakfast US$9; 🖳) The former Hotel Michelle is under new management by Backpacker Tours, and rates include breakfast next door and a free half-hour of internet access.

Hotel Augusta (☎ 995-1654, 0414-886-0168; Calle Bolívar; s/d/tr/q US$14/17/19/23) Palm trees soar up from the courtyard of this pleasant hotel. The 21 fan-cooled rooms have hot water and a cheerful tropical decor.

Hotel San Marcos Rodríguez (☎ 995-1611, 0414-185-2614; Calle Raúl Leoni; s/d/tr US$21/23/26; P ✗) Twenty clean and modern rooms with comfy beds, hot water, fridge, towels and a surplus of reminder signs affixed to the walls.

Hotel Lucrecia (☎ 995-1105; hotellucrecia@cantv.net; Av Perimetral; d/tr US$23/28; P ✗ 🖳) Fifteen rooms with hot water radiate around a lush garden veranda. There's a midsized pool tucked out back, and breakfast and dinner are available for groups.

Eco Inn Anaconda (☎ 995-1459, 0416-787-5505; www.ecoinnsantaelenadeuairen.com; Vía Brasil; r incl breakfast US$65-74; P ✗ 🖳) Santa Elena gets a big bite of luxury with a swanky new hotel. Ground-floor rooms have small patios with hammocks, and all rooms have a safe, a mini-bar fridge and cable TV. A discotheque and casino will be opening soon. For US$12 non-guests can eat lunch at the restaurant and frolic in the cascade-fed pool.

Eating

Inversiones Lakshmy (Calle Icabarú; ⊙ 8am-noon & 3-7pm Mon-Sat) A small health-food store and bakery with fabulous vegan (can you *believe* it?) empanadas (US$1), dried fruit and bags of TVP (texturized vegetable protein) that vegetarians covet on Roraima treks.

Kamadac (☎ 995-1408; Calle Urdaneta; pizza US$2) This tour operator also runs a yummy pizza parlor. And after a Roraima trek, the flan is a decadent indulgence.

Restaurant Michelle (☎ 995-1415; Calle Urdaneta; mains US$2-4; ☺ 11am-10pm) Dig into huge portions at this popular and centrally located Chinese restaurant. Family-size patio tables are great for people-watching.

Alfredo's Restaurant (☎ 995-1628; Av Perimetral; pasta & pizza US$4-8, mains US$8-19; ☒) One of the best restaurants in town, Alfredo's has a lengthy menu, gourmet meals and tortellini with ricotta and spinach that melts in your mouth. Their filling lunch *menú* is a bargain at US$4.

Restaurant Nova Opção (☎ 995-1013; Plaza Bolívar; buffet per kilo US$7; ☺ 11am-5pm Mon-Sat) A budget self-service Brazilian restaurant with buffet food by weight. Most of the entrees are heavy meat and potato dishes, but it sometimes has a few tasty vegetarian options. When the heat drives you to drink, revitalize with an enormous fresh juice.

Restaurant Nova Opção Sucursal I (☎ 995-1615; cnr Calles Urdaneta & Roscio; buffet per kilo US$7; ☺ 6:30am-10pm Mon-Sat) In addition to the buffet, Nova Opção's newer branch has table service and longer hours.

Looking for a fabulous *cachapa*? Scoop up a perfect savory corn pancake – with or without a mountain of shredded cheese, chicken or pork – from the doorway stand at the Rivas Manrique **carnecería** (cnr Calles Roscio & Icabarú; cachapa US$3-7).

Entertainment

If you're in the mood for a movie, **Victoria Video** (☎ 995-2997; Calle Zea; per person US$1.50; ☺ 10am-9pm Tue-Sat) has 5000 DVDs of classics and, ahem, *very* recent blockbusters that you can watch in air-conditioned cell-like cubicles.

Getting There & Away

TO/FROM BRAZIL

Venezuelan and Brazilian immigration control points are at the border, nicknamed La Línea, 15km south of Santa Elena. Going as far as Pacaraima, the Brazilian border town, there is no need for a visa (if required for nationals of your country) but you must show your passport and proof of yellow fever vaccination.

Onward travelers will need to get a passport exit stamp from the Venezuelan immigration point and then a Brazilian entry stamp a few blocks over. You can no longer buy tickets for Brazil in Santa Elena. From the Pacaraima bus station there are three daily buses to Boa Vista (three to four hours, 223km); two of these continue on to Manaus (12 hours, 758km). Brazilian bus companies in Pacaraima check passport stamps before selling tickets.

In Santa Elena taxis (US$12 to US$14) to Pacaraima congregate in front of the bus terminal and will wait at both immigration checks before dropping you off at the terminal in Brazil. From the Santa Elena city center, cheaper por puestos (US$2) leave from Calle Icabarú but go only as far as the Venezuelan immigration point.

AIR

The tiny airport is 7km southwest of town, off the road to the border with Brazil. There are no buses; taxis cost around US$5. Not the busiest landing strip you'll see; tour operators often wait for incoming flights and offer free lifts to town in the hope of selling tours. Rutaca has flights on five-seater Cessnas to Ciudad Bolívar (US$155), often via Canaima (US$145).

BUS

Santa Elena has a small, sparkling bus terminal on the Ciudad Guayana highway about 2km east of the town's center. There are no local buses, but tour agencies will often provide free transfers. Because it is a border town, before departures you must present your luggage to the customs desk; they will mark and tape it shut before you get on the bus. A US$0.50 departure tax is paid outside just prior to boarding.

There are almost a dozen daily departures to Ciudad Bolívar (US$16 to US$19, 10 to 12 hours, 716km), and they all pass through Ciudad Guayana (US$14 to US$16, nine to 11 hours, 601km). Be warned that night buses stop up to five times per trip for comically useless identification checks. Keep your passport handy, and if rudely awakened, remember: don't swear at men with guns.

EL PAUJÍ
pop 280

Urban newcomers started moving to this isolated area in the 1980s in order to form a more laid-back arts community, and the town evolved into a rural hotspot. The current demographics are a mash-up of Venezuelan New Agers, artisans, miners and indigenous Pemón, and the grass-covered field they call the Plaza Bolívar has large stones representing the cardinal directions. Partly by design, but also by necessity, there's an emphasis on off-the-grid and sustainable living; electricity is hit-and-miss and there is no regular phone service.

There's a lot of creativity and industry in residence for such a small place. Family-run businesses produce honey, hibiscus products and incense from local tree sap. A majestic dance space hosts exciting though infrequent events, and a sizeable group of artists concentrate on their work while bringing up their young families.

Visitors often stay here for a spell, and a number of natural attractions make it worthwhile. Vistas of the Amazon basin are within easy hiking distance at **El Abismo**, and the delectable swimming spots at **Salto Cathedral** and **Pozo Esmeralda** are a great place to visit. In addition, the adjacent tabletop mountain of **El Altar** is a beautiful place to go backpacking.

An orange dirt road charges over hills and valleys to reach the town, continuing on to Icabarú, though the runoff from rainstorms can make progress difficult. On the drive in, you can occasionally see stands of skeletal trees killed by mercury runoff – the scars of the land's wildcat gold-mining history.

Sleeping & Eating

Tacamajaca (www.tacamajaca.com; tent US$5, plus per person US$0.50, meals or kitchen use US$2) An incredibly popular and communal gathering place. Isabel and Paulista craft incense and emphasize sustainable practices, like their composting toilet; work exchanges are available.

Campamento Amariba (amaribapauji@yahoo.com; r US$9, with meals US$16, kitchen use US$2) Creative though rickety cabañas and a huge open dance studio reached by way of a painfully long and bumpy 4WD road.

Campamento Manoa (☎ 0212-414-8998; d/tr US$23/28, camping for up to 3 tents US$28) Just off the main road at the start of town, with six nicely decorated cabañas with water but no electricity, a comfortable comedor hangout, and a free shelter house for campers stuck outside in the rain. Meals are available for groups upon demand; barbeque grills are also available.

Maripak (☎ 0416-802-4882, 0212-234-3661; mari paktepuy@hotmail.com; per person incl breakfast & dinner US$23-37, per person camping US$2) Six beautiful cabañas with private bathrooms and tasty meals.

Getting There & Away

A 10-seater por puesto jeep (US$14, 2½ to three hours, 73km) leaves from Calle Icabarú in Santa Elena de Uairén every morning at around 7am. It departs when full, so show up early to assure a spot. A second vehicle runs later in the morning if there are enough passengers. Because of illegal mining concerns, independent visitors to El Paují must obtain a special authorization permit (free) beforehand at the Santa Elena DIEX office. Have your passport on hand for checkpoints, and be prepared for a possible bag search.

AMAZONAS

Sparsely populated by humans but teeming with diverse and exotic animal and plant species, the southernmost state of Amazonas is Venezuela's untamed jungle wilderness. Predominantly a thick rainforest, the road-forsaken region is crisscrossed by rivers and inhabited by a mosaic of indigenous communities, whose primary form of transportation is the dugout canoe called a *bongo*.

The current indigenous population, estimated at 40,000 (half of what it was in 1925), comprises three main groups – the Piaroa, Yanomami and Guajibo – and a number of smaller communities, among them the Yekuana (Maquiritare), Curripaco and Piapoco. Following a checkered history of mistreatment by Spanish missionaries and successive Creole governments, the Venezuelan constitution was amended in 1999 to accord special status to the nation's indigenous peoples. There are now guarantees of political, cultural, economic and language rights, as well as the recognition of collective ownership of their lands.

Amazonas covers an area of 180,000 sq km – one-fifth of the national territory – yet it's home to less than 1% of the country's population. Despite its name, most of the region lies in the Orinoco basin, while the Amazon basin occupies only the southwestern portion of the state. The two basins are linked by the unusual 320km-long Brazo Casiquiare,

GUAYANA

a natural channel that sends a portion of the water from the Orinoco to Río Negro and down to the Amazon. Amazonas boasts four large national parks that cover 30% of the state area.

In contrast to the central Amazon basin in Brazil, Venezuelan Amazonas is quite diverse topographically, with towering tepuis.

Though not as numerous or as classical as those in the Gran Sabana, they do give the green carpet of rainforest a distinctive and spectacular appearance.

At the southernmost part of the Amazonas, along the border with Brazil, is the Serranía de la Neblina, a scarcely explored and virtually unknown mountain range. The highest peak

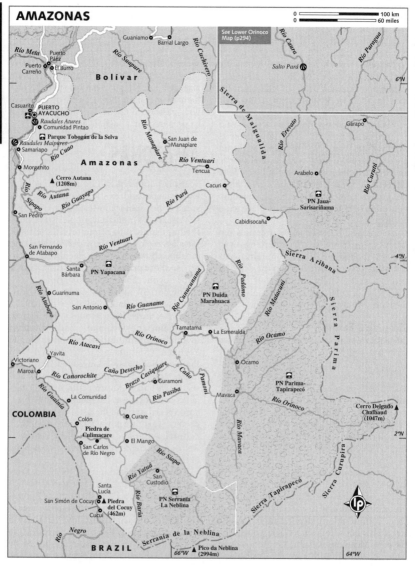

AMAZONAS

0 —————— 100 km
0 —————— 60 miles

INDIGENOUS AMAZONAS: DO NOT DISTURB

In order to protect indigenous land and culture, most of Amazonas is off limits to tourism. Europeans first entered Amazonas during the colonial period, and missionaries went to great (and often violent) lengths to convert the local people, pressing many into forced labor. And during the regional gold rush of the 1980s, mining prospectors trespassed onto indigenous lands, bringing disease and environmental damage.

Based on this history, a 1989 law designated eight permissible tourism routes within Amazonas. Outside of these areas, visitors must obtain a government permit, in addition to consent from specific indigenous communities to be visited or affected.

These routes are:

- El Burro – Puerto Ayacucho – Samariapo (northwest)
- Samariapo – San Fernando de Atabapo (northwest)
- San Fernando de Atabapo – Yavita – Maroa (central west)
- San Fernando de Atabapo – San Antonio – La Esmeralda (central/west)
- The mouth of the Río Ventuari (in the Río Orinoco) – Tencua (north/northeast)
- The Río Manapiare valley (north central)
- Río Guainía – Río Negro (Maroa – San Carlos de Río Negro – San Simón del Cocuy; southwest)
- The Brazo Casiquiare from Tamatama to the Río Negro (central/southwest)

However, Amazonas is a vast region, which makes enforcement and monitoring difficult.

---

reaches 2994m, making it the tallest mountain range on the continent east of the Andean chain, and the canyon running through its middle is one of the world's deepest. La Neblina has some of the richest endemic plant life in the world.

The climate is not uniform throughout the region. At the northern edge there's a distinctive dry season from December to April; April is the hottest month. Heading south, the dry season becomes shorter and not so dry, and eventually disappears. Accordingly, the southern part of Amazonas is wet year-round. The best time to explore the region is from October to December, when the river level is high but rains are already easing.

Getting Around

Amazonas is an enormous region with very few roads, and almost all transportation is by air or riverway. Other than a few short hops from Puerto Ayacucho, there are no regular passenger boats. Independent travel is difficult, if not impossible, but tour operators in Puerto Ayacucho can take you just about everywhere – at a price, of course. Note that you need government permits to visit the majority of Amazonas, as many areas are restricted to indigenous residents (see the boxed text above).

PUERTO AYACUCHO
☎ 0248 / pop 55,000

The hot and humid capital of evocative Amazonas, the gateway city of Puerto Ayacucho has an unhurried tempo born of isolation and the contemplation of colossal distances. Residents saunter through the dreamy heat, their daily rhythms decelerating as the mercury rises. Umbrellas do double-time as sun shades between hot-water rainstorms, and even a quick downpour turns the streets to rivers. Pedestrians must duck around the ubiquitous drizzle of window-box air-conditioners, and safe nighttime streets fade to black during frequent power outages.

Puerto Ayacucho was founded as a river port in 1924, together with another port, Samariapo, 63km upriver (south). The towns were linked by road to bypass a non-navigable stretch of the Orinoco cut by a series of rapids; this enabled timber to be shipped from the upper Amazonas down to the country's center. For a long time the two ports were obscure and isolated villages as the only road connection to the rest of the country was just a rough track. Only in the late 1980s, when this track was improved and surfaced, did Puerto Ayacucho start to grow dramatically. Ironically, the port, which was responsible for the town's birth and initial growth, has

THE RUTA HUMBOLDT

A true Renaissance man, Alexander von Humboldt (1769–1859) was a scientist, explorer, geographer, artist and diplomat. He was a celebrity of his time, hobnobbing with Napoleon Bonaparte and directly influencing the work of Charles Darwin. Born to Prussian nobility, he set sail from Europe at the age of 30 to explore Latin America, accompanied by French botanist Aimé Bonpland. The epic voyage lasted from 1799 to 1804. Over a four-month period, they navigated the Orinoco River and mapped the uncharted Brazo Casiquiare, which connects the Orinoco to the Amazon River.

It wasn't a comfortable cruise, and Humboldt's extensive writings chronicle his misery and discomforts. Biting swarms forced the party to travel by night and spend daylight sleeping in mosquito nets. Notwithstanding such trials, they collected and cataloged a voluminous number of tropical plants. In addition to his scientific observations, Humboldt's journals are a candid snapshot of life under Spanish colonial rule, noting the cruelty of overzealous missionaries.

Libertador Simon Bolívar credited him with being the true discoverer of the New World, declaring that the sum of 'his scientific contributions had given America more than all the conquistadores combined.'

lost its importance as most cargo is now carried by road.

Puerto Ayacucho is the only significant urban center in Amazonas state, and it's set on a colorful section of the Orinoco, just down from the spectacular rapids of Raudales Atures. The town is the regional tourist center, home to a dozen tour companies that can take you up the Orinoco and its tributaries, and deep into the jungle. It is also a transit point on the adventurous back routes to Colombia and Brazil. The town itself has a few interesting sights, including an indigenous craft market and an ethnographic museum.

Orientation

Puerto Ayacucho is a small city with a lot of small-scale commercial activity. The main thoroughfare is the Av Orinoco, which begins to the north at the *muelle* (dock). The town of Causarito, Colombia is a short distance across the Río Orinoco. Passing a wetlands overrun by dive-bombing birds, the road continues on, becoming busier as it approaches the city's main intersection at Av 23 de Enero. From here, sidewalk vendors camp out under sun-obscuring tarps and sheets, building a continuous arcade a block or so south past the Mercadito stalls. Further south, large bulbous hills seem to pop out of nowhere, and the Raudales Atures churn up the Orinoco.

The bus terminal is 6km east of the center and the airport is almost 6km south. It's rare for a taxi ride anywhere in town to cost more than US$1.

Information

EMERGENCY
Emergency Center (☎ 171)

IMMIGRATION
Colombian Consulate (☎ 521-0789; Calle Yapacana, Quinta Beatriz; 7am-1pm Mon-Fri)
DIEX (☎ 521-0198; Av Aguerrevere; 8am-noon & 2-5:30pm Mon-Fri) You must have your passport stamped here when leaving or entering Venezuela. No fee.

INTERNET ACCESS
CANTV has the best internet connection in town. Access costs about US$1 per hour.
Biblionet (Biblioteca Pública, Av Río Negro; 8:30am-4:30pm Mon-Fri) Half-hour free access.
M&M.com (Centro Comercial Maniglia, Av Orinoco)
Intercyber (Av Aguerrevere)
Windows PC (Centro Comercial Rapagna, Av Orinoco) Very slow connection.

LAUNDRY
Lavandería Aquario (Av Aguerrevere)

MONEY
Banco de Venezuela (Av Orinoco)
Banco Provincial (Calle La Guardia)
Banesco (Av Orinoco)

TELEPHONE
CANTV (Av Río Negro) Fast internet also available. There's another branch on Av Orinoco.
Movistar (Av Orinoco) Blissfully cold air-con.

TOURIST INFORMATION
Dirección de Turismo (☎ 521-0033; www.fondomixtoamazonas.com; Plaza Bolívar; 8am-noon & 2-5:30pm

Mon-Fri) On the ground floor of the Gobernación (government offices). Don't expect much.

Sights

A fascinating display of regional indigenous culture, the **Museo Etnológico de Amazonas** (Av Río Negro; admission US$0.50; ⏰ 8:30-11:30am & 2:30-6pm Tue-Fri, 9am-noon & 3-6pm Sat, 9am-1pm Sun) is one place you absolutely shouldn't miss. There are several exhibition rooms, with each one displaying personal items and model housing replicas of the Piaroa, Guajibo, Yekuana and Yanomami groups. Maybe a photo of Yanomami men blowing *yoppo* (a hallucinogenic snuff drug), through a 1m-plus-long wooden pipe will be motivation enough to visit.

Across the street from the museum, the **Mercado Indígena** (Av Río Negro) sells indigenous crafts, but you need to pick through a bit in order to find anything worthwhile, like handmade hammocks and human figures carved in wood. Nearby on the shady Plaza Bolívar, the **Catedral de María Auxiliadora** (Av Río Negro) has a colorful interior worth seeing.

You don't get a true sense of the city and its river history until you get a bird's-eye view. The **Cerro Perico**, just southwest of the town's center, provides good views over Río Orinoco and the town. Another hill, Cerro El Zamuro, commonly known as **El Mirador**, 1.5km south of the center, overlooks the **Raudales Atures**, the feisty rapids that defy river navigation. The rapids are most impressive in the wet season,

GUAYANA

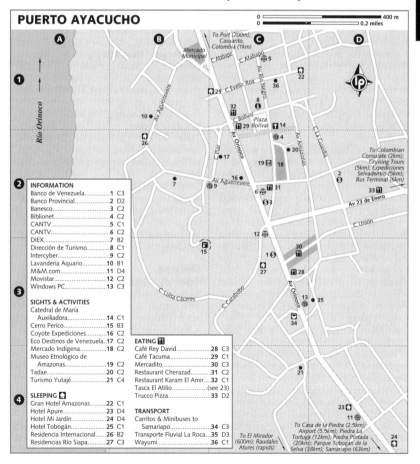

PUERTO AYACUCHO

0 — 400 m
0 — 0.2 miles

INFORMATION
Banco de Venezuela	1 C3
Banco Provincial	2 D2
Banesco	3 C2
Biblionet	4 C2
CANTV	5 C1
CANTV	6 C2
DIEX	7 B2
Dirección de Turismo	8 C1
Intercyber	9 C2
Lavandería Aquario	10 B1
M&M.com	11 D4
Movistar	12 C2
Windows PC	13 C3

SIGHTS & ACTIVITIES
Catedral de María Auxiliadora	14 C1
Cerro Perico	15 B3
Coyote Expediciones	16 C2
Eco Destinos de Venezuela	17 C2
Mercado Indígena	18 C2
Museo Etnológico de Amazonas	19 C2
Tadae	20 C2
Turismo Yutajé	21 C4

SLEEPING
Gran Hotel Amazonas	22 C1
Hotel Apure	23 D4
Hotel Mi Jardín	24 D4
Hotel Tobogán	25 C1
Residencia Internacional	26 B2
Residencias Río Siapa	27 C3

EATING
Café Rey David	28 C3
Café Tacuma	29 C1
Mercadito	30 C3
Restaurant Cherazad	31 C2
Restaurant Karam El Amir	32 C1
Tasca El Atilio	(see 23)
Trucco Pizza	33 D2

TRANSPORT
Carritos & Minibuses to Samariapo	34 C3
Transporte Fluvial La Roca	35 D3
Wayumi	36 C1

To Port (700m); Casuarito, Colombia (1km)

To Colombian Consulate (2km); Cruising Tours (5km); Expediciones Selvadentro (5km); Bus Terminal (6km)

To Casa de la Piedra (2.5km); Piedra La Tortuga (12km); Piedra Pintada (20km); Parque Tobogán de la Selva (38km); Samariapo (63km)

To El Mirador (600m); Raudales Atures (rapids)

when the water is high, and they encompass a sprawling chain of wooded islands with gorgeous boulder beaches.

To the southeast and closer to the airport, the **Casa de la Piedra** (Av La Florida, Urb La Florida) is a cute little house built on two boulders; it looks like the building fell from the sky and landed there.

Tours

Although Puerto Ayacucho is the only major city in Amazons, it doesn't get a reliable stream of tourists, so you need to plan ahead in order to visit off-the-beaten-path destinations. Unless you want to do a standard tour like Cerro Autana, you should book in advance, as most of the tour operators fashion individualized trips. Amazonas covers a huge amount of territory, and tour operators can develop all sorts of itineraries according to your interests and time.

Among the popular shorter tours are a three-day trip up the Río Cuao and a three-day trip up the Sipapo and Autana Rivers to the foot of Cerro Autana. Expect to pay from US$60 to US$75 per person per day all-inclusive, and try to negotiate bonus side trips to Piedra Pintada, La Tortuga and/or Parque Tobogán.

The Ruta Humboldt, following the route of the great explorer Alexander von Humboldt (see the boxed text p330), is a longer and more adventurous trip. It goes along the Orinoco, Brazo Casiquiare and Guainía Rivers up to Maroa. The boat is then transported overland to Yavita, and returns down the Atabapo and Orinoco rivers to Puerto Ayacucho. This trip can take from 10 to 15 days and will cost around US$125 to US$200 per person per day. Tour operators don't usually do the whole loop, but only its most attractive fragments, including Brazo Casiquiare, skipping over the less interesting parts by plane.

Much of Amazonas is not open to independent travelers. The far southeastern part of Amazonas beyond La Esmeralda, including basically all the Parque Nacional Parima-Tapirapecó, where the Yanomami live, is a restricted area; you need special permits that are virtually impossible to get. Some agents get around the ban by visiting Yanomami villages on the Río Siapa off Brazo Casiquiare. Some exceptions seem to be made for scholarly research groups, but resident indigenous com-

munities have the right to deny visits to their area. For adventurous river journeys, tour companies will acquire any required permits necessary. Make sure you carry your passport and tourist permit on all trips.

Recommended tour operators:

Coyote Expediciones (☎ 521-4583, 0416-448-7125; coyotexpedition@cantv.net; Av Aguerrevere) A busy and popular outfit operating here for 15 years, it specializes in three-day trips to Autana (US$180 per person) and has frequent departures.

Cruising Tours (☎ 414-5036, 0416-785-5033; cruisingtours@hotmail.com; Valle Verde Triángulo) A 25-year veteran of the region, Axel Keleman can arrange all kinds of expeditions throughout Amazonas and has wonderful stories to tell. Tour participants can stay in his self-catering guesthouse the night before and after trips. The office is 5km east of the center.

Eco Destinos de Venezuela (☎ 521-3964, 0416-448-6394; henryamazonas@hotmail.com; Calle Piar) Specializes in Cerro Autana trips; a minimum of three people needed.

Expediciones Selvadentro (☎ 414-7458; www .selvadentro.com; Vía Alto Carinagua) Long, adventurous trips to distant destinations (around US$140 to US$150 per person per day) aboard the *Iguana*, its 17m-long comfortable catamaran with toilet and kitchen, personally guided by the experienced manager Lucho Navarro. The office is 5km east of the center.

Tadae (☎ 521-4882, 0414-486-5923; tadaevenezuela@ hotmail.com; Av Río Negro) Apart from the staple Autana and Cuao tours, Tadae offers rafting on the Raudales Atures (US$28).

Turismo Yutajé (☎ 521-0664, 0416-747-8234; www .mipagina.cantv.net/turismoamazonas; Barrio Monte Bello) An experienced, responsible and long-established company with good prices and experience. Manager Virgilio Limpias works with small groups of tourists and researchers, and hires guides from local indigenous communities.

Sleeping

Residencia Internacional (☎ 521-0242; Av Aguerrevere; d with fan US$14-19, d/tr with air-con US$37/46; [P] [icon]) This friendly, family-operated place on a quiet residential street has a rainbow palette of 20 simple rooms arrayed along a long courtyard. Borrow a candle and wait out the frequent city power outages on the rooftop terrace.

Hotel Tobogán (☎ 521-0320; Av Orinoco; d/tr/q US$14/19/23; [P] [icon]) The larger four-person rooms flirt with antiseptic hospital-ward decor. Get a room away from Av Orinoco, which can be slightly noisy.

Residencias Río Siapa (☎ 521-0138; Calle Carabobo; d/tr US$14/16/19; [P] [icon]) Clean, basic and good-sized rooms close to the middle of town but still quiet. Look for the hotel sign written in paving stones on the driveway wall.

Hotel Mi Jardín (☎ 521-4647; hotelmijardin@hotmail .com; Av Orinoco; d US$28-37, tr/q US$51/56; P ❄) A bit south of the center, this well-designed five-story hotel has 66 rooms with windows that catch the breeze and take in views of nearby hills. Enjoy the night air in the large open-air courtyard crawling with bougainvillea.

Hotel Apure (☎ 521-4443; fax 521-0049; Av Orinoco; d US$28-40, tr/q US$46/58; P ❄) Slightly sterile but spotlessly clean, the Apure has 27 good-sized rooms with air-con and cable TV. Comfy lounges and a dramatic wooden entryway add nice touches, and the tasca restaurant downstairs (see below) is wonderful and convenient.

Gran Hotel Amazonas (☎ 809-0099, 521-5633; aya cucho-liz@hotmail.com; cnr Avs Evelio Roa & Amazonas; d/tr US$46/56; P ❄ ☐) Puerto Ayacucho's finest, the recently remodeled Gran Amazonas has a lodge-like atrium, a large pool and a good (but ridiculously slow) tasca restaurant. All 20 rooms are done up in tasteful tropical colors and wicker furniture, with refrigerators and nicely tiled bathrooms.

Eating

Café Tacuma (cnr Av Orinoco & Calle Bolívar; pastries US$1; ☽ 7am-10pm Mon-Sat, 7am-2pm & 6-10pm Sun) On a tranquil section of Av Orinoco, this *panadería* has excellent coffee, savory pastries and sidewalk seating that's just right for people-watching.

Café Rey David (Av Orinoco; mains US$3-7; ☽ 7-11am & 3-7pm) A streetside café right in the thick of it all, serving a bit of everything – whole roasted chickens, *arepas*, pizza, ice-cream bars – whatever you can dream up.

Restaurant Karam El Amir (☎ 521-1610; Av Orinoco; sandwiches US$5, mains US$7; ☽ 10:30am-10:30pm) A relaxed Middle Eastern eatery that stays open all day, cooking up decent falafels and filling shawarma sandwiches.

Trucco Pizza (☎ 521-4721; Av 23 de Enero; pizza US$6; ☽ lunch & dinner) A small fan-cooled patio eatery set back from the road, it makes calzones, burgers and delicious pizza.

Restaurant Cherazad (☎ 521-5679; cnr Avs Aguerrevere & Río Negro; mains US$6-9) The swanky drapes border on kitsch and the textured ceiling resembles stalactites, but the menu offers a large selection of cuisines. Choose from a cornucopia of Arabic food, pizzas, pastas and grilled meats.

Tasca El Atilio (☎ 521-3569; Hotel Apure, Av Orinoco; mains US$8-12, set meal US$11; ☽ noon-11pm) An at-tractive wood interior gives this tasca restaurant a homey feel. It stocks a good selection of wines to wash down your choice of pastas (US$5 to US$6) or an extravagant *paella valenciana* (US$13).

For an inexpensive meal or a quick empanada fix, duck into the **Mercadito** (Av Orinoco), or visit one of the basic criollo eateries next door on the Av Amazonas.

Getting There & Away
TO/FROM COLOMBIA
The Colombian town of Casuarito is just across the Orinoco, and a small ferry (US$1.50 to Colombia, free return) makes the 10-minute trip all day long from the Puerto Ayacucho dock. Bring your passport to register at the port control office, and sign in again in Casuarito. If you're just doing a day trip, check back with both offices as you return.

From Casuarito, boats depart daily at 7am and 4pm (Colombian time, one hour behind) for Puerto Carreño, Colombia (US$11, one to 1½ hours). Puerto Carreño is a long, one-street town with an airport, a half-dozen budget hotels and a few eateries. Pick up a passport entry stamp at the DAS office (Colombian immigration), one block west of the main plaza.

Alternatively, Puerto Carreño can be reached from the Venezuelan village of Puerto Páez (US$3) via buses bound for San Fernando de Apure. The trip includes a ferry crossing of the Orinoco from El Burro to Puerto Páez. You then take a boat from the village's wharf across the Río Meta to Puerto Carreño (US$1); the boat runs regularly during the day. **Satena** (www.satena.com) has four flights per week from here to Bogotá (US$160). Buses go only in the dry season, roughly from mid-December to mid-March, but they are not advised because of the strong presence of guerrillas in the region.

Make sure to get an exit stamp from the DIEX office in Puerto Ayacucho if you're going further than Casuarito.

TO/FROM BRAZIL
Get an exit stamp at the DIEX office in Puerto Ayacucho, and make sure you have yellow fever certification to enter Brazil. Fly south to San Carlos de Río Negro, where irregular boats will take you to San Simón de Cocuy, on the border. From here you must take a 12-hour boat ride (over one or two days) to São Gabriel da Cachoeira (Brazil).

All gas here is imported, so boat prices can be as high as US$500 to US$600; if you have time to wait, you may be able to hitch. Get an entrance stamp in São Gabriel. There are flights to Manaus (US$280) or you can take a week-long boat trip (US$150). Most of Puerto Ayacucho's tour companies can tailor a tour that concludes in San Carlos de Río Negro, or even escort you to São Gabriel.

AIR
The airport is 6km southeast of town; taxis charge US$2 to US$3 to get there and the departure tax is US$3. Conviasa handles flights to Caracas (US$90) every day but Saturday, and the military airline, **Ruta Social Aérea** (☎ 0243-808-7502, 0416-643-9602; airport terminal), flies to San Fernando de Apure (US$20) and Maracay (US$40) on Tuesday and Thursday. **Wayumi** (☎ 521-0635; Calle Evelio Roa) operates daily flights to San Juan de Manapiare (US$70), and two weekly stops at both San Carlos de Río Negro (US$140) and Maroa (US$90). It also flies pricey charters to San Fernando de Atabapo and La Esmeralda.

BOAT
Transporte Fluvial La Roca (☎ 809-1595, 0416-240-1428; Pasaje Orinoco, Centro Comercial Rapagna, Av Orinoco) runs daily services to San Fernando de Atabapo (US$19, three hours) on a 28-person boat.

BUS
The bus terminal sits 6km east of the center, on the outskirts of town. City buses go there from Av 23 de Enero, or take a taxi (US$2). Buses to Ciudad Bolívar (US$13 to US$15, 10 to 12 hours, 728km) depart regularly throughout the day. There are a few morning departures and one night bus daily to San Fernando de Apure (US$15, seven hours, 299km), from where you can connect with buses to Caracas, Maracay, Valencia, Barinas and San Cristóbal. Carritos to Samariapo (US$14, 1¼ hours, 63km), as well as cheaper minibuses (US$1.50), depart from Av Orinoco in front of the Panadería Barahona.

AROUND PUERTO AYACUCHO
The **Piedra La Tortuga** is an enormous boulder that looks like a giant turtle submerged partway into the earth. There are great views from the apex of the shell. Register at the nearby Inparques office before climbing, and you need to set out before 2pm. The rock for-

mation is very close to the Samariapo road, and por puestos or taxis can drop you off at Inparques.

Another massive rock called the **Piedra Pintada** boasts pre-Columbian petroglyphs carved high above the ground in a virtually inaccessible place. They include a 40m-long serpent and a 10m-long centipede. From Puerto Ayacucho, take the Ruta 17 bus from Av Orinoco to the village of Comunidad Pintao, 17km south of the city on the Samariapo road, and then take a side road left (east) for 3km. The monument is a 10-minute walk from the village.

A smooth and elongated stone surface flushed by a swift creek, the **Parque Tobogán de la Selva** is a popular natural water slide and picnic spot 32km south and 6km east of Puerto Ayacucho. There's no public transportation all the way to the park, but the Ruta 17 bus (which also goes to Piedra Pintada) will drop you at the road fork just 2km away from the park before it continues to the village of Comunidad Coromoto. The park was closed for renovation at the time of research, but was expected to reopen by publication time. In the past, you could camp or hang your tent here for a small fee.

The best known and most commonly visited tepui in Amazonas is **Cerro Autana**, about 80km south of Puerto Ayacucho. It is the sacred mountain of the Piaroa peoples, who consider it the birthplace of the universe. From one side the tepui looks like a gigantic tree trunk, growing 700m above the surrounding plains (1208m above sea level). About 200m below the top is the mouth of an enormous cave system, with a labyrinth that passes all the way through the tepui.

SAN FERNANDO DE ATABAPO
☎ 0248 / pop 4500
The former state capital of Amazonas, San Fernando de Atabapo was founded as a mission settlement in the 18th century. Located where the Orinoco, Guaviare and Atabapo rivers meet, in the summer dry season (approximately January to March) the black waters of the Río Atabapo recede, baring beautiful white-sand beaches not generally found in the jungle.

In 1800 Alexander von Humboldt (see the boxed text, p330) visited here during his epic trip through Latin America, but the town is mostly known as an important producer of *balatá* (rubber). San Fernando was the epicenter of the regional rubber boom that began at the end of the 19th century.

For years, the river town was dominated by a despised and blood-thirsty *caudillo* (dictator) named José Tomás Funes. In an infamous 1913 bloodbath he killed the state governor, assumed power and ordered the massacre of hundreds of local rubber tappers. He is also held responsible for the deaths of thousands of indigenous people. In 1921 he finally paid the price for his crimes and was executed in the Plaza Bolívar; a plaque marks the site.

Interestingly, oral histories have kept his vicious reputation alive. When Yekuana women see lightning during thunderstorms, they scare children by saying 'Here come the Creoles, here comes Funes!'

Sleeping & Eating

Posada Atabapo (☎ 808-1033, 541-1139; Calle Piar; d US$19-33, breakfast US$5, lunch US$7, dinner US$7; ✷) A comfortable 11-room posada with traditional details, private bathrooms and a *comedor* for guests.

Posada Turística Pendare (Plaza Bolívar; d US$28-37) A convenient 10-room posada right on Plaza Bolívar, next to Casa Funes.

Getting There & Away
AIR
From Puerto Ayacucho, **Wayumi** (☎ 521-0635; Calle Evelio Roa) runs charter flights. All prices for the flight (40 minutes) are based on same-day roundtrip flights, and depend on the total number of passengers. Per person roundtrip fares are about US$270 in a full three-seater and US$140 per person in a full six-seater plane.

BOAT
Transporte Fluvial La Roca (☎ 809-1595, 0416-240-1428; Pasaje Orinoco, Centro Comercial Rapagna, Av Orinoco), in Puerto Ayacucho, runs a daily morning service to San Fernando de Atabapo (US$19, three hours) on a 28-person boat.

GUAYANA

Directory

CONTENTS

ACCOMMODATIONS

Hotels are not hard to come by in Venezuela and there are budget and midrange options in most towns (though Caracas is conspicuously short on quality budget accommodations). Popular tourist areas like Isla de Margarita and Canaima can become quite full on major holidays, but it is almost always possible to find a vacant room. Camp grounds are rare, but you can rough it in the countryside. Camping on the beach is popular, but be cautious and don't leave your tent unattended. Venezuela has almost no youth hostels. Be aware that urban budget hotels may double as hourly-rates love motels, particularly in Caracas.

PRACTICALITIES

- Venezuela uses the metric system for weights and measures.
- Electrical current is 110V, 60 cycles AC throughout the country. Plugs are the US type with two flat prongs.
- The two leading Caracas newspapers *El Universal* and *El Nacional* have country-wide distribution; both have reasonable coverage of national and international affairs, sports, economics and culture. The *Daily Journal* is the main English-language newspaper published in Venezuela, but it's hard to get outside Caracas.
- Many hotels have cable TV, bringing some English-language stations to your hotel room.

A good choice of accommodations is the posada, a small, family-run guesthouse. These have mushroomed over past decades in the cities and, particularly, in the smaller towns and the countryside. They usually have more character then hotels and offer more personalized attention. Most posadas are budget places but there are also some midrange and a few top-end posadas.

Another kind of countryside lodging are the *campamentos* (literally 'camps'), which have sprung up even in the most remote areas. Not to be confused with campsites, *campamentos* can be anything from a rustic shelter with a few hammocks to a smart country lodge with a swimming pool and its own airstrip. More commonly, though, it will be a collection of cabañas plus a restaurant. *Campamentos* provide accommodations, food and usually tours, sometimes selling these services as all-inclusive packages.

Places to stay can legally charge a 16% VAT on top of the room price, though few budget hotels or posadas actually do it. The prices listed in this book have included this tax already. Most top-end hotels will accept payment by credit card, but this is rarely offered in budget places so make sure you have cash at hand. As in most developing countries, prices are not set in stone and can change due to the day of the week or if the person at the front desk feels like it. Never count on being able to use a credit card – even if they say that they accept plastic.

Hotels in the popular holiday destinations (eg Isla de Margarita) increase their rates during holiday periods. On the other hand, in the slow season it's possible to bargain, both in the budget and five-star hotels, but always try to do it in a friendly and easygoing manner.

Budget

In this book, budget category generally covers places where a double room costs about US$20 or less (this rises to about US$30 or US$40 in areas like Caracas and Gran Roque). Budget places to stay have a variety of names, such as *hotel, residencia, hospedaje,* posada and *pensión.* The last two are meant to be small, family-run guesthouses, but don't jump to conclusions by just looking at the sign out the front; check inside.

Budget hotels tend to be grouped together in certain areas, usually around the market and bus terminal and in the backstreets of the city center. Most of the cheapies have a private bathroom, which includes a toilet and shower. Note that cheap hotel plumbing can't cope with toilet paper, so throw it in the wastebasket that is normally provided. Venezuelans love TV, so most budget hotels provide TVs in the rooms.

As most of the country lies in the lowland tropics, rooms have either a fan or air-con, but there's no hot water. Air-con may not always be advantageous. The equipment often dates from oil-rich years and, after decades of use, it may be in a desperate state of disrepair and very noisy. There's usually only the on/off switch, and it's not always clear which is better. Sometimes they're *very* efficient and turn the room into a freezer; other times they don't cool at all.

BOOK ACCOMMODATIONS ONLINE

For more accommodations reviews and recommendations by Lonely Planet authors, check out the online booking service at www.lonelyplanet.com. You'll find the true, insider lowdown on the best places to stay. Reviews are thorough and independent. Best of all, you can book online.

Always have a look at the room and check the fan or air-con before you book in and pay.

Few budget hotels have single or twin rooms, but many do have *matrimoniales* (rooms with a double bed intended for couples). This type of room usually costs the same for one person as for two, so traveling as a couple significantly reduces the cost of accommodations. Single travelers are at a disadvantage. In this guide, price ranges given for doubles will include prices for *matrimoniales*.

Many cheap hotels double as 'love hotels' (that rent rooms by the hour), and it may be impossible to avoid staying in one from time to time.

Midrange

In this guide, midrange covers the places where double rooms and/or *matrimoniales* generally cost between US$20 and US$50.

Many of the midrange hotels nestle conveniently in city centers – you'll often find a few of them in the environs of the local Plaza Bolívar. Some of them can be booked online and paid for by credit card, but most still follow traditional style – reserve by phone and pay in cash.

Although sometimes lacking in character, midrange hotels usually provide better rooms and more facilities than budget establishments, and virtually every room will have a TV, often with cable. They will almost always have private bathrooms and air-con, and the air-con will usually be quieter than those in the cheapies. That said, it's a good idea to inspect the room in these hotels before you commit yourself.

Midrange hotels in tourism destinations with a lower number of accommodations, such as Canaima or Los Roques, or those in Caracas, can have prices on par with top-end hotels in the rest of Venezuela.

Top End

Any hotel with double rooms costing US$50 or more is considered top end. By and large, top-end hotels are outside downtown areas, in greener and wealthier residential suburbs, sometimes quite a way from the center. After all, if you have money enough to stay in such places, you'll also have some change for a taxi to get around.

Standards of these hotels vary, but you can expect silent, central air-con; hot water; a reception desk open around the clock; and proper facilities to safeguard guests' valuables. An increasing number of these hotels have internet connections in rooms or in a business center, and you can usually book these hotels online. However, keep in mind that they are likely to charge you the full price online, while walk-in rates off the street can be much lower.

Prices vary greatly and don't always reflect quality. You can normally grab quite a good double with facilities for somewhere between $50 and $100, except in Caracas and Isla de Margarita, where prices are generally higher. Los Roques also has higher prices, but due to development restrictions (it's in national park land), there are no five-star accommodations – though the bill might look like it comes from a world-class hotel. Only Caracas and Isla de Margarita, and to a lesser extent Puerto La Cruz and Maracaibo, have a choice of five-star hotels. Sometimes top-end hotels have much lower weekend rates.

ACTIVITIES

Venezuela has much to offer those who love the great outdoors. Mérida (p185), in particular, is known as Venezuela's adventure-sports capital.

Fishing

Los Roques (p103) is renowned as one of the world's finest areas for game fishing, particularly for bonefish. You can also go piranha fishing in the *hatos* (large cattle ranches typical of Los Llanos; p222) and trout fishing in the mountain lakes around Mérida (p191).

Hiking & Trekking

Many of Venezuela's 40-odd national parks provide a choice of walks ranging from easy, well-signposted trails to wild jungle paths. Parque Nacional El Ávila (p96), near Caracas, offers some of the best easy walking trails, while Mérida's surrounds (p190) offer fabulous opportunities for high-mountain trekking. Other hiking possibilities include Parque Nacional Guatopo (p109), Parque Nacional Henri Pittier (p119), Parque Nacional San Esteban (p139), Sierra de San Luis (p153), Parque Nacional Península de Paria (p282) and one of the most adventurous and fascinating treks, to the top of Roraima (p319).

Mountain Biking

The region around Mérida is excellent for mountain biking, and the tour operators in the city organize biking trips and rent out bikes (see p191).

Paragliding

Mérida (p190) is the best place in Venezuela to go paragliding. Double gliders are available, so even greenhorns can try this breathtaking experience.

Rafting & Canyoning

Rafting trips are run on some Andean rivers (arranged in Mérida; p190) and in the Parque Nacional Mochima (arranged in Mochima; p264). There are new rafting opportunities opening in the Amazonas region too (ask travel agencies in Puerto Ayacucho; p329). The Mérida region is also the home of canyoning (climbing, rappeling and hiking down a river canyon), the rapidly growing adventure craze.

Snorkeling & Scuba Diving

Venezuela has excellent snorkeling and scuba diving around the offshore archipelagos such as Los Roques (p103). There's also some good snorkeling and diving around the islands closer to the mainland, including in Parque Nacional Mochima (p260) and Parque Nacional Morrocoy (p155). In all these places, local operators offer courses and diving trips, and rent equipment.

Spelunking

Spelunkers can explore some of Venezuela's several hundred caves. The most famous and among the most spectacular is the Cueva del Guácharo (p285). There are about 20 other lesser-known caves in the same area.

Wildlife- & Bird-Watching

Los Llanos is one of the best regions to see wild animals, including caimans, capybaras (aquatic rodents), anacondas, anteaters and birds. Wildlife safaris are organized from the *hatos* (p222) and from Mérida (p191). If you are particularly interested in bird-watching, consider Parque Nacional Henri Pittier (p119) and Parque Nacional Yacambú (p169). There are also some good bird-watching spots around Mérida (p191) and along La Escalera (p317) on the Ciudad Guayana–Santa Elena road.

Windsurfing & Kitesurfing

Venezuela has some windsurfing and kitesurfing areas of international reputation, including

Adícora (p151) and El Yaque (p253). There is also fine windsurfing at Los Roques (p103).

BUSINESS HOURS

Fixed business hours may exist theoretically in Venezuela, but, in practice, opening and closing hours are relatively fluid. The working day is supposedly eight hours, from 8am to noon and 2pm to 6pm, Monday to Friday, but many businesses work shorter hours. Almost all offices, including tourist offices, are closed on Saturday and Sunday.

Usual shopping hours are 9am to 6pm or 7pm weekdays, and a half-day on Saturday (9am to 1pm). Many shops close for lunch but some work without a lunchtime break. Restaurants normally open from around noon to 9pm or 11pm, but many are closed on Sunday.

Most museums are open on Sunday but closed on Monday.

For opening hours of banks, post offices, telephone centers and internet cafés, see the respective sections in this chapter (for banks, see Money).

CHILDREN

Very few foreigners travel with children in Venezuela, but any visiting parents will easily find plenty of local companions for their kids. Venezuelan culture is very family oriented and children will likely be welcomed in most locations.

Children enjoy numerous privileges on local transportation and in accommodations and entertainment. Age limits for discounts or freebies vary from place to place, but are rarely rigidly enforced. Officially children can ride free on buses and the Caracas metro if they don't occupy a separate seat.

In most major Venezuelan cities there are usually quite a few shops devoted to kids' clothing, shoes and toys, and you can buy disposable diapers (nappies) and baby food in most supermarkets and pharmacies. For more information, see Lonely Planet's *Travel with Children*.

CLIMATE CHARTS

See p14 for general information about climate and p340 for various climate charts. Venezuela is close to the equator, so average temperatures vary little throughout the year. They do, however, change with altitude, dropping about 42°F with every 1000m increase. Since over 90%

of Venezuela lies below 1000m, you'll experience temperatures between 70°F and 85°F in most places. The Andean and coastal mountain ranges have more moderate temperatures.

COURSES

Venezuela is not known as a major destination for Spanish-language schools, but it does have programs in most big cities. You can also find an independent teacher and arrange individual classes. Possibly the best place in Venezuela to learn Spanish is Mérida (p191), which has plenty of language-teaching facilities and a welcoming local culture, and is one of the most affordable places to study. You can also study Spanish in Caracas (p73) and in Pampatar on Isla de Margarita (p249).

CUSTOMS

Customs regulations don't differ much from those in other South American countries. You are allowed to bring in personal belongings and presents you intend to give to Venezuelan residents, as well as personal and professional camera gear, camping equipment, sports accessories, a personal computer and the like.

According to Venezuelan law, possession, trafficking and consumption of drugs are all serious offenses subject to heavy penalties. The government is trying to stem the flow of drug trafficking from neighboring countries. There are random searches of vehicles and buses inside the borders too.

DANGERS & ANNOYANCES

Venezuela is a reasonably safe place to travel. However, theft, robbery and common crime are on the increase, particularly in major cities. Caracas is, far and away, the most dangerous place in the country, and you should take care while strolling around the streets, particularly at night (see p61).

The most common methods of theft are snatching your daypack, camera or watch; taking advantage of a moment's inattention

---

COPIES

All important documents (passport, credit cards, travel insurance policy, air tickets, driver's license etc) should be photocopied before you leave home. Leave one copy at home and keep another with you, separate from the originals.

to pick up your gear and run away; or pick-pocketing. Thieves often work in pairs or groups; one or more will distract you, while an accomplice does the deed. Theft from hotel rooms, cars and unattended tents are also potential dangers.

If you can, leave your money and valuables somewhere safe before walking the streets. In practice, it's good to carry a decoy bundle of small notes, the equivalent of US$5 to US$10, ready to hand over in case of an assault; if you don't have anything, robbers can become frustrated and unpredictable.

Armed hold-ups in the cities can occur even in upmarket suburbs. If you are accosted by robbers, it is best to give them what they are after. Don't try to escape or struggle, and don't count on any help from passers-by. There have been reports of armed robbery on remote hiking trails and deserted beaches or even in a few posadas in tourist towns, but they are considerably less frequent. Also be aware of your surrounding when withdrawing cash from an ATM at any time of the day.

When traveling around the country, there are plenty of *alcabalas* (checkpoints), though not all are actually operating. They check the identity documents of passengers, and occasionally the luggage as well. In the cities, police checks are uncommon, but they do occur, so always have your passport with you. If you don't, you may end up at the police station. Police are not necessarily trustworthy (though many are), so do not blindly accept the demands of these authority figures.

If your passport, valuables or other belongings are stolen, go to the nearest Policía Técnica Judicial (PTJ) office to make a *denuncia* (report). The officer on duty will write a statement according to what you tell them. It should include the description of the events and the list of stolen articles. Pay attention to

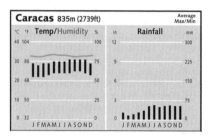

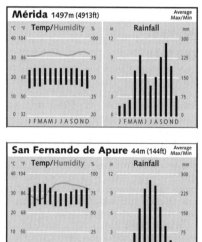

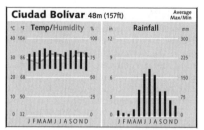

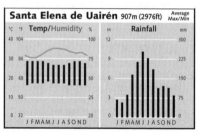

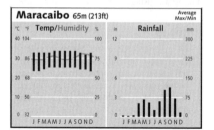

TEN BASIC PRECAUTIONS AGAINST THEFT & ROBBERY

■ Keep your money and documents as secure as possible, preferably in a money belt next to your skin.

■ Distribute your valuables about your person and luggage to avoid the risk of losing everything in one fell swoop.

■ Don't venture into poor suburbs, desolate streets or suspicious-looking surroundings, especially after dark.

■ Wear casual and inexpensive dress, preferably in plain, sober tones rather than in bright colors.

■ Don't wear jewelry or wristwatches, and keep your camera out of sight as much as possible.

■ Behave confidently on the street; don't look lost or stand with a blank expression in the middle of the street.

■ Before arriving in a new place, make sure you have a map or at least a rough idea about orientation.

■ Use taxis if this seems the appropriate way to avoid walking through risky or unknown areas.

■ Look around to see whether you're being observed or followed, especially while leaving a bank, *casa de cambio* (money-exchange office) or an ATM.

■ Have good travel insurance just in case something goes wrong.

---

the wording you use, make sure you include every stolen item and document, and carefully check the statement before signing it to ensure it contains exactly what you've said. They will give you a copy of the statement, which serves as a temporary identity document, and you will need to present it to your insurer in order to make a claim. Don't expect your things to be found, as the police are unlikely to do anything about it. Stolen cars and motorcycles should also be reported at the PTJ.

All said, your biggest dangers are the standard risks of international travel: sunburn, food-borne illness and traffic-related concerns.

DISCOUNT CARDS

Students and senior citizens can get small discounts on airfares with some domestic carriers and on ferry tickets to Isla de Margarita, but that's about it. There are no discounts on intercity bus fares, urban transportation or cinema tickets, and most museums have free admission anyway.

EMBASSIES & CONSULATES
Venezuelan Embassies & Consulates

Venezuelan embassies abroad include the following:

Australia (☎ 2-6290-2967, 6290-2968; www.venezuela -emb.org.au; 7 Culgoa Circuit O'Malley, Canberra, ACT, 2606)

Canada (☎ 613-235-5151, 235-0551; www.misionven ezuela.org; 32 Range Rd, Ottawa, Ontario K1N 4J8)

Colombia (☎ 1-640-1213; www.embaven.org.co; Carrera 11 No 87-51, Bogotá)

France (☎ 01-45-53-29-98, 01-47-55-00-11; www .embavenez-paris.com; 11 rue Copernic, Paris 75116)

Germany (☎ 030-832-24-00; www.botschaft-ven ezuela.de; Schillstrasse 9-10, 10785 Berlin)

Italy (☎ 068-07-97-97, 068-07-94-64; embaveit@iol.it; Via Nicolo Tartaglia 11, 00197 Rome)

Japan (☎ 0334-091-501; embavene@interlink.or.jp; 38 Kowa Bldg, 12-24 Nishi Azabu, 4 Chrome, Minato Ku, Tokyo 106)

Netherlands (☎ 0703-65-12-56, 0703-63-38-05; embavene@xs4all.nl; Nassaulaan 2, 2514 JS The Hague)

Spain (☎ 01-598-12-00; embvenez@teleline.es; Edificio Eurocentro, Calle Capitan Haya No 1, 28020 Madrid)

Trinidad & Tobago (☎ 627-9821; embaveneztt@ carib-link.net; Venezuelan Center, 16 Victoria Av, Port of Spain)

UK (☎ 020-7581-2776, 7584-4206; www.venezuela.em bassyhomepage.com; 1 Cromwell Rd, London SW7 2HW)

USA (☎ 202-342-2214; www.embavenez-us.org; 1099 30th St NW, Washington DC 20007)

Embassies & Consulates in Venezuela

The following embassies are located in Caracas. Consulates are at the same address as the embassies unless otherwise noted. If you can't find your home embassy, check a Caracas phone directory.

DIRECTORY

YOUR OWN EMBASSY

It's important to realize what your own embassy – the embassy of the country of which you are a citizen – can and can't do to help if you get into trouble. Generally speaking, it won't be much help if the trouble you're in is remotely your own fault. Remember that you are bound by the laws of the country you are in. Your embassy will not be sympathetic if you end up in jail after committing a crime locally, even if such actions are legal in your own country.

In genuine emergencies you might get some assistance, but only if other channels have been exhausted. For example, if you need to get home urgently, a free ticket home is exceedingly unlikely – the embassy would expect you to have insurance. If all your money and documents are stolen, it should assist you with getting a new passport, but a loan for onward travel is out of the question. See also Legal Matters, p344.

Brazil (Map p70; ☎ 0212-261-5505; www.embaja dabrasil.org.ve; Centro Gerencial Mohedano, cnr Calle Los Chaguaramos & Av Mohedano, La Castellana, Caracas; Ⓜ Chacao); Consulate in Santa Elena de Uairén (Map p323; ☎ 0289-995-1256; Av Gran Mariscal)
Canada (Map p70; ☎ 0212-264-0833, 266-7176; crcas@dfait-maeci.gc.ca; cnr Avs Francisco de Miranda & Sur Altamira, Altamira, Caracas; Ⓜ Altamira)
Colombia (Map p80; ☎ 0212-261-5584; Torre Credival, cnr 2a Av de Campo Alegre & Av Francisco de Miranda, Campo Alegre, Caracas; Ⓜ Chacaíto); Consulate in Maracaibo (☎ 0261-792-1483; Av 3Y No 70-16); Consulate in Puerto Ayacucho (☎ 0248-521-0789; Calle Yapacana off Av Rómulo Gallegos)
France (Map p80; ☎ 0212-909-6500; www.francia.org .ve; Edificio Embajada de Francia, cnr Calle Madrid & Av La Trinidad, Las Mercedes, Caracas)
Germany Consulate (Map p70; ☎ 0212-261-0181; diplogermacara@cantv.net; Torre La Castellana, Av Princi pal de la Castellana, La Castellana, Caracas; Ⓜ Altamira)
Guyana (☎ 0212-977-1158; embaguy@caracas-office .org.ve; Quinta Roraima, Av El Paseo, Prados del Este, Caracas)
Israel (Map pp56-7; ☎ 0212-239-4921; Centro Empre sarial Miranda, cnr Av Francisco de Miranda & Av Principal de los Ruices, Los Ruices, Caracas; Ⓜ Los Cortijos)
Italy (Map p80; ☎ 0212-952-7311; ambcara@italamb .org.ve; Edificio Atrium, Calle Sorocaima; El Rosal, Caracas; Ⓜ Chacao)
Japan Consulate (Map p70; ☎ 0212-261-8333; csjapon@genesisbci.net; Edificio Bancaracas, Plaza La Castellana, La Castellana, Caracas; Ⓜ Altamira)
Netherlands Consulate (Map p70; ☎ 0212-263-3076, 263-3622; Edificio San Juan, cnr 2a Transversal & Av San Juan Bosco, Altamira, Caracas; Ⓜ Altamira)
Spain (Map pp56-7; ☎ 0212-263-2855; espanve@cantv .net; Quinta Marmolejo, Av Mohedano btwn 1a & 2a Transversal, La Castellana, Caracas)
Suriname (Map p70; ☎ 0212-261-2724; embsur1@cantv.net; Quinta Los Milagros, 4a Av btwn 7a & 8a Transversal, Altamira, Caracas)

Trinidad & Tobago (Map p70; ☎ 0212-261-3748; embassytt@cantv.net; Quinta Serrana, 4a Av btwn 7a & 8a Transversal, Altamira, Caracas)
UK (Map p70; ☎ 0212-263-8411; www.britain.org.ve; Torre La Castellana, Av Principal de la Castellana, La Castel lana, Caracas; Ⓜ Altamira)
USA (Map pp56-7; ☎ 0212-975-6411, 975-7811; www .embajadausa.org.ve; cnr Calle F & Calle Suapure, Colinas del Valle Arriba, Caracas)

FESTIVALS & EVENTS

Given the strong Catholic character of Venezuela, many feasts and celebrations follow the Church calendar – Christmas, Carnaval, Easter and Corpus Christi are celebrated all over the country. The religious calendar is dotted with saints' days, and every village and town has its own patron saint and will hold a celebratory feast on that day.

One of Venezuela's most colorful festivals is the Diablos Danzantes (see p108). It's held on Corpus Christi in San Francisco de Yare, located about 70km southeast of Caracas. The ceremony consists of a spectacular parade and the dance of the devils, performed by dancers wearing elaborate masks and costumes.

Cultural events such as festivals of theater, film or classical music are almost exclusively confined to Caracas. Venezuela's main religious and cultural festivals and events are listed below. See the respective sections for more information.

JANUARY
Feria de San Sebastián Main event of San Cristóbal, taking place in the second half of January (p214).
Fiesta Patronales de la Divina Pastora Barquisime to's major feast, held in mid-January (p163).
Paradura del Niño Celebrated for the whole month in Mérida state (p192).

FEBRUARY/MARCH

Carnaval Celebrated throughout the country on the Monday and Tuesday prior to Ash Wednesday; particularly elaborate in Mérida, El Callao and Carúpano.

MARCH/APRIL

Festival Internacional de Teatro Cultural festival held in Caracas on even years (p74).

Semana Santa Easter week (the week leading up to Easter Sunday) sees solemn celebrations in the churches all around the country and processions on Maundy Thursday and Good Friday.

MAY/JUNE

Festival de los Diablos Danzantes Colorful dancing devils invade San Francisco de Yare, Chuao and some other villages in the northern-central region on Corpus Christi (60 days after Easter, in May or June; see p108).

SEPTEMBER

Fiesta de la Virgen de Coromoto Major pilgrimage gathering in Guanare on September 8, to honor the anniversary of the Virgin's appearance (p231).

Fiesta de la Virgen del Valle Another focus of religious fervor, on September 8 at Valle del Espíritu Santo on Isla de Margarita (p249).

NOVEMBER

Feria de la Chinita Maracaibo's major annual bash, held for a week and culminating with the coronation of Zulia's patron saint on November 18 (p176).

FOOD

See the Food & Drink chapter (p48) to see what you can eat, where and when. In this guide we have divided eating sections into budget, mid-range and top end in major cities such as Caracas. Expect main dishes to cost under US$5 in a budget eatery, US$5 to US$10 in a midranger, and over US$10 in a top-end place (more so in Caracas and top tourist spots).

GAY & LESBIAN TRAVELERS

Homosexuality isn't illegal in Venezuela, but the overwhelmingly Catholic society tends to both deny and suppress it. The gay and lesbian movement is at present still very underdeveloped. Caracas has the largest gay and lesbian community and the most open gay life, and is the best place to make contacts and get to know what's going on (see the boxed text p88). Get as much information there as you can, because elsewhere in Venezuela it can be difficult to contact the gay community.

Caracas' contacts include the **Movimiento Ambiente de Venezuela** (☎ 0212-321-9470) and the gay 'what's on' guide **En Ambiente** (☎ 0414-219-1837; enambiente@latinmail.com). Also check local website www.rumbacaracas.com (in Spanish).

HOLIDAYS

Keep in mind that Venezuelans usually take holidays over Christmas, Carnaval (several days prior to Ash Wednesday) and Semana Santa (the week before Easter Sunday). In these periods, you'll have to plan ahead as it can be tricky to find a place to stay in more popular destinations. The upside is that they really come alive with holiday merrymakers.

Official public holidays include:

Año Nuevo (New Year's Day) January 1

Carnaval Monday and Tuesday prior to Ash Wednesday, February/March.

Pascua (Easter) Maundy Thursday and Good Friday, March/April.

Declaración de Independencia (Declaration of Independence) April 19

Labor Day May 1

Batalla de Carabobo (Battle of Carabobo) June 24

Día de Independecia (Independence Day) July 5

Cumpleaños de Bolívar (Bolívar's Birthday) July 24

Discovery of America October 12

Navidad (Christmas Day) December 25

INSURANCE

A travel insurance policy to cover theft, loss and medical problems is a good idea. Some policies specifically exclude 'dangerous activities,' which can include scuba diving, motorcycling, even trekking. You may prefer a policy which pays doctors or hospitals directly rather than you having to pay on the spot and claim later. If you have to claim later make sure you keep all documentation. Check that the policy covers ambulances or an emergency flight home. See p358 for more details.

INTERNET ACCESS

Virtually all cities and most towns have cybercafés. An hour of internet access will cost between US$0.50 and US$2, depending on the region, city and particular place. Mérida and Caracas have the most widespread number of cybercafés and some of the best prices. Also note that CANTV and Movistar, the two major local telephone operators (see the Telephone section under each town), often provide internet facilities.

Many cybercafés in major cities now have *banda ancha* (broadband), so connection is fast. Opening hours of cybercafés vary, but many are open 9am to 9pm or longer. In the larger cities, you'll usually find a place open till 11pm or longer, and there may be some open round the clock. Most cybercafés provide a range of related facilities, such as printing, scanning and faxing, and some offer cheap international phone calls via the internet.

Wireless internet connections are rare, but are increasing in popularity. Mérida and Caracas offer the best chance of finding a hotel with wireless access, although it can be found elsewhere.

LEGAL MATTERS

Venezuelan police are to be treated with respect, but with a healthy dose of caution too. Cases of police corruption, abuse of power and use of undue force are unfortunately common. The military is less suspect, but is still to be regarded with caution. Do not expect any 'just cause' or 'due process' that may exist in your home country.

Some travelers associate the tropics with open and relaxed drug policy. That is far from the truth in Venezuela. Penalties for trafficking, possessing and using illegal drugs are some of the heaviest in all of Latin America (and probably heavier than in your home country). Soldiers often stop and search buses on the highways. They are looking for drugs (mainly cocaine) and are known to hand search every piece of luggage on the bus – even at 3am. It is in your best interest to keep your passport on hand for identification purposes.

Venezuelan prisons are not the most pleasant places you've ever seen. Also be aware that your embassy is of limited help if you get into trouble with the law – foreigners here, as elsewhere, are subject to the laws of the host country.

While your embassy or consulate is the best stop in any emergency, bear in mind that there are some things it cannot do for you. These include getting local laws or regulations waived because you're a foreigner, investigating a crime, providing legal advice or representation in civil or criminal cases, getting you out of jail, and lending you money. An embassy or consulate can, however, issue emergency passports, contact relatives and friends, advise on how to transfer funds, provide lists of reliable local doctors, lawyers and interpreters, and visit you if you've been arrested or jailed.

MAPS

The best general map of Venezuela (scale 1:1,750,000) is published by International Travel Maps (Canada). Within Venezuela, folded road maps of the country are produced by several local publishers and are available in tourism offices, some hotels and stores that cater to foreign visitors.

MONEY

The unit of Venezuelan currency is the *bolívar*, abbreviated to B. There are 50-, 100- and 500-*bolívar* coins, and paper notes of 1000, 2000, 5000, 10,000, 20,000 and 50,000 *bolívares*. (See the boxed text below on the intended renaming and redemonination of the *bolívar* announced in March 2007.) Watch carefully the notes you pay and receive because some notes of various denominations have similar colors and are easily confused.

By far the most popular foreign currency is the US dollar, so stick strictly to the greenback. For this reason, all the prices quoted in this guide are in US dollars unless specified.

For exchange rates, see the Quick Reference page on the inside front cover of this guide. For information on costs in Venezuela, see p14.

ATMs & Banks

Cajeros automáticos (ATMs) are the easiest way of getting cash. ATMs can be found at most major banks, including Banco de Venezuela, Banco Mercantil, Banco Provincial and Banesco (these are listed under individual towns). ATMs are normally open 24 hours. Always have a backup option as some machines will eat cards. A lost or damaged

---

A STRONGER BOLÍVAR?

In March 2007 President Chávez announced his intention to rename the *bolívar* to 'bolívar fuerte' and to remove three zeros from the currency, so that one *bolívar fuerte* would equal 1000 *bolívares*. Chávez has indicated that this change, intended for January 2008, would ease growing inflation problems – a big ask given the highly unstable nature of the currency presently (see the boxed text p15).

bankcard can cause some major disruptions to your trip.

Some ATMs will ask you to enter the first few digits of your national ID document in order to process the transaction. The first two numbers of your passport will usually suffice.

Most ATMs are linked to Cirrus and Plus and should accept international Visa and MasterCard, though some don't. If this is the case, go inside the bank and get a cash advance from the cashier. The usual opening hours of banks are 8:30am to 3:30pm Monday to Friday countrywide. Venezuelan banks are almost always crowded, inefficient and painfully slow. Remember that your bank at home will usually charge a fee for each foreign ATM and cashier transaction.

Black Market

There is a thriving black market for US dollars and euros and many people will ask you to change currency in airports, bus stations or the center of towns. You can get a much better rate with these money traders, but do so at a higher risk of getting ripped off. Make sure that you are familiar with current Venezuelan currency before wading into the black market, so you don't come away with obsolete bills. Consider dealing with someone who works out of a storefront (car dealership, restaurant, hotel, whatever) so you can track them down later if there is any issue.

Cash

The usual official place to change your cash is at a *casa de cambio* (an authorized money-exchange office). They exist in most major cities and buy foreign currency (but don't sell it) at the official exchange rate. There are a number of them in Caracas, Puerto La Cruz and Porlamar, but there may be just one or two in other large cities. Italcambio is the biggest and best-known company, with branches all over the country.

By far the most popular foreign currency is the US dollar. Other internationally known currencies, such as the euro or pound sterling, can be exchanged in a *casa de cambio,* but not all will accept them and the rates are usually poor.

US dollars are normally accepted by tour operators as payment for tours, and hotels may also accept dollars.

Credit Cards

Visa and MasterCard are the most useful credit cards in Venezuela. Both are accepted as a means of payment for goods and services (though many tour operators may refuse payment by credit card or charge 10% more for the service). They are also useful for taking cash advances from banks or ATMs. Make sure you know the number to call if you lose your credit card, and be quick to cancel it if it's lost or stolen. Also remember that just because an establishment claims that it takes credit cards, doesn't mean that their machine functions correctly.

Traveler's Checks

American Express is the most recognized traveler's check brand. Corp Banca or a *casa de cambio* (try Italcambio) will cash your check, but it can be difficult to find one of these locations. Same *casas de cambio* will charge a commission of about 3% or more. Some tour operators will accept traveler's checks as payment, but cash is generally preferred.

POST

The postal service is run by **Ipostel** (www.ipostel .gob.ve in Spanish), which has post offices throughout the country. The usual opening hours are 8am to noon and 1pm to 4:30pm Monday to Friday, with regional variations. Some offices in the main cities may open longer hours and on Saturday. Airmailing a letter up to 20g costs US$0.50 to anywhere in the Americas, US$0.60 to Europe or Africa and US$0.70 to the rest of the world. Sending a package of up to 500g will cost US$6/8/10, respectively.

The service is unreliable and slow. Airmail to Europe can take up to a month to arrive, if it arrives at all.

Ipostel also handles poste restante (general delivery mail). This service is also slow and not very reliable. Letters sent to Venezuela from abroad take a long time to be delivered and sometimes simply never make it. If you decide to use poste restante, stick to the main offices in major cities.

SHOPPING

A quick perusal of street stalls in Caracas would lead you to believe that Venezuela sold little more than pirated DVDs or t-shirts with portraits of *reggaetón* stars or Chávez with the tagline: Patria o Muerte (Fatherland or Death). In fact, Venezuela offers varied, good-quality craftwork. It's particularly renowned for its fine basketry, pottery and woodcarving, which differs significantly from region to region. Other attractive crafts include handwoven hammocks of the Guajiros, papier-mâché devil masks from San Francisco de Yare and woolen ponchos from the Andes.

Try to buy crafts in their region of origin, ideally from the artisans themselves: not only are the crafts more authentic, but they are also cheaper, and the money goes directly to the artisan. If you can't get to the remote communities, shop in the markets in nearby towns. However, don't ignore handicraft shops in the large cities, particularly in Caracas, where you can find the best collections and best-quality crafts from around the country.

If you are interested in local music (*joropo, gaita,* salsa), the Caracas CD shops have the best selection. The price of locally produced CDs ranges from about US$8 to US$15.

Venezuela is noted for gold and diamonds, but don't expect to find great bargains everywhere. Possibly the cheapest place to buy gold jewelry is El Callao, but you'll find better quality in Ciudad Bolívar and Caracas.

SOLO TRAVELERS

While traveling on your own, you need to be more alert to what's going on around you and more cautious about where you go. You also face more potential risks, whether you're walking the city streets or trekking remote mountains. Solo females may face an additional problem of being the target of unwanted attention; see Women Travelers (p348).

Traveling solo is likely to be more expensive, principally due to the higher accommodations costs. Few hotels have single rooms, so you will need to pay for a *matrimonial* or double.

Mérida, Puerto Colombia, Canaima and other major destinations are more accustomed to solo travelers and are generally easier to navigate by one's self.

TELEPHONE

Venezuela's telephone system is operated by CANTV and is largely automated for both domestic and international connections. All phone numbers in the country are seven digits and area codes are three digits. A three-minute local call within a city costs about US$0.10. The cost of long-distance calls is around US$0.25 per minute, and it doesn't depend on the distance, so calling the neighboring city costs the same as calling anywhere within the country.

Area Codes

Area codes are listed under the headings of the relevant destinations throughout this guide.

The country code for Venezuela is ☎ 58. To call Venezuela from abroad, dial the international access code of the country you're calling from, Venezuela's code (☎ 58), the area code (drop the initial 0) and the local phone number.

If making an international call from Venezuela, dial the international access code (00), the country code, the area code (without the initial 0), then the local number.

Cell Phones

Those who plan to stay a longer period of time in Venezuela may opt to purchase a cell phone or buy a local SIM card for their own handset. The malls all have numerous competing cellphone offices. Generally the less expensive services have poorer reception, especially in areas outside of Caracas. **Movistar** (numbers begin with ☎ 0414) is the major operator of mobile telephone services, followed by **Movilnet** (☎ 0416) and **Digitel** (☎ 0412). Venezuela has one of the highest cell-phone-per-capita ratios in Latin America. Note that calling cellular numbers is expensive and eats quickly into a phonecard.

Public Phones

Bright blue CANTV public phones are everywhere, though only about 50% of them work.

Phone cards for these phones come in a few different values and can be purchased at most stores and kiosks.

During the day, entrepreneurs set up small tables on street corners with a few cell phones chained to the table top. They charge by the minute for calls. This can be more convenient than using a card in a public phone, but can get expensive unless you are calling a domestic number.

Phone Centers

Long-distance and international calls can be made from public phones or from the communication offices of CANTV and Movistar. In large cities, these centers are everywhere, from downtown to the suburbs, and most of them also offer fast internet connections. Telephone centers are normally open from about 7am to 9pm daily, with some regional variations, and are listed in the Information sections of each town.

Sample per-minute phone rates of CANTV/ Movistar are US$0.15/0.10 to the USA, US$0.45/0.35 to the UK and US$0.80/0.75 to Australia. At the time of writing, Chávez called for the nationalization of CANTV which may or may not happen and would have an unknown effect on the quality of communications services in Venezuela.

TIME

All of Venezuela lies within the same time zone, four hours behind Greenwich Mean Time. There's no daylight saving time. When it's noon in Venezuela, it's 11am in New York, 8am in San Francisco, 4pm in London and 2am next day in Sydney (add one hour to these times during daylight saving).

TOILETS

Since there are no self-contained public toilets in Venezuela, use the toilets of establishments such as restaurants, hotels, museums, shopping malls and bus terminals. The most common word for toilet is *baño*. Men's toilets will usually bear a label reading *señores* or *caballeros*, whereas women's toilets will be marked *señoras* or *damas*.

You can't rely on bathrooms being stocked with toilet paper (particularly in more remote areas), so it is worth carrying a small stash with you. Some toilets charge fees (normally not exceeding US$0.20), for which you receive a piece of toilet paper. If it doesn't seem like enough, don't hesitate to ask for more.

Except for toilets in upmarket establishments, the plumbing might not be of a standard you are accustomed to. The tubes are narrow and water pressure is weak, so toilets can't cope with toilet paper. A wastebasket is normally provided.

TOURIST INFORMATION

Inatur (Instituto Autónomo de Turismo de Aragua; www .inatur.gob.ve) is the Caracas-based government agency that promotes tourism and provides tourist information; see p61 for contact details. Outside the capital, tourist information is handled by regional tourist bodies which have offices in their respective state capitals and in some other cities. Some are better than others, but on the whole they lack city maps and brochures, and the staff members rarely speak English.

TRAVELERS WITH DISABILITIES

Venezuela offers very little to people with disabilities. Wheelchair ramps are available only at a few upmarket hotels and restaurants, and public transportation will be a challenge for any person with mobility limitations. Hardly any office, museum or bank provides special facilities for disabled persons, and wheelchair-accessible toilets are virtually nonexistent.

VISAS

Nationals of the US, Canada, Australia, New Zealand, Japan, the UK and most of Western and Scandinavian Europe don't need a visa to enter Venezuela; a free Tarjeta de Ingreso (Tourist Card, officially denominated DEX-2) is all that is required. The card is normally valid for 90 days (unless immigration officers note on the card a shorter period) and can be extended. Airlines flying into Venezuela provide these cards to passengers while on the plane. Overland visitors bearing passports of the countries listed above can obtain the card from the immigration official at the border crossing (it's best to check this beforehand at the nearest consulate).

On entering Venezuela, your passport and tourist card will be stamped (make sure this happens) by Dirección de Identificación y Extranjería (DIEX or DEX) border officials. Keep the yellow copy of the tourist card while traveling in Venezuela (you may be asked for it during passport controls), and return it to immigration officials when leaving the country (although not all are interested in collecting the cards).

Visa and tourist-card extensions are handled by Onidex in Caracas (p58).

WOMEN TRAVELERS

Like most of Latin America, Venezuela is very much a man's country. Women travelers will attract more curiosity, attention and advances from local men than they would from men in North America or Western Europe. Local males will quickly pick you out in a crowd and are not shy to show their admiration through whistles, endearments and flirtatious comments. These advances are usually lighthearted, though they can seem rude (or actually be rude).

The best way to deal with unwanted attention is simply to ignore it. Dressing modestly will make you less conspicuous to the local piranhas. Even though Venezuelan women wear revealing clothes, they are a lot more aware of the culture and the safety of their surroundings. A cheap, fake wedding band is also a good trick to quickly end awkward chat-ups.

WORK

Travelers looking for a paid job in Venezuela will almost always be disappointed. The economy is not strong enough to take on foreigners for casual jobs. Qualified English teachers have the best chance of getting a job, yet it's still hard to arrange work once in the country. Try English-teaching institutions such as the **British Council** (www.britishcouncil .com), private language schools or linguistic departments at universities. Note that you need a work visa to work legally in Venezuela. Sure it's possible to get a job without a visa, but you run the risk of exploitation or refusal to pay by your employer with no legal recourse.

Transportation

GETTING THERE & AWAY

ENTERING THE COUNTRY

Entering Venezuela by air, sea or land is pretty straightforward. Most visitors from Western countries don't need a visa, just a *tarjeta de ingreso* (tourist card), officially known as DEX-2, which is free and will be provided upon entry to the country. Fill the card in and present it, along with your valid passport, to the immigration officials, who will then stamp the passport and card and give you a yellow carbon copy of the card. For information on visas, see p347.

Upon departure, you need to return the tourist card to the immigration officials, though not all are interested in collecting them. Make sure they put an exit stamp in your passport; without one you may have problems entering Venezuela next time. All travelers, at both airports and road crossings, are charged a US$17.50 *impuesto de salida* (departure tax). The international air departure tax is a hefty US$44.

AIR
Airports & Airlines

Most international visitors arrive at Caracas' **Aeropuerto Internacional 'Simón Bolívar'** (www.aeropuerto-maiquetia.com.ve in Spanish) in Maiquetía, 26km

from Caracas. Venezuela has several other airports servicing international flights, but these change frequently and unexpectedly. Isla de Margarita's airport is used by charter flights bringing international package tourists, but few independent travelers fly in here.

Following is a list of national and international airlines flying to/from Venezuela (the addresses and phone numbers listed are in Caracas). Aeropostal is the country's largest airline with the widest international coverage serving Bogotá, Guayaquil, Havana, Lima, Miami, Madrid, Port of Spain, Quito and Santo Domingo.

Aerolíneas Argentinas (Map p80; ☎ 0212-951-3005; www.aerolineas.com.ar; Calle Guaicaipuro, Torre Hener 1-A, El Rosal; Ⓜ Chacaíto)
Aeropostal (Map p70; ☎ 0800-337-8466, 0212-266-1059; www.aeropostal.com; 1st fl, Torre ING Bank, Av Eugenio Mendoza, La Castellana; Ⓜ Altamira)
Air Canada (☎ 0212-993-4960; www.aircanada.ca; Maiquetía airport)
Air Europa (☎ 0212-951-1155; www.air-europa.com; 9th floor, Torre Europa, Av Francisco de Miranda)
Air France (Map p70; ☎ 0212-283-5855, 0800-100-3459; www.airfrance.com; 2nd fl, Torre Este, Parque Cristal, Av Francisco de Miranda, Los Palos Grandes)
Alitalia (Map p70; ☎ 0212-208-4120, 208-4111; www.alitalia.it; 5th fl, Edificio Atlantic, Av Andrés Bello, Los Palos Grandes; Ⓜ Altamira)
American Airlines (Map p70; ☎ 0212-209-8000; www.aa.com; 7th fl, Torre ING Bank, Av Eugenio Mendoza, La Castellana; Ⓜ Altamira)
Aserca (Map p80; ☎ 0800-648-8356; www.asercaairlines.com; ground fl, Edificio Taeca, Calle Guaicaipuro, El Rosal; Ⓜ Chacaíto)

THINGS CHANGE

The information in this chapter is particularly vulnerable to change. Check directly with the airline or a travel agent to make sure you understand how a fare (and ticket you may buy) works and be aware of the security requirements for international travel. Shop carefully. The details given in this chapter should be regarded as pointers and are not a substitute for your own careful, up-to-date research.

Avianca (Map p80; ☎ 0212-200-5725; www.avi anca.com; Av Venezuela, cnr Calle Mohedano, El Rosal; Ⓜ Chacaíto)

BWIA/Caribbean Airlines (Map p80; ☎ 0212-953-6666; www.bwee.com; 8th fl, Edificio EXA, No 803-4, Avs Libertador & Alameda, El Rosal; Ⓜ Chacaíto)

Continental Airlines (☎ 0800-359-2600, 0212-953-3107; www.continental.com) El Rosal (Map p80; Centro Lido, Nivel Miranda, No M-22, Av Francisco de Miranda; Ⓜ Chacaíto) Las Mercedes (Map p80; Tamanaco InterContinental Caracas, Av Principal de las Mercedes)

Conviasa (www.conviasa.aero) Maiquetía Airport (☎ 0212-355-2704); Parque Central (Map pp64–5; ☎ 0212-507-8866; 49th floor, Torre Oeste, Av Lecuna)

Copa Airlines (www.copaair.com) Maiquetía Airport (☎ 0800-8267200) El Rosal (Map p80; ☎ 0212-952-2510; 6th floor, Centro Lido, Torre E, Av Francisco de Miranda; Ⓜ Chacaíto)

Cubana (Map p70; ☎ 0212-286-9890; www.cubana.cu; 4th fl, Edificio Atlantic, Av Andrés Bello, Los Palos Grandes; Ⓜ Altamira)

Delta Airlines (www.delta.com) Maiquetía Airport (☎ 0800-100-3453); El Rosal (Map p80; ☎ 0212-958-1000; 8th floor, Centro Lido, Torre E, Av Francisco de Miranda; Ⓜ Chacaíto)

Dutch Antilles Express (☎ 0212-232-0453, www .flydae.com; 4th floor, Multicentro Paseo El Parral, Urban- ización El Parral, Av Río Orinoco, cnr Calle 119)

Iberia (Map p70; ☎ 0212-284-0044; www.iberia.com; 9th floor, Parque Cristal, Av Francisco de Miranda, Los Palos Grandes; Ⓜ Parque del Este)

KLM (Map p70; ☎ 0212-285-3333; www.klm.com; Torre KLM, Av Rómulo Gallegos, Altamira; Ⓜ Parque del Este)

Lan (Map p80; ☎ 0212-267-9526; www.lan.com; 3rd floor, Centro San Ignacio, Torre Kepler, Av Blandín, La Castellana; Ⓜ Chacao)

Lufthansa (Map p70; ☎ 0212-210-2111; www .lufthansa.com; 1st fl, Torre Centro Coinasa, Av San Felipe 16, La Castellana; Ⓜ Altamira)

Santa Bárbara (Map p80; ☎ 0212-952-9658; www .santabarbaraairlines.com; Miranda level, Centro Lido, Av Francisco de Miranda)

TAP Air Portugal (Map p80; ☎ 0212-951-0511; www .flytap.com; Edificio Canaima, Av Francisco de Miranda, El Rosal; Ⓜ Chacaíto)

TACA/LACSA (Map p80; ☎ 800-100-8222; www.taca .com; 2nd floor, Torre C, Centro Comercial Ciudad Taman- aco, Av Ernesto Blohm, Chuao)

Varig (☎ 0212-202-2811; www.varig.com.br; 3rd floor, Centro Empresarial Los Ruices, Av Principal Los Ruices)

Tickets

Venezuela is not a good place to buy interna- tional air tickets – avoid arriving on a one-way ticket as you may be disappointed: airfares to Europe and Australia are high, and there are virtually no discounted tickets available. It's

---

CLIMATE CHANGE & TRAVEL

Climate change is a serious threat to the ecosystems that humans rely upon, and air travel is the fastest-growing contributor to the problem. Lonely Planet regards travel, overall, as a global bene- fit, but believes we all have a responsibility to limit our personal impact on global warming.

Flying & Climate Change

Pretty much every form of motor travel generates $CO2$ (the main cause of human-induced climate change) but planes are far and away the worst offenders, not just because of the sheer distances they allow us to travel, but because they release greenhouse gases high into the atmosphere. The statistics are frightening: two people taking a return flight between Europe and the US will contribute as much to climate change as an average household's gas and electricity consump- tion over a whole year.

Carbon Offset Schemes

Climatecare.org and other websites use 'carbon calculators' that allow jetsetters to offset the greenhouse gases they are responsible for with contributions to energy-saving projects and other climate-friendly initiatives in the developing world – including projects in India, Honduras, Kazakhstan and Uganda.

Lonely Planet, together with Rough Guides and other concerned partners in the travel industry, supports the carbon offset scheme run by climatecare.org. Lonely Planet offsets all of its staff and author travel.

For more information check out our website: www.lonelyplanet.com

DEPARTURE TAX

Venezuela's international *tasa aeroportuaria* (airport tax) is US$44. On top of it, an additional *impuesto de salida* (departure tax) of US$17.50 must be paid by all visitors. The taxes are payable in either US dollars or *bolívares*, but not by credit card. Children over the age of two must pay fees the same as adults. Check the Caracas airport website (www.aeropuerto-maiquetia.com.ve in Spanish) for possible increases.

always better to have the whole route covered by a ticket bought at home.

Just about every travel agency in Caracas will sell you tickets for flights with most airlines and, consequently, will know which is the cheapest carrier on a particular route. When it comes to more complex intercontinental connections, however, not all agencies are experts, so shop around or use online sources.

It may be cheapest to fly to Miami and take one of the relatively cheap transatlantic flights to Europe (eg with United Airlines). Some Caracas travel agencies will sell combined tickets for the whole route.

The following websites are recommended for online bookings:
Cheap Tickets (www.cheaptickets.com)
Expedia (www.expedia.com)
Kayak (www.kayak.com)
Orbitz (www.orbitz.com)
STA (www.sta.com)
Travelocity (www.travelocity.com)

Australia & New Zealand
The shortest route between Australia and South America goes over the South Pole. You can fly with either Lan to Santiago or Aerolíneas Argentinas to Buenos Aires. Both carriers fly from Sydney through Auckland and have connections to Caracas. Expect to pay between A$2200 and A$2800 for the Sydney–Caracas roundtrip flight, depending on the length of stay and the season. The Auckland–Caracas fare will be only marginally lower.

Another possible route goes via Los Angeles and Miami, and will cost much the same as those via Chile or Argentina, though you will probably need to change planes twice, in both LA and Miami. You can also fly to Venezuela through Europe – it's the longest route, but not as absurd as it may sound. You can stop in London, Amsterdam or Paris, and the total fare may be comparable to or even lower than traveling via Los Angeles. Finally, you can buy a RTW (round-the-world) ticket that includes South America, or at least Miami, from where you can make a side trip to Venezuela.

The following are well-known agents for cheap fares:
Flight Centre Australia (☎ 133-133; www.flightcentre .com.au); New Zealand (☎ 0800-243-544; www.flight centre.co.nz)
STA Travel Australia (☎ 1300-733-035; www.statravel .com.au); New Zealand (☎ 0508-782-872; www.statravel .co.nz)
Travel.com (www.travel.com.au)

Canada
Air Canada flies from Toronto to Caracas. Tickets range from CA$500 to CA$1400 depending on time of year. **Travel CUTS** (☎ 800-667-2887; www.travelcuts.com) is Canada's national student travel agency.

Caribbean
NETHERLANDS ANTILLES
Dutch Caribbean Airlines (DCA) flies between Caracas and Aruba, Curaçao and Bonaire. It also has flights between Maracaibo and Aruba and Curaçao, and between Las Piedras (Punto Fijo) and Curaçao. Aeropostal serves Aruba and Curaçao from Caracas. Aserca and Avior fly between Caracas and Aruba. Aerocaribe Coro has flights between Coro and Curaçao and between Las Piedras and Aruba. Expect to pay roughly US$120 to US$140 one way, and US$100 to US$150 roundtrip for any of the routes. Discount fares are available on seven- and 14-day roundtrip flights.

TRINIDAD
Aeropostal and BWIA fly daily between Port of Spain and Caracas (one way US$150, 21-day roundtrip US$205). Aeropostal and Rutaca fly between Porlamar and Port of Spain (one way US$110, 21-day roundtrip US$155).

South America
BRAZIL
Flying between Brazil and Venezuela is expensive. The Varig flight from São Paulo or Rio de Janeiro to Caracas will cost around US$840 one way and US$890 for a 60-day roundtrip. There are no direct flights between Manaus

TRANSPORTATION

and Caracas, nor between Boa Vista and Santa Elena de Uairén.

COLOMBIA

Avianca and Aeropostal fly between Bogotá and Caracas (one way from US$200, round-trip from US$300). Most flights between the two countries require you to fly through Caracas or Bogotá, regardless of whether this takes you out of your way. If you have sufficient time and are already traveling near the border it's much more affordable to cross the border by land and then take a domestic flight from the first major border city to your desired destination.

GUYANA

There are no direct flights between Venezuela and Guyana. You need to fly via Port of Spain (Trinidad) with BWIA ($257 one way, $347 for a 30-day roundtrip).

UK

Caracas is usually the cheapest South American destination from the UK, with prices for discounted flights from London to Caracas starting at around UK£250 one way and UK£400 roundtrip. Bargain hunters should have little trouble finding even lower prices. Discount air travel is big in London. Advertisements for many travel agencies appear in weekend newspapers, and in *Time Out*, *Evening Standard* and the free magazine *TNT*. Recommended ticket agencies:

Flight Centre (☎ 0870-890-8099; www.flightcentre .co.uk)

Journey Latin America (☎ 020-8747-3108; www .journeylatinamerica.co.uk)

STA Travel (☎ 0870-160-0599; www.statravel.co.uk)

Trailfinders (☎ 020-7937-1234; www.trailfinders .co.uk)

Travel Bag (☎ 0870-890-1456; www.travelbag.co.uk)

USA

The major US gateway for Venezuela is Miami, from where several carriers, including American Airlines, Lan and Aeropostal, fly to Caracas. Roundtrip tickets normally costs US$400 to US$600, but Aeropostal may offer cut-down airfares. Other US cities serving direct flights to Caracas include Atlanta (Delta Airlines), Houston and New York (both Continental Airlines).

STA Travel (☎ 800-781 4040; www.sta-travel.com) is one of the most reputable discount travel agencies in the USA. See also the online booking agencies listed on p351.

LAND

Venezuela has road connections with Brazil and Colombia only. There is no road link with Guyana; you must go via Brazil.

Brazil

Only one major road connects Brazil and Venezuela; it leads from Manaus through Boa Vista (Brazil) to Santa Elena de Uairén (Venezuela) and continues to Ciudad Guayana; see p326.

You can also enter Venezuela from Manaus via the Río Negro at San Simón de Cocuy. This is an adventurous river/road route seldom used by travelers; see p333.

Colombia

You can enter Venezuela from Colombia at four border crossings. In the northwest is a fairly popular coastal route between Maicao in Colombia and Maracaibo in Venezuela (see p179). Further south is the most popular border crossing, between Cúcuta and San Antonio del Táchira (see p219). There is a crossing from Arauca to El Amparo de Apure, but it is inconvenient and dangerous (because of Colombian guerrilla activity) and is rarely used.

Finally, there's an uncommon but interesting outback route from Puerto Carreño in Colombia to Puerto Páez in Venezuela (see p333).

Remember to wind your watch forward one hour when crossing from Colombia to Venezuela.

SEA

Weekly passenger boats operate between Güiria in Venezuela and Port of Spain on Trinidad (p282), but there are no longer ferries between Venezuela and Netherlands Antilles.

GETTING AROUND

AIR

Venezuela has a number of airlines and a reasonable network of air routes. Caracas (or, more precisely, Maiquetía, where Caracas' airport is located) is the country's major aviation hub and handles flights to most airports around the country. Cities most frequently serviced from Caracas include Porlamar, Maracaibo and Puerto Ordaz (Ciudad Guayana). The most popular destinations with travelers are Mérida, Ciudad Bolívar, Canaima and Porlamar.

Fares vary between carriers (sometimes substantially), so if the route you're flying is serviced by several airlines, check all fares before buying your ticket. Approximate fares are given in the relevant sections in the book; see p91 for fares on the main routes out of Caracas. The fares listed in this book include the domestic airport tax (US$9), which you normally pay when purchasing your ticket.

Some airlines offer discount fares for students and/or senior citizens, but these change

frequently and may apply only to Venezuelans; check with the airlines or agencies. Reconfirm your flight at least 72 hours before departure and arm yourself with patience, as not all flights depart on time.

Airlines in Venezuela

Venezuela has half a dozen major commercial airlines servicing main domestic routes, and a dozen minor provincial carriers that cover regional and remote routes on a regular or charter basis. The big cities are served mostly by large modern jets, while light planes fly to obscure destinations. The airline safety record is appreciably good – you can check www.airsafe.com/index.html for statistical data.

AIR FARES

Full, one-way prices are listed in US dollars.

The airline situation changes frequently. Always check with a reliable travel agency as the companies come and go and their routes and schedules are malleable.

Venezuelan airlines include the following (the listed addresses and phone numbers are for Caracas):

Aeropostal (Map p70; ☎ 0800-337-8466, 0212-266-1059; www.aeropostal.com; 1st fl, Torre ING Bank, Av Eugenio Mendoza, La Castellana; **M** Altamira) The country's largest airline, with flights to most major domestic destinations, including Barcelona, Barquisimeto, Maracaibo, Maturín, Porlamar, Puerto Ordaz (Ciudad Guayana), San Antonio del Táchira and Valencia.

Aserca (Map p80; ☎ 0800-648-8356, 0212-905-5333; www.asercaairlines.com; ground fl, Edificio Taeca, Calle Guaicaipuro, El Rosal; **M** Chacaíto) Airline operating jet flights between several major airports, including Caracas, Barcelona, Maracaibo, Porlamar and San Antonio del Táchira.

Avensa (domestic ☎ 0212-355-1609, international ☎ 0212-355-1889; www.avensa.com.ve in Spanish; Maiquetía airport)

Avior (Map p69; ☎ 0212-761-1621; www.avior.com.ve; Lincoln Suites, Av Francisco Solano, Sabana Grande; **M** Sabana Grande) Young, progressive carrier flying on fairly new propeller crafts to many airports around the country, including Caracas, Barcelona, Barinas, Barquisimeto, Canaima, Ciudad Bolívar, Coro, Cumaná, Maturín, Mérida, Porlamar and Valera.

LAI (☎ 0212-355-2333, 355-2322; Maiquetía airport)

Laser (☎ 0212-202-0011; www.laser.com.ve in Spanish; Maiquetía airport) Carrier focusing on a few main cities, including Caracas, Maracaibo and Porlamar.

Rutaca (www.rutaca.com.ve in Spanish) Maiquetía Airport ☎ 0212-355-1838); Caracas (☎ 0212-235-6035; Centro Seguros La Paz, Av Francisco de Miranda) Small but expanding airline with planes ranging from old Cessnas to new jets, serving Caracas, Canaima, Ciudad Bolívar, Porlamar, San Antonio del Táchira and Santa Elena de Uairén.

Santa Bárbara (Map p80; ☎ 0212-952-9658; www.santabarbaraairlines.com; Miranda level, Centro Lido, Av Francisco de Miranda) A young but already well-established airline serving Caracas, Cumaná, Las Piedras, Maracaibo, Mérida, Puerto Ayacucho and San Antonio del Táchira.

BICYCLE

Unfortunately, Venezuela is not the best place for cyclists. There are almost no bike tracks, bike rentals or any other facilities. Drivers don't show much courtesy to cyclists either. Cycling is not a popular means of transportation among locals, and foreign travelers with their own bikes are a rarity. Mérida is cur-rently one of the few places where mountain biking tours are organized and bikes can be hired (see p191).

BOAT

Venezuela has many islands off its Caribbean coast, but only Isla de Margarita is serviced by regular boats and ferries; see p240.

The Río Orinoco is the country's major in-land waterway. It's navigable from its mouth up to Puerto Ayacucho, but there's no regular passenger service on any part of it.

BUS & POR PUESTO

As there is no passenger train service in Ven-ezuela, most traveling is done by bus. Buses are generally fast, and they run regularly day and night between major population cent-ers. Bus transportation is reasonably cheap in Venezuela; you probably won't go wrong if you allow US$1.50 to US$2 per hour (or roughly 60km) on a bus.

Venezuela's dozens of bus companies own buses ranging from archaic pieces of junk to the most recent models. All major compan-ies offer *servicio ejecutivo* in comfortable air-conditioned buses, which now cover virtually all the major long-distance routes and are the dominant means of intercity transportation. Still better is the so-called *bus-cama*, where seats can be reclined almost into beds. These buses are the most comfy means of transpor-tation – they have air-conditioning, TV and often a toilet. Note that the air-con is often very efficient, so have plenty of warm clothing at hand to avoid freezing.

If various companies operate the same route, fares are much the same though some may offer discounts. Figures given in the re-gional sections of this book are approximate minimum-to-maximum fares you are likely to pay on a given route.

All intercity buses depart from and arrive at the *terminal de pasajeros* (bus terminal). Every city has such a terminal, usually outside the city center, but always linked to it by local transportation. Caracas is the most important transportation hub, handling buses to just about every corner of the country. In general, there's no need to buy tickets in advance for major routes, except around Christmas, Car-naval and Easter.

Many short-distance regional routes are served by por puesto (literally 'by the seat'), a cross between a bus and a taxi. Por puestos are usually large US-made cars (less often minibuses) of the '60s and '70s vintages that ply fixed routes and depart when all seats are filled. They cost about 40% to 80% more than buses, but they're faster and usually more comfortable. On some routes, they are the dominant or even the exclusive means of transportation. Depending on the region and the kind of vehicle, por puestos may also be called carros or carritos.

CAR & MOTORCYCLE

Traveling by car is a comfortable and attractive way of getting around Venezuela. The country is reasonably safe, and the network of roads is extensive and usually in acceptable shape. Gas stations are numerous and fuel is just about the cheapest in the world – US$0.03 to US$0.06 per liter, depending on the octane level. You can fill up your tank for a dollar!

This rosy picture is slightly obscured by Venezuelan traffic and local driving manners. Traffic in Venezuela, especially in Caracas, is wild, chaotic, noisy, polluting and anarchic.

Bringing a car to Venezuela (or to South America in general) is expensive and time-consuming and involves plenty of paperwork, and few people do it. It's much more convenient and cheaper to rent a car locally.

Rental

A number of international and local car-rental companies, including Hertz, Avis and Budget, operate in Venezuela. They have offices at major airports and in city centers, often in top-end hotels. See individual destinations for details. As a rough guide, a small car will cost US$40 to US$60 per day, with discount rates applying for a full week or longer. A 4WD vehicle is considerably more expensive and difficult to obtain.

Rental agencies require a credit card and driver's license (your home-country license is valid in Venezuela). You need to be at least 21 years of age to rent a car, although renting some cars (particularly 4WDs and luxury models) may require you to be at least 23 or 25 years. Some companies also have a maximum age of about 65 years.

Read the rental contract carefully before signing (most contracts are in Spanish only). Pay close attention to any theft clause, as it will probably load any loss onto the renter. Look at the car carefully, and insist on listing any defects (including scratches) on the rental

form. Check the spare tire, and take note of whether there is a jack.

This said, it's a good idea to contact the international rental companies at home before your trip and check what they can offer in Venezuela. It's likely to be more convenient and cheaper to book at home rather than in Venezuela, and you can be pretty sure that the car will be waiting for you upon arrival.

Road Rules

Watching Venezuela's crazy traffic, reminiscent of Formula One racing, you'd never suspect that there are speed limits, but they do legally exist. Unless traffic signs say otherwise, the maximum speed limit in urban areas is 40km/h, and outside built-up areas it's 80km/h. Officially, traffic coming from the right has priority, unless indicated otherwise by signs. In practice, however, it seems that right-of-way depends on the size of vehicle rather than the regulations.

Cars must be equipped with seat belts for front seats (which always have to be used), and they must have a spare tire, wheel block, jack and a special reflector triangle, which in case of accident or breakdown has to be placed 50m behind the car. Motorcyclists have to wear a crash helmet, and motorcycles cannot be ridden at night. However, once again, all this is theoretical.

Like the rest of the Americas, Venezuela uses right-hand drive.

HITCHHIKING

Hitchhiking is never entirely safe in any country and is not recommended. Travelers who decide to hitchhike should understand that they are taking a small, but potentially serious risk. People who do choose to hitchhike will be safer if they travel in pairs and let someone know where they are planning to go. Women traveling on their own should not hitchhike at all.

Safety apart, Venezuela is not good for hitchhiking. Although many people have cars, they are reluctant to stop to pick up strangers. As bus transportation is fast, efficient and relatively cheap, it's probably not worth wasting time hitchhiking.

LOCAL TRANSPORTATION
Bus & Metro

All cities and many major towns have their own urban transportation systems, which in most places are small buses or minibuses.

Depending on the region, these are called busetas, carros, carritos, micros or camionetas, and fares are usually no more than US$0.20. In many larger cities you can also find urban por puestos, swinging faster than buses through the chaotic traffic. Caracas is the only city in Venezuela with a subway system.

Taxi

Taxis are inexpensive and worth considering, particularly for transportation between the bus terminal and city center when you are carrying luggage. Taxis don't have meters, so always fix the fare with the driver before boarding the cab. It's a good idea to find out the correct fare from a terminal official or a hotel reception desk beforehand.

TOURS

Independent travelers who've never taken an organized tour in their lives will find themselves signing up with a group in Venezuela. As vast areas of the country are virtually inaccessible by public transportation (eg the Delta del Orinoco or Amazon Basin) or because a solitary visit to scattered sights in a large territory (eg the Gran Sabana) may be inconvenient, time-consuming and expensive, tours are a standard option in Venezuelan travel.

Although under some circumstances it makes sense to prebook tours from Caracas (as when stringing together various tours in a short period of time), it is most cost effective to arrange a tour from the regional center closest to the area you are going to visit.

Tour Companies

Some Caracas-based agencies (the so-called *mayoristas*, or wholesalers) simply sell tours organized by other companies. Many agencies use some of the services of selected regional operators, adding their own guides and transfers, and sometimes altering routes and upgrading lodging facilities. Some Caracas operators, though, organize the entire trip themselves, using their own camps and means of transportation. Some companies can prepare tailor-made trips, which will cost considerably more than standard tours. Prices vary significantly depending on the number of people in the tour.

The following companies focus on responsible tourism and offer English-speaking guides (some also have guides that speak German and/or French):

Akanan Travel & Tours (Map p80; ☎ 0212-264-2769; www.akanan.com; Edificio Grano de Oro, Ground fl, Av Bolívar, Chacao, Caracas; Ⓜ Chacao) This company specializes in quality adventure trips, including treks to the top of Auyantepui (eight days) and Roraima (eight days), as well as bicycle trips from La Paragua to Canaima (five days). It's worth stopping in to browse the voluminous library and maps collection.

Alpitour (Map pp56-7; ☎ 0212-283-1433, www.alpi -group.com; 1st fl, Torre Centro, No 11, Centro Parque Boyacá, Av Sucre, Los Dos Caminos) This company specializes in fishing trips, but also offers a range of mainstream packages and some adventurous tours in the Amazonas.

Cacao Travel Group (☎ 0212-977-1234; www.cacao travel.com; Quinta Orquidea, Calle Andrómeda, Urbanización El Peñón, Caracas) This agency, 2.5km south of Las Mercedes, has expertise in Río Caura tours (five days in total, US$412 per person from Ciudad Bolívar, minimum four persons), where it has its own lodge. It also has a lodge in the Amazonas, serving as a base for boat trips in the region.

Cóndor Verde (☎ 0212-975-4306; www.condorverde travel.com; Av Río Caura, Torre Humboldt, Mezzanina 3, Prados del Este, Caracas) This German-run agency, 2km south of Las Mercedes, offers one of the widest ranges of tours, from beach holidays on Isla de Margarita to adventurous boat trips in the Amazonas, plus special-interest packages such as fishing, diving and golf. Tours include Delta del Orinoco (three days), Gran Sabana (four days), Roraima (seven days) and Río Caura (five days).

Osprey Expeditions (Map p69; ☎ 0212-762-5974; www.ospreyvenezuela.com; Edificio La Paz, office 51, Av Casanova at 2a Av de Bello Monte, Bello Monte, Caracas; Ⓜ Sabana Grande) Small, personable, Venezuelan-owned agency attuned to a budget traveler's perspective. It can organize tours to most parts of the country but it's particularly strong on Los Roques, Canaima and the Delta del Orinoco.

Tucaya (Map pp56-7; ☎ 0212-234-9401; www.tucaya .com; Quinta Santa Marta, 1a Av Urbanización Campo Claro, Los Dos Caminos, Caracas) Caters principally to French-speaking clientele, but also organizes English-speaking tours. Major destinations include the Andes (four days, US$255 per person), Los Llanos (four days, US$400) and Delta del Orinoco (three days, US$204).

ANGEL FALLS TOUR OPERATORS

Angel Falls (Salto Angel) is one of Venezuela's top tourist attractions, so many Caracas tour companies (including most listed earlier) have it in their program. You can also find a couple of agencies in the domestic terminal at Maiquetía airport. See Ciudad Bolívar (p298) for more tour options. **Hoturvensa** (☎ 0212-976-0530; www.hoturvensa.com.ve in Spanish; Av Río Caura, Torre

Humboldt, Nivel Mezzanina 1 & 2, Prados del Este, Caracas), 2km south of Las Mercedes, is an offspring of Avensa airlines and owns the Campamento Canaima (p314). A three-day trip to Canaima costs US$295/210 per adult/child, which includes room and board at the Canaima camp plus one excursion; an all-day tour to Angel Falls costs an additional US$200. The Caracas–Canaima flight costs extra, as do any flights over the falls (about US$80). This is one of the more expensive offers on the market. You can buy these packages at Avensa offices and in most travel agencies.

LOS ROQUES TOUR OPERATORS
Archipiélago Los Roques is serviced from Maiquetía airport's auxiliary terminal by a number of small airlines. Besides the flight-only option, the following offer tours as well.

AeroEjecutivos (☎ 0212-793-0668; www.aeroejecutivos.com.ve)

Avior (☎ 0212-955-3811, 0501-2846-7737; www.aviorairlines.com)

Transavén Airlines (☎ 0212-355-1965, 355-1349)

Sol de América (☎ 0212-267-2424; www.sol-america.com)

LOS LLANOS TOUR OPERATORS
If you plan on taking tours to the *hatos* (ranches) in Los Llanos (see p222), note that some may require you to book and pay beforehand through a Caracas agent.

Hato El Cedral (Map p69; ☎ 0212-781-8995; www.elcedral.com; 5th fl, Edificio Pancho, Av La Salle, Los Caobos, Caracas; Ⓜ Plaza Venezuela)

Hato La Fe (☎ 0414-325-4188; www.posadahatolafe.com)

Hato Piñero (Map pp56-7; ☎ 0212-991-8935; www.hatopinero.com; 6th fl, Edificio General, No 6-B, Av La Estancia, Chuao, Caracas)

Excursion Centers
An alternative to tour companies, *centros excursionistas* (excursion centers) are associations of outdoor-minded people who organize independent excursions in their spare time. These are essentially one- or two-day weekend trips around Caracas and the central states,

but longer journeys to other regions are often scheduled for long weekends and holiday periods. The focus is usually on nature and walking, though cultural sights are often part of the program. Each trip is prepared by a member of the group, who then serves as a guide. The *excursionistas* use public transportation and take their own food and camping gear if necessary. Foreign travelers are welcome, and you can usually find a companion for conversation in English, German etc.

Centro Excursionista Caracas (CEC; www.mipagina.cantv.net/centroexcursionista in Spanish) Founded in 1929, this is the oldest and best-known club of its kind. It organizes regular weekend trips to places like Parque Nacional El Ávila, Mérida and Parque Nacional Henri Pittier, and its members include people of all ages. To find out about forthcoming trips and how you can participate, contact Hans Schwarzer (nortron@internet.ve) or Fritz Werner (☎ 0212-945-0946), both of whom speak German and English.

Centro Excursionista Universitario (CEU; www.ucv.ve/ceu.htm in Spanish; infoceu@ucv.edu.ve) The CEU bands together mostly university students for relatively low-key Sunday hikes to Ávila or, during vacation periods, more ambitious week-long excursions to places like the Parque Nacional Sierra Nevada near Mérida. It also offers rock-climbing courses. Contact persons include Roberto González (☎ 0212-762-0424), Mirna Carolina Ríos (☎ 0212-661-5644, 0416-827-9552; caimandelorinoco@hotmail.com) and English-speaking José Daniel Santana (☎ 0212-371-1871; 0414-253-2384; duendeaventura@yahoo.es). The club meets on Tuesday at 6pm in the Edificio de Deportes ground floor, alongside the Judo Club, at the Universidad Central de Venezuela.

Guides
Asociación Venezolana de Instructores y Guías de Montaña (☎ 0416-614-1969; www.avigm.com in Spanish) An association consisting of 50 or so experienced guides for mountaineering, rock climbing and trekking, most of whom are listed on the website with their email addresses.

Explora Treks (☎ 0212-283-3260, 0416-631-1960; www.exploratreks.com) A federation of seven highly seasoned Venezuelan climbers that can organize and guide expeditions to several tepuis (flat-topped sandstone mountains with vertical flanks), including a 12-day strenuous trek to the top of Auyantepui in Parque Nacional Canaima, with a descent by rappel alongside Angel Falls.

Health Dr David Goldberg

Prevention is the key to staying healthy while abroad. Travelers who receive the recommended vaccines and follow common-sense precautions usually come away with nothing more than a little diarrhea.

BEFORE YOU GO

Most vaccines don't produce immunity until at least two weeks after they're given, so visit a physician four to eight weeks before departure. Ask your doctor for an International Certificate of Vaccination (otherwise known as the yellow booklet), which will list all the vaccinations you've received. This is mandatory for countries that require proof of yellow-fever vaccination upon entry, but it's a good idea to carry it wherever you travel.

INSURANCE

If your health insurance does not cover you for medical expenses abroad, consider supplemental insurance. Check the Bookings & Services section of the **Lonely Planet website** (www.lonelyplanet.com/travel_services) for more information. Find out in advance if your insurance plan will make payments directly to providers or reimburse you later for overseas health expenditures.

MEDICAL CHECKLIST

- acetaminophen/paracetamol (Tylenol) or aspirin
- adhesive or paper tape
- antibacterial ointment (eg Bactroban) for cuts and abrasions
- antibiotics
- antidiarrheal drugs (eg loperamide)
- antihistamines (for hay fever and allergic reactions)
- anti-inflammatory drugs (eg ibuprofen)
- bandages, gauze, gauze rolls
- DEET-containing insect repellent for the skin
- iodine tablets (for water purification)
- oral rehydration salts
- permethrin-containing insect spray for clothing, tents and bed nets
- pocket knife
- scissors, safety pins, tweezers
- steroid cream or cortisone (for poison ivy and other allergic rashes)
- sunblock
- syringes and sterile needles
- thermometer

INTERNET RESOURCES

There is a wealth of travel-health advice on the internet. For further information, the **Lonely Planet website** (www.lonelyplanet.com) is a good place to start. A superb book called *International Travel and Health*, which is revised annually and available online at no cost, is published by the **World Health Organization** (www.who.int/ith/).

Another health website of general interest is **MD Travel Health** (www.mdtravelhealth.com), which provides a complete set of travel-health recommendations for every country. The site is updated daily and is also available at no charge.

It is usually a good idea to consult your own country's government travel health website before departure, if one is available.

Australia (www.dfat.gov.au/travel/)
Canada (www.hc-sc.gc.ca/pphb-dgspsp/tmp-pmv/pub _e.html)
UK (www.doh.gov.uk/traveladvice/index.htm)
USA (www.cdc.gov/travel/)

FURTHER READING

For further information, see *Healthy Travel Central & South America*, published by Lonely Planet. If you're traveling with children, Lonely Planet's *Travel with Children* may also be useful. The *ABC of Healthy Travel*, by E Walker et al, and *Medicine for the Outdoors*, by Paul S Auerbach, are other valuable resources.

IN TRANSIT

DEEP VEIN THROMBOSIS (DVT)

Blood clots may form in the legs during plane flights, chiefly because of prolonged immobility. The longer the flight, the greater the risk. Though most blood clots are reabsorbed uneventfully, some may break off and travel through the blood vessels to the lungs, where they could cause life-threatening complications.

The chief symptom of deep vein thrombosis (DVT) is swelling or pain of the foot, ankle or calf, usually but not always on just one side. When a blood clot travels to the lungs, it may cause chest pain and difficulty breathing. Travelers with any of these symptoms should immediately seek medical attention.

To prevent the development of DVT on long flights you should walk about the cabin, perform isometric compressions of the leg muscles (ie contract the leg muscles while sitting), drink plenty of fluids, and avoid alcohol and tobacco.

JET LAG & MOTION SICKNESS

Jet lag is common when crossing more than five time zones, and can result in insomnia, fatigue, malaise or nausea. To avoid jet lag try drinking plenty of fluids (nonalcoholic) and eating light meals. Upon arrival, get exposure to natural sunlight and readjust your schedule (for meals, sleep etc) as soon as possible.

RECOMMENDED VACCINATIONS

There are no required vaccines for Venezuela, but a number are recommended. Note that some of these are not approved for use by children or pregnant women – check with your physician.

Vaccine	Recommended for	Dosage	Side effects
chickenpox	travelers who've never had chickenpox	2 doses 1 month apart	fever; mild case of chickenpox
hepatitis A	all travelers	1 dose before trip; booster 6-12 months later	soreness at injection site; headaches; body aches
hepatitis B	long-term travelers in close contact with the local population	3 doses over 6 months	soreness at injection site; low-grade fever
measles	travelers who have never had measles or completed a vaccination course	1 dose	fever; rash; joint pain; allergic reactions
rabies	travelers who may have contact with animals and may not have access to medical care	3 doses over 3-4 weeks	soreness at injection site; headaches; body aches
tetanus-diphtheria	all travelers who haven't had booster within 10 years	1 dose lasts 10 years	soreness at injection site
typhoid	all travelers	4 capsules orally, 1 taken every other day	abdominal pain; nausea; rash
yellow fever	travelers to all areas, but especially rural areas of the following states: Apure, Amazonas, Barinas, Bolívar, Sucre, Táchira, Delta Amacuro, Angel Falls	1 dose lasts 10 years	headaches; body aches; severe reactions are rare

Bring medications in their original containers, clearly labeled. A signed, dated letter from your physician describing all medical conditions and medications, including generic names, is also a good idea. If carrying syringes or needles, be sure to have a physician's letter documenting their medical necessity.

Antihistamines such as dimenhydrinate (Dramamine) and meclizine (Antivert or Bonine) are usually the first choice for treating motion sickness. Their main side effect is drowsiness. A herbal alternative is ginger, which works like a charm for some people.

IN VENEZUELA

AVAILABILITY & COST OF HEALTH CARE

Good medical care is available in Caracas, but may be difficult to find in rural areas. Public hospitals are free, but the quality of medical care is better in private facilities. For an online list of physicians, dentists and other health-care providers, most of whom speak English, go to the US embassy website (http://embajadausa.org.ve/wwwh005.html). Many doctors and hospitals expect payment in cash, regardless of whether you have travel health insurance.

For an ambulance in Venezuela, call ☎ 171. If you develop a life-threatening medical problem, you'll probably want to be evacuated to a country with state-of-the-art medical care. Since this may cost tens of thousands of dollars, be sure you have insurance to cover this before you depart. You can find a list of medical evacuation and travel insurance companies on the US state department website (www.travel.state.gov/medical.html).

Venezuelan *farmacias* (pharmacies) are identifiable by a red light in the store window. The quality and availability of medication is comparable to that in most other countries. The pharmacies keep a rotating schedule of 24-hour availability, so that different pharmacies are open on different nights. To find a late-night pharmacy, you can either look in the local newspaper under 'Turnos,' call ☎ 800-88766 (that is, 800-TURNO), check the list posted on most pharmacy doors or search for a pharmacy with its red light still on.

INFECTIOUS DISEASES
Brucellosis

This is an infection of domestic and wild animals that may be transmitted to humans through direct animal contact or by consumption of unpasteurized dairy products from infected animals. In Venezuela, most human cases are related to infected cattle. Symptoms may include fever, malaise, depression, loss of appetite, headache, muscle ache and back pain. Complications may include arthritis, hepatitis, meningitis and endocarditis (heart-valve infection).

Cholera

Cholera is an intestinal infection acquired through ingestion of contaminated food or water. The main symptom is profuse, watery diarrhea, which may be so severe that it causes life-threatening dehydration. The key treatment is drinking an oral rehydration solution. Antibiotics are also given, usually tetracycline or doxycycline, though quinolone antibiotics such as ciprofloxacin and levofloxacin are also effective.

Cholera sometimes occurs in Venezuela, but it's rare among travelers. Cholera vaccine is no longer required, and is in fact no longer available in some countries, including the US, because the old vaccine was relatively ineffective and caused side effects. There are new vaccines that are safer and more effective, but they're not available in many countries and are only recommended for those at particularly high risk.

Dengue Fever (Breakbone Fever)

Dengue fever is a viral infection found throughout South America. In Venezuela, large numbers of cases are reported each year, especially from the states of Barinas, Amazonas, Aragua, Mérida, Táchira and Lara, and the Caracas district. Dengue is transmitted by aedes mosquitoes, which bite preferentially during the daytime and are usually found close to human habitations, often indoors. They breed primarily in artificial water containers, such as jars, barrels, cans, cisterns, metal drums, plastic containers and discarded tires. As a result, dengue is especially common in densely populated, urban environments.

Dengue usually causes flu-like symptoms, including fever, muscle ache, joint pain, headache, nausea and vomiting, often followed by a rash. The body aches may be quite uncomfortable, but most cases resolve uneventfully in a few days. Severe cases usually occur in children under the age of 15 who are experiencing their second dengue infection.

There is no treatment as yet for dengue fever, except to take analgesics such as acetaminophen/paracetamol (Tylenol) and drink plenty of fluids. Severe cases may require hospitalization for intravenous fluids and supportive care. There is no vaccine. The cornerstone of prevention is protecting against insect bites, see p364.

Hepatitis A

Hepatitis A is the second most common travel-related infection (after travelers' diarrhea). It's a viral infection of the liver that is usually acquired by ingestion of contaminated water, food or ice, though it may also be acquired by direct contact with infected persons. The illness occurs throughout the world, but the incidence is higher in developing nations. Symptoms may include fever, malaise, jaundice, nausea, vomiting and abdominal pain. Most cases resolve without complications, though hepatitis A occasionally causes severe liver damage. There is no treatment.

The vaccine for hepatitis A is extremely safe and highly effective. If you get a booster six to 12 months later, it lasts for at least 10 years. You really should get it before you go to Venezuela or any other developing nation. Because the safety of hepatitis A vaccine has not been established for pregnant women or children under the age of two, they should instead be given a gammaglobulin injection.

Hepatitis B

Like hepatitis A, hepatitis B is a liver infection that occurs worldwide, but is more common in developing nations. Unlike hepatitis A, the disease is usually acquired by sexual contact or by exposure to infected blood, generally through blood transfusions or contaminated needles. The vaccine is recommended only for long-term travelers (on the road more than six months) who expect to live in rural areas or have close physical contact with the local population. Additionally, the vaccine is recommended for anyone who anticipates sexual contact with the local inhabitants or a possible need for medical, dental or other treatments while abroad, especially if a need for transfusions or injections is expected.

Hepatitis B vaccine is safe and highly effective. A total of three injections however, are necessary to establish full immunity. Several countries added hepatitis B vaccine to the list of routine childhood immunizations in the 1980s, so many young adults are already protected.

HIV/AIDS

This has been reported in all South American countries. Be sure to use condoms for all sexual encounters.

Leishmaniasis

This disease occurs in the mountains and jungles of all South American countries except Chile, Uruguay and the Falkland Islands. In Venezuela it is widespread in rural areas, especially the west-central part of the country. The infection is transmitted by sand flies, which are about one-third the size of mosquitoes. Leishmaniasis may be particularly severe in those with HIV. There is no vaccine. To protect yourself from sand flies, follow the same precautions as for mosquitoes (p364), except that netting must be finer mesh (at least 18 holes to the linear inch).

Malaria

Malaria occurs in every South American country except Chile, Uruguay and the Falkland Islands. It's transmitted by mosquito bites, usually between dusk and dawn. The main symptom is high-spiking fevers, which may be accompanied by chills, sweats, headache, body aches, weakness, vomiting or diarrhea. Severe cases may involve the central nervous system and lead to seizures, confusion, coma and death.

Taking malaria pills is strongly recommended for those visiting Angel Falls and for rural areas in the states of Apure, Amazonas, Barinas, Bolívar, Delta Amacuro, Sucre, Táchira and Zulia. In general, the risk of malaria is greatest between February and August, especially after the onset of the rainy season in late May.

There is a choice of three malaria pills, all of which work equally well. Mefloquine (Lariam) is taken once weekly in a dosage of 250mg, starting one to two weeks before arriving in Venezuela and continuing until four weeks after departure. A certain percentage of people (the number is controversial) develop neuropsychiatric side effects, which may range from mild to severe. Atovaquone/proguanil (Malarone) is a newly approved combination pill; it's taken once daily with food, starting two days before arrival and continuing until seven days after departure. Side effects are typically mild. Doxycycline is a third alternative, but may cause an exaggerated sunburn reaction.

In general, Malarone seems to cause fewer side effects than Lariam and is becoming more popular. The chief disadvantage is that it has to be taken daily. For longer trips, it's probably worth trying Lariam; for shorter trips,

Malarone will be the drug of choice for most people.

Protecting yourself against mosquito bites (see p364), is just as important as taking malaria pills since none of the pills are 100% effective.

Since you may not have access to medical care while traveling, you should bring along additional pills for emergency self-treatment; take these if you can't reach a doctor and you develop symptoms that suggest malaria, such as high-spiking fevers. One self-treatment option is to take four tablets of Malarone once daily for three days. However, Malarone should not be used for treatment if you're already taking it for prevention. An alternative is to take 650mg quinine three times daily and 100mg doxycycline twice daily for one week. If you start self-medication, see a doctor at the earliest possible opportunity.

If you develop a fever after returning home, see a physician, as malaria symptoms may not occur for months.

Measles

All travelers should be sure they have had either two measles vaccinations or a blood test proving they're immune. Although measles immunization usually doesn't begin until the age of 12 months, children between six and 11 months should probably receive an initial dose of measles vaccine before traveling to Venezuela.

Rabies

Rabies is a viral infection of the brain and spinal cord that is almost always fatal. The rabies virus is carried in the saliva of infected animals and is typically transmitted through an animal bite, though contamination of any break in the skin with infected saliva may result in rabies. Rabies occurs in all South American countries. In Venezuela, most cases are related to dog bites.

Rabies vaccine is safe, but a full series requires three injections and is quite expensive. Those at high risk for rabies, such as animal handlers and spelunkers (cave explorers), should certainly get the vaccine. In addition, those at lower risk for animal bites should consider asking for the vaccine if they might be traveling to remote areas and might not have access to appropriate medical care if needed. The treatment for a possibly rabid bite consists of rabies vaccine with rabies

immune globulin. It's effective, but must be given promptly. Most travelers don't need rabies vaccine.

All animal bites and scratches must be promptly and thoroughly cleansed with large amounts of soap and water, and local health authorities contacted to determine whether or not further treatment is necessary.

Schistosomiasis

This parasitic infection is acquired by exposure to contaminated fresh water, and is reported from isolated spots in the north-central part of the country, including the areas around Caracas (but not Caracas) and the states of Aragua, Carabobo, Guárico and Miranda. When traveling in these areas, you should avoid swimming, wading, bathing or washing in bodies of fresh water, including lakes, ponds, streams and rivers. Salt water and chlorinated pools carry no risk of schistosomiasis.

Tick-Borne Relapsing Fever

This fever, which may be transmitted by either ticks or lice, is caused by bacteria that is closely related to those that cause Lyme disease and syphilis. The illness is characterized by periods of fever, chills, headache, body aches, muscle aches and coughs, alternating with periods when the fever subsides and the person feels relatively well. To minimize the risk of relapsing fever, follow tick precautions as outlined on p364 and practice good personal hygiene at all times.

Typhoid Fever

Typhoid is caused by ingestion of food or water contaminated by a species of salmonella known as *Salmonella typhi*. Fever occurs in virtually all cases. Other symptoms may include headache, malaise, muscle aches, dizziness, loss of appetite, nausea and abdominal pain. Either diarrhea or constipation may occur. Possible complications include intestinal perforation, intestinal bleeding, confusion, delirium or (rarely) coma.

Unless you expect to take all your meals in major hotels and restaurants, typhoid vaccine is a good idea. It's usually given orally, but is also available as an injection. Neither vaccine is approved for use in children under the age of two.

The drug of choice for typhoid fever is usually a quinolone antibiotic such as ciprofloxacin (Cipro) or levofloxacin (Levaquin), which many travelers carry for treatment of traveler's diarrhea. However, if you self-treat for typhoid fever, you may also need to self-treat for malaria, since the symptoms of the two diseases may be indistinguishable.

Venezuelan Equine Encephalitis

This viral infection, transmitted by mosquitoes, reached epidemic levels in 1995 after unusually heavy rainfalls, especially in the northwestern states of Zulia, Lara, Falcón, Yaracuy, Carabobo and Trujillo. The greatest incidence was reported among the Warao population. Cases still occur, but in smaller numbers, chiefly in the west between the Península de la Guajira and the Río Catatumbo. This illness comes on suddenly and symptoms are malaise, fevers, rigors, severe headache, photophobia and myalgias. Possible complications can include convulsions, coma, and paralysis.

Yellow Fever

Yellow fever is a life-threatening viral infection transmitted by mosquitoes in forested areas. The illness begins with flu-like symptoms, which may include fever, chills, headache, muscle aches, backache, loss of appetite, nausea and vomiting. These symptoms usually subside in a few days, but one person in six enters a second, toxic phase characterized by recurrent fever, vomiting, listlessness, jaundice, kidney failure and hemorrhage, leading to death in up to half of the cases. There is no treatment except for supportive care.

Yellow fever is still present in Venezuela and the yellow-fever vaccine is strongly recommended for all travelers (except pregnant women), especially anyone traveling beyond Caracas and the northern coast.

Yellow-fever vaccine is given only in approved yellow-fever vaccination centers, which provide validated International Certificates of Vaccination (yellow booklets). The vaccine should be given at least 10 days before any potential exposure to yellow fever, and remains effective for approximately 10 years. Reactions to the vaccine are generally mild and may include headache, muscle ache, low-grade fevers or discomfort at the injection site. Severe, life-threatening reactions have been described, but are extremely rare. In general, the risk of becoming ill from the vaccine is far less than the risk of becoming ill from yellow

fever, and you're strongly encouraged to get the vaccine.

Taking measures to protect yourself from mosquito bites (p364) is an essential part of preventing yellow fever.

TRAVELER'S DIARRHEA

To prevent diarrhea, avoid tap water unless it has been boiled, filtered or chemically disinfected (iodine tablets); only eat fresh fruit or vegetables if cooked or peeled; be wary of dairy products that might contain unpasteurized milk; and be highly selective when eating food from street vendors.

If you develop diarrhea, be sure to drink plenty of fluids, preferably an oral rehydration solution containing lots of salt and sugar. A few loose stools don't require treatment but, if you start having more than four or five stools a day, you should start taking an antibiotic (usually a quinolone drug) and an antidiarrheal agent (such as loperamide). If diarrhea is bloody or persists for more than 72 hours or is accompanied by fever, shaking chills or severe abdominal pain, you should seek medical attention.

ENVIRONMENTAL HAZARDS
Altitude Sickness

Altitude sickness may develop in those who ascend rapidly to altitudes greater than 2500m. Being physically fit offers no protection. Those who have experienced altitude sickness in the past are prone to future episodes. The risk increases with faster ascents, higher altitudes and greater exertion. Symptoms may include headaches, nausea, vomiting, dizziness, malaise, insomnia and loss of appetite. Severe cases may be complicated by fluid in the lungs (high-altitude pulmonary edema) or swelling of the brain (high-altitude cerebral edema).

The best treatment for altitude sickness is descent. If you are exhibiting symptoms, do not ascend. If symptoms are severe or persistent, descent immediately.

One option for the prevention of altitude sickness is to take acetazolamide (Diamox). The recommended dosage ranges from 125mg (twice daily) to 250mg (three times daily). It should be taken 24 hours before ascent and continued for 48 hours after arrival at altitude. Possible side effects include increased urinary volume, numbness, tingling, nausea, drowsiness, myopia and temporary impotence.

HEALTH

HEALTH

TRADITIONAL MEDICINE

The following are some traditional remedies for common travel-related conditions.

Problem	Treatment
altitude sickness	gingko
jet lag	melatonin
motion sickness	ginger
mosquito-bite prevention	oil of eucalyptus or soybean

Acetazolamide should not be given to pregnant women or anyone with a history of sulfa allergy. For those who cannot tolerate acetazolamide, the next best option is 4mg of dexamethasone taken four times daily. Unlike acetazolamide, dexamethasone must be tapered gradually upon arrival at altitude, since there is a risk that altitude sickness will occur as the dosage is reduced. Dexamethasone is a steroid, so it should not be given to diabetics or anyone for whom steroids are contraindicated. A natural alternative is gingko, which some people find quite helpful.

When traveling to high altitudes, it's also important to avoid overexertion, eat light meals and abstain from alcohol.

If your symptoms are more than mild or don't resolve promptly, see a doctor. Altitude sickness should be taken seriously; it can be life threatening when severe.

Insect Bites
MOSQUITOES
To prevent mosquito bites, wear long sleeves, long pants, hats and shoes (rather than sandals). Bring along a good insect repellent, preferably one containing DEET, which should be applied to exposed skin and clothing, but not to eyes, mouth, cuts, wounds or irritated skin. Products containing lower concentrations of DEET are as effective, but for shorter periods of time. In general, adults and children over 12 years of age should use preparations containing 25% to 35% DEET, which usually lasts about six hours. Children between two and 12 years of age should use preparations containing no more than 10% DEET, applied sparingly, which will usually last about three hours. Neurological toxicity has been reported from using DEET, especially in children, but appears to be extremely

uncommon and generally related to overuse. DEET-containing compounds should not be used on children under the age of two.

Insect repellents containing certain botanical products, including oil of eucalyptus and soybean oil, are effective but last only 1½ to two hours. DEET-containing repellents are preferable for areas where there is a high risk of malaria or yellow fever. Citronella-based products are not effective.

For additional protection, you can apply permethrin to clothing, shoes, tents and bed nets. Permethrin treatments are safe and remain effective for at least two weeks, even when items are laundered. Permethrin should not be applied directly to skin.

Don't sleep with the window open unless there is a screen. If sleeping outdoors or in accommodations that allow entry of mosquitoes, use a bed net, preferably treated with permethrin, with edges tucked in under the mattress. The mesh size should be less than 1.5mm. If the sleeping area is not otherwise protected, use a mosquito coil, which will fill the room with insecticide through the night. Repellent-impregnated wristbands are not effective.

TICKS
To protect yourself from tick bites, follow the same precautions as for mosquitoes, except that boots are preferable to shoes, with pants tucked in. Be sure to perform a thorough tick check at the end of each day. You'll generally need the assistance of a friend or mirror for a full examination. Ticks should be removed with tweezers, grasping them firmly by the head. Insect repellents based on botanical products (described under Mosquitoes, left) have not been adequately studied for insects other than mosquitoes and cannot be recommended to prevent tick bites.

Snake Bites
Snakes and leeches are a hazard in some areas of South America. In the event of a venomous snake bite, place the victim at rest, keep the bitten area immobilized, and move the victim immediately to the nearest medical facility. Avoid tourniquets, which are no longer recommended.

Sun
To protect yourself from excessive sun exposure, you should stay out of the midday

sun, wear sunglasses and a wide-brimmed sun hat, and apply sunblock with SPF 15 or higher, with both UVA and UVB protection. Sunblock should be generously applied to all exposed parts of the body approximately 30 minutes before sun exposure, and should be reapplied after swimming or vigorous activity. Travelers should also drink plenty of fluids and avoid strenuous exercise when the temperature is high.

Water

Tap water in Venezuela is not safe to drink – buying bottled water is your best bet. If you have the means, vigorous boiling for one minute is the most effective means of water purification. At altitudes greater than 2000m, boil for three minutes. Another option is to disinfect water with iodine pills: add 2% tincture of iodine to 1L of water (five drops to clear water, 10 drops to cloudy water) and let stand for 30 minutes. If the water is cold, longer times may be required.

TRAVELING WITH CHILDREN

Children under nine months should not be taken to areas where yellow fever occurs, since the vaccine is not safe for this age group. Although measles immunization doesn't begin until the age of 12 months, children between the ages six and 11 months should probably receive an initial dose of measles vaccine before traveling to Venezuela.

When traveling with young children, be particularly careful about what you allow them to eat and drink, because diarrhea can be especially dangerous in this age group and because the vaccines for hepatitis A and typhoid fever are not approved for use in children under the age of two.

The two main malaria medications, Lariam and Malarone, may be given to children, but insect repellents must be applied in lower concentrations.

WOMEN'S HEALTH

There are English-speaking obstetricians in Venezuela, listed on the **US embassy website** (http://embajadausa.org.ve/wwwh005.html). However, medical facilities will probably not compare favorably to those in your home country. It's safer to avoid travel to Venezuela late in pregnancy, so that you don't have to deliver here. Yellow-fever vaccine should not be given during pregnancy because the vaccine contains a live virus that may infect the fetus.

Also it isn't advisable for pregnant women to spend time at altitudes where the air is thin. If you need to take malaria pills, mefloquine (Lariam) is the safest during pregnancy.

HEALTH

Language

CONTENTS

Spanish is Venezuela's official language, and with the exception of some of the more remote areas, it's spoken throughout the country. There are also more than 25 indigenous languages spoken in Venezuela. English speakers can be found in large urban centers, but it's certainly not a commonly understood or widely spoken language, even though it's taught as a mandatory second language in the public school system.

Spanish is quite easy to learn and a predeparture language course can considerably enhance your stay in Venezuela. Courses are also available once you're there; Caracas (p73) and Mérida (p191) have the most options, but Pamapatar (p249) on Isla de Margarita has some facilities too. Even if classes are impractical, you should make the effort to at least learn a few pleasantries. Don't hesitate to practice your new skills – in general, Latin Americans meet any attempts to communicate in their language with enthusiasm and appreciation.

Lonely Planet's *Latin American Spanish Phrasebook* is a worthwhile addition to your backpack. Another useful resource is the *University of Chicago Spanish-English, English-Spanish Dictionary* – its small size, light weight and thorough entries make it ideal for travel. It also makes a great gift for any new friends upon your departure.

SPANISH IN VENEZUELA

Throughout Latin America, the Spanish language is referred to as *castellano* more often than *español*. Probably the most notable difference between the sound of Latin American Spanish and the principal language of Spain is that the letters **c** and **z** are never lisped; attempts to do so could well provoke amusement or even scorn.

Venezuelan Spanish is not the clearest or easiest to understand. Venezuelans (except those from the Andes) speak more rapidly than most other South Americans and tend to drop some endings, especially plurals.

The use of the forms *tú* (informal 'you') and *usted* (polite 'you') is very flexible in Venezuela. Both are used, but with regional variations. Either is OK, though it's best to answer using the same form in which you are addressed. Always use the *usted* form when talking to the police and the Guardia Nacional.

Greetings in Venezuela are more elaborate than in Spain. The short Spanish *hola* has given way to a number of expressions, which are exchanged at the beginning of a conversation. Listen to how the locals greet people, and you'll quickly pick up on some of their local idiom.

Although Venezuelans don't seem to be devoutly religious, the expressions *si Dios quiere* (God willing) and *gracias a Dios* (thanks to God) are frequently heard in conversation.

PRONUNCIATION

Spanish spelling is phonetically consistent, meaning that there's a clear and consistent relationship between what you see in writing and how it's pronounced.

Vowels

a	as in 'father'
e	as in 'met'
i	as in 'marine'
o	as in 'or' (without the 'r' sound)
u	as in 'rule;' the 'u' is not pronounced after **q** and in the letter combinations **gue** and **gui**, unless it's marked with a diaeresis (eg *argüir*), in which case it's pronounced as English 'w'

y   at the end of a word or when it stands alone, it's pronounced as the Spanish **i** (eg *ley*); between vowels within a word it's as the 'y' in 'yonder'

Consonants

As a rule, Spanish consonants resemble their English counterparts. You should be aware that while the consonants **ch**, **ll** and **ñ** are generally considered distinct letters, **ch** and **ll** are now often listed alphabetically under **c** and **l** respectively. The letter **ñ** is still treated as a separate letter and comes after **n** in dictionaries.

b	similar to English 'b,' but softer; referred to as 'b larga'
c	as in 'celery' before **e** and **i**; otherwise as English 'k'
ch	as in 'church'
d	as in 'dog,' but between vowels and after **l** or **n**, the sound is closer to the 'th' in 'this'
g	as the 'ch' in the Scottish *loch* before **e** and **i** ('kh' in our guides to pronunciation); elsewhere, as in 'go'
h	invariably silent; if your name begins with this letter, listen carefully if you're waiting for public officials to call you
j	as the 'ch' in the Scottish *loch* (written as 'kh' in our guides to pronunciation)
ll	as the 'y' in 'yellow'
ñ	as the 'ni' in 'onion'
r	a short **r** except at the beginning of a word, and after **l**, **n** or **s**, when it's often rolled
rr	very strongly rolled
v	similar to English 'b,' but softer; referred to as 'b corta'
x	as in 'taxi' except for a very few words, when it's pronounced as **j**
z	as the 's' in 'sun'

Semiconsonant

The Spanish **y** is a semiconsonant; it's pronounced as the Spanish **i** when it stands alone or appears at the end of a word. Normally, **y** is pronounced like the 'y' in 'yesterday'; however, in some regions it may be pronounced as the 's' in 'pleasure' or even the 'j' in 'jacket.' Hence, *yo me llamo* can sound like 'joe meh jahm-oh.'

Word Stress

In general, words ending in vowels or the letters **n** or **s** have stress on the next-to-last syllable, while those with other endings have stress on the last syllable. Written accents denote stress, and override these rules, eg *sótano* (basement), *América* and *porción* (portion).

GENDER & PLURALS

In Spanish, nouns are either masculine or feminine, and there are rules to help determine gender – with exceptions, of course! Feminine nouns generally end with -**a** or with the groups -**ción**, -**sión** or -**dad**. Other endings typically signify a masculine noun. Endings for adjectives also change to agree with the gender of the noun they modify (masculine/feminine -**o**/-**a**). Where both masculine and feminine forms are included in this language guide, they are separated by a slash, with the masculine form first.

If a noun or adjective ends in a vowel, the plural is formed by adding **s** to the end. If it ends in a consonant, the plural is formed by adding **es** to the end.

ACCOMMODATIONS

I'm looking for ...	*Estoy buscando ...*	e·stoy boos·kan·do ...
Where is ...?	*¿Dónde hay ...?*	don·de ai ...
a hotel	*un hotel*	oon o·tel
a guesthouse	*una pensión/ casa de huéspedes*	oo·na pen·syon/ ka·sa de we·spe·des
a camping ground	*un terreno de cámping*	oon te·re·no de kam·peen
a youth hostel	*un albergue juvenil*	oon al·ber·ge khoo·ve·neel
I'd like a ... room.	*Quisiera una habitación ...*	kee·sye·ra oo·na a·bee·ta·syon ...
single	*sencilla*	sen·see·la
double	*doble*	do·ble
twin	*con dos camas*	kon dos ka·mas
How much is it per ...?	*¿Cuánto cuesta por ...?*	kwan·to kwes·ta por ...
night	*noche*	no·che
person	*persona*	per·so·na
week	*semana*	se·ma·na
private/shared bathroom	*baño privado/ compartido*	ba·nyo pree·va·do/ kom·par·tee·do
full board	*pensión completa*	pen·syon kom·ple·ta

MAKING A RESERVATION

(for phone or written requests)

To ...	A ...
From ...	De ...
Date	Fecha
I'd like to book ...	Quisiera reservar ... (see 'Accommodations' on p367 for bed and room options)
in the name of ...	en nombre de ...
for the nights of ...	para las noches del ...
credit card ...	tarjeta de crédito ...
number	número
expiry date	fecha de vencimiento
Please confirm ...	Puede confirmar ...
availability	la disponibilidad
price	el precio

too expensive	demasiado caro	de·ma·sya·do ka·ro
cheaper	más barato/ económico	mas ba·ra·to/ e·ko·no·mee·ko
discount	descuento	des·kwen·to

May I see the room?
¿Puedo ver la habitación? — pwe·do ver la a·bee·ta·syon
I don't like it.
No me gusta. — no me goos·ta
It's fine. I'll take it.
OK. La alquilo. — o·kay la al·kee·lo
Does it include breakfast?
¿Incluye el desayuno? — een·kloo·ye el de·sa·yoo·no
I'm leaving now.
Me voy ahora. — me voy a·o·ra

CONVERSATION & ESSENTIALS

In their public behavior, South Americans are very conscious of civilities, sometimes to the point of ceremoniousness. Never approach a stranger for information without extending a greeting and use only the polite form of address, especially with the police and public officials. Young people may be less likely to expect this, but it's best to stick to the polite form unless you're quite sure you won't offend by using the informal mode. The polite form is used in all cases in this guide; where options are given, the form is indicated by the abbreviations 'pol' and 'inf.'

Hello.	Hola.	o·la
Good morning.	Buenos días.	bwe·nos dee·as
Good afternoon.	Buenas tardes.	bwe·nas tar·des
Good evening/ night.	Buenas noches.	bwe·nas no·ches
Goodbye.	Adiós.	a·dyos
See you soon.	Hasta luego.	as·ta lwe·go
Yes.	Sí.	see
No.	No.	no
Please.	Por favor.	por fa·vor
Thank you.	Gracias.	gra·syas
Many thanks.	Muchas gracias.	moo·chas gra·syas
You're welcome.	De nada.	de na·da
Pardon me.	Perdón.	per·don
Excuse me.	Permiso.	per·mee·so
(used when asking permission)		
Forgive me.	Disculpe.	dees·kool·pe
(used when apologizing)		

How are things?
¿Qué tal? — ke tal
What's your name?
¿Cómo se llama? — ko·mo se ya·ma (pol)
¿Cómo te llamas? — ko·mo te ya·mas (inf)
My name is ...
Me llamo ... — me ya·mo ...
It's a pleasure to meet you.
Mucho gusto. — moo·cho goos·to
The pleasure is mine.
El gusto es mío. — el goos·to es mee·o
Where are you from?
¿De dónde es/eres? — de don·de es/e·res (pol/inf)
I'm from ...
Soy de ... — soy de ...
Where are you staying?
¿Dónde está alojado? — don·de es·ta a·lo·kha·do (pol)
¿Dónde estás alojado? — don·de es·tas a·lo·kha·do (inf)
May I take a photo?
¿Puedo sacar una foto? — pwe·do sa·kar oo·na fo·to

DIRECTIONS

How do I get to ...?
¿Cómo puedo llegar a ...? — ko·mo pwe·do lye·gar a ...
I'm lost.
Estoy perdido/a. — es·toy per·dee·do/a
Can you show me (on the map)?
¿Me lo podría indicar (en el mapa)? — me lo po·dree·a een·dee·kar (en el ma·pa)
Is it far?
¿Está lejos? — es·ta le·khos
Go straight ahead.
Siga/Vaya derecho. — see·ga/va·ya de·re·cho
Turn left.
Voltée a la izquierda. — vol·te·e a la ees·kyer·da
Turn right.
Voltée a la derecha. — vol·te·e a la de·re·cha

LANGUAGE

SIGNS

Entrada	Entrance
Salida	Exit
Información	Information
Abierto	Open
Cerrado	Closed
Prohibido	Prohibited
Comisaria	Police Station
Servicios/Baños	Toilets
Hombres/Varones	Men
Señoras/Damas	Women

north	*norte*	*nor·te*
south	*sur*	soor
east	*este/oriente*	*es·te/o·ryen·te*
west	*oeste/occidente*	*o·es·te/ok·see·den·te*
here	*aquí*	*a·kee*
there	*allí*	*a·yee*
avenue	*avenida*	*a·ve·nee·da*
block	*cuadra*	*kwa·dra*
street	*calle/paseo*	*ka·lye/pa·se·o*

HEALTH

I'm sick.
Estoy enfermo/a.   *es·toy* en·*fer*·mo/a
I need a doctor.
Necesito un médico.   ne·se·*see*·to oon *me*·dee·ko
Where's the hospital?
¿Dónde está el hospital?   *don*·de es·*ta* el os·pee·*tal*
I'm pregnant.
Estoy embarazada.   es·*toy* em·ba·ra·*sa*·da
I've been vaccinated.
Estoy vacunado/a.   es·*toy* va·koo·*na*·do/a

I'm allergic to ...	*Soy alérgico/a a ...*	soy a·*ler*·khee·ko/a a ...
antibiotics	*los antibióticos*	los an·tee·*byo*·tee·kos
penicillin	*la penicilina*	la pe·nee·see·*lee*·na
nuts	*las fruta secas*	las *froo*·tas *se*·kas
I'm ...	*Soy ...*	soy ...
asthmatic	*asmático/a*	as·*ma*·tee·ko/a
diabetic	*diabético/a*	dya·*be*·tee·ko/a
epileptic	*epiléptico/a*	e·pee·*lep*·tee·ko/a
I have ...	*Tengo ...*	*ten*·go ...
altitude sickness	*soroche*	so·*ro*·che
diarrhea	*diarrea*	dya·*re*·a
nausea	*náusea*	*now*·se·a
a headache	*un dolor de cabeza*	oon do·*lor* de ka·*be*·sa
a cough	*tos*	tos

EMERGENCIES

Help!	*¡Socorro!*	so·*ko*·ro
Fire!	*¡Incendio!*	een·*sen*·dyo
I've been robbed.	*Me robaron.*	me ro·*ba*·ron
Go away!	*¡Déjeme!*	*de*·khe·me
Get lost!	*¡Váyase!*	*va*·ya·se
Call ...!	*¡Llame a ...!*	*ya*·me a...
an ambulance	*una ambulancia*	oo·na am·boo·*lan*·sya
a doctor	*un médico*	oon *me*·dee·ko
the police	*la policía*	la po·lee·*see*·a

It's an emergency.
Es una emergencia.   es oo·na e·mer·*khen*·sya
Could you help me, please?
¿Me puede ayudar,   me *pwe*·de a·yoo·*dar*
por favor?   por fa·*vor*
I'm lost.
Estoy perdido/a.   es·*toy* per·*dee*·do/a
Where are the toilets?
¿Dónde están los baños?   *don*·de es·*tan* los *ba*·nyos

LANGUAGE DIFFICULTIES

Do you speak (English)?
¿Habla/Hablas (inglés)?   *a*·bla/*a*·blas (een·*gles*) (pol/inf)
Does anyone here speak English?
¿Hay alguien que hable   ai al·*gyen* ke *a*·ble
inglés?   een·*gles*
I (don't) understand.
Yo (no) entiendo.   yo (no) en·*tyen*·do
How do you say ...?
¿Cómo se dice ...?   *ko*·mo se *dee*·se ...
What does ...mean?
¿Qué quiere decir ...?   ke *kye*·re de·*seer* ...

Could you please ...?	*¿Puede ..., por favor?*	*pwe*·de ... por fa·*vor*
repeat that	*repetirlo*	re·pe·*teer*·lo
speak more slowly	*hablar más despacio*	a·*blar* mas des·*pa*·syo
write it down	*escribirlo*	es·kree·*beer*·lo

NUMBERS

1	*uno*	*oo*·no
2	*dos*	dos
3	*tres*	tres
4	*cuatro*	*kwa*·tro
5	*cinco*	*seen*·ko
6	*seis*	says
7	*siete*	*sye*·te
8	*ocho*	*o*·cho

9	nueve	nwe·ve
10	diez	dyes
11	once	on·se
12	doce	do·se
13	trece	tre·se
14	catorce	ka·tor·se
15	quince	keen·se
16	dieciséis	dye·see·says
17	diecisiete	dye·see·sye·te
18	dieciocho	dye·see·o·cho
19	diecinueve	dye·see·nwe·ve
20	veinte	vayn·te
21	veintiuno	vayn·tee·oo·no
30	treinta	trayn·ta
31	treinta y uno	trayn·ta ee oo·no
40	cuarenta	kwa·ren·ta
50	cincuenta	seen·kwen·ta
60	sesenta	se·sen·ta
70	setenta	se·ten·ta
80	ochenta	o·chen·ta
90	noventa	no·ven·ta
100	cien	syen
101	ciento uno	syen·to oo·no
200	doscientos	do·syen·tos
1000	mil	meel
5000	cinco mil	seen·ko meel
10,000	diez mil	dyes meel
50,000	cincuenta mil	seen·kwen·ta meel
100,000	cien mil	syen meel
1,000,000	un millón	oon mee·yon

SHOPPING & SERVICES

I'd like to buy ...
   Quisiera comprar ... kee·sye·ra kom·prar
I'm just looking.
   Sólo estoy mirando. so·lo es·toy mee·ran·do
May I look at it?
   ¿Puedo mirar(lo/la)? pwe·do mee·rar·(lo/la)
How much is it?
   ¿Cuánto cuesta? kwan·to kwes·ta
That's too expensive for me.
   Es demasiado caro es de·ma·sya·do ka·ro
   para mí. pa·ra mee
Could you lower the price?
   ¿Podría bajar un poco po·dree·a ba·khar oon po·ko
   el precio? el pre·syo
I don't like it.
   No me gusta. no me goos·ta
I'll take it.
   Lo llevo. lo ye·vo

**Do you ¿Aceptan ...? a·sep·tan...
accept ...?**
   **American dólares do·la·res
   dollars americanos a·me·ree·ka·nos**

credit cards	tarjetas de	tar·khe·tas de
	crédito	kre·dee·to
traveler's	cheques de	che·kes de
checks	viajero	vya·khe·ro

less	menos	me·nos
more	más	mas
large	grande	gran·de
small	pequeño/a	pe·ke·nyo/a

I'm looking	Estoy buscando ...	es·toy boos·kan·do...
for (a/the) ...		
ATM	un cajero	oon ka·khe·ro
	automático	ow·to·ma·tee·ko
bank	el banco	el ban·ko
bookstore	una librería	oo·na lee·bre·ree·a
embassy	la embajada	la em·ba·kha·da
exchange	una casa de	oo·na ka·sa de
house	cambio	kam·byo
general store	la tienda	la tyen·da
laundry	la lavandería	la la·van·de·ree·a
market	el mercado	el mer·ka·do
pharmacy/	la farmacia/	la far·ma·sya/
chemist	la botica	la bo·tee·ka
post office	el correo	el ko·re·o
public	un teléfono	oon te·le·fo·no
telephone	público	poob·lee·ko
supermarket	el supermercado	el soo·per·
		mer·ka·do
tourist office	la oficina de	la o·fee·see·na de
	turismo	too·rees·mo

What time does it open/close?
   ¿A qué hora abre/cierra? a ke o·ra a·bre/sye·ra
I want to change some money/traveler's checks.
   Quiero cambiar dinero/ kye·ro kam·byar dee·ne·ro/
   cheques de viajero. che·kes de vya·khe·ro
What is the exchange rate?
   ¿Cuál es el tipo de kwal es el tee·po de
   cambio? kam·byo
I want to call ...
   Quiero llamar a ... kye·ro lya·mar a ...

airmail	correo aéreo	ko·re·o a·e·re·o
black market	mercado (negro/	mer·ka·do (ne·gro/
	paralelo)	pa·ra·le·lo)
collect call	llamada a cobro	ya·ma·da a ko·bro
	revertido	re·ver·tee·do
email	correo electrónico	ko·re·yo
		e·le·tro·nee·ko
letter	carta	kar·ta
local call	llamada local	ya·ma·da lo·kal
long-distance	llamada de larga	ya·ma·da de lar·ga
call	distancia	dis·tan·sa
parcel	paquete	pa·ke·te

person to	persona a	per·so·na a
person	persona	per·so·na
postcard	postal	pos·tal
registered mail	certificado	ser·tee·fee·ka·do
stamps	estampillas	es·tam·pee·lyas

TIME & DATES

The time is expressed by saying *la* or *las* followed by the hour number and how far it is past or until the hour. Thus, eight o'clock is *las ocho*, while 8:30 is *las ocho y treinta* (eight and thirty) or *las ocho y media* (eight and a half). However, 7:45 is *las ocho menos quince* (eight minus fifteen) or *las ocho menos cuarto* (eight minus a quarter).

Times are modified by morning *(de la mañana)* or afternoon *(de la tarde)* instead of am or pm. Use of the 24-hour clock, or military time, is also common, especially with transportation schedules.

What time is it?	¿Qué hora es?	ke o·ra es
It's one o'clock.	Es la una.	es la oo·na
It's two/three ... (etc) o'clock.	Son las dos/tres ...	son las dos/tres ...
At three o'clock.	A las tres.	a las tres
midnight	medianoche	me·dya·no·che
noon	mediodía	me·dyo·dee·a
half past two	dos y media	dos ee me·dya

now	ahora	a·o·ra
today	hoy	oy
tonight	esta noche	es·ta no·che
tomorrow	mañana	ma·nya·na
yesterday	ayer	a·yer

Monday	lunes	loo·nes
Tuesday	martes	mar·tes
Wednesday	miércoles	myer·ko·les
Thursday	jueves	khwe·ves
Friday	viernes	vyer·nes
Saturday	sábado	sa·ba·do
Sunday	domingo	do·meen·go

January	enero	e·ne·ro
February	febrero	fe·bre·ro
March	marzo	mar·so
April	abril	a·breel
May	mayo	ma·yo
June	junio	khoo·nyo
July	julio	khoo·lyo
August	agosto	a·gos·to
September	septiembre	sep·tyem·bre
October	octubre	ok·too·bre
November	noviembre	no·vyem·bre
December	diciembre	dee·syem·bre

GEOGRAPHICAL EXPRESSIONS

The expressions below are among the most common you'll encounter in Spanish-language maps and guides.

avenida	avenue
bahía	bay
calle	street
camino	road
campo/finca/fundo/ hacienda	farm
carretera/camino/ruta	highway
cascada/salto	waterfall
cerro	hill/mount
cordillera	mountain range
estancia/granja/rancho	ranch
estero	marsh, estuary
lago	lake
montaña	mountain
parque nacional	national park
paso	pass
playa	beach
puente	bridge
río	river
seno	sound
valle	valley

TRANSPORTATION
Public Transportation

airport	el aeropuerto	el a·e·ro·pwer·to
bus stop	la parada de autobuses	la pa·ra·da de ow·to·boo·ses
bus terminal	la terminal de pasajeros	la tair·mee·nal de pa·sa·khe·ros
luggage check room	guardería/ equipaje	gwar·de·ree·a/ e·kee·pa·khe
ticket office	la boletería	la bo·le·te·ree·a
train station	la estación de ferrocarril	la es·ta·syon de fe·ro·ka·reel

What time does ... leave/arrive?	¿A qué hora ... sale/llega?	a ke o·ra ... sa·le/ye·ga
the boat	el bongo/ la lancha/ el bote	el bon·go/ la lan·cha/ el bo·te
the bus	el autobus	el ow·to·boos
the plane	el avión	el a·vyon
the ship	el barco/buque	el bar·ko/boo·ke
the small bus	el por puesto/ la buseta/ el carrito	el por·pwes·to/ la boo·se·ta/ el ka·ree·to
the train	el tren	el tren

LANGUAGE

I'd like a ticket to ...
Quiero un boleto a ...   kye·ro oon bo·*le*·to a ...
What's the fare to ...?
¿Cuánto cuesta hasta ...?   kwan·to *kwes*·ta *a*·sta ...

1st class	*primera clase*	pree·me·ra *kla*·se
2nd class	*segunda clase*	se·*goon*·da *kla*·se
single/one-way	*ida*	ee·da
return/roundtrip	*ida y vuelta*	ee·da ee *vwel*·ta
taxi	*taxi*	tak·see

Private Transportation

pickup (truck)	*camioneta*	ka·myo·*ne*·ta
truck	*camión*	ka·myon
hitchhike	*hacer dedo/*	a·ser de·do/
	pedir una cola	pe·*deer* oon *ko*·la

I'd like to	*Quisiera*	kee·*sye*·ra
hire a/an ...	*alquilar ...*	al·kee·*lar* ...
4WD	*un todo terreno*	oon *to*·do te·*re*·no
car	*un auto/carro*	oon *ow*·to/*ka*·ro
motorcycle	*una moto*	*oo*·na mo·to
bicycle	*una bicicleta*	*oo*·na bee·*see*·*kle*·ta

Is this the road to (...)?
¿Se va a (...) por   se va a (...) por
esta carretera?   *es*·ta ka·re·*te*·ra
Where's a petrol station?
¿Dónde hay una   don·de ai oo·na
gasolinera/un grifo?   ga·so·lee·*ne*·ra/oon *gree*·fo
Please fill it up.
Lleno, por favor.   ye·no por fa·*vor*
I'd like (20) liters.
Quiero (veinte) litros.   kye·ro (vayn·te) lee·tros

diesel	*diesel*	dee·sel
leaded (regular)	*gasolina con*	ga·so·*lee*·na kon
	plomo	*plo*·mo
petrol (gas)	*gasolina*	ga·so·*lee*·na
unleaded	*gasolina sin*	ga·so·*lee*·na seen
	plomo	*plo*·mo

(How long) Can I park here?
¿(Por cuánto tiempo)   (por *kwan*·to *tyem*·po)
Puedo aparcar aquí?   pwe·do a·par·kar a·kee
Where do I pay?
¿Dónde se paga?   don·de se *pa*·ga
I need a mechanic.
Necesito un mecánico.   ne·se·*see*·to oon me·*ka*·nee·ko
The car has broken down (in ...).
El carro se ha averiado   el *ka*·ro se a a·ve·*rya*·do
(en ...).   (en ...)
The motorbike won't start.
No arranca la moto.   no a·*ran*·ka la *mo*·to

ROAD SIGNS

Keep in mind that traffic signs will invariably be in Spanish and may not be accompanied by internationally recognized symbols. Pay especially close attention to *Peligro* (Danger), *Ceda el Paso* (Yield/Give Way; especially prevalent on one-lane bridges), and *Hundimiento* (Dip; this is often a euphemistic term for 'axle-breaking sinkhole'). Disregarding these warnings could result in disaster.

Acceso	Entrance
Alto	Stop
Aparcamiento	Parking
Ceda el Paso	Yield/Give Way
Curva Peligrosa	Dangerous Curve
Derrumbes en la Vía	Landslides/Rockfalls
Despacio	Slow
Desvío	Detour
Dirección Única	One-way
Hundimiento	Dip
Mantenga Su Derecha	Keep to the Right
No Adelantar/No Rebase	No Passing
No Estacionar	No Parking
No Hay Paso	No Entrance
Peaje	Toll
Peligro	Danger
Prohibido Aparcar/	No Parking
No Estacionar	
Prohibido el Paso	No Entry
Pare/Stop	Stop
Salida de Autopista	Freeway Exit
Trabajos en la Vía	Roadwork
Tránsito Entrando	Entering Traffic

I have a flat tyre.
Tengo un pinchazo.   ten·go oon peen·*cha*·so
I've run out of petrol.
Me quedé sin gasolina.   me ke·*de* seen ga·so·*lee*·na
I've had an accident.
Tuve un accidente.   *too*·ve oon ak·see·*den*·te

TRAVEL WITH CHILDREN

I need ...
Necesito ...   ne·se·*see*·to ...
Do you have ...?
¿Hay ...?   ai ...
  a car baby seat
  un asiento de seguridad   oon a·*syen*·to de se·goo·ree·*da*
  para bebés   pa·ra be·*bes*
  a child-minding service
  un servicio de cuidado   oon ser·*vee*·syo de kwee·*da*·do
  de niños   de *nee*·nyos

a children's menu
una carta infantil   oona *kar*·ta een·fan·*teel*
a creche
una guardería   oo·na gwar·de·*ree*·a
(disposable) diapers/nappies
pañoles (de usar y tirar)   pa·*nyo*·les (de oo·*sar* ee tee·*rar*)
an (English-speaking) babysitter
una niñera   oo·na nee·*nye*·ra
  (de habla inglesa)   (de *a*·bla een·*gle*·sa)
formula (milk)
leche en polvo   *le*·che en *pol*·vo

a highchair
una trona   oo·na *tro*·na
a potty
una pelela   oo·na pe·*le*·la
a pusher/stroller
un cochecito   oon ko·che·*see*·to

Do you mind if I breast-feed here?
  ¿Le molesta que dé   le mo·*les*·ta ke de
    de pecho aquí?   de *pe*·cho a·*kee*
Are children allowed?
  ¿Se admiten niños?   se ad·*mee*·ten *nee*·nyos

Also available from Lonely Planet:
Latin American Spanish Phrasebook

Glossary

See the Food & Drink chapter (p48) for useful words and phrases dealing with food and dining. See the Language chapter (p366) for general-use words and phrases.

abasto – small rural store selling anything from bread and batteries to sunblock and beer

acure – hare-sized rodent, species of agouti

adobe – sun-dried brick made of mud and straw, used in traditional rural constructions

alcabala – road checkpost operated by the Guardia Nacional

alcaldía – mayor's office

andino/a – inhabitant of the Andes

araguaney – trumpet tree *(Tabebuia chrysantha)*, a large tree with yellow flowers; Venezuela's national tree

arepa – hamburger-sized corn pancake stuffed with juicy fillings

arepera – restaurant selling *arepas*

atarraya – traditional circular fishing net used on the coast and rivers

ateneo – cultural center

autopista – freeway

azulejos – ornamental handmade tiles brought to South America from Spain and Portugal in colonial times

baba – spectacled caiman, the smallest of the family of local crocodiles

baloncesto – basketball

bandola – four-string, pear-shaped guitar-type instrument used by some *joropo* bands instead of the harp

barrio – shantytown built of *ranchos* around the big city centers; particularly numerous and extensive in Caracas

béisbol – baseball

bodega – warehouse; also used to mean 'grocery,' especially in small localities and rural areas

bolo – informal term for the *bolívar* (Venezuela's currency); see also *real*

bolas criollas – Venezuelan form of lawn bowling

bonche – party (informal)

bongo – large dugout canoe; traditionally hand-hewn, today usually equipped with outboard motor

buhonero – street vendor

bus-cama – long-distance bus with seats almost reclining into a bed; the most comfy means of intercity transportation

buseta – small bus, frequently used in city transportation

cabalgata – horseback ride

cabaña – cabin, found mostly on the coast and in the mountains

cachicamo – armadillo

caimán – caiman, or American crocodile; similar to alligators, but with a more heavily armored belly

cajero automático – automated teller machine (ATM)

calle – street

callejón – alley or narrow, short street

caminata – trek, hike

camioneta – minibus

campamento – countryside lodging facility, usually in cabins, with its own food services and often a tour program

campesino/a – rural dweller, usually of modest economic means; subsistence farmer

caney – palm-thatched open-sided large hut

canoa – a dugout canoe

canotaje – rafting

CANTV – the national telecommunications company

caño – natural water channel

capybara – a tailless largely aquatic South American rodent; also called *chigüire*

carabobeño/a – inhabitant of Carabobo state, particularly Valencia

Caracazo – violent Caracas riots of February 27–29, 1989, in which more than 300 people died

caraqueño/a – person born and/or residing in Caracas

cardón – columnar type of cactus typical of the Península de Paraguaná

carrito – term used for por puesto

casa – house; used for anything from a rustic hut to a rambling colonial mansion

casa de cambio – money-exchange office

cascabel – rattlesnake

caserío – hamlet

casona – large, rambling old mansion; stately home

castillo – fort

catire – person of light complexion

caudillo – South American dictator, normally a military man who assumes power by force and is noted for autocratic rule; caudillos governed Venezuela from 1830 to 1958

CC – common abbreviation for Centro Comercial, or shopping mall

cédula – identity document of Venezuelan citizens and residents

ceiba – common tree of the tropics that can reach a huge size

cepillada – shaved ice

chalana – flatbed river ferry for people and vehicles

chaguaramo – popular term for royal palm

chamo/a – boy/girl, young person, friend, pal, mate (informal)

cheque viajero – traveler's check
chévere – good, fine (informal)
chigüire – capybara, the world's largest rodent
chinchorro – hammock woven of cotton threads or palm fiber like a fishing net; typical of many indigenous groups, including the Warao and Guajiro
churuata – traditional palm-thatched, large, circular hut
ciénaga – shallow lake or lagoon
cinemateca – arthouse cinema that focuses on screening films of a high artistic quality
coleo – form of rodeo practiced in Los Llanos, also known as *toros coleadoss*; the aim is to overthrow a bull by grabbing its tail from a galloping horse
colibrí – hummingbird
comida criolla – typical Venezuelan cuisine
cónchale – informal tag word, used on its own or added to the beginning of a sentence to emphasize emotional involvement
conuco – small cultivated plot, usually obtained by slashing-and-burning
corrida – bullfight
costeño/a – inhabitant of the coastal regions
criollo/a – Creole, a person of European (especially Spanish) ancestry but born in the Americas
crucero – highway crossroad
cuadra – city block
cuatro – a small four-stringed guitar, used in *joropo* and *gaita* music
cuñado – literally 'brother-in-law'; pal, friend, mate (informal)
curiara – small dugout canoe
Curripaco – indigenous community living in Amazonas state

danta – tapir; large hoofed mammal of tropical and subtropical forests
denuncia – official report/statement to the police
DIEX or DEX – Dirección Nacional de Identificación y Extranjería, the Venezuelan immigration authority

embalse – reservoir formed by a dam built for hydroelectric or water-supply purposes
embarcadero – landing dock
epa – hey
esquina – street corner
estacionamiento (vigilado) – (guarded) car park
estera – a type of mat constructed from a papyrus-like reed

farmacia – pharmacy
ferretería – hardware store
flamenco – flamingo
flor de mayo – species of orchid that is Venezuela's national flower
fortín – small fort

frailejón – *espeletia*; a species of plant typical of the *páramo*
franela – literally 'flannel'; commonly refers to a T-shirt
fuerte – fort
fundo – country estate
fútbol – soccer
furruco – musical instrument consisting of a drum and a wooden pole piercing the drumhead; used in some kinds of popular music including the *gaita*. The sound is produced via striking the drumhead by moving the pole up and down.

gaita – popular music played in Zulia state
gallera – cockfight ring
garimpeiro – illegal gold miner
garza – heron
gavilán – sparrow hawk
gringo/a – any white foreigner; sometimes, not always, derogatory
guacamaya – macaw
guácharo – oilbird, a species of nocturnal bird living in caves
Guajibo – indigenous group living in parts of Los Llanos and Amazonas along the frontier with Colombia
Guajiro – Venezuela's most numerous indigenous group, living in Zulia state (Venezuela) and Península de la Guajira (Colombia)
guardaequipaje – left-luggage office; checkroom
guardaparque – national-park ranger
Guardia Nacional – military police responsible for security
guarupa – jacaranda; a tall tropical tree with lavender-blue blossoms

hacienda – country estate
hato – large cattle ranch, typical of Los Llanos
hospedaje – cheap hotel

iglesia – church
impuesto – tax
impuesto de salida – departure tax
invierno – literally 'winter'; refers to the rainy season
Ipostel – company operating a network of post offices
isla – island
IVA – *impuesto de valor agregado*, a value-added sales tax (VAT)

jején – species of small biting gnat that infests the Gran Sabana and, to a lesser extent, some other regions
joropo – typical music of Los Llanos, today widespread throughout the country; considered Venezuelan national rhythm

lanchero – boatman
lapa – species of agouti, a rabbit-sized rodent whose brown skin is dotted with white spots

lavandería – launderette
liqui liqui – men's traditional costume, typical of most of the Caribbean; a white or beige suit comprising trousers and a shirt with a collar, usually accompanied by white hat and shoes
llanero/a – inhabitant of Los Llanos
(Los) Llanos – literally 'plains'; Venezuela's vast central region
loro – parrot

mal de páramo – altitude sickness
malecón – waterfront boulevard
manatí – manatee; a cetaceous herbivore living in calm rivers. Manatees can reach up to 5m in length.
manga de coleo – place where *coleos* are held
manta – long, loose, usually colorful dress worn by Guajiro women
mapanare – venomous snake common in Venezuela
Maquiritare – see *Yekuana*
maracas – gourd rattles; an indispensable accompanying instrument of *joropo*
maracucho/a – person from Maracaibo; often extended to mean anyone from the Zulia state
margariteño/a – person from the Isla de Margarita
matrimonial – hotel room with a double bed intended for couples
médanos – sand dunes near Coro
menú del día – set lunch or dinner
merengue – musical rhythm originating from the Dominican Republic, today widespread throughout the Caribbean
merú – Pemón word for 'waterfall'
mestizo/a – person of mixed European–American Indian blood
micro – in some regions, a term for a minibus or van used as local transportation
mirador – lookout, viewpoint
mochilero – backpacker
módulo – dormitory-style accommodations, popular with school groups
monedero – originally a term referring to a public telephone operated by coins, but now extended to any public phone
moreno/a – person of dark complexion; usually a mix of black and white ancestry
morichale – palm grove (see also *moriche*)
moriche – oily palm common in Los Llanos and the Delta del Orinoco, used by indigenous people for construction, food, household items, handicrafts etc
morrocoy – tortoise typical of some regions, including Los Llanos and Guayana
mosquitero – mosquito net
mucuposadas – traditional rural lodges
muelle – pier, wharf
mulatto – a person of mixed European-African ancestry

Navidad – Christmas
nevado – snowcapped peak

Onidex – Oficina Nacional de Identificación y Extranjería (see also DIEX)
orquídea – orchid
oso hormiguero – anteater

palafito – house built on stilts over the water; a typical Warao dwelling in the Delta del Orinoco. Also found in Zulia state, especially in Laguna de Sinamaica.
palos – literally 'sticks'; drinks (informal)
pana – pal, mate (informal)
panadería – bakery
paño – small towel, the one you'll get in cheap hotels
parada – bus stop
páramo – open highland above about 3300m; typical of Venezuela, Colombia and Ecuador
parapente – paragliding
pardo/a – mulatto; person of mixed European and African descent
parrilla – mixed grill
paseo – promenade
pastelería – pastry shop
paují – a black bird that inhabits cloud forest in the north and west of Venezuela
Pemón – indigenous group inhabiting the Gran Sabana and neighboring areas
peñero – open fishing boat made from wood
pereza – sloth
Piapoco – indigenous community living in Amazonas state
Piaroa – indigenous community living in Amazonas state
piscina – swimming pool
playa – beach
plaza de toros – bullfight ring
por puesto – cross between a bus and taxi that plies fixed routes and departs when full
por rato – love motel
posada – small, family-run guesthouse
pozo – pond
primo – literally 'cousin'; pal, brother (informal)
propina – tip
puri-puri – small biting sand flies, similar to *jejenes*

quebrada – a steep ravine which may or may not have a creek or river at the bottom of it
quinta – house with a garden; *quintas* originally took up a fifth of a city block – hence the name

ranchería – Indian hamlet
rancho or **ranchito** – ramshackle dwelling built of waste materials
raudales – rapids
real – informal term for the *bolívar* (Venezuela's currency)

redoma – traffic circle, roundabout
refugio – rustic shelter in a remote area, mostly in the mountains
reggaetón – form of music fusing hip-hop with a hybrid of reggae, dancehall (a contemporary offshoot of reggae with faster, digital beats and an MC) and traditional Latin-music beats; much of it comes from Puerto Rico
residencia – cheap hotel or, more often, apartment building
río – river
roqueño/a – inhabitants of the Archipiélago Los Roques
rumba – party
rústico – jeep

salinas – seaside salt pans or shallow lagoons used for extraction of salt
sapito – tiny frog
Semana Santa – Holy Week, the week before Easter Sunday
shabono – large circular house typical of the Yanomami
SIDA – AIDS
sifrino/a – yuppie (informal)
sima – sinkhole; depression in the ground, usually circular and deep, with vertical walls

tambora – large wooden drum
tarjeta de crédito – credit card
tarjeta de ingreso – tourist card
tasa aeroportuaria – airport tax
tasca – Spanish-style bar-restaurant
teleférico – cable car
teléfono público – public telephone
telenovela – TV soap opera

tepui – also spelled *tepuy*; a flat-topped sandstone mountain with vertical flanks; the term is derived from the Pemón word for 'mountain'
terminal de pasajeros – bus terminal
tienda – small store that sells food, toiletries, batteries etc
tigre – jaguar
tonina – freshwater dolphin
toros coleados – see *coleo*
trapiche – traditional sugarcane mill
turpial – small black, red and yellow bird; Venezuela's national bird

urbanización – suburb

vaina – thing (colloquial)
vallenato – typical Colombian music, now widespread throughout Venezuela
vaquero – cowboy of Los Llanos
vená – Pemón word for 'high waterfall'
verano – literally 'summer'; used in the sense of 'dry season'
viajero – traveler

Warao – indigenous group living in the Delta del Orinoco

yagrumo – tree with large palmate silver-colored leaves
Yanomami – indigenous group living in the Venezuelan and Brazilian Amazon
Ye'Kwana/Yekuana – also referred to as Maquiritare; an indigenous group inhabiting parts of Amazonas and Bolívar states

zambo/a – person of mixed American Indian-African ancestry
zona libre – duty-free zone

Behind the Scenes

THIS BOOK

This 5th edition of *Venezuela* was researched and written by Thomas Kohnstamm (coordinating author), Sandra Bao, Beth Kohn, Jens Porup and Daniel C Schechter. Dr David Goldberg MD also contributed. The 4th edition was written by Krzysztof Dydyński and Charlotte Beech. The first three editions were also written by Krzysztof Dydyński. This guidebook was commissioned in Lonely Planet's Oakland office, and produced by the following:

Commissioning Editor David Zingarelli
Coordinating Editor Fionnuala Twomey
Coordinating Cartographer Helen Rowley
Coordinating Layout Designer Carlos Solarte
Managing Editors Imogen Bannister, Barbara Delissen
Managing Cartographers David Connolly, Alison Lyall
Assisting Editors Andrea Dobbin, Chris Girdler, Kate James, Rowan McKinnon
Assisting Cartographer Diana Duggan

Assisting Layout Designers David Kemp, Wibowo Rusli
Cover Designer Annika Roojun
Project Managers Rachel Imeson, Kate McLeod
Language Content Coordinator Quentin Frayne

Thanks to David Burnett, Sin Choo, Sally Darmody, Laura Jane, Raphael Richards, Cara Smith, Celia Wood

THANKS
THOMAS KOHNSTAMM
Thanks to Sandra, Beth, Jens and Daniel for their hard work. Thanks to David Zingarelli for putting me on the project.

SANDRA BAO
Thanks to the many Venezuelans, travelers and expats who tolerated numerous and seemingly inane questions throughout this research trip. Folks who especially helped me out include Claudia Beckmann in Puerto Colombia, Gina Malpica

---

LONELY PLANET: TRAVEL WIDELY, TREAD LIGHTLY, GIVE SUSTAINABLY

The Lonely Planet Story
The story begins with a classic travel adventure: Tony and Maureen Wheeler's 1972 journey across Europe and Asia to Australia. There was no useful information about the overland trail then, so Tony and Maureen published the first Lonely Planet guidebook to meet a growing need.

From a kitchen table, Lonely Planet has grown to become the largest independent travel publisher in the world, with offices in Melbourne (Australia), Oakland (USA) and London (UK). Today Lonely Planet guidebooks cover the globe. There is an ever-growing list of books and information in a variety of media. Some things haven't changed. The main aim is still to make it possible for adventurous individuals to get out there – to explore and better understand the world.

The Lonely Planet Foundation
The Lonely Planet Foundation proudly supports nimble nonprofit institutions working for change in the world. Each year the foundation donates 5% of Lonely Planet company profits to projects selected by staff and authors. Our partners range from Kabissa, which provides small nonprofits across Africa with access to technology, to the Foundation for Developing Cambodian Orphans, which supports girls at risk of falling victim to sex traffickers.

Our nonprofit partners are linked by a grass-roots approach to the areas of health, education or sustainable tourism. Many projects we support choose to focus on women and children as one of the most effective ways to support the whole community.

Sometimes foundation assistance is as simple as restoring a local ruin like the Minaret of Jam in Afghanistan; this incredible monument now draws intrepid tourists to the area and its restoration has greatly improved options for local people.

Just as travel is often about learning to see with new eyes, so many of the groups we work with aim to change the way people see themselves and the future for their children and communities.

in Puerto La Cruz, Emilio José in Río Caribe and Chris Morgado in the Mochima area. Meeting fellow travelers was also a treat – a big thanks to Hans and Heinz, the German sailors, for a delicious meal in Mochima. And a big 'grazie' to Marco Avellino, the kind Italian-German who returned my passport on Margarita and saved me a trip to Caracas! Thanks always to my family for their love and support – my father and mother, David and Fung Bao, and my brother Daniel. And especially to my husband Ben, who puts up with me leaving for weeks on end, and in the meantime keeps our love nest in good order (for the most part).

BETH KOHN

So many people shared their love of Venezuela and their encyclopedic knowledge of the way things work. A big thank you to Ricardo and Luis Guillermo of Adrenaline, Francisco Alvarez, Andrea Mata Escobar, Axel Keleman, Virgilio Limpias, Jaime Rodriguez, Saul Silva and the state tourism office in Ciudad Bolívar. Closer to home, Michael Zap, Lourdes Castillo, Julia Brashares and Michael Read all contributed invaluable support at crucial times, and David Zingarelli trusted me with a country he adores. A shout out to all the fabulous travelers who trekked and swam with me along the way, especially Julie and Dave Osborne, Ignacio Fabo and Daniel Jimenez Urmenta. Special thanks to Stefan Lisowski, Sandra Bao and the very patient Thomas Kohnstamm, and un abrazo for Claude Moller.

JENS PORUP

What could have been a very difficult first research trip for Lonely Planet was made delightful by the many wonderful people in Venezuela who went out of their way to help me, sometimes bending over backwards to find difficult-to-impossible-to-find information. The following people deserve my warmest thanks: Gustavo and his rocks, Joe and his hummingbirds, the crowd at Tun Tun, Ernesto in the hills, Carlos and Kledy on the coast, and, of course, mi torita mágica who was there when I got back.

DANIEL C SCHECHTER

Caracas can be a tough place but the tremendously good-natured caraqueños smoothed my passage every step of the way. Here's my chance to show my appreciation for their efforts. Even before I touched down, Ben Rodríguez was making arrangements for my arrival, and his estimable cohort, Don Eustoquio Ferrer, ushered me into the capital. Once I had my feet on the ground, Theresa

León and her pals Geraldine and Melesio initiated me into the rituals of Caracas nightlife, and Jojo Farrell, Leo Lameda, Draichir Cabello, Tania Adler and Carlos Moscoso shared their voluminous knowledge of, and unflappable affection for, their city. Honorable mention also goes to these others who pitched in with contacts and contexts before and after Venezuela: Ilan Adler, Jeffrey A Wright and Rossana Torres, and Thomas Kohnstamm. And thanks again, Myra, for helping out in so many ways.

OUR READERS

Many thanks to the travelers who used the last edition and wrote to us with helpful hints, useful advice and interesting anecdotes:

A Duncan Allen, Michael Altenberger **B** Jonathan Barach, Sylvie Barbier, Peter Barman, Alison Barton, Christian Berggren, John Blagg, Martin Bolkovac, Rowan Braybrook, Andrea Bruni, Sandra Buchanan **C** Tessa Carroll, Lisa Carvalhal, Mario Castillo, Daniel Castro, A Charlebois, Chateau du Moret, Jon & Karen Cheek, Jenny Chua, Christina Cox **D** Bill Damon, Jennifer Davitt, Eduardo Delgado, Lisa Dervin, Krzysztof Dydyński **E** Jane Edmondson, Daniel Egli, Johanna Ekblom, Troy Emberton **F** Macdara Ferris, Claudia Fliegner, Rolf Forster, Melissa Foster, Mike Fox, Stefan Fuchs, Nick Fuegi, Peter Fumberger **G** Laura Garcia, Michael Gebelein, Anita Glynn, William Golden, Rupert Griffiths **H** Allen Hancock, Annette

---

SEND US YOUR FEEDBACK

We love to hear from travelers – your comments keep us on our toes and help make our books better. Our well-traveled team reads every word on what you loved or loathed about this book. Although we cannot reply individually to postal submissions, we always guarantee that your feedback goes straight to the appropriate authors, in time for the next edition. Each person who sends us information is thanked in the next edition – and the most useful submissions are rewarded with a free book.

To send us your updates – and find out about Lonely Planet events, newsletters and travel news – visit our award-winning website: **www.lonelyplanet.com/contact**.

Note: we may edit, reproduce and incorporate your comments in Lonely Planet products such as guidebooks, websites and digital products, so let us know if you don't want your comments reproduced or your name acknowledged. For a copy of our privacy policy visit www.lonelyplanet.com/privacy.

Hartmetz, Adrian Hawkins, Siobhan Healy, Claus Hecking, Mieke Hermans, Clementina Hernandez, Catherine Hogue, Tim & Nia Holding, Niels Hollum, Mariann Howell **I** Karl Ike **J** Steffen Janz, Eugene Joseph, Marianna Judd **K** Harold Kollmeier **L** Nicolas Lanquetin, Katrin Lauff, Peter Laustetter, Simon Lee, Sune Lolk, Simona Di Lorenzo **M** Remco Maat, Charlotte Skrubbeltrang Madsen, Federico Maiardi, Yossi Margoninsky, Francesco Marino, Tony Martin, Peter Meier, Christian Melliger, Dany Mertens, Silvia Meyer, Ted Miller, Richard Millhiser, Kjell Mittag, Kirsten & Johs Mondrup, Paolo Morazzi, Andreas Mugler, Raphael Müller **N** Danny Newman, Grant Nielsen **O** Elio Ohep, Frances Osborn, Wilco Otte **P** Roberto Pozo, Nikolas Pratt **R** Mieke Rener, Florian Rickert, Noe Rojas **S** Dean Sammut, Ezequiel Santos, Katrin Sauer, Mirjam Schmidt, Christoph Schneider, Nicolas Serre, Joe Shahda, Julie Sion, Aidan Skoyles, Karen Slater, Janiece Smith, Stephanie Smith, Piotr Sobczak, Birgit Sonnerer, Mark Southworth, Paul Stanley, Jonas Stockhecke, Steven Strange, Jacob Sykes **T** Birgit Tantner, Michael Tappe, Lieven de Temmerman, Alexander Thoener, Linda Thomson, Lincoln Tucker, Rhonda Tupper **V** Joris van Empel, Oscar van de Pas, Kevin Verbist, James Vessey, Rita Voegeli **W** Fabio Weissert, Amy L White, Corinna Wiesner-Rau, Nigel & Deisy Williams **Z** Reiner Zeisig, Kerstin Zimmermann, Yotam Ben Zvi

ACKNOWLEDGMENTS

Many thanks to the following for the use of their content:

Globe on title page ©Mountain High Maps 1993 Digital Wisdom, Inc.

Index